Spanish Verb Workbook

Frank H. Nuessel, Ph.D.

University of Louisville

BARRON'S

All inquiries should be addressed to:
Barron's Educational Series, Inc.
250 Wireless Boulevard
Hauppauge, New York 11788
http://www.barronseduc.com

ISBN-13: 978-0-7641-3052-6
ISBN-10: 0-7641-3052-8
Library of Congress Control Number: 2005044261

Library of Congress Cataloging-in-Publication Data

Nuessel, Frank H.
    Spanish verb workbook / Frank Nuessel.
        p. cm.
    ISBN 0-7641-3052-8 (alk. paper)
    1. Spanish language—Verb—Handbooks, manuals, etc. I. Title.

    PC4271.N84   2005
    468.2'421—dc22   2005044261

Printed in the United States of America

10

10%
POST-CONSUMER
WASTE
Paper contains a minimum
of 10% post-consumer
waste (PCW). Paper used
in this book was derived
from certified, sustainable
forestlands.

Contents

Part Three
The Future and Conditional Tenses 203

Part Four
The Subjunctive Tenses   251

Part Five
Other Verb Forms   319

Introduction

Many people feel a sense of anxiety when starting to learn a new language. Too many conjugations! Too many uses! But verbs are crucial to the effective learning of a new language. It cannot be avoided. These feelings are normal and this book will help you to overcome these feelings very quickly.

This book is an in-depth and comprehensive manual on how to conjugate and use Spanish verbs. Its simple method is designed to help you learn the basics of Spanish verbs in an effortless way. All you need is this book, no matter at what stage of learning you find yourself. It can thus be used profitably by:

- Those who know some Spanish, but who wish to improve their knowledge of Spanish verbs in a comprehensive and intensive, but user-friendly, way.

- Students enrolled in a Spanish language course, in a high school, college, or university, who feel that they need more practice with Spanish verbs.

- Beginners of the language.

If you are a true beginner, you will find that this book makes no assumptions. You will learn about the other aspects of Spanish grammar as you work your way through it. If you are someone who already possesses some knowledge of Spanish, you will find this book particularly helpful, since it also reviews the other aspects of grammar, connecting them to the Spanish verbal system.

Thus, whether you are just beginning your study of Spanish or have had some training in the language, this book is for you. Previous knowledge has not been taken for granted in these pages; definitions and explanations are concise and clear, and examples use and reuse a core of basic vocabulary.

You should not skip any chapter, especially if you are a beginner. The book is designed to be sequential and coherent. It builds on notions and vocabulary introduced in previous chapters. By the end, you will be in a position to grasp the fundamentals of the Spanish verb system. You can also use this book as a reference manual, consulting the table of contents to guide you to the areas of Spanish verb conjugation and use for information or practice.

Finally, we ask that you consult maps of those countries where Spanish is an official language so that you can visualize these places. You will see that Spanish is truly a worldwide language.

¡Diviértete! (*Have fun!*)

How to Use This Book

This book is divided into five main parts, each consisting of a number of chapters. Part 1 covers the present indicative tenses, Part 2 covers the past indicative tenses, part 3 the future and conditional tenses, Part 4 the subjunctive tenses, and Part 5 the imperative and the passive voice.

Overview Units

Before starting to do the exercises and activities in the chapters of a specific part, read the overview unit at the beginning, especially if you are unsure about grammatical terms or concepts. This unit explains the relevant technical terms used in each part, in a non-technical and easy-to-follow way—what is a *conjugation*, what is a verb *tense*, what is the *subjunctive*, and so on.

Conjugation Information at the Beginning of a Chapter

Each of the chapters is organized around a specific tense or problematic verb (or verbs). There are several recurring sections and features in each chapter.

In the introductory section, you are given all of the information you will need on how to conjugate verbs in a specific tense and mood. This is followed by exercises that, although they may appear mechanical, are nevertheless necessary. These are akin to scales and arpeggios in musical practice. A student will never become a good pianist or violinist without mastery over them. Correspondingly, you will need to do your exercises consistently and faithfully so as to gain mastery over Spanish verbs.

Vocabulary

Words constitute the building blocks of any language. In order to facilitate the successful completion of the exercises, we have a comprehensive English-Spanish vocabulary at the end of the book for easy reader reference.

Uses and Features

This section contains a summary of how the verb or verb tense is to be used and what its features are. Exercises focusing on usage follow. Many of these involve translating from English to Spanish. In this area of grammar, there is no better way to grasp differences in usage than by comparing how the two languages express certain things. The exercises should be pronounced aloud. It really works!

Tips, Notes, Grammar

Throughout a chapter, tips on how to use a verb, notes on aspects of grammar that are relevant to the chapter, charts introducing new vocabulary, and the like are interspersed throughout.

Crossword Puzzle

Each chapter ends with a crossword puzzle that is designed to provide an entertaining format for reinforcing what you have learned in the chapter. The clues provided will vary in nature and level of difficulty.

Review Chapters

At the end of each of the five parts, you will find a review chapter that allows you to reinforce what you have learned through the conjugation and usage exercises. Each review contains two parts: (1) conjugation review and (2) usage review.

Vocalization

It is important to vocalize all of the exercises in each chapter. This will help you use the verbs.

1. Say each exercise aloud. In some exercises, you are asked to produce a verb form. After you have done this, make up a complete sentence (based on the vocabulary that you already know).
2. Articulate each sentence that you have to translate from English to Spanish. This will help you remember what you have done and it will give you confidence.

Back Matter

At the back of the book, you will find the answers to the exercises of all chapters and an English-Spanish vocabulary of all the words that you have been using in this book.

Part One

The Present Indicative and the Present Progressive

The Present: An Overview

What Are Verbs?

Verbs are words that indicate the action performed by the subject of a sentence. For this reason, they agree with the *person* (first, second, third) and *number* (singular or plural) of the subject.

Ella	canta
She	sings

↑	↑
3rd person singular subject pronoun	3rd person singular form of verb **cantar** / *to sing*

Los amigos	cantan
The friends	sing

↑	↑
3rd person plural subject pronoun	3rd person plural form of verb **cantar** / *to sing*

Infinitives and Conjugations

The *infinitive* is the form of a verb not inflected (modified) for a person or number. In English, it is commonly preceded by *to—to sing, to eat*, and so on. In a dictionary, verbs are listed in their infinitive form, the form that ends in -r.

Spanish verbs are divided into three conjugations according to their infinitive endings. A *conjugation* is the systematic arrangement of the verb forms according to tense and mood. The infinitive endings in Spanish are **-ar** (first conjugation), **-er** (second conjugation), and **-ir** (third conjugation).

TIP

The infinitive endings allow you to determine which person and number endings a verb must take when you conjugate it. Learn these now!

pagar / *to pay*	beber / *to drink*	vivir / *to live*
↑	↑	↑
first conjugation	second conjugation	third conjugation

Tense

A verb tense indicates the time an action occurred—now (present tense), before (past tense), after (future tense).

1. Present tense:
   La <u>como</u> ahora. / *I'm eating it now.*

2. Past tense:
   La <u>comí</u> ayer. / *I ate it yesterday.*

3. Future tense:
   La <u>comeré</u> mañana. / *I will eat it tomorrow.*

Mood

Not only do verbs allow you to express the time an action took place, but they also allow you to convey the manner of thinking, point of view, etc. This aspect is known as *mood*:

1. Indicative mood = statement:
   Pedro <u>lee</u> esa novela. / *Peter is reading that novel.*

2. Imperative mood = command:
   Inés, ¡<u>lee</u> esa novela! / *Inés, read that novel!*

3. Subjunctive mood = probability:
   Es probable que Jorge <u>lea</u> esa novela. / *It is probable that George is reading that novel.*

Regular and Irregular Verbs

A *regular verb* is one that is conjugated according to a recurring pattern. A verb that is not conjugated in this way is known as *irregular*.

The Present Indicative

The present indicative, called the **presente de indicativo**, allows you to express, indicate, or refer to actions that are ongoing, permanent, or imply present time in some way. It is the most commonly used tense in everyday conversation.

The Present Progressive

The second main present tense is the present progressive, called the presente progresivo in Spanish. It is an alternative to the present indicative, allowing you to zero in on an ongoing action. It will be dealt with in Chapter 6.

Subject Pronouns

The subject pronouns are shown below.

Singular		Plural	
1st person	(yo) / *I*	1st person	(nosotros) / *we* (nosotras) / *we*
2nd person	(tú) / *you* (fam. sg.)	2nd person	(vosotros) / *you* (fam. pl.) (vosotras) / *you* (fam. pl.) Used in Spain.
3rd person	(él) / *he* (ella) / *she* (usted) / *you* (pol. sg.)	3rd person	(ellos) / *they* (ellas) / *they* (ustedes) / *you* (pol. pl) General plural in Latin America.

USAGE NOTES

As you can see, there are both familiar (fam.) and polite (pol.) forms of address in Spanish. These are not to be used alternatively! If you address someone incorrectly, it might be taken as rudeness! So, be careful.

Simply put, the familiar forms are used to address people with whom you are on familiar terms: members of the family, friends, etc. If you call someone by a first name, then you are obviously on familiar terms.

· Remember that the plural for the singular (sg.) forms tú (fam.) and usted (pol.) in this hemisphere is ustedes. This is the usage that you are most likely to hear unless you are in Spain. In Spain, the plural (pl.) for tú is vosotros/vosotras and the plural for usted is ustedes. In the exercises in this book, we will use the vosotros/vosotras forms, but you must remember that they are used only in Spain. The following chart illustrates this point:

Spain:	Singular		Plural
	tú	→	vosotros, vosostras
	usted	→	ustedes

Latin America:	Singular		Plural
	tú	→	ustedes
	usted	→	ustedes

Remember also that usted has the following abbreviations: Ud. and Vd. Likewise, ustedes has the following common abbreviations: Uds. and Vds.

Notice also that we have placed the first and second persons singular (yo, tú) and plural (nosotros, nosotras, vosotros, vosotras) within parentheses ( ) to call to your attention the fact that these forms are normally used for emphasis. We will follow this convention throughout the book as appropriate.

What Are Sentences?

A *sentence* is an organized sequence of words that allows you to make a statement, ask a question, express a thought, offer an opinion, etc. In writing, a sentence is easily identified because it starts with a capitalized word and ends with a period, a question mark, or an exclamation point. Remember, however, that in Spanish, you introduce a question with an "upside down" question mark: ¿. Likewise, you introduce a command with an "upside down" exclamation point: ¡.

1. Affirmative sentence:
    Él es español. / *He is Spanish.*

2. Interrogative sentence:
    ¿Quién es ese hombre? / *Who is that man?*

3. Imperative sentence:
    Margarita, ¡ven acá! / *Margarita, come here!*

Sentences have two basic parts: a *subject* and a *predicate*. A subject is "who" or "what" the sentence is about. It is often the first element in a simple sentence:

    <u>Gloria</u> habla español. / *Gloria speaks Spanish.*
    <u>Ella</u> es boliviana. / *She is Bolivian.*

But be careful! The subject is not necessarily always the first word:

    Sí, también <u>Roberto</u> habla español. / *Yes, Roberto also speaks Spanish.*
    No, quizás <u>Clara</u> no venga. / *No, perhaps Clara is not coming.*

A *predicate* is the remaining part of the sentence. It provides information about the subject. In many simple sentences, you will find it after the subject.

    Mario <u>habla español.</u> / *Mario speaks Spanish.*
    Él <u>es mexicano.</u> / *He is Mexican.*

A Note About Tense and Verb Form Names

In this book, you will learn and practice the commonly used Spanish tenses. There are 7 simple tenses and 6 compound tenses in this volume. The names of these tenses in English and Spanish follow.

Simple Tenses

English Name	Spanish Name
1. Present indicative	El presente de indicativo
2. Preterit	El pretérito
3. Imperfect indicative	El imperfecto de indicativo
4. Future	El futuro
5. Conditional	El potencial simple
6. Present subjunctive	El presente de subjuntivo
7. Imperfect subjunctive	El imperfecto de subjuntivo

Compound Tenses

English Name	Spanish Name
1. Present perfect indicative	El perfecto de indicativo
2. Pluperfect or past perfect indicative	El pluscuamperfecto de indicativo
3. Future perfect	El futuro perfecto
4. Conditional perfect	El potencial perfecto
5. Present perfect subjunctive	El perfecto de subjuntivo
6. Pluperfect or past perfect subjunctive	El pluscuamperfecto de subjuntivo

The Progressive Verb Forms

You will learn the following progressive verb forms: (1) present progressive and (2) imperfect progressive.

English Name	Spanish Name
1. Present progressive	El presente progresivo
2. Imperfect progressive	El imperfecto progresivo

Other Verb Forms

There are other verb forms in Spanish that are called non-finite forms. This means that they do not indicate the person (first, second, and third person), number (singular, plural), tense (present, past, future, conditional), or the mood (indicative, subjunctive, imperative). The following chart provides the names of these forms in English and Spanish.

English Name	Spanish Name
1. Infinitive	Infinitivo
2. Present participle	Gerundio
3. Past participle	Participio

Additional Verb Forms

There are two other verb forms. The first is the imperative or command form. The second is the passive voice.

English Name	Spanish Name
1. Imperative/Command	Imperativo/Mandato
2. Passive voice	La voz pasiva

You are now ready to start learning how to conjugate and use Spanish verbs!

1
The Present Indicative (*el presente de indicativo*) of Regular Verbs

Uses and Features

The presente de indicativo / *present indicative* is used in everyday conversation to refer to actions, events, and ideas that imply the present situation or some permanent or habitual situation. Specifically, it is used:

1. To indicate an action or state of being that is taking place at the present time:
   <u>Hablo</u> con Isabel en este momento. / *I am speaking with Isabel at this moment.*
   <u>Miro</u> una telenovela ahora. / *I am watching a soap opera now.*

2. To indicate an action or state of being that is permanent or continuous:
   <u>Hablo</u> español también. / *I speak Spanish too.*
   Ella lo <u>comprende</u> todo. / *She understands everything.*

3. To emphasize something in the present time:
   Sí, ¡lo <u>comprendo</u>! / *Yes, I understand!*
   No, ¡no <u>miro</u> nada! / *No, I don't look at anything!*

4. To indicate a habitual action:
   <u>Toco</u> la guitarra todos los días. / *I play the guitar every day.*
   Los lunes, <u>limpiamos</u> la casa. / *On Mondays, we clean the house.*

5. To convey a general truth:
   Las tiendas <u>abren</u> a las siete y media. / *The stores open at 7:30 A.M.*
   Los españoles <u>trabajan</u> mucho. / *Spaniards work hard.*

6. To express an action that will occur in the near future:
   Él <u>llega</u> mañana. / *He will arrive tomorrow.*
   Dentro de poco, <u>escribo</u> un correo electrónico. / *In a little bit, I will write an e-mail.*

First Conjugation Verbs

As you learned in the preceding unit, the infinitives of regular Spanish verbs end in -ar, -er, or -ir. Those ending in -ar are first conjugation verbs. To form the present indicative of such verbs, called the presente de indicativo, do the following:

1. Drop the infinitive ending, -ar. This produces the "verb stem," as it is called. The verb stem contains the basic meaning of the verb.

    hablar / *to speak* → habl-

2. Add the following *endings* to the stem:

(yo)	-o
(tú)	-as
(él, ella, Ud.)	-a
(nosotros/-as)	-amos
(vosotros/-as)	-áis
(ellos/-as, Uds.)	-an

3. Here's the result:

hablar / *to speak*

Subject Pronoun	Verb Form	Meaning
(yo)	habl+o	*I speak, I am speaking, I do speak*
(tú)	habl+as	*you (fam. sg.) speak, you are speaking, you do speak*
(él, ella, Ud.)	habl+a	*he, she, you (pol. sg.) speak(s), he, she, you is/are speaking, he, she, you does/do speak*
(nosotros/-as)	habl+amos	*we speak, we are speaking, we do speak*
(vosotros/-as)	habl+áis	*you (fam. pl.) speak, you are speaking, you do speak*
(ellos/-as, Uds.)	habl+an	*they, you (pol. pl.) speak, they, you are speaking, they, you do speak*

TIP

You should note that the following endings are associated with the following verb forms in Spanish.

Person	Ending
(tú)	-s*
(nosotros/-as)	-mos
(vosotros/-as)	-is
(Uds., ellos/-as)	-n

*The preterit tense (see Chapter 7) is the one exception to this rule. It does not have an ending in -s for the tú / *you* form as you will discover.

To make a sentence negative in Spanish, just put no before the predicate (no / *no*; sí / *yes*).

Affirmative	Negative
Sí, Raquel habla español. / *Yes, Raquel speaks Spanish.*	No, Raquel <u>no</u> habla español. / *No, Rachel does not speak Spanish.*
Sí, ellos llegan mañana. / *Yes, they are arriving tomorrow.*	No, ellos <u>no</u> llegan mañana. / *No, they are not arriving tomorrow.*

TIP

Notice that the presente de indicativo is rendered by three English verb forms:

hablo	=	I speak
		I am speaking
		I do speak

The present tense may also be used to convey the immediate future, i.e., to an event that will take place very soon.

Hablo español esta tarde. / *I will speak Spanish this afternoon.*

USAGE NOTES

Note that the pronouns yo, tú, nosotros, nosotras, vosotros, vosotras are normally used to make an emphatic statement. In this book, we will place these forms in parentheses as a reminder that they should only be used for emphasis: (yo), (tú), (nosotros), (nosotras), (vosotros), (vosotras).

Observe the difference between the following two sentences:

Hablo español. / *I speak Spanish.* = Matter of fact statement.
Yo hablo español. / *I speak Spanish.* = Very emphatic statement (with raised voice in English).

English normally requires a subject pronoun, but in the Spanish verb system the ending tells us who is doing the speaking.

In the third person singular and plural, the subject pronouns are often used because one verb form corresponds to several possible subjects in Spanish:

Él habla. / *He speaks.*
Ella habla. / *She speaks.*
Ud. habla. / *You (pol. sg.) speak.*
Ellos hablan. / *They (men, or men and women) speak.*
Ellas hablan. / *They (women) speak.*
Uds. hablan. / *You (pol. pl. in this hemisphere, also plural of the familiar form **tú**) speak.*

In Spanish the -s form of the verb corresponds to tú / you (fam. sg.). In English the -s form of the verb of the present tense signifies the third person singular:

Spanish:

(Tú) canta<u>s</u>. / *You sing.*
Él canta. / *He sing<u>s</u>.*

In Spanish, when you include yourself (yo) and at least one other person, you must use the -mos form of the verb.

Javier y yo hablamos español. / *Javier and I speak Spanish.*
Amparo, Enrique y yo hablamos inglés. / *Amparo, Enrique and I speak English.*

Common Verbs

Below are some common regular first conjugation verbs that will come in handy for basic communication.

abrazar	*to embrace, to hug*	hablar	*to speak*
acabar	*to finish, to complete*	hallar	*to find*
admirar	*to admire*	limpiar	*to clean*
andar	*to walk*	llamar	*to call*
bailar	*to dance*	llegar (a)	*to arrive*
besar	*to kiss*	llevar	*to wear, to carry*
buscar	*to look for*	mandar	*to send*
caminar	*to walk*	manejar	*to drive*
cantar	*to sing*	mirar	*to look at, to watch*
charlar	*to chat*	nadar	*to swim*
cocinar	*to cook*	necesitar	*to need*
comprar	*to buy*	pagar	*to pay for*
conjugar	*to conjugate*	pasar	*to spend (time)*
cuidar	*to care for*	pintar	*to paint*
dejar	*to leave (something)*	preparar	*to prepare*
descansar	*to rest*	regresar	*to return*
desear	*to want*	terminar	*to complete, to finish*
entrar (en)	*to enter*	tocar	*to play (an instrument), to touch*
escuchar	*to listen to*	tomar	*to take (food)*
esperar	*to wait for, to hope*	trabajar	*to work*
estudiar	*to study*	viajar	*to travel*
gastar	*to spend (money)*	visitar	*to visit*
gritar	*to shout*		

GRAMMAR NOTE

Certain verbs have characteristic prepositions. This means that if there is a following noun or in many cases a following infinitive, it is necessary to include this so-called characteristic preposition. In the list above, entrar (en) is one example of this type of verb. By convention, the characteristic preposition usually appears in parentheses ( ). It is used when there is a following noun: Entro <u>en</u> la biblioteca / *I enter the library.* As we progress in this book, there will be many more such verbs.

VOCABULARY NOTE

The verb acabar / *to finish, to complete* has the special idiomatic meaning *"to have just"* when used with the preposition de and an infinitive as shown below.

Acabo de estudiar.
I have just studied.

TIP

Some commonly used verbs have a preposition in their basic meaning:

buscar	*to look for*
escuchar	*to listen to*
esperar	*to wait for*
pagar	*to pay for*

It is not necessary to add an extra word for these prepositions; it is built-in!

GRAMMAR NOTE

Spanish nouns are either masculine or feminine. You can usually identify the noun's gender by the ending. If it ends in -o, the noun is (generally) masculine; if it ends in -a, it is (generally) feminine. There are exceptions to the previous rule and several commonly used nouns are among these exceptions. Also, if the word refers to people, it will be masculine or feminine if it refers to a man or a woman. Dictionaries usually indicate the gender of a noun with the following notations: (*m.*) for masculine and (*f.*) for feminine.

Masculine	*Feminine*
minut<u>o</u> / *minute*	hij<u>a</u> / *daughter*

Note the forms of the definite article ("*the*") introduced above:

<u>el</u> = with a masculine singular noun:

<u>el</u> hij<u>o</u> / *the son*

la = with a feminine singular noun:

<u>la</u> hij<u>a</u> / *the daughter*

NOTE

The word ¿verdad? in Spanish is used as a tag question. Its precise meaning is determined by the context as shown below.

Estudias español, ¿<u>verdad</u>? / *You study Spanish, <u>don't you?</u>*

Ellos beben café, ¿<u>verdad</u>? / *They drink coffee, <u>don't they?</u>*

EXERCISE Set 1-1

A. Supply the missing Spanish verb ending and then give the English equivalent.

EXAMPLE: *él habl_*   =   _____

   él habla   =   *he speaks, he is speaking, he does speak*

1. (yo) toc_   =   *yo toco   I play*
2. (tú) esper__   =   *Tú esperas   you wait for*
3. (nosotros) prepar__   =   *nosotros preparamos - we prepare*
4. (ellos) llev__   =   *ellos llevan - they wear*
5. (vosotros) pag__   =   *vosotros pagais - you pay for*
6. (Ud.) trabaj__   =   *ud trabaja   you work*
7. (ellas) mir__   =   *ellas miran - they look*
8. (Uds.) estud__   =   *uds estudian - they study*
9. (yo) viaj__   =   *yo viajo - I travel*
10. (tú) bail__   =   *tú bailas - you dance*
11. (nosotras) cant__   =   *nosotras cantamos - we sing*
12. (él) compr__   =   *el compra - he buys*
13. (ellas) habl__   =   *ellas hablan - they speak*
14. (Ud.) entr__   =   *ud entra - you enter*
15. (Uds.) busc__   =   *uds buscan - they look for*

B. How do you say the following sentences in Spanish? Remember that sg. = singular, pl. = plural, fam. = familiar, pol. = polite. The material in parentheses tells you what verb form to use, or it provides cultural information.

1. Excuse me, do you (pol. sg.) speak English?

   Perdon habla ud Ingles
   Desculpa me, ud habla Ingles ¿

2. Yes, I speak English very well.

   Si hablo Ingles muy bien.

3. They do not speak Spanish very well.

Ellos no hablan español muy bien

4. We speak Spanish a little bit.

nosotras hablamos español un poco

5. Rafael, you (fam. sg.) also speak Spanish, don't you?

Rafael, tú hablas español también ¿verdad?

6. I do not speak Spanish, but my daughter speaks Spanish very well.

Yo no hablo español pero mi hija habla español (mucho bueno) muy bien

7. No, it is not true. The bus is not arriving now.

No es verdadero. El autobús no es llega ahora

8. Thank you, you are very kind (pol. sg.). I do not speak Spanish well.

Gracias, ud. es muy amable. no hablo español bien

9. Alejandro plays the cello like *Pablo Casals*[1] and Claudia paints like *Diego Velázquez*[2].

Alejandro toca violoncello como Pablo Casals y Claudia pinta como Diego Velázquez

10. She listens to the radio too much.

Ella Escucha la radio muc demasiado

11. I want to watch the bullfight[3] on TV.

Deseo miro la corrida de toros en la televisión

12. They play the piano well.

ellos tocan el piano bien

13. You (fam. sg.) are always watching television.

tú Siempre mirar la televisione

14. You (pol. sg.) are wearing a new jacket, aren't you?

ud lleva una chaqueta nueva, verdad

15. You (pol. pl.) are waiting for the bus, aren't you?

uds esperan el autobus verdad

[1]Renowned Spanish cellist, 1876–1973; [2]Renowned Spanish painter, 1599–1660; [3]Regular afternoon program in Madrid.

Second Conjugation Verbs

Infinitives ending in -er are classified as second conjugation verbs. To form the present indicative of these verbs, do exactly the same thing you did with first conjugation verbs:

1. Drop the infinitive ending, -er. This produces the "verb stem," as it is called.

    comer / *to eat* → com-

2. Add the following endings to the stem:

(yo)	-o
(tú)	-es
(él, ella, Ud.)	-e
(nosotros/-as)	-emos
(vosotros/-as)	-éis
(ellos/-as, Uds.)	-en

3. Here's the result:

                            comer / *to eat*

Subject Pronoun	Verb Form	Meaning
(yo)	com+o	*I eat, I am eating, I do eat*
(tú)	com+es	*you (fam. sg.) eat, you are eating, you do eat*
(él, ella, Ud.)	com+e	*he, she, you (pol. sg.) eat(s), he, she, you is/are eating, he, she, you does/do eat*
(nosotros/-as)	com+emos	*we eat, we are eating, we do eat*
(vosotros/-as)	com+éis	*you (fam. pl.) eat, you are eating, you do eat*
(ellos/-as, Uds.)	com+en	*they, you (pol. pl.) eat, they, you are eating, they, you do eat*

Common Verbs
Below are some common regular second conjugation verbs for basic communication.

aprender (a)	*to learn*	leer	*to read*
beber	*to drink*	meter (en)	*to put (into)*
comer	*to eat*	poseer	*to possess*
comprender	*to understand*	romper	*to break*
correr	*to run*	temer	*to fear*
creer	*to believe*	vender	*to sell*
deber	*ought, should, to owe*		

TIP

Note that if there are two verbs together, it is the first one that is conjugated, whereas the second one is usually an infinitive:

Juan <u>debe</u> leer. / *John must read.*
Carmen <u>necesita</u> estudiar. / *Carmen needs to study.*

GRAMMAR NOTES

Note the forms of the indefinite article ("*a/an*") introduced below:

un   =   with a masculine singular noun:
<u>un</u> corre<u>o</u> electrónic<u>o</u> / *an e-mail*
una   =   with a feminine noun:
un<u>a</u> amig<u>a</u> mexican<u>a</u> / *a Mexican female friend*

The plural of the indefinite article ("*a/an*") means "*some*" as shown below:

un<u>os</u> amig<u>os</u> mexican<u>os</u> / *some Mexican friends*
un<u>as</u> amig<u>as</u> mexican<u>as</u> / *some female Mexican friends*

Note: The descriptive adjective generally follows the noun and agrees with the noun also: either masculine or feminine, singular or plural. Note also that adjectives of nationality are not capitalized in Spanish.

EXERCISE Set 1-2

A. Supply the missing Spanish verb and then give the English equivalent.

EXAMPLE: *él corr__*   =   _____

   él corre   =   *he runs, he is running, he does run*

1. (yo) aprend. *o*   =   *I learn*

2. (tú) comprend *es*   =   *you understand*

3. (nosotros) cre *mos*   =   *we believe*

4. (ellos) met *en*   =   *to put (into) they*

5. (vosotros) corr *éis*   =   *to run you*

6. (Ud.) le *e*   =   *to read you*

7. (mi amiga) tem *e*   =   *to fear my*

8. (ellas) romp_EN_   =   they break

9. (yo) deb_o_   =   I ought, should

10. (tú) beb_e_   =   you drink

11. (nosotras) vend_EMOS_ =   we sell

12. (Uds.) com_EN_   =   you eat, are eating, do eat

13. (él) aprend_E_   =   he is learning, does learn

14. (ellos) comprend_EN_ =   they understand, are understanding

15. (Ud.) cre_e_   =   you believe, are believing, do believe

B. How do you say the following things in Spanish? Note: sg. = singular, pl. = plural, fam. = familiar, pol. = polite). You do not have to translate material in parentheses; this information tells you what verb form to use, or it provides cultural information.

1. Are you (fam. sg.) reading *Don Quijote*[1]?

    Lees don Quijote

2. I'm not reading. I'm sending an e-mail.

    Yo soy non leo. Yo soy mando correo electronico

3. Excuse me, are you (pol. sg.) sending an e-mail in Spanish?

    Perdona? manda un correo electronico en espanol

4. Yes, because my friend (f.) speaks, reads and writes Spanish very well.

    Si porque mi amiga habla, lee y escribe Espanol muy bien

5. Good-bye. Do you (pol. pl.) understand?

    Adios. ¿ comprenden uds?

6. I should send an e-mail in twenty minutes.

    debo mando un correo electronica en veinte minutos veinte

7. My friend (f.) is not selling the *Seat*[2].

    Mi amiego(a) no vende el Seat

8. My grandmother drinks a lot of coffee.

Mi abuela bebe mucho café

9. I fear Spanish tests.

Temo los exámenes de español

10. My brother is selling the car.

Mi hermano vende su coche

11. My sister is always breaking something.

Mi hermana siempre rompe algo

12. My Mexican friend (f.) reads *El País*[3] frequently.

Mi mexicana amiga lee El País con frecuencia

13. My son should read more.

Mi hijo debe leer más

14. My daughter is learning to speak Spanish at the *University of Salamanca*[4].

Mi hija aprende habla español

15. Do you (fam. sg.) eat a lot?

comes mucho

[1]Famous novel by Miguel de Cervantes, 1547–1616; [2]Car manufactured in Spain; [3]Major newspaper in Spain;
[4]Famous Spanish university founded in 1218 by *Alfonso IX* [1171–1230], one of the oldest universities in Europe.

Third Conjugation Verbs

Infinitives ending in -ir are called third-conjugation verbs.

1. Drop the infinitive ending, -ir. This produces the "verb stem," as it is called.

   abrir / *to open* → abr-

2. Add the following endings to the stem:

(yo)	-o
(tú)	-es
(él, ella, Ud.)	-e
(nosotros/-as)	-imos
(vosotros/-as)	-ís
(ellos/-as, Uds.)	-en

3. Here's the result:

abrir / *to open*

Subject Pronoun	Verb Form	Meaning
(yo)	abr+o	*I open, I am opening, I do open*
(tú)	abr+es	*you (fam. sg.) open, you are opening, you do open*
(él, ella, Ud.)	abr+e	*he, she, you (pol. sg.) open(s), he, she, you (pol. sg.) is/are opening, he, she, you does/do open*
(nosotros/-as)	abr+imos	*we open, we are opening, we do open*
(vosotros/-as)	abr+ís	*you (fam. pl.) open, you are opening, you do open*
(ellos/-as, Uds.)	abr+en	*they, you (pol. pl.) open, they, you are opening, they, you do open*

Common Verbs

Below are some common regular second conjugation verbs for basic communication.

abrir	*to open*	escribir	*to write*
admitir	*to admit*	existir	*to exist*
asistir (a)	*to attend*	partir	*to leave*
cubrir	*to cover*	permitir	*to permit*
decidir	*to decide*	recibir	*to receive*
describir	*to describe*	subir (a)	*to go up, climb*
descubrir	*to discover*	sufrir	*to suffer*
discutir	*to discuss*	vivir	*to live*

GRAMMAR NOTES

Nouns in Spanish that end in a vowel are made plural by adding an -s.

Singular	*Plural*
amigo (*m.*) / *male friend*	amigos / *male friends*
amiga (*f.*) / *female friend*	amigas / *female friends*

Nouns in Spanish that end in a consonant are made plural by adding an -es.

Singular	*Plural*
animal (*m.*) / *animal*	animales / *animals*
universidad (*f.*) / *university*	universidades / *universities*

Note that nouns that end in -ión do not have the graphic accent in the plural.

Singular	*Plural*
nación (*f.*) / *nation*	naciones / *nations*

EXERCISE Set 1-3

A. Supply the missing Spanish verb and then give the English equivalent.

EXAMPLE: *él abr___*   =   _____

   él abre   =   *he opens, he is opening, he does open*

1. (yo) viv___   =   *vivo   I live is living does live*

2. (tú) asist___   =   *asistes "attend" attending do attend*

3. (nosotros) describ___   =   *describimos - we describe*

4. (ellos) cubr ___   =   *cubren. They cover*

5. (vosotros) sufr___   =   *sufrís you suffer*

6. (Ud.) admit ___   =   *admite You admit*

7. (mi amiga) discut___   =   *my friend discute (discusses)*

8. (ellas) viv___   =   *viven They live*

9. (yo) permit ___   =   *permito I permit*

10. (tú) part___   =   *partes you leave*

11. (nosotras) sub___   =   *subimos we go up - climb*

12. (Uds.) exist___   =   *existen you exist*

13. (él) escrib___   =   *escribe - he writes*

14. (ellos) decid___   =   *deciden - They decide*

15. (Ud.) recib___   =   *recibe you receive*

B. How do you say the following things in Spanish? Note: sg. = singular, pl. = plural, fam. = familiar, pol. = polite. You do not have to translate material in parentheses; this information tells you what verb form to use, or it provides cultural information.

1. Do you (fam. sg.) receive a lot of e-mail?

recibir   ¿recibes mucho de correo electrónico

2. They are discussing the movie by *Luis Buñuel*[1] now.

_____

3. We are attending the class now.

   _____

4. She leaves for (*para*) *Málaga*[2] tomorrow.

   _____

5. You (pol. pl.) live nearby.

   _____

6. I write, read and send a lot of e-mail.

   _____

7. I need to attend class every day.

   _____

8. They are describing the painting by (de) *Francisco de Goya*[3] now.

   _____

9. Many people suffer today.

   _____

10. You (fam. pl.) decide to discuss the matter.

    _____

11. Marta and I open the windows.

    _____

12. I discover many secrets in class.

    _____

13. My husband writes like *Calderón de la Barca*[4].

    _____

14. Do fairies exist?

    _____

15. You (fam. sg.) cover the table.

---

[1]Spanish film director, 1900–1983; [2]City in Southern coastal Spain; [3]Spanish painter, 1746–1828; [4]Spanish dramatist, 1600–1681.

C. Which of the following two options, **a** or **b,** is the correct one? Say the question aloud and then say the answer out loud also. Use this and every opportunity to practice Spanish as a spoken language.

1. ¿A qué hora abren las tiendas aquí?

> **a.** A las siete y media.
> **b.** A las veinte.

2. ¿Llegas tarde?

> **a.** Sí, llego tarde.
> **b.** Sí, llegamos tarde.

3. Muchos estadounidenses … español.

> **a.** hablan
> **b.** habláis

4. ¿Toca Ud. la guitarra?

> **a.** No, no toco la guitarra.
> **b.** Sí, tocamos la guitarra.

5. Mis amigos argentinos …. muchos periódicos.

> **a.** leemos
> **b.** leen

6. ¿A qué hora … los amigos de Ignacio?

> **a.** trabajan
> **b.** trabajamos

7. Sí, (yo) … muchos regalos.

> **a.** recibe
> **b.** recibo

8. Mis amigos … español.

> **a.** estudian
> **b.** estudiamos

9. Jorge debe … mucho.

> **a.** estudias
> **b.** estudiar

10. Mi amiga … para Argentina mañana.

> **a.** parte
> **b.** partes

11. Ellos ... en Barcelona.

    a. vives
    b. viven

12. ¿Escriben Uds. muchas cartas?

    a. Sí, escribimos muchas.
    b. Sí, escribís muchas.

13. ¿Beben Uds. mucho café?

    a. No, no bebéis mucho.
    b. No, no bebemos mucho.

14. ¿Hablan Uds. español mucho?

    a. Sí, hablamos español mucho.
    b. No, no hablo español mucho.

VOCABULARY TIP

The present indicative is often used with words and expressions such as:

a esta hora	*at this time*
ahora mismo	*right now*
ahora	*now*
cada	*every*
en este momento	*at this moment*
hoy en día	*nowadays*
mañana	*tomorrow*

Asking Questions

In written Spanish, an interrogative sentence always has an "upside question mark" (¿) at the beginning of the sentence and a regular question mark at the end (?). The two most common methods of turning an affirmative sentence into an interrogative one are:

1. Simply put an upside down question mark (¿) at the beginning and a regular one (?) at the end in writing. In speaking, raise the tone of your voice.
    ¿Manolo habla español? / *Does Manolo speak Spanish?*

2. Put the subject at the end of the sentence, adding the appropriate dual question marks at the beginning and end in writing or raising your tone of voice when speaking.
    ¿Habla español Beatriz? / *Does Beatriz speak Spanish?*

   Interrogative sentences can also be formed with interrogative adjectives and pronouns when certain information is required. Again, you must remember to use an upside down question mark (¿) at the beginning of an interrogative sentence and a regular question mark (?) at the end.

    ¿Quién habla español aquí? / *Who speaks Spanish here?*
    ¿Dónde vive José? / *Where does José live?*

VOCABULARY NOTE

The following question words (interrogative pronouns and adjectives) are used to ask questions. When you use these question words, you normally place the subject of the sentence at the end. Note that all of these words bear a graphic accent.

¿cuál?	*which (one)?*
¿cuáles?	*which (ones)?*
¿cuándo?	*when?*
¿cuánto/a?	*how much?*
¿cuántos/as?	*how many?*
¿dónde?	*where?*
¿por qué?	*why?*
¿qué?	*what?*
¿quién?	*who? (one person)*
¿quiénes?	*who? (more than one person)*

Note that ¿cuánto?, ¿cuánta?, ¿cuántos?, ¿cuántas? agree with the noun they modify. This means that their endings agree in number (singular or plural) and gender (masculine or feminine) with the noun:

Masculine Singular ¿<u>Cuánto</u> dinero necesitas? / *How much money do you need?*	*Masculine Plural* ¿<u>Cuántos</u> libros compras? / *How many books are you buying?*

Feminine Singular ¿<u>Cuánta</u> leche compras? / *How much milk do you buy?*	*Feminine Plural* ¿<u>Cuántas</u> clases necesitas? / *How many classes do you need?*

Use ¿verdad? to seek approval, consent, or agreement when asking a rhetorical question.

Amparo habla español, ¿<u>verdad</u>? / *Amparo speaks Spanish, doesn't she?*
Enrique habla muy bien, ¿<u>verdad</u>? / *Henry speaks very well, doesn't he?*
Mis amigos son muy simpáticos, ¿<u>verdad</u>? / *My friends are very nice, aren't they?*

Familiar and Polite Forms of Address

Remember that in the singular, the tú form is used for familiar address (this verb form ends in -s), and the usted form for polite address (this verb form corresponds to the third person singular). Also, recall that usted has two common abbreviations: Ud. and Vd. We will use Ud. in this book.

¿Qué <u>necesitas</u>? / *What do you (fam. sg.) need?*
¿Qué <u>necesita</u> Ud.? / *What do you (pol. sg.) need?*

The ustedes form, which requires the third person plural form of the verb, is used for the plural of both tú and usted in this hemisphere. Thus, in this hemisphere, the ustedes form (abbreviated as Uds.) is the only plural form for both tú and usted.

¿<u>Miran</u> Uds. la televisión? / *Are you watching TV?*
¿Dónde <u>viven</u> Uds.? / *Where do you live?*

In Spain, the plural of **tú** is **vosotros** (all men or a group of men and women) or **vosotras** (all women). This usage is thus more geographically limited in its usage.

¿<u>Habláis</u> español mucho? / *Do you speak Spanish a lot?*
¿<u>Necesitáis</u> estudiar español mucho? / *Do you need to study Spanish a lot?*

Odds and Ends

Recall from the previous overview unit that subject pronouns are optional. Note that the subject pronoun "it" (plural "they") is not normally expressed when referring to things. Likewise, when referring to people, it is not necessary to repeat the third person pronoun (**él, ella, Ud., ellos, ellas, Uds.**) once the reference has been established in a conversation.

<u>Abre</u> a las siete y media. / *It opens at seven thirty.*
<u>Abren</u> a las siete y media. / *They open at seven thirty.*

The English equivalent for "Sara's friends," "my friend's guitar," etc. is rendered in Spanish with the preposition **de**:

Los amigos <u>de</u> Sara necesitan café. / *Sara's friends need coffee.*
Toco la guitarra <u>de</u> mi hija. / *I play my daughter's guitar.*

Remember: there is no 's in Spanish. You must use the preposition **de** / *of* to join two nouns in Spanish. <u>Mary's house</u> = la casa de María.

EXERCISE Set 1-4

A. Missing from each of the following sentences is the verb. The missing verbs are given to you in their infinitive forms. Put each verb, in its correct form, in each sentence according to the sense.

Verbs: comprender, escuchar, hablar, limpiar, llegar, mirar, partir, tocar, vivir.

1. Mi hermana _____ el violoncelo muy bien.

2. Mis amigos _____ para España.

3. Ahora (nosotros) _____ en México porque deseamos hablar muy bien el español.

4. En este momento, ellos _____ la televisión.

5. ¿A qué hora _____ los amigos de Pablo?

6. Cada día mi esposa y yo _____ la casa.

7. (Yo) _____ francés un poco.

8. Mi hermano siempre _____ la radio.

9. ¿ _____ (tú) el español?

B. Choose the appropriate answer to each question. You should also say the question out loud and provide the answer out loud. This will help you to remember the words.

1. ¿Dónde vives?

    a. Deseo mirar la televisión.
    b. En Sevilla.

2. ¿Miran Uds. la televisión?

    a. Sí, miráis la televisión.
    b. Sí, miramos la televisión.

3. ¿Habla Miguel español?

    a. Sí, lee y habla español.
    b. Sí, leemos y escribimos español.

4. ¿Trabaja aquí Miranda?

    a. No, no trabaja aquí.
    b. No, no trabajan aquí.

5. ¿Qué lee Mario?

    a. Lee una novela.
    b. Leo una novela.

6. ¿Cuándo llegan ellos?

    a. A las siete y media.
    b. No llegamos.

7. ¿Por qué estudian Uds. español?

    a. Deseamos hablar la lengua.
    b. Deseo hablar la lengua.

8. ¿Cuánto café bebes?

    a. Bebemos mucho.
    b. Bebo poco (little).

9. ¿Cuántos libros (books) compran Uds.?

    a. Compro los libros.
    b. Compramos muchos (many).

C. Each question is given to you in the familiar form. Change each one to the polite form. Say the question aloud.

EXAMPLE: ¿Qué bebes?
¿Qué bebe Ud.?

¿Dónde vivís? (Spain)
¿Dónde viven Uds.?

1. ¿Bailas el tango muy bien también?   _____

2. ¿Qué leéis en este momento? **(Spain)**   _____

3. ¿Qué estudias?   _____

4. ¿Por qué miras la televisión tanto **(so much)**? _____

5. ¿Necesitáis estudiar mucho? **(Spain)**   _____

D. Change the following sentences from the singular to the plural. In the first two sentences, assume you are in Spain. In the remaining three sentences, assume you are in this hemisphere.

1. Vives en Madrid.   _____

2. Ud. vive en Barcelona.   _____

3. Bebes mucho café.   _____

4. Hablas español muy bien. _____

5. Ud. canta muy bien.   _____

Crossword Puzzle 1

Fill in the blanks. All of the clues both vertical and horizontal are English verbal expressions that correspond to a single verb in Spanish.

Horizontales
1. you (fam. sg.) believe
3. I fear
4. I sell
6. they speak
9. we understand
10. we leave

Verticales
1. she runs
2. we study
5. they prepare
7. he breaks
8. you (Spain, fam. pl.) read

2
The Present Indicative of Stem-Changing Verbs

Stem-Changing Verbs

Stem-changing verbs have one difference from the regular verbs that we studied in the previous chapter. They have an alternation or change of the form of the vowel in their stem and this is why they are called stem-changing verbs. Recall from Chapter 1 that the stem of a verb is the form of the verb that remains after you remove the infinitive ending as shown below.

1. First conjugation verbs (-ar verbs).
   hablar / *to speak* → habl-

2. Second conjugation verbs (-er verbs).
   comer / *to eat* → com-

3. Third conjugation verbs (-ir verbs).
   abrir / *to open* → abr-

Stem-changing verbs, as just noted, have a change or alternation of the vowel in the stem. There are several patterns and we will examine each type in this chapter.

TIP

The endings of stem-changing verbs are exactly the same as those for the regular verbs that we studied in the previous chapter. The only difference is a change in the stem in certain verb forms (first, second, third person singular, and third person plural).

The best way to remember where the stem changes occur in stem-changing verbs is to remember a tried-and-true mnemonic technique. These verbs are called "shoe" verbs because the outline of where the changes occur looks like the profile of a shoe when these verbs are conjugated. We have created two profiles below to help you remember.

Shoe Pattern of Stem-Changing Verbs	
✔ Vowel change	
✔ Vowel change	
✔ Vowel change	✔ Vowel change

To emphasize where the stem-vowel changes and where it remains the same, we provide the following additional chart to help you see these changes. There is another important fact to remember about all stem-changing verbs: <u>The stem changes occur when the vowel in the stem receives primary stress</u>.

Location of Stem Changes in the Conjugation Format	
✔ (vowel stressed)	No Change
✔ (vowel stressed)	No Change
✔ (vowel stressed)	✔ (vowel stressed)

TIP

You will need to remember which verbs are stem-changing when you learn new verbs. Dictionaries usually list the type of stem change in parentheses after the verb entry. In the following pattern (e → ie), you will see the verb entender / *to understand* in the format of a typical dictionary entry:

entender (ie) / *to understand*

It is important to remember which verbs change stems because not all verbs follow this pattern. For example, the verb comprender / *to understand* does not have a stem change.

Remember also that some verbs have a "characteristic preposition." In a typical dictionary entry, the verb comenzar / *to begin* would have the following format:

comenzar (ie) (a) / *to begin*

The first parenthetical item means that this verb (ie) changes its stem (e → ie). The second parenthetical item (a) means that if there is a following infinitive, you must use the preposition a. The following example illustrates this point.

Comienzo a estudiar. / *I'm beginning to study.*

Verbs that have the stem changes (o → ue) and (e → i) will also have similar entries. We will discuss these verbs below.

mostrar (ue) / *to show*
servir (i) / *to serve*

Stem-Changing Verbs (e → ie)

Now that we have established where the changes occur, we will examine the three patterns of stem-changing verbs to see how these verbs work. The first type of stem change is e → ie. Remember, these verbs change their stem in all of the forms except for **nosotros** /-as / *we* and **vosotros/-as** / *you* forms. We have highlighted the stem changes with italic type.

Remember that these changes may occur in first conjugation (-ar), second conjugation (-er), and third conjugation (-ir) verbs. The following three verbs illustrate this pattern.

cerrar (ie) / *to close*

Subject Pronoun	Verb Form	Meaning
(yo)	cierr+o	*I close, I am closing, I do close*
(tú)	cierr+as	*you (fam. sg.) close, you are closing, you do close*
(él, ella, Ud.)	cierr+a	*he, she, you (pol. sg.) close(s), he, she, you is/are closing, he, she, you does/do close*
(nosotros/-as)	cerr+amos	*we close, we are closing, we do close*
(vosotros/-as)	cerr+áis	*you (fam. pl.) close, you are closing, you do close*
(ellos/-as, Uds.)	cierr+an	*they, you (pol. pl.) close, they, you are closing, they, you do close*

querer (ie) / *to want*

Subject Pronoun	Verb Form	Meaning
(yo)	quier+o	*I want, I am wanting, I do want*
(tú)	quier+es	*you (fam. sg.) want, you are wanting, you do want*
(él, ella, Ud.)	quier+e	*he, she, you (pol. sg.) want(s), he, she, you is/are wanting, he, she, you does/do want*
(nosotros/-as)	quer+emos	*we want, we are wanting, we do want*
(vosotros/-as)	quer+éis	*you (fam. pl.) want, you are wanting, you do want*
(ellos/-as, Uds.)	quier+en	*they, you (pol. pl.) want, they, you are wanting, they, you do want*

sugerir (ie) / *to suggest*

Subject Pronoun	Verb Form	Meaning
(yo)	sugier+o	*I suggest, I am suggesting, I do suggest*
(tú)	sugier+es	*you (fam. sg.) suggest, you are suggesting, you do suggest*
(él, ella, Ud.)	sugier+e	*he, she, you (pol. sg.) suggest(s), he, she, you is/are suggesting, he, she, you does/do suggest*
(nosotros/-as)	suger+imos	*we suggest, we are suggesting, we do suggest*
(vosotros/-as)	suger+ís	*you (fam. pl.) suggest, you are suggesting, you do suggest*
(ellos/-as, Uds.)	sugier+en	*they, you (pol. pl.) suggest, they, you are suggesting, they, you do suggest*

Common Verbs

Below are some common e → ie stem-changing verbs that will come in handy for basic communication.

advertir (ie)	*to warn*	fregar (ie)	*to scrub, to wash (dishes)*
cerrar (ie)	*to close*	hervir (ie)	*to boil*
comenzar (ie) (a)	*to begin*	mentir (ie)	*to lie*
confesar (ie)	*to confess*	negar (ie)	*to deny*
consentir (ie)	*to consent*	pensar (ie) (en)	*to think (about)*
convertir (ie)	*to convert*	perder (ie)	*to lose*
defender (ie)	*to defend*	preferir (ie)	*to prefer*
empezar (ie) (a)	*to begin*	querer (ie)	*to want, to wish, to love*
encender (ie)	*to light, to turn on*	sentir (ie)	*to feel, to regret*
entender (ie)	*to understand*	sugerir (ie)	*to suggest*

TIP

Remember that it is always the <u>last</u> vowel in the stem (what is left after you remove the infinitive marker [-ar, -er, -ir]) that has a vowel change. The following examples illustrate this point. We have indicated the vowel that changes with an underline and italic type.

rec*o*rdar / to remember → rec*o*rd-
ent*e*nder / to understand → ent*e*nd-
comp*e*tir / to compete → comp*e*t-

NOTE

The verb pensar + an infinitive has the meaning of *"to plan"* or *"to intend."*

Pienso estudiar. / *I plan to study / I intend to study.*

GRAMMAR NOTE

Remember that when there are two verbs in a row, it is the first one that is conjugated ,whereas the second one is usually an infinitive, as the examples below illustrate.

Quiero estudiar mucho. / *I want to study a lot.*
Prefiero beber café. / *I prefer to drink coffee.*

When a verb has a characteristic preposition, it goes before the infinitive:

Empiezo a fregar los platos. / *I begin to clean the plates.*

EXERCISE Set 2-1

A. Supply the missing indicative forms of the verb **empezar (ie)**, giving the English equivalent.

EXAMPLE: *él* _____   =   _____

             él empieza   =   *he begins, he is beginning, he does begin*

1. (yo) _____   =   _____

2. (tú) _____   =   _____

3. (nosotros) _____ =   _____

4. (ellos) _____   =   _____

5. (vosotros) _____ =   _____

6. (Ud.) _____   =   _____

Now, supply the missing present indicative forms of the verb **entender (ie)**, giving the English equivalent.

1. (yo) _____   =   _____

2. (Raquel y yo) _____ =   _____

3. (Uds.) _____   =   _____

4. (ellos) _____   =   _____

5. (vosotros) _____   =   _____

6. (tú) _____   =   _____

Now, supply the missing present indicative forms of the verb **mentir (ie)**, giving the English equivalent.

1. (yo) _____   =   _____

2. (tú) _____   =   _____

3. (nosotros) _____ =   _____

4. (ellos) _____   =   _____

5. (vosotros) _____ =   _____

6. (Ud.) _____   =   _____

B. How do you say the following sentences in Spanish?

1. I am beginning to read the poetry of *Alfonsina Storni*[1].

   _____

2. Do you (fam. sg.) want to read the novels of *Eduardo Mallea*[2].

   _____

3. We turn on the light every night.

   _____

4. Do you (pol. sg.) understand the question?

   _____

5. Do you (fam. sg.) regret not reading *El túnel*[3] by (**de**) *Ernesto Sábato*[4].

   _____

6. We lose our keys a lot.

   _____

7. She confesses that (**que**) she watches many soap operas.

   _____

8. We want to read *Mafalda*[5].

   _____

9. They prefer to go to *Calle Florida*[6] in order to buy clothes.

   _____

10. He suggests the book by (**de**) *Ana María Shua*[7].

    _____

11. You (fam. sg.) do not lie.

    _____

[1]Argentinean poet, 1892–1938; [2]Argentinean novelist, 1903–1982; [3]Famous Argentinean novel, 1948; [4]Author of *El túnel*, 1911– ;
[5]Argentinean cartoon about a mischievous little girl by Quino, pseudonym of Joaquín Salvador Lavado, 1932– ;
[6]Traditional shopping area in Buenos Aires; [7]Argentinean novelist, 1951– .

Stem-Changing Verbs (o → ue)

The second type of stem change is o → ue. Remember that these verbs change their stem in all of the forms except for nosotros/nosotras and vosotros/vosotras. These changes may occur in first conjugation (-ar), second conjugation (-er), and third conjugation (-ir) verbs. The following verbs illustrate this. We have highlighted the stem changes with italic type.

mostrar (ue) / *to show*

Subject Pronoun	Verb Form	Meaning
(yo)	m*ue*str+o	*I show, I am showing, I do show*
(tú)	m*ue*str+as	*you (fam. sg.) show, you are showing, you do show*
(él, ella, Ud.)	m*ue*str+a	*he, she, you (pol. sg.) show(s), he, she, you is/are showing, he, she, you does/do show*
(nosotros/-as)	mostr+amos	*we show, we are showing, we do show*
(vosotros/-as)	mostr+áis	*you (fam. pl.) show, you are showing, you do show*
(ellos/-as, Uds.)	m*ue*str+an	*they, you (pol. pl.) show, they, you are showing, they, you do show*

volver (ue) (a) / *to return*

Subject Pronoun	Verb Form	Meaning
(yo)	v*ue*lv+o	*I return, I am returning, I do return*
(tú)	v*ue*lv+es	*you (fam. sg.) return, you are returning, you do return*
(él, ella, Ud.)	v*ue*lv+e	*he, she, you (pol. sg.) return(s), he, she, you is/are returning, he, she, you does/do return*
(nosotros/-as)	volv+emos	*we return, we are returning, we do return*
(vosotros/-as)	volv+éis	*you (fam. pl.) return, you are returning, you do return*
(ellos/-as, Uds.)	v*ue*lv+en	*they, you (pol. pl.) return, they, you are returning, they, you do return*

dormir (ue) / *to sleep*

Subject Pronoun	Verb Form	Meaning
(yo)	d*ue*rm+o	*I sleep, I am sleeping, I do sleep*
(tú)	d*ue*rm+es	*you (fam. sg.) sleep, you are sleeping, you do sleep*
(él, ella, Ud.)	d*ue*rm+e	*he, she, you (pol. sg.) sleep(s), he, she, you is/are sleeping, he, she, you does/do sleep*
(nosotros/-as)	dorm+imos	*we sleep, we are sleeping, we do sleep*
(vosotros/-as)	dorm+ís	*you (fam. pl.) sleep, you are sleeping, you do sleep*
(ellos/-as, Uds.)	d*ue*rm+en	*they, you (pol. pl.) sleep, they, you are sleeping, they, you do sleep*

Common Verbs

Below are some common o → ue stem-changing verbs that will come in handy for basic communication.

almorzar (ue)	*to eat lunch*	mover (ue)	*to move*
aprobar (ue)	*to approve*	poder (ue)	*can, be able*
colgar (ue)	*to hang (up)*	probar (ue)	*to prove, to taste, to test*
contar (ue) (con)	*to count (on)*	recordar (ue)	*to remember*
costar (ue)	*to cost*	resolver (ue)	*to solve*
devolver (ue)	*to return (something)*	rogar (ue)	*to request, to beg*
dormir (ue)	*to sleep*	soler (ue)	*to be in the habit of*
encontrar (ue)	*to find*	soñar (ue) (con)	*to dream (of)*
envolver (ue)	*to wrap (up)*	sonar (ue)	*to ring, to sound*
morder (ue)	*to bite*	tostar (ue)	*to toast*
morir (ue)	*to die*	volar (ue)	*to fly*
mostrar (ue)	*to show*	volver (ue) (a)	*to return*

NOTE

The verb volver + a + an infinitive means *to … again*.

Vuelvo a estudiar. / *I study again.*

Stem-Changing Verbs (u → ue)

There is a single Spanish verb that has the change u → ue. Because it is a commonly used verb jugar (ue) (a) / *to play (a game)*, it is important to learn it. We have indicated the changes with italic type.

jugar (ue) (a) / *to play (a game)*

Subject Pronoun	Verb Form	Meaning
(yo)	*jueg*+o	*I play, I am playing, I do play*
(tú)	*jueg*+as	*you (fam. sg.) play, you are playing, you do play*
(él, ella, Ud.)	*jueg*+a	*he, she, you (pol. pl.) play(s), he, she, you is/are playing, he, she, you does/do play*
(nosotros/-as)	*jug*+amos	*we play, we are playing, we do play*
(vosotros/-as)	*jug*+áis	*you (fam. pl.) play, you are playing, you do play*
(ellos/-as, Uds.)	*jueg*+an	*they, you (pol. pl.) play, they, you are playing, they, you do play*

Remember that jugar (ue) (a) means *to play a game* and tocar means *to play a musical instrument* or *to touch*. When you specify the game that you play, the name of the game is normally preceded by al, a los, or a las. The following are some common games that you may play.

jugar al ajedrez	*to play chess*	jugar al golf	*to play golf*
jugar al baloncesto	*to play basketball*	jugar al hockey	*to play hockey*
jugar al béisbol	*to play baseball*	jugar a un juego	*to play a game*
jugar al billar	*to play pool*	jugar a los naipes	*to play cards*
jugar a las damas	*to play checkers*	jugar al tenis	*to play tennis*
jugar al fútbol	*to play soccer*		
jugar al fútbol americano	*to play football*		

A. Supply the missing indicative forms of the verb **encontrar (ue)**, giving the English equivalent.

EXAMPLE: *él* _____   =   _____

                    él encuentra =   *he finds, he is finding, he does find*

1. (yo) _____   =   _____

2. (tú) _____   =   _____

3. (nosotras) _____ =   _____

4. (ellos) _____   =   _____

5. (Uds.) _____   =   _____

6. (Ud.) _____   =   _____

   Now, supply the missing present indicative forms of the verb **devolver (ue)**, giving the English equivalent.

1. (yo) _____   =   _____

2. (Javier y yo) _____ =   _____

3. (ellas) _____   =   _____

4. (Uds.) _____   =   _____

5. (vosotros) _____   =   _____

6. (tú) _____   =   _____

   Now, supply the missing present indicative forms of the verb **morir (ue)**, giving the English equivalent.

1. (yo) _____   =   _____

2. (tú) _____   =   _____

3. (nosotros) _____ =   _____

4. (ellos) _____   =   _____

5. (vosotros) _____   =   _____

6. (Ud.) _____   =   _____

B. How do you say the following sentences in Spanish?

1. A T-bone steak costs a lot at *La Cabaña*[1].

_____

2. You (pol. pl.) can read *El puente*[2] by (**de**) *Carlos Gorostiza*[3].

_____

3. She finds the car keys in the sofa.

_____

4. We are flying to *Ushuaia*[4] tomorrow.

_____

5. You (fam. sg.) dream of winning the lottery.

_____

6. They sleep late if they can.

_____

7. I hang up the phone if they are selling something.

_____

8. We are returning to *Mendoza*[5] tomorrow on *Aerolíneas Argentinas*[6].

_____

9. He remembers the essay by (**de**) *Domingo Faustino Sarmiento*[7].

_____

10. The telephone rings constantly.

_____

[1]Famous restaurant in Buenos Aires that serves world-famous Argentinean beef; [2]Drama by Carlos Gorostiza, 1963; [3]Renowned Argentinean playwright, 1920– ; [4]Southernmost town of Argentina; [5]City south of Buenos Aires; [6]Argentina's national airline; [7]Argentinean essayist, 1811–1888.

Stem-Changing Verbs (e → i)

The third type of stem change is e → i. Remember that these verbs change their stem in all of the forms except for nosotros/-as and vosotros/-as. It is important to remember that the change e → i occurs only with third conjugation (-ir) verbs. We have highlighted the stem changes with italic type.

servir (i) / *to serve*

Subject Pronoun	Verb Form	Meaning
(yo)	sirv+o	*I serve, I am serving, I do serve*
(tú)	sirv+es	*you (fam. sg.) serve, you are serving, you do serve*
(él, ella, Ud.)	sirv+e	*he, she, you (pol. sg.) serve(s), he, she, you is/are serving, he, she, you does/do serve*
(nosotros/-as)	serv+imos	*we serve, we are serving, we do serve*
(vosotros/-as)	serv+ís	*you (fam. pl.) serve, you are serving, you do serve*
(ellos/-as, Uds.)	sirv+en	*they, you (pol. pl.) serve, they, you are serving, they, you do serve*

Note that some e → i verbs have a spelling change (<u>not a sound change</u>) in the stem. The changes depend upon whether the following vowel is e or i (gu spelling) or an o (g spelling). Review the introductory pronunciation and spelling guide.

seguir (i) / *to follow*

Subject Pronoun	Verb Form	Meaning
(yo)	sig+o	*I follow, I am following, I do follow*
(tú)	sigu+es	*you (fam. sg.) follow, you are following, you do follow*
(él, ella, Ud.)	sigu+e	*he, she, you (pol. sg.) follow(s), he, she, you is/are following, he, she, you does/do follow*
(nosotros/-as)	segu+imos	*we follow, we are following, we do follow*
(vosotros/-as)	segu+ís	*you (fam. pl.) follow, you are following, you do follow*
(ellos/-as, Uds.)	sigu+en	*they, you (pol. pl.) follow, they, you are following, they, you do follow*

Note that some e → i stem-changing verbs have a written accent. This is to indicate that there is no diphthong. Reír / *to laugh* and freír / *to fry* are two such verbs. We have indicated the changes with italic type.

reír / *to laugh*

Subject Pronoun	Verb Form	Meaning
(yo)	rí+o	*I laugh, I am laughing, I do laugh*
(tú)	rí+es	*you (fam. sg.) laugh, you are laughing, you do laugh*
(él, ella, Ud.)	rí+e	*he, she, you (pol. sg.) laugh(s), he, she, you is/are laughing, he, she, you does/do laugh*
(nosotros/-as)	re+ímos	*we laugh, we are laughing, we do laugh*
(vosotros/-as)	re+ís	*you (fam. pl.) laugh, you are laughing, you do laugh*
(ellos/-as, Uds.)	rí+en	*they, you (pol. pl.) laugh, they, you are laughing, they, you do laugh*

Common Verbs

Below are some common e → i stem-changing verbs that will come in handy for basic communication.

competir (i)	*to compete*	medir (i)	*to measure*
conseguir (i)	*to obtain, to get*	pedir (i)	*to ask for, to request, to order*
corregir (i)	*to correct*	reír (i)	*to laugh*
despedir (i)	*to fire*	repetir (i)	*to repeat*
elegir (i)	*to elect*	seguir (i)	*to follow*
freír (i)	*to fry*	servir (i)	*to serve*
impedir (i)	*to prevent, to hinder*		

SPELLING TIP

Verbs that end in -ger and -gir have a first person singular form (yo) as follows:

proteger / *to protect* → protejo / *I protect*
elegir / *to elect* → elijo / *I elect*

There will be more about these spelling changes in Chapter 4.

EXERCISE Set 2-3

A. Supply the missing indicative forms of the verb **competir (i)**, giving the English equivalent.

EXAMPLE: *él* _____ = _____

él compite = *he competes, he is competing, he does compete*

1. (yo) _____ = _____

2. (tú) _____ = _____

3. (nosotras) _____ = _____

4. (ellos) _____ = _____

5. (Uds.) _____ = _____

6. (Ud.) _____ = _____

Now, supply the missing present indicative forms of the verb **medir (i)**, giving the English equivalent.

1. (yo) _____ = _____

2. (ellos) _____ = _____

3. (Lidia y yo) _____ = _____

4. (Uds.) _____ = _____

5. (nosotros) _____ = _____

6. (tú) _____ = _____

Now, supply the missing present indicative forms of the verb **seguir (i)**, giving the English equivalent.

1. (yo) _____ = _____

2. (Ud.) _____ = _____

3. (nosotros) _____ = _____

4. (ellos) _____   =   _____

5. (vosotros) _____   =   _____

6. (Joaquín y yo) _____   =   _____

B. How do you say the following sentences in Spanish?

1. They are competing for the prize.

   _____

2. The teachers need to correct the exams today.

   _____

3. I always follow the rules.

   _____

4. I ask for *churrasco*[1] in *Dora*[2].

   _____

5. When you (fam. sg.) repeat the words aloud, you remember.

   _____

6. She measures the ingredients carefully.

   _____

7. They serve excellent wine in the restaurant.

   _____

8. He fires the employees.

   _____

9. You (pol. pl.) laugh a lot.

   _____

10. They always fry the eggs here.

   _____

[1]Thick grilled steak; [2]Well-known restaurant in downtown Buenos Aires.

EXERCISE Set 2-4

A. Missing from each of the following sentences is the verb. The missing verbs are given to you in their infinitive forms. Put each verb, in its correct form, in each sentence according to the sense.

Verbs: cerrar, competir, entender, fregar, preferir, servir, soñar (con), volar, volver.

1. (Yo) _____ estudiar en casa.

2. (Uds.) _____ la pregunta.

3. (Concepción y yo) no _____ la puerta.

4. En este momento, (él) _____ los platos.

5. ¿Con qué _____ (tú)?

6. (Yo) _____ a casa tarde.

7. (Nosotros) _____ cuando jugamos al fútbol.

8. (Ella) _____ a Mendoza en *Aerolíneas Argentinas*.

9. (Ellos) _____ una buena *parrillada*[1].

[1]A mixed grill with roast meat and sausages.

B. Which of the following two options, **a** or **b**, is the correct one? You should say the question out loud and provide the answer out loud. This will help you to remember the words.

1. ¿Pierdes tus llaves mucho?

   a. Nunca pierdo mis llaves.
   b. Siempre perdemos nuestras llaves.

2. ¿Encienden Uds. las luces cuando duermen?

   a. Sí, enciendo las luces cuando duermo.
   b. Sí, encendemos las luces cuando dormimos.

3. ¿Cierras la puerta cuando estudias?

   a. Sí, cierro la puerto cuando estudio.
   b. Sí, cerramos la puerta cuando estudiamos.

4. ¿Quieren Uds. partir para Buenos Aires ahora?

   a. No, no quiero partir.
   b. No, no queremos partir.

5. ¿Puede Marisol empezar a cocinar ahora?

   a. Sí, puedes comenzar.
   b. Sí, puede comenzar.

6. ¿Sirven bife de costilla (T-bone) aquí?

    a. No sirve.
    b. Sí, sirven bife de costilla excelente.

7. ¿Piden Uds. un buen vino cuando comen en un restaurante?

    a. Siempre pedimos un buen vino.
    b. Siempre piden un buen vino.

8. ¿Sigues la misma rutina todos los días?

    a. No, seguimos la misma rutina.
    b. Sí, siempre sigo la misma rutina.

9. ¿Prefieres estudiar o jugar al béisbol?

    a. Preferimos jugar al béisbol.
    b. Prefiero estudiar.

C. Change the following sentences from the plural to the singular. Pronounce the original sentence and then say the new sentence aloud. This will help you to remember the words and you will gain confidence by verbalizing them.

1. Volvemos a Buenos Aires. _____

2. Almorzamos en *Güerrín*[1]. _____

3. Cerramos las puertas. _____

4. Seguimos la misma ruta. _____

5. Empezamos a estudiar. _____

[1]Well-known and inexpensive restaurant in Buenos Aires.

GRAMMAR NOTE

Adverbs of manner end in -mente corresponding (in general) to the English -*ly*. To construct such an adverb, change the -o of an adjective to -a and then add on -mente. For all other adjectives, you just add -mente as the following examples illustrate.

    perfecto → perfecta + mente = perfectamente / *perfectly*
    fácil → fácil + mente = fácilmente / *easily*
    prudente → prudente + mente = prudentemente / *prudently*

    Remember: If there is a written accent on the adjective, it also remains on the adverb.

Crossword Puzzle 2

Fill in the blanks. All of the clues, both vertical and horizontal, are English verbal expressions that correspond to a single verb in Spanish.

Horizontales
2. We follow
4. We play
7. They lie
8. We fly

Verticales
1. They are closing
3. I am showing
5. You (fam. sg.) serve
6. They are eating

3

The Present Indicative of *Ser, Estar, Hay, Tener, Hacer, Saber,* and *Conocer*

Conjugation of *Ser*

The verb ser / *to be* is an irregular verb. Unlike the verbs that you have learned to conjugate in the first chapter, you cannot predict its forms on the basis of the infinitive. You will simply have to memorize them.

ser / *to be*

Subject Pronoun	Verb Form	Meaning
(yo)	soy	*I am*
(tú)	eres	*you (fam. sg.) are*
(él, ella, Ud.)	es	*he, she, you (pol. sg.) is/are*
(nosotros/-as)	somos	*we are*
(vosotros/-as)	sois	*you (fam. pl.) are*
(ellos/-as, Uds.)	son	*they, you (pol. pl.) are*

Uses of Ser

The verb ser / *to be* has a variety of uses, which we illustrate here.

Ser is used in the following situations	Examples
1. To indicate nationality.	Eperanza es cubana. / *Esperanza is Cuban.*
2. To indicate profession or vocation.	Carlos es abogado. / *Carlos is a lawyer.*
3. To indicate place of origin (with de).	Pilar es de Uruguay. / *Pilar is from Uruguay.*
4. To indicate the material from which something is made (with de).	¿De qué es la casa? / *What is the house made of?* La casa es de ladrillo. / *The house is made of brick.*
5. To indicate the time.	Es la una. / *It's one o'clock.* Son las nueve. / *It's nine o'clock.*
6. To indicate the date.	Es el dos de noviembre. / *It's November 2nd.*
7. To indicate possession (with de).	¿De quién es el libro? / *Whose book is it?* El libro es de Antonio. / *The book is Antonio's.* (Remember: There is no *'s* in Spanish.)
8. To identify basic characteristics of people or things.	Berta es simpática. / *Berta is nice.*
9. To indicate a generalization or an impersonal statement.	Es importante estudiar. / *It's important to study.*
10. To indicate the time or location of an event.	El concierto es a las nueve. / *The concert takes place at nine.*

Adjectives of Nationality

Item 3 above points out that ser / *to be* is used to indicate nationality. The following adjectives of nationality will be used throughout this book, so we are introducing them here.

americano	*American*	guatemalteco	*Guatemalan*
argentino	*Argentinean*	hondureño	*Honduran*
boliviano	*Bolivian*	mexicano	*Mexican*
chileno	*Chilean*	nicaragüense	*Nicaraguan*
colombiano	*Colombian*	panameño	*Panamanian*
costarricense	*Costa Rican*	paraguayo	*Paraguayan*
cubano	*Cuban*	peruano	*Peruvian*
dominicano	*Dominican*	puertorriqueño	*Puerto Rican*
ecuatoriano	*Ecuadorean*	salvadoreño	*Salvadoran*
español	*Spanish*	uruguayo	*Uruguayan*
estadounidense	*person from the U.S.*	venezolano	*Venezuelan*

GRAMMAR NOTE

Adjectives of nationality are not capitalized in Spanish (as they are in English). See the following example:

Elena es <u>u</u>ruguaya. / *Elena is <u>U</u>ruguayan.*

GRAMMAR NOTE

There are two types of adjectives in Spanish. The first type is called limiting (definite and indefinite articles, possessive adjectives "my," "your," "his," and so forth, and demonstrative adjectives "this" and "that"; see below and Chapter 6). These go before the noun they modify as illustrated below. This is similar to English usage.

el hombre / *the man*
una mujer / *a woman*
mi esposa / *my wife*
este libro / *this book*

The other type of adjective, and the one that is of interest here, is the descriptive adjective. A descriptive adjective provides information about the noun such as size, shape, color, and nationality, to name but a few examples. Normally, these adjectives go after the noun to which they refer. This is a different pattern from English, where the descriptive adjective goes before the noun. We will use adjectives of nationality to show this pattern. We have underlined these adjectives to highlight their position relative to the noun they modify.

el hombre <u>español</u> / *the <u>Spanish</u> man*
la mujer <u>chilena</u> / *the <u>Chilean</u> woman*
los hombres <u>cubanos</u> / *the <u>Cuban</u> men*
las mujeres <u>paraguayas</u> / *the <u>Paraguayan</u> women*

Telling Time

We saw that ser / *to be* is used to tell time. We will now discuss this in more detail.

To ask what time it is, you say:

¿Qué hora es? / *What time is it?*

You use the verb form es for one o'clock.

Es la una. / *It is one o'clock.*
Es la una y cuarto. / *It's a quarter past one.*

For all other hours, you use the verb son.

Son las tres. / *It is three o'clock.*

To indicate time up to the half-hour, you <u>add</u> the minutes up to the half-hour as illustrated below.

Es la una y quince. / *It's one fifteen.*
Es la una y cuarto. / *It's one fifteen.*
Son las tres y veinte. / *It's three twenty.*
Son once y treinta. / *It's eleven thirty.*
Son las once y media. / *It's eleven thirty.*

To indicate the time after the half-hour, you <u>subtract</u> the minutes from the following hour as shown below.

Son las tres menos quince. / *It's two forty-five. (It's a quarter to three.)*
Son las nueve menos cuarto. / *It's eight forty-five. (It's a quarter to nine.)*
Es la una menos diez. / *It's twelve fifty (It's ten to one.)*

Another common time expression is the following:

Son las cinco en punto. / *It's five o'clock on the dot.*

Remember that in countries outside the United States there is a twenty-four-hour clock, especially for public transportation and business hours as illustrated below.

Es la una. / *It's one* A.M.
Son las trece. / *It's one* P.M.

In conversation, the twenty-four-hour clock is not used. In order to specify A.M. or P.M., the following expressions are used:

Es la una <u>de la tarde.</u> / *It's one* P.M. *(in the afternoon).*
Son las siete <u>de la mañana.</u> / *It's seven* A.M. *(in the morning).*
Son las diez <u>de la noche.</u> / *It's ten* P.M. *(in the evening).*

To express midnight and noon, you may say the following:

Es la medianoche. / *It's midnight.*
Es el mediodía. / *It's noon.*

Cardinal Numbers

You need to know the following cardinal numbers to tell time.

Cardinal Numbers 1-31

1	uno	17	diecisiete
2	dos	18	dieciocho
3	tres	19	diecinueve
4	cuatro	20	veinte
5	cinco	21	veintiuno
6	seis	22	veintidós
7	siete	23	veintitrés
8	ocho	24	veinticuatro
9	nueve	25	veinticinco
10	diez	26	veintiséis
11	once	27	veintisiete
12	doce	28	veintiocho
13	trece	29	veintinueve
14	catorce	30	treinta
15	quince	31	treinta y uno
16	dieciséis		

Descriptive Adjectives with Ser

Previously, we noted that ser / *to be* is used to indicate characteristics and qualities of a person or object. The following is a selected list of common descriptive adjectives used with ser.

Common Descriptive Adjectives Used with Ser

COLORS

amarillo	*yellow*	marrón	*brown*
anaranjado	*orange*	negro	*black*
azul	*blue*	rojo	*red*
blanco	*white*	rosado	*pink*
gris	*gray*	verde	*green*

APPEARANCE

alto	*tall*	hermoso	*beautiful*
atractivo	*attractive*	joven	*young*
bajo	*short*	lindo	*pretty*
delgado	*slender*	moreno	*brunette*
elegante	*elegant*	pelirrojo	*red-haired*
feo	*ugly*	rubio	*blond*
gordo	*fat*	viejo	*old*

PERSONALITY

activo	*active*	mentiroso	*lying*
antipático	*unpleasant*	perezoso	*lazy*
bueno	*good*	responsable	*responsible*
cómico	*funny*	serio	*serious*
egoísta	*selfish*	simpático	*nice*
generoso	*generous*	sincero	*sincere*
inteligente	*intelligent*	tonto	*foolish*
irresponsable	*irresponsible*	trabajador	*hardworking*
malo	*bad, evil*		

Possessive Adjectives

Possessive adjectives allow you to express possession. They go <u>before</u> the noun they modify just as in English. They all agree in <u>number</u> (singular, plural). Nuestro and vuestro also agree in <u>gender</u> (masculine, feminine).

Singular		Plural	
1st person	mi / *my*	1st person	nuestro / *our*
2nd person	tu / *your* (fam. sg.)	2nd person	vuestro / *your* (fam. pl.)
3rd person	su / *his, her, your* (pol. sg.)	3rd person	su / *their, your* (pol. pl.)

TIP

Remember: <u>Possessive adjectives agree with the item possessed and **NOT** the possessor.</u> Possessive adjectives always agree in number (singular, plural). Only nuestro/-a / *our* and vuestro/-a / *your* (fam. pl.) agree in gender also. The following selected examples illustrate this point.

> mi libro / *my book*
> mis libros / *my books*
> nuestra casa / *our house*
> nuestras casas / *our houses*

Note that the subject pronoun tú / *you* (fam. sg.) has a written accent but the possessive adjective tu / *your* (fam. sg.) does not.

GRAMMAR NOTE

Note that the preposition de / *of* and the masculine singular definite article el / *the* contract to the single form del / *of the* in Spanish, as shown below.

> ¿<u>De</u> quién es <u>el</u> libro? / *Whose book is it?*
> El libro es <u>del</u> hombre. / *It's the man's book.*

EXERCISE Set 3-1

A. Supply the missing forms of the Spanish verb **ser**, and then give the English equivalent.

EXAMPLE: *él* ____   =   _____

                    él es   =   *he is*

1. (yo) _____   =   _____

2. (tú) _____   =   _____

3. (nosotros) _____   =   _____

4. (ellos) _____   =   _____

5. (vosotros) _____   =   _____

6. (Ud.) _____   =   _____

B. Give the indicated times.

EXAMPLE: 2:45 A.M.
                    Son las tres menos cuarto de la mañana.
                    2:45 P.M.
                    Son las tres menos quince de la tarde.

¿Qué hora es?

1. 8:20 P.M.   _____

2. 7:30 A.M.   _____

3. 4:45 P.M.   _____

4. 10:18 A.M.   _____

5. 11:35 P.M.   _____

6. 9:00 A.M. sharp   _____

7. 2:10 P.M.   _____

8. 4:30 A.M.   _____

C. How do you say the following sentences in Spanish? You do not have to translate material in parentheses; this information tells you what verb form to use, or it provides cultural information.

1. Where are you (fam. sg.) from?

   _____

2. My wife is from Uruguay, but I am from Spain.

   _____

3. They are Uruguayan and they are nice.

   _____

4. The Spanish woman is blond.

   _____

5. What is the red pen made of? It's plastic.

   _____

6. Whose watch is it? It's Pilar's. (Remember: No 's in Spanish!)

   _____

7. It is important to study Spanish today.

   _____

8. Silvia is red-haired and tall.

   _____

9. My home is made of wood.

   _____

10. The movie is at 8 P.M.

    _____

Conjugation of *Estar*

The verb estar / *to be* is an irregular verb. Unlike the verbs that you have learned to conjugate in the first chapter, you cannot predict its forms on the basis of the infinitive. You will simply have to memorize them. Note that there are several forms (tú, él, ella, Ud., vosotros/vosotras, and ellos/-as, Uds.) that have a written accent.

estar / *to be*

Subject Pronoun	Verb Form	Meaning
(yo)	estoy	*I am*
(tú)	estás	*you (fam. sg.) are*
(él, ella, Ud.)	está	*he, she, you (pol. pl.) is/are*
(nosotros/-as)	estamos	*we are*
(vosotros/-as)	estáis	*you (fam. pl.) are*
(ellos/-as, Uds.)	están	*they, you (pol. pl.) are*

Uses of Estar

The verb estar / *to be* has a variety of uses, which we illustrate here.

Estar is used in the following situations	Examples
1. To indicate location.	Carmen está en casa. / *Carmen is at home.*
2. To indicate health.	Roberto está enfermo. / *Robert is sick.*
3. To indicate certain conditions with some adjectives.	Mónica está preocupada. / *Mónica is worried.*
4. Estar is used in certain idiomatic expressions.	Jorge está para salir. / *Jorge is about to leave.*
5. Estar is used with present participles (gerunds) to form the present progressive tense (see Chapter 6).	Alicia está cantando. / *Alicia is singing (at this very moment).*

Descriptive Adjectives with Estar

Items 2 and 3 indicate that estar / *to be* is used with certain adjectives to indicate health and well-being. The following is a selected list of common descriptive adjectives used with estar.

HEALTH AND WELL-BEING

enfermo	*sick*	vivo	*alive*
cansado	*tired*	muerto	*dead*

OTHER ADJECTIVES WITH *ESTAR*

alegre	*happy*	enojado	*angry*
ausente	*absent*	listo para	*ready to*
casado (con)	*married*	lleno	*full*
cubierto (de)	*covered with*	sentado	*sitting*
divorciado	*divorced*	vestido (de)	*dressed (in)*

IDIOMS WITH *ESTAR*

estar de acuerdo (con)	*to be in agreement*	estar de pie	*to be standing*
estar de buen humor	*to be in a good mood*	estar seguro (de)	*to be sure (of)*
estar de mal humor	*to be in a bad mood*	estar de vacaciones	*to be on vacation*
estar de guardia	*to be on call*		

Uses of Ser *and* Estar

Thus far, we have looked at the specific uses of ser / *to be* and estar / *to be* in isolation. We will now see that these two verbs may be used with the same adjectives. When this happens, there is a change of meaning. The following is a list of some common adjectives with changing meanings when they are used with either ser or estar.

Adjective	With Ser	With Estar
aburrido/-a	*boring*	*bored*
bueno/-a	*good (by nature)*	*in good health*
callado/-a	*quiet*	*silent*
cansado/-a	*tiring*	*tired*
completo/-a	*exhaustive*	*not lacking anything*
despierto/-a	*alert*	*awake*
divertido/-a	*entertaining*	*amused*
listo/-a	*clever, witty*	*ready*
malo/-a	*bad, evil*	*sick*
nuevo/-a	*brand-new*	*like new*
seguro/-a	*safe (reliable), sure to happen*	*certain, sure*
verde	*green*	*ripe*
vivo/-a	*lively, bright (in color)*	*alive*

EXERCISE Set 3-2

A. Supply the missing forms of the Spanish verb estar, and then give the English equivalent.

EXAMPLE: *él* ____   =   _____

  él está   =   *he is*

1. (tú) _____   =   _____

2. (yo) _____   =   _____

3. (nosotras) _____   =   _____

4. (ellas) _____   =   _____

5. (vosotros) _____   =   _____

6. (Uds.) _____   =   _____

B. How do you say the following sentences in Spanish?

1. I am at home now, because I am sick.

   _____

2. My husband is about to leave for Montevideo.

   _____

3. She is tired because she works a lot.

   _____

4. My sister is married to a nice man.

   _____

5. I agree with Pablo.

   _____

6. We are on vacation in Uruguay now.

   _____

7. Blanca, you (fam. sg.) are tired because you are standing so much.

   _____

8. When I study a lot, I am in a good mood because I am learning.

   _____

9. I am bored because I am not on vacation.

   _____

10. This color is very bright.

    _____

The Verb *Hay*

Uses of Hay

Hay has only one form in the present tense. The verb **hay** means *there is* or *there are*. Its meaning depends on the noun that follows. It is used to call attention to the presence or existence of someone or something. The following examples illustrate this point.

> Hay muchas personas aquí. / *There are many persons here.*
> Hay mucho dinero en el banco. / *There is a lot of money in the bank.*

There is an idiomatic expression that is used with the verb **hay: hay que**. It means *one must* or *it is necessary to* and it is followed by an infinitive. The following examples illustrate this point.

> Hay que estudiar. / *One must study.*
> Hay que dormir. / *It is necessary to sleep.*

EXERCISE Set 3-3

A. How do you say the following sentences in Spanish?

1. There are six books here.

   _____

2. There is a Uruguayan woman in the class.

   _____

3. One must be here at 8:00 A.M.

   _____

4. It is necessary to go to Montevideo.

   _____

5. There are many students in class.

   _____

Conjugation of *Tener*

The verb **tener** / *to have* is an irregular verb. **Tener** is a stem-changing verb. There is one exception, however. The first person singular (yo) has an irregularity. Otherwise, it follows the usual conjugation format for a stem-changing verb (e → ie) in the present indicative tense. All of the endings are regular.

tener / *to have*

Subject Pronoun	Verb Form	Meaning
(yo)	<u>teng</u>+o	*I have, I do have*
(tú)	<u>tien</u>+es	*you (fam. sg.) have, you do have*
(él, ella, Ud.)	<u>tien</u>+e	*he, she, you (pol. sg.) has/have, he, she, you does/do have*
(nosotros/-as)	<u>ten</u>+emos	*we have, we do have*
(vosotros/-as)	<u>ten</u>+éis	*you (fam. pl.) have, you are having*
(ellos/-as, Uds.)	<u>tien</u>+en	*they, you (pol. pl.) do have; they, you do have*

Tener has the basic meaning of *to have* or *to possess*. **Tener** also appears in many idiomatic expressions, many of which relate to bodily experiences such as experiencing hunger, thirst, cold, heat, and so forth. It should be noted that if you use the adverb *very*, you have to use the adjective **mucho** / *much* in Spanish. Remember that in English these expressions use the verb *to be*, whereas in Spanish you must use *to have*.

IDIOMATIC EXPRESSIONS WITH *TENER*

tener (mucha) hambre	*to be (very) hungry*	tener ganas (de)	*to feel like*
tener (mucha) sed	*to be (very) thirsty*	tener (mucho) sueño	*to be (very) sleepy*
tener (mucho) frío	*to be (very) cold*	tener razón	*to be right*
tener (mucho) calor	*to be (very) warm*	no tener razón	*to be wrong*
tener (mucho) miedo		tener vergüenza (de)	*to be ashamed (of)*
(de)	*to be (very) afraid (of)*	tener … años	*to be … years old*
tener (mucha) suerte	*to be (very) lucky*	tener que (+ infinitive)	*to have to*
tener (mucha) prisa	*to be (very much) in a hurry*		

CARDINAL NUMBERS

40	cuarenta	300	trescientos
50	cincuenta	400	cuatrocientos
60	sesenta	500	quinientos
70	setenta	600	seiscientos
80	ochenta	700	setecientos
90	noventa	800	ochocientos
100	cien, ciento	900	novecientos
200	doscientos	1,000	mil

EXERCISE Set 3-4

A. Supply the missing forms of the Spanish verb tener, and then give the English equivalent.

EXAMPLE: *él* ____   =   _____

         él tiene • =   *he has, he does have*

1. (ella) _____   =   _____

2. (yo) _____   =   _____

3. (tú) _____   =   _____

4. (ellas) _____   =   _____

5. (Ud.) _____   =   _____

6. (Uds.) _____   =   _____

B. How do you say the following sentences in Spanish? You do not have to translate material in parentheses; this information tells you what verb form to use, or it provides cultural information.

1. I feel like going to the (al) *Museo del Gaucho y de la Moneda*[1].

_____

2. When I am in the casino, I am very lucky.

_____

3. He is 50 years old.

_____

4. She is ashamed of her actions.

_____

5. You (pol. pl.) have to eat at *La Silenciosa*[2].

_____

6. I am very thirsty today and I want to drink water.

_____

7. When I am very hungry, I eat sausages.

_____

8. I am afraid of spiders.

_____

9. I am always in a big hurry when I have to work.

_____

10. She is very sleepy and she needs to sleep.

_____

[1]Excellent museum of Uruguayan _gaucho_ culture and currency in Montevideo; [2]Excellent restaurant in Montevideo.

Conjugation of _Hacer_

The verb hacer / _to do, to make_ is an irregular verb. This verb has one irregular form in the first person singular (yo) of the present indicative tense. Otherwise, it follows the usual conjugation for a regular -er verb. The endings are all regular.

hacer / _to do, to make_

Subject Pronoun	Verb Form	Meaning
(yo)	<u>hag</u>+o	_I do, I am doing, I do do_
(tú)	<u>hac</u>+es	_you (fam. sg.) do, you are doing, you do do_
(él, ella, Ud.)	<u>hac</u>+e	_he, she, you (pol. sg.) does/do, he, she, you is/are doing, he, she, you does/do do_
(nosotros/-as)	<u>hac</u>+emos	_we do, we are doing, we do do_
(vosotros/-as)	<u>hac</u>+éis	_you (fam. pl.) do, you are doing, you do do_
(ellos/-as, Uds.)	<u>hac</u>+en	_they, you (pol. pl.) do, they, you are doing, they, you do do._

Uses of Hacer

The verb hacer is used to express weather conditions. The following are common meteorological expressions with the verb hacer / _to do, to make_.

¿Qué tiempo hace?	_What's the weather like?_
Hace (muy) buen tiempo.	_It's (very) good weather._
Hace (muy) mal tiempo.	_It's (very) bad weather._
Hace (mucho) frío.	_It's (very) cold._
Hace (mucho) calor.	_It's (very) hot._
Hace (mucho) sol.	_It's (very) sunny._
Hace (mucho) viento.	_It's (very) windy._
Hace fresco.	_It's cool._

The following are additional weather expression with the verb estar / *to be*.

Está (muy) húmedo.	*It's (very) humid.*
Está (muy) nublado.	*It's (very) cloudy.*
Está (muy) lluvioso.	*It's (very) rainy.*

The following are additional weather expressions with other verbs.

Llueve.	*It's raining.*
Llovizna.	*It's drizzling.*
Nieva.	*It's snowing.*
Relampaguea.	*It's lightning.*
Truena.	*It's thundering.*

There are a number of important idiomatic expressions with the verb hacer. The following are a few of them.

hacer caso a	*to pay attention to*
hacer el papel de	*to play the role of*
hacer un viaje	*to take a trip*

GRAMMAR NOTE

The verb hacer / *to do, to make* may appear in a special idiomatic construction with the present tense as illustrated below. This construction indicates that a specified activity began in the past and continues into the present.

¿Cuánto tiempo hace que estudias español? / *How long have you been studying Spanish?*
Hace un año que estudio español. / *I have been studying Spanish for a year.*

The above question and answer may be expressed in a different way as seen below.

¿Desde cuándo estudias español? / *How long have you been studying Spanish?*
Estudio español desde hace un año. / *I have been studying Spanish for a year.*

Dates

Indicating days is a simple process in Spanish. You use the cardinal numbers for 2–31. For the first, however, you use the ordinal number primero / *first* to indicate the first day of the month.

¿Cuál es la fecha de hoy? / *What's today's date?*
Hoy es el primero de diciembre. / *Today is the first of December.*
Hoy es el 5 de abril. / *Today is April fifth.*
Mañana es el primero de agosto. / *Tomorrow is August 1st.*

DAYS (día, *m.*) OF THE WEEK (semana, *f.*)

lunes	*Monday*	viernes	*Friday*
martes	*Tuesday*	sábado	*Saturday*
miércoles	*Wednesday*	domingo	*Sunday*
jueves	*Thursday*		

MONTHS (mes, *m.*) OF THE YEAR (año, *m.*)

enero	*January*	julio	*July*
febrero	*February*	agosto	*August*
marzo	*March*	septiembre	*September*
abril	*April*	octubre	*October*
mayo	*May*	noviembre	*November*
junio	*June*	diciembre	*December*

SEASONS (estación, *f.*) OF THE YEAR (año, *m.*)

la primavera (*f.*)	*spring*	el otoño (*m.*)	*fall*
el verano (*m.*)	*summer*	el invierno (*m.*)	*winter*

EXERCISE Set 3-5

A. Supply the missing forms of the Spanish verb hacer, and then give the English equivalent.

EXAMPLE: *él* ____   =   _____

              él hace   =   *he does/makes, he is doing/making, he does do/make*

1. (tú) _____   =   _____

2. (yo) _____   =   _____

3. (nosotras) _____   =   _____

4. (ellas) _____   =   _____

5. (vosotros) _____   =   _____

6. (Uds.) _____   =   _____

B. How do you say the following sentences in Spanish?

1. How long have you (fam. sg.) been studying Spanish?

_____

2. I have been studying Spanish for an hour.

_____

3. It is cold in Montevideo in June.

_____

4. When it rains, it is cloudy.

_____

5. I pay attention to verbs when I study Spanish.

_____

6. It is hot in Montevideo in December.

_____

7. I am taking a trip to *Punta del Este*[1].

_____

8. It always snows in winter.

_____

9. It is always very good weather in June.

_____

10. It is very windy in Chicago.

_____

11. It is March 31, 2006.

_____

[1]Resort area of Uruguay.

Conjugation of *Saber*

The verb **saber** / *to know* is an irregular verb. This verb has one irregular form in the first person singular (**yo**) of the present indicative tense. Otherwise, it follows the usual conjugation for a regular -er verb. The endings are all regular.

saber / *to know*

Subject Pronoun	Verb Form	Meaning
(yo)	sé	*I know, I do know*
(tú)	sab+es	*you (fam. sg.) know, you do know*
(él, ella, Ud.)	sab+e	*he, she, you (pol. sg.) knows/know, he, she, you does/do know*
(nosotros/-as)	sab+emos	*we know, we do know*
(vosotros/-as)	sab+éis	*you (fam. pl.) know, you do know*
(ellos/-as, Uds.)	sab+en	*they, you (pol. pl.) know, they, you do know*

Uses of Saber

The verb **saber**/ *to know* has a variety of uses that we will illustrate here. **Saber** / *to know* has the basic meaning of *to know something* (information, facts, ideas, etc.) or *how to do something* (to speak Spanish, to swim, etc.).

Saber is used in the following situations	Examples
1. To indicate that you know a fact.	**Marco sabe la dirección de Juana.** / *Marco knows Juana's address.*
2. To indicate that you know how to do something.	**Ella sabe hablar español.** / *She knows how to speak Spanish.*
3. To indicate that you *know that* …	**Sé que Irene está aquí.** / *I know that Irene is here.*

EXERCISE Set 3-6

A. Supply the missing forms of the Spanish verb **saber**, and then give the English equivalent.

EXAMPLE: *él* _____   =   _____

      él sabe   =   *he knows, he does know*

1. (tú) _____   =   _____

2. (yo) _____   =   _____

3. (nosotras) _____   =   _____

4. (ellas) _____   =   _____

5. (vosotros) _____   =   _____

6. (Uds.) _____   =   _____

B. How do you say the following sentences in Spanish?

1. You (fam. sg.) know how to swim well.

   _____

2. She knows that (**que**) Raquel is here.

   _____

3. I know that (**que**) it is necessary to sleep 8 hours.

   _____

4. We know that (que) it is cold in January.

_____

5. You (pol. pl.) know that (que) I have to be in Montevideo tomorrow.

_____

6. You (fam. sg.) know today's date. (Remember: No 's in Spanish.)

_____

7. He knows that (que) I am tired.

_____

8. You (pol. sg.) know that the tango is very popular in Montevideo.

_____

9. We know that (que) *Piriápolis*[1] is in Uruguay.

_____

10. They know that (que) I am in a good mood.

_____

[1] Famous Uruguayan resort.

Conjugation of *Conocer*

The verb **conocer** / *to know* is an irregular verb. This verb has one irregular form in the first person singular (**yo**) of the present indicative tense. Otherwise, it follows the usual conjugation for a regular -er verb. The endings are all regular. See Chapter 4 for a list of additional **-cer** (preceded by a vowel) verbs that are conjugated like **conocer** / *to know*.

conocer / *to know*

Subject Pronoun	Verb Form	Meaning
(yo)	<u>conozc</u>+o	*I know, I do know*
(tú)	<u>conoc</u>+es	*you (fam. sg.) know, you do know*
(él, ella, Ud.)	<u>conoc</u>+e	*he, she, you (pol. sg.) knows/know, he, she, you does/do know*
(nosotros/-as)	<u>conoc</u>+emos	*we know, we do know*
(vosotros/-as)	<u>conoc</u>+éis	*you (fam. pl.) know, you do know*
(ellos/-as, Uds.)	<u>conoc</u>+en	*they, you (pol. pl.) know, they, you do know*

Uses of Conocer

The verb conocer / *to know* has a variety of uses that we will illustrate here. Conocer / *to know* means to know a person or to be familiar with a place.

Conocer is used in the following situations	Examples
1. To indicate that you know someone. 2. To indicate that you are familiar with something, such as a location.	Conozco a Juan. / *I know John.* Gloria conoce bien Mercado del Puerto. / *Gloria is very familiar with Mercado del Puerto*[1].

[1]Restaurant in Montevideo.

GRAMMAR NOTE

In Spanish, when the direct object (the recipient of the action of the verb) refers to a person or persons, you must place the "personal a" immediately before the direct object. There is no such form in English, which means that you must remember to place it there. The following examples illustrate the "personal a."

> Quiero a Rosa. / *I love Rosa.*
> Veo a mi amigo. / *I see my friend.*

If there is a series of names, you must place the "personal a" before each name.

> Veo a Margarita y a Jesús. / *I see Margarita and Jesús.*

If you ask a question with ¿quién? / *whom?* (sg.) or ¿quiénes? / *whom?* (pl.), when it is a direct object, you must use the "personal a" as seen in the following examples.

> ¿A quién ves? / *Who(m) do you see?*
> ¿A quiénes admiras? / *Who(m) do you admire?*

You can even use the "personal a" with your pets.

> Quiero a mi perro. / *I love my dog.*

You use the "personal a" with the following verbs that have an implicit preposition.

> Miro a Juan. / *I look at John.*
> Buscas a Magadalena. / *You are looking for Magdalena.*
> Uds. esperan a Jorge. / *You are waiting for Jorge.*

Finally, you do not use the "personal a" with the verbs ser / *to be*, tener / *to have*, and hay / *there is, there are*, as illustrated in the following examples.

> Alba es doctora. / *Alba is a doctor.*
> Tengo tres hermanos. / *I have three brothers.*
> Hay muchos estudiantes aquí. / *There are many students here.*

The "personal a" is a concept that you will need to remember later in this book.

EXERCISE Set 3-7

A. Supply the missing forms of the Spanish verb conocer, and then give the English equivalent.

EXAMPLE: *él* ____ = _____

él conoce = *he knows, he does know*

1. (tú) _____ = _____

2. (yo) _____ = _____

3. (nosotras) _____ = _____

4. (ellas) _____ = _____

5. (vosotros) _____ = _____

6. (Uds.) _____ = _____

B. How do you say the following sentences in Spanish?

1. I know a good restaurant in *Punta del Este*[1].

_____

2. I know Julio Rodríguez well.

_____

3. I am familiar with the short stories of *Horacio Quiroga*[2].

_____

4. He knows the Hernández family (los Hernández).

_____

5. I know the city of Montevideo very well.

_____

[1]Resort area in Uruguay; [2]Famous Uruguayan writer of suspense and horror stories, 1879–1937.

EXERCISE Set 3-8

A. How do you say the following sentences in Spanish? This set of exercises includes all of the materials in this chapter. Most of these sentences contain the English verb *to be*. ¡Ojo! (*watch out!*). There are many ways to express *to be* in Spanish.

1. I am sure that I am right.

   _____

2. I know that it is cold today.

   _____

3. I have to be here at six P.M. sharp.

   _____

4. It is necessary to be nice.

   _____

5. They are sleepy and they are tired.

   _____

6. We are Argentinean but they are Uruguayan.

   _____

7. It is 1:15 P.M.

   _____

8. I am twenty years old and I am a student.

   _____

9. Cristina Aguilera is blond and pretty.

   _____

10. When it is hot, I am very thirsty.

   _____

Crossword Puzzle 3

Fill in the blanks. The clues contain expressions that will indicate which forms of the verbs **ser, estar, tener, hacer, saber,** and **conocer** you should use.

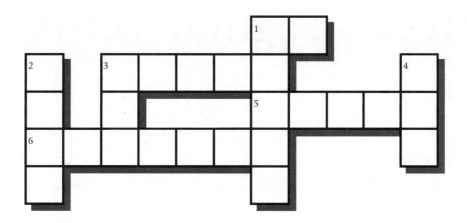

Horizontales
  1. ____ el 31 de agosto.
  3. (Tú) ____ la fecha.
  5. (Yo) ____ que estudiar.
  6. (Yo) ____ a Rosa.

Verticales
  1. (Yo) ____ aquí.
  2. ____ frío.
  3. ____ las dos de la noche.
  4. (Yo) ____ inteligente.

4

The Present Indicative of More Irregular Verbs

Irregular Verbs

We have already studied seven irregular verbs in Chapter 3. Now we will examine eight more common irregular verbs: **Dar** / *to give*, **decir** / *to say/to tell*, **ir (a)** / *to go*, **oír** / *to hear*, **poner** / *to put, to place*, **salir (de)** / *to leave*, **venir** / *to come*, **ver** / *to see*. Later in this chapter, we will also see some other irregular verbs that follow certain common patterns.

dar / *to give*

Subject Pronoun	Verb Form	Meaning
(yo)	<u>d</u>+oy	*I give , I am giving, I do give*
(tú)	<u>d</u>+as	*you (fam. sg.) give, you are giving, you do give*
(él, ella, Ud.)	<u>d</u>+a	*he, she, you (pol. sg.) give(s), he, she, you is/are giving, he, she, you does/do give*
(nosotros/-as)	<u>d</u>+amos	*we give, we are giving, we do give*
(vosotros/-as)	<u>d</u>+ais	*you (fam. pl.) give, you are giving, you do give*
(ellos/-as, Uds.)	<u>d</u>+an	*they, you (pol. pl.) give, they, you are giving, they, you do give*

decir (i) / *to say, to tell*

Subject Pronoun	Verb Form	Meaning
(yo)	<u>dig</u>+o	*I say/tell, I am saying/telling, I do say/tell*
(tú)	<u>dic</u>+es	*you (fam. sg.) say/tell, you are saying/telling, you do say/tell*
(él, ella, Ud.)	<u>dic</u>+e	*he, she, you (pol. sg.) say(s)/tell(s), he, she, you is/are saying/telling, he, she, you does/do say/tell*
(nosotros/-as)	<u>dec</u>+imos	*we say/tell, we are saying/telling, we do say/tell*
(vosotros/-as)	<u>dec</u>+ís	*you (fam. pl.) say/tell, you are saying/telling, you do say/tell*
(ellos/-as, Uds.)	<u>dic</u>+en	*they, you (pol. pl.) say/tell, they, you are saying/telling, they, you do say/tell*

ir (a) / *to go*

Subject Pronoun	Verb Form	Meaning
(yo)	<u>v</u>+oy	*I go, I am going, I do go*
(tú)	<u>v</u>+as	*you (fam. sg.) go, you are going, you do go*
(él, ella, Ud.)	<u>v</u>+a	*he, she, you (pol. sg.) go(es), he, she, you is/are going, he, she, you does/do go*
(nosotros/-as)	<u>v</u>+amos	*we go, we are going, we do go*
(vosotros/-as)	<u>v</u>+ais	*you (fam. pl.) go, you are going, you do go*
(ellos/-as, Uds.)	<u>v</u>+an	*they, you (pol. pl.) go, they, you are going, they, you do go*

oír / *to hear*

Subject Pronoun	Verb Form	Meaning
(yo)	<u>oig</u>+o	*I hear, I am hearing, I do hear*
(tú)	<u>oy</u>+es	*you (fam. sg.) hear, you are hearing, you do hear*
(él, ella, Ud.)	<u>oy</u>+e	*he, she, you (pol. sg.) hear(s), he, she, you is/are hearing, he, she, you does/do hear*
(nosotros/-as)	<u>o</u>+ímos	*we hear, we are hearing, we do hear*
(vosotros/-as)	<u>o</u>+ís	*you (fam. pl.) hear, you are hearing, you do hear*
(ellos/-as, Uds.)	<u>oy</u>+en	*they, you (pol. pl.) hear, they, you are hearing, they, you do hear*

poner / *to put, to place*

Subject Pronoun	Verb Form	Meaning
(yo)	<u>pong</u>+o	*I put/place, I am putting/placing, I do put/place*
(tú)	<u>pon</u>+es	*you (fam. sg.) put/place, you are putting/placing, you do put/place*
(él, ella, Ud.)	<u>pon</u>+e	*he, she, you (pol. sg.) put(s)/place(s), he, she, you is/are putting/placing, he, she, you does/do put/place*
(nosotros/-as)	<u>pon</u>+emos	*we put/place, we are putting/placing, we do put/place*
(vosotros/-as)	<u>pon</u>+éis	*you (fam. pl.) put/place, you are putting/placing, you do put/place*
(ellos/-as, Uds.)	<u>pon</u>+en	*they, you (pol. pl.) put/place, they, you are putting/placing, they, you do put/place*

salir (de) / *to leave*

Subject Pronoun	Verb Form	Meaning
(yo)	<u>salg</u>+o	*I leave, I am leaving, I do leave*
(tú)	<u>sal</u>+es	*you (fam. sg.) leave, you are leaving, you do leave*
(él, ella, Ud.)	<u>sal</u>+e	*he, she, you (pol. sg.) leave(s), he, she, you is/are leaving, he, she, you does/do leave*
(nosotros/-as)	<u>sal</u>+imos	*we leave, we are leaving, we do leave*
(vosotros/-as)	<u>sal</u>+ís	*you (fam. pl.) leave, you are leaving, you do leave*
(ellos/-as, Uds.)	<u>sal</u>+en	*they, you (pol. pl.) leave, they, you are leaving, they, you do leave*

venir / *to come*

Subject Pronoun	Verb Form	Meaning
(yo)	<u>veng</u>+o	*I come, I am coming, I do come*
(tú)	<u>vien</u>+es	*you (fam. sg.) come, you are coming, you do come*
(él, ella, Ud.)	<u>vien</u>+e	*he, she, you (pol. sg.) come(s), he, she, you is/are coming, he, she, you does/do come*
(nosotros/-as)	<u>ven</u>+imos	*we come, we are coming, we do come*
(vosotros/-as)	<u>ven</u>+ís	*you (fam. pl.) come, you are coming, you do come*
(ellos/-as, Uds.)	<u>vien</u>+en	*they, you (pol. pl.) come, they, you are coming, they, you do come*

ver / *to see*

Subject Pronoun	Verb Form	Meaning
(yo)	<u>ve</u>+o	*I see, I am seeing, I do see*
(tú)	<u>v</u>+es	*you (fam. sg.) see, you are seeing, you do see*
(él, ella, Ud.)	<u>v</u>+e	*he, she, you (pol. sg.) see(s), he, she, you is/are seeing, he, she, you does/do see*
(nosotros/-as)	<u>v</u>+emos	*we see, we are seeing, we do see*
(vosotros/-as)	<u>v</u>+eis	*you (fam. pl.) see, you are seeing, you do see*
(ellos/-as, Uds.)	<u>v</u>+en	*they, you (pol. pl.) see, they, you are seeing, they, you do see*

Several of these verbs (**dar** / *to give*, **ir** / *to go*, **poner** / *to put/to place*, and **salir** / *to leave*) are used in idiomatic expressions. Following are some of the more common ones.

Idioms with Dar, Ir, Poner, *and* Salir

dar un paseo	*to take a walk*
dar una carcajada	*to burst out laughing*
dar igual	*to make no difference*
dar la mano	*to shake hands*
dar saltos	*to jump about*
dar voces	*to scream*
darse cuenta (de)	*to realize*
ir de compras	*to go shopping*
ir al centro	*to go downtown*
poner la mesa	*to set the table*
salir (con)	*to go out with*
salir (de)	*to leave (from a building)*

GRAMMAR NOTES

When you use the preposition a / *to* with the masculine singular definite article in Spanish, these two words contract to al / *to the*, as shown below.

Voy al parque. / *I'm going to the park.*
Voy al centro. / *I'm going downtown.*

The verb ir / *to go* may be used with an infinitive to indicate that you are going to do something. It is, thus, a substitute for the future as seen below.

Voy a cantar. / *I'm going to sing.*
Magdalena va a estudiar español. / *Magdalena is going to study Spanish.*

EXERCISE Set 4-1

A. Supply the missing indicative forms of the verb **salir**, giving the English equivalent.

EXAMPLE: *él* _____   =   _____

            él sale   =   *he leaves, he is leaving, he does leave*

1. (yo) _____   =   _____

2. (tú) _____   =   _____

3. (ella y yo) _____   =   _____

4. (ellos) _____   =   _____

5. (vosotras) _____   =   _____

6. (Ud.) _____   =   _____

Now, supply the missing present indicative forms of the verb **ir**, giving the English equivalent.

1. (yo) _____   =   _____

2. (Isabel y yo) _____   =   _____

3. (Uds.) _____   =   _____

4. (ellas) _____   =   _____

5. (nosotros) _____   =   _____

6. (tú) _____   =   _____

Now, supply the missing present indicative forms of the verb **venir**, giving the English equivalent.

1. (yo) _____   =   _____

2. (tú) _____   =   _____

3. (Ignacio y yo) _____   =   _____

4. (ellos) _____   =   _____

5. (vosotros) _____   =   _____

6. (Uds.) _____   =   _____

Now, supply the missing present indicative forms of the verb **dar**, giving the English equivalent.

1. (yo) _____   =   _____

2. (tú) _____   =   _____

3. (nosotros) _____   =   _____

4. (ellos) _____   =   _____

5. (vosotros) _____   =   _____

6. (Uds.) _____   =   _____

Now, supply the missing present indicative forms of the verb **oír**, giving the English equivalent.

1. (yo) _____   =   _____

2. (tú) _____   =   _____

3. (nosotros) _____   =   _____

4. (ellas) _____   =   _____

5. (vosotros) _____   =   _____

6. (Uds.) _____   =   _____

Now, supply the missing present indicative forms of the verb **decir (i)**, giving the English equivalent.

1. (yo) _____   =   _____

2. (tú) _____   =   _____

3. (Isabel y yo) _____   =   _____

4. (ellos) _____   =   _____

5. (vosotros) _____   =   _____

6. (Uds.) _____   =   _____

Now, supply the missing present indicative forms of the verb **poner**, giving the English equivalent.

1. (yo) _____   =   _____

2. (tú) _____   =   _____

3. (nosotros) _____   =   _____

4. (ellos) _____   =   _____

5. (vosotros) _____   =   _____

6. (Uds.) _____   =   _____

Now, supply the missing present indicative forms of the verb **ver**, giving the English equivalent.

1. (yo) _____   =   _____

2. (tú) _____   =   _____

3. (nosotros) _____   =   _____

4. (ellos) _____   =   _____

5. (vosotros) _____   =   _____

6. (Uds.) _____   =   _____

B. How do you say the following sentences in Spanish?

1. I take a walk in the park every day.

   _____

2. I go out with my friends on Fridays.

   _____

3. I frequently come late to the university.

   _____

4. I see the *Museo de Arte Indígena*[1] now.

   _____

5. I put my money in my wallet.

   _____

6. I'm going to the (al) *Chaco*[2] tomorrow.

   _____

7. I hear the sounds of the jungle (selva).

   _____

8. I don't tell lies.

   _____

[1]Museum of Indigenous Art in Asunción; [2]Farm area in Paraguay and home to Mennonite settlers and indigenous peoples.

C. Choose the appropriate verb, **a**, **b**, or **c**, according to the meaning.

1. Cada año … a España.

   a. doy
   b. veo
   c. voy

2. ¿Cuándo … tu amigo? ¡Es tarde!

   a. viene
   b. dice
   c. oye

3. ¿A qué hora ... ellos de casa?

   a. ven
   b. salen
   c. dan

4. Ellos ... la mesa.

   a. vienen
   b. van
   c. ponen

5. ¿Con quién ... (tú) hoy?

   a. ves
   b. vas
   c. das

6. (Nosotros) ... al mar por las vacaciones.

   a. decimos
   b. vemos
   c. vamos

Additional Irregular Verbs

Verbs Ending in -cer *Preceded by a Vowel*

Verbs that end in -cer preceded by a vowel have an irregular yo form. You have already seen an example of such a verb in Chapter 3 with the verb conocer / *to know*. These verbs have the yo form in -zco. All other forms of the verb in the present indicative tense have regular endings. We provide an example of the verb establecer/ *to establish*.

establecer / *to establish*

Subject Pronoun	Verb Form	Meaning
(yo)	establezc+o	*I establish, I am establishing, I do establish*
(tú)	establec+es	*you (fam. sg.) establish, you are establishing, you do establish*
(él, ella, Ud.)	establec+e	*he, she, you (pol. sg.) establish(es), he, she, you is/are establishing, he, she, you does/do establish*
(nosotros/-as)	establec+emos	*we establish, we are establishing, we do establish*
(vosotros/-as)	establec+éis	*you (fam. pl.) establish, you are establishing, you do establish*
(ellos/-as, Uds.)	establec+en	*they, you (pol. pl.) establish, they, you are establishing, they, you do establish*

Common -cer Verbs Preceded by a Vowel

Below are some common -cer verbs that will come in handy for basic communication. All of these verbs have the irregular yo form in -zco.

agradecer	*to thank*	obedecer	*to obey*
aparecer	*to appear*	ofrecer	*to offer*
conocer	*to know*	parecer	*to seem*
crecer	*to grow*	pertenecer (a)	*to belong*
desaparecer	*to disappear*	reconocer	*to recognize*
establecer	*to establish*	yacer	*to lie down*
merecer	*to merit, to deserve*		

Verbs Ending in -ucir

Verbs that end in -ucir also have an irregular yo form. We provide the example here with the verb conducir / *to drive*. These verbs have the yo form in -zco. All other present indicative tense forms are regular.

conducir / *to drive*

Subject Pronoun	Verb Form	Meaning
(yo)	<u>conduzc</u>+o	*I drive, I am driving, I do drive*
(tú)	<u>conduc</u>+es	*you (fam. sg.) drive, you are driving, you do drive*
(él, ella, Ud.)	<u>conduc</u>+e	*he, she, you (pol. sg.) drive(s), he, she, you is/are driving, he, she, you does/do drive*
(nosotros/-as)	<u>conduc</u>+imos	*we drive, we are driving, we do drive*
(vosotros/-as)	<u>conduc</u>+ís	*you (fam. pl.) drive, you are driving, you do drive*
(ellos/-as, Uds.)	<u>conduc</u>+en	*they, you (pol. pl.) drive, they, you are driving, they, you do drive*

Common -ucir Verbs

Below are some common -cir verbs that will come in handy for basic communication. All of these verbs have the irregular yo form in -zco.

conducir	*to drive*	lucir	*to light up, to display*
deducir	*to deduce*	producir	*to produce*
inducir	*to induce, to persuade*	reducir	*to reduce*
introducir	*to introduce*	traducir	*to translate*

Other Irregular Verbs—Verbs Ending in -er

The following verb also has irregularities in the yo form. Other verbs listed below follow this pattern. All other present indicative tense forms are regular. We provide an example of the verb caer / *to fall*.

caer / *to fall*

Subject Pronoun	Verb Form	Meaning
(yo)	<u>caig</u>+o	*I fall, I am falling, I do fall*
(tú)	<u>ca</u>+es	*you (fam. sg.) fall, you are falling, you do fall*
(él, ella, Ud.)	<u>ca</u>+e	*he, she, you (pol. sg.) fall(s), he, she, you is/are falling, he, she, you does/do fall*
(nosotros/-as)	<u>ca</u>+emos	*we fall, we are falling, we do fall*
(vosotros/-as)	<u>ca</u>+éis	*you (fam. pl.) fall, you are falling, you do fall*
(ellos/-as, Uds.)	<u>ca</u>+en	*they, you (pol. pl.) fall, they, you are falling, they, you do fall*

Common -er Verbs

Below are some common -er verbs that will come in handy for basic communication. All of these verbs have the irregular yo form in -aigo.

atraer	*to attract*	retraer	*to bring back*
caer	*to fall*	sustraer	*to subtract*
contraer	*to contract*	traer	*to bring*

Verbs Ending in -uir

The following verbs that end in -uir have a y inserted in the stem of the first, second, and third person singular, and the third person plural. We provide an example of the verb concluir / *to conclude*.

concluir / *to conclude*

Subject Pronoun	Verb Form	Meaning
(yo)	<u>concluy</u>+o	*I conclude, I am concluding, I do conclude*
(tú)	<u>concluy</u>+es	*you (fam. sg.) conclude, you are concluding, you do conclude*
(él, ella, Ud.)	<u>concluy</u>+e	*he, she, you (pol. sg.) conclude(s), he, she, you is/are concluding, he, she, you does/do conclude*
(nosotros/-as)	<u>conclu</u>+imos	*we conclude, we are concluding, we do conclude*
(vosotros/-as)	<u>conclu</u>+ís	*you (fam. pl.) conclude, you are concluding, you do conclude*
(ellos/-as, Uds.)	<u>concluy</u>+en	*they, you (pol. pl.) conclude, they, you are concluding, they, you do conclude*

Common -uir Verbs

Below are some common -uir verbs that will come in handy for basic communication. All of these verbs have a -y- inserted in the first, second, and third person singular, and third person plural forms between the stem and the ending.

concluir	*to conclude*	huir	*to flee*
construir	*to build*	incluir	*to include*
contribuir	*to contribute*	influir	*to influence*
destruir	*to destroy*	sustituir	*to substitute*
fluir	*to flow*		

Spelling Change Verbs

There are some common verbs that undergo a spelling change according to the type of vowel that appears in the ending. When the ending vowel is -o or -a, it is preceded by a -z-. When the vowel is -e or -i, there is a -c- in the stem. In this hemisphere, the -z- and the -c- are pronounced as "s," as in the initial sound of the English word <u>sit</u>. We provide an example here of the verb convencer / *to convince*. This change occurs with verbs that end in -cer or -cir <u>when they are preceded by a consonant</u>.

Verbs Ending in -cer or -cir Preceded by a Consonant

Verbs that end in -cer or -cir, and that are preceded by a consonant, have a spelling change to -z- in the first person singular of the present indicative as illustrated below.

convencer / *to convince*

Subject Pronoun	Verb Form	Meaning
(yo)	<u>convenz</u>+o	*I convince, I am convincing, I do convince*
(tú)	<u>convenc</u>+es	*you (fam. sg.) convince, you are convincing, you do convince*
(él, ella, Ud.)	<u>convenc</u>+e	*he, she, you (pol. sg.) convince(s), he, she, you is/are convincing, he, she, you does/do convince*
(nosotros/-as)	<u>convenc</u>+emos	*we convince, we are convincing, we do convince*
(vosotros/-as)	<u>convenc</u>+éis	*you (fam. pl.) convince, you are convincing, you do convince*
(ellos/-as, Uds.)	<u>convenc</u>+en	*they, you (pol. pl.) convince, they, you are convincing, they, you do convince*

zurcir / *to mend, to darn*

Subject Pronoun	Verb Form	Meaning
(yo)	zur*z*+o	*I mend/darn, I am mending/darning, I do mend/darn*
(tú)	zur*c*+es	*you (fam. sg.) mend/darn, you are mending/darning, you do mend/darn*
(él, ella, Ud.)	zur*c*+e	*he, she, you (pol. sg.) mend(s)/darn(s), he, she, you is/are mending/darning, he, she, you does/do mend/darn*
(nosotros/-as)	zur*c*+imos	*we mend/darn, we are mending/darning, we do mend/darn*
(vosotros/-as)	zur*c*+ís	*you (fam. pl.) mend/darn, you are mending/darning, you do mend/darn*
(ellos/-as, Uds.)	zur*c*+en	*they, you (pol. pl.) mend/darn, they, you are mending/darning, they, you do mend/darn*

Common -cer *and* -cir *Verbs Preceded by a Consonant*

The following are some common verbs that have the spelling changes mentioned above. Again, these verbs are all preceded by a consonant.

convencer	*to convince*	vencer	*to conquer, to defeat*
ejercer	*to exert, to exercise*	zurcir	*to mend, to darn*
esparcir	*to scatter, to spread*		

Other Verbs with Spelling Changes

There are other common verbs that undergo a spelling change according to the type of vowel that appears in the ending. When there is a following -o or -a, there is a -j- in the stem. When the following vowel is -e or -i, there is a -g- in the stem. The -j- and the -g- are always pronounced as "h," as in the initial sound of the English word <u>h</u>it. We provide an example here of the verb **escoger** / *to select*.

Verbs Ending in -ger *and* -gir

For verbs that end in -ger, there is a spelling change for the sound *h* (as in <u>h</u>it). There is a spelling change to -j- before a following -o in the present indicative tense as illustrated below. Before a following -e, however, the sound *h* is spelled with a -g-.

escoger / *to select*

Subject Pronoun	Verb Form	Meaning
(yo)	esco*j*+o	*I select, I am selecting, I do select*
(tú)	esco*g*+es	*you (fam. sg.) select, you are selecting, you do select*
(él, ella, Ud.)	esco*g*+e	*he, she, you (pol. sg.) select(s), he, she, you is/are selecting, he, she, you does/do select*
(nosotros/-as)	esco*g*+emos	*we select, we are selecting, we do select*
(vosotros/-as)	esco*g*+éis	*you (fam. pl.) select, you are selecting, you do select*
(ellos/-as, Uds.)	esco*g*+en	*they, you (pol. pl.) select, they, you are selecting, they, you do select*

Other -ger and -gir Verbs

The following are some common verbs that have the spelling changes mentioned above.

coger	*to grasp, to seize*	exigir	*to demand, to require*
corregir (i)	*to correct*	fingir	*to pretend*
dirigir	*to direct*	proteger	*to protect*
elegir (i)	*to elect, to choose*	recoger	*to pick up*
escoger	*to select*	surgir	*to surge, to spur*

EXERCISE Set 4-2

A. Supply the missing indicative forms of the verb ofrecer, giving the English equivalent.

EXAMPLE: *él* _____   =   _____

              él ofrece   =   *he offers, he is offering, he does offer*

1. (yo) _____   =   _____

2. (tú) _____   =   _____

3. (ella y yo) _____   =   _____

4. (ellos) _____   =   _____

5. (vosotras) _____   =   _____

6. (Ud.) _____   =   _____

Now, supply the missing present indicative forms of the verb producir, giving the English equivalent.

1. (yo) _____   =   _____

2. (nosotras) _____   =   _____

3. (Uds.) _____   =   _____

4. (ellas) _____   =   _____

5. (nosotros) _____   =   _____

6. (tú) _____   =   _____

Now, supply the missing present indicative forms of the verb **traer**, giving the English equivalent.

1. (yo) _____   =   _____

2. (Ignacio y yo) _____ =   _____

3. (Uds.) _____   =   _____

4. (ellas) _____   =   _____

5. (nosotros) _____   =   _____

6. (tú) _____   =   _____

Now, supply the missing present indicative forms of the verb **incluir**, giving the English equivalent.

1. (yo) _____   =   _____

2. (nosotros) _____   =   _____

3. (Uds.) _____   =   _____

4. (ellos) _____   =   _____

5. (ella) _____   =   _____

6. (tú) _____   =   _____

Now, supply the missing present indicative forms of the verb **vencer**, giving the English equivalent.

1. (yo) _____   =   _____

2. (Jorge y yo) _____ =   _____

3. (Uds.) _____   =   _____

4. (ellas) _____   =   _____

5. (nosotros) _____   =   _____

6. (tú) _____   =   _____

Now, supply the missing present indicative forms of the verb **proteger**, giving the English equivalent.

1. (yo) _____   =   _____

2. (nosotros) _____   =   _____

3. (Uds.) _____   =   _____

4. (ellas) _____   =   _____

5. (él) _____   =   _____

6. (tú) _____   =   _____

B. How do you say the following sentences in Spanish?

1. I know the city of Asunción well.

   _____

2. This book belongs to Carmen.

   _____

3. I'm translating poetry from Guaraní to Spanish.

   _____

4. I'm going to reduce my work hours.

   _____

5. I'm bringing my books to the office today.

   _____

6. I'm including a chapter about (**sobre**) Paraguayan literature.

   _____

7. They defeat their enemies with praise.

   _____

8. I protect my children.

   _____

C. Choose the appropriate verb, **a**, **b**, or **c**, according to the meaning.

1. (Yo) … cuando nieva.

   a. traigo
   b. caigo
   c. atraigo

2. Ellos … a la policía.

   a. parecen
   b. producen
   c. obedecen

3. (Tú) … a tus amigos.

   a. esparces
   b. zurces
   c. convences

4. (Yo) … la cosecha (crop).

   a. recojo
   b. exijo
   c. finjo

5. (Nosotros) … del inglés al español.

   a. conducimos
   b. traducimos
   c. deducimos

6. Uds. … de sus enemigos.

   a. influyen
   b. contribuyen
   c. huyen

Crossword Puzzle 4

Fill in the blanks. All of the clues both vertical and horizontal are English verbal expressions that correspond to a single verb in Spanish. Use the following verbs in your answers: **conducir, construir, corregir, dar, decir, ir, obedecer, salir, traer.**

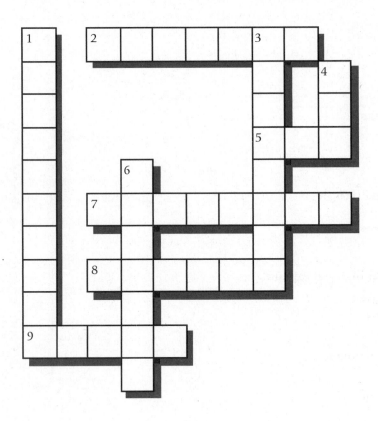

Horizontales
  2. Mis amigos y yo _____ la verdad.
  5. (Yo) _____ un paseo en el parque.
  7. (Yo) _____ a la universidad.
  8. (Yo) _____ mis libros a clase.
  9. (Yo) _____ de la universidad

Verticales
  1. (Tú) _____ una casa nueva.
  3. (Yo) _____ a mis padres.
  4. (Yo) _____ a estudiar.
  6. El profesor _____ los exámenes.

5

The Present Indicative
of Reflexive Verbs

Conjugation of Reflexive Verbs

A verb is reflexive when it has an identical subject and direct object, as in _She dressed herself_. The object is expressed as a reflexive pronoun. Reflexive verbs are thus conjugated in exactly the same manner as nonreflexive verbs, but with reflexive pronouns.

Here are the Spanish reflexive pronouns:

Singular		Plural	
1st person	me / _myself_	1st person	nos / _ourselves_
2nd person	te / _yourself_ (fam. sg.)	2nd person	os / _yourselves_ (fam. pl.)
3rd person	se / _himself, herself, yourself_ (pol. sg.)	3rd person	se / _themselves, yourselves_ (pol. pl.)

The following sentences exemplify typical sentences with reflexive verbs.

> <u>Me</u> lav<u>o</u> por la mañana. / <u>I</u> wash <u>myself</u> in the morning.
> <u>Te</u> diviert<u>es</u> en el cine. / <u>You</u> enjoy <u>yourself</u> at the movies.

NOTE

A reflexive verb is identifiable by the ending -se (_oneself_) attached to the infinitive.

> lavar<u>se</u> / _to wash oneself_
> ver<u>se</u> / _to see oneself_
> divertir<u>se</u> (ie) / _to entertain oneself_

Reflexive pronouns are placed in front of conjugated verbs.

Reflexive verbs are conjugated in exactly the same manner as other verbs with, of course, the addition of reflexive pronouns.

1. Drop the reflexive ending, -arse; -erse; -irse.
     lavarse / _to wash oneself_
     ponerse / _to put on (clothing)_
     divertirse (ie) / _to entertain oneself_

2. Add the endings in the usual manner (Chapter 1).

3. Don't forget to add the reflexive pronouns.

lavarse / *to wash oneself*

Subject Pronoun	Reflexive Pronoun	Conjugated Verb	Meaning
(yo)	me	<u>lav</u>+o	*I wash myself, I am washing myself, I do wash myself*
(tú)	te	<u>lav</u>+as	*you (fam. sg.) wash yourself, you are washing yourself, you do wash yourself*
(él, ella, Ud.)	se	<u>lav</u>+a	*he, she, you (pol. sg.) wash(es) himself/herself/ yourself, he, she, you is/are washing himself/herself/ yourself, he, she, you does/do wash himself/ herself/yourself*
(nosotros/-as)	nos	<u>lav</u>+amos	*we wash ourselves, we are washing ourselves, we do wash ourselves*
(vosotros/-as)	os	<u>lav</u>+áis	*you (fam. pl.) wash yourselves, you are washing yourselves, you do wash yourselves*
(ellos/-as, Uds.)	se	<u>lav</u>+an	*they, you (pol. pl.) wash themselves/yourselves, they, you are washing themselves/ yourselves, they, you do wash themselves/ yourselves*

The verb verse / *to see oneself* has an irregular first person singular form, as seen in Chapter 4.

verse / *to see oneself*

Subject Pronoun	Reflexive Pronoun	Conjugated Verb	Meaning
(yo)	me	<u>ve</u>+o	*I see myself, I am seeing myself, I do see myself*
(tú)	te	<u>v</u>+es	*you (fam. sg.) see yourself, you are seeing yourself, you do see yourself*
(él, ella, Ud.)	se	<u>v</u>+e	*he, she, you (pol. sg.) see(s) himself/herself/yourself, he, she, you is/ are seeing himself/herself/yourself, he, she, you does/do see himself/herself/yourself*
(nosotros/-as)	nos	<u>v</u>+emos	*we see ourselves, we are seeing ourselves, we do see ourselves*
(vosotros/-as)	os	<u>v</u>+eis	*you (fam. pl.) see yourselves, you are seeing yourselves, you do see yourselves*
(ellos/-as, Uds.)	se	<u>v</u>+en	*they, you (pol. pl.) see themselves/ yourselves, they, you are seeing themselves/yourselves, they, you do see themselves/yourselves*

The verb divertirse (ie) / *to entertain oneself* is a stem-changing verb. See Chapter 2 for a complete discussion of these verbs. Remember that the endings for stem-changing verbs are regular.

divertirse (ie) / *to entertain oneself*

Subject Pronoun	Reflexive Pronoun	Conjugated Verb	Meaning
(yo)	me	<u>diviert</u>+o	*I entertain myself, I am entertaining myself, I do entertain myself*
(tú)	te	<u>diviert</u>+es	*you (fam. sg.) entertain yourself, you are entertaining yourself, you do entertain yourself*
(él, ella, Ud.)	se	<u>diviert</u>+e	*he, she, you (pol. sg.) entertain(s) himself/herself/ yourself, he, she, you is/are entertaining himself/ herself/yourself, he, she, you does/do entertain himself/ herself/yourself*
(nosotros/-as)	nos	<u>divert</u>+imos	*we entertain ourselves, we are entertaining ourselves, we do entertain ourselves*
(vosotros/-as)	os	<u>divert</u>+ís	*you (fam. pl.) entertain yourselves, you are entertaining yourselves, you do entertain yourselves*
(ellos/-as, Uds.)	se	<u>diviert</u>+en	*they, you (pol. pl.) entertain themselves/yourselves, they, you are entertaining themselves/yourselves, they, you do entertain themselves/ yourselves*

Common Reflexive Verbs

Below are some common reflexive verbs that will come in handy for basic communication.

acordarse (ue) (de)	*to remember*	lavarse	*to wash oneself*
acostarse (ue)	*to go to bed*	levantarse	*to get up*
afeitarse	*to shave oneself*	llamarse	*to call oneself / to be named*
bañarse	*to bathe oneself*	mirarse	*to look at oneself*
cansarse	*to get tired*	peinarse	*to comb one's hair*
casarse (con)	*to get married / to marry*	ponerse (la ropa)	*to put on clothing*
cepillarse	*to brush oneself*	preocuparse (por)	*to worry (about)*
despertarse (ie)	*to wake up*	quedarse	*to remain, to stay*
desvestirse (i)	*to get undressed*	quitarse	*to take off (clothing)*
divertirse (ie)	*to entertain oneself*	secarse	*to dry oneself*
dormirse (ue)	*to fall asleep*	sentarse (ie)	*to sit down*
ducharse	*to take a shower*	sentirse (ie)	*to feel (emotions, physical well-being)*
enfermarse	*to get sick*		
enojarse	*to get angry*	verse	*to see oneself*
irse	*to go away*	vestirse (i)	*to dress oneself*

GRAMMAR NOTE

Reflexive pronouns may also be used in a construction known as the "reciprocal reflexive." It is restricted to the plural and its common English translation is "each other," or "one another." The following examples show this usage.

Mis amigos se abrazan. / *My friends embrace one another.*
Los amantes se besan. / *The lovers kiss each other.*

NOTE ON MEANING

Some verbs may have two forms: a non-reflexive version and a reflexive version. In the former case, this means that you are performing the action of the verb on someone else. In the latter version, you are performing the action on yourself. The following examples illustrate this usage. The first example in each pair is non-reflexive; the second is reflexive.

Baño a mi hijo. / *I bathe my child.*
<u>Me</u> baño. / *I take a bath (I bathe myself).*

Despierto a mis hijos. / *I wake up my children.*
<u>Me</u> despier<u>to</u>. / *I wake up.*

Many, but not all, reflexive verbs have these two meanings.

GRAMMAR NOTES

Certain verbs are followed directly by infinitives or by a preposition and an infinitive (see Chapter 2). With these verbs, you may place the reflexive pronoun either before the main verb (the first verb) or immediately following the infinitive and attached to it (the second verb). The following examples illustrate these two possibilities.

Before:
¿<u>Te</u> quieres divertir? / *Do you want to have fun?*
Uds. <u>se</u> pueden despertar tarde. / *You can wake up late.*

After:
¿Quieres divertir<u>te</u>? / *Do you want to have have a good time?*
Uds. pueden despertar<u>se</u> tarde. / *You can wake up late.*

EXERCISE Set 5-1

A. Supply the missing indicative forms of the verb **levantarse**, giving the English equivalent.

EXAMPLE: *él _____*   =   _____

él se levanta   =   *he gets up, he is getting up, he does get up*

1. (yo) _____   =   _____

2. (tú) _____   =   _____

3. (nosotros) _____   =   _____

4. (ellos) _____   =   _____

5. (vosotros) _____   =   _____

6. (Ud.) _____   =   _____

Now, supply the missing present indicative forms of the verb despertarse (ie), giving the English equivalent.

1. (yo) _____   =   _____

2. (Isabel y yo) _____ =   _____

3. (Uds.) _____   =   _____

4. (ellos) _____   =   _____

5. (nosotros) _____ =   _____

6. (tú) _____   =   _____

Now, supply the missing present indicative forms of the verb vestirse (i), giving the English equivalent.

1. (yo) _____   =   _____

2. (tú) _____   =   _____

3. (nosotros) _____ =   _____

4. (ellos) _____   =   _____

5. (vosotros) _____ =   _____

6. (Uds.) _____   =   _____

B. Choose the appropirate verb form, **a**, **b**, or **c**, according to the meaning.

1. Generalmente, … cuando miro la televisión.

   a. me duermo
   b. me llamo
   c. me levanto

2. Tu amigo regularmente … cuando mira una película **(film)**.

   a. se llama
   b. se divierte
   c. se casa

3. ¿(Tú) … de todo?

   a. te despiertas
   b. te acuerdas
   c. te duermes

4. Uds. … cuando hay problemas.

   a. se duchan
   b. se peinan
   c. se enojan

5. Señora, ¿cómo ... Ud.?

    a. se llama
    b. se levanta
    c. se sienta

6. Ellos ... en el cuarto de baño todos los días.

    a. se enojan
    b. se duchan
    c. se llaman

7. (Yo) ... en el espejo.

    a. me preocupo
    b. me duermo
    c. me miro

C. How do you say the following sentences in Spanish?

1. Ana goes to bed very early.

_____

2. The author of *Raza de bronce*[1] is named *Alcides Arguedas*[2].

_____

3. Margarita wants to get married in La Paz.

_____

4. In the morning I wake up, I get up, I shower, and I get dressed.

_____

5. When I study Spanish verbs a lot, I get tired.

_____

6. After I take a bath, I dry myself.

_____

7. I feel happy when I learn Spanish verbs.

_____

8. I worry when I have a test.

_____

9. They fall asleep at 11 P.M.

_____

10. Guillermo looks at himself in the mirror in the morning.

_____

[1]Novel about the mistreatment of Indians in Bolivia, 1919; [2]Famed Bolivian author, 1879–1946.

Crossword Puzzle 5

Fill in the blanks. All of the clues, both vertical and horizontal, are English verbal expressions that correspond to a single verb in Spanish. Use the following verbs in your answers: acostarse, afeitarse, casarse, levantarse, llamarse, preocuparse, quitarse, sentirse, verse.

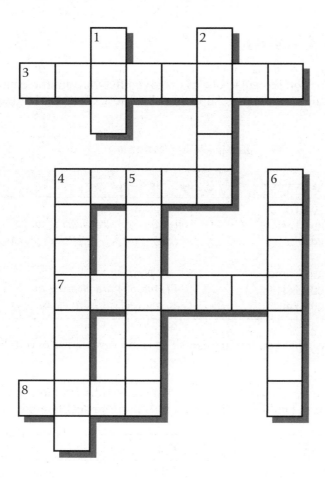

Horizontales
  3. Ud. se . . . por todo.
  4. Ella se . . . Mónica.
  7. Los hombres se . . . todos los días.
  8. Jorge se . . . con Elena.

Verticales
  1. Me . . . en el espejo.
  2. Él se . . . el sombrero.
  4. ¿A qué hora te . . . por la mañana?
  5. Ella se . . . tarde por la noche.
  6. Ellos no se . . . bien.

6

Gustar-Type Constructions and the Present Progressive (*el presente progresivo*)

Conjugation of *Gustar*

The verb gustar / *to be pleasing to, to like* is another important and very common verb. Its present indicative forms are given below. Its formation is regular, but its usage is different from the English verb *to like*. Gustar is almost always used in the third person singular or plural because of its special usage and basic meaning of *to be pleasing to*.

gustar / *to be pleasing to*

Subject Pronoun	Verb Form	Meaning
(yo)	<u>gust</u>+o	*I am pleasing to*
(tú)	<u>gust</u>+as	*you (fam. sg.) are pleasing to*
(él, ella, Ud.)	<u>gust</u>+a	*he, she, you (pol. sg.) is/are pleasing to*
(nosotros/-as)	<u>gust</u>+amos	*we are pleasing to*
(vosotros/-as)	<u>gust</u>+áis	*you (fam. pl.) are pleasing to*
(ellos/-as, Uds.)	<u>gust</u>+an	*they, you (pol. pl.) are pleasing to*

This verb allows you to express what you *like* in Spanish. It is, however, a tricky verb because it really means *to be pleasing to*.

1. In order to use it appropriately, you will first need to know the indirect object pronouns *to me, to you*, etc. We will discuss the usage of the indirect object pronouns in more detail below.

Singular		Plural	
1st person	me / *to me*	1st person	nos / *to us*
2nd person	te / *to you* (fam. sg.)	2nd person	os / *to you* (fam. pl.)
3rd person	le / *to him, to her, to you* (pol. sg.)	3rd person	les / *to them, to you* (pol. pl.)

2. The best initial learning strategy is to rephrase the English expression in your mind as shown below. Notice that the indirect object pronouns precede the verb.

English Expression	Rephrase to	Spanish Expression
↓	↓	↓
I like the book.	"To me is pleasing the book"	Me gusta el libro.
We like these books.	"To us are pleasing the books"	Nos gustan los libros.

3. If the indirect object is not a pronoun, use the preposition a before it. Note that when you are talking about someone, you will also need to use the indirect object pronoun le or les.

English Expression	Rephrase to	Spanish Expression
↓	↓	↓
Elena likes the book.	"To Elena is pleasing the book"	<u>A Elena</u> <u>le</u> gusta el libro.
My friends like those books.	"To my friends are pleasing the books"	<u>A mis amigos</u> <u>les</u> gustan los libros.

NOTE

When gustar is used with persons, it means *I am attracted to*. If you want to say that you like someone, you need to use the expression caer bien a / *to like*. The following examples show this usage.

Me caes bien. / *I like you.*

Compare the above usage to the gustar expression with a person.

Me gustas. / *I am attracted to you.*

Prepositional Pronouns

You need to know another set of pronouns. These are pronouns for use after prepositions, hence their name "prepositional pronouns." These are especially useful for the gustar-type verbs we just discussed. You will note that, except for mí / *me* and ti / *you* (fam.), the forms are just like the <u>subject pronouns</u> discussed in Part 1. Here the Spanish direct object pronouns are used after a preposition. Note, however, the following two prepositional pronous: conmigo / *with me*, contigo / *with you*.

Prepositional pronouns are used with third person singular (le) and third person plural (les) indirect object pronouns to clarify ambiguous forms that may mean *to him*, *to her*, *to you* (pol. sg.), *to them* (m. or f.), and *to you* (pol. pl.). When we discuss indirect object pronouns, we will see once again that it is important to know the prepositional pronouns.

Singular		Plural	
1st person	mí / *me*	1st person	nosotros / *us* nosotras / *us*
2nd person	ti / *you* (fam. sg.)	2nd person	vosotros / *you* (fam. pl.) vosotras / *you* (fam. pl.)
3rd person	él/ *him* ellas / *her* Ud. / *you* (pol. sg.)	3rd person	ellos / *them* ellas / *them* Uds. / *you* (pol. pl.)

GRAMMAR NOTE

If you use a third person indirect pronoun, you will need to include a clarifying pronominal phrase as shown below. We have underlined the clarifying phrase and the indirect object pronoun in the following examples.

A él le gusta la casa. / *He likes the house.*
A ella le gusta la casa. / *She likes the house.*
A Ud. le gusta la casa. / *You like the house.*
A ellos les gusta la casa. / *They like the house.*
A ellas les gusta la casa. /*They like the house.*
A Uds. les gusta la casa. / *You like the house.*

You may use the first- and second-person singular and plural prepositional objects with gustar-type constructions, but they are emphatic as seen in the examples below.

Me gusta leer libros. / *I like to read books.* (ordinary statement)
A mí me gusta leer libros. / *I like to read books.* (very emphatic statement)

Nos gusta Santiago. / *We like Santiago.* (ordinary statement)
A nosotros nos gusta Santiago. / *We like Santiago.* (very emphatic statement)

NOTE

If you want to make a gustar construction negative, you must place the word no immediately before the indirect object pronoun as shown below. This placement of no is true for all object pronouns (reflexive, direct, and indirect).

No me gustan los libros. / *I do not like the books.*
A ella no le gusta la casa. / *She doesn't like the house.*

GRAMMAR NOTE

Demonstrative adjectives, the words that express *this / that, these / those* generally appear before the noun they modify. You will need to remember a few things about them as shown here. We have indicated the agreement (number and gender) with an underline.

> est<u>e</u> libr<u>o</u> / *this book*
> est<u>os</u> libr<u>os</u> / *these books*
> est<u>a</u> cas<u>a</u> / *this house*
> est<u>as</u> cas<u>as</u> / *these houses*

There are two demonstrative adjectives for *that* and *those* in Spanish. To indicate *that / those* relatively near the speaker and hearer, use the forms of the demonstrative adjective **ese**.

> es<u>e</u> libr<u>o</u> / *that book*
> es<u>os</u> libr<u>os</u> / *those books*
> es<u>a</u> cas<u>a</u> / *that house*
> es<u>as</u> cas<u>as</u> / *those houses*

To indicate *that / those* relatively far away from the speaker and hearer, use the forms of the demonstrative adjective **aquel**. Note that the l is doubled (l → ll) in the feminine and plural forms (indicated in italic type).

> aque<u>l</u> libr<u>o</u> / *that book*
> aque<u>llos</u> libr<u>os</u> / *those books*
> aque<u>lla</u> cas<u>a</u> / *that house*
> aque<u>llas</u> cas<u>as</u> / *those houses*

You may use the demonstrative forms without a following noun. In this case, they function as pronouns (*pro* means "in the place of"). When there is no following noun, it is necessary to write a graphic accent over the next to the last vowel (except for **aquél** / *that one*).

Rule of Thumb

As you can see, **gustar** can be confusing for anyone accustomed to the English verb *to like*. The following rule of thumb might help you to use this important verb more easily.

As the verb is often used with indirect object pronouns, just think of the pronouns as subjects; then make the verb agree with direct object.

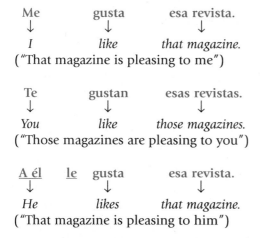

Me   gusta   esa revista.
↓   ↓   ↓
I   *like*   *that magazine.*
("That magazine is pleasing to me")

Te   gustan   esas revistas.
↓   ↓   ↓
You   *like*   *those magazines.*
("Those magazines are pleasing to you")

<u>A él</u>   <u>le</u>   gusta   esa revista.
↓   ↓   ↓
He   *likes*   *that magazine.*
("That magazine is pleasing to him")

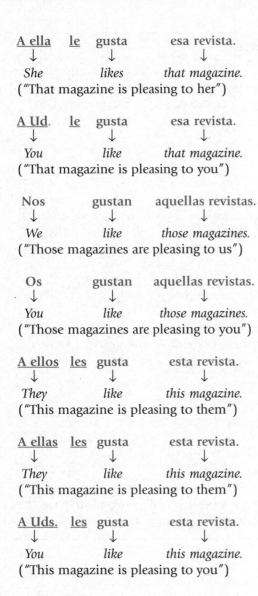

A ella   le   gusta   esa revista.
 ↓   ↓   ↓
She   *likes*   *that magazine.*
("That magazine is pleasing to her")

A Ud.   le   gusta   esa revista.
 ↓   ↓   ↓
You   *like*   *that magazine.*
("That magazine is pleasing to you")

Nos   gustan   aquellas revistas.
 ↓   ↓   ↓
We   *like*   *those magazines.*
("Those magazines are pleasing to us")

Os   gustan   aquellas revistas.
 ↓   ↓   ↓
You   *like*   *those magazines.*
("Those magazines are pleasing to you")

A ellos   les   gusta   esta revista.
 ↓   ↓   ↓
They   *like*   *this magazine.*
("This magazine is pleasing to them")

A ellas   les   gusta   esta revista.
 ↓   ↓   ↓
They   *like*   *this magazine.*
("This magazine is pleasing to them")

A Uds.   les   gusta   esta revista.
 ↓   ↓   ↓
You   *like*   *this magazine.*
("This magazine is pleasing to you")

Remember that in the third person singular and plural, you use a prepositional pronoun phrase and indirect object to indicate "<u>what</u> is pleasing <u>to whom</u>."

EXERCISE Set 6-1

A. Rephrase each sentence as shown, and then give its Spanish equivalent.

EXAMPLE: I like the book.
               "The book is pleasing to me" → *Me gusta el libro.*

1. I like this book.

2. My friends like that (over there) restaurant.

_____

3. You (fam. sg.) like to watch soap operas.

_____

4. We like that program.

_____

5. She likes this film.

_____

6. They like these magazines.

_____

7. He likes to visit *Antofagasta*[1].

_____

8. Rosa likes *Concepción*[2].

_____

9. Do you (pol. sg.) like Chilean food?

_____

10. They like to travel to *Punta Arenas*[3].

_____

11. I am attracted to you (fam. sg.).

_____

12. We are attracted to her.

_____

13. I like you.

_____

14. I like to go to the *Museo de Santiago*[4].

_____

15. You (pol. pl.) like to swim in the sea.

_____

[1]Largest city in Northern Chile and site of two universities; also a major port; [2]Third largest city in Chile, founded in 1515, place where Bernardo O'Higgins declared independence from Spain in 1818; [3]Southernmost city in Chile, founded in 1843; [4]Museum of Santiago's history, covers the conquest period through the present.

Summary

As mentioned above, in order to use the verb **gustar** correctly, you must always think of what it really means.

I like the movie.

Me	gusta	la película
↓	↓	↓
To me	is pleasing	the movie

I like the movies.

Me	gustan	las películas
↓	↓	↓
To me	are pleasing	the movies

If you think that way, you will always be correct. Notice the preferred word order.

She likes the book.

A ella le	gusta	el libro
↓	↓	↓
To her	is pleasing	the book

She likes the books.

A ella le	gustan	los libros
↓	↓	↓
To her	are pleasing	the books

Other Verbs with Similar Features

The following verbs exhibit the same "grammatical behavior" of gustar / *to be pleasing to*—that is, they require frequent usage of indirect object pronouns and they may be rephrased mentally in analogous ways.

The best learning strategy, once again, is to rephrase the English expression in your mind:

English Expression	Rephrase to	Spanish Expression
↓	↓	↓
My head aches.	"To me is aching the head"	Me duele la cabeza.
We need the money.	"To us is lacking the money"	Nos falta el dinero.
You (fam. sg.) *are interested in the magazines.*	"To you are interesting the magazines"	Te interesan las revistas.

The following are verbs that function like gustar / *to be pleasing to*.

agradar	*to please*	faltar	*to be lacking to, to be missing to*
apetecer	*to be appetizing, to appeal to (food)*	fascinar	*to be fascinating to*
bastar	*to be sufficient, to be enough*	importar	*to be important to*
caer bien	*to be liked, to create a good impression*	interesar	*to be interesting to*
convenir (ie)	*to suit one's interest, to be good for*	molestar	*to bother, to annoy*
doler (ue)	*to be painful, to ache*	parecer	*to seem, to appear to*
encantar	*to be enchanting to*	sobrar	*to be left over, to be in surplus*

EXERCISE Set 6-2

A. The following exercise contains verbs that function like gustar. Rephrase each sentence as shown, and then give its Spanish equivalent.

EXAMPLE: I am interested in the book.
"The book is interesting to me" → *Me interesa el libro.*

1. Her tooth (diente) aches.

_____

2. I like you (fam. sg.).

_____

3. I need twenty *pesos*.

_____

4. I am interested in old books.

_____

5. Chilean art is important to me.

_____

6. Foolish people bother him.

_____

7. *Valdivia* is interesting to the tourists.

_____

8. It suits your (fam. sg.) interest to work hard now.

_____

B. Each question is given to you in the familiar form (singular or plural). Change each one to its corresponding polite form.

1. ¿Te gusta la literatura chilena?

_____

2. ¿Te gustan los museos de Santiago?

_____

3. ¿Te interesa ir al teatro chileno?

_____

4. ¿Te bastan 100 pesos?

_____

5. ¿Te importa leer *La Nación*?

_____

6. ¿Te conviene dormir tarde todos los días?

_____

Conjugation of *Estar*

In order to learn how to use the present progressive, called the presente progresivo, you will have to review the forms of the verb estar / *to be*. We have already learned the forms of the irregular verb estar / *to be* in Chapter 3, and we will review it here.

estar / *to be*

Subject Pronoun	Verb Form	Meaning
(yo)	estoy	*I am*
(tú)	estás	*you (fam. sg.) are*
(él, ella, Ud.)	está	*he, she, you (pol. sg.) is/are*
(nosotros/-as)	estamos	*we are*
(vosotros/-as)	estáis	*you (fam. pl.) are*
(ellos/-as, Uds.)	están	*they, you (pol. pl.) are*

The Present Progressive

The present progressive, called the presente progresivo in Spanish, is formed with the present tense of the verb estar and the present participle or the gerund of the verb, in that order.

It is very important to be aware that when we speak English, the normal verb form is the present progressive as seen below.

> What <u>are you doing</u>?
> <u>I am studying</u> Spanish.

In Spanish, however, the normal verb form is NOT the present progressive. In Spanish, the present progressive is rarely used, and when it is used, it is only to indicate what you are doing at the precise moment that you are speaking. The above interchange in English would be as follows.

> ¿Qué haces? / *What are you doing?*
> Estudio español. / *I am studying Spanish.*

When you want to know what a person is doing at the precise moment you are conversing with that person, you use the present progressive as illustrated below.

> ¿Qué <u>estás haciendo</u> ahora mismo? / *What are you doing right now?*
> <u>Estoy leyendo</u> un libro en este momento. / *I am writing a book at this moment.*

To form the present participle, or gerund, known as the gerundio in Spanish, of regular verbs:

1. Drop the infinitive ending of the verb:

hablar / *to speak*	→	habl-
comer / *to eat*	→	com-
vivir / *to live*	→	viv-

2. Add the following endings (-ando for -ar verbs; and -iendo for -er and -ir verbs) to the resulting stems:

habl+ando / *speaking*
com+iendo / *eating*
viv+iendo / *living*

hablar / *to speak*

Subject Pronoun	Estar	Present Participle	Meaning
(yo)	estoy	<u>habl</u>+ando	*I am speaking*
(tú)	estás	<u>habl</u>+ando	*you (fam. sg.) are speaking*
(él, ella, Ud.)	está	<u>habl</u>+ando	*he, she, you (pol. sg.) is/are speaking*
(nosotros/-as)	estamos	<u>habl</u>+ando	*we are speaking*
(vosotros/-as)	estáis	<u>habl</u>+ando	*you (fam. pl.) are speaking*
(ellos/-as, Uds.)	están	<u>habl</u>+ando	*they/you (pol. pl.) are speaking*

comer / *to eat*

Subject Pronoun	Estar	Present Participle	Meaning
(yo)	estoy	<u>com</u>+iendo	*I am eating*
(tú)	estás	<u>com</u>+iendo	*you (fam. sg.) are eating*
(él, ella, Ud.)	está	<u>com</u>+iendo	*he, she, you (pol. sg.) is/are eating*
(nosotros/-as)	estamos	<u>com</u>+iendo	*we are eating*
(vosotros/-as)	estáis	<u>com</u>+iendo	*you (fam. pl.) are eating*
(ellos/-as, Uds.)	están	<u>com</u>+iendo	*they/you (pol. pl.) are eating*

vivir / *to live*

Subject Pronoun	Estar	Present Participle	Meaning
(yo)	estoy	<u>viv</u>+iendo	*I am living*
(tú)	estás	<u>viv</u>+iendo	*you (fam. sg.) are living*
(él, ella, Ud.)	está	<u>viv</u>+iendo	*he, she, you (pol. sg.) is/are living*
(nosotros/-as)	estamos	<u>viv</u>+iendo	*we are living*
(vosotros/-as)	estáis	<u>viv</u>+iendo	*you (fam. pl.) are living*
(ellos/-as, Uds.)	están	<u>viv</u>+iendo	*they/you (pol.. pl.) are living*

The Present Progressive of Reflexive Verbs

Reflexive verbs always use reflexive pronouns in the present progressive tense as shown below. There are, in fact, two ways of placing the reflexive pronoun. The first example shows the placement of the reflexive pronoun before the verb estar / *to be*. The second example shows the placement of the reflexive pronoun following the present participle (gerund) and attached to it. You will also note that there is a written accent over the final vowel of the present participle (gerund) ending, to indicate that the accent is retained in its original position. We indicate this with italic type in the second example.

Reflexive Pronoun Before Estar

lavarse / *to wash oneself*

Subject Pronoun	Reflexive Pronoun	Estar	Past Participle	Meaning
(yo)	me	estoy	lav+ando	*I am washing myself*
(tú)	te	estás	lav+ando	*you (fam. sg.) are washing yourself*
(él, ella, Ud.)	se	está	lav+ando	*he, she, you (pol. sg.) is/are washing himself/herself/ yourself*
(nosotros/-as)	nos	estamos	lav+ando	*we are washing ourselves*
(vosotros/-as)	os	estáis	lav+ando	*you (fam. pl.) are washing yourselves*
(ellos/-as, Uds.)	se	están	lav+ando	*they, you (pol. pl.) are washing themselves/yourselves*

Reflexive Pronoun Following and Attached to Present Participle (Gerund)

lavarse / *to wash oneself*

Subject Pronoun	Estar	Present Participle	Meaning
(yo)	estoy	lav+ándo+me	*I am washing myself*
(tú)	estás	lav+ándo+te	*you (fam. sg.) are washing yourself*
(él, ella, Ud.)	está	lav+ándo+se	*he, she, you (pol. sg.) is/are washing himself/herself/yourself*
(nosotros/-as)	estamos	lav+ándo+nos	*we are washing ourselves*
(vosotros/-as)	estáis	lav+ándo+os	*you (fam. pl.) are washing yourselves*
(ellos/-as, Uds.)	están	lav+ándo+se	*they/you (pol. pl.) are washing themselves/yourselves*

Spelling Changes in Present Participles (Gerunds)

When there is a vowel in the stem of an -er or -ir verb, you change the -i- of the present participle (gerund) ending to a -y-. The following verbs show this change. We have indicated the change in the present participle (gerund) with an underline.

atraer / *to attract*	→ atra<u>y</u>endo
caer / *to fall*	→ ca<u>y</u>endo
construir / *to construct*	→ constru<u>y</u>endo
contribuir / *to contribute*	→ contribu<u>y</u>endo
creer / *to believe*	→ cre<u>y</u>endo
destruir / *to destroy*	→ destru<u>y</u>endo
huir / *to flee*	→ hu<u>y</u>endo
incluir / *to include*	→ inclu<u>y</u>endo
influir / *to influence*	→ influ<u>y</u>endo

oír / *to hear*	→ oy̲endo
poseer / *to possess*	→ posey̲endo
retraer / *to bring back*	→ retray̲endo
sustituir / *to substitute*	→ sustituy̲endo
sustraer / *to subtract*	→ sustray̲endo
traer / *to bring*	→ tray̲endo

GRAMMAR NOTES

The verb **ir** / *to go* has the present participle (gerund) **yendo** / *going*. This occurs because the complete infinitive (ir) corresponds to the verb ending (-ir). As a result, once the verb ending is removed, the -yendo addition becomes the gerund itself.

Stem-changing verbs in -ar and -er do not change their stem in the present participle (gerund) as shown below.

almorzar (ue) / *to have lunch* → almo̲rzando / *having lunch*
pensar (ie) / *to think* → pe̲nsando / *thinking*
entender (ie) / *to understand* → ente̲ndiendo / *understanding*
volver (ue) / *to return* → vo̲lviendo / *returning*

TIP

There are a few adverbial expressions that indicate that the present progressive is an appropriate verb tense to use. The following are some of the more common expressions.

ahora mismo / *right now*
en este momento / *at this moment*

Stem Changes in Present Participles (Gerunds)

The present participle (gerund) for -ir stem-changing verbs has a vowel change in the stem. The following are the three patterns. Refer to Chapter 2 to review stem-changing verbs. The dictionary entry for this group of verbs includes a second vowel in parentheses to indicate this change as follows: **dormir (ue, u)** / *to sleep*, **sentir (ie, i)** / *to regret*, and **pedir (i, i)** / *to ask for/to request*.

1. Third conjugation (-ir) verbs with the stem change o → ue verbs have a change of o → u in the present participle (gerund). We have underlined the stem change in the present participle (gerund).

    dormir (ue, u) → du̲rmiendo / *sleeping*
    morir (ue, u) → mu̲riendo / *dying*

2. Third conjugation (-ir) verbs with the stem change e → ie verbs have a change of e → i in the present participle (gerund). We have underlined the stem change in the present participle (gerund).

    advertir (ie, i) → advi̲rtiendo / *warning*
    consentir (ie, i) → consi̲ntiendo / *consenting*
    hervir (ie, i) → hi̲rviendo / *boiling*
    mentir (ie, i) → mi̲ntiendo / *lying*
    preferir (ie, i) → prefi̲riendo / *preferring*
    sentir (ie, i) → si̲ntiendo / *feeling*
    sugerir (ie, i) → sugi̲riendo / *suggesting*

3. Third conjugation (-ir) verbs with the stem change e → i verbs have a change of e → i in the present participle (gerund). We have underlined the stem change in the present participle (gerund).

competir (i, i) → comp<u>i</u>tiendo / *competing*
conseguir (i, i) → consi<u>g</u>uiendo / *obtaining*
decir (i, i) → d<u>i</u>ciendo / *saying, telling*
medir (i, i) → m<u>i</u>diendo / *measuring*
pedir (i, i) → p<u>i</u>diendo / *requesting, asking for*
reír (i, i) → r<u>i</u>endo / *laughing*
repetir (i, i) → rep<u>i</u>tiendo / *repeating*
seguir (i, i) → s<u>i</u>guiendo / *following*
servir (i, i) → s<u>i</u>rviendo / *serving*

GRAMMAR NOTE

Many dictionaries include a convention in their notation to alert the reader to the fact that -ir stem-changing verbs undergo a vowel change in the present participle (gerund). There are two parenthetical vowels in the dictionary entry, the first indicates a change in the present tense, and the second indicates a change in the present participle (gerund) <u>and</u> in certain forms of the preterite tense (see Chapter 7), the present subjunctive (see Chapter 15), and the past subjunctive (see Chapter 16) as illustrated below.

dormir (ue, u) / *to sleep*
mentir (ie, i) / *to lie*
pedir (i, i) / *to request, to order, to ask for*

It should be noted that decir (i, i) / *to say, to tell* is irregular in the preterite and does not have this change in that tense. From now on, we will use this convention in this book.

NOTE

Verb with the change u → ue. Jugar (ue) / *to play (a game)* is the only verb that has this change.

Jugar (ue) / *to play (a game)* → j<u>u</u>gando / *playing (a game)*

EXERCISE Set 6-3

A. Supply the missing present progressive forms of the verb escribir, giving the English equivalent.

EXAMPLE: *él* _____ = _____

él está escribiendo = *he is writing*

1. (yo) _____ = _____

2. (tú) _____ = _____

3. (nosotros) _____   =   _____

4. (ellos) _____   =   _____

5. (vosotros) _____   =   _____

6. (Ud.) _____   =   _____

Now, supply the missing present progressive forms of the verb leer, giving the English equivalent.

1. (yo) _____   =   _____

2. (Isabel y yo) _____   =   _____

3. (Uds.) _____   =   _____

4. (ellos) _____   =   _____

5. (nosotros) _____   =   _____

6. (tú) _____   =   _____

Now, supply the missing present progressive forms of the verb servir (i, i), giving the English equivalent.

1. (yo) _____   =   _____

2. (tú) _____   =   _____

3. (nosotros) _____   =   _____

4. (ellos) _____   =   _____

5. (vosotros) _____   =   _____

6. (Uds.) _____   =   _____

Now, supply the missing present progressive forms of the verb morir (ue, u), giving the English equivalent.

1. (yo) _____   =   _____

2. (tú) _____   =   _____

3. (nosotros) _____   =   _____

4. (ellos) _____   =   _____

5. (vosotros) _____   =   _____

6. (Uds.) _____   =   _____

Now, supply the missing present progressive forms of the verb bañarse, giving the English equivalent. In this case, place the reflexive pronouns before the verb estar / *to be*.

1. (yo) _____   =   _____

2. (tú) _____   =   _____

3. (nosotros) _____   =   _____

4. (ellos) _____   =   _____

5. (vosotros) _____   =   _____

6. (Uds.) _____   =   _____

Now, supply the missing present progressive forms of the verb bañarse, giving the English equivalent. In this case, place the reflexive pronoun following the present participle (gerund) and attached to it. Remember to include the written accent mark on the last vowel of the present participle ending.

1. (yo) _____   =   _____

2. (tú) _____   =   _____

3. (nosotros) _____   =   _____

4. (ellos) _____   =   _____

5. (vosotros) _____   =   _____

6. (Uds.) _____   =   _____

B. How do you say the following sentences in Spanish?

1. She's studying for her exam right now.

_____

2. They are practicing Spanish at this moment.

_____

3. We are serving the dinner to our friends.

_____

4. I am playing soccer at this moment.

_____

5. You (fam. sg.) are sleeping right now.

_____

6. I am telling the truth.

_____

7. He is eating the Chilean food now.

_____

Direct Object Pronouns

In Chapter 4, you learned about reflexive pronouns. Remember that a pronoun stands in the place of a noun, i.e., it substitutes for a noun. Now you will learn about direct object pronouns. Just like reflexive pronouns, direct object pronouns come immediately before a conjugated verb. Direct objects answer the question *whom?* or *what?* as shown below (the direct object pronouns are underlined).

<u>Whom</u> do you see?
I see <u>Mary</u>. <u>Mary</u> is the direct object.

<u>What</u> do you wear?
I wear <u>new shoes</u>. <u>New shoes</u> is the direct object.

Here are the Spanish direct object pronouns:

Singular		Plural	
1st person	me / *me*	1st person	nos / *us*
2nd person	te / *you* (fam. sg.)	2nd person	os / *you* (fam. sg.)
3rd person	lo / *him, you* (m. pol. sg.)	3rd person	los / *them, you* (m. pol. pl.)
	la / *her, you* (f. pol. sg.)		las / *them, you* (f. pol. pl.)

The English direct object pronoun *it* (or plural *them*) is expressed by the third person direct object pronoun forms above. Be careful! Choose the pronoun according to the gender and number of the noun that has been replaced. The following examples illustrate the process of changing direct objects to direct object pronouns (the direct objects and direct object pronouns are underlined).

Eva compra <u>el libro.</u> / *Eva is buying the book.*

Eva <u>lo</u> compra. / *Eva is buying it.*

Jorge compra <u>los boletos.</u> / *Jorge is buying the tickets.*

Jorge <u>los</u> compra. / *Jorge is buying them.*

Berta compra la <u>revista.</u> / *Berta is buying the magazine.*

Berta <u>la</u> compra. / *Berta is buying it.*

Jorge compra <u>las revistas.</u> / *Jorge is buying the magazines.*

Jorge <u>las</u> compra. / *Jorge is buying them.*

The placement of object pronouns relative to the verb (reflexive pronouns, direct object pronouns, indirect object pronouns) follows set patterns. As we have already noted, object pronouns must appear immediately before a conjugated verb. The situation is different, however, when there is an infinitive or a present participle (gerund) as shown below. In these two cases, the object pronoun may follow and be attached to the infinitive/present participle (gerund), or it may also go immediately before the conjugated verb.

It is precisely because of their close association with verbs that we pay so much attention to object pronouns. You will use them frequently in conversation and in writing, so you need to know how to use them. We have underlined the direct objects.

A. INFINITIVES
Eva necesita comprar <u>el libro.</u> / *Eva needs to buy the book.*
Eva necesita comprar<u>lo.</u> / *Eva needs to buy it.*
Eva <u>lo</u> necesita comprar. / *Eva needs to buy it.*

B. PRESENT PARTICIPLES
Eva está comprando <u>el libro.</u> / *Eva is buying the book.*
Eva está comprándo<u>lo.</u> / *Eva is buying it.*
Eva <u>lo</u> está comprando. / *Eva is buying it.*

EXERCISE Set 6-4

A. Replace the direct objects with direct object pronouns. Remember that there are two options with infinitives and present participles (gerunds). In these cases, write both possibilities.

EXAMPLE: Rosa hace <u>el trabajo</u>.
            Rosa <u>lo</u> hace.

            Rosa no quiere hacer <u>el trabajo</u>.
            Rosa no quiere hacer<u>lo</u>.
            Rosa no <u>lo</u> quiere hacer.

            Rosa está haciendo <u>el trabajo</u>.
            Rosa está haciéndo<u>lo</u>.
            Rosa <u>lo</u> está haciendo.

1. Pablo lee <u>las revistas</u>.

2. Pilar está bebiendo <u>el café</u>.

_____

_____

3. Quiero cantar <u>la canción</u>.

_____

_____

4. Excribimos <u>las cartas</u>.

_____

5. Ella come <u>los frijoles</u>.

_____

B. Provide the Spanish for the following sentences. Use a direct object pronoun in your answer. If there are two ways of writing the answer, please do so.

1. I see her in the car.

_____

2. You (fam. sg.) want to watch it (soap opera).

_____

3. She is reading it (the book) right now.

_____

4. They need it (money) now.

_____

C. Answer the following questions in Spanish. Use a direct object pronoun in your answer. If there are two ways of writing the answer, please do so.

1. ¿Lees los poemas de *Gabriela Mistral*[1]?

_____

2. ¿Necesitas hacer el trabajo ahora?

_____

3. ¿Están Uds. estudiando el libro de texto?

_____

[1]Chilean poet, 1889–1957; winner of the Nobel Prize, 1945.

Indirect Object Pronouns

By now, you are probably telling yourself that you have had enough of Spanish pronouns! What you need to remember is that once you learn the pronouns and the rules for their use, you will be able to use them throughout the rest of this book and in your daily communication in Spanish. They are always used in association with verbs, so you need to know how to use them. Because the third person singular (**le**) and third person plural (**les**) forms are ambiguous, it is necessary to use clarifying prepositional pronouns (with the preposition **a** / *to*) to specify the reference for these two pronominal forms. We have already seen their use with **gustar**-type constructions previously. We reproduce the indirect object pronouns here for your reference.

Singular		Plural	
1st person	me / *to me*	1st person	nos / *to us*
2nd person	te / *to you* (fam. sg.)	2nd person	os / *to you* (fam. pl.)
3rd person	le / *to him, to her, to you* (pol. sg.)	3rd person	les / *to them, to you* (pol. pl.)

Indirect object pronouns normally occur with verbs of communication and verbs of giving and transmitting (see the list on the next page). Again, just like other object pronouns (direct and reflexive), indirect object pronouns come immediately before a conjugated verb. Indirect object pronouns answer the question *to whom?* or *for whom?* (the indirect objects are underlined).

> **To whom** are you speaking?
> I am speaking **to Mary**. **To Mary** is the indirect object.

> **For whom** are you buying the book?
> I am buying the book **for Mary**. **For Mary** is the indirect object.

Indirect object pronouns appear in the same positions as reflexive pronouns and direct object pronouns, i.e., immediately before a conjugated verb but optionally following and attached to an infinitive or present participle (gerund). The following examples illustrate this. But first, the third person singular (**le**) and plural (**les**) indirect object pronoun must always be used even though it seems unnecessary to English speakers. For this reason, it is called the "redundant indirect object pronoun." You will also note that the examples include prepositional pronouns (those that are used after a preposition).

1. Conjugated verb.

Le doy el libro <u>a él</u>. / *I give the book to him.*

2. Infinitive.

Quiero decir<u>le</u> la verdad <u>a ella</u>. / *I want to tell the truth to her.*
<u>Le</u> quiero decir la verdad <u>a ella</u>. / *I want to tell the truth to her.*

3. Present participle (gerund).

Estoy escribiéndo<u>les</u> la carta <u>a ellos.</u> / *I am writing the letter to them.*
<u>Les</u> estoy escribiendo la carta <u>a ellos</u>. / *I am writing the letter to them.*

Common Verbs of Communication

contar (ue)	*to tell (a story)*	gritar	*to shout*
decir (i)	*to say, to tell*	hablar	*to speak*
escribir	*to write*		

Common Verbs of Giving or Transmitting

dar	*to give*	mostrar (ue)	*to show*
entregar	*to hand over*	vender	*to sell*
mandar	*to send*		

GRAMMAR NOTE

If you add two pronouns to an infinitive, you must write a graphic accent mark on the place where the stress original fell to indicate that it is maintained there as illustrated below.

Voy a mostrártelo. / *I am going to show it to you.*

If you add one or two pronouns to a present participle, you must write a graphic accent mark on the place where the stress originally fell to indicate that it is maintained there as we illustrate below.

.Estoy haciéndolo. / *I am doing it.*
Estoy dándotelo. / *I am giving it to you.*

EXERCISE Set 6-5

A. Provide the Spanish for the following sentences. Use an indirect object pronoun in your answer. Remember to use the redundant indirect object pronoun in the third person singular and plural. If there are two ways of writing the answer, please do so.

1. I tell the truth to her.

   _____

2. They have to write the letter to them (our friends).

   _____

   _____

3. They are speaking in Spanish to us.

   _____

   _____

B. Answer the following questions in Spanish. Use an indirect object pronoun in your answer. If there are two ways of writing the answer, please do so.

1. ¿Le das los libros a Magdalena?

   _____

2. ¿Prefieres darle los regalos a tu novia?

   _____

   _____

3. ¿Estás entregándole el paquete a Manolo?

   _____

   _____

Double Object Pronouns

It is possible to make pronouns of both indirect and direct objects in Spanish as exemplified here. When there are two object pronouns, the order is always: INDIRECT + DIRECT.

> Alba *me* da <u>el libro</u>. / *Alba gives me the book.* →
> Alba *me* <u>lo</u> da. / *Alba gives it to me.*

> Alberto *te* manda <u>la carta</u>. / *Alberto sends you the letter.* →
> Alberto *te* <u>la</u> manda. / *Albert sends it to you.*

When you use two object pronouns and one of them is either le or les, you must change the indirect object pronoun to se as shown below.

> le + direct object → se + direct object
> les + direct object → se + direct object

The following examples illustrate this change.

> Alicia *le* habla <u>español</u> a Félix. / *Alicia speaks Spanish to Félix.* →
> Alicia *se* <u>lo</u> habla *a él.* / *Alicia speaks it to him.*

> Guillermo *les* canta <u>las canciones chilenas</u> a Teresa y a Tomás. / *Guillermo sings the Chilean songs to Teresa and Tomás.* →
> Guillermo *se* <u>las</u> canta *a ellos.* / *Guillermo sings them (songs) to them.*

When you use two object pronouns with an infinitive, you may place them before the conjugated verb or after it, as illustrated below.

> Gustavo no quiere decir*le* <u>la verdad</u> a Julia. / *Gustavo doesn't want to tell the truth to Julia.*
> Gustavo no quiere decír*se*la *a ella.* / *Gustavo doesn't want to tell it to her.*
> Gustavo no *se* <u>la</u> quiere decir *a ella.* / *Gustavo doesn't want to tell it to her.*

When you use two object pronouns with a present participle (gerund), you may place them before the conjugated verb or after it, as illustrated below.

> Gustavo está diciéndo*le* <u>la verdad</u> a Julia. / *Gustavo is telling the truth to Julia.*
> Gustavo está diciéndo*se*la *a ella.* / *Gustavo is telling it to her.*
> Gustavo *se* <u>la</u> está diciendo *a ella.* / *Gustavo is telling it to her.*

EXERCISE Set 6-6

A. Replace the indirect and direct objects with indirect and direct object pronouns. Remember that there are two options with infinitives and present participles (gerunds). In these cases, write both possibilities. Remember that the order of these pronouns is always INDIRECT + DIRECT. If there are two ways of writing the answer, please do so.

EXAMPLES: Gustavo *le* dice <u>la verdad</u> *a Julia.*
Gustavo *se* <u>la</u> dice *a ella.*

Gustavo no quiere decir*le* <u>la verdad</u> *a Julia.*
Gustavo no quiere decír*se*<u>la</u> *a ella.*
Gustavo no *se* <u>la</u> quiere decir *a ella.*

Gustavo está diciéndo*le* <u>la verdad</u> *a Julia.*
Gustavo está diciéndo*se*<u>la</u> *a ella.*
Gustavo *se* <u>la</u> está diciendo *a ella.*

1. Aristófanes les escribe muchas cartas a sus padres.

   _____

2. Irene está contándole el cuento a Luisa.

   _____

   _____

3. Francisco necesita venderle la casa a Marina.

   _____

   _____

4. Ellas están dándoles el dinero a sus amigos.

   _____

   _____

5. Carlos me muestra la casa.

   _____

B. Provide the Spanish for the following sentences. Use an indirect object pronoun and a direct object in your answer. If there are two ways of writing the answer, please do so.

1. They sell them (books) to us.

   _____

2. We want to show them (photos) to them (our friends).

   _____

   _____

3. He is giving it (gift) to her.

   _____

   _____

C. Answer the following questions in Spanish. Use an indirect object and a direct object pronoun in your answer.

1. ¿Le muestras las joyas a tu novia?

   _____

2. ¿Vas a escribirles una carta a tus padres?

   _____

   _____

3. ¿Estás dándole el coche a tu hermano?

   _____

   _____

Crossword Puzzle 6

Fill in the blanks. The clues indicate the verb tenses.

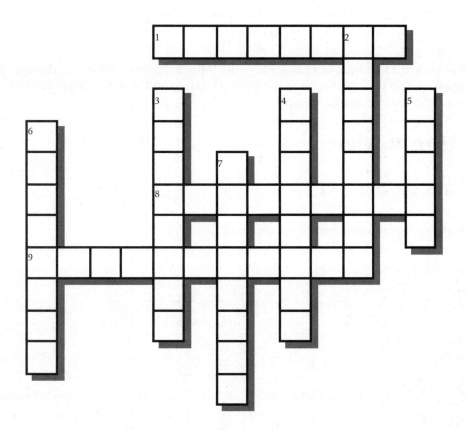

Horizontales

1. ¿Qué estás . . . (drinking)?
8. Está . . . (raining) ahora.
9. Uds. están . . . (learning) español ahora.

Verticales

2. ¿Qué estás . . . (saying) ahora?
3. En este momento, están . . . (dancing).
4. ¿Qué estás . . . (doing) ahora?
5. Yo . . . (am) trabajando ahora.
6. Él está . . . (singing) ahora.
7. Ella está . . . (eating).

Review 1
(Chapters 1–6)

This review will allow you to go over and reinforce your ability to conjugate verbs in the present indicative and present progressive, and to recognize their use in conversation and writing. There are, thus, two types of exercises: (1) *Conjugation Review* and (2) *Usage Review*.

Conjugation Review

Review Exercise Set 1-1

A. Conjugate the following regular verbs in the present indicative:

1. hablar

(yo)   _____

(tú)   _____

(él, ella, Ud.)   _____

(nosotros/-as)   _____

(vosotros/-as)   _____

(ellos/-as, Uds.)   _____

2. beber

(yo)   _____

(tú)   _____

(él, ella, Ud.)   _____

(nosotros/-as)   _____

(vosotros/-as)   _____

(ellos/-as, Uds.)   _____

3. vivir

(yo)   _____

(tú)   _____

118

(él, ella, Ud.) _____

(nosotros/-as) _____

(vosotros/-as) _____

(ellos/-as, Uds.) _____

B. Conjugate the following irregular verbs in the present indicative:

1. ser

    (yo) _____

    (tú) _____

    (él, ella, Ud.) _____

    (nosotros/-as) _____

    (vosotros/-as) _____

    (ellos/-as, Uds.) _____

2. estar

    (yo) _____

    (tú) _____

    (él, ella, Ud.) _____

    (nosotros/-as) _____

    (vosotros/-as) _____

    (ellos/-as, Uds.) _____

3. tener

    (yo) _____

    (tú) _____

    (él, ella, Ud.) _____

    (nosotros/-as) _____

    (vosotros/-as) _____

    (ellos/-as, Uds.) _____

4. hacer

    (yo) _____

    (tú) _____

    (él, ella, Ud.) _____

    (nosotros/-as) _____

    (vosotros/-as) _____

    (ellos/-as, Uds.) _____

5. conocer

    (yo) _____

    (tú) _____

    (él, ella, Ud.) _____

    (nosotros/-as) _____

    (vosotros/-as) _____

    (ellos/-as, Uds.) _____

6. saber

    (yo) _____

    (tú) _____

    (él, ella, Ud.) _____

    (nosotros/-as) _____

    (vosotros/-as) _____

    (ellos/-as, Uds.) _____

7. poner

    (yo) _____

    (tú) _____

    (él, ella, Ud.) _____

    (nosotros/-as) _____

    (vosotros/-as) _____

    (ellos/-as, Uds.) _____

8. ir

(yo) _____

(tú) _____

(él, ella, Ud.) _____

(nosotros/-as) _____

(vosotros/-as) _____

(ellos/-as, Uds.) _____

9. decir (i, i)

(yo) _____

(tú) _____

(él, ella, Ud.) _____

(nosotros/-as) _____

(vosotros/-as) _____

(ellos/-as, Uds.) _____

10. ver

(yo) _____

(tú) _____

(él, ella, Ud.) _____

(nosotros/-as) _____

(vosotros/-as) _____

(ellos/-as, Uds.) _____

11. dar

(yo) _____

(tú) _____

(él, ella, Ud.) _____

(nosotros/-as) _____

(vosotros/-as) _____

(ellos/-as, Uds.) _____

12. salir

(yo) _____

(tú) _____

(él, ella, Ud.) _____

(nosotros/-as) _____

(vosotros/-as) _____

(ellos/-as, Uds.) _____

13. venir

(yo) _____

(tú) _____

(él, ella, Ud.) _____

(nosotros/-as) _____

(vosotros/-as) _____

(ellos/-as, Uds.) _____

14. ofrecer

(yo) _____

(tú) _____

(él, ella, Ud.) _____

(nosotros/-as) _____

(vosotros/-as) _____

(ellos/-as, Uds.) _____

15. producir

(yo) _____

(tú) _____

(él, ella, Ud.) _____

(nosotros/-as) _____

(vosotros/-as) _____

(ellos/-as, Uds.) _____

16. atraer

    (yo) _____

    (tú) _____

    (él, ella, Ud.) _____

    (nosotros/-as) _____

    (vosotros/-as) _____

    (ellos/-as, Uds.) _____

17. huir

    (yo) _____

    (tú) _____

    (él, ella, Ud.) _____

    (nosotros/-as) _____

    (vosotros/-as) _____

    (ellos/-as, Uds.) _____

C. Conjugate the following stem-changing verbs in the present indicative:

1. cerrar (ie)

    (yo) _____

    (tú) _____

    (él, ella, Ud.) _____

    (nosotros/-as) _____

    (vosotros/-as) _____

    (ellos/-as, Uds.) _____

2. almorzar (ue)

    (yo) _____

    (tú) _____

    (él, ella, Ud.) _____

    (nosotros/-as) _____

(vosotros/-as) _____

(ellos/-as, Uds.) _____

3. perder (ie)

(yo) _____

(tú) _____

(él, ella, Ud.) _____

(nosotros/-as) _____

(vosotros/-as) _____

(ellos/-as, Uds.) _____

4. pedir (i, i)

(yo) _____

(tú) _____

(él, ella, Ud.) _____

(nosotros/-as) _____

(vosotros/-as) _____

(ellos/-as, Uds.) _____

D. Conjugate the following reflexive verbs in the present indicative:

1. levantarse

(yo) _____

(tú) _____

(él, ella, Ud.) _____

(nosotros/-as) _____

(vosotros/-as) _____

(ellos/-as, Uds.) _____

2. vestirse (i, i)

(yo) _____

(tú) _____

(él, ella, Ud.) _____

(nosotros/-as) _____

(vosotros/-as) _____

(ellos/-as, Uds.) _____

3. **despertarse (ie)**

(yo) _____

(tú) _____

(él, ella, Ud.) _____

(nosotros/-as) _____

(vosotros/-as) _____

(ellos/-as, Uds.) _____

E. Conjugate the following verbs in the present progressive tense:

1. **cantar**

(yo) _____

(tú) _____

(él, ella, Ud.) _____

(nosotros/-as) _____

(vosotros/-as) _____

(ellos/-as, Uds.) _____

2. **comer**

(yo) _____

(tú) _____

(él, ella, Ud.) _____

(nosotros/-as) _____

(vosotros/-as) _____

(ellos/-as, Uds.) _____

3. escribir

(yo) _____

(tú) _____

(él, ella, Ud.) _____

(nosotros/-as) _____

(vosotros/-as) _____

(ellos/-as, Uds.) _____

Usage Review

Review Exercise Set 1-2

A. Choose the appropriate verb form **a** or **b** according to the meaning:

1. (Nosotros) … la televisón.
    a. miramos
    b. jugamos

2. Mi hermano … el trabajo.
    a. toca
    b. hace

3. Mis tíos … tocar la guitarra.
    a. saben
    b. conoce

4. ¿Que hora es?
    a. Llegan a las ocho.
    b. Son las dos de la tarde.

5. Hoy … el doce de junio.
    a. está
    b. es

6. Mario … mucha hambre.
    a. tiene
    b. es

7. ¿Cuántos años tienes?
    a. Es 2005.
    b. Tengo veintiún años.

8. Ellos … nadar.
   a. saben
   b. conocen

9. Ud. … a mi profesora de español, ¿verdad?
   a. sabe
   b. conoce

10. Dolores, ¿te … este libro?
    a. gusta
    b. gustan

11. Julio, ¿Qué … ahora?
    a. estás dando
    b. estás bebiendo

12. ¿Qué tiempo … hoy?
    a. tiene
    b. hace

13. … a ir a la fiesta.
    a. Voy
    b. Tengo

14. Carla, ¿Qué … hacer hoy?
    a. quieres
    b. hablas

15. Ellos … ir al banco.
    a. tienen que
    b. conocen

16. Ignacio … en el baño.
    a. se acuesta
    b. se afeita

17. ¿Dónde …
    a. te llamas?
    b. te vistes?

18. Elena … su bolígrafo.
    a. busca
    b. influye

19. A las dos mujeres les … ese libro.
    a. gustan
    b. gusta

20. En invierno … mucho.
    a. nieva
    b. hace buen tiempo

B. Missing from the following sentences are the indicated verbs. Insert them in the spaces provided according to the meaning.

> *Verbs:* comer, conocer, estar, gustar, hablar, ir, jugar, leer, limpiar, llegar, saber,
> salir, ser, tener, vender

1. Ellos _____ al fútbol muy bien.

2. Mi abuelo _____ su coche mañana.

3. El lunes (nosotros) _____ la casa.

4. Ud. _____ las novelas de ciencia ficción.

5. Él _____ español también.

6. (Yo) _____ que estudiar los verbos españoles ahora.

7. Marta, ¿ _____ (tú) la fecha?

8. (Nosotras) _____ un buen restaurante.

9. Me _____ el libro *Conjugating and Using Spanish Verbs*.

10. Mis amigos y yo _____ el sábado por la noche.

11. La señora González siempre _____ a clase tarde.

12. ¿Qué hora _____ ?

13. Generalmente, (yo) _____ cuando miro la televisión.

14. (Yo) _____ a estudiar mañana.

15. Ella _____ enferma.

Part Two

The Past Indicative Tenses

The Past Indicative Tenses: An Overview

What Is a Past Tense?

A past tense is any tense indicating time gone by or some former action or state. There are four main indicative past tenses in Spanish:

1. The preterit, called the **pretérito**:

> **Gloria comió pescado ayer.** / *Gloria ate fish yesterday.*
> **Bebimos mucho café ayer.** / *We drank a lot of coffee yesterday.*

This tense shows that an event was completed at the time of speaking. It is equivalent to *I spoke* or *I did speak*.

2. The imperfect tense, called the **imperfecto de indicativo**:

> **Reinaldo comía pescado muchas veces.** / *Reinaldo used to eat fish often.*
> **Viajábamos a España muchas veces.** / *We used to travel to Spain often.*

This tense is used to indicate incomplete, continued, or customary past actions. English has no "true" imperfect tense, but some constructions, such as *she was studying* and *he used to study* render the meaning of imperfect verbs in Spanish in a fairly accurate way.

3. The present perfect, or the **perfecto de indicativo**:

> **Teresa ha ido a Venezuela.** / *Teresa has gone to Venezuela.*
> **Ellos han estudiado mucho en casa.** / *They have studied a lot at home.*

The present perfect is used to indicate an action that was completed prior to the present time and that has some bearing on the present time. It is equivalent to *I have gone, I have returned.*

4. The pluperfect, also known as the past perfect, or the **pluscuamperfecto de indicativo**:

> **Salvador había perdido las llaves.** / *Salvador had lost the keys.*
> **Habías encontrado a tu amigo en el centro cuando estabas en el parque.** / *You had found your friend downtown when you were in the park.*

The pluperfect (past perfect) is used to indicate that an action was completed prior to some other action that may be implied or expressed in a sentence. It is equivalent to *I had talked, I had eaten.*

Compound Tenses

The present perfect and the pluperfect (past perfect) are compound tenses. This means that they are verbs constructed of two parts, an auxiliary verb and a past participle, in that order:

1. Present Perfect Tense

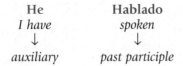

2. Past Perfect or Pluperfect Tense

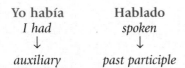

In Spanish, the tense of the auxiliary verb, present or imperfect, determines the tense of the compound verb, either present perfect, or pluperfect (past perfect).

7

The Preterit
(*el pretérito*)

Uses and Features of the Preterit

The preterit describes the past as a completed action. The preterit may report on past events as complete units of time. It may focus on the beginning, the end, or the entire event.

1. The preterit may focus on the beginning of an action:
    > **Pablo empezó la nueva lección a las ocho.** / *John began the new lesson at 8 o'clock.*

2. The preterit may focus on the end of an action:
    > **Teresa terminó la novela ayer.** / *Teresa finished the novel yesterday.*

3. The preterit may view a period of time as a completed unit of time:
    > **En España la guerra civil duró tres años.** / *In Spain, the Civil War lasted three years.*

Regular Verbs

First Conjugation Verbs

As you learned in the preceding unit, the infinitives of regular Spanish verbs end in **-ar**, **-er**, or **-ir**. Those ending in **-ar** are first-conjugation verbs. To form the preterit, called the **pretérito**, of such verbs in Spanish, do the following:

1. Drop the infinitive ending, **-ar**. This produces the verb stem.
    > <u>habl</u>**ar** / *to speak* → **habl-**

2. Add the following endings to the stem:

(yo)	-é
(tú)	-aste
(él, ella, Ud.)	-ó
(nosotros/-as)	-amos
(vosotros/-as)	-asteis
(ellos/-as, Uds.)	-aron

3. Here's the result:

hablar / to speak

Subject Pronoun	Verb Form	Meaning
(yo)	<u>habl</u>+é	*I spoke, I did speak*
(tú)	<u>habl</u>+aste	*you (fam. sg.) spoke, you did speak*
(él, ella, Ud.)	<u>habl</u>+ó	*he, she, you (pol. sg.) spoke, he, she, you did speak*
(nosotros/-as)	<u>habl</u>+amos	*we spoke, we did speak*
(vosotros/-as)	<u>habl</u>+asteis	*you (fam. pl.) spoke, you did speak*
(ellos/-as, Uds.)	<u>habl</u>+aron	*they, you (pol. pl.) spoke, they, you did speak*

Second Conjugation Verbs

Those verbs ending in -er are second conjugation verbs. To form the preterit, called the pretérito, of such verbs in Spanish, do the following:

1. Drop the infinitive ending, -er. This produces the verb stem.
<u>com</u>er / to eat → com-

2. Add the following endings to the stem:

(yo)	-í
(tú)	-iste
(él, ella, Ud.)	-ió
(nosotros/-as)	-imos
(vosotros/-as)	-isteis
(ellos/-as, Uds.)	-ieron

3. Here's the result:

comer / to eat

Subject Pronoun	Verb Form	Meaning
(yo)	<u>com</u>+í	*I ate, I did eat*
(tú)	<u>com</u>+iste	*you (fam. sg.) ate, you did eat*
(él, ella, Ud.)	<u>com</u>+ió	*he, she, you (pol. sg.) ate, he, she, you did eat*
(nosotros/-as)	<u>com</u>+imos	*we ate, we did eat*
(vosotros/-as)	<u>com</u>+isteis	*you (fam. pl.) ate, you did eat*
(ellos/-as, Uds.)	<u>com</u>+ieron	*they, you (pol. pl.) ate, they, you did eat*

Third Conjugation Verbs

Those verbs ending in -ir are third conjugation verbs. To form the preterit, called the pretérito, of such verbs in Spanish, do the following:

1. Drop the infinitive ending, -ir. This produces the verb stem.

   <u>escrib</u>ir / *to write* → escrib-

2. Add the following endings to the stem:

(yo)	-í
(tú)	-iste
(él, ella, Ud.)	-ió
(nosotros/-as)	-imos
(vosotros/-as)	-isteis
(ellos/-as, Uds.)	-ieron

3. Here's the result:

escribir / *to write*

Subject Pronoun	Verb Form	Meaning
(yo)	<u>escrib</u>+í	*I wrote, I did write*
(tú)	<u>escrib</u>+iste	*you (fam. sg.) wrote, you did write*
(él, ella, Ud.)	<u>escrib</u>+ió	*he, she, you (pol. sg.) wrote, he, she, you did write*
(nosotros/-as)	<u>escrib</u>+imos	*we wrote, we did write*
(vosotros/-as)	<u>escrib</u>+isteis	*you (fam. pl.) wrote, you did write*
(ellos/-as, Uds.)	<u>escrib</u>+ieron	*they, you (pol. pl.) wrote, they, you did write*

You have, by now, noted that the endings for second and third conjugation verbs in the preterit are <u>identical</u>. When you learn a new tense, however, it is useful to see how the endings for each conjugation work.

TIP

You will note that the nosotros, nosotras / *we* form of the first conjugation and the third conjugation are identical in the present indicative and the preterit tenses, as shown below. You can often distinguish the tense by the context and by the presence of adverbs of time.

Hablamos español ahora. / *We speak Spanish now.*
Hablamos español ayer. / *We spoke Spanish yesterday.*

Vivimos en Lima hoy. / *We live in Lima today.*
Vivimos en Lima hace diez años. / *We lived in Lima ten years ago.*

The Preterit Tense of Reflexive Verbs

Reflexive verbs always use reflexive pronouns in the preterit, as shown below. They always appear immediately before the conjugated verb, as they do in the present tense and all other tenses.

lavarse / *to wash oneself*

Subject Pronoun	Reflexive Pronoun	Conjugated Verb	Meaning
(yo)	me	lav+é	*I washed myself, I did wash myself*
(tú)	te	lav+aste	*you (fam. sg.) washed yourself, you did wash yourself*
(él, ella, Ud.)	se	lav+ó	*he, she, you (pol. sg.) washed himself/herself/yourself, he, she, you did wash himself/herself/yourself*
(nosotros/-as)	nos	lav+amos	*we washed ourselves, we did wash ourselves*
(vosotros/-as)	os	lav+asteis	*you (fam. pl.) washed yourselves, you did wash yourselves*
(ellos/-as, Uds.)	se	lav+aron	*they, you (pol. pl.) washed themselves/yourselves, they, you did wash themselves/yourselves*

GRAMMAR NOTE

Hace (from the verb hacer / *to do, to make* may be used with the preterit tense to mean *ago*, as shown in the following examples.

Construí la casa hace dos años. / *I built the house two years ago.*
Estudié esa lección hace dos semanas. / *I studied that lesson two weeks ago.*

TIP

Certain adverbial expressions of time are often used with the preterit tense. The following is a list of some of the more common ones.

anoche / *last night*
ayer / *yesterday*
anteayer / *day before yesterday*
la semana pasada / *last week*
el mes pasado / *last month*
el año pasado / *last year*

EXERCISE Set 7-1

A. Supply the missing preterit forms of the verb **cantar**, giving the English equivalent.

| EXAMPLE: | *él* _____ | = | _____ |
| | *él cantó* | = | *he sang, he did sing* |

1. (yo) _____   =   _____

2. (tú) _____   =   _____

3. (nosotros) _____   =   _____

4. (ellos) _____   =   _____

5. (vosotros) _____   =   _____

6. (Ud.) _____   =   _____

Now, supply the missing preterit forms of the verb **vender**, giving the English equivalent.

1. (yo) _____   =   _____

2. (Raquel y yo) _____   =   _____

3. (Uds.) _____   =   _____

4. (ellos) _____   =   _____

5. (vosotros) _____   =   _____

6. (tú) _____   =   _____

Now, supply the missing preterit forms of the verb **vivir**, giving the English equivalent.

1. (yo) _____   =   _____

2. (tú) _____   =   _____

3. (nosotros) _____   =   _____

4. (ellos) _____   =   _____

5. (vosotros) _____   =   _____

6. (Ud.) _____   =   _____

Now, supply the missing preterit forms of the verb **bañarse**, giving the English equivalent. Be sure to place the reflexive pronoun immediately before the conjugated verb.

1. (yo) _____   = _____

2. (tú) _____   = _____

3. (nosotros) _____ = _____

4. (ellos) _____   = _____

5. (vosotros) _____ = _____

6. (Ud.) _____   = _____

B. How do you say the following sentences in Spanish?

1. I traveled from *Lima* to *Cuzco*[1].

_____

2. They ate and drank at *Antaño*[2].

_____

3. We visited *Arequipa*[3] in the south of Peru.

_____

4. I lived in that neighborhood two years ago.

_____

5. She sang the same song last night.

_____

6. I bought a new car yesterday morning.

_____

7. You (fam. sg.) wrote an e-mail last night.

_____

8. You (pol. sg.) opened the door.

_____

9. I drank a lot of coffee this morning.

_____

10. Did you (fam. sg.) receive the gift from Elena yesterday?

_____

11. I liked the trip to *Huancayo*[4].

_____

12. His head ached last night.

_____

[1]Capital city of the Incan empire in southern Peru; [2]Restaurant with typical Peruvian food in Central Lima; [3]Tourist center located near Lake Titicaca; [4]Central Andean city known for its natural beauty and local handicrafts.

Stem-Changing Verbs

First conjugation (-ar) and second conjugation (-er) stem-changing verbs (see Chapter 2) do not have stem changes in the preterit tense. Third conjugation stem-changing verbs, however, do have stem changes that occur in the <u>third person singular and plural</u>. There are two patterns: o → u, and e → i. We will illustrate these patterns below. We will indicate where the stem changes with underlined italic type. The endings for stem-chaning verbs are regular.

When you look up these verbs in a dictionary, you will find in parentheses the following standard notations.

> dormir (ue, u) / *to sleep*
> mentir (ie, i) / *to lie*
> servir (i, i) / *to serve*

Remember that the first vowel(s) mean(s) that there is a stem change in present tense in the form of a shoe (see Chapter 2). The second vowel means that there is also a stem change in the preterit tense in the third person singular and plural, as well as the present participle (gerund; see Chapter 6). We will see examples of all three of these verbs.

dormir (ue, u) / *to sleep*

Subject Pronoun	Verb Form	Meaning
(yo)	<u>dorm</u>+í	*I slept, I did sleep*
(tú)	<u>dorm</u>+iste	*you (fam. sg.) slept, you did sleep*
(él, ella, Ud.)	<u>durm</u>+ió	*he, she, you (pol. sg.) slept, he, she, you did sleep*
(nosotros/-as)	<u>dorm</u>+imos	*we slept, we did sleep*
(vosotros/-as)	<u>dorm</u>+isteis	*you (fam. pl.) slept, you did sleep*
(ellos/-as, Uds.)	<u>durm</u>+ieron	*they, you (pol. pl.) slept, they, you did sleep*

The following verbs follow this pattern:

dormir (ue, u)	*to sleep*	morir (ue, u)	*to die*

mentir (ie, i) / *to lie*

Subject Pronoun	Verb Form	Meaning
(yo)	<u>ment</u>+í	*I lied, I did lie*
(tú)	<u>ment</u>+iste	*you (fam. sg.) lied, you did lie*
(él, ella, Ud.)	<u>mint</u>+ió	*he, she, you (pol. sg.) lied, he, she, you did lie*
(nosotros/-as)	<u>ment</u>+imos	*we lied, we did lie*
(vosotros/-as)	<u>ment</u>+isteis	*you (fam. pl.) lied, you did lie*
(ellos/-as, Uds.)	<u>mint</u>+ieron	*they, you (pol. pl.) lied, they, you did lie*

The following verbs follow this pattern:

advertir (ie, i)	*to notice*	sentir(se) (ie, i)	*to feel sorry, to regret*
mentir (ie, i)	*to lie*	sugerir (ie, i)	*to suggest*
preferir (ie, i)	*to prefer*		

servir (i, i) / *to serve*

Subject Pronoun	Verb Form	Meaning
(yo)	<u>serv</u>+í	*I served, I did serve*
(tú)	<u>serv</u>+iste	*you (fam. sg.) served, you did serve*
(él, ella, Ud.)	<u>sirv</u>+ió	*he, she, you (pol. sg.) served, he, she, you did serve*
(nosotros/-as)	<u>serv</u>+imos	*we served, we did serve*
(vosotros/-as)	<u>serv</u>+isteis	*you (fam. pl.) served, you did serve*
(ellos/-as, Uds.)	<u>sirv</u>+ieron	*they, you (pol. pl.) served, they, you did serve*

The following verbs have this pattern:

despedir (i, i)	*to fire*	pedir (i, i)	*to request, to ask for, to order*
elegir (i, i)	*to elect*	reír (i, i)	*to laugh*
freír (i, i)	*to fry*	repetir (i, i)	*to repeat*
impedir (i, i)	*to impede, to hinder*	seguir (i, i)	*to follow*
medir (i, i)	*to measure*	servir (i, i)	*to serve*

EXERCISE Set 7-2

A. Supply the missing preterit forms of the verb morir (ue, u), giving the English equivalent.

EXAMPLE: *él* _____   =   _____

                él murió   =   *he died, he did die*

1. (yo) _____   =   _____

2. (tú) _____   =   _____

3. (Marta y yo) _____   =   _____

4. (ellas) _____   =   _____

5. (vosotros) _____   =   _____

6. (Ud.) _____   =   _____

Now, supply the missing preterit forms of the verb preferir (ie, i), giving the English equivalent.

1. (yo) _____   =   _____

2. (nosotros) _____   =   _____

3. (Uds.) _____   =   _____

4. (ellos) _____   =   _____

5. (vosotros) _____   =   _____

6. (tú) _____   =   _____

Now, supply the missing preterit forms of the verb repetir (i, i), giving the English equivalent.

1. (yo) _____   =   _____

2. (nosotras) _____   =   _____

3. (Uds.) _____   =   _____

4. (ellos) _____   =   _____

5. (vosotros) _____   =   _____

6. (tú) _____   =   _____

B. How do you say the following sentences in Spanish?

1. They served a good meal in *Pisco*[1].

_____

2. Inés slept very late today.

_____

3. My friends preferred to go to the *Museo de la Nación*[2] in Lima.

_____

4. I repeated the conjugation of the preterit.

_____

5. I measured the room last night.

_____

6. He followed the teacher (m.) to the classroom.

_____

7. His grandfather died last night.

_____

8. They fried the meat in olive oil.

_____

9. He fired the employee two days ago.

_____

10. My parents never lied.

_____

[1]Town on the Southern coast of Peru; [2]Museum of aboriginal art in Lima.

Irregular Preterits

The preterit tense has some irregular forms characterized by an irregular stem and irregular endings. There are two basic patterns that we will now illustrate. It should be noted that irregular preterit verbs do not have written accents.

Irregular Preterit: Pattern 1

1. Learn the irregular preterit stem to which you add the Pattern-1 irregular preterit endings. We list them below.

> andar / *to walk* → anduv-
> caber / *to fit* → cup-
> estar / *to be* → estuv-
> haber / *to have* (auxiliary) → hub-
> hacer / *to do, to make* → hic- (hiz- in third person singular)
> poder / *can, to be able* → pud-
> poner / *to put, to place* → pus-
> querer / *to want* → quis-
> saber / *to know* → sup-
> tener / *to have* → tuv-
> venir / *to come* → vin-

2. Add the following irregular preterit tense endings to the irregular stems listed above. You will note that there are no written accents on these endings.

(yo)	-e
(tú)	-iste
(él, ella, Ud.)	-o
(nosotros/-as)	-imos
(vosotros/-as)	-isteis
(ellos/-as, Uds.)	-ieron

3. Here's the result:

venir / *to come*

Subject Pronoun	Verb Form	Meaning
(yo)	vin+e	*I came, I did come*
(tú)	vin+iste	*you (fam. sg.) came, you did come*
(él, ella, Ud.)	vin+o	*he, she, you (pol. sg.) came, he, she, you did come*
(nosotros/-as)	vin+imos	*we came, we did come*
(vosotros/-as)	vin+isteis	*you (fam. pl.) came, you did come*
(ellos/-as, Uds.)	vin+ieron	*they, you (pol. pl.) came, they, you did come*

Irregular Preterit: Pattern 2

The second pattern of irregular preterits is slightly different. All of the stems of these irregular preterits end in j-, and the third person plural form is -eron.

1. Learn the irregular preterit stem to which you add the Pattern-2 irregular preterit endings. We list them below. All of these verbs have an irregular stem that ends in a j-.

> atraer / *to attract* → atraj-
> conducir / *to drive* → conduj-
> decir / *to say, to tell* → dij-
> deducir / *to deduce, to infer* → deduj-
> distraer / *to distract* → distraj-
> introducir / *to introduce* → introduj-
> producir / *to produce* → produj-
> retraer / *to bring back, to dissuade* → retraj-
> sustraer / *to subtract, to take away* → sustraj-
> traducir / *to translate* → traduj-
> traer / *to bring* → traj-

2. Add the following irregular preterit tense endings to the irregular stems listed above. You will note that there are no written accents on these endings. The only difference between irregular preterit Pattern-1 and Pattern-2 endings is in the third person plural form. Pattern-2 endings have no -i- in this ending (-eron).

(yo)	-e
(tú)	-iste
(él, ella, Ud.)	-o
(nosotros/-as)	-imos
(vosotros/-as)	-isteis
(ellos/-as, Uds.)	-eron

3. Here's the result:

decir / *to say, to tell*

Subject Pronoun	Verb Form	Meaning
(yo)	dij+e	*I said, told, I did say, tell*
(tú)	dij+iste	*you (fam. sg.) said, told, you did say, tell*
(él, ella, Ud.)	dij+o	*he, she, you (pol. sg.) said, told, he, she, you did say, tell*
(nosotros/-as)	dij+imos	*we said, told, we did say, tell*
(vosotros/-as)	dij+isteis	*you (fam. pl.) said, told, you did say, tell*
(ellos/-as, Uds.)	dij+eron	*they, you (pol. pl.) said, told, they, you did say, tell*

> **TIP**
>
> You will note that the <u>third person singular</u> of the preterit tense ends in a stressed -ó for regular verbs and an unstressed -o for irregular verbs. Do not confuse this verb form with the unstressed -o of the present indicative tense that stands for the first person singular (yo). Consider the following examples:
>
> habl<u>o</u> / *I speak, I am speaking, I do speak*
> habl<u>ó</u> / *he, she, you spoke, he, she, you did speak*
>
> tuv<u>e</u> / *I had, I did have*
> tuv<u>o</u> / *he, she, you had, he, she, you did have*

The Preterit of Ir / *to go and* Ser / *to be*

The preterit of the verbs ir / *to go* and ser / *to be* are identical. You will also note that the first and third persons singular are different from the irregular preterit patterns noted above. We will provide conjugations of both verbs here. You will need context to distinguish the meaning.

ir / *to go*

Subject Pronoun	Verb Form	Meaning
(yo)	<u>fu</u>+i	*I went, I did go*
(tú)	<u>fu</u>+iste	*you (fam. sg.) went, you did go*
(él, ella, Ud.)	<u>fu</u>+e	*he, she, you (pol. sg.) went, he, she, you did go*
(nosotros/-as)	<u>fu</u>+imos	*we went, we did go*
(vosotros/-as)	<u>fu</u>+isteis	*you (fam. pl.) went, you did go*
(ellos/-as, Uds.)	<u>fu</u>+eron	*they, you (pol. pl.) went, they, you did go*

ser / *to be*

Subject Pronoun	Verb Form	Meaning
(yo)	<u>fu</u>+i	*I was*
(tú)	<u>fu</u>+iste	*you (fam. sg.) were*
(él, ella, Ud.)	<u>fu</u>+e	*he, she, you (pol. sg.) was, were*
(nosotros/-as)	<u>fu</u>+imos	*we were*
(vosotros/-as)	<u>fu</u>+isteis	*you (fam. pl.) were*
(ellos/-as, Uds.)	<u>fu</u>+eron	*they, you (pol. pl.) were*

The Preterit of Dar / to give and Ver / to see

There are two more verbs that have a slightly different pattern from preceding ones. They are the verbs dar / *to give* and ver / *to see*. The endings for the first and third person singular are distinct.

dar / *to give*

Subject Pronoun	Verb Form	Meaning
(yo)	<u>d</u>+i	*I gave, I did give*
(tú)	<u>d</u>+iste	*you (fam. sg.) gave, you did give*
(él, ella, Ud.)	<u>d</u>+io	*he, she, you (pol. sg.) gave, he, she, you did give*
(nosotros/-as)	<u>d</u>+imos	*we gave, we did give*
(vosotros/-as)	<u>d</u>+isteis	*you (fam. pl.) gave, you did give*
(ellos/-as, Uds.)	<u>d</u>+ieron	*they, you (pol. pl.) gave, they, you did give*

ver / *to see*

Subject Pronoun	Verb Form	Meaning
(yo)	<u>v</u>+i	*I saw, I did see*
(tú)	<u>v</u>+iste	*you (fam. sg.) saw, you did see*
(él, ella, Ud.)	<u>v</u>+io	*he, she, you (pol. sg.) saw, he, she, you did see*
(nosotros/-as)	<u>v</u>+imos	*we saw, we did see*
(vosotros/-as)	<u>v</u>+isteis	*you (fam. pl.) saw, you did see*
(ellos/-as, Uds.)	<u>v</u>+ieron	*they, you (pol. pl.) saw, they, you did see*

The Preterit of Hay / there is, there are

The preterit of the verb hay / *there is, there are* is hubo / *there was, there were*. It is used to refer to a situation as it existed in the past, but which no longer exists. The following sentences illustrate its use.

> Hubo una plaga en el pasado. / *There was a plague in the past.*
> Hubo guerras terribles en el pasado. / *There were terrible wars in the past.*

Remember also that the idiomatic form hay que / *it is necessary, one must* may also appear in the preterit as hubo que / *it was necessary*. The following sentence illustrates this usage.

> Hubo que ir a clase. / *It was necessary to go to class.*

EXERCISE Set 7-3

A. Supply the missing preterit forms of the verb **tener**, giving the English equivalent.

EXAMPLE: *él* _____   =   _____

       él tuvo   =   *he had, he did have*

1. (yo) _____   =   _____

2. (tú) _____   =   _____

3. (Marta y yo) _____   =   _____

4. (ellas) _____   =   _____

5. (vosotros) _____   =   _____

6. (Ud.) _____   =   _____

Now, supply the missing preterit forms of the verb **querer (ie)**, giving the English equivalent.

1. (yo) _____   =   _____

2. (nosotros) _____   =   _____

3. (Uds.) _____   =   _____

4. (ellos) _____   =   _____

5. (vosotros) _____   =   _____

6. (tú) _____   =   _____

Now, supply the missing preterit forms of the verb **hacer**, giving the English equivalent.

1. (yo) _____   =   _____

2. (tú) _____   =   _____

3. (nosotras) _____   =   _____

4. (Uds.) _____   =   _____

5. (vosotros) _____   =   _____

6. (Ud.) _____   =   _____

Now, supply the missing preterit forms of the verb **estar**, giving the English equivalent.

1. (yo) _____ = _____

2. (tú) _____ = _____

3. (nosotras) _____ = _____

4. (Uds.) _____ = _____

5. (vosotros) _____ = _____

6. (Ud.) _____ = _____

Now, supply the missing preterit forms of the verb **poder (ue)**, giving the English equivalent.

1. (yo) _____ = _____

2. (tú) _____ = _____

3. (nosotras) _____ = _____

4. (Uds.) _____ = _____

5. (vosotros) _____ = _____

6. (Ud.) _____ = _____

Now, supply the missing preterit forms of the verb **venir**, giving the English equivalent.

1. (yo) _____ = _____

2. (tú) _____ = _____

3. (nosotras) _____ = _____

4. (Uds.) _____ = _____

5. (vosotros) _____ = _____

6. (Ud.) _____ = _____

Now, supply the missing preterit forms of the verb **ser**, giving the English equivalent.

1. (yo) _____ = _____

2. (tú) _____ = _____

3. (nosotros) _____ = _____

4. (Uds.) _____   =   _____

5. (vosotros) _____   =   _____

6. (Ud.) _____   =   _____

Now, supply the missing preterit forms of the verb traducir, giving the English equivalent.

1. (yo) _____   =   _____

2. (tú) _____   =   _____

3. (nosotros) _____   =   _____

4. (Uds.) _____   =   _____

5. (vosotros) _____   =   _____

6. (Ud.) _____   =   _____

Now, supply the missing preterit forms of the verb ir, giving the English equivalent.

1. (yo) _____   =   _____

2. (tú) _____   =   _____

3. (nosotros) _____   =   _____

4. (Uds.) _____   =   _____

5. (vosotros) _____   =   _____

6. (Ud.) _____   =   _____

Now, supply the missing preterit forms of the verb conducir, giving the English equivalent.

1. (yo) _____   =   _____

2. (tú) _____   =   _____

3. (nosotros) _____   =   _____

4. (Uds.) _____   =   _____

5. (vosotros) _____   =   _____

6. (Ud.) _____   =   _____

B. How do you say the following sentences in Spanish?

1. We drove from *Lima* to *Tacna*[1].

   _____

2. I gave the money to my friend.

   _____

3. Raquel and I went downtown to eat dinner.

   _____

4. They took a walk in *Parque Kennedy*[2].

   _____

5. I came to class late.

   _____

6. I fell in the street.

   _____

7. I told the truth to Marco.

   _____

8. I translated the verbs from English to Spanish.

   _____

9. We were at home when I saw her.

   _____

10. I was president of the organization last year.

    _____

11. Yesterday it was bad weather because it rained a lot.

    _____

12. It was very cold in February because it snowed a lot.

    _____

[1]City in Southern Peru near the Chilean border; [2]Beautiful park in the suburban Miraflores section of Lima.

Spelling Changes in the Preterit

Certain verbs have spelling changes in some forms of the preterit tense. There are three types of spelling changes as shown here. It must be remembered that the endings for each verb are completely regular and that they all follow the pattern for regular -ar preterit verbs.

1. Verbs that end in -gar, the first person singular (yo) form is -gué.
2. Verbs that end in -car, the first person singular (yo) form is -qué.
3. Verbs that end in -zar, the first person singular (yo) form is -cé.

We will now look at a conjugation in the preterit for each verb category. We will also provide a list of common verbs for each of these verb types.

llegar / *to arrive*

Subject Pronoun	Verb Form	Meaning
(yo)	lle*gu*+é	*I arrived, I did arrive*
(tú)	lleg+aste	*you (fam. sg.) arrived, you did arrive*
(él, ella, Ud.)	lleg+ó	*he, she, you (pol. sg.) arrived, he, she, you did arrive*
(nosotros/-as)	lleg+amos	*we arrived, we did arrive*
(vosotros/-as)	lleg+asteis	*you (fam. pl.) arrived, you did arrive*
(ellos/-as, Uds.)	lleg+aron	*they, you (pol. pl.) arrived, they, you did arrive*

The following verbs have this pattern.

conjugar	*to conjugate*	regar (ie)	*to water (a plant)*
llegar	*to arrive*	tragar	*to swallow*
jugar (ue)	*to play (a game)*	vagar	*to wander*
pagar	*to pay for*		

buscar / *to look for*

Subject Pronoun	Verb Form	Meaning
(yo)	bus*qu*+é	*I looked for, I did look for*
(tú)	busc+aste	*you (fam. sg.) looked for, you did look for*
(él, ella, Ud.)	busc+ó	*he, she, you (pol. sg.) looked for, he, she, you did look for*
(nosotros/-as)	busc+amos	*we looked for, we did look for*
(vosotros/-as)	busc+asteis	*you (fam. pl.) looked for, you did look for*
(ellos/-as, Uds.)	busc+aron	*they, you (pol. pl.) looked for, they, you did look for*

The following verbs have this pattern.

buscar	*to look for*	practicar	*to practice*
clasificar	*to classify*	sacar	*to take, to take a photo*
destacar	*to stand out*	tocar	*to touch, to play (an instrument)*
justificar	*to justify*		

organizar / *to organize*

Subject Pronoun	Verb Form	Meaning
(yo)	<u>organic</u>+é	*I organized, I did organize*
(tú)	<u>organiz</u>+aste	*you (fam. sg.) organized, you did organize*
(él, ella, Ud.)	<u>organiz</u>+ó	*he, she, you (pol. sg.) organized, he, she, you did organize*
(nosotros/-as)	<u>organiz</u>+amos	*we organized, we did organize*
(vosotros/-as)	<u>organiz</u>+asteis	*you (fam. pl.) organized, you did organize*
(ellos/-as, Uds.)	<u>organiz</u>+aron	*they, you (pol. pl.) organized, they, you did organize*

The following verbs have this pattern.

autorizar	*to authorize*	rezar	*to pray*
comenzar (ie)	*to begin*	trazar	*to trace*
empezar (ie)	*to begin*	tropezarse (ie) (con)	*to stumble (into)*

Verbs with i → y Change in the Preterit

There is another group of verbs that have the change i → y in the preterit in the third person singular and plural. This change occurs because the unstressed i appears between two vowels. The following conjugation illustrates this spelling change. Note that in all of the other forms of the verb, there is a written accent over the í.

leer / *to read*

Subject Pronoun	Verb Form	Meaning
(yo)	<u>le</u>+í	*I read, I did read*
(tú)	<u>le</u>+íste	*you (fam. sg.) read, you did read*
(él, ella, Ud.)	<u>le</u>+yó	*he, she, you (pol. sg.) read, he, she, you did read*
(nosotros/-as)	le+ímos	*we read, we did read*
(vosotros/-as)	le+ísteis	*you (fam. pl.) read, you did read*
(ellos/-as, Uds.)	<u>le</u>+yeron	*they, you (pol. pl.) read, they, you did read*

The following verbs have this pattern.

caer	*to fall*	oír	*to hear*
caerse	*to fall down*	poseer	*to possess*
creer	*to believe*	proveer	*to provide*

There is another slightly different verbal pattern in the preterit in which i → y. This group of verbs ends in -uir. This group is different from the previous one because the written accent occurs only over the yo form of the verb (í). The vowel -i- in the remaining verbal endings (second person singular, first and second person plural) does not receive a written accent. The following conjugation illustrates this spelling change.

huir / *to flee*

Subject Pronoun	Verb Form	Meaning
(yo)	hu+í	*I fled, I did flee*
(tú)	hu+iste	*you (fam. sg.) fled, you did flee*
(él, ella, Ud.)	hu+yó	*he, she, you (pol. sg.) fled, he, she, you did flee*
(nosotros/-as)	hu+imos	*we fled, we did flee*
(vosotros/-as)	hu+isteies	*you (fam. pl.) fled, you did flee*
(ellos/-as, Uds.)	hu+yeron	*they, you (pol. pl.) fled, they, you did flee*

The following verbs have this pattern.

construir	*to build*	fluir	*to flow*
contribuir	*to contribute*	incluir	*to include*
destruir	*to destroy*	influir	*to influence*

EXERCISE Set 7-4

A. Supply the missing preterit forms of the verb jugar (ue), giving the English equivalent.

EXAMPLE: *él* _____   =   _____

               él jugó   =   *he played, he did play*

1. (yo) _____   =   _____

2. (tú) _____   =   _____

3. (nosotras) _____   =   _____

4. (Uds.) _____   =   _____

5. (vosotros) _____   =   _____

6. (Ud.) _____   =   _____

Now, supply the missing preterit forms of the verb tocar, giving the English equivalent.

1. (yo) _____   =   _____

2. (tú) _____   =   _____

3. (nosotras) _____   =   _____

4. (Uds.) _____   =   _____

5. (vosotros) _____   =   _____

6. (Ud.) _____   =   _____

Now, supply the missing preterit forms of the verb **empezar (ie)**, giving the English equivalent.

1. (yo) _____   =   _____

2. (tú) _____   =   _____

3. (nosotras) _____   =   _____

4. (Uds.) _____   =   _____

5. (vosotros) _____   =   _____

6. (Ud.) _____   =   _____

Now, supply the missing preterit forms of the verb **oír**, giving the English equivalent.

1. (yo) _____   =   _____

2. (tú) _____   =   _____

3. (nosotras) _____   =   _____

4. (Uds.) _____   =   _____

5. (vosotros) _____   =   _____

6. (Ud.) _____   =   _____

Now, supply the missing preterit forms of the verb **construir**, giving the English equivalent.

1. (yo) _____   =   _____

2. (tú) _____   =   _____

3. (nosotras) _____   =   _____

4. (Uds.) _____   =   _____

5. (vosotros) _____   =   _____

6. (Ud.) _____   =   _____

B. How do you say the following sentences in Spanish?

1. I ate lunch with my friend (m.) in a good Peruvian restaurant.

   _____

2. I read *La República*[1] early this morning.

   _____

3. I contributed 100 *soles* yesterday.

   _____

4. We heard the woman in the street.

   _____

5. They built an expensive home.

   _____

6. The guilty man fled from the police.

   _____

7. It began to rain yesterday.

   _____

8. He stumbled into the chair.

   _____

9. I played the guitar for my sister.

   _____

10. The storm destroyed my home.

    _____

[1] Peruvian newspaper.

C. Provide the corresponding preterit forms for the following verbs in the present indicative tense.

1. hablamos _____

2. tienen _____

3. van _____

4. somos _____

5. estás _____

6. dice _____

7. comemos _____

8. vivimos _____

9. me acuesto _____

10. soy _____

11. duermen _____

12. pide _____

13. hace _____

14. tienes _____

15. entiendo _____

16. puedo _____

17. quieren _____

18. empiezo _____

Meaning Change in Preterit Verbs

There is a small group of verbs that has a change of meaning when they are used in the preterit. The following is a list of these verbs.

Verb	Meaning in Present Tense	Meaning in Preterit Tense
conocer	to know (a person)	Conocí a Luis ayer. / I <u>met</u> Louis yesterday.
poder	to be able	Pude ir a Trujillo. I <u>managed</u> to go to Trujillo.
no poder	not to be able	No pude estudiar español anoche. / I <u>failed</u> to study Spanish last night.
querer	to want	Quise visitar Iquitos. / I <u>tried</u> to visit Iquitos.
no querer	not to want	No quise leer el libro. / I <u>refused</u> to read the book.
saber	to know (a fact)	Supe la verdad. / I <u>found out</u> the truth.
tener	to have	Tuve una carta de mi familia. / I received a letter from my family.

EXERCISE Set 7-5

A. How do you say the following sentences in Spanish?

1. I received a gift from my mother last night.

    _____

2. I failed to conjugate all of the Spanish verbs.

    _____

3. He met his wife in an elevator.

    _____

4. We discovered the truth last year.

    _____

5. I managed to find my book at home.

    _____

6. They tried to study but they failed.

    _____

Crossword Puzzle 7

Fill in the blanks. Use the following verbs in the preterit tense in your answers: andar, beber, conocer, decir, estar, gustar, hacer, ir, leer, perder.

Horizontales
2. . . . mucho calor ayer.
5. Félix y Juana . . . el libro anoche.
6. (Tú) . . . la bolsa.
9. Me . . . los libros.
10. Ellos . . . a Marta en la fiesta.

Verticales
1. ¿ . . . (tú) la verdad?
3. Marisol . . . en el parque ayer.
4. (Nosotros) . . . mucho café ayer.
7. . . . nublado ayer.
8. Laura y yo . . . al centro.

8

The Imperfect Indicative (*el imperfecto de indicativo*) and the Imperfect Progressive (*el imperfecto progresivo*)

Uses and Features

"Imperfect indicative" means incomplete. The imperfect indicative is, thus, a tense used to express or describe an action, event, or state of being that was incomplete, continuous, or habitual in the past. Specifically, it is used:

1. To express an action in the past that went on simultaneously with another action:

> Mientras que mi madre leía, mi padre miraba la televisión. / *While my mother was reading, my father was watching TV.*
> Mientras que mi madre estaba leyendo, mi padre estaba mirando la televisión. / *While my mother was reading, my father was watching TV.*

2. To express an action that was ongoing while another action occurred in the past:

> Mi hermana escuchaba un disco cuando llamé por teléfono. / *My sister was listening to a CD when I telephoned.*
> Mi hermana estaba escuchando un disco cuando llamé por teléfono. / *My sister was listening to a CD when I telephoned.*

3. To indicate a past action, desire, condition, etc. that took place habitually:

> Cuando estábamos en Ecuador, íbamos con frecuencia al mar. / *When we were in Ecuador, we frequently went to the sea.*
> De niño, yo siempre quería comer las alcachofas. / *As a child, I always wanted to eat artichokes.*

4. To describe a former, earlier, or bygone mental, emotional, or physical condition or situation. The most common verbs used in this way are:

> **creer** / *to think*, **estar** / *to be*, **pensar** / *to think*, **poder** / *to be able*, **preferir** / *to prefer*, **querer** / *to want*, **saber** / *to know*, **sentir** / *to feel*, **ser** / *to be*, **tener** / *to have*.

> **De niña, ella tenía el pelo rubio.** / *As a child, she had blonde hair.*
> **De niño, yo sabía hablar dos idiomas.** / *As a child, I knew how to speak two languages.*

5. To refer to routine time of the day in the past:

> **¿A qué hora tenías la clase de español?** / *At what time did you use to have Spanish class?*

6. To quote someone directly in the past:

> **Carlos dijo que él iba a la fiesta.** / *Carlos said that he was going to the party.*

7. To express time and age:

> **Eran las cinco de la tarde cuando regresé a casa.** / *It was 5 P.M. when I returned home.*
> **Yo tenía treinta años el año pasado.** / *I was thirty last year.*

Regular -ar Verbs

To form the imperfect indicative, called the **imperfecto de indicativo**, of regular -ar verbs, do the following:

1. Drop the -ar from the infinitive:
   hablar / *to speak* → habl-

2. Add the following endings to the stem according to person and number (note that the **nosotros/-as** / *we* form has a graphic accent):

(yo)	-aba
(tú)	-abas
(él, ella, Ud.)	-aba
(nosotros/-as)	-ábamos
(vosotros/-as)	-abais
(ellos/-as, Uds.)	-aban

3. Here's the result:

hablar / *to speak*

Subject Pronoun	Verb Form	Meaning
(yo)	habl+aba	*I was speaking, I used to speak*
(tú)	habl+abas	*you (fam. sg.) were speaking, you used to speak*
(él, ella, Ud.)	habl+aba	*he, she, you (pol. sg.) was/were speaking, he, she, you used to speak*
(nosotros/-as)	habl+ábamos	*we were speaking, we used to speak*
(vosotros/-as)	habl+abais	*you (fam. pl.) were speaking, you used to speak*
(ellos/-as, Uds.)	habl+aban	*they, you (pol. pl.) were speaking, they, you used to speak*

Regular -er and -ir Verbs

To form the imperfect indicative of regular -er and -ir verbs, called the imperfecto de indicativo, do the following:

1. Drop the -er and -ir from the infinitive (the endings are the same for second and third conjugation verbs in the imperfect tense):

    <u>com</u>er / *to eat* → com-
    <u>abr</u>ir / *to open* → abr-

2. Add the following endings to the stem according to person and number:

(yo)	-ía
(tú)	-ías
(él, ella, Ud.)	-ía
(nosotros/-as)	-íamos
(vosotros/-as)	-íais
(ellos/-as, Uds.)	-ían

3. Here's the result:

comer / *to eat*

Subject Pronoun	Verb Form	Meaning
(yo)	<u>com</u>+ía	*I was eating, I used to eat*
(tú)	<u>com</u>+ías	*you (fam. sg.) were eating, you used to eat*
(él, ella, Ud.)	<u>com</u>+ía	*he, she, you (pol. sg.) was/were eating, he, she, you used to eat*
(nosotros/-as)	<u>com</u>+íamos	*we were eating, we used to eat*
(vosotros/-as)	<u>com</u>+íais	*you (fam. pl.) were eating, you used to eat*
(ellos/-as, Uds.)	<u>com</u>+ían	*they, you (pol. pl.) were eating, they, you used to eat*

abrir / *to open*

Subject Pronoun	Verb Form	Meaning
(yo)	<u>abr</u>+ía	*I was opening, I used to open*
(tú)	<u>abr</u>+ías	*you (fam. sg.) were opening, you used to open*
(él, ella, Ud.)	<u>abr</u>+ía	*he, she, you (pol. sg.) was/were opening, he, she, you used to open*
(nosotros/-as)	<u>abr</u>+íamos	*we were opening, we used to open*
(vosotros/-as)	<u>abr</u>+íais	*you (fam. pl.) were opening, you used to open*
(ellos/-as, Uds.)	<u>abr</u>+ían	*they, you (pol. pl.) were opening, they, you used to open*

The Imperfect Indicative of Reflexive Verbs

Reflexive verbs always use reflexive pronouns in the imperfect indicative as shown below. They always appear immediately before the conjugated verb as they do in all tenses.

lavarse / *to wash oneself*

Subject Pronoun	Reflexive Pronoun	Conjugated Verb	Meaning
(yo)	me	<u>lav</u>+aba	*I was washing myself, I used to wash myself*
(tú)	te	<u>lav</u>+abas	*you (fam. sg.) were washing yourself, you used to wash yourself*
(él, ella, Ud.)	se	<u>lav</u>+aba	*he, she, you (pol. sg.) was/were washing himself/ herself/yourself, he, she, you used to wash himself/ herself/yourself*
(nosotros/-as)	nos	<u>lav</u>+ábamos	*we were washing ourselves, we used to wash ourselves*
(vosotros/-as)	os	<u>lav</u>+abais	*you (fam. pl.) were washing yourselves, you used to wash yourselves*
(ellos/-as, Uds.)	se	<u>lav</u>+aban	*they, you (pol. pl.) were washing themselves/yourselves, they, you used to wash themselves/yourselves*

Irregular Imperfect Indicative Verbs

You will be delighted to learn that there are only three irregular imperfect indicative verbs: **ir** / *to go*, **ser** / *to be*, and **ver** / *to see*. Their conjugations in the imperfect indicative follow.

ir / *to go*

Subject Pronoun	Verb Form	Meaning
(yo)	<u>ib</u>+a	*I was going, I used to go*
(tú)	<u>ib</u>+as	*you (fam. sg.) were going, you used to go*
(él, ella, Ud.)	<u>ib</u>+a	*he, she, you (pol. sg.) was/were going, he, she, you used to go*
(nosotros/-as)	<u>íb</u>+amos	*we were going, we used to go*
(vosotros/-as)	<u>ib</u>+ais	*you (fam. pl.) were going, you used to go*
(ellos/-as, Uds.)	<u>ib</u>+an	*they, you (pol. pl.) were going, they, you used to go*

ser / *to be*

Subject Pronoun	Verb Form	Meaning
(yo)	<u>er</u>+a	*I was, I used to be*
(tú)	<u>er</u>+as	*you (fam. sg.) were, you used to be*
(él, ella, Ud.)	<u>er</u>+a	*he, she, you (pol. sg.) was/were, he, she, you used to be*
(nosotros/-as)	<u>ér</u>+amos	*we were, we used to be*
(vosotros/-as)	<u>er</u>+ais	*you (fam. pl.) were, you used to be*
(ellos/-as, Uds.)	<u>er</u>+an	*they, you (pol. pl.) were, they, you used to be*

ver / *to see*

Subject Pronoun	Verb Form	Meaning
(yo)	<u>ve</u>+ía	*I was seeing, I used to see*
(tú)	<u>ve</u>+ías	*you (fam. sg.) were seeing, you used to see*
(él, ella, Ud.)	<u>ve</u>+ía	*he, she, you (pol. sg.) was/were seeing, he, she, you used to see*
(nosotros/-as)	<u>ve</u>+íamos	*we were seeing, we used to see*
(vosotros/-as)	<u>ve</u>+íais	*you (fam. pl.) were seeing, you used to see*
(ellos/-as, Uds.)	<u>ve</u>+ían	*they, you (pol. pl.) were seeing, they, you used to see*

TIP

There are no stem changes in the imperfect indicative tense. So you don't have to worry about remembering!

NOTE

You have probably noticed that the first person singular (yo) and third person singular (él, ella, Ud.) forms of the imperfect tense are identical in form. For this reason, you must normally use the subject pronoun yo / *I* to distinguish these forms.

GRAMMAR NOTE

The verb hacer / *to do, to make* may appear in a special idiomatic construction with the imperfect indicative tense as illustrated below. This construction indicates that a specified activity began in the past and continued in the past.

¿Cuánto tiempo hacía que estudiabas español? / *How long had you been studying Spanish?*
Hacía un año que yo estudiaba español. / *I had been studying Spanish for a year.*

The above question and answer may be expressed in a different way as seen below.

¿Desde cuándo estudiabas español? / *How long had you been studying Spanish?*
Yo estudiaba español desde hacía un año. / *I had been studying Spanish for a year.*

EXERCISE Set 8-1

A. Supply the missing imperfect indicative forms of the verb **cantar**, giving the English equivalent.

EXAMPLE: *él* _____   =   _____

                 él cantaba   =   *he was singing, he used to sing*

1. (yo) _____   =   _____

2. (tú) _____   =   _____

3. (nosotros) _____   =   _____

4. (ellos) _____   =   _____

5. (vosotros) _____   =   _____

6. (Ud.) _____   =   _____

Now, supply the missing imperfect indicative forms of the verb **tener**, giving the English equivalent.

1. (yo) _____   =   _____

2. (Rachel y yo) _____   =   _____

3. (Uds.) _____   =   _____

4. (ellos) _____   =   _____

5. (vosotros) _____   =   _____

6. (tú) _____   =   _____

Now, supply the missing imperfect indicative forms of the verb **decir (i, i)**, giving the English equivalent.

1. (yo) _____   =   _____

2. (tú) _____   =   _____

3. (nosotros) _____   =   _____

4. (ellos) _____   =   _____

5. (vosotros) _____   =   _____

6. (Ud.) _____   =   _____

Now, supply the missing imperfect indicative forms of the verb ser, giving the English equivalent.

1. (yo) _____   =   _____

2. (tú) _____   =   _____

3. (nosotros) _____   =   _____

4. (ellos) _____   =   _____

5. (vosotros) _____   =   _____

6. (Ud.) _____   =   _____

Now, supply the missing imperfect indicative forms of the verb ir, giving the English equivalent.

1. (yo) _____   =   _____

2. (tú) _____   =   _____

3. (nosotros) _____   =   _____

4. (ellos) _____   =   _____

5. (vosotros) _____   =   _____

6. (Ud.) _____   =   _____

Now, supply the missing imperfect indicative forms of the verb ver, giving the English equivalent.

1. (yo) _____   =   _____

2. (tú) _____   =   _____

3. (nosotros) _____   =   _____

4. (ellos) _____   =   _____

5. (vosotros) _____   =   _____

6. (Ud.) _____   =   _____

Now, supply the missing imperfect indicative forms of the verb levantarse, giving the English equivalent.

1. (yo) _____   =   _____

2. (tú) _____   =   _____

3. (nosotros) _____   =   _____

4. (ellos) _____   =   _____

5. (vosotros) _____   =   _____

6. (Ud.) _____   =   _____

B. How do you say the following sentences in Spanish?

1. I used to live in Quito.

   _____

2. I was very nice as a child.

   _____

3. It was 9 P.M.

   _____

4. We used to go to school every day.

   _____

5. As a child, Isabel had blond hair.

   _____

6. It was raining and it was cloudy.

   _____

7. They wanted to see the latest movie.

   _____

8. I liked to read the books of *Jorge Icaza*[1].

   _____

9. Were you (fam. sg.) playing soccer?

   _____

10. I used to work in that store.

_____

11. They were studying in the library.

_____

[1]Ecuadorean novelist, 1906–1978; author of *Huasipungo*, 1934.

Imperfect Indicative of Hay

The imperfect indicative of hay / *there is, there are* is había / *there was, there were*. It is used in the same way that hay is used, except that it is in the imperfect indicative tense. The following sentences illustrate this point.

> Había mucho papel en la calle. / *There was a lot of paper in the street.*
> Había muchas personas en la fiesta. / *There were a lot of people at the party.*

The imperfect indicative of the idiomatic expression hay que / *one must, it is necessary to* is había que / *it was necessary to*. The following sentence illustrates this usage.

> Había que ir a Quito para estudiar la literatura ecuatoriana. / *It was necessary to go to Quito to study Ecuadorean literature.*

Imperfect Progressive

The imperfect progressive, called the imperfecto progresivo in Spanish, is an alternative to the imperfect indicative. It corresponds, basically, to the present progressive (Chapter 6), allowing you to zero in on an action in the past that was ongoing at the time (usually relative to another action):

> Ayer, mientras mi hermana estaba comiendo, yo estaba mirando la televisión. / *Yesterday, while my sister was eating, I was watching TV.*

The imperfect progressive is formed with the imperfect indicative tense of estar / *to be* and the present participle of the verb. Review Chapter 6 for the formation of the present participle (gerund) and for its irregular forms.

Here are three verbs conjugated in the imperfect progressive:

hablar / *to speak*

Subject Pronoun	Estar	Present Participle	Meaning
(yo)	est+aba	habl+ando	*I was speaking*
(tú)	est+abas	habl+ando	*you (fam. sg.) were speaking*
(él, ella, Ud.)	est+aba	habl+ando	*he, she, you (pol. sg.) was/were speaking*
(nosotros/-as)	est+ábamos	habl+ando	*we were speaking*
(vosotros/-as)	est+abais	habl+ando	*you (fam. pl.) were speaking*
(ellos/-as, Uds.)	est+aban	habl+ando	*they, you (pol. pl.) were speaking*

comer / to eat

Subject Pronoun	Estar	Present Participle	Meaning
(yo)	est+aba	com+iendo	I was eating
(tú)	est+abas	com+iendo	you (fam. sg.) were eating
(él, ella, Ud.)	est+aba	com+iendo	he, she, you (pol. sg.) was/were eating
(nosotros/-as)	est+ábamos	com+iendo	we were eating
(vosotros/-as)	est+abais	com+iendo	you (fam. pl.) were eating
(ellos/-as, Uds.)	est+aban	com+iendo	they, you (pol. pl.) were eating

vivir / to live

Subject Pronoun	Estar	Present Participle	Meaning
(yo)	est+aba	viv+iendo	I was living
(tú)	est+abas	viv+iendo	you (fam. sg.) were living
(él, ella, Ud.)	est+aba	viv+iendo	he, she, you (pol. sg.) was/were living
(nosotros/-as)	est+ábamos	viv+iendo	we were living
(vosotros/-as)	est+abais	viv+iendo	you (fam. pl.) were living
(ellos/-as, Uds.)	est+aban	viv+iendo	they, you (pol. pl.) were living

The Imperfect Progressive of Reflexive Verbs

Reflexive verbs always also use reflexive pronouns in the imperfect progressive tense. As we noted in our discussion of the present progressive of reflexive verbs (see Chapter 6), there are, in fact, two ways of placing the reflexive pronoun. We illustrate both possibilities here. The first example shows the placement of the reflexive pronoun before the verb estar / to be. The second example shows the placement of the reflexive pronoun following and attached to the present participle. In the latter case, you will note that there is a written accent over the final vowel of the present participle ending, to indicate that the accent is retained in its original position. We have highlighted the graphic accent with italics in the second example.

Reflexive Pronoun Before Estar

lavarse / to wash oneself

Subject Pronoun	Reflexive Pronoun	Estar	Past Participle	Meaning
(yo)	me	est+aba	lav+ando	I was washing myself
(tú)	te	est+abas	lav+ando	you (fam. sg.) were washing yourself
(él, ella, Ud.)	se	est+aba	lav+ando	he, she, you (pol. sg.) was/were washing himself/ herself/ yourself
(nosotros/-as)	nos	est+ábamos	lav+ando	we were washing ourselves
(vosotros/-as)	os	est+abais	lav+ando	you (fam. pl.) were washing yourselves
(ellos/-as, Uds.)	se	est+aban	lav+ando	they, you (pol. pl.) were washing themselves/yourselves

Reflexive Pronoun Following and Attached to Present Participle (Gerund)

lavarse / *to wash oneself*

Subject Pronoun	Estar	Present Participle	Meaning
(yo)	<u>est</u>+aba	<u>lav</u>+*á*ndo+me	*I was washing myself*
(tú)	<u>est</u>+abas	<u>lav</u>+*á*ndo+te	*you (fam. sg.) were washing yourself*
(él, ella, Ud.)	<u>est</u>+aba	<u>lav</u>+*á*ndo+se	*he, she, you (pol. sg.) was/were washing himself/herself/yourself*
(nosotros/-as)	<u>est</u>+*á*bamos	<u>lav</u>+*á*ndo+nos	*we were washing ourselves*
(vosotros/-as)	<u>est</u>+abais	<u>lav</u>+*á*ndo+os	*you (fam. pl.) were washing yourselves*
(ellos/-as, Uds.)	<u>est</u>+aban	<u>lav</u>+*á*ndo+se	*they, you (pol. pl.) were washing themselves/yourselves*

EXERCISE Set 8-2

A. Replace the imperfect indicative forms of the given verbs with the corresponding imperfect progressive forms.

EXAMPLE: *él comía*   = _____

   él estaba comiendo =   *he was eating*

1. yo pagaba   = _____

2. empezabas   = _____

3. comíamos   = _____

4. ellos preferían   = _____

5. jugabais   = _____

6. Ud. estudiaba   = _____

7. ellas cantaban   = _____

8. dábamos   = _____

9. yo creía   = _____

10. Uds. hacían   = _____

11. escribíamos   = _____

12. yo salía   =   _____

13. te levantabas (2 ways) =   _____

                              =   _____

B. How do you say the following sentences in Spanish? Use the imperfect progressive in your answers.

1. You (fam. sg.) were reading *Hoy*[1].

_____

2. Sofía was studying Spanish verbs.

_____

3. Roberto and I were watching television.

_____

4. My friends were playing soccer.

_____

5. He was preparing the meal.

_____

[1]Daily newspaper in Quito.

VOCABULARY TIP

Certain adverbs of time are commonly used with the imperfect indicative because they express repeated or habitual action.

a menudo / *often*	siempre / *always*
con frecuencia / *frequently*	todas las noches / *every night*
de niño/-a / *as a child*	todas las semanas / *every week*
frecuentemente / *frequently*	todos los años / *every year*
generalmente / *generally*	todos los días / *every day*
muchas veces / *often*	todos los meses / *every month*

A Comparison of the Meaning of Selected Verbs in the Imperfect Indicative and the Preterit

There is a small group of verbs that has a change of meaning when they are used in the preterit (see Chapter 7). The following is a list of the meanings of these verbs in the imperfect indicative and the preterite tenses.

Verb	Meaning in Imperfect Tense	Meaning in Preterite Tense
Conocer / to know a person	Yo conocía a Luis. / I used to know Luis.	Conocí a Luis. / I _met_ Luis.
Poder / to be able, can	Yo podía ir a Cuenca. / I was able to go to Cuenca.	Pude ir a Cuenca. / I _managed_ to go to Cuenca.
no poder / not to be able, can	Yo no podía estudiar español anoche. / I could not study Spanish last night.	No pude estudiar español anoche. / I _failed_ to study Spanish last night.
querer / to want	Yo quería visitar Otavalo. / I wanted to visit Otavalo.	Quise visitar Otavalo. / I _tried_ to visit Otavalo.
no querer / not to want	Yo no quería leer el libro. / I did not want to read the book.	No quise leer el libro. / I _refused_ to read the book.
saber / to know (a fact)	Yo sabía la verdad. / I knew the truth.	Supe la verdad. / I _found out_ the truth.
tener / to have	Yo tenía una carta de mi familia. / I had a letter from my family.	Tuve una carta de mi familia. / I _received_ a letter from my family.

A Comparison of the Uses of the Imperfect Indicative and the Preterit Tenses

The imperfect indicative and the preterit tenses may be described in general terms in the following way.

Imperfect Indicative Uses

Imperfect Indicative Uses	Examples
1. Repeated or habitual past action	Vicente estudiaba todos los días. / Vincent studied every day.
2. To tell time	Eran las dos de la tarde. / It was 2 P.M.
3. To express the English phrase "used to," i.e., a repeated activity in the past	Clara iba a la universidad por la mañana. / Clara used to go to the university in the morning.
4. To express the English past progressive "was … -ing"	Cuando Ricardo llegó, Teresa salía. / When Richard arrived, Teresa was leaving.
5. To express (1) mental, (2) physical, or (3) emotional activity	Pilar pensaba que llovía. / Pilar thought that it was raining. Fernando estaba cansado. / Fernando was tired. Bernardo quería mucho a Gloria. / Bernard loved Gloria a lot.
6. To refer to two actions that occur simultaneously in the past	Mientras Carla bailaba, Ignacio hablaba con Antonio. / While Carla was dancing, Ignacio was speaking with Antonio.
7. To refer to an activity in progress in the past while something else took place	Mientras Inés preparaba la comida, Jorge terminó su tarea. / While Inés was preparing the meal, George completed his homework.

Preterit Uses

Uses	Examples
1. To express a completed past action	Rosa leyó toda la novela. / *Rosa read the entire novel.*
2. To describe a series of completed past actions	Beatriz se despertó, se levantó, se duchó y se vistió. / *Beatriz woke up, got up, took a shower, and got dressed.*
3. To indicate the beginning of an activity	Alvaro empezó a mirar televisión. / *Alvaro began to watch television.*
4. To indicate the end of an actvity	Margarita cesó de fumar. / *Margarita stopped smoking.*
5. To describe a change of state	Laura se puso enferma cuando vio el examen. / *Laura became ill when she saw the test.*

EXERCISE Set 8-3

A. Provide the corresponding preterit and imperfect indicative forms for the following verbs in the present indicative tense.

1. hablamos

2. tengo

3. vamos

4. somos

5. estoy

6. digo

7. comemos

8. vivimos

9. se acuesta

10. son

11. dormimos

12. pides

13. hace

14. tienen

15. entiende

16. puede

17. queremos   _____   _____

18. empiezo   _____   _____

B. How do you say the following sentences in Spanish? Use the imperfect indicative or preterit according to the meaning of the sentence.

1. I used to study when you (fam. sg.) went to school.

   _____

2. Gloria was taking a shower when the telephone rang.

   _____

3. I went to the store while it was raining.

   _____

4. Francisco was reading a magazine when María entered the house.

   _____

5. My father used to drink coffee when it was snowing.

   _____

C. Fill in the blanks with the appropriate form of the verb in the preterit or imperfect indicative according to the context.

1. De niña, yo (**estudiar**) _____ mucho.

2. Nicolás (**afeitarse**) _____ esta mañana.

3. Pilar y yo (**llegar**) _____ a las ocho en punto.

4. (**Ser**) _____ las nueve de la mañana cuando yo (**levantarse**) _____ .

5. Ella siempre (**tocar**) _____ la guitarra.

6. Mi hermano (**leer**) _____ toda la novela anoche.

Crossword Puzzle 8

Supply the correct form of the imperfect indicative tense according to the meaning. Use the following verbs in your answers: **beber, cantar, comer, estar, llover, hablar, ir, saber, ser.**

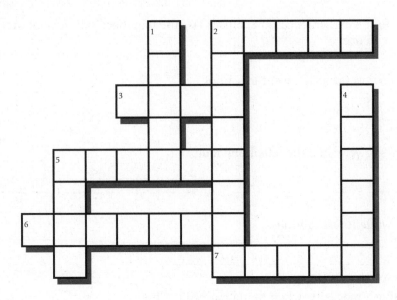

Horizontales

2. Él . . . la pizza.

3. De niños, ellos . . . al mar.

5. Ud. . . . muy cansado.

6. Mi amigo siempre . . ..

7. Yo . . . tocar el piano.

Verticales

1. Yo . . . mucho café.

2. Tú siempre . . . mi canción favorita.

4. . . . mucho.

5. . . . las ocho de la mañana.

9

The Present
Perfect Indicative
(*el perfecto de indicativo*)

Past Participles

A regular past participle, called **participio**, is formed in the following way:

1. Drop the infinitive ending:

    <u>habl</u>ar / *to speak* → **habl-**
    <u>com</u>er / *to eat* → **com-**
    <u>viv</u>ir / *to live* → **viv-**

2. Add the appropriate past participle ending to the stem: **-ado** for **-ar** verbs and **-ido** for **-er** and **-ir** verbs:

    habl + ado → **hablado** / *spoken*
    com + ido → **comido** / *eaten*
    viv + ido → **vivido** / *lived*

Irregular Past Participles

There are a number of irregular past participles in Spanish. The following is a list of the most common ones. Most of these end in **-to**. Two (**decir** / *to tell*, **hacer** / *to do*) end in **-cho**, and one (**pudrir** / *to rot*) has a change in the stem, **podrido** / *rotten*.

abrir / *to open*	abierto	**morir (ue, u)** / *to die*	muerto
cubrir / *to cover*	cubierto	**oponer** / *to oppose*	opuesto
describir / *to describe*	descrito	**poner** / *to put, to place*	puesto
descubrir / *to discover*	descubierto	**proveer** / *to provide*	provisto
devolver (ue) / *to return*	devuelto	**pudrir** / *to rot*	podrido
envolver (ue) / *to wrap*	envuelto	**resolver** / *to resolve*	resuelto
escribir / *to write*	escrito	**romper** / *to break*	roto
freír (i, i) / *to fry*	frito	**ver** / *to see*	visto
hacer / *to do, to make*	hecho	**volver (ue)** / *to return*	vuelto

Additional Irregular Past Participles

Regular -er and -ir verbs with a vowel immediately preceding the past participle ending -ido have a graphic accent. The following is a list of the common verbs.

atraer / to attract	atraído	oír / to hear	oído
caer / to fall	caído	poseer / to possess	poseído
creer / to believe	creído	reír / to laugh	reído
leer / to read	leído	traer / to bring	traído

GRAMMAR NOTE

The past participle of derived verbs will have the same past participle of the basic verb. The following examples illustrate this.

volver / to return → vuelto / returned
devolver / to return (something) → devuelto / returned
envolver / to wrap → envuelto / wrapped

EXERCISE Set 9-1

A. Give the past participle of the following verbs.

1. llegar   =   _____

2. comer   =   _____

3. recibir   =   _____

4. ser   =   _____

5. estar   =   _____

6. tener   =   _____

7. hacer   =   _____

8. saber   =   _____

9. conocer   =   _____

10. mentir   =   _____

11. perder   =   _____

12. poder   =   _____

13. ofrecer   = _____

14. seguir   = _____

15. corregir   = _____

16. empezar   = _____

17. querer   = _____

18. almorzar   = _____

B. Now give the infinitive of the following past participles.

1. roto   = _____

2. escrito   = _____

3. visto   = _____

4. abierto   = _____

5. puesto   = _____

6. frito   = _____

7. dicho   = _____

8. podrido   = _____

9. muerto   = _____

10. caído   = _____

11. hecho   = _____

12. vuelto   = _____

13. envuelto   = _____

14. resuelto   = _____

15. descubierto = _____

16. creído   = _____

17. devuelto   = _____

18. provisto   = _____

The Present Perfect Indicative Tense

The present perfect indicative, called **el perfecto de indicativo** in Spanish, is a tense that talks about the past and continues into the present. The present perfect indicative may refer to an action that started in the past and that may be ongoing in the present. The sentence "**Siempre he comido a las seis** / *I have always eaten at six*" means that you did this in the past and you still do it today. At the same time, the present perfect indicative may refer to a recently completed action, as "**He estudiado todo el capítulo** / *I have studied the entire chapter*" illustrates.

Uses and Features

The present perfect indicative is a compound tense that uses the present tense of the auxiliary verb **haber** / *to have* and the past participle in that order. You use the present perfect indicative in the following situations.

1. To refer to a situation that was true in the past and remains true in the present.

> He comido la comida colombiana toda mi vida. / *I have eaten Colombian cuisine my entire life.*

2. To indicate a recently completed action.

> He conjugado los verbos en el perfecto de indicativo. / *I have conjugated the verbs in the present perfect.*

To form the present perfect indicative of regular verbs, this is what you have to do:

1. Use the present tense of the auxiliary verb **haber** / *to have*, which we provide here. Remember that **haber** is an auxiliary verb. It does not mean *to have* in the sense of *to possess*. To indicate that you have or possess something, you must use the verb **tener** / *to have*.

haber / *to have*

Subject Pronoun	Verb Form	Meaning
(yo)	he	*I have*
(tú)	has	*you (fam. sg.) have*
(él, ella, Ud.)	ha	*he, she, you (pol. sg.) has/have*
(nosotros/-as)	hemos	*we have*
(vosotros/-as)	habéis	*you (fam. pl.) have*
(ellos/-as, Uds.)	han	*they, you (pol. pl.) have*

2. Place the past participle after present tense of the auxiliary verb **haber** / *to have*. The following conjugations of **-ar**, **-er**, and **-ir** verbs illustrate the format of the present perfect indicative tense.

hablar / *to talk*

Subject Pronoun	Haber	Past Participle	Meaning
(yo)	he	habl+ado	*I have spoken*
(tú)	has	habl+ado	*you (fam. sg.) have spoken*
(él, ella, Ud.)	ha	habl+ado	*he, she, you (pol. sg.) has/have spoken*
(nosotros/-as)	hemos	habl+ado	*we have spoken*
(vosotros/-as)	habéis	habl+ado	*you (fam. pl.) have spoken*
(ellos/-as, Uds.)	han	habl+ado	*they, you (pol. pl.) have spoken*

comer / *to eat*

Subject Pronoun	Haber	Past Participle	Meaning
(yo)	he	<u>com</u>+ido	*I have eaten*
(tú)	has	<u>com</u>+ido	*you (fam. sg.) have eaten*
(él, ella, Ud.)	ha	<u>com</u>+ido	*he, she, you (pol. sg.) has/have eaten*
(nosotros/-as)	hemos	<u>com</u>+ido	*we have eaten*
(vosotros/-as)	habéis	<u>com</u>+ido	*you (fam. pl.) have eaten*
(ellos/-as, Uds.)	han	<u>com</u>+ido	*they, you (pol. pl.) have eaten*

vivir / *to live*

Subject Pronoun	Haber	Past Participle	Meaning
(yo)	he	<u>viv</u>+ido	*I have lived*
(tú)	has	<u>viv</u>+ido	*you (fam. sg.) have lived*
(él, ella, Ud.)	ha	<u>viv</u>+ido	*he, she, you (pol. sg.) has/have lived*
(nosotros/-as)	hemos	<u>viv</u>+ido	*we have lived*
(vosotros/-as)	habéis	<u>viv</u>+ido	*you (fam. pl.) have lived*
(ellos/-as, Uds.)	han	<u>viv</u>+ido	*they, you (pol. pl.) have lived*

The Present Perfect Indicative of Reflexive Verbs

Reflexive verbs always use reflexive pronouns in the present perfect indicative as shown below. Remember that you must place the reflexive pronoun immediately before the conjugated auxiliary verb **haber** / *to have.*

lavarse / *to wash oneself*

Subject Pronoun	Reflexive Pronoun	Haber	Past Participle	Meaning
(yo)	me	he	<u>lav</u>+ado	*I have washed myself*
(tú)	te	has	<u>lav</u>+ado	*you (fam. sg.) have washed yourself*
(él, ella, Ud.)	se	ha	<u>lav</u>+ado	*he, she, you (pol. sg.) has/have washed himself/herself/yourself*
(nosotros/-as)	nos	hemos	<u>lav</u>+ado	*we have washed ourselves*
(vosotros/-as)	os	habéis	<u>lav</u>+ado	*you (fam. pl.) have washed yourselves*
(ellos/-as, Uds.)	se	han	<u>lav</u>+ado	*they, you (pol. pl.) have washed themselves/yourselves*

The Present Perfect Indicative of Hay

The present perfect indicative form of **hay** / *there is, there are* is **ha habido** / *there has been, there have been.* The following examples illustrate this usage.

> **Ha habido mucha lluvia.** / *There has been a lot of rain.*
> **Ha habido muchos exámenes.** / *There have been a lot of tests.*

The present perfect of the idiomatic expression **hay que** / *one must, it is necessary to* is **ha habido que** / *it has been necessary to.* The following sentence illustrates this usage.

> **Ha habido que ir a Colombia para estudiar la cultura colombiana.** / *It has been necessary to go to Colombia to study Colombian culture.*

EXERCISE Set 9-2

A. Supply the missing present perfect indicative forms of the verb **cantar**, giving the English equivalent.

EXAMPLE: *él* _____   =   _____

              él ha cantado   =   *he has sung*

1. (yo) _____   =   _____

2. (tú) _____   =   _____

3. (nosotros) _____   =   _____

4. (ellos) _____   =   _____

5. (vosotros) _____   =   _____

6. (Ud.) _____   =   _____

   Now, supply the missing present perfect indicative forms of the verb **vender**, giving the English equivalent.

1. (yo) _____   =   _____

2. (Raquel y yo) _____   =   _____

3. (Uds.) _____   =   _____

4. (ellos) _____   =   _____

5. (vosotros) _____   =   _____

6. (tú) _____   =   _____

Now, supply the missing present perfect indicative forms of the verb recibir, giving the English equivalent.

1. (yo) _____   =   _____

2. (tú) _____   =   _____

3. (nosotros) _____   =   _____

4. (ellos) _____   =   _____

5. (vosotros) _____   =   _____

6. (Ud.) _____   =   _____

Now, supply the missing present perfect indicative forms of the verb bañarse, giving the English equivalent.

1. (yo) _____   =   _____

2. (tú) _____   =   _____

3. (nosotros) _____   =   _____

4. (ellos) _____   =   _____

5. (vosotros) _____   =   _____

6. (Ud.) _____   =   _____

Now, supply the missing present perfect indicative forms of the verb volver (ue), giving the English equivalent.

1. (yo) _____   =   _____

2. (tú) _____   =   _____

3. (nosotros) _____   =   _____

4. (ellos) _____   =   _____

5. (vosotros) _____   =   _____

6. (Ud.) _____   =   _____

Now, supply the missing present perfect indicative forms of the verb estar, giving the English equivalent.

1. (yo) _____   =   _____

2. (tú) _____   =   _____

3. (nosotros) _____   =   _____

4. (ellos) _____   =   _____

5. (vosotros) _____   =   _____

6. (Ud.) _____   =   _____

Now, supply the missing present perfect indicative forms of the verb **ser**, giving the English equivalent.

1. (yo) _____   =   _____

2. (tú) _____   =   _____

3. (nosotros) _____   =   _____

4. (ellos) _____   =   _____

5. (vosotros) _____   =   _____

6. (Ud.) _____   =   _____

B. How do you say the following sentences in Spanish?

1. I have visited Bogotá often.

    _____

2. We have been in *Cartagena*[1].

    _____

3. Have you (fam. sg.) taken a shower?

    _____

4. Have you (pol. sg.) seen my wife?

    _____

5. It has rained a lot.

    _____

6. Have they resolved their problems?

    _____

7. You (pol. pl.) have been thirsty all day.

    _____

8. We have seen *Leticia*[2].

_____

8. She has told the truth.

_____

10. I have always liked this beach.

_____

11. You (fam. sg.) have had to work hard.

_____

12. He has been very nice.

_____

13. You (pol. pl.) have opened all the doors.

_____

14. I have provided the food.

_____

15. They have gotten dressed.

_____

16. We have always believed our son.

_____

17. You (fam. sg.) have taken a trip to *Cali*[3].

_____

18. We have read the writings of *José Eustacio Rivera*[4].

_____

19. Why hasn't she returned?

_____

20. The telephone has rung all night and I have not been able to sleep.

_____

21. There have been many tests in this book.

_____

[1]Colonial resort city on Colombia's Northern Caribbean coast; [2]Located in the Amazon region on the border with Peru and Brazil; [3]Second city located in Southwestern Colombia; founded in 1536; [4]Colombian writer, 1889–1928, author of _La vorágine_, 1924.

The Present Perfect Indicative with Object Pronouns

We have already seen that reflexive pronouns appear in the same place as in other tenses, namely, immediately before the conjugated verb, in this case the auxiliary verb haber / _to have_. You must remember that all object pronouns (direct, indirect, and reflexive) follow the same rules. They are placed immediately before the conjugated auxiliary verb haber / _to have_. Likewise, the order of the object pronouns (indirect and direct) is the same: INDIRECT OBJECT + DIRECT OBJECT. The following selected sentences show these patterns.

> He leído <u>la novela</u>. / _I have read the novel._
>
> <u>La</u> he leído. / _I have read it._
>
> _Le_ he dado <u>los libros</u> a Pablo. / _I have given the books to Pablo._
>
> _Se_ <u>los</u> he dado a él. / _I have given the books to him._

When you use the infinitive form of the auxiliary verb, the object pronouns (reflexive, indirect, direct) may follow and be attached to the infinitive or they may appear immediately before the conjugated verb, as illustrated below.

1. Reflexive Verbs
   Debo haber<u>me</u> despertado temprano. / _I should have woken up early._
   <u>Me</u> debo haber despertado temprano. / _I should have woken up early._

2. Direct Object Pronouns
   Debo haber comprado <u>el libro</u>. / _I should have bought the book._
   Debo haber<u>lo</u> comprado. / _I should have bought it._
   <u>Lo</u> debo haber comprado. / _I should have bought it._

3. Indirect Object Pronouns
   Debo haber<u>le</u> dado el coche a Marta. / _I should have given the car to Marta._
   _Le_ debo haber dado el coche a Marta. / _I should have given the car to Marta._
   Debo haber<u>le</u> dado el coche a ella. / _I should have given the car to her._
   _Le_ debo haber dado el coche a ella. / _I should have given the car to her._

4. Double Object Constructions
   Debo haber<u>le</u> dado <u>el coche</u> a Marta. / _I should have given the car to Marta._
   Debo habér<u>selo</u> dado a ella. / _I should have given it to her._
   _Se_ <u>lo</u> debo haber dado a ella. / _I should have given it to her._

EXERCISE Set 9-3

A. Replace the direct objects with direct object pronouns. Remember that there are two options for pronoun placement with infinitives. In these cases, write both possibilities.

1. He leído <u>los libros</u>.

   _____

2. Pilar ha bebido <u>el café</u>.

   _____

3. Debo haber cantado <u>la canción</u>.

   _____

4. Ella ha escrito <u>la carta</u>.

   _____

B. Replace both indirect and direct objects with indirect and direct object pronouns. You will need to use prepositional pronouns to "clarify" the reference (see Chapter 6). Remember that there are two options with infinitives and present participles. In such cases, write both possibilities. Remember also that you need the "redundant indirect object pronoun" with the indirect object in the third person singular and plural. And finally, remember that the order of these pronouns is always INDIRECT + DIRECT.

1. Ramón le ha hablado español a Rosalba.

   _____

2. Marina debe haber escrito la carta a su hijo.

   _____

3. Uds. les han dicho la verdad a sus amigos.

   _____

C. Provide the Spanish for the following sentences. Use an indirect object pronoun in your answer. Remember to use the redundant indirect object pronoun in the third person singular and plural. If there are two ways of writing the answer, please do so.

1. I have sold the car to my brother.

   _____

2. They should have spoken to us.

   _____

D. Replace the indirect and direct objects with indirect and direct object pronouns. Remember the order of these pronouns is always INDIRECT + DIRECT.

1. Vicente le ha mandado el paquete a Raquel.

   _____

2. Le he leído el cuento a mi hija.

   _____

3. Le hemos dicho la verdad a Antonio.

   _____

4. Berta le ha enseñado toda la lección a su amigo.

   _____

E. Provide the Spanish for the following sentences. Use an indirect object pronoun and a direct object in your answer. Remember to use the redundant indirect object pronoun.

1. You (fam. sg.) have sent it to him (the letter).

   _____

2. We have given them (books) to them (our cousins).

   _____

3. They have sold it (the car) to her.

   _____

F. Answer the following questions in Spanish. Use an indirect object and a direct object pronoun in your answer. Remember to use the redundant indirect object pronoun.

1. ¿Le has dado los regalos a Marta?

   _____

2. ¿Les has hablado español a tus amigos?

   _____

3. ¿Le has servido el té a tu amiga?

   _____

EXERCISE Set 9-4

A. Provide the corresponding preterit, imperfect, and present perfect indicative forms for the following verbs in the present indicative tense.

1. comemos   _____   _____   _____

2. tiene   _____   _____   _____

3. voy   _____   _____   _____

4. soy   _____   _____   _____

5. estoy   _____   _____   _____

6. decimos   _____   _____   _____

7. vivimos   _____   _____   _____

8. hacemos   _____   _____   _____

9. se baña   _____   _____   _____

10. hay   _____   _____   _____

11. muere   _____   _____   _____

12. piden   _____   _____   _____

13. hace   _____   _____   _____

14. tienen   _____   _____   _____

15. entiendes   _____   _____   _____

16. pueden

17. quiero

18. empieza

Crossword Puzzle 9

Fill in the blanks. All of the clues both vertical and horizontal require that you use the appropriate past participle form.

Horizontales
  5. Ud. ha . . . (escuchar) la música.
  6. Ellos han . . . (abrir) las ventanas.
  8. Uds. han . . . (decir) la verdad.
  9. Él ha . . . (ser) generoso.

Verticales
  1. ¿Qué tiempo ha . . . (hacer)?
  2. Ella ha . . . (estar) enferma.
  3. He . . . (escribir) un libro.
  4. ¿A qué hora te has . . . (levantarse)?
  7. ¿Quién ha . . . (romper) el plato?

10

The Pluperfect (Past Perfect) Indicative (*el pluscuamperfecto de indicativo*)

The Conjugation of the Pluperfect (Past Perfect) Indicative Tense

The pluperfect tense, sometimes called the past perfect tense, and known as the pluscuamperfecto de indicativo in Spanish, is a compound tense. Therefore, it is conjugated with the auxiliary verb haber / *to have*. See Chapter 9 for the relevant details regarding past participles. In the pluperfect, the auxiliary verbs are in the imperfect tense.

The pluperfect indicative (past perfect indicative) refers to an action that took place before another action or event. You use the pluperfect indicative (past perfect indicative) to refer to an event prior in time to another event in the past. The following sentences illustrate this point.

> Yo ya había bebido el café cuando Dolores entró. / *I had already drunk the coffee when Dolores entered.*
> Después de que ella había llegado, me llamó por teléfono. / *After she had arrived, she phoned me.*

To form the pluperfect indicative (past perfect indicative) tense of regular verbs, this is what you have to do:

1. Use the imperfect tense of the auxiliary verb haber / *to have* that we provide here. Remember that haber is an auxiliary verb. It does not mean *to have* in the sense of *to possess*. To indicate that you have or possess something, you must use the verb tener / *to have, to possess*.

haber / *to have*

Subject Pronoun	Verb Form	Meaning
(yo)	<u>hab</u>+ía	*I had*
(tú)	<u>hab</u>+ías	*you (fam. sg.) had*
(él, ella, Ud.)	<u>hab</u>+ía	*he, she, you (pol. sg.) had*
(nosotros/-as)	<u>hab</u>+íamos	*we had*
(vosotros/-as)	<u>hab</u>+íais	*you (fam. pl.) had*
(ellos/-as, Uds.)	<u>hab</u>+ían	*they, you (pol. pl.) had*

2. Place the past participle after the imperfect form of the auxiliary verb **haber** / *to have*. The following are examples of -ar, -er, and -ir verbs.

hablar / *to talk*

Subject Pronoun	Haber	Past Participle	Meaning
(yo)	hab+ía	habl+ado	*I had spoken*
(tú)	hab+ías	habl+ado	*you (fam. sg.) had spoken*
(él, ella, Ud.)	hab+ía	habl+ado	*he, she, you (pol. sg.) had spoken*
(nosotros/-as)	hab+íamos	habl+ado	*we had spoken*
(vosotros/-as)	hab+íais	habl+ado	*you (fam. pl.) had spoken*
(ellos/-as, Uds.)	hab+ían	habl+ado	*they, you (pol. pl.) had spoken*

comer / *to eat*

Subject Pronoun	Haber	Past Participle	Meaning
(yo)	hab+ía	com+ido	*I had eaten*
(tú)	hab+ías	com+ido	*you (fam. sg.) had eaten*
(él, ella, Ud.)	hab+ía	com+ido	*he, she, you (pol. sg.) had eaten*
(nosotros/-as)	hab+íamos	com+ido	*we had eaten*
(vosotros/-as)	hab+íais	com+ido	*you (fam. pl.) had eaten*
(ellos/-as, Uds.)	hab+ían	com+ido	*they, you (pol. pl.) had eaten*

vivir / *to live*

Subject Pronoun	Haber	Past Participle	Meaning
(yo)	hab+ía	viv+ido	*I had lived*
(tú)	hab+ías	viv+ido	*you (fam. sg.) had lived*
(él, ella, Ud.)	hab+ía	viv+ido	*he, she, you (pol. sg.) had lived*
(nosotros/-as)	hab+íamos	viv+ido	*we had lived*
(vosotros/-as)	hab+íais	viv+ido	*you (fam. pl.) had lived*
(ellos/-as, Uds.)	hab+ían	viv+ido	*they, you (pol. pl.) had lived*

The Pluperfect Indicative (Past Perfect Indicative) of Reflexive Verbs

Reflexive verbs always use reflexive pronouns in the pluperfect indicative (past perfect indicative) tense as shown below. Remember that you must place the reflexive pronoun immediately before the conjugated auxiliary verb haber / *to have*.

lavarse / *to wash oneself*

Subject Pronoun	Reflexive Pronoun	Haber	Past Participle	Meaning
(yo)	me	hab+ía	lav+ado	*I had washed myself*
(tú)	te	hab+ías	lav+ado	*you (fam. sg.) had washed yourself*
(él, ella, Ud.)	se	hab+ía	lav+ado	*he, she, you (pol. sg.) had washed himself/herself/yourself*
(nosotros/-as)	nos	hab+íamos	lav+ado	*we had washed ourselves*
(vosotros/-as)	os	hab+íais	lav+ado	*you (fam. pl.) had washed yourselves*
(ellos/-as, Uds.)	se	hab+ían	lav+ado	*they, you (pol. pl.) had washed themselves/yourselves*

NOTE

You have probably noticed that the first person singular (yo) and third person singular (él, ella, Ud.) are identical in form. For this reason, you must normally use the subject pronoun yo / *I* to distinguish these forms. You will recall that this was necessary in the imperfect tense, and since the pluperfect indicative (past perfect indicative) uses the imperfect of the auxiliary verb haber / *to have*, this is simply a continuation of that usage.

The Pluperfect Indicative (Past Perfect Indicative) of Hay

The pluperfect indicative (past perfect indicative) form of hay / *there is, there are* is había habido / *there had been*. The following examples illustrate this usage.

Había habido mucha nieve. / *There had been a lot of snow.*
Había habido muchas tormentas. / *There had been many storms.*

The pluperfect (past perfect) of the idiomatic expression hay que / *one must, it is necessary to* is había habido que / *it had been necessary to*. The following sentence illustrates this usage.

Había habido que conjugar los verbos en el pluscuamperfecto. / *It had been necessary to conjugate the verbs in the pluperfect.*

EXERCISE Set 10-1

A. Supply the missing pluperfect indicative (past perfect indicative) forms of the verb dar, giving the English equivalent.

EXAMPLE: *él* _____   =   _____

             él había dado   =   *he had given*

1. (yo) _____   =   _____

2. (tú) _____   =   _____

3. (nosotros) _____   =   _____

4. (ellos) _____   =   _____

5. (vosotros) _____   =   _____

6. (Ud.) _____   =   _____

Now, supply the missing pluperfect indicative (past perfect indicative) forms of the verb **aprender**, giving the English equivalent.

1. (yo) _____   =   _____

2. (Raquel y yo) _____   =   _____

3. (Uds.) _____   =   _____

4. (ellos) _____   =   _____

5. (vosotros) _____   =   _____

6. (tú) _____   =   _____

Now, supply the missing pluperfect indicative (past perfect indicative) forms of the verb **sufrir**, giving the English equivalent.

1. (yo) _____   =   _____

2. (tú) _____   =   _____

3. (nosotros) _____   =   _____

4. (ellos) _____   =   _____

5. (vosotros) _____   =   _____

6. (Ud.) _____   =   _____

Now, supply the missing pluperfect indicative (past perfect indicative) forms of the verb vestirse (i, i), giving the English equivalent.

1. (yo) _____   =   _____

2. (tú) _____   =   _____

3. (nosotros) _____   =   _____

4. (ellos) _____   =   _____

5. (vosotros) _____   =   _____

6. (Ud.) _____   =   _____

Now, supply the missing pluperfect indicative (past perfect indicative) forms of the verb cubrir, giving the English equivalent.

1. (yo) _____   =   _____

2. (tú) _____   =   _____

3. (nosotros) _____   =   _____

4. (ellos) _____   =   _____

5. (vosotros) _____   =   _____

6. (Ud.) _____   =   _____

Now, supply the missing pluperfect indicative (past perfect indicative) forms of the verb estar, giving the English equivalent.

1. (yo) _____   =   _____

2. (tú) _____   =   _____

3. (nosotros) _____   =   _____

4. (ellos) _____   =   _____

5. (vosotros) _____   =   _____

6. (Ud.) _____   =   _____

Now, supply the missing pluperfect indicative (past perfect indicative) forms of the verb ser, giving the English equivalent.

1. (yo) _____ = _____

2. (tú) _____ = _____

3. (nosotros) _____ = _____

4. (ellos) _____ = _____

5. (vosotros) _____ = _____

6. (Ud.) _____ = _____

B. How do you say the following sentences in Spanish?

1. I had seen the *Museo Bolivariano*[1] in Caracas.

_____

2. I had heard the folkloric music of Venezuela.

_____

3. I had purchased *El Diario de Caracas*[2].

_____

4. There had been many houses there.

_____

5. It had rained last night.

_____

6. Pablo had lived in Madrid before coming to Venezuela.

_____

7. I had seen the latest Venezuelan movie.

_____

8. I had played the guitar.

_____

9. I had traveled to *Mérida*[3].

_____

10. I had gotten up very late.

_____

11. You (fam. sg.) had studied Spanish verbs a lot.

_____

12. We had entered the capital of Venezuela.

_____

13. It had begun to rain.

_____

14. They had driven to Maracaibo[4].

_____

15. Where had he found the money?

_____

16. I had done the puzzle.

_____

17. You (pol. sg.) had had the book before.

_____

18. Had you (pol. pl.) discovered the secret?

_____

19. The flowers had died in the fall.

_____

20. She had laughed a lot.

_____

[1]Museum for Simón Bolívar, 1783–1830, Venezuelan soldier and South American liberator; [2]Daily newspaper in Caracas; [3]Colonial city founded in 1558 in Western Venezuela; [4]Oil producing center in Northwestern Venezuela; second largest city.

EXERCISE **Set 10-2**

A. Provide the corresponding present perfect indicative and pluperfect indicative (past perfect indicative) forms for the following verbs in the present indicative tense.

1. vivimos _____ _____

2. llueve _____ _____

3. va _____ _____

4. eres _____ _____

5. estamos _____ _____

6. dicen _____ _____

7. bebemos _____ _____

8. hago _____ _____

9. se ducha _____ _____

10. hay _____ _____

11. muere _____ _____

12. pide _____ _____

13. hace _____ _____

14. tengo _____ _____

15. entiendes _____ _____

16. puede _____ _____

17. quieres _____ _____

18. comienza _____ _____

Crossword Puzzle 10

Fill in the blanks. All of the clues both vertical and horizontal require that you use the appropriate past participle form.

Horizontales
  4. Habías . . . (poner) la mesa.
  5. Mi amigo y yo habíamos . . .
       (resolver) el problema.
  9. Habíamos . . . (entrar) en casa.
  10. Ud. había . . . (oír) la música.
  11. Había . . . (hacer) buen tiempo.

Verticales
  1. Yo había . . . (ver) la película.
  2. Habías . . . (ir) a casa.
  3. Ella se había . . . (despertarse) tarde.
  6. Jorge había . . . (estar) cansado.
  7. Ellos habían . . . (traer) los libros.
  8. Elena había . . . (comer) la comida.

Review 2

(Chapters 7–10)

This review chapter will allow you to go over and reinforce your ability to conjugate verbs in the past indicative tenses and to recognize their use in conversation and in writing. There are, as in the first review chapter, two specific types of exercises: (1) *Conjugation Review* and (2) *Usage Review*.

Conjugation Review

Review Exercise Set 2-1

A. Give the past participles of the following verbs:

1. abrir

2. atraer

3. beber

4. cantar

5. creer

6. cubrir

7. decir

8. describir

9. descubrir

10. devolver

11. envolver

12. escribir

13. estar

14. freír

15. hacer

16. morir

17. oír

_____

18. oponer

_____

19. poner

_____

20. proveer

_____

21. pudrir

_____

22. resolver

_____

23. romper

_____

24. ser

_____

25. tener

_____

26. ver

_____

27. volver

_____

B. Conjugate the following verbs in the preterit tense:

1. comprar, correr, abrir

(yo)			
(tú)			
(él, ella, Ud.)			
(nosotros/-as)			
(vosotros/-as)			
(ellos/-as, Uds.)			

2. dormir, mentir, pedir

(yo)			
(tú)			
(él, ella, Ud.)			
(nosotros/-as)			
(vosotros/-as)			
(ellos/-as, Uds.)			

3. estar, tener, haber

(yo)

(tú)

(él, ella, Ud.)

(nosotros/-as)

(vosotros/-as)

(ellos/-as, Uds.)

4. poder, poner, saber

(yo)

(tú)

(él, ella, Ud.)

(nosotros/-as)

(vosotros/-as)

(ellos/-as, Uds.)

5. hacer, querer, venir

(yo)

(tú)

(él, ella, Ud.)

(nosotros/-as)

(vosotros/-as)

(ellos/-as, Uds.)

6. ir, dar, decir

(yo)		
(tú)		
(él, ella, Ud.)		
(nosotros/-as)		
(vosotros/-as)		
(ellos/-as, Uds.)		

7. buscar, llegar, comenzar

(yo)		
(tú)		
(él, ella, Ud.)		
(nosotros/-as)		
(vosotros/-as)		
(ellos/-as, Uds.)		

C. Conjugate the following verbs in the imperfect indicative:

1. estudiar, creer, cubrir

(yo)		
(tú)		
(él, ella, Ud.)		
(nosotros/-as)		
(vosotros/-as)		
(ellos/-as, Uds.)		

2. ir, ser, ver

(yo)		
(tú)		
(él, ella, Ud.)		
(nosotros/-as)		
(vosotros/-as)		
(ellos/-as, Uds.)		

D. Conjugate the following verbs in the present perfect indicative:

buscar, vender, vestirse

(yo)		
(tú)		
(él, ella, Ud.)		
(nosotros/-as)		
(vosotros/-as)		
(ellos/-as, Uds.)		

E. Conjugate the following verbs in the past perfect (pluperfect) tense:

bailar, temer, sentirse

(yo)		
(tú)		
(él, ella, Ud.)		
(nosotros/-as)		
(vosotros/-as)		
(ellos/-as, Uds.)		

Usage Review

Review Exercise Set 2-2

A. Choose the appropriate verb form **a** or **b** according to the meaning:

1. ¿Qué hora ... cuando llegaste?
   a. fue
   b. era

2. ¿De niño, te ... los dulces?
   a. gustaban
   b. había gustado

3. ¿A qué hora ... tus amigos anoche?
   a. llegaron
   b. llegaban

4. ¿Qué tiempo ... el lunes pasado?
   a. hizo
   b. hacía

5. ¿Qué hacías cuando ...?
   a. yo entré
   b. yo entraba

6. Yo ... mucho café todos los días.
   a. bebí
   b. bebía

7. Aurelio ... la novela en un día.
   a. leía
   b. leyó

8. Él siempre ... a sus padres.
   a. creía
   b. creyó

9. En aquel momento, Aurora ... a escuchar la música.
   a. empezaba
   b. empezó

10. Mis amigos siempre ... a la universidad a la misma hora.
    a. iban
    b. fueron

B. Missing from the following sentences are the indicated verbs. Insert them in the spaces provided according to the meaning.

Verbs: acostarse, comprar, correr, estudiar, hacer, ir, llover, mirar, nacer, trabajar

1. ¿ _____ (tú) en la tienda anoche?

2. Cervantes _____ en 1547.

3. Yo _____ mis lecciones todas las noches.

4. Aquel día _____ mucho frío.

5. Elena _____ en el parque todos los días.

6. _____ mucho en abril.

7. Yo _____ la televisión mucho en la universidad.

8. Uds. _____ un buen coche.

9. Juanita y yo _____ al concierto anoche.

10. Yo _____ muy tarde ayer.

Part Three
The Future and Conditional Tenses

The Future and the Conditional: An Overview

What Is the Future Tense?

In English, the *future* tense is expressed by the "modal" form *will* to indicate something that will take place in the time to come. In Spanish, the same tense is constructed with endings added on to the stem base of the infinitive:

> Mañana llamaré a Marta por teléfono. / *Tomorrow I will phone Marta.*
> Estudiaremos la lección mañana. / *We will study the lesson tomorrow.*

There is also a *future perfect* tense in English and Spanish that is used to express or indicate past time with respect to some point in future time, as in:

> La semana próxima ya habrás partido. / *Next week you will have left already.*
> Habré leído todo el libro para mañana. / *I shall have read the entire book by tomorrow.*

As you can see, it is a compound tense made up of an auxiliary verb in the future tense and the past participle of the verb.

What Is the Conditional Tense?

In English, the *conditional* tense is expressed by the modal form *would* to indicate or make reference to conditions. In Spanish the same tense is constructed with endings added on to the base of the infinitive:

> Yo iría a la casa de Laura, pero ella no está allí. / *I would go Laura's home, but she isn't there.*
> Iríamos a España, pero no tenemos el dinero. / *We would go to Spain, but we don't have the money.*

There is also a *conditional perfect* tense in English and Spanish that is used to express or indicate an action or event that would have taken place under certain conditions:

> Yo habría hecho el trabajo, pero yo no tenía el tiempo. / *I would have done the work, but I did not have the time.*
> Marco habría pagado la cuenta, pero él no tenía su cartera. / *Marco would have paid the bill, but he didn't have his wallet.*

As you can see, it is also a compound tense made up of an auxiliary verb in the conditional tense and the past participle of the verb.

11
The Future
(*el futuro*)

Uses and Features

The simple future is used most of the time as follows:

1. To express an action or state of being that will take place at some time in the future:
   Mañana iré al cine. / *Tomorrow I will go the movies.*
   Lo haré si tengo el tiempo. / *I will do it if I have the time.*

2. To express probability:
   ¿Qué hora será? / *I wonder what time it is?*
   Serán las ocho. / *It is probably eight o'clock.*

3. To express conjecture (wondering, guessing):
   ¿Quién llamará a esta hora? / *I wonder who is calling at this hour?*

Regular Verbs

To form the future tense, called the futuro in Spanish, do the following:

1. Use the entire infinitive as the stem: <u>hablar</u> / *to speak*, <u>comer</u> / *to eat*, and <u>vivir</u> / *to live*.

2. Add the following endings to the stem. Note that there is a single set of endings for the future tense:

(yo)	-é
(tú)	-ás
(él, ella, Ud.)	-á
(nosotros/-as)	-emos
(vosotros/-as)	-éis
(ellos/-as, Uds.)	-án

3. Here's the result:

hablar / *to speak*

Subject Pronoun	Verb Form	Meaning
(yo)	hablar+é	*I will speak*
(tú)	hablar+ás	*you (fam. sg.) will speak*
(él, ella, Ud.)	hablar+á	*he, she, you (pol. sg.) will speak*
(nosotros/-as)	hablar+emos	*we will speak*
(vosotros/-as)	hablar+éis	*you (fam. pl.) will speak*
(ellos/-as, Uds.)	hablar+án	*they, you (pol. pl.) will speak*

comer / *to eat*

Subject Pronoun	Verb Form	Meaning
(yo)	comer+é	*I will eat*
(tú)	comer+ás	*you (fam. sg.) will eat*
(él, ella, Ud.)	comer+á	*he, she, you (pol. sg.) will eat*
(nosotros/-as)	comer+emos	*we will eat*
(vosotros/-as)	comer+éis	*you (fam. pl.) will eat*
(ellos/-as, Uds.)	comer+án	*they, you (pol. pl.) will eat*

vivir / *to live*

Subject Pronoun	Verb Form	Meaning
(yo)	vivir+é	*I will live*
(tú)	vivir+ás	*you (fam. sg.) will live*
(él, ella, Ud.)	vivir+á	*he, she, you (pol. sg.) will live*
(nosotros/-as)	vivir+emos	*we will live*
(vosotros/-as)	vivir+éis	*you (fam. pl.) will live*
(ellos/-as, Uds.)	vivir+án	*they, you (pol. pl.) will live*

The Future Tense of Reflexive Verbs

Reflexive verbs always use reflexive pronouns in the future, as shown below. They always appear immediately before the conjugated verb, as they do in the present and all other tenses.

lavarse / *to wash oneself*

Subject Pronoun	Reflexive Pronoun	Conjugated Verb	Meaning
(yo)	me	lavar+é	*I will wash myself*
(tú)	te	lavar+ás	*you (fam. sg.) will wash yourself*
(él, ella, Ud.)	se	lavar+á	*he, she, you (pol. sg.) will wash himself/herself/yourself*
(nosotros/-as)	nos	lavar+emos	*we will wash ourselves*
(vosotros/-as)	os	lavar+éis	*you (fam. pl.) will wash yourselves*
(ellos/-as, Uds.)	se	lavar+án	*they, you (pol. pl.) will wash themselves/yourselves*

NOTE

Notice that the future generally is rendered in English by the following two translations:

Ella llegará mañana. = *She will arrive tomorrow.*
= *She will be arriving tomorrow.*

You will be pleased to know that there are no stem changes in the future tense.

TIP

There are no stem changes in the future tense. There are, however, twelve verbs that have an irregular stem to which the regular future tense endings are added. These verbs appear right after the following exercises.

EXERCISE Set 11-1

A. Supply the missing future forms of the verb **estudiar**, giving the English equivalent.

EXAMPLE: *él* _____   =   _____

él estudiará =   he will study

1. (yo) _____   =   _____

2. (tú) _____   =   _____

3. (nosotros) _____   =   _____

4. (ellos) _____   =   _____

5. (vosotros) _____   =   _____

6. (Ud.) _____   =   _____

Now, supply the missing future forms of the verb **aprender**, giving the English equivalent.

1. (yo) _____   =   _____

2. (Raquel y yo) _____ =   _____

3. (Uds.) _____   =   _____

4. (ellos) _____   =   _____

5. (vosotros) _____   =   _____

6. (tú) _____   =   _____

Now, supply the missing future forms of the verb escribir, giving the English equivalent.

1. (yo) _____   =   _____

2. (tú) _____   =   _____

3. (nosotros) _____   =   _____

4. (ellos) _____   =   _____

5. (vosotros) _____   =   _____

6. (Ud.) _____   =   _____

Now, supply the missing future forms of the verb sentarse (ie), giving the English equivalent.

1. (yo) _____   =   _____

2. (tú) _____   =   _____

3. (nosotros) _____   =   _____

4. (ellos) _____   =   _____

5. (vosotros) _____   =   _____

6. (Ud.) _____   =   _____

B. How do you say the following sentences in Spanish?

1. I will travel to *David*[1].

_____

2. That program will begin at 8 P.M.

_____

3. She will take a shower tomorrow.

_____

4. Rosalba and I will buy our books tomorrow.

_____

5. I will get up late tomorrow.

_____

6. I will see the *Museo afro-antillano*[2] on Friday.

_____

7. She will not like that movie.

_____

8. He will sleep until noon.

_____

9. I will attend the university next year.

_____

10. They will arrive at 1 P.M.

_____

[1]Panama's southwestern province on the border of Costa Rica, noted for its natural beauty; [2]Museum dedicated to Panama's West Indian community, located in Panama City.

Irregular Future Tense Verbs

There are twelve irregular verbs in the future tense. What makes these verbs irregular is the fact that they have an irregular stem. As we noted earlier, there is a single set of regular endings for the future tense.

Irregular Future Stems: Pattern 1

Learn the irregular future stem to which you add the future tense endings. In this group, you take the infinitive and you delete the vowel in the infinitive ending: -er → -r-. We list them below.

> caber / *to fit, to be contained* → cabr-
> haber / *to have (auxiliary verb)* → habr-
> poder / *can, to be able* → podr-
> querer / *to want* → querr-
> saber / *to know, to know how* → sabr-

Irregular Future Stems: Pattern 2

Learn the irregular future stem, to which you add the future tense endings. In this group, you take the infinitive and you delete the vowel in the infinitive ending. Then you insert the consonant -d-: -er → -dr-. We list them below.

poner / *to put, to place* → pondr-
salir / *to leave* → saldr-
tener / *to have* → tendr-
valer / *to be worth* → valdr-
venir / *to come* → vendr-

Irregular Future Stems: Pattern 3

Learn the irregular future stem, to which you add the future tense endings. In this group, a completely different stem is used. We list them below:

decir (i, i) / *to say, to tell* → dir-
hacer / *to do, to make* → har-

To each of these irregular stems, you add the regular future tense endings that we reproduce here:

(yo)	-é
(tú)	-ás
(él, ella, Ud.)	-á
(nosotros/-as)	-emos
(vosotros/-as)	-éis
(ellos/-as, Uds.)	-án

We now provide one conjugation from each of the three categories we just saw.

querer / *to want*

Subject Pronoun	Verb Form	Meaning
(yo)	querr+é	*I will want*
(tú)	querr+ás	*you (fam. sg.) will want*
(él, ella, Ud.)	querr+á	*he, she, you (pol. sg.) will want*
(nosotros/-as)	querr+emos	*we will want*
(vosotros/-as)	querr+éis	*you (fam. pl.) will want*
(ellos/-as, Uds.)	querr+án	*they, you (pol. pl.) will want*

tener / *to have*

Subject Pronoun	Verb Form	Meaning
(yo)	tendr+é	*I will have*
(tú)	tendr+ás	*you (fam. sg.) will have*
(él, ella, Ud.)	tendr+á	*he, she, you (pol. sg.) will have*
(nosotros/-as)	tendr+emos	*we will have*
(vosotros/-as)	tendr+éis	*you (fam. pl.) will have*
(ellos/-as, Uds.)	tendr+án	*they, you (pol. pl.) will have*

hacer / *to do, to make*

Subject Pronoun	Verb Form	Meaning
(yo)	<u>har</u>+é	*I will do/make*
(tú)	<u>har</u>+ás	*you (fam. sg.) will do/make*
(él, ella, Ud.)	<u>har</u>+á	*he, she, you (pol. sg.) will do/make*
(nosotros/-as)	<u>har</u>+emos	*we will do/make*
(vosotros/-as)	<u>har</u>+éis	*you (fam. pl.) will do/make*
(ellos/-as, Uds.)	<u>har</u>+án	*they, you (pol. pl.) will do/make*

GRAMMAR NOTE

There are several verbs derived from these twelve verbs that also have an irregular future stem. The following are some common ones.

1. <u>hacer</u> / *to do, to make* → <u>har</u>-
   des<u>hacer</u> / *to undo, to untie (a knot)* → deshar-

2. <u>poner</u> / *to put, to place* → <u>pondr</u>-
   com<u>poner</u> / *to compose* → compondr-
   o<u>ponerse</u> / *to oppose* → opondr-
   su<u>poner</u> / *to suppose* → supondr-

3. <u>tener</u> / *to have* → <u>tendr</u>-
   con<u>tener</u> / *to contain, to hold* → contendr-
   de<u>tener</u> / *to detain, to arrest* → detendr-
   man<u>tener</u> / *to maintain* → mantendr-
   ob<u>tener</u> / *to obtain* → obtendr-
   sos<u>tener</u> / *to sustain, to support* → sostendr-

Future Tense of Hay

The future of hay / *there is, there are* is habrá / *there will be*. It is used in the same way that hay is used, except that it is in the future tense. The following sentences illustrate this point.

Habrá un examen mañana. / *There will be an exam tomorrow.*
Habrá muchas tareas mañana. / *There will be many chores tomorrow.*

The future of the idiomatic expression hay que / *one must, it is necessary to* is habrá que / *it will be necessary to*. The following sentence illustrates this usage.

Habrá que ir a la Ciudad de Panamá mañana. / *It will be necessary to go to Panama City tomorrow.*

EXERCISE Set 11-2

A. Supply the missing the missing future forms of the verb **caber**, giving the English equivalent.

EXAMPLE: *él _____*   =   _____

él cabrá   =   he will fit

1. (yo) _____   =   _____

2. (tú) _____   =   _____

3. (nosotros) _____   =   _____

4. (ellos) _____   =   _____

5. (vosotros) _____   =   _____

6. (Ud.) _____   =   _____

Now, supply the missing future forms of the verb **salir**, giving the English equivalent.

1. (yo) _____   =   _____

2. (Raquel y yo) _____   =   _____

3. (Uds.) _____   =   _____

4. (ellos) _____   =   _____

5. (vosotros) _____   =   _____

6. (tú) _____   =   _____

Now, supply the missing future forms of the verb **decir (i, i)**, giving the English equivalent.

1. (yo) _____   =   _____

2. (tú) _____   =   _____

3. (nosotros) _____   =   _____

4. (ellos) _____   =   _____

5. (vosotros) _____   =   _____

6. (Ud.) _____   =   _____

Now, supply the missing future forms of the auxiliary verb **haber**, giving the English equivalent.

1. (yo) _____ = _____

2. (tú) _____ = _____

3. (nosotros) _____ = _____

4. (ellos) _____ = _____

5. (vosotros) _____ = _____

6. (Ud.) _____ = _____

Now, supply the missing future forms of the verb **poder**, giving the English equivalent.

1. (yo) _____ = _____

2. (tú) _____ = _____

3. (nosotros) _____ = _____

4. (ellos) _____ = _____

5. (vosotros) _____ = _____

6. (Ud.) _____ = _____

Now, supply the missing future forms of the verb **venir**, giving the English equivalent.

1. (yo) _____ = _____

2. (tú) _____ = _____

3. (nosotros) _____ = _____

4. (ellos) _____ = _____

5. (vosotros) _____ = _____

6. (Ud.) _____ = _____

Now, supply the missing future forms of the verb **saber**, giving the English equivalent.

1. (yo) _____ = _____

2. (tú) _____ = _____

3. (nosotros) _____ = _____

4. (ellos) _____ = _____

5. (vosotros) _____ = _____

6. (Ud.) _____ = _____

Now, supply the missing future forms of the verb **poner**, giving the English equivalent.

1. (yo) _____ = _____

2. (tú) _____ = _____

3. (nosotros) _____ = _____

4. (ellos) _____ = _____

5. (vosotros) _____ = _____

6. (Ud.) _____ = _____

B. How do you say the following sentences in Spanish?

1. When will Elena arrive?

   _____

2. It will be six o'clock soon.

   _____

3. There will be many people there.

   _____

4. They will have to be here.

   _____

5. You (fam. sg.) will leave tomorrow.

   _____

6. We will come at 11 A.M.

   _____

7. Cristina will know the answer.

   _____

8. My parents will want to see the photos of Panama.

_____

9. The *balboa*[1] will be worth more in the future.

_____

10. You (pol. pl.) will place the books on the table.

_____

11. It will be cold in December.

_____

12. They will go to *Isla Contadora*[2].

_____

13. It will be cloudy tomorrow.

_____

14. I will tell the truth.

_____

[1]Unit of money in Panama, though the U.S. dollar is commonly used. *Balboa* = Vasco Núñez de Balboa, Spanish explorer, 1475–1517; [2]Best known of the Pearl Islands, about fifty miles off Panama's coast.

EXERCISE Set 11-3

A. Match the two columns logically.

1. ¿Qué tiempo …?	a.	haré
2. (Yo) … un viaje a Panamá.	b.	conjugarás
3. ¿Qué hora …?	c.	diremos
4. ¿… los verbos mañana?	d.	cantará
5. (Tú) … a casa más tarde.	e.	será
6. (Nosotros) … la verdad.	f.	hará
7. Ud. … esa canción.	g.	vendrán
8. Ellos … tarde.	h.	irás

B. How do you say the following sentences in Spanish?

1. I wonder where he will be?

   _____

2. It will be necessary to conjugate more verbs.

   _____

3. They will leave tomorrow.

   _____

4. I will have to work in the evening.

   _____

5. You (fam. sg.) will want to see the latest film.

   _____

6. There will be many students in this class.

   _____

7. We will tell her the truth.

   _____

8. You (pol. pl.) will have to buy more food.

   _____

9. I wonder what day it is.

   _____

10. I will go to Pablo's house.

   _____

C. Provide the corresponding future forms for the following verbs in the present indicative tense.

1. llegan _____

2. rompo _____

3. cubres _____

4. es _____

5. están _____

6. va _____

7. tengo _____

8. hay _____

9. sé _____

10. conozco _____

11. podemos _____

12. quiere _____

13. hace _____

14. digo _____

15. vale _____

16. salgo _____

17. venimos _____

18. te vistes _____

Crossword Puzzle 11

Fill in the blanks. All of the clues both vertical and horizontal require that you use the appropriate future form.

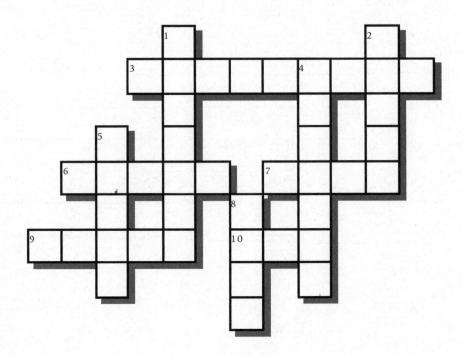

Horizontales
3. Juanita y yo . . . (venir) mañana.
6. . . . (haber) muchas personas en casa.
7. . . . (hacer) calor mañana.
9. . . . (ser) las ocho.
10. Elena . . . (ir) a la fiesta.

Verticales
1. Ellos . . . (beber) café.
2. Ud. . . . (poder) hacer la tarea.
4. Ellos . . . (estar) aquí.
5. Él . . . (saber) la verdad.
8. (Yo) te lo . . . (decir) mañana.

12

The Future Perfect (*el futuro perfecto*)

Uses and Features

The future perfect is used to refer to an action that occurred before another simple future action (Chapter 11):

Cuando habré comido la cena, iré al cine. / *When I will have eaten, I will go to the movies.*

And, like the simple future, it can be used to convey probability.

Habrá habido un accidente. / *There must have been an accident.*
Él habrá mentido en la corte. / *He must have lied in court.*

The Conjugation of the Future Perfect Tense

The future perfect, called the futuro perfecto in Spanish, is a compound tense. Therefore, it is conjugated with the auxiliary verb haber / *to have*, and the past participle of the verb, in that order. See Chapter 9 for the relevant details regarding past participles.

To form the future perfect tense of regular verbs, this is what you have to do:

1. Use the future tense of the auxiliary verb haber / *to have* which we provide here. Remember that haber is an auxiliary verb. It does not mean *to have* in the sense of *to possess*. To indicate that you have or possess something, you must use the verb tener / *to have, to possess*.

haber / *to have*

Subject Pronoun	Verb Form	Meaning
(yo)	habr+é	*I will have*
(tú)	habr+ás	*you (fam. sg.) will have*
(él, ella, Ud.)	habr+á	*he, she, you (pol. sg.) will have*
(nosotros/-as)	habr+emos	*we will have*
(vosotros/-as)	habr+éis	*you (fam. pl.) will have*
(ellos/-as, Uds.)	habr+án	*they, you (pol. pl.) will have*

2. The combination of the future tense of the auxiliary verb **haber** / *to have* and the past participle of a verb produces the following results:

hablar / *to talk*

Subject Pronoun	Haber	Past Participle	Meaning
(yo)	habr+é	habl+ado	*I will have spoken*
(tú)	habr+ás	habl+ado	*you (fam. sg.) will have spoken*
(él, ella, Ud.)	habr+á	habl+ado	*he, she, you (pol. sg.) will have spoken*
(nosotros/-as)	habr+emos	habl+ado	*we will have spoken*
(vosotros/-as)	habr+éis	habl+ado	*you (fam. pl.) will have spoken*
(ellos/-as, Uds.)	habr+án	habl+ado	*they, you (pol. pl.) will have spoken*

comer /·*to eat*

Subject Pronoun	Haber	Past Participle	Meaning
(yo)	habr+é	com+ido	*I will have eaten*
(tú)	habr+ás	com+ido	*you (fam. sg.) will have eaten*
(él, ella, Ud.)	habr+á	com+ido	*he, she, you (pol. sg.) will have eaten*
(nosotros/-as)	habr+emos	com+ido	*we will have eaten*
(vosotros/-as)	habr+éis	com+ido	*you (fam. pl.) will have eaten*
(ellos/-as, Uds.)	habr+án	com+ido	*they, you (pol. pl.) will have eaten*

vivir / *to live*

Subject Pronoun	Haber	Past Participle	Meaning
(yo)	habr+é	viv+ido	*I will have lived*
(tú)	habr+ás	viv+ido	*you (fam. sg.) will have lived*
(él, ella, Ud.)	habr+á	viv+ido	*he, she, you (pol. sg.) will have lived*
(nosotros/-as)	habr+emos	viv+ido	*we will have lived*
(vosotros/-as)	habr+éis	viv+ido	*you (fam. pl.) will have lived*
(ellos/-as, Uds.)	habr+án	viv+ido	*they, you (pol. pl.) will have lived*

The Future Perfect of Reflexive Verbs

Reflexive verbs always use reflexive pronouns in the future perfect tense, as shown below. They always appear immediately before the conjugated verb, as they do in the present and all other tenses.

lavarse / *to wash oneself*

Subject Pronoun	Reflexive Pronoun	Haber	Past Participle	Meaning
(yo)	me	habr+é	lav+ado	*I will have washed myself*
(tú)	te	habr+ás	lav+ado	*you (fam. sg.) will have washed yourself*
(él, ella, Ud.)	se	habr+á	lav+ado	*he, she, you (pol. sg.) will have washed himself/herself/yourself*
(nosotros/-as)	nos	habr+emos	lav+ado	*we will have washed ourselves*
(vosotros/-as)	os	habr+éis	lav+ado	*you (fam. pl.) will have washed yourselves*
(ellos/-as, Uds.)	se	habr+án	lav+ado	*they, you (pol. pl.) will have washed themselves/yourselves*

The Future Perfect of Hay

The future perfect form of hay / *there is, there are* is habrá habido / *there will have been*. The following examples illustrate this usage.

> Habrá habido una tormenta para mañana. / *There will have been a storm by tomorrow.*
> Habrá habido muchas tormentas. / *There will have been many storms.*

The future perfect of the idiomatic expression hay que / *one must, it is necessary to* is habrá habido que / *it will have been necessary to*. The following sentence illustrates this usage.

> Habrá habido que ir a San José. / *It will have been necessary to go to San Jose.*

VOCABULARY TIP

The future perfect is often used with words and expressions such as:

cuando / *when*
ya / *already*

EXERCISE Set 12-1

A. Supply the missing future forms of the verb **trabajar**, giving the English equivalent.

EXAMPLE: *él* _____ = _____

él habrá trabajado = *he will have worked*

1. (yo) _____ = _____

2. (tú) _____ = _____

3. (nosotros) _____ = _____

4. (ellos) _____ = _____

5. (vosotros) _____ = _____

6. (Ud.) _____ = _____

Now, supply the missing future perfect forms of the verb **creer**, giving the English equivalent.

1. (yo) _____ = _____

2. (Raquel y yo) _____ = _____

3. (Uds.) _____ = _____

4. (ellos) _____ = _____

5. (vosotros) _____ = _____

6. (tú) _____ = _____

Now, supply the missing future perfect forms of the verb **decidir**, giving the English equivalent.

1. (yo) _____ = _____

2. (tú) _____ = _____

3. (nosotros) _____ = _____

4. (ellos) _____ = _____

5. (vosotros) _____ = _____

6. (Ud.) _____ = _____

Now, supply the missing future perfect forms of the verb **afeitarse**, giving the English equivalent.

1. (yo) _____   =   _____

2. (tú) _____   =   _____

3. (nosotros) _____   =   _____

4. (ellos) _____   =   _____

5. (vosotros) _____   =   _____

6. (Ud.) _____   =   _____

Now, supply the missing future perfect forms of the verb **ser**, giving the English equivalent.

1. (yo) _____   =   _____

2. (tú) _____   =   _____

3. (nosotros) _____   =   _____

4. (ellos) _____   =   _____

5. (vosotros) _____   =   _____

6. (Ud.) _____   =   _____

Now, supply the missing future perfect forms of the verb **estar**, giving the English equivalent.

1. (yo) _____   =   _____

2. (tú) _____   =   _____

3. (nosotros) _____   =   _____

4. (ellos) _____   =   _____

5. (vosotros) _____   =   _____

6. (Ud.) _____   =   _____

Now, supply the missing future perfect forms of the verb **hacer**, giving the English equivalent.

1. (yo) _____   =   _____

2. (tú) _____   =   _____

3. (nosotros) _____   =   _____

4. (ellos) _____   = _____

5. (vosotros) _____   = _____

6. (Ud.) _____   = _____

B. How do you say the following sentences in Spanish?

1. When they will have married, they will live in San José.

   _____

2. When you (pol. pl.) will have graduated, where will you work?

   _____

3. When I will have learned many Spanish verbs, I will be able to speak Spanish.

   _____

4. They will have arrived tomorrow morning.

   _____

5. He will have read the book by tomorrow.

   _____

C. Provide the corresponding future and future perfect forms for the following verbs in the present indicative tense.

1. veo   _____   _____

2. cubres   _____   _____

3. abren   _____   _____

4. son   _____   _____

5. estoy   _____   _____

6. digo   _____   _____

7. vendemos   _____   _____

8. escribimos   _____   _____

9. te bañas   _____   _____

10. tenéis

11. piden

12. volvemos

13. hace

14. tienen

15. cierras

16. muere

17. pongo

18. hay

Crossword Puzzle 12

Fill in the blanks. All of the clues both vertical and horizontal require that you use the appropriate past participle form. Supply the appropriate auxiliary verb in the future tense.

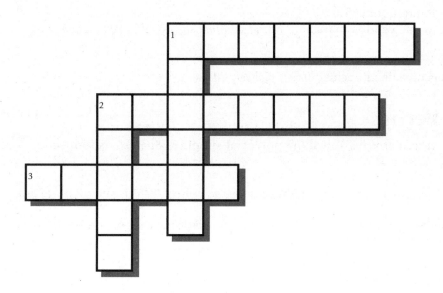

Horizontales
1. (Vosotros) . . . vuelto.
2. (Nosotros) . . . estudiado mucho.
3. (Tú) . . . dicho la verdad.

Verticales
1. Ellos . . . sido buenos.
2. (Yo) . . . estado en casa.

13

The Conditional
(*el potencial simple*)

Uses and Features

The conditional is used most of the time as follows:

1. To express a conditional, potential, or hypothetical action:
   Yo iría al teatro pero no tengo el tiempo. / *I would go to the theater but I don't have the time.*

2. To convey courtesy or politeness:
   ¿Me podría Ud. ayudar? / *Could you help me?*
   ¿Qué querría Ud.? / *What would you like?*

3. To express an indirect quotation:
   María dijo que vendría mañana. / *María said that she would be coming tomorrow.*

4. To express probability:
   Serían las diez de la noche. / *It was probably 10 P.M.*

Regular Verbs

The conditional of regular verbs, called the **potencial simple** in Spanish, is formed in a similar manner to the future tense (Chapter 11).

1. Use the entire infinitive as the stem: <u>hablar</u> / *to speak*, <u>comer</u> / *to eat*, and <u>vivir</u> / *to live*.

2. Add the following endings to the stem. Note that there is a single set of endings for the conditional tense:

(yo)	-ía
(tú)	-ías
(él, ella, Ud.)	-ía
(nosotros/-as)	-íamos
(vosotros/-as)	-íais
(ellos/-as, Uds.)	-ían

3. Here's the result:

hablar / *to speak*

Subject Pronoun	Verb Form	Meaning
(yo)	hablar+ía	*I would speak*
(tú)	hablar+ías	*you (fam. sg.) would speak*
(él, ella, Ud.)	hablar+ía	*he, she, you (pol. sg.) would speak*
(nosotros/-as)	hablar+íamos	*we would speak*
(vosotros/-as)	hablar+íais	*you (fam. pl.) would speak*
(ellos/-as, Uds.)	hablar+ían	*they, you (pol. pl.) would speak*

comer / *to eat*

Subject Pronoun	Verb Form	Meaning
(yo)	comer+ía	*I would eat*
(tú)	comer+ías	*you (fam. sg.) would eat*
(él, ella, Ud.)	comer+ía	*he, she, you (pol. sg.) would eat*
(nosotros/-as)	comer+íamos	*we would eat*
(vosotros/-as)	comer+íais	*you (fam. pl.) would eat*
(ellos/-as, Uds.)	comer+ían	*they, you (pol. pl.) would eat*

vivir / *to live*

Subject Pronoun	Verb Form	Meaning
(yo)	vivir+ía	*I would live*
(tú)	vivir+ías	*you (fam. sg.) would live*
(él, ella, Ud.)	vivir+ía	*he, she, you (pol. sg.) would live*
(nosotros/-as)	vivir+íamos	*we would live*
(vosotros/-as)	vivir+íais	*you (fam. pl.) would live*
(ellos/-as, Uds.)	vivir+ían	*they, you (pol. pl.) would live*

The Conditional Tense of Reflexive Verbs

Reflexive verbs always use reflexive pronouns in the conditional, as shown below. They always appear immediately before the conjugated verb, as they do in the present and all other tenses.

lavarse / *to wash oneself*

Subject Pronoun	Reflexive Pronoun	Conjugated Verb	Meaning
(yo)	me	lavar+ía	*I would wash myself*
(tú)	te	lavar+ías	*you (fam. sg.) would wash yourself*
(él, ella, Ud.)	se	lavar+ía	*he, she, you (pol. sg.) would wash herself/yourself*
(nosotros/-as)	nos	lavar+íamos	*we would wash ourselves*
(vosotros/-as)	os	lavar+íais	*you (fam. pl.) would wash yourselves*
(ellos/-as, Uds.)	se	lavar+ían	*they/you (pol. pl.) would wash themselves/yourselves*

TIP

While there are no stem changes in the conditional tense, there are, however, twelve verbs that have irregular stems. You will learn these forms in the next section. These irregular stems are exactly the same as those for the future tense (Chapter 11).

NOTE

You have probably noticed that the first person singular (yo) and third person singular (él, ella, Ud.) are identical in form in the conditional tense. For this reason, you must normally use the subject pronoun yo / I to distinguish these forms in the conditional.

TIP

Notice that the conditional is rendered in English generally by the following two translations:

Alfonso llegaría ...   = *Alfonso would arrive ...*
                       = *Alfonso would be arriving ...*

EXERCISE Set 13-1

A. Supply the missing conditional forms of the verb **entrar**, giving the English equivalent.

EXAMPLE: *él* _____   =   _____

            él entraría   =   *he would enter*

1. (yo) _____   =   _____

2. (tú) _____   =   _____

3. (nosotros) _____   =   _____

4. (ellos) _____   =   _____

5. (vosotros) _____   =   _____

6. (Ud.) _____   =   _____

Now, supply the missing conditional forms of the verb **temer**, giving the English equivalent.

1. (yo) _____   =   _____

2. (Raquel y yo) _____   =   _____

3. (Uds.) _____   =   _____

4. (ellos) _____   =   _____

5. (vosotros) _____   =   _____

6. (tú) _____   =   _____

Now, supply the missing conditional forms of the verb **descubrir**, giving the English equivalent.

1. (yo) _____   =   _____

2. (tú) _____   =   _____

3. (nosotros) _____   =   _____

4. (ellos) _____   =   _____

5. (vosotros) _____   =   _____

6. (Ud.) _____   =   _____

Now, supply the missing conditional forms of the verb **casarse (con)**, giving the English equivalent.

1. (yo) _____   =   _____

2. (tú) _____   =   _____

3. (nosotros) _____   =   _____

4. (ellos) _____   =   _____

5. (vosotros) _____   =   _____

6. (Ud.) _____   =   _____

VOCABULARY TIP

The conditional is often followed by the conjunction **pero** / *but*.

Concepción estudaría, pero no tiene su libro. / *Concepción would study but she doesn't have her book.*

B. How do you say the following sentences in Spanish?

1. I would speak Spanish more, but I must study the verbs.

_____

2. Would you (fam. sg.) come here, please?

_____

3. They would pay for the coffee, but they have no money.

_____

4. Where would you (fam. sg.) find an open store at this hour?

_____

5. Who would see it?

_____

6. They would go to the _Reserva Natural Volcán Mombacho_[1].

_____

7. I would go shopping, but I don't have money.

_____

8. Would you (fam. sg.) give me that newspaper?

_____

9. Would he marry Carmen?

_____

10. I would like to learn more Spanish verbs.

_____

[1]Government-protected natural reserve with a volcano that was last active in 1570; biodiversity area.

Irregular Verbs

There are twelve irregular verbs in the conditional tense. What makes these verbs irregular is the fact that they have an irregular stem. As we said before, there is a single set of endings for the conditional tense. Also, you will be pleased to know that the verbs with irregular stems in the conditional tense are the same as for those in the future tense (see Chapter 11), so you will not have to learn new forms. You will simply add the single set of conditional endings to these forms. We repeat the three groups of irregular conditional stems for your convenience.

Irregular Conditional Stems: Pattern 1

Learn the irregular conditional stem to which you add the conditional tense endings. In this group, you take the infinitive and you delete the vowel in the infinitive ending: -er → -r-. We list them below.

>   caber / _to fit, to be contained_ → cabr-
>   haber / _to have (auxiliary verb)_ → habr-
>   poder / _can, to be able_ → podr-
>   querer / _to want_ → querr-
>   saber / _to know, to know how_ → sabr-

Irregular Conditional Stems: Pattern 2

Learn the irregular conditional stem to which you add the conditional tense endings. In this group, you take the infinitive and you delete the vowel in the infinitive ending. Then you insert the consonant -d-: -er → -dr-. We list them below.

poner / *to put, to place* → pondr-
salir / *to leave* → saldr-
tener / *to have* → tendr-
valer / *to be worth* → valdr-
venir / *to come* → vendr-

Irregular Conditional Stems: Pattern 3

Learn the irregular conditional stem to which you add the conditional tense endings. In this group, a completely different stem is used. We list them below:

decir / *to say, to tell* → dir-
hacer / *to do, to make* → har-

To each of these irregular stems, you add the conditional tense endings that we reproduce here:

(yo)	-ía
(tú)	-ías
(él, ella, Ud.)	-ía
(nosotros/-as)	-íamos
(vosotros/-as)	-íais
(ellos/-as, Uds.)	-ían

We now provide one conjugation from each of the three categories we just saw.

saber/ *to know*

Subject Pronoun	Verb Form	Meaning
(yo)	sabr+ía	*I would know*
(tú)	sabr+ías	*you (fam. sg.) would know*
(él, ella, Ud.)	sabr+ía	*he, she, you (pol. sg.) would know*
(nosotros/-as)	sabr+íamos	*we would know*
(vosotros/-as)	sabr+íais	*you (fam. pl.) would know*
(ellos/-as, Uds.)	sabr+ían	*they, you (pol. pl.) would know*

salir / *to leave*

Subject Pronoun	Verb Form	Meaning
(yo)	saldr+ía	*I would leave*
(tú)	saldr+ías	*you (fam. sg.) would leave*
(él, ella, Ud.)	saldr+ía	*he, she, you (pol. sg.) would leave*
(nosotros/-as)	saldr+íamos	*we would leave*
(vosotros/-as)	saldr+íais	*you (fam. pl.) would leave*
(ellos/-as, Uds.)	saldr+ían	*they, you (pol. pl.) would leave*

decir / *to say, to tell*

Subject Pronoun	Verb Form	Meaning
(yo)	<u>dir</u>+ía	*I would say/tell*
(tú)	<u>dir</u>+ías	*you (fam. sg.) would say/tell*
(él, ella, Ud.)	<u>dir</u>+ía	*he, she, you (pol. sg.) would say/tell*
(nosotros/-as)	<u>dir</u>+íamos	*we would say/tell*
(vosotros/-as)	<u>dir</u>+íais	*you (fam. pl.) would say/tell*
(ellos/-as, Uds.)	<u>dir</u>+ían	*they, you (pol. pl.) would say/tell*

Conditional of Hay

The conditional of hay / *there is, there are* is habría / *there would be*. It is used in the same way that hay is used, except that it is in the conditional tense. The following sentences illustrate this point.

Habría más dinero pero no tuve empleo entonces. / *There would be more money but I had no job then.*
Habría más muebles pero no tuvimos el dinero. / *There would be more furniture but we didn't have the money.*

The conditional of the idiomatic expression hay que / *one must, it is necessary to* is habría que / *it would be necessary to*. The following sentence illustrates this usage.

Habría que ir a Managua. / *It would be necessary to go to Managua.*

EXERCISE Set 13-2

A. Supply the missing conditional forms of the verb **querer (ie)**, giving the English equivalent.

EXAMPLE: *él* _____   =   _____

            él querría   =   *he would want*

1. (yo) _____   =   _____

2. (tú) _____   =   _____

3. (nosotros) _____   =   _____

4. (ellos) _____   =   _____

5. (vosotros) _____   =   _____

6. (Ud.) _____   =   _____

Now, supply the missing conditional forms of the verb caber, giving the English equivalent.

1. (yo) _____   =   _____

2. (Raquel y yo) _____   =   _____

3. (Uds.) _____   =   _____

4. (ellos) _____   =   _____

5. (vosotros) _____   =   _____

6. (tú) _____   =   _____

Now, supply the missing conditional forms of the verb hacer, giving the English equivalent.

1. (yo) _____   =   _____

2. (tú) _____   =   _____

3. (nosotros) _____ =   _____

4. (ellos) _____   =   _____

5. (vosotros) _____ =   _____

6. (Ud.) _____   =   _____

Now, supply the missing conditional forms of the verb haber, giving the English equivalent.

1. (yo) _____   =   _____

2. (tú) _____   =   _____

3. (nosotros) _____ =   _____

4. (ellos) _____   =   _____

5. (vosotros) _____ =   _____

6. (Ud.) _____   =   _____

Now, supply the missing conditional forms of the verb poder (ue), giving the English equivalent.

1. (yo) _____   =   _____

2. (tú) _____   =   _____

3. (nosotros) _____ =   _____

4. (ellos) _____   =   _____

5. (vosotros) _____   =   _____

6. (Ud.) _____   =   _____

Now, supply the missing conditional forms of the verb **venir**, giving the English equivalent.

1. (yo) _____   =   _____

2. (tú) _____   =   _____

3. (nosotros) _____   =   _____

4. (ellos) _____   =   _____

5. (vosotros) _____   =   _____

6. (Ud.) _____   =   _____

Now, supply the missing conditional forms of the verb **tener**, giving the English equivalent.

1. (yo) _____   =   _____

2. (tú) _____   =   _____

3. (nosotros) _____   =   _____

4. (ellos) _____   =   _____

5. (vosotros) _____   =   _____

6. (Ud.) _____   =   _____

B. How do you say the following sentences in Spanish?

1. I would do the exercises, but I am very tired.

_____

2. She would be able to do that job.

_____

3. We would put the plates on the table.

_____

4. I would leave in the evening.

   _____

5. You (pol. sg.) would know the answer.

   _____

6. He would say that it is late.

   _____

7. You (pol. pl.) would have to be here on time.

   _____

8. The car would be worth 10.000 *córdobas*[1].

   _____

9. Would you (fam. sg.) want to go to the theater?

   _____

10. It would rain in the evening.

    _____

11. You (fam. sg.) would tell the truth.

    _____

12. The books would fit on the shelf.

    _____

13. We would know how to conjugate the conditional tense.

    _____

14. It would be necessary to get up early.

    _____

[1]Unit of money in Nicaragua.

EXERCISE Set 13-3

A. How do you say the following sentences in Spanish?

1. It was probably five P.M. when Lidia arrived.

_____

2. It would be necessary to work all night.

_____

3. What would you (fam. sg.) do during a storm?

_____

4. It probably would cost a lot of money.

_____

5. I would buy another car, but I don't have the money.

_____

B. Provide the corresponding conditional forms for the following verbs in the present indicative tense.

1. van   _____

2. hago   _____

3. dices   _____

4. son   _____

5. estoy   _____

6. canta   _____

7. tienes   _____

8. hay   _____

9. sé   _____

10. encuentro _____

11. puede   _____

12. queremos _____

13. hace _____

14. cierro _____

15. vale _____

16. salen _____

17. vengo _____

18. te afeitas _____

Crossword Puzzle 13

Fill in the blanks. Supply the corresponding conditional tense form for the present tense indicative form given in the clue.

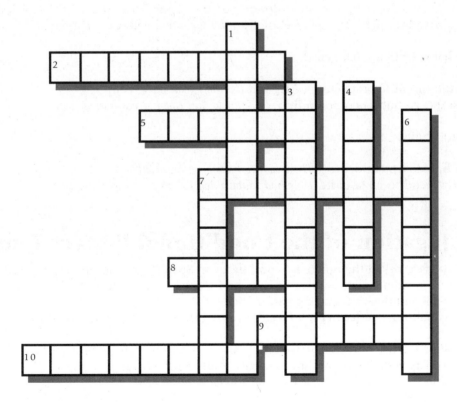

Horizontales
2. Beben
5. Cabe
7. Valen
8. Dice
9. Puede
10. Quieres

Verticales
1. Hay
3. Salimos
4. Hacéis
6. Cantas
7. Vive

14
The Conditional Perfect
(*el potencial compuesto*)

Uses and Features

The conditional perfect is used most of the time as follows:

1. To express an action that would have occurred if something else had been possible.

   Ella habría cantado, pero tenía un dolor de garganta. / *She would have sung, but she had a sore throat.*
   Ellos habrían ido, pero no tenían el tiempo. / *They would have gone, but they didn't have the time.*

2. To express what would have happened.

   Él me dijo que él habría venido. / *He said that he would have come.*
   Él sabía que yo habría comprendido. / *He knew that I would have understood.*

3. To convey probability.

   Habría habido un accidente. / *There had to have been an accident.*
   Él habría mentido en la corte. / *He had to have lied in court.*

The Conjugation of the Conditional Perfect Tense

The conditional perfect, called the potencial compuesto in Spanish, is a compound tense. Therefore, it is conjugated with the auxiliary verb haber / *to have*, and the past participle of the verb, in that order. See Chapter 9 for the relevant details regarding past participles.

   To form the conditional perfect tense of regular verbs, this is what you have to do:

1. Use the conditional tense of the auxiliary verb haber / *to have*, which we provide here. Remember that haber is an auxiliary verb. It does not mean *to have* in the sense of *to possess*. To indicate that you have or possess something, you must use the verb tener / *to have, to possess*.

haber / *to have*

Subject Pronoun	Verb Form	Meaning
(yo)	habr+ía	*I would have*
(tú)	habr+ías	*you (fam. sg.) would have*
(él, ella, Ud.)	habr+ía	*he, she, you (pol. sg.) would have*
(nosotros/-as)	habr+íamos	*we would have*
(vosotros/-as)	habr+íais	*you (fam. pl.) would have*
(ellos/-as, Uds.)	habr+ían	*they, you (pol. pl.) would have*

The combination of the conditional tense of the auxiliary verb haber / *to have* produces the following results:

hablar / *to talk*

Subject Pronoun	Haber	Past Participle	Meaning
(yo)	habr+ía	habl+ado	*I would have spoken*
(tú)	habr+ías	habl+ado	*you (fam. sg.) would have spoken*
(él, ella, Ud.)	habr+ía	habl+ado	*he, she, you (pol. sg.) would have spoken*
(nosotros/-as)	habr+íamos	habl+ado	*we would have spoken*
(vosotros/-as)	habr+íais	habl+ado	*you (fam. pl.) would have spoken*
(ellos/-as, Uds.)	habr+ían	habl+ado	*they, you (pol. pl.) would have spoken*

comer / *to eat*

Subject Pronoun	Haber	Past Participle	Meaning
(yo)	habr+ía	com+ido	*I would have eaten*
(tú)	habr+ías	com+ido	*you (fam. sg.) would have eaten*
(él, ella, Ud.)	habr+ía	com+ido	*he, she, you (pol. sg.) would have eaten*
(nosotros/-as)	habr+íamos	com+ido	*we would have eaten*
(vosotros/-as)	habr+íais	com+ido	*you (fam. pl.) would have eaten*
(ellos/-as, Uds.)	habr+ían	com+ido	*they, you (pol. pl.) would have eaten*

vivir / *to live*

Subject Pronoun	Haber	Past Participle	Meaning
(yo)	habr+ía	viv+ido	*I would have lived*
(tú)	habr+ías	viv+ido	*you (fam. sg.) would have lived*
(él, ella, Ud.)	habr+ía	viv+ido	*he, she, you (pol. sg.) would have lived*
(nosotros/-as)	habr+íamos	viv+ido	*we would have lived*
(vosotros/-as)	habr+íais	viv+ido	*you (fam. pl.) would have lived*
(ellos/-as, Uds.)	habr+ían	viv+ido	*they, you (pol. pl.) would have lived*

The Conditional Perfect of Reflexive Verbs

Reflexive verbs always use reflexive pronouns in the conditional perfect tense, as shown below. They always appear immediately before the conjugated verb, as they do in the present and all other tenses.

lavarse / *to wash oneself*

Subject Pronoun	Reflexive Pronoun	Haber	Past Participle	Meaning
(yo)	me	habr+ía	lav+ado	*I would have washed myself*
(tú)	te	habr+ías	lav+ado	*you (fam. sg.) would have washed yourself*
(él, ella, Ud.)	se	habr+ía	lav+ado	*he, she, you (pol. sg.) would have washed himself/herself/yourself*
(nosotros/-as)	nos	habr+íamos	lav+ado	*we would have washed ourselves*
(vosotros/-as)	os	habr+íais	lav+ado	*you (fam. pl.) would have washed yourselves*
(ellos/-as, Uds.)	se	habr+ían	lav+ado	*they, you (pol. pl.) would have washed themselves/yourselves*

NOTE

You have probably noticed that the first person singular (yo) and third person singular (él, ella, Ud.) are identical in form in the conditional perfect tense. For this reason, you must normally use the subject pronoun yo / *I* to distinguish these forms in the conditional.

TIP

Notice that the conditional perfect is rendered in English generally by the following translation:

Alfonso habría dicho ...   = *Alfonso would have said ...*

The Conditional Perfect of Hay

The conditional perfect form of hay / *there is, there are* is habría habido / *there would have been*. The following examples illustrate this usage.

Habría habido un problema, pero no pasó nada. / *There would have been a problem, but nothing happened.*
Habría habido muchos estudiantes allí, pero llovió. / *There would have been many students there, but it rained.*

The conditional perfect of the idiomatic expression hay que / *one must, it is necessary to* is habría habido que / *it would have been necessary to*. The following sentence illustrates this usage.

Habría habido que ir a Tegucigalpa. / *It would have been necessary to go to Tegucigalpa.*

VOCABULARY TIP

As is the case with the conditional tense (Chapter 13), the conditional perfect tense is often followed by the conjunction pero / *but*:

Julio se habría levantado temprano, pero estaba muy cansado. / *Julio would have gotten up early, but he was very tired.*

EXERCISE Set 14-1

A. Supply the missing conditional perfect forms of the verb llegar, giving the English equivalent.

EXAMPLE: *él* _____   =   _____

él habría llegado   =   *he would have arrived*

1. (yo) _____   =   _____

2. (tú) _____   =   _____

3. (nosotros) _____   =   _____

4. (ellos) _____   =   _____

5. (vosotros) _____   =   _____

6. (Ud.) _____   =   _____

Now, supply the missing conditional perfect forms of the verb comprender, giving the English equivalent.

1. (yo) _____   =   _____

2. (Raquel y yo) _____   =   _____

3. (Uds.) _____   =   _____

4. (ellos) _____   =   _____

5. (vosqtros) _____   =   _____

6. (tú) _____   =   _____

Now, supply the missing conditional perfect forms of the verb **discutir**, giving the English equivalent.

1. (yo) _____ = _____

2. (tú) _____ = _____

3. (nosotros) _____ = _____

4. (ellos) _____ = _____

5. (vosotros) _____ = _____

6. (Ud.) _____ = _____

Now, supply the missing conditional perfect forms of the verb **quitarse**, giving the English equivalent.

1. (yo) _____ = _____

2. (tú) _____ = _____

3. (nosotros) _____ = _____

4. (ellos) _____ = _____

5. (vosotros) _____ = _____

6. (Ud.) _____ = _____

Now, supply the missing conditional perfect forms of the verb **ser**, giving the English equivalent.

1. (yo) _____ = _____

2. (tú) _____ = _____

3. (nosotros) _____ = _____

4. (ellos) _____ = _____

5. (vosotros) _____ = _____

6. (Ud.) _____ = _____

Now, supply the missing conditional perfect forms of the verb estar, giving the English equivalent.

1. (yo) _____   =   _____

2. (tú) _____   =   _____

3. (nosotros) _____ =   _____

4. (ellos) _____   =   _____

5. (vosotros) _____ =   _____

6. (Ud.) _____   =   _____

Now, supply the missing conditional perfect forms of the verb hacer, giving the English equivalent.

1. (yo) _____   =   _____

2. (tú) _____   =   _____

3. (nosotros) _____ =   _____

4. (ellos) _____   =   _____

5. (vosotros) _____ =   _____

6. (Ud.) _____   =   _____

B. How do you say the following sentences in Spanish?

1. I would have gone to the party, but I didn't have the time.

    _____

2. My parents would have gone to Honduras, but they didn't have the money.

    _____

3. I would have gone with them, but I had to study.

    _____

4. They would have gotten up early, but they slept late.

    _____

5. He would have bought the car, but it cost too much.

    _____

C. Provide the corresponding conditional and conditional perfect forms for the following verbs in the present indicative tense.

1. voy

2. escribes

3. dicen

4. sois

5. están

6. dice

7. comemos

8. vivimos

9. te lavas

10. tengo

11. mueren

12. vuelvo

13. vienes

14. sé

15. conozco

16. resuelvo

17. ponemos

18. hay

Crossword Puzzle 14

Fill in the blanks. All of the clues both vertical and horizontal require that you use the appropriate past participle form.

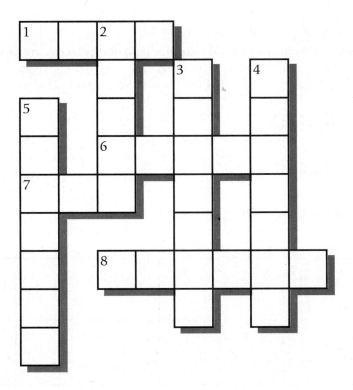

Horizontales
1. Ud. habría . . . (ser) bueno.
6. Ella lo habría . . . (hacer).
7. Mis amigos habrían . . . (ir).
8. Yo habría . . . (estar) allí.

Verticales
2. (Vosotros) habríais . . . (decir) la verdad.
3. (Nosotros) habríamos . . . (escribir) la tarea.
4. Habría . . . (llover).
5. (Tú) habrías . . . (abrir) la puerta.

Review 3
(Chapters 11–14)

This review chapter will allow you to go over and reinforce your ability to conjugate verbs in the future and conditional tenses and to recognize their use in conversation and writing. There are, as in the previous review chapters, two specific types of exercise: (1) *Conjugation Review* and (2) *Usage Review*.

Conjugation Review

Review Exercise Set 3-1

A. Conjugate the following verbs in the future tense.

1. bailar, leer, asistir

(yo)		
(tú)		
(él, ella, Ud.)		
(nosotros/-as)		
(vosotros/-as)		
(ellos/-as, Uds.)		

2. contar (ue), perder (ie), sugerir (i, i)

(yo)		
(tú)		
(él, ella, Ud.)		
(nosotros/-as)		
(vosotros/-as)		
(ellos/-as, Uds.)		

3. caber, poner, decir (i, i)

    (yo)

    (tú)

    (él, ella, Ud.)

    (nosotros/-as)

    (vosotros/-as)

    (ellos/-as, Uds.)

4. haber, salir, hacer

    (yo)

    (tú)

    (él, ella, Ud.)

    (nosotros/-as)

    (vosotros/-as)

    (ellos/-as, Uds.)

5. ser, estar, bañarse

    (yo)

    (tú)

    (él, ella, Ud.)

    (nosotros/-as)

    (vosotros/-as)

    (ellos/-as, Uds.)

B. Conjugate the following verbs in the future perfect.

hacer, ser, estar

(yo)		
(tú)		
(él, ella, Ud.)		
(nosotros/-as)		
(vosotros/-as)		
(ellos/-as, Uds.)		

C. Conjugate the following verbs in the conditional.

1. buscar, meter, sufrir

(yo)		
(tú)		
(él, ella, Ud.)		
(nosotros/-as)		
(vosotros/-as)		
(ellos/-as, Uds.)		

2. poder (ue), tener, querer (ie)

(yo)		
(tú)		
(él, ella, Ud.)		
(nosotros/-as)		
(vosotros/-as)		
(ellos/-as, Uds.)		

3. saber, venir, ser

(yo)			
(tú)			
(él, ella, Ud.)			
(nosotros/-as)			
(vosotros/-as)			
(ellos/-as, Uds.)			

D. Conjugate the following verbs in the conditional perfect.

estar, tener, ser

(yo)			
(tú)			
(él, ella, Ud.)			
(nosotros/-as)			
(vosotros/-as)			
(ellos/-as, Uds.)			

Usage Review

Review Exercise Set 3-2

A. Choose the appropriate verb form, **a** or **b**, according to the grammar and the meaning:

1. ¿Qué tiempo … mañana?
   - **a.** hará
   - **b.** dirá

2. ¿De dónde … ?
   - **a.** estará
   - **b.** será

3. ¿Cuántos años … tu primo?
   - **a.** tendrá
   - **b.** será

4. ¿A qué hora … Uds. mañana?
   a. saldrán
   b. habrán

5. Según él, ella … nicaragüense.
   a. tendría
   b. sería

6. Ella dijo que … mañana.
   a. llegaría
   b. llegará

7. Mencioné que yo … a la fiesta.
   a. habría ido
   b. habría sido

8. Uds. … a San Salvador mañana.
   a. viajarán
   b. entrarán

9. ¿Me … la verdad?
   a. dirás
   b. tendrás

10. Él ya … para la Ciudad de Panamá.
    a. habrá partido
    b. habría sabido

B. Missing from the following sentences are the indicated verbs. Insert them in the spaces in their correct future or conditional form according to the meaning.

   Verbs: **asistir, estar, estudiar, hacer, ir, regresar, tener, valer**

1. ¿Cuánto _____ cien colones costarricenses en dólares estadounidenses?

2. ¿Adónde _____ ellos para las vacaciones?

3. _____ mucho frío mañana.

4. _____ nublado por la tarde.

5. Juan _____ veinte años.

6. Dijo que _____ a la clase.

7. Ellos _____ de Nicaragua mañana.

8. Yo _____ pero no tengo el tiempo.

Part Four
The Subjunctive Tenses

The Subjunctive Tenses: An Overview

What Is the Subjunctive?

The subjunctive is a mood that allows you to express a point of view—fear, doubt, hope, possibility—in sum, anything that is not a fact. In a way, the subjunctive is a counterpart to the indicative, the mood that allows you to convey facts and information.

The main thing to note about the subjunctive is that it is used, primarily, in a subordinate clause. What is a subordinate clause, you might ask?

A complex sentence has at least one subordinate clause—a clause, by the way, is a group of related words that contains a subject and predicate and is part of the main sentence. The subjunctive is used, as mentioned, mainly in a subordinate clause, generally introduced by que / *that, which, who.* So, when expressing something that is a doubt, etc. with a verb in the main clause (the verb to the left of que), put the verb in the subordinate clause (the verb to the right of que) in the subjunctive:

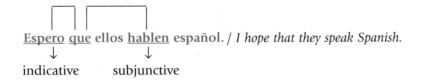

Espero que ellos hablen español. / *I hope that they speak Spanish.*

    indicative   subjunctive

Subjunctive vs. Indicative

Not all verbs in subordinate clauses (those after que) are necessarily to be put in the subjunctive—only those connected with a main clause verb that expresses a "nonfact" (fear, supposition, anticipation, wish, hope, doubt, etc.).

Indicative	Subjunctive
<u>Sé</u> que <u>es</u> la verdad. / *I know that it is the truth.*	<u>Quiero</u> que <u>sea</u> la verdad. / *I want it to be the truth.*
<u>Es cierto</u> que él <u>paga</u>. / *It's certain that he is paying.*	<u>Es probable</u> que él <u>pague</u>. / *It's probable that he is paying.*

15

The Present Subjunctive (*el presente de subjuntivo*)

Uses and Features

The subjunctive allows you to convey a point of view, emotion, doubt, hope, possibility—anything that is not a fact or certainty.

There is a useful memory tool to help you to remember when to use the subjunctive. It is the acronym WEDDING. This acronym stands for the various situations in which the subjunctive is used.

Will
Emotion
Desire
Doubt
Impersonal expression
Negative
Generalized Characteristics

The WEDDING acronym thus covers noun clauses introduced by verbs of volition, emotion, desire, doubt, and impersonal expressions. Likewise, it covers the use of the subjunctive with negative or indefinite antecedents.

Will (verbs of volition such as **preferir (ie, i)** / *to prefer*, and so forth).

<u>Prefiero</u> que Jorge <u>llegue</u> a tiempo./ *I prefer that Jorge arrive on time.*

Emotion (verbs and verbal expressions of emotion such as **sentir (ie, i)** / *to regret*, and so forth).

<u>Siento</u> que María <u>esté</u> enferma. / *I regret that María is sick.*

Desire (verbs such as **querer (ie)** / *to want*, and so forth).

<u>Quiero</u> que Juan <u>escriba</u> la carta. / *I want Juan to write the letter.*

Doubt (verbs such as **dudar** / *to doubt*, and so forth).

Dudo que llueva hoy. / *I doubt that it will rain today.*

Impersonal expression (verbal expressions such as **es posible** / *it is possible*, and so forth).

<u>Es posible</u> que <u>haya</u> mucha gente allí. / *It is possible that there will be a lot of people there.*

Negative (clauses with negative antecedents such as nadie / *no one*, and so forth).

> No hay nadie que pueda trabajar el domingo. / *There is no one that can work on Sunday.*

Generalized characteristics (clauses with unspecified antecedents).

> ¿Hay <u>alguien</u> que <u>tenga</u> la tarea de hoy? / *Is there someone who has today's homework?*

Formation of the Present Subjunctive

To form the present subjunctive of regular verbs, called the presente de subjuntivo in Spanish, do the following:

1. Take the first person singular of the present indicative. You need to note that this includes all regular and irregular verbs, with the exception of six irregular verbs (see further in this chapter) and stem-changing -ir verbs. We include selective examples of each type of verb here.

   hablo / *I speak*
   como / *I eat*
   vivo / *I live*
   tengo / *I have*
   hago / *I do/make*
   salgo / *I leave*
   concluyo / *I conclude*
   caigo / *I fall*

2. Remove the -o ending:
   habl+o → habl-
   com+o → com-
   viv+o → viv-
   teng+o → teng-
   hag+o → hag-
   salg+o → salg-
   concluy+o → concluy-
   caig+o → caig-

3. Add the following endings for -ar verbs (we use suspension points […] to indicate that verbs in the subjunctive appear in subordinate clauses, and we will use this convention in the remaining chapters of this section):

. . . (yo)	-e
. . . (tú)	-es
. . . (él, ella, Ud.)	-e
. . . (nosotros/-as)	-emos
. . . (vosotros/-as)	-éis
. . . (ellos/-as, Uds.)	-en

4. Add the following endings for -er and -ir verbs:

. . . (yo)	-a
. . . (tú)	-as
. . . (él, ella, Ud.)	-a
. . . (nosotros/-as)	-amos
. . . (vosotros/-as)	-áis
. . . (ellos/-as, Uds.)	-an

5. Here's the result for the examples given above:

<u>habl</u>+e
<u>com</u>+a
<u>viv</u>+a
<u>teng</u>+a
<u>hag</u>+a
<u>salg</u>+a
<u>concluy</u>+a
<u>caig</u>+a

We now provide exemplary and complete conjugations of the verb types used above. Again, we remind you that we use suspension points (...) in all examples to indicate that the subjunctive appears in subordinate clauses.

hablar / *to speak*

Subject Pronoun	Verb Form	Meaning
...(yo)	<u>habl</u>+e	...I speak, I am speaking, I may speak
...(tú)	<u>habl</u>+es	...you (fam. sg.) speak, you are speaking, you may speak
...(él, ella, Ud.)	<u>habl</u>+e	...he, she, you (pol. sg.) speak(s), he, she, you is/are speaking, he, she, you may speak
...(nosotros/-as)	<u>habl</u>+emos	...we speak, we are speaking, we may speak
...(vosotros/-as)	<u>habl</u>+éis	...you (fam. pl.) speak, you are speaking, you may speak
...(ellos/-as, Uds.)	<u>habl</u>+en	...they, you (pol. pl.) speak, they, you are speaking, they, you may speak

comer / *to eat*

Subject Pronoun	Verb Form	Meaning
...(yo)	<u>com</u>+a	...I eat, I am eating, I may eat
...(tú)	<u>com</u>+as	...you (fam. sg.) eat, you are eating, you may eat
...(él, ella, Ud.)	<u>com</u>+a	...he, she, you (pol. sg.) eat(s), he, she, you is/are eating, he, she, you may eat
...(nosotros/-as)	<u>com</u>+amos	...we eat, we are eating, we may eat
...(vosotros/-as)	<u>com</u>+áis	...you (fam. pl.) eat, you are eating, you may eat
...(ellos/-as, Uds.)	<u>com</u>+an	...they, you (pol. pl.) eat, they, you are eating, they, you may eat

vivir / *to live*

Subject Pronoun	Verb Form	Meaning
...(yo)	viv+a	...*I live, I am living, I may live*
...(tú)	viv+as	...*you (fam. sg.) live, you are living, you may live*
...(él, ella, Ud.)	viv+a	...*he, she, you (pol. sg.) live(s), he, she, you is/are living, he, she, you may live*
...(nosotros/-as)	viv+amos	...*we live, we are living, we may live*
...(vosotros/-as)	viv+áis	...*you (fam. pl.) live, you are living, you may live*
...(ellos/-as, Uds.)	viv+an	...*they, you (pol. pl.) live, they, you are living, they, you may live*

tener / *to have*

Subject Pronoun	Verb Form	Meaning
...(yo)	teng+a	...*I have, I am having, I may have*
...(tú)	teng+as	...*you (fam. sg.) have, you are having, you may have*
...(él, ella, Ud.)	teng+a	... *he, she, you (pol. sg.) has/have, he, she, you is/are having, he, she, you may have*
...(nosotros/-as)	teng+amos	...*we have, we are having, we may have*
...(vosotros/-as)	teng+áis	...*you (fam. pl.) have, you are having, you may have*
...(ellos/-as, Uds.)	teng+an	...*they, you (pol. pl.) have, they, you are having, they, you may have*

hacer / *to do, to make*

Subject Pronoun	Verb Form	Meaning
...(yo)	hag+a	...*I do/make, I am doing/making, I may do/make*
...(tú)	hag+as	...*you (fam. sg.) do/make, you are doing/making, you may do/make*
...(él, ella, Ud.)	hag+a	...*he, she, you (pol. sg.) does/do, makes/make, he, she, you is/are doing/making, he, she, you may do/make*
...(nosotros/-as)	hag+amos	...*we do/make, we are doing/making, we may do/make*
...(vosotros/-as)	hag+áis	...*you (fam. pl.) do/make, you are doing/making, you may do/make*
...(ellos/-as, Uds.)	hag+an	...*they, you (pol. pl.) do/make, they, you are doing/making, they, you may do/make*

salir / *to leave*

Subject Pronoun	Verb Form	Meaning
...(yo)	<u>salg</u>+a	...*I leave, I am leaving, I may leave*
...(tú)	<u>salg</u>+as	...*you (fam. sg.) leave, you are leaving, you may leave*
...(él, ella, Ud.)	<u>salg</u>+a	...*he, she, you (pol. sg.) leave(s), he, she, you is/are leaving, he, she, you may leave*
...(nosotros/-as)	<u>salg</u>+amos	...*we leave, we are leaving, we may leave*
...(vosotros/-as)	<u>salg</u>+áis	...*you (fam. pl.) leave, you are leaving, you may leave*
...(ellos/-as, Uds.)	<u>salg</u>+an	... *they, you (pol. pl.) leave, they, you are leaving, they, you may leave*

concluir / *to conclude*

Subject Pronoun	Verb Form	Meaning
...(yo)	<u>concluy</u>+a	...*I conclude, I am concluding, I may conclude*
...(tú)	<u>concluy</u>+as	...*you (fam. sg.) conclude, you are concluding, you may conclude*
...(él, ella, Ud.)	<u>concluy</u>+a	...*he, she, you (pol. sg.) conclude(s), he, she, you is/are concluding, he, she, you may conclude*
...(nosotros/-as)	<u>concluy</u>+amos	...*we conclude, we are concluding, we may conclude*
...(vosotros/-as)	<u>concluy</u>+áis	...*you (fam. pl.) conclude, you are concluding, you may conclude*
...(ellos/-as, Uds.)	<u>concluy</u>+an	...*they, you (pol. pl.) conclude, they, you are concluding, they, you may conclude*

caer / *to fall*

Subject Pronoun	Verb Form	Meaning
...(yo)	<u>caig</u>+a	...*I fall, I am falling, I may fall*
...(tú)	<u>caig</u>+as	...*you (fam. sg.) fall, you are falling, you may fall*
...(él, ella, Ud.)	<u>caig</u>+a	...*he, she, you (pol. sg.) fall(s), he, she, you is/are fallling, he, she, you may fall*
...(nosotros/-as)	<u>caig</u>+amos	...*we fall, we are falling, we may fall*
...(vosotros/-as)	<u>caig</u>+áis	...*you (fam. pl.) fall, you are falling, you may fall*
...(ellos/-as, Uds.)	<u>caig</u>+an	...*they, you (pol. pl.) fall, they, you are falling, they, you may fall*

NOTE

The English translation of the present subjunctive is often the same as the English translation of the present indicative. In English, the subjunctive has virtually disappeared from everyday usage. It is used rarely in such expressions as "*If he be*" and "*I prefer that he be here.*" Nevertheless, it remains a viable form in Spanish even though its English translation does not reflect this grammatical fact.

The Present Subjunctive of Reflexive Verbs

Reflexive verbs always use reflexive pronouns in the present subjunctive, as shown below. They always appear immediately before the conjugated verb, as they do in all other tenses.

lavarse / *to wash oneself*

Subject Pronoun	Reflexive Pronoun	Conjugated Verb	Meaning
...(yo)	me	lav+e	...I wash myself, I am washing myself, I may wash myself
...(tú)	te	lav+es	...you (fam. sg.) wash yourself, you are washing yourself, you may wash yourself
...(él, ella, Ud.)	se	lav+e	...he, she, you (pol. sg.) wash(es) himself, herself, yourself, he, she, you does/do wash himself/herself/yourself, he, she, you may wash himself/herself/yourself
...(nosotros/-as)	nos	lav+emos	...we wash ourselves, we are washing ourselves, we may wash ourselves
...(vosotros/-as)	os	lav+éis	...you (fam. pl.) wash yourselves, you are washing yourselves, you may wash yourselves
...(ellos/-as, Uds.)	se	lav+en	...they, you (pol. pl.) wash themselves/yourselves, they, you are washing themselves/yourselves, they, you may wash themselves/yourselves

Stem-Changing Verbs

Stem-changing verbs have the same changes in the stem as they do in the present indicative (see Chapter 2 to review this pattern). We provide two selected examples (**cerrar (ie)** / *to close* and **volver (ue)** / *to return*) of this type of verb in the present subjunctive. You will note that the subjunctive endings are the same as for regularly formed subjunctive verbs.

cerrar (ie) / *to close*

Subject Pronoun	Verb Form	Meaning
...(yo)	cierr+e	...I close, I am closing, I may close
...(tú)	cierr+es	...you (fam. sg.) close, you are closing, you may close
...(él, ella, Ud.)	cierr+e	...he, she, you (pol. sg.) close(s), he, she, you is/are closing, he, she, you may close
...(nosotros/-as)	cerr+emos	...we close, we are closing, we may close
...(vosotros/-as)	cerr+éis	...you (fam. pl.) close, you are closing, you may close
...(ellos/-as, Uds.)	cierr+en	... they, you (pol. pl.) close, they, you are closing, they, you may close

volver (ue) (a) / *to return*

Subject Pronoun	Verb Form	Meaning
…(yo)	<u>vuelv</u>+a	…*I return, I am returning, I may return*
…(tú)	<u>vuelv</u>+as	…*you (fam. sg.) return, you are returning, you may return*
…(él, ella, Ud.)	<u>vuelv</u>+a	…*he, she, you (pol. sg.) return(s), he, she, you is/are returning, he, she, you may return*
…(nosotros/-as)	<u>volv</u>+amos	…*we return, we are returning, we may return*
…(vosotros/-as)	<u>volv</u>+áis	…*you (fam. pl.) return, you are returning, you may return*
…(ellos/-as, Uds.)	<u>vuelv</u>+an	… *they, you (pol. pl.) return, they, you are returning, they, you may return*

Stem-Changing -*ir* Verbs

Third conjugation stem-changing verbs (-ir) also have a stem change in the nosotros/-as / *we* and vosotros/-as / *you* (fam. pl.) forms. Verbs such as medir (i, i) / *to measure* have an -i- in these forms, and verbs such as dormir (ue, u) / *to sleep* have a -u- in these forms. We provide conjugations of each one below.

medir (i, i) / *to measure*

Subject Pronoun	Verb Form	Meaning
…(yo)	<u>mid</u>+a	…*I measure, I am measuring, I may measure*
…(tú)	<u>mid</u>+as	…*you (fam. sg.) measure, you are measuring, you may measure*
…(él, ella, Ud.)	<u>mid</u>+a	…*he, she, you (pol. sg.) measure(s), he, she, you is/are measuring, he, she, you may measure*
…(nosotros/-as)	<u>mid</u>+amos	…*we measure, we are measuring, we may measure*
…(vosotros/-as)	<u>mid</u>+áis	…*you (fam. pl.) measure, you are measuring, you may measure*
…(ellos/-as, Uds.)	<u>mid</u>+an	…*they, you (pol. pl.) measure, they, you are measuring, they, you may measure*

dormir (ue, u) / *to sleep*

Subject Pronoun	Verb Form	Meaning
…(yo)	<u>duerm</u>+a	…*I sleep, I am sleeping, I may sleep*
…(tú)	<u>duerm</u>+as	…*you (fam. sg.) sleep, you are sleeping, you may sleep*
…(él, ella, Ud.)	<u>duerm</u>+a	…*he, she, you (pol. sg.) sleep(s), he, she, you is/are sleeping, he, she, you may sleep*
…(nosotros/-as)	<u>durm</u>+amos	…*we sleep, we are sleeping, we may sleep*
…(vosotros/-as)	<u>durm</u>+áis	… *you (fam. pl.) sleep, you are sleeping, you may sleep*
…(ellos/-as, Uds.)	<u>duerm</u>+an	…*they, you (pol. pl.) sleep, they, you are sleeping, they, you may sleep*

> **TIP**
>
> Remember that third conjugation verbs have a parenthetical -i- or a -u- in their dictionary entry to indicate this additional change. In the case of e → i verbs, it is the second i that indicates the change in the present subjunctive.
>
> servir (i, i) / *to serve*
> dormir (ue, u) / *to sleep*
>
> Recall also that the second vowel in these stem-changing -ir verbs means that there is a change in the present participle (gerund; see Chapter 6) and the preterit tense (see Chapter 7).

Irregular Verbs

As noted previously, there are six verbs that are irregular in the present subjunctive. There is a useful memory aid to help you remember them. The acronym DISHES spells out the first letter of each of these irregular verbs as illustrated below:

<u>D</u>ar / *to give*
<u>I</u>r / *to go*
<u>Se</u>r / *to be*
<u>H</u>aber / *to have*
<u>E</u>star / *to be*
<u>Sa</u>ber / *to know*

We provide a complete conjugation of each of these verbs here:

dar / *to give*

Subject Pronoun	Verb Form	Meaning
…(yo)	<u>d</u>+é	…*I give, I am giving, I may give*
…(tú)	<u>d</u>+es	…*you (fam. sg.) give, you are giving, you may give*
…(él, ella, Ud.)	<u>d</u>+é	…*he, she, you (pol. sg.) give(s), he, she, you is/are giving, he, she, you may give*
…(nosotros/-as)	<u>d</u>+emos	…*we give, we are giving, we may give*
…(vosotros/-as)	<u>d</u>+eis	…*you (fam. pl.) give, you are giving, you may give*
…(ellos/-as, Uds.)	<u>d</u>+en	…*they, you (pol. pl.) give, they, you are giving, they, you may give*

ir / *to go*

Subject Pronoun	Verb Form	Meaning
…(yo)	<u>vay</u>+a	…*I go, I am going, I may go*
…(tú)	<u>vay</u>+as	…*you (fam. sg.) go, you are going, you may go*
…(él, ella, Ud.)	<u>vay</u>+a	…*he, she, you (pol. sg.) go(es), he, she, you is/are going, he, she, you may go*
…(nosotros/-as)	<u>vay</u>+amos	…*we go, we are going, we may go*
…(vosotros/-as)	<u>vay</u>+áis	…*you (fam. pl.) go, you are going, you may go*
…(ellos/-as, Uds.)	<u>vay</u>+an	…*they, you (pol. pl.) go, they, you are going, they, you may go*

ser / *to be*

Subject Pronoun	Verb Form	Meaning
…(yo)	<u>se</u>+a	…*I am, I may be*
…(tú)	<u>se</u>+as	…*you (fam. sg.) are, you may be*
…(él, ella, Ud.)	<u>se</u>+a	…*he, she, you (pol. sg.) is/are, he, she, you may be*
…(nosotros/-as)	<u>se</u>+amos	…*we are, we may be*
…(vosotros/-as)	<u>se</u>+áis	…*you (fam. pl.) are, you may be*
…(ellos/-as, Uds.)	<u>se</u>+an	…*they, you (pol. pl.) are, they, you may be*

haber / *to have*

Subject Pronoun	Verb Form	Meaning
…(yo)	<u>hay</u>+a	…*I have, I may have*
…(tú)	<u>hay</u>+as	…*you (fam. sg.) have, you may have*
…(él, ella, Ud.)	<u>hay</u>+a	…*he, she, you (pol. sg.) has/have, he, she, you may have*
…(nosotros/-as)	<u>hay</u>+amos	…*we have, we may have*
…(vosotros/-as)	<u>hay</u>+áis	…*you (fam. pl.) have, you may have*
…(ellos/-as, Uds.)	<u>hay</u>+an	…*they, you (pol. pl.) have, they, you may have*

estar / *to be*

Subject Pronoun	Verb Form	Meaning
…(yo)	<u>est</u>+é	…*I am, I may be*
…(tú)	<u>est</u>+és	…*you (fam. sg.) are, you may be*
…(él, ella, Ud.)	<u>est</u>+é	…*he, she, you (pol. sg.) is/are, he, she, you may be*
…(nosotros/-as)	<u>est</u>+emos	… *we are, we may be*
…(vosotros/-as)	<u>est</u>+éis	… *you (fam. pl.) are, you may be*
…(ellos/-as, Uds.)	<u>est</u>+én	…*they, you (pol. pl.) are, they, you may be*

saber / *to know*

Subject Pronoun	Verb Form	Meaning
...(yo)	<u>sep</u>+a	...*I know, I am knowing, I may know*
...(tú)	<u>sep</u>+as	...*you (fam. sg.) know, you are knowing, you may know*
...(él, ella, Ud.)	<u>sep</u>+a	...*he, she, you (pol. sg.) know(s), he, she, you is/are knowing, he, she, you may know*
...(nosotros/-as)	<u>sep</u>+amos	...*we know, we are knowing, we may know*
...(vosotros/-as)	<u>sep</u>+áis	...*you (fam. pl.) know, you are knowing, you may know*
...(ellos/-as, Uds.)	<u>sep</u>+an	...*they, you (pol. pl.) know, they, you are knowing, they, you may know*

Spelling Change in the Present Subjunctive

Certain verbs have spelling changes in the present subjunctive (see Chapter 4 and Chapter 7 for spelling changes in the present indicative and preterit tenses, respectively). These spelling changes do not affect the pronunciation; they are simply spelling conventions. We provide examples of each type and lists of verbs that follow these spelling patterns. It should be remembered that the present subjunctive endings will follow one of the two patterns noted above, namely, one set of endings for **-ar** verbs and another for **-er** and **-ir** verbs.

There are five types of spelling changes shown here.

1. Verbs that end in -gar, the -g- changes to -gu-.
2. Verbs that end in -car, the -c- changes to -qu-.
3. Verbs that end in -zar, the -z- changes to -c-.
4. Verbs that end in -ger or -gir, the -g- changes to -j-.
5. Verbs that end in -cer or -cir preceded by a consonant, the -c- changes to a -z-.

We will now look at a conjugation in the present subjunctive for each one of these five verb types.

Verbs Ending in -gar

Verbs that end in -gar have a spelling change to -gu- in the present subjunctive, as illustrated below.

llegar / *to arrive*

Subject Pronoun	Verb Form	Meaning
...(yo)	<u>llegu</u>+e	...*I arrive, I am arriving, I may arrive*
...(tú)	<u>llegu</u>+es	...*you (fam. sg.) arrive, you are arriving, you may arrive*
...(él, ella, Ud.)	<u>llegu</u>+e	...*he, she, you (pol. sg.) arrive(s), he, she, you is/are arriving, he, she, you may arrive*
...(nosotros/-as)	<u>llegu</u>+emos	...*we arrive, we are arriving, we may arrive*
...(vosotros/-as)	<u>llegu</u>+éis	...*you (fam. pl.) arrive, you are arriving, you may arrive*
...(ellos/-as, Uds.)	<u>llegu</u>+en	...*they, you (pol. pl.) arrive, they, you are arriving, they, you may arrive*

The following verbs have this pattern.

conjugar	*to conjugate*	regar (ie)	*to water (a plant)*
llegar	*to arrive*	tragar	*to swallow*
jugar (ue)	*to play (a game)*	vagar	*to wander*
pagar	*to pay for*		

Verbs Ending in -car

Verbs that end in -car have a spelling change to -qu- in the present subjunctive, as illustrated below.

buscar / *to look for*

Subject Pronoun	Verb Form	Meaning
...(yo)	bus*qu*+e	...I look for, I am looking for, I may look for
...(tú)	bus*qu*+es	... you (fam. sg.) look for, you are looking for, you may look for
...(él, ella, Ud.)	bus*qu*+e	...he, she, you (pol. sg.) look(s) for, he, she, you is/are looking for, he, she, you may look for
...(nosotros/-as)	bus*qu*+emos	...we look for, we are looking for, we may look for
...(vosotros/-as)	bus*qu*+éis	...you (fam. pl.) look for, you are looking for, you may look for
...(ellos/-as, Uds.)	bus*qu*+en	...they, you (pol. pl.) look for, they, you are looking for, they, you may look for

The following verbs have this pattern.

buscar	*to look for*	practicar	*to practice*
clasificar	*to classify*	sacar	*to take, to take a photo*
destacar	*to stand out*	tocar	*to touch, to play (an instrument)*
justificar	*to justify*		

Verbs Ending in -zar

Verbs that end in -zar have a spelling change to -c- in the present subjunctive, as illustrated below.

organizar / *to organize*

Subject Pronoun	Verb Form	Meaning
...(yo)	organi*c*+e	...I organize, I am organizing, I may organize
...(tú)	organi*c*+es	...you (fam. sg.) organize, you are organizing, you may organize
...(él, ella, Ud.)	organi*c*+e	...he, she, you (pol. sg.) organize(s), he, she, you is/are organizing, he, she, you may organize
...(nosotros/-as)	organi*c*+emos	...we organize, we are organizing, we may organize
...(vosotros/-as)	organi*c*+éis	...you (fam. pl.) organize, you are organizing, you may organize
...(ellos/-as, Uds.)	organi*c*+en	...they, you (pol. pl.) organize, they, you are organizing, they, you may organize

The following verbs have this pattern.

autorizar	to authorize	rezar	to pray
comenzar (ie) (a)	to begin	trazar	to trace
empezar (ie) (a)	to begin	tropezar (ie) (con)	to stumble (into)

Verbs Ending in -ger and -gir

Verbs that end in -ger and -gir have a spelling change to -j- in the present subjunctive, as illustrated below.

proteger / to protect

Subject Pronoun	Verb Form	Meaning
...(yo)	protej+a	...I protect, I am protecting, I may protect
...(tú)	protej+as	...you (fam. sg.) protect, you are protecting, you may protect
...(él, ella, Ud.)	protej+a	...he, she, you (pol. sg.) protect(s), he, she, you is/are protecting, he, she, you may protect
...(nosotros/-as)	protej+amos	...we protect, we are protecting, we may protect
...(vosotros/-as)	protej+áis	...you (fam. pl.) protect, you are protecting, you may protect
...(ellos/-as, Uds.)	protej+an	...they, you (pol. pl.) protect, they, you are protecting, they, you may protect

corregir (i, i) / to correct

Subject Pronoun	Verb Form	Meaning
...(yo)	corrij+a	...I correct, I am correcting, I may correct
...(tú)	corrij+as	...you (fam. sg.) correct, you are correcting, you may correct
...(él, ella, Ud.)	corrij+a	...he, she, you (pol. sg.) correct(s), he, she, you is/are correcting, he, she, you may correct
...(nosotros/-as)	corrij+amos	...we correct, we are correcting, we may correct
...(vosotros/-as)	corrij+áis	...you (fam. pl.) correct, you are correcting, you may correct
...(ellos/-as, Uds.)	corrij+an	...they, you (pol. pl.) correct, they, you are correcting, they, you may correct

The following verbs have this pattern.

coger	to grasp, to seize	fingir	to pretend
corregir (i, i)	to correct	proteger	to protect
dirigir	to direct	regir (i, i)	to rule
elegir (i, i)	to elect, to choose	recoger	to pick up
escoger	to select	surgir	to surge, to spur
exigir (i, i)	to demand, to require		

Verbs Ending in -cer or -cir Preceded by a Consonant

Certain verbs that end in -cer or -cir that are preceded by a consonant have a spelling change to -z- in the present subjunctive, as illustrated below.

convencer / *to convince*

Subject Pronoun	Verb Form	Meaning
…(yo)	<u>convenz</u>+a	…*I convince, I am convincing, I may convince*
…(tú)	<u>convenz</u>+as	…*you (fam. sg.) convince, you are convincing, you may convince*
…(él, ella, Ud.)	<u>convenz</u>+a	…*he, she, you (pol. sg.) convince(s), he, she, you is/are convincing, he, she, you may convince*
…(nosotros/-as)	<u>convenz</u>+amos	…*we convince, we are convincing, we may convince*
…(vosotros/-as)	<u>convenz</u>+áis	…*you (fam. pl.) convince, you are convincing, you may convince*
…(ellos/-as, Uds.)	<u>convenz</u>+an	…*they, you (pol. pl.) convince, they, you are convincing, they, you may convince*

zurcir / *to mend, to darn*

Subject Pronoun	Verb Form	Meaning
…(yo)	<u>zurz</u>+a	…*I mend/darn, I am mending/darning, I may mend/darn*
…(tú)	<u>zurz</u>+as	…*you (fam. sg.) mend/darn, you are mending/darning, you may mend/darn*
…(él, ella, Ud.)	<u>zurz</u>+a	…*he, she, you (pol. sg.) mend(s)/darn(s), he, she, you is/are mending/darning, he, she, you may mend/darn*
…(nosotros/-as)	<u>zurz</u>+amos	…*we mend/darn, we are mending/darning, we may mend/darn*
…(vosotros/-as)	<u>zurz</u>+áis	…*you (fam. pl.) mend/darn, you are mending/darning, you may mend/darn*
…(ellos/-as, Uds.)	<u>zurz</u>+an	…*they, you (pol. pl.) mend/darn, they, you are mending/darning, they, you may mend/darn*

The following verbs have this same pattern.

convencer	*to convince*	vencer	*to defeat, to conquer*
ejercer	*to exercise*	zurcir	*to mend, to darn*
esparcir	*to scatter, to spread*		

NOTE

You have probably noticed that the first person singular (yo) and third person singular (él, ella, Ud.) are identical in form in the present subjunctive. For this reason, you must use the subject pronoun yo / *I* to distinguish these forms in the present subjunctive.

EXERCISE **Set 15-1**

A. Supply the missing present subjunctive forms of the verb **mirar**, giving the English equivalent.

EXAMPLE: … *él* _____   =   _____

                … *él mire*   =   *… he looks at, he is looking at, he may look at*

Es necesario que …

1. (yo) _____   =   _____

2. (tú) _____   =   _____

3. (nosotros) _____   =   _____

4. (ellos) _____   =   _____

5. (vosotros) _____   =   _____

6. (Ud.) _____   =   _____

   Now, supply the missing present subjunctive forms of the verb **creer**, giving the English equivalent.

1. (yo) _____   =   _____

2. (Raquel y yo) _____   =   _____

3. (Uds.) _____   =   _____

4. (ellos) _____   =   _____

5. (vosotros) _____   =   _____

6. (tú) _____   =   _____

   Now, supply the missing present subjunctive forms of the verb **discutir**, giving the English equivalent.

1. (yo) _____   =   _____

2. (tú) _____   =   _____

3. (nosotros) _____   =   _____

4. (ellos) _____   =   _____

5. (vosotros) _____   =   _____

6. (Ud.) _____   =   _____

Now, supply the missing present subjunctive forms of the verb ducharse, giving the English equivalent.

1. (yo) _____   =   _____

2. (tú) _____   =   _____

3. (nosotros) _____   =   _____

4. (ellos) _____   =   _____

5. (vosotros) _____   =   _____

6. (Ud.) _____   =   _____

Now, supply the missing present subjunctive forms of the verb contar (ue), giving the English equivalent.

1. (yo) _____   =   _____

2. (tú) _____   =   _____

3. (nosotros) _____   =   _____

4. (ellos) _____   =   _____

5. (vosotros) _____   =   _____

6. (Ud.) _____   =   _____

Now, supply the missing present subjunctive forms of the verb negar (ie), giving the English equivalent.

1. (yo) _____   =   _____

2. (tú) _____   =   _____

3. (nosotros) _____   =   _____

4. (ellos) _____   =   _____

5. (vosotros) _____   =   _____

6. (Ud.) _____   =   _____

Now, supply the missing present subjunctive forms of the verb morir (ue, u), giving the English equivalent.

1. (yo) _____   =   _____

2. (tú) _____   =   _____

3. (nosotros) _____   =   _____

4. (ellos) _____   =   _____

5. (vosotros) _____   =   _____

6. (Ud.) _____   =   _____

Now, supply the missing present subjunctive forms of the verb **conseguir** (i, i), giving the English equivalent.

1. (yo) _____   =   _____

2. (tú) _____   =   _____

3. (nosotros) _____   =   _____

4. (ellos) _____   =   _____

5. (vosotros) _____   =   _____

6. (Ud.) _____   =   _____

Now, supply the missing present subjunctive forms of the verb **regir** (i, i), giving the English equivalent.

1. (yo) _____   =   _____

2. (tú) _____   =   _____

3. (nosotros) _____   =   _____

4. (ellos) _____   =   _____

5. (vosotros) _____   =   _____

6. (Ud.) _____   =   _____

Now, supply the missing present subjunctive forms of the verb **obtener**, giving the English equivalent.

1. (yo) _____   =   _____

2. (tú) _____   =   _____

3. (nosotros) _____   =   _____

4. (ellos) _____   =   _____

5. (vosotros) _____   =   _____

6. (Ud.) _____   =   _____

Now, supply the missing present subjunctive forms of the verb componer, giving the English equivalent.

1. (yo) _____ = _____

2. (tú) _____ = _____

3. (nosotros) _____ = _____

4. (ellos) _____ = _____

5. (vosotros) _____ = _____

6. (Ud.) _____ = _____

Now, supply the missing present subjunctive forms of the verb ser, giving the English equivalent.

1. (yo) _____ = _____

2. (tú) _____ = _____

3. (nosotros) _____ = _____

4. (ellos) _____ = _____

5. (vosotros) _____ = _____

6. (Ud.) _____ = _____

Now, supply the missing present subjunctive forms of the verb estar, giving the English equivalent.

1. (yo) _____ = _____

2. (tú) _____ = _____

3. (nosotros) _____ = _____

4. (ellos) _____ = _____

5. (vosotros) _____ = _____

6. (Ud.) _____ = _____

Now, supply the missing present subjunctive forms of the verb vencer, giving the English equivalent.

1. (yo) _____ = _____

2. (tú) _____ = _____

3. (nosotros) _____ = _____

4. (ellos) _____ = _____

5. (vosotros) _____   =   _____

6. (Ud.) _____   =   _____

Use of the Subjunctive

As mentioned in the previous overview unit, the subjunctive is used in subordinate clauses, and it is generally introduced by que / *that*. So, when expressing something that is in doubt, hope, fear, and so forth with a verb in the main clause (the verb to the left of que), put the verb in the subordinate clause (the verb to the right of que) in the subjunctive.

The best way to learn which main clause verbs require the subjunctive is to memorize the most commonly used ones. These verbs form "meaning classes," or verbs that share a common meaning. The following are the common meaning classes: verbs of desire (preferir (ie, i) / *to prefer*, querer (ie) / *to want*, desear / *to wish*), verbs of command (mandar / *to order*), verbs of emotion (temer / *to fear*), verbs of doubt and denial (dudar / *to doubt*, negar (ie) / *to deny*), and many impersonal expressions (es importante / *it is important*). We shall discuss each group now. We will also provide selected lists of verbs for each category.

Verbs of Desire

The following sentences exemplify this group of verbs. These verbs indicate that you exert your will over someone else.

> Prefiero que Inés me devuelva el dinero. / *I prefer that Inés return the money to me.*
> Jorge quiere que Emilia haga la tarea. / *Jorge wants Emilia to do the homework.*
> Matilde desea que Gaspar mire la televisión menos. / *Matilde wants Gaspar to look at the TV less.*

The following is a list of verbs that belong to this class.

desear	*to desire*	querer (ie)	*to want*
preferir (ie, i)	*to prefer*		

Verbs of Command

Notice that in these sentences, you use an indirect object to specify the subject of the subordinate clause. Recall also the use of the redundant indirect object pronoun.

> Le mando a Carlos que regrese a casa. / *I order Carlos to return home.*
> Les mando a mis amigos que canten una canción. / *I order my friends to sing a song.*

aconsejar	*to advise*	preferir (ie, i)	*to prefer*
exigir	*to demand*	recomendar (ie)	*to recommend*
mandar	*to order*	rogar (ue)	*to pray, to beg*
pedir (i, i)	*to request*	sugerir (ie, i)	*to suggest*

Verbs of Emotion

Verbs of emotion constitute another meaning class.

<u>Temo</u> que Roberto no <u>llegue</u> a tiempo. / *I fear that Roberto may not arrive on time.*
Teresa <u>siente</u> que Ricardo no <u>esté</u> aquí. / *Teresa regrets that Ricardo isn't here.*

The following are some common verbs in this category.

alegrarse (de)	*to be glad*	sentir (ie, i)	*to regret*
esperar	*to hope*	temer	*to fear*
lamentar	*to regret*		

Verbs of Doubt and Denial

The following examples belong to the meaning class of doubt and denial.

<u>Dudo</u> que Tomás <u>venga</u>. / *I doubt that Tomás is coming.*
Esmeralda <u>niega</u> que él <u>sea</u> generoso. / *Esmeralda denies that he is generous.*

The following verbs belong to this category.

no creer	*not to believe*	no estar seguro/a	*not to be sure*
dudar	*to doubt*	de que	
no estar convencido	*not to be*	negar (ie)	*to deny*
de que	*convinced*	no pensar (ie)	*not to think*

GRAMMAR NOTE

With the affirmative version of verbs of doubt, you use the indicative because you are asserting a fact, as illustrated below.

<u>Creo</u> que mis amigos <u>son</u> simpáticos. / *I believe that my friends are nice.*
<u>Estoy seguro/a de</u> que <u>hace</u> viento. / *I am sure that it is windy.*
<u>Pienso</u> que Amparo <u>está</u> cansada. / *I think that Amparo is tired.*
<u>Estoy convencido/a</u> de que <u>tienes</u> razón. / *I am convinced that you are right.*

Impersonal Expressions

The following impersonal expressions are followed by the subjunctive.

<u>Es importante</u> que Silvia <u>trabaje</u> más. / *It is important that Silvia work more.*
<u>Es fácil</u> que Raúl <u>sepa</u> la verdad. / *It is likely that Raúl knows the truth.*

The following are some common impersonal expressions.

conviene	*it is advisable*	es increíble	*it is incredible*
es (una) lástima	*it is a pity*	es mejor	*it is better*
es difícil	*it is unlikely*	es necesario	*it is necessary*
es fácil	*it is likely*	es posible	*it is possible*
es fantástico	*it is fantastic*	es probable	*it is probable*
es importante	*it is important*	es ridículo	*it is ridiculous*
es imposible	*it is impossible*	puede ser	*it may be*

GRAMMAR NOTE

There are a few impersonal expressions listed below that are followed by the indicative. The indicative is used because these expressions introduce information that is factual. You use the indicative when these sentences are in the affirmative.

Es verdad que Claudia habla español. / *It is true that Claudia speaks Spanish.*
Es obvio que José está aquí. / *It is obvious that José is here.*
Es cierto que Pilar sabe mucho. / *It is certain that Pilar knows a lot.*
Es evidente que hay un problema. / *It is evident that there is a problem.*

When these impersonal expressions are negative, you use the subjunctive, as illustrated below.

No es verdad que Claudia hable español. / *It is not true that Claudia speaks Spanish.*
No es obvio que José esté aquí. / *It is not obvious that José is here.*
No es cierto que Pilar sepa mucho. / *It is not certain that Pilar knows a lot.*
No es evidente que haya un problema. / *It is not evident that there is a problem.*

TIP

When you use the verbs from the different "meaning classes" or groups discussed above, you must always use a word that connects the main clause with the subordinate clause. This word is que / *that*. The following sentences illustrate this usage.

Dudo que vaya a llover. / *I doubt that it is going to rain.*
Es posible que Blanca lea el libro. / *It is possible that Blanca is reading the book.*

In English, it is possible to omit the word "that" as shown below.

I don't think (that) he's coming.

The word que / *that* can never be deleted in Spanish, as shown below.

No creo que él venga. / *I don't think (that) he's coming.*

> **GRAMMAR NOTE**
>
> When there is a change of subject with various meaning classes of verbs, you always use the subjunctive. However, when there is <u>no change of subject</u>, you use the <u>infinitive</u> (-r) form of the verb, as shown below.
>
> Quiero <u>ver</u> esa película. / *I want to see that film.*
> Prefieres <u>dar</u> un paseo en el parque. / *You prefer to take a stroll in the park.*

More Information About the Use of the Subjunctive

In this section, we shall discuss additional cases when you use the subjunctive. The first involves indefinite and negative references. This means that the person or thing referred to is vague or uncertain, or does not exist. The second involves what are called conjunctions. As the name implies, these are words that connect, or conjoin, two clauses. The third involves some miscellaneous expressions that require the subjunctive.

Indefinite or Negative Reference

The subjunctive is used when there is an indefinite or negative antecedent in a sentence. The following sentences illustrate this usage. We have indicated the antecedent noun in the main clause and the verb in the subjunctive in the subordinate clause with an underline. The first case is an example of an indefinite antecedent. We do not know if such a person exists. The second sentence illustrates a negative antecedent. The person does not exist.

Busco <u>un empleado</u> que <u>trabaje</u> mucho. / *I am looking for an employee who works hard.*

No hay <u>nadie</u> que <u>toque</u> la guitarra. / *There is no one who plays the guitar.*

Adverbial Conjunctions

The subjunctive is used after certain adverbial conjunctions, or connectors, in Spanish. These are words that you use to connect two sentences. Some of them indicate the time when an action is occurring. Others indicate purpose. Still others, by their very meaning, involve uncertainty. We shall look at each group now.

Conjunctions of Time

The following adverbs of time take the subjunctive when the time referred to has not yet taken place. We have indicated the adverb of time and the verb in the subjunctive with an underline.

Él vendrá <u>cuando</u> <u>pueda</u>. / *He will come when he can.*
<u>En cuanto</u> <u>haga</u> buen tiempo, iré a la playa. / *As soon as the weather is nice, I will go to the beach.*

The following are some common adverbs of time.

cuando	*when*	hasta que	*until*
en cuanto	*as soon as*	tan pronto como	*as soon as*

GRAMMAR NOTE

Cuando / *when* takes the subjunctive if the action has not yet occurred, as shown below.

> Voy a hablar con Amparo cuando ella llegue. / *I am going to speak with Amparo when she arrives.*

If you are speaking about a regularly occurring activity, you use the indicative as illustrated below. In this usage, cuando / *when* often has the meaning of "whenever."

> Cuando Mauricio enseña, él habla en voz alta. / *When Mauricio teaches, he speaks in a loud voice.*

Another conjunction, aunque / *even if/although/even though*, uses the subjunctive when the action of the verb has not yet occurred, as illustrated below.

> Aunque Sofía llegue tarde, iremos al cine. / *Even though Sofía may arrive late, we will go to the movies.*

Other Conjunctions

Certain conjunctions always take the subjunctive. The following sentences show how these work. We have indicated the conjunction and the verb in the subjunctive with an underline.

> A menos que vayas a clase, no puedes aprender. / *Unless you go to class, you can't learn.*
> Para que ganes más, debes buscar otro empleo. / *In order for you to earn more, you ought to look for another job.*

The following are some common conjunctions that always take the subjunctive.

a menos que	*unless*	en caso de que	*in case that*
antes de que	*before*	para que	*in order that*
con tal de que	*provided that*	sin que	*without*

There is a useful memory aid to help you remember these words. It is the acronym ESCAPA, which is the first letter of each conjunction, as illustrated below.

> En caso de que / *in case that*
> Sin que / *without*
> Con tal de que / *provided that*
> Antes de que / *before*
> Para que / *in order that*
> A menos que / *unless*

Miscellaneous Expressions

There are a few other expressions that require the subjunctive because they express uncertainty. These are the words for "perhaps," namely, **acaso** (usually reserved for writing), **quizá(s)**, and **tal vez**. The following sentences illustrate this usage. Note that **quizá** is more commonly used now.

> <u>Quizá(s)</u> él <u>esté</u> aquí. / *Perhaps he is here.*
> <u>Tal vez</u> ellos <u>sean</u> simpáticos. / *Perhaps they are nice.*

There is another expression, **ojalá** / *I hope that*, that derives from the Arabic word meaning "may Allah grant that" that takes the subjunctive, as shown below.

> <u>Ojalá</u> que no <u>llueva</u>. / *I hope that it doesn't rain.*

Present Subjunctive of Hay

The present subjunctive of **hay** / *there is, there are* is …**haya** / *…there is, there are, there may be*. It is used in the same way that **hay** is used, except that it is in the present subjunctive. The following sentences illustrate this point. This form of **hay** always appears in a subordinate clause, i.e., it is to the right of the word **que**.

> <u>Temo</u> que <u>haya</u> un examen. / *I fear that there is an exam.*
> <u>Espero</u> que no <u>haya</u> muchas tareas. / *I hope that there aren't many chores.*

The present subjunctive of the idiomatic expression **hay que** / *one must, it is necessary to* is …**haya que** / *…it is necessary to, it may be necessary to*. The following sentence illustrates this usage.

> <u>Dudo</u> que <u>haya que</u> ir a San Salvador. / *I doubt that it is necessary to go to San Salvador.*

EXERCISE Set 15-2

A. How do you say the following sentences in Spanish?

1. Concepción doubts that it is going to snow.

   _____

2. I want Oscar to be here at 9 P.M.

   _____

3. You (fam. sg.) regret that the test is tomorrow.

   _____

4. Unless we work hard, we will never finish.

   _____

5. It is likely that Rosa has the book.

_____

6. He doesn't believe that there are many students there today.

_____

7. I hope that Julio reads the novel.

_____

8. There is no one that knows how to use this computer.

_____

9. She will write the composition before she watches television.

_____

10. It is possible that he pays the bill.

_____

11. As soon as I arrive in San Salvador, I will go to the _Museo Nacional de Antropología David J. Guzmán_[1].

_____

12. They are not sure that their parents are in El Salvador.

_____

13. It is unlikely that Laura knows Enrique.

_____

14. I want Salvador to see this program.

_____

15. My parents insist that my brother attend class.

_____

[1]Excellent museum that houses El Salvador's major archaelogical finds.

EXERCISE Set 15-3

A. Change the verbs into the subjunctive by adding the indicated expression to the given sentence.

1. Ellos van a San Salvador este año (Es probable que …)

   _____

2. Tengo sueño (Mi esposa niega que …)

   _____

3. Mis amigos beben mucha cerveza (Temo que …)

   _____

4. Este libro es muy bueno (Espero que …)

   _____

5. Pablo estudia demasiado (No creo que …)

   _____

6. Mis niños están enfermos (Es una lástima que …)

   _____

7. Ellos juegan al fútbol (Prefiero que …)

   _____

8. Aurora viene mañana (Tal vez …)

   _____

9. Voy a El Salvador (Es fácil que …)

   _____

10. Hace calor (No pienso que …)

    _____

EXERCISE Set 15-4

A. How do you say the following sentences in Spanish?

1. Provided it is cool, we will swim in *La Libertad*[1].

   _____

2. Perhaps they are going to Central America. Do you (fam. sg.) know?

   _____

3. It's possible that it is cloudy.

   _____

4. It may be that she is tired.

   _____

5. I will go to the library when Mario arrives.

   _____

6. I want him to write a letter.

   _____

7. He doesn't believe that there is a storm.

   _____

8. I fear that Esperanza may not know the answer.

   _____

[1]Beach closest to the capital of El Salvador.

EXERCISE Set 15-5

A. Provide the corresponding present subjunctive forms for the following verbs in the present indicative tense.

1. tiene _____

2. ponemos _____

3. pedís _____

4. son _____

5. estás _____

6. van _____

7. sé _____

8. conocemos _____

9. dormimos _____

10. corrigen _____

11. hay _____

12. decimos _____

13. traes _____

14. te bañas _____

15. busco _____

16. salen _____

17. viene _____

18. hace _____

Crossword Puzzle 15

Change the following verbs in the present indicative to their corresponding present subjunctive forms.

Horizontales
  4. Practico
  5. Conoces
  7. Vas
  8. Hay

Verticales
  1. Dormimos
  2. Decimos
  3. Somos
  4. Proteges
  6. Hace

16

The Imperfect Subjunctive (*el imperfecto de subjuntivo*)

Uses and Features

The imperfect subjunctive is used in subordinate clauses for the same reasons as for the present subjunctive (see Chapter 15). The main difference between the use of the present subjunctive and the imperfect subjunctive is the time of the action.

1. If the main clause is in the present tense, and if the subordinate clause refers to the past, then the imperfect subjunctive in the dependent clause is normally called for.

    <u>Es posible</u> que mis amigos <u>fueran</u> al espectáculo. / *It's possible that my friends went to the show.*
    <u>Niego</u> que Matilde <u>estuviera</u> aquí ayer. / *I deny that Matilde was here yesterday.*

2. If the main clause is in the past tense, then the past subjunctive in the subordinate clause is normally called for.

    Yo <u>quería</u> que mis amigos <u>fueran</u> al espectáculo. / *I wanted my friends to go to the show.*
    <u>Era necesario</u> que Juanita <u>dijera</u> la verdad. / *It was necessary that Juanita tell the truth.*

3. In contrary-to-fact clauses (si clauses), use the imperfect subjunctive if the main clause is in the conditional tense.

    Si yo <u>fuera</u> rico, yo <u>compraría</u> un palacio. / *If I were rich, I would buy a palace.*
    Si ella <u>tuviera</u> mucho tiempo, <u>iría</u> a Guatemala por un año. / *If she had a lot of time, she would go to Guatemala for a year.*

4. You use the imperfect subjunctive in main clauses if you want to make a polite request. This usage is normally restricted to the imperfect subjunctive of two verbs: querer / *to want* and poder / *can, be able.*

    ¿<u>Pudiera</u> Ud. ayudarme? / *Could you help me?*
    Yo <u>quisiera</u> ir al teatro. / *I would like to go to the theater.*

5. In *as if* clauses (como si), use the imperfect subjunctive.

    Él <u>estudia</u> como si <u>tuviera</u> un examen. / *He is studying as if he had a test.*
    Ella <u>vivió</u> como si <u>estuviera</u> muy contenta. / *She lived as if she were very happy.*

Regular Verbs

To form the imperfect subjunctive, or the imperfecto de subjuntivo in Spanish, do the following:

1. Take the third person plural of the preterit tense of <u>all</u> verbs.

> hablaron
> comieron
> vivieron
> midieron
> durmieron
> quisieron
> dijeron
> fueron

2. Remove the -ron to get the stem for the imperfect subjunctive tense.

> <u>habla</u>ron → habla-
> <u>comie</u>ron → comie-
> <u>vivie</u>ron → vivie-
> <u>midie</u>ron → midie-
> <u>durmie</u>ron → durmie-
> <u>quisie</u>ron → quisie-
> <u>dije</u>ron → dije-
> <u>fue</u>ron → fue-

3. Add the following endings to form the imperfect subjunctive endings. You should note that the nosotros/-as / *we* form of the verb has an accent (´) on the vowel that precedes the ending for the imperfect subjunctive (-´ramos): <u>hablá</u>ramos, <u>comié</u>ramos, <u>vivié</u>ramos.

(yo)	-ra
(tú)	-ras
(él, ella, Ud.)	-ra
(nosotros/-as)	-´ramos
(vosotros/-as)	-rais
(ellos/-as, Uds.)	-ran

4. There is an alternative set of endings for the imperfect subjunctive. These endings are added to the same stem as noted in 2 above. These endings tend to be found in literary works. Nevertheless, you may hear them in use in some parts of the Spanish-speaking world. Both are interchangeable and there is no meaningful difference between the two. We will provide the endings here, but we will only use the following endings for the exercises in this book: -ra, -ras, -ra, ´ramos, -rais, -ran. We provide the alternative set of endings for your reference. You should also note that the nosotros/-as / *we* form of the verb of this set of endings has an accent (´) on the vowel that precedes the ending for the imperfect subjunctive (-´semos): <u>hablá</u>semos, <u>comié</u>semos, <u>vivié</u>semos.

(yo)	-se
(tú)	-ses
(él, ella, Ud.)	-se
(nosotros/-as)	- semos
(vosotros/-as)	-seis
(ellos/-as, Uds.)	-sen

5. Here's the result. We will provide the -se forms (in parentheses) in the first three verb conjugations so that you may become familiar with these forms. Both have the same translations.

hablar / *to speak*

Subject Pronoun	Verb Form	Meaning
...(yo)	habla+ra (habla+se)	...*I spoke, I was speaking, I might speak*
...(tú)	habla+ras (habla+ses)	...*you (fam. sg.) spoke, you were speaking, you might speak*
...(él, ella, Ud.)	habla+ra (habla+se)	...*he, she, you (pol. sg.) spoke, he, she, you was/were speaking, he, she, you might speak*
...(nosotros/-as)	hablá+ramos (hablá+semos)	...*we spoke, we were speaking, we might speak*
...(vosotros/-as)	habla+rais (habla+seis)	...*you (fam. pl.) spoke, you were speaking, you might speak*
...(ellos/-as, Uds.)	habla+ran (habla+sen)	...*they, you (pol. pl.) spoke, they, you were speaking, they, you might speak*

comer / *to eat*

Subject Pronoun	Verb Form	Meaning
...(yo)	comie+ra (comie+se)	...*I ate, I was eating, I might eat*
...(tú)	comie+ras (comie+ses)	...*you (fam. sg.) ate, you were eating, you might eat*
...(él, ella, Ud.)	comie+ra (comie+se)	...*he, she, you (pol. sg.) ate, he, she, you was/were eating, he, she you might eat*
...(nosotros/-as)	comié+ramos (comié+semos)	...*we ate, we were eating, we might eat*
...(vosotros/-as)	comie+rais (comie+seis)	...*you (fam. pl.) ate, you were eating, you might eat*
...(ellos/-as, Uds.)	comie+ran (comie+sen)	...*they, you (pol. pl.) ate, they, you were eating, they, you might eat*

vivir / *to live*

Subject Pronoun	Verb Form	Meaning
…(yo)	<u>vivie</u>+ra (<u>vivie</u>+se)	…I lived, I was living, I might live
…(tú)	<u>vivie</u>+ras (<u>vivie</u>+ses)	…you (fam. sg.) lived, you were living, you might live
…(él, ella, Ud.)	<u>vivie</u>+ra (<u>vivie</u>+se)	…he, she, you (pol. sg.) lived, he, she, you was/were living, he, she, you might live
…(nosotros/-as)	<u>vivié</u>+ramos (<u>vivié</u>+semos)	…we lived, we were living, we might live
…(vosotros/-as)	<u>vivie</u>+rais (<u>vivie</u>+seis)	…you (fam. pl.) lived, you were living, you might live
…(ellos/-as, Uds.)	<u>vivie</u>+ran (<u>vivie</u>+sen)	…they, you (pol. pl.) lived, they, you were living, they, you might live

The Imperfect Subjunctive of Reflexive Verbs

Reflexive verbs always use reflexive pronouns in the imperfect subjunctive, as shown below. They always appear immediately before the conjugated verb, as they do in the present subjunctive and all other tenses.

lavarse / *to wash oneself*

Subject Pronoun	Reflexive Pronoun	Conjugated Verb	Meaning
…(yo)	me	<u>lava</u>+ra	…I washed myself, I was washing myself, I might wash myself
…(tú)	te	<u>lava</u>+ras	…you (fam. sg.) washed yourself, you were washing yourself, you might wash yourself
…(él, ella, Ud.)	se	<u>lava</u>+ra	…he, she, you (pol. sg.) washed himself/herself/ yourself, he, she, you was/were washing himself/ herself/yourself, he, she, you might wash himself/ herself/yourself
…(nosotros/-as)	nos	<u>lavá</u>+ramos	…we washed ourselves, we were washing ourselves, we might wash ourselves
…(vosotros/-as)	os	<u>lava</u>+rais	…you (fam. pl.) washed yourselves, you were washing yourselves, you might wash yourselves
…(ellos/-as, Uds.)	se	<u>lava</u>+ran	…they, you (pol. pl.) washed themselves/yourselves, they, you were washing themselves/yourselves, they, you might wash themselves/yourselves

GRAMMAR NOTE

Remember to write the graphic accent on the **nosotros/-as** / *we* form of the verb in the past subjunctive.

habláramos   comiéramos   viviéramos

GRAMMAR REMINDER

Remember to determine the stem to which you add the imperfect subjunctive endings by removing the **-ron** (third person plural) form of the preterit tense. Then add the imperfect subjunctive endings (see 1 and 2 under "Regular Verbs" in this chapter). See Chapter 7 for a list of the preterit tense forms with an irregular stem.

NOTE

You have probably noticed that the first person singular (**yo**) and third person singular (**él, ella, Ud.**) are identical in form in the imperfect subjunctive. For this reason, you must use the subject pronoun **yo** / *I* to distinguish these forms in the imperfect subjunctive.

EXERCISE Set 16-1

A. Supply the missing imperfect subjunctive forms of the verb **pagar**, giving the English equivalent.

EXAMPLE: … *él* _____   =   _____

   … *él pagara*   =   … *he paid, he was paying, he might pay*

Era difícil que …

1. (yo) _____   =   _____

2. (tú) _____   =   _____

3. (nosotros) _____   =   _____

4. (ellos) _____   =   _____

5. (vosotros) _____   =   _____

6. (Ud.) _____   =   _____

Now, supply the missing imperfect subjunctive forms of the verb **cometer**, giving the English equivalent.

1. (yo) _____   =   _____

2. (Raquel y yo) _____ = _____

3. (Uds.) _____ = _____

4. (ellos) _____ = _____

5. (vosotros) _____ = _____

6. (tú) _____ = _____

Now, supply the missing imperfect subjunctive forms of the verb **permitir**, giving the English equivalent.

1. (yo) _____ = _____

2. (tú) _____ = _____

3. (nosotros) _____ = _____

4. (ellos) _____ = _____

5. (vosotros) _____ = _____

6. (Ud.) _____ = _____

Now, supply the missing imperfect subjunctive forms of the verb **quitarse**, giving the English equivalent.

1. (yo) _____ = _____

2. (tú) _____ = _____

3. (nosotros) _____ = _____

4. (ellos) _____ = _____

5. (vosotros) _____ = _____

6. (Ud.) _____ = _____

Now, supply the missing imperfect subjunctive forms of the verb **confesar (ie)**, giving the English equivalent.

1. (yo) _____ = _____

2. (tú) _____ = _____

3. (nosotros) _____ = _____

4. (ellos) _____ = _____

5. (vosotros) _____ = _____

6. (Ud.) _____ = _____

Now, supply the missing imperfect subjunctive forms of the verb volar (ue), giving the English equivalent.

1. (yo) _____   =   _____

2. (tú) _____   =   _____

3. (nosotros) _____ =   _____

4. (ellos) _____   =   _____

5. (vosotros) _____ =   _____

6. (Ud.) _____   =   _____

Now, supply the missing imperfect subjunctive forms of the verb medir (i, i), giving the English equivalent.

1. (yo) _____   =   _____

2. (tú) _____   =   _____

3. (nosotros) _____ =   _____

4. (ellos) _____   =   _____

5. (vosotros) _____ =   _____

6. (Ud.) _____   =   _____

Now, supply the missing imperfect subjunctive forms of the verb morir (ue, u), giving the English equivalent.

1. (yo) _____   =   _____

2. (tú) _____   =   _____

3. (nosotros) _____ =   _____

4. (ellos) _____   =   _____

5. (vosotros) _____ =   _____

6. (Ud.) _____   =   _____

Now, supply the missing imperfect subjunctive forms of the verb ser, giving the English equivalent.

1. (yo) _____   =   _____

2. (tú) _____   =   _____

3. (nosotros) _____ = _____

4. (ellos) _____ = _____

5. (vosotros) _____ = _____

6. (Ud.) _____ = _____

Now, supply the missing imperfect subjunctive forms of the verb tener, giving the English equivalent.

1. (yo) _____ = _____

2. (tú) _____ = _____

3. (nosotros) _____ = _____

4. (ellos) _____ = _____

5. (vosotros) _____ = _____

6. (Ud.) _____ = _____

Now, supply the missing imperfect subjunctive forms of the verb hacer, giving the English equivalent.

1. (yo) _____ = _____

2. (tú) _____ = _____

3. (nosotros) _____ = _____

4. (ellos) _____ = _____

5. (vosotros) _____ = _____

6. (Ud.) _____ = _____

Now, supply the missing imperfect subjunctive forms of the verb ir, giving the English equivalent.

1. (yo) _____ = _____

2. (tú) _____ = _____

3. (nosotros) _____ = _____

4. (ellos) _____ = _____

5. (vosotros) _____ = _____

6. (Ud.) _____ = _____

Now, supply the missing imperfect subjunctive forms of the verb estar, giving the English equivalent.

1. (yo) _____   =   _____

2. (tú) _____   =   _____

3. (nosotros) _____   =   _____

4. (ellos) _____   =   _____

5. (vosotros) _____   =   _____

6. (Ud.) _____   =   _____

Now, supply the missing imperfect subjunctive forms of the verb conducir, giving the English equivalent.

1. (yo) _____   =   _____

2. (tú) _____   =   _____

3. (nosotros) _____   =   _____

4. (ellos) _____   =   _____

5. (vosotros) _____   =   _____

6. (Ud.) _____   =   _____

Tense and the Imperfect Subjunctive

We will discuss the cases in which the imperfect subjunctive is used and we will provide illustrations for each instance.

Main Verb in the Present Tense and Subordinate Verb in the Past

The imperfect subjunctive is used when the main clause is in the present and there is a past tense in the subordinate clause (see Chapter 15 for when to use the subjunctive). You will notice that in the indicative mood, there are two simple past tenses: the preterit (see Chapter 7) and the imperfect (see Chapter 8). With the imperfect subjunctive, there is only one simple past tense. Even though there are two different forms, these forms have the same meaning. For this reason, the imperfect subjunctive may correspond, depending on the context of the sentence, to the preterit or imperfect indicative. The following are selected examples.

Es posible que lloviera. / *It's possible that it was raining.*
Dudo que Ramón se levantara temprano. / *I doubt that Ramón got up early.*

Main Clause in the Past Tense

If there is a past tense in the main clause, then the verb in the subordinate clause will be in the past (imperfect subjunctive). The following are selected examples.

> Pilar <u>quería</u> que Camilo <u>fuera</u> a la tienda. / *Pilar wanted Camilo to go to the store.*
> <u>Era probable</u> que Mónica <u>diera</u> un paseo en el parque. / *It was probable that Mónica took a walk in the park.*

Imperfect Subjunctive of Hay

The imperfect subjunctive of hay / *there is, there are* is ...hubiera / *there was/there were, there might be*. It is used in the same way that hay is used, except that it is in the past subjunctive. The following sentences illustrate this point. This form of hay (...hubiera) always appears in a subordinate clause, that is, it is to the right of the word que.

> <u>Dudábamos</u> que <u>hubiera</u> un examen. / *We feared that there was an exam.*
> Ella <u>temía</u> que no <u>hubiera</u> bebidas en la fiesta. / *She feared that there were no drinks at the party.*

The imperfect subjunctive of the idiomatic expression hay que / *one must, it is necessary to* is ...hubiera que / *...it was necessary to, it might be necessary to*. The following sentence illustrates this usage.

> Yo <u>no creía</u> que <u>hubiera que</u> conjugar los verbos españoles. / *I didn't think that it was necessary to conjugate Spanish verbs.*

If Clauses

Clauses that begin with si / *if* are sometimes called contrary-to-fact clauses, counterfactuals, or hypothetical statements, because they refer to a situation that has not yet occurred. We will look at two examples of "if clauses." The first group is in the present and does not use the subjunctive, as illustrated below. In these examples, the si clause verb is in the present indicative tense and the main clause verb is in the future tense.

> Si <u>tengo</u> el dinero, <u>iré</u> a Guatemala. / *If I have the money, I will go to Guatemala.*
> Si <u>veo</u> a Roberto, le <u>daré</u> el dinero a él. / *If I see Roberto, I will give him the money.*

In the second type of "if clause," commonly called contrary-to-fact sentences, the "if clause" is in the imperfect subjunctive and the main clause is in the conditional tense. A typical example in English is "*If I were rich, I would travel more.*" It is clear that the verb in the "if clause" is in the subjunctive because of the subjunctive form of the verb *to be*. The meaning of this sentence is hypothetical because the conditions for it to be true have not been met. Therefore, the past subjunctive is used. The following sentences illustrate this usage.

> Si yo <u>tuviera</u> mucho dinero, yo <u>iría</u> a la Ciudad de Guatemala. / *If I had a lot of money, I would go to Guatemala City.*
> Si <u>hiciera</u> calor, yo <u>nadaría</u> en el Mar Caribe. / *If it were hot, I would swim in the Caribbean.*
> Eva <u>compraría</u> un coche nuevo, si ella <u>tuviera</u> un empleo. / *Eva would buy a new car, if she had a job.*

EXERCISE Set 16-2

A. How do you say the following sentences in Spanish?

1. If I had the money, I would buy a lottery ticket.

   _____

2. I would read *El señor presidente*[1] by (**de**) *Miguel Ángel Asturias*,[2] if I had the time.

   _____

3. If it weren't so hot, I would run in the park.

   _____

4. If I weren't so tired, I would clean the house.

   _____

5. She would come, if she could.

   _____

6. We would buy the house if it weren't so expensive.

   _____

7. We would go to *Quetzaltenango*,[3] if we didn't work.

   _____

8. If she were here, she would be happy.

   _____

9. If you (pol. pl.) saw *Chichecastenango*,[4] you wouldn't leave.

   _____

10. If there were more time, I would go to Guatemala more often.

    _____

[1]Novel written in 1946 by Miguel Ángel Asturias, 1899–1974; [2]Nobel Prize winner in 1967; [3]Mayan city located in the Western highlands of Guatemala; also known as Xela; [4]Important Cakchiquel commercial center before the arrival of the Spaniards, still a center of trade for Mayan Indians.

B. Change the verb into the subjunctive by adding the indicated expression.

EXAMPLE: María leía una novela (Era posible que…)

María leía una novela (Era posible que…)

Era posible que María leyera una novela.

1. Yo empezaba a estudiar (Ellos dudaban que…)

_____

2. Querías ir a Guatemala (Él temía que…)

_____

3. No hacía mucho frío (Esperábamos que …)

_____

4. Ud. tenía razón (Yo no estaba seguro/a de que…)

_____

5. Ellos no miraban la televisión (Era increíble que…)

_____

6. Yo sabía hablar español (Ella no creía que…)

_____

7. Íbamos a la capital de Guatemala (Era fácil que…)

_____

8. Llovía mucho (Yo no pensaba que…)

_____

Querer / *to want* and Poder/ *can, be able*

The verbs querer / *to want* and poder / *can, be able* may be used in the imperfect subjunctive tense. They may be used alone and they don't have to be in a subordinate clause. When they are used this way, they are "polite" ways of making a request. In English, for example, it is possible to make requests in a very direct fashion that some people may perceive to be impolite or even ill-mannered. We have all heard people say "I want a hamburger," or "Give me a hamburger." These same requests can be phrased in English by saying "Could you please give me a hamburger," or "I would like to have a hamburger." In Spanish, you can also use the verbs querer / *want* and poder / *can, be able* in the imperfect to make a polite request, as shown below.

¿<u>Pudiera</u> traerme la sopa del día? / *Could you bring me the soup of the day?*
Yo <u>quisiera</u> una cerveza. / *I would like a beer.*

A. How do you say the following sentences in Spanish?

1. Where would you (fam. sg.) like to go?

   _____

2. Would you (pol. sg.) show me the novel by (de) the new Guatemalan writer?

   _____

3. Could you (pol. sg.) drive me to the university?

   _____

4. My wife would like to see the Mayan ruins.

   _____

5. Could (pol. sg.) you repeat the question?

   _____

Como si / *as if*

The imperfect subjunctive is used after the phrase como si / *as if*. The main clause may be in the present, the conditional, or the past tense, as illustrated below.

> Ellos <u>corrieron</u> como si <u>fueran</u> culpables. / *They are ran as if they were guilty.*
> Carlos <u>habló</u> como si él lo <u>supiera</u> todo. / *Carlos spoke as if he knew everything.*
> <u>Canté</u> como si yo <u>fuera</u> Julio Iglesias. / *I sang as if I were Julio Iglesias.*

A. How do you say the following sentences in Spanish?

1. I felt as if I were sick.

   _____

2. I played the guitar as if I were *Andrés Segovia*[1].

   _____

3. He paints as if he were *Pablo Picasso*[2].

_____

4. I used to write as if I were *Miguel Angel Asturias*[3].

_____

5. You (fam. sg.) speak as if you were from Guatemala.

_____

6. He drove as if he were drunk.

_____

[1]Classical Spanish guitarist, 1893–1987; [2]Spanish painter, 1881–1973; [3]Guatemalan writer and Nobel Prize winner (1967); 1899–1974.

EXERCISE Set 16-5

A. Provide the corresponding present subjunctive and imperfect subjunctive forms for the following verbs in the present indicative tense.

1. compra   _____   _____

2. creen   _____   _____

3. vivimos   _____   _____

4. somos   _____   _____

5. estoy   _____   _____

6. va   _____   _____

7. conozco   _____   _____

8. sé   _____   _____

9. morís   _____   _____

10. dicen   _____   _____

11. hay   _____   _____

12. corriges   _____   _____

13. cae   _____   _____

14. se ducha   _____   _____

15. pongo   _____   _____

16. salimos   _____   _____

17. vienes   _____   _____

18. hace   _____   _____

Crossword Puzzle 16

Change the verb in the following sentences to the appropriate imperfect subjunctive form.

Era fácil que...

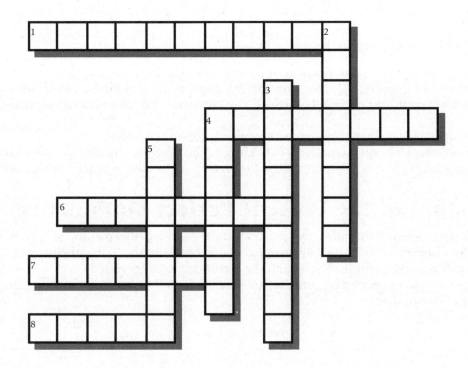

Horizontales
  1. Es probable que tú . . . (entender).
  4. No creo que mi amigo . . . (dormir).
  6. Ella esperaba que no . . . (llover).
  7. Yo temía que . . . (hacer) mal tiempo.
  8. Era posible que él . . . (ser) mexicano.

Verticales
  2. Yo quería que (tú) . . . (saber) hablar español.
  3. Era mejor que Enrique . . . (trabajar).
  4. Era fácil que mis amigos . . . (decir) la verdad.
  5. Yo negaba que ella . . . (tener) frío.

17

The Present Perfect Subjunctive (*el perfecto de subjuntivo*)

Uses and Features

The present perfect subjunctive corresponds to the present perfect in temporal usage. The difference is that it comes after a verb, a conjunction, or an expression that requires the subjunctive mood (see Chapter 15 for a discussion of the various uses of the subjunctive). The following examples illustrate these uses.

> <u>Espero</u> que Mauricio <u>haya llegado</u>. / *I hope that Mauricio has arrived.*
> <u>Busco</u> un estudiante que <u>haya leído</u> la lección. / *I'm looking for a student who has studied the lesson.*
> <u>Voy a esperar</u> hasta que Berta <u>haya llegado</u>. / *I am going to wait until Berta has arrived.*

Conjugation of the Present Perfect Subjunctive

The present perfect subjunctive, called the perfecto de subjuntivo in Spanish, is a compound tense. Therefore, it is conjugated with the auxiliary verb haber / *to have*, and the past participle. See Chapter 9 for the relevant details regarding past participles and the use of the auxiliary verb.

In the case of the present perfect subjunctive, the auxiliary verb haber / *to have* is conjugated in the present subjunctive as shown here.

haber / *to have*

Subject Pronoun	Verb Form	Meaning
…(yo)	<u>hay</u>+a	…*I have, I may have*
…(tú)	<u>hay</u>+as	…*you (fam. sg.) have, you may have*
…(él, ella, Ud.)	<u>hay</u>+a	…*he, she, you (pol. sg.) has/have, he, she, you may have*
…(nosotros/-as)	<u>hay</u>+amos	…*we have, we may have*
…(vosotros/-as)	<u>hay</u>+áis	…*you (fam. pl.) have, you may have*
…(ellos/-as, Uds.)	<u>hay</u>+an	…*they, you (pol. pl.) have, they, you may have*

hablar / *to talk*

Subject Pronoun	Haber	Past Participle	Meaning
…(yo)	<u>hay</u>+a	<u>habl</u>+ado	…I have spoken, I may have spoken
…(tú)	<u>hay</u>+as	<u>habl</u>+ado	…you (fam. sg.) have spoken, you may have spoken
…(él, ella, Ud.)	<u>hay</u>+a	<u>habl</u>+ado	…he, she, you (pol. sg.) has/have spoken, he, she, you may have spoken
…(nosotros/-as)	<u>hay</u>+amos	<u>habl</u>+ado	…we have spoken, we may have spoken
…(vosotros/-as)	<u>hay</u>+áis	<u>habl</u>+ado	…you (fam. pl.) have spoken, you may have spoken
…(ellos/-as, Uds.)	<u>hay</u>+an	<u>habl</u>+ado	…they, you (pol. pl.) have spoken, they, you may have spoken

comer / *to eat*

Subject Pronoun	Haber	Past Participle	Meaning
…(yo)	<u>hay</u>+a	<u>com</u>+ido	…I have eaten, I may have eaten
…(tú)	<u>hay</u>+as	<u>com</u>+ido	…you (fam. sg.) have eaten, you may have eaten
…(él, ella, Ud.)	<u>hay</u>+a	<u>com</u>+ido	…he, she, you (pol. sg.) has/have eaten, he, she, you may have eaten
…(nosotros/-as)	<u>hay</u>+amos	<u>com</u>+ido	…we have eaten, we may have eaten
…(vosotros/-as)	<u>hay</u>+áis	<u>com</u>+ido	…you (fam. pl.) have eaten, you may have eaten
…(ellos/-as, Uds.)	<u>hay</u>+an	<u>com</u>+ido	…they, you (pol. pl.) have eaten, they, you may have eaten

vivir / *to live*

Subject Pronoun	Haber	Past Participle	Meaning
…(yo)	<u>hay</u>+a	<u>viv</u>+ido	…I have lived, I may have lived
…(tú)	<u>hay</u>+as	<u>viv</u>+ido	…you (fam. sg.) have lived, you may have lived
…(él, ella, Ud.)	<u>hay</u>+a	<u>viv</u>+ido	…he, she, you (pol. sg.) has/have lived, he, she, you may have lived
…(nosotros/-as)	<u>hay</u>+amos	<u>viv</u>+ido	…we have lived, we may have lived
…(vosotros/-as)	<u>hay</u>+áis	<u>viv</u>+ido	…you (fam. pl.) have lived, you may have lived
…(ellos/-as, Uds.)	<u>hay</u>+an	<u>viv</u>+ido	… they, you (pol. pl.) have lived, they, you may have lived

The Present Perfect Subjunctive of Reflexive Verbs

Reflexive verbs always use reflexive pronouns in the present perfect subjunctive, as shown below. They always appear immediately before the conjugated verb, as they do in the present subjunctive and all other tenses.

lavarse / *to wash oneself*

Subject Pronoun	Reflexive Pronoun	Haber	Past Participle	Meaning
…(yo)	me	hay+a	lav+ado	…*I have washed myself, I may have washed myself*
…(tú)	te	hay+as	lav+ado	…*you (fam. sg.) have washed yourself, you may have washed yourself*
…(él, ella, Ud.)	se	hay+a	lav+ado	…*he, she, you (pol. sg.) has/have washed himself/herself/yourself, he she, you may have washed himself/herself/yourself*
…(nosotros/-as)	nos	hay+amos	lav+ado	…*we have washed ourselves, we may have washed ourselves*
…(vosotros/-as)	os	hay+áis	lav+ado	…*you (fam. pl.) have washed yourselves, you may have washed yourselves*
…(ellos/-as, Uds.)	se	hay+an	lav+ado	…*they, you (pol. pl.) have washed themselves/yourselves, they, you may have washed themselves/yourselves*

NOTE

You have probably noticed that the first person singular (yo) and third person singular (él, ella, Ud.) are identical in form. For this reason, you must normally use the subject pronoun yo / *I* to distinguish these forms.

TIP

The present perfect subjunctive corresponds to the present perfect in temporal usage and overall features (see Chapter 9). For a review of the formation of past participles, see Chapter 9. For a review of the uses of the subjunctive, see Chapter 15. Essentially, it expresses a completed action, usually a recently completed one.

The Present Perfect Subjunctive of Hay

The present perfect subjunctive form of hay / *there is, there are* is …haya habido / …*there has been, there have been*. The following examples illustrate this usage.

Es increíble que haya habido tanta lluvia. / *It is unbelievable that there has been so much rain.*
Dudo que no haya habido exámenes. / *I doubt that there have been no tests.*

The present perfect subjunctive of the idiomatic expression **hay que** / *one must, it is necessary to* is …**haya habido que** / *…it has been necessary to, it may have been necessary to*. The following sentence illustrates this usage.

Él <u>teme</u> que <u>haya habido que</u> estudiar más. / *He fears that it may have been necessary to study more.*

EXERCISE Set 17-1

A. Supply the missing present perfect subjunctive forms of the verb **estudiar**, giving the English equivalent.

EXAMPLE: … *él* _____   =   _____

                … *él haya estudiado*   =   *… he has studied, he may have studied*

Es posible que …

1. (yo) _____   =   _____

2. (tú) _____   =   _____

3. (nosotros) _____   =   _____

4. (ellos) _____   =   _____

5. (vosotros) _____   =   _____

6. (Ud.) _____   =   _____

Now, supply the missing present perfect subjunctive forms of the verb **correr**, giving the English equivalent.

1. (yo) _____   =   _____

2. (Raquel y yo) _____   =   _____

3. (Uds.) _____   =   _____

4. (ellos) _____   =   _____

5. (vosotros) _____   =   _____

6. (tú) _____   =   _____

Now, supply the missing present perfect subjunctive forms of the verb **sufrir**, giving the English equivalent.

1. (yo) _____   =   _____

2. (tú) _____   =   _____

3. (nosotros) _____ = _____

4. (ellos) _____ = _____

5. (vosotros) _____ = _____

6. (Ud.) _____ = _____

Now, supply the missing present perfect subjunctive forms of the verb **afeitarse**, giving the English equivalent.

1. (yo) _____ = _____

2. (tú) _____ = _____

3. (nosotros) _____ = _____

4. (ellos) _____ = _____

5. (vosotros) _____ = _____

6. (Ud.) _____ = _____

B. How do you say the following sentences in Spanish?

1. It is unlikely that she has read *El laberinto de la soledad*[1] by (de) *Octavio Paz*[2].

_____

2. I doubt that Eulalia has arrived.

_____

3. Antonio doesn't know anyone who has seen that movie.

_____

4. In case that Clara has arrived, I will have to go to the airport.

_____

5. You (fam. sg.) fear that she has already returned home.

_____

6. It is possible that they have eaten all of the sweets.

_____

7. I don't think that Benito has done his homework.

_____

8. They deny that Blas has gone to México.

_____

9. I hope that Gloria has not been sick.

_____

10. César doesn't believe that Amalia has done the work.

_____

[1]Essays published in 1950; [2]Winner of the Nobel Prize, 1990; 1914–1998.

C. Choose **a** (present subjunctive) or **b** (present perfect subjunctive) according to the meaning.

1. Es probable que ella … Jorge mañana.
   a. se case con
   b. se haya casado con

2. Niego que Juana ya …
   a. parta
   b. haya partido

3. Quiero que Marina … la verdad.
   a. diga
   b. haya dicho

4. Es probable que Ramón ya se …
   a. despierte
   b. haya despertado

5. Temo que Teresa no … todavía.
   a. llegue
   b. haya llegado

EXERCISE Set 17-2

A. Change the verb to the present perfect subjunctive by adding the indicated expression.

1. He comenzado a estudiar (Es fantástico que…)

_____

2. Mi hermana ha llegado (Dudo que…)

_____

3. Ha hecho mal tiempo (Temo que...)

_____

4. He leído esos poemas (Mi esposo niega que...)

_____

5. Mi amiga ha visto esa película (Espero que...)

_____

6. Ha estado nublado (Es posible que...)

_____

7. Me he divertido mucho (Ella no cree que...)

_____

8. Mi hermano ha pagado la cuenta (Es increíble que...)

_____

9. Te has levantado muy tarde (Es improbable que...)

_____

10. Ellos han estado aquí por dos semanas (Puede ser que...)

_____

EXERCISE Set 17-3

A. Provide the corresponding present perfect subjunctive forms for the following verbs in the present indicative tense.

1. tenemos   _____

2. podéis   _____

3. pide   _____

4. soy   _____

5. estamos   _____

6. voy   _____

7. saben   _____

8. conozco   _____

9. duermes   _____

10. rompe   _____

11. hay   _____

12. digo   _____

13. traen   _____

14. se ducha   _____

15. cree   _____

16. abro   _____

17. cubres   _____

18. hace   _____

Crossword Puzzle 17

The auxiliary form of the verb **haber** / *to have* for the present perfect subjunctive is missing in each sentence.

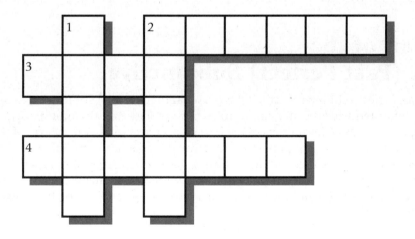

Horizontales
  2. No creo que (vosotros) . . . visto a Juan.
  3. Es probable que . . . nevado.
  4. Ella teme que Enrique y yo no . . .
     estudiado poco.

Verticales
  1. Dudo que ellos . . . hecho la tarea.
  2. Espero que (tú) . . . escrito la carta.

18

The Pluperfect (Past Perfect) Subjunctive (*el pluscuamperfecto de subjuntivo*)

Uses and Features

The pluperfect (past perfect) subjunctive corresponds to the pluperfect (past perfect) indicative. The difference is that it comes after a verb, conjunction, or expression that requires the subjunctive mood in the subordinate clause.

> <u>Era posible</u> que ellos <u>hubieran venido</u>. / *It was possible that they had come.*
> Si yo no <u>hubiera visto</u> a Matilde, yo la <u>habría llamado</u>. / *If I hadn't seen Matilde, I would have called her.*

Conjugation of the Pluperfect (Past Perfect) Subjunctive

The pluperfect or past perfect subjunctive, called the pluscuamperfecto de subjuntivo in Spanish, is a compound tense. It is conjugated with the auxiliary verb haber / *to have* and the past participle of the verb, in that order. See Chapter 9 for the relevant details regarding past participles and the use of the auxiliary verb.

In the case of the pluperfect, or past perfect subjunctive, the auxiliary verb haber / *to have* is conjugated in the imperfect subjunctive. Again, there are two forms of haber / *to have* in the imperfect subjunctive. The first set has endings in -ra, -ras, -ra, -´ramos, -rais, -ran shown below. Remember that the nosotros/-as / *we* form of this verb has an accent (´) on the vowel that precedes the ending for the imperfect subjunctive (-´ramos): <u>hubié</u>ramos.

haber / *to have* (-ra endings)

Subject Pronoun	Verb Form	Meaning
…(yo)	<u>hubie</u>+ra	…*I had, I might have*
…(tú)	<u>hubie</u>+ras	…*you (fam. sg.) had, you might have*
…(él, ella, Ud.)	<u>hubie</u>+ra	…*he, she, you (pol. sg.) had, he, she, you might have*
…(nosotros/-as)	<u>hubié</u>+ramos	…*we had, we might have*
…(vosotros/-as)	<u>hubie</u>+rais	…*you (fam. pl.) had, you might have*
…(ellos/-as, Uds.)	<u>hubie</u>+ran	…*they, you (pol. pl.) had, they, you might have*

The second set's endings are -se, -ses, -se, -´semos, -seis, -sen. Remember that the nosotros/-as / *we* form of this verb has an accent (´) on the vowel that precedes the ending for the imperfect subjunctive (-´semos): <u>hubié</u>semos. In this book, we will only use the first set of endings for the exercises.

haber / to have (-se endings)

Subject Pronoun	Verb Form	Meaning
...(yo)	<u>hubie</u>+se	...*I had, I might have*
...(tú)	<u>hubie</u>+ses	...*you (fam. sg.)had, you might have*
...(él, ella, Ud.)	<u>hubie</u>+se	...*he, she, you (pol. sg.) had, he, she, you might have*
...(nosotros/-as)	<u>hubié</u>+semos	...*we had, we might have*
...(vosotros/-as)	<u>hubie</u>+seis	...*you (fam. pl.) had, you might have*
...(ellos/-as, Uds.)	<u>hubie</u>+sen	...*they, you (pol. pl.) had, they, you might have*

hablar / to talk

Subject Pronoun	Haber	Past Participle	Meaning
...(yo)	<u>hubie</u>+ra	<u>habl</u>+ado	...*I had spoken, I might have spoken*
...(tú)	<u>hubie</u>+ras	<u>habl</u>+ado	...*you (fam. sg.) had spoken, you might have spoken*
...(él, ella, Ud.)	<u>hubie</u>+ra	<u>habl</u>+ado	...*he, she, you (pol. sg.) had spoken, he, she, you might have spoken*
...(nosotros/-as)	<u>hubié</u>+ramos	<u>habl</u>+ado	...*we had spoken, we might have spoken*
...(vosotros/-as)	<u>hubie</u>+rais	<u>habl</u>+ado	...*you (fam. pl.) had spoken, you might have spoken*
...(ellos/-as, Uds.)	<u>hubie</u>+ran	<u>habl</u>+ado	...*they, you (pol. pl.) had spoken, they, you might have spoken*

comer / to eat

Subject Pronoun	Haber	Past Participle	Meaning
...(yo)	<u>hubie</u>+ra	<u>com</u>+ido	...*I had eaten, I might have eaten*
...(tú)	<u>hubie</u>+ras	<u>com</u>+ido	...*you (fam. sg.) had eaten, you might have eaten*
...(él, ella, Ud.)	<u>hubie</u>+ra	<u>com</u>+ido	...*he, she, you (pol. sg.) had eaten, he, she, you might have eaten*
...(nosotros/-as)	<u>hubié</u>+ramos	<u>com</u>+ido	...*we had eaten, we might have eaten*
...(vosotros/-as)	<u>hubie</u>+rais	<u>com</u>+ido	...*you (fam. pl.) had eaten, you might have eaten*
...(ellos/-as, Uds.)	<u>hubie</u>+ran	<u>com</u>+ido	...*they, you (pol. pl.) had eaten, they, you might have eaten*

vivir / *to live*

Subject Pronoun	Haber	Past Participle	Meaning
...(yo)	hubie+ra	viv+ido	...I had lived, I might have lived
...(tú)	hubie+ras	viv+ido	...you (fam. sg.) had lived, you might have lived
...(él, ella, Ud.)	hubie+ra	viv+ido	...he, she, you (pol. sg.) had lived, he, she, you might have lived
...(nosotros/-as)	hubié+ramos	viv+ido	...we had lived, we might have lived
...(vosotros/-as)	hubie+rais	viv+ido	...you (fam. pl.) had lived, you might have lived
...(ellos/-as, Uds.)	hubie+ran	viv+ido	... they, you (pol. pl.) had lived, they, you might have lived

The Pluperfect (Past Perfect) Subjunctive of Reflexive Verbs

Reflexive verbs always use reflexive pronouns in the pluperfect (past perfect) subjunctive, as shown below. They always appear immediately before the conjugated verb, as they do in the present subjunctive and all other tenses.

lavarse / *to wash oneself*

Subject Pronoun	Reflexive Pronoun	Haber	Past Participle	Meaning
...(yo)	me	hubie+ra	lav+ado	...I had washed myself, I might have washed myself
...(tú)	te	hubie+ras	lav+ado	...you (fam. sg.) had washed yourself, you might have washed yourself
...(él, ella, Ud.)	se	hubie+ra	lav+ado	...he, she, you (pol. sg.) had washed himself/herself/yourself, he, she, you might have washed himself/herself/yourself
...(nosotros/-as)	nos	hubié+ramos	lav+ado	...we had washed ourselves, we might have washed ourselves
...(vosotros/-as)	os	hubie+rais	lav+ado	...you (fam. pl.) had washed yourselves, you might have washed yourselves
...(ellos/-as, Uds.)	se	hubie+ran	lav+ado	...they, you (pol. pl.) had washed themselves/yourselves, they, you might have washed themselves/yourselves

---

> **NOTE**
>
> You have probably noticed that the first person singular (yo) and third person singular (él, ella, Ud.) are identical in form. For this reason, you must normally use the subject pronoun yo / *I* to distinguish these forms.

The Pluperfect (Past Perfect) Subjunctive

The pluperfect (past perfect) subjunctive corresponds to the pluperfect (past perfect) indicative (Chapter 10) in usage and overall features. It allows you to express a past action that occurred before another past action. We will discuss the cases in which the pluperfect (past perfect) subjunctive is used and we will provide illustrations for each instance.

> Era fácil que él hubiera dicho la verdad. / *It was likely that he had told the truth.*
> Temíamos que Víctor hubiera entrado en la cueva. / *We feared that Víctor had entered the cave.*
> Esperando que hubiera llovido mucho, llevamos botas. / *Assuming that it had rained a lot, we wore boots.*

If Clauses

As was the case with the imperfect subjunctive (see Chapter 16), the pluperfect (past perfect) subjunctive is also used after si / *if* contrary-to-fact clauses (sometimes known as counterfactual or hypothetical statements). In this case, it is used when the main clause verb is in the conditional perfect.

> Si Miguel se hubiera levantado a tiempo, él no habría llegado a la universidad tarde. / *If Miguel had gotten up on time, he wouldn't have arrived at the university late.*
> Si yo hubiera tenido el dinero, yo habría comprado la casa. / *If I had had the money, I would have bought the house.*

The Pluperfect (Past Perfect) Subjunctive of Hay

The pluperfect (past perfect) subjunctive form of hay / *there is, there are* is ...hubiera habido / *...there had been*. The following examples illustrate this usage.

> Era difícil que hubiera habido un problema. / *It was unlikely that there had been a problem.*
> Yo dudaba que no hubiera habido muchos problemas. / *I doubted that there had been many problems.*

The present perfect subjunctive of the idiomatic expression hay que / *one must, it is necessary to* is ...hubiera habido que / *...it had been necessary to, it might have been necessary to*. The following sentence illustrates this usage.

> Él temía que hubiera habido que estudiar más. / *He feared that it might have been necessary to study more.*

EXERCISE Set 18-1

A. Supply the missing pluperfect (past perfect) subjunctive forms of the verb dudar, giving the English equivalent.

EXAMPLE: ... *él* _____   =   _____

                   ... *él hubiera dudado*   =   *... he had doubted, he might have doubted*

Era posible que...

1. (yo) _____   =   _____

2. (tú) _____   =   _____

3. (nosotros) _____   =   _____

4. (ellos) _____   =   _____

5. (vosotros) _____   =   _____

6. (Ud.) _____   =   _____

   Now, supply the missing pluperfect (past perfect) subjunctive forms of the verb beber, giving the English equivalent.

1. (yo) _____   =   _____

2. (Raquel y yo) _____ =   _____

3. (Uds.) _____   =   _____

4. (ellos) _____   =   _____

5. (vosotros) _____   =   _____

6. (tú) _____   =   _____

   Now, supply the missing pluperfect (past perfect) subjunctive forms of the verb escribir, giving the English equivalent.

1. (yo) _____   =   _____

2. (Raquel y yo) _____ =   _____

3. (Uds.) _____   =   _____

4. (ellos) _____   =   _____

5. (vosotros) _____ = _____

6. (Ud.) _____ = _____

Now, supply the missing pluperfect (past perfect) subjunctive forms of the verb ducharse, giving the English equivalent.

1. (yo) _____ = _____

2. (tú) _____ = _____

3. (nosotros) _____ = _____

4. (ellos) _____ = _____

5. (vosotros) _____ = _____

6. (Ud.) _____ = _____

B. How do you say the following sentences in Spanish?

1. I doubted that you (fam. sg.) had read *Tres tristes tigres*[1] by (de) *Guillermo Cabrera Infante*[2].

   _____

2. Was it likely that they had seen my sister?

   _____

3. I did not believe that Beatriz had visited Havana.

   _____

4. The teacher hoped that his students had conjugated the verbs in the pluperfect subjunctive.

   _____

5. You (fam. sg.) denied that I had been in Cuba.

   _____

6. There was no one who had seen the news on TV.

   _____

7. It was unlikely that Julio had been very busy.

   _____

8. It was possible that my parents had arrived late.

_____

9. Inés didn't believe that my brother had broken the dishes.

_____

10. It was probable that there had been an accident there.

_____

[1]Novel published in 1967; [2]Famous Cuban novelist, 1929–2005.

C. How do you say the following sentences in Spanish?

1. If I had had the time, I would have gone to Cuba.

_____

2. Bárbara would have driven to the university if she had known how to drive.

_____

3. If I had known of the test, I would have read the book.

_____

4. If Oscar had bought a ticket, he would have won the lottery.

_____

5. If Rosa hadn't been tired, she would not have had an accident.

_____

6. If it hadn't rained so much, we would have gone to the party.

_____

7. If Raúl hadn't lied, he wouldn't have gone to jail.

_____

8. If you (fam. sg.) had told me the truth, I wouldn't have been so angry.

_____

9. If there hadn't been so many problems, we would have arrived on time.

_____

10. If I had remembered my wallet, I would have been able to pay the bill.

_____

EXERCISE Set 18-2

A. Provide the corresponding present perfect and pluperfect (past perfect) subjunctive forms for the following verbs in the present indicative tense.

1. tenéis

2. canto

3. hace

4. están

5. somos

6. van

7. sé

8. conoce

9. mueres

10. abrimos

11. hay

12. dices

13. cae

14. se baña

15. cree

16. abro

17. cubren

18. mido

Crossword Puzzle 18

The auxiliary form of the verb **haber** / *to have* for the pluperfect (past perfect) subjunctive is missing from each verb.

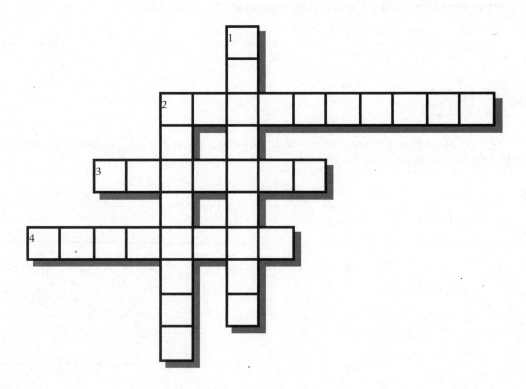

Horizontales

2. Él temía que (nosotros) . . . escuchado.
3. Yo no creía que ella ya . . . llegado.
4. Si (tú) . . . tenido el dinero, habrías comprado el coche.

Verticales

1. Yo esperaba que (vosotros) . . . ganado.
2. Era difícil que ellos . . . llegado.

Review 4
(Chapters 15–18)

This review chapter will allow you to go over and reinforce your ability to conjugate verbs in the subjunctive tenses and to recognize their use in conversation and writing. There are, as in the previous review chapters, two specific types of exercise: (1) *Conjugation Review* and (2) *Usage Review*.

Conjugation Review

Review Exercise Set 4-1

A. Conjugate the following verbs in the present subjunctive tense.

1. tomar, vender, abrir

...(yo)		
...(tú)		
...(él, ella, Ud.)		
...(nosotros/-as)		
...(vosotros/-as)		
...(ellos/-as, Uds.)		

2. tener, salir, ver

...(yo)		
...(tú)		
...(él, ella, Ud.)		
...(nosotros/-as)		
...(vosotros/-as)		
...(ellos/-as, Uds.)		

3. dar, ir, saber

    ...(yo)

    ...(tú)

    ...(él, ella, Ud.)

    ...(nosotros/-as)

    ...(vosotros/-as)

    ...(ellos/-as, Uds.)

4. haber, estar, ser

    ...(yo)

    ...(tú)

    ...(él, ella, Ud.)

    ...(nosotros/-as)

    ...(vosotros/-as)

    ...(ellos/-as, Uds.)

5. dormir, pedir, vestirse

    ...(yo)

    ...(tú)

    ...(él, ella, Ud.)

    ...(nosotros/-as)

    ...(vosotros/-as)

    ...(ellos/-as, Uds.)

6. pagar, sacar, rezar

...(yo)

...(tú)

...(él, ella, Ud.)

...(nosotros/-as)

...(vosotros/-as)

...(ellos/-as, Uds.)

7. recoger, fingir, seguir

...(yo)

...(tú)

...(él, ella, Ud.)

...(nosotros/-as)

...(vosotros/-as)

...(ellos/-as, Uds.)

B. Conjugate the following verbs in the imperfect subjunctive.

1. cantar, correr, escribir

...(yo)

...(tú)

...(él, ella, Ud.)

...(nosotros/-as)

...(vosotros/-as)

...(ellos/-as, Uds.)

2. hacer, ser, estar

...(yo)

...(tú)

...(él, ella, Ud.)

...(nosotros/-as)

...(vosotros/-as)

...(ellos/-as, Uds.)

3. decir, ir, querer

...(yo)

...(tú)

...(él, ella, Ud.)

...(nosotros/-as)

...(vosotros/-as)

...(ellos/-as, Uds.)

C. Conjugate the following verbs in the present perfect subjunctive.

1. correr, admitir

...(yo)

...(tú)

...(él, ella, Ud.)

...(nosotros/-as)

...(vosotros/-as)

...(ellos/-as, Uds.)

D. Conjugate the following verbs in the past perfect subjunctive.

1. bailar, comer

...(yo)

...(tú)

...(él, ella, Ud.)

...(nosotros/-as)

...(vosotros/-as)

...(ellos/-as, Uds.)

Usage Review

Review Exercise Set 4-2

A. Choose the appropriate verb form, **a** or **b**, according to the grammar and the meaning:

1. Es importante que él ... la verdad.
     a. dice
     b. diga

2. Si yo ... un coche, yo conduciría a México.
     a. tuviera
     b. tenga

3. Temo que ya ... llovido.
     a. haya
     b. hubiera

4. Si yo ... visto esa película, yo habría estado contento/a.
     a. hubiera
     b. haya

5. Es increíble que Uds. ... hecho el trababajo.
     a. hayan
     b. hubieran

6. Ojalá que no ... hoy.
     a. lloviera
     b. llueva

7. Yo dudaba que ... posible.
     a. fuera
     b. sea

8. En caso de que Marta no ..., iré solo.
     a. llegue
     b. llega

B. Put the indicated verbs in their correct subjunctive form (present, imperfect, present perfect, pluperfect) according to the meaning.

1. Espero que él (poder) _____ venir.

2. Yo esperaba que él (poder) _____ venir.

3. Es probable que ella (tener) _____ mucho dinero.

4. Era probable que ella (tener) _____ mucho dinero.

5. Dudo que Uds. (saber) _____ la respuesta.

6. Yo dudaba que Uds. (saber) _____ la respuesta.

7. Si yo (poder) _____ , yo iría a Guatemala.

8. Si yo (poder) _____ , yo habría ido a Cuba.

Part Five

Other Verb Forms

Other Verb Forms:
An Overview

What Is the Imperative?

The imperative is a verbal mood that allows you to express a command, request, or warning. The request may be affirmative or negative and it may be familiar or polite. It may also include yourself (*let's* command).

> ¡Abre la boca! / *Open your mouth!* (fam. sg.)
> ¡No abras la boca! / *Don't open your mouth!* (fam. sg.)
>
> ¡Comed la fruta! / *Eat the fruit!* (fam. pl.)
> ¡No comáis la fruta! / *Don't eat the fruit!* (fam. pl.)
>
> ¡Diga la verdad! / *Tell the truth!* (pol. sg.)
> ¡No diga la verdad! / *Don't tell the truth!* (pol. sg.)
>
> ¡Trabajen más! / *Work more!* (pol. pl.)
> ¡No trabajen tanto! / *Don't work so much!* (pol. pl.)
>
> ¡Estudiemos los verbos españoles! / *Let's study Spanish verbs!* (*Let's* command)
> ¡No estudiemos los verbos españoles! / *Let's not study Spanish verbs!* (*Let's* command).

Notice that there is no first person singular form in the imperative, for it would make no sense.

What Is the Passive?

All the sentences and exercises that have preceded this unit have been *active* in their form. The verb in such sentences expresses the action performed by the subject. But for many active sentences there are corresponding *passive* ones in which the action is performed on the subject.

Active Sentence	Passive Sentence
<u>María</u> compra <u>el coche</u>. / *María buys the car.*	<u>El coche</u> es comprado por <u>María</u>. / *The car is bought by María.*

An alternative to the passive voice is the use of the pronoun se + verb in the third person singular or third person plural, as illustrated below.

<u>Se vende</u> tobaco aquí. / *Tobacco is sold here (one sells tobacco here).*
<u>Se venden</u> coches aquí. / *Cars are sold here (one sells cars here).*

What Is a Non-Finite Verb Form?

A verb in a *non-finite* form such as an infinitive, gerund, or past participle allows you to express an action that does not specify the subject. The following are examples of expressions with an infinitive (= a verbal noun), a present participle (= a verbal adverb), and a past participle (= a verbal adjective).

1. Infinitive

   El <u>comer</u> es necesario para <u>vivir</u>. / *Eating is necessary to live.*

2. Present Participle

   Marina llegó <u>cantando</u> canciones populares. / *Marina arrived singing popular songs.*

3. Past Participle

   <u>Hecha</u> la tarea, el estudiante cerró el libro. / *With the homework completed, the student closed the book.*

19

The Imperative
(*el imperativo*)

Imperative Forms of Regular Verbs

The imperative of regular verbs is called the imperativo in Spanish. This form is also called the command form of the verb, known as mandato in Spanish. The imperative is a mood and not a tense.

The imperative, or command form, of the verb has two forms. The first is the familiar imperative (tú / *you* [fam. sg.], and vosotros-as / *you* [fam. pl.]). The second is the polite imperative (Ud. / *you* [pol. sg.], and Uds. / *you* [pol. pl.]). We shall discuss all of these imperative forms in this chapter. Finally, we shall discuss the *let's* imperative in Spanish.

It will be helpful to review Chapter 15 (Present Subjunctive) since many of the imperative forms are the same as certain present subjunctive forms. Review, also, the section on spelling changes in verbs in that same chapter.

The imperative forms follow specific rules for their formation. Likewise, the placement of object pronouns (reflexive, indirect, direct) also follow a certain order depending on whether or not the imperatives are affirmative or negative. At first, the rules for formation of the two imperative forms (familiar, polite) and the placement of object pronouns with relation to these imperative forms may seem complex. If you follow the step-by-step discussion below, you will have no problems. Remember that the imperative forms in Spanish use an upside down exclamation point (¡) at the beginning of the sentence.

We shall examine imperative forms in the following step-by-step order:

Familiar Imperative

1. Affirmative familiar singular imperative
2. Affirmative familiar plural imperative
3. Negative familiar singular imperative
4. Negative familiar plural imperative
5. Irregular affirmative familiar singular imperative
6. Irregular negative familiar singular imperative
7. Affirmative familiar singular imperative with object pronouns
8. Negative familiar singular imperative with object pronouns
9. Affirmative familiar plural imperative with object pronouns
10. Negative familiar plural imperative with object pronouns

Polite Imperative

1. Affirmative polite singular imperative
2. Affirmative polite plural imperative
3. Negative polite singular imperative
4. Negative polite plural imperative
5. Irregular affirmative polite singular and plural imperative
6. Irregular negative polite singular and plural imperative
7. Affirmative polite singular imperative with object pronouns
8. Negative polite singular imperative with object pronouns
9. Affirmative polite plural imperative with object pronouns
10. Negative polite plural imperative with object pronouns

Let's Imperative

1. Affirmative *let's* imperative
2. Negative *let's* imperative
3. Affirmative *let's* imperative with object pronouns
4. Negative *let's* imperative with object pronouns

Familiar Imperative Forms

Affirmative Familiar Singular Imperative

The affirmative familiar singular imperative form (tú / *you*) of regular verbs is formed as follows:

The tú / *you* imperative form is the same as the third person singular present indicative as illustrated below.

> ¡Entra! / *Enter!*
> ¡Come! / *Eat!*
> ¡Escribe! / *Write!*
> ¡Cierra! / *Close!*
> ¡Vuelve! / *Return!*
> ¡Pide! / *Order!*

Affirmative Familiar Plural Imperative

The plural of the affirmative familiar imperative (vosotros/as / *you*) is very simple to form.

1. With the exception of the reflexive verbs (see below), the stem for the familiar plural imperative form is achieved by dropping the -r from the infinitive, as illustrated.

> entrar / *to enter* → entra-
> comer / *to eat* → come-
> escribir / *to write* → escribi-
> cerrar (ie) / *to close* → cerra-
> volver (ue) / *to return* → volve-
> pedir (i, i) / *to order* → pedi-

2. Add **-d** to the stem indicated in 1 above.

    entra- → ¡Entrad! / *Enter!*
    come- → ¡Comed! / *Eat!*
    escribi- → ¡Escribid! / *Write!*
    cerra- → ¡Cerrad! / *Close!*
    volve- → ¡Volved! / *Return!*
    pedi- → ¡Pedid! / *Order!*

Negative Familiar Singular Imperative

The negative form of the familiar singular imperative (tú / you) is formed by using the second person singular form of the present subjunctive (see Chapter 15) plus the negative word **no** before the verb, as illustrated below.

    ¡No entres! / *Don't enter!*
    ¡No comas! / *Don't eat!*
    ¡No escribas! / *Don't write!*
    ¡No cierres! / *Don't close!*
    ¡No vuelvas! / *Don't return!*
    ¡No pidas! / *Don't order!*

Negative Familiar Plural Imperative

The negative form of the familiar plural imperative (vosotros/-as / *you*) is formed by using the second person plural form of the present subjunctive (see Chapter 15) plus the negative word **no** before the verb, as illustrated below.

    ¡No entréis! / *Don't enter!*
    ¡No comáis! / *Don't eat!*
    ¡No escribáis! / *Don't write!*
    ¡No cerréis! / *Don't close!*
    ¡No volváis! / *Don't return!*
    ¡No pidáis! / *Don't order!*

Irregular Affirmative Familiar Singular Imperative

The affirmative familiar singular imperative has a few irregular forms. These irregularities are limited to the tú / *you* form only. In all other respects, these forms follow the rules outlined above. The following are the most common irregular (tú / *you*) imperative forms.

    decir (i, i) / *to say/to tell* → ¡Di!
    hacer / *to do/to make* → ¡Haz!
    ir / *to go* → ¡Ve!
    poner / *to put/to place* → ¡Pon!
    salir / *to leave* → ¡Sal!
    ser / *to be* → ¡Sé!
    tener / *to have* → ¡Ten!
    venir / *to come* → ¡Ven!

Irregular Negative Familiar Singular Imperative

The negative familiar singular imperatives (tú / *you*) for the previous verbs are completely regular, i.e., you use the second person singular present subjunctive of the verb preceded by the word no. Nevertheless, we illustrate them below to help you become familiar with them.

decir (i, i) / *to say/to tell* → ¡No digas!
hacer / *to do/to make* → ¡No hagas!
ir / *to go* → ¡No vayas!
poner / *to put/to place* → ¡No pongas!
salir / *to leave* → ¡No salgas!
ser / *to be* → ¡No seas!
tener / *to have* → ¡No tengas!
venir / *to come* → ¡No vengas!

EXERCISE Set 19-1

A. Supply the missing affirmative familiar singular imperative (tú) forms of comprar, beber, abrir, tener, salir, giving the English equivalents.

1. _____ = _____

2. _____ = _____

3. _____ = _____

4. _____ = _____

5. _____ = _____

B. Supply the missing negative familiar singular imperative (tú) forms of preparar, correr, cubrir, hacer, venir, giving the English equivalents.

1. _____ = _____

2. _____ = _____

3. _____ = _____

4. _____ = _____

5. _____ = _____

C. Supply the missing affirmative familiar plural imperative (vosotros/-as) forms of comprar, beber, abrir, tener, salir, giving the English equivalents.

1. _____ = _____

2. _____ = _____

3. _____ = _____

4. _____ = _____

5. _____ = _____

D. Supply the missing negative familiar plural imperative (vosotros/-as) forms of preparar, correr, cubrir, hacer, venir, giving the English equivalents.

1. _____ = _____

2. _____ = _____

3. _____ = _____

4. _____ = _____

5. _____ = _____

Affirmative Familiar Singular Imperative with Object Pronouns

As with other verb forms, the familiar singular imperative (tú / *you*) may be used with object pronouns (reflexive, indirect, direct). In this section, we shall consider first the affirmative familiar imperatives.

With affirmative familiar imperatives, the object pronouns follow and are attached to the familiar imperative form (see Chapter 6 for the section on object pronouns). We provide examples with direct object pronouns, indirect object pronouns, combinations of indirect and direct object pronouns (in that order), and reflexive pronouns below.

You will note that when you add one or two pronouns to a multi-syllable affirmative familiar singular imperative verb form (tú), you must write an accent mark over <u>the next to the last syllable</u> of the base imperative form (the verb before you add object pronoun(s)).

If the affirmative familiar singular imperative (tú) has only one syllable, and you add only one object pronoun, it is not necessary to write a graphic accent. We have examples of these cases below. The written accent means that you retain the stress in its original position. We have indicated the base imperative form of the verb, minus the object pronoun(s), with an underline. We have also used italic type to indicate the syllable that receives a written stress mark.

1. *Direct object pronoun*
    ¡<u>Ciérra</u>la! / *Close it!*
    ¡<u>Cóme</u>la! / *Eat it!*
    ¡<u>Ábre</u>la! / *Open it!*
    ¡<u>Haz</u>lo! / *Do it!* (Single syllable; no written accent)
    ¡<u>Pon</u>lo aquí! / *Put it here!* (Single syllable; no written accent)

2. *Indirect object pronoun*
    ¡<u>Hábla</u>me! / *Speak to me!*
    ¡<u>Muéstra</u>me! / *Show me!*

3. *Indirect and direct object pronouns*
    ¡<u>Dí</u>melo! / *Tell it to me!* (Single syllable; two object pronouns added)
    ¡<u>Cánta</u>mela! / *Sing it to me!*

4. *Reflexive pronoun.*
    ¡<u>Leván</u>tate! / *Get up!*
    ¡<u>Vís</u>tete! / *Get dressed!*

TIP

1. If a word ends in a vowel, n or s, the stress falls on the next to the last syllable as shown below. No written accent is necessary.

> h<u>a</u>blo / *I speak*
> h<u>a</u>blas / *you (fam. sg.) speak*
> h<u>a</u>bla / *he, she, you (pol. sg.) speak(s)*

2. If a word ends in a consonant other than n or s, the stress falls on the last syllable as shown below. No written accent is necessary.

> habl<u>a</u>r / *to speak*
> ¡Habl<u>a</u>d! / *Speak!*

If you add extra syllables (object pronouns), you will need to indicate that the stress is retained in its original place with a written accent.

Negative Familiar Singular Imperative with Object Pronouns

To form the negative familiar singular imperative (tú / *you*) of the above verb examples, you use the second person singular present subjunctive (fam. sg.). First you place the negative word no before the verb. Next, you place the object pronoun(s) immediately before the imperative form. The order would thus be: No + object pronoun(s) + verb.

The order of the words in a negative familiar singular imperative is the following: No + object pronoun(s) + second person singular present subjunctive. We reproduce the examples from the previous section, but in a negative format. We use an underline to indicate the imperative form.

1. *Direct object pronoun*
   ¡No la <u>cierres</u>! / *Don't close it!*
   ¡No la <u>comas</u>! / *Don't eat it!*
   ¡No la <u>abras</u>! / *Don't open it!*
   ¡No lo <u>hagas</u>! / *Don't do it!*
   ¡No lo <u>pongas</u> aquí! / *Don't put it here!*

2. *Indirect object pronoun*
   ¡No me <u>hables</u>! / *Don't speak to me!*
   ¡No me <u>muestres</u>! *Don't show me!*

3. *Indirect and direct object pronouns.*
   ¡No me lo <u>digas</u>! / *Don't tell it to me!*
   ¡No me la <u>cantes</u>! / *Don't sing it to me!*

4. *Reflexive pronoun*
   ¡No te <u>levantes</u>! / *Don't get up!*
   ¡No te <u>vistas</u>! / *Don't get dressed!*

Affirmative Familiar Plural Imperative with Object Pronouns

As with other verbs, the affirmative familiar plural imperative (**vosotros-as** / *you*) may be used with object pronouns (reflexive, indirect, direct). In this section, we shall consider first the affirmative familiar plural imperatives. With affirmative familiar plural imperatives, the object pronouns follow and are attached to the familiar imperative form (see Chapter 6 for the section on object pronouns). We provide examples with direct object pronouns, indirect object pronouns, combinations of indirect and direct object pronouns (in that order), as well as reflexive pronouns below.

You will note that with the affirmative familiar plural imperative (**vosotros-as** / *you*), <u>you drop the -d from the stem before you add the reflexive pronoun</u>. We have indicated the base imperative form with an underline.

We use the same verbs from the previous section, but this time they are in the **vosotros-as** / *you* form. We have indicated the base imperative form with an underline.

1. *Direct object pronoun*
   ¡<u>Cerrad</u>la! / *Close it!*
   ¡<u>Comed</u>la! / *Eat it!*
   ¡<u>Abrid</u>la! / *Open it!*
   ¡<u>Haced</u>lo! / *Do it!*
   ¡<u>Poned</u>lo aquí! / *Put it here!*

2. *Indirect object pronoun*
   ¡<u>Hablad</u>me! / *Speak to me!*
   ¡<u>Mostrad</u>me! / *Show me!*

3. *Indirect and direct object pronouns*
   ¡<u>Decíd</u>melo! / *Tell it to me!* (Written accent because you have added two syllables)
   ¡<u>Cantád</u>mela! / *Sing it to me!* (Written accent because you have added two syllables)

4. *Reflexive pronoun*
   ¡<u>Levanta</u>os! / *Get up!*
   ¡<u>Vestí</u>os! / *Get dressed!* (Written accent to indicate two separate syllables)

Negative Familiar Plural Imperative with Object Pronouns

Finally, to form the negative familiar plural imperative (**vosotros/as** / *you*) of the verb examples just seen, you use the second person plural present subjunctive (fam. pl.). First you place the negative word no before the verb. Next, you place the object pronouns immediately before the imperative form. The order of the words in a negative familiar plural imperative is the following: No + object pronoun(s) + Verb. We reproduce the examples from the previous section, but in a negative format. We have indicated the imperative form with an underline.

1. *Direct object pronoun*
   ¡No la <u>cerréis</u> ! / *Don't close it!*
   ¡No la <u>comáis</u>! / *Don't eat it!*
   ¡No la <u>abráis</u>! / *Don't open it!*
   ¡No lo <u>hagáis</u>! / *Don't do it!*
   ¡No lo <u>pongáis</u> aquí! / *Don't put it here!*

2. *Indirect object pronoun*
   ¡No me <u>habléis</u>! / *Don't speak to me!*
   ¡No me <u>mostréis</u>! / *Don't show me!*

3. *Indirect and direct object pronouns*
    ¡No me lo <u>digáis</u>! / *Don't tell it to me!*
    ¡No me la <u>cantéis</u>! / *Don't sing it to me!*

4. *Reflexive pronoun*
    ¡No os <u>levantéis</u>! / *Don't get up!*
    ¡No os <u>vistáis</u>! / *Don't get dressed!*

EXERCISE Set 19-2

A. How do you say the following sentences in Spanish? Use the tú imperatives. Pay attention to the placement of the object pronouns (reflexive, indirect, direct).

1. Shave!

   _____

2. Don't give it (book) to me!

   _____

3. Study it (lesson)!

   _____

4. Read it (book) to me!

   _____

5. Don't go to bed!

   _____

6. Don't tell it (truth) to me!

   _____

7. Don't read it (novel)!

   _____

8. Buy it (car)!

   _____

Polite Imperative Forms of Regular Verbs

In this section, we deal with the polite imperative (Ud. / *you* [pol. sg.], and Uds. / *you* [pol. pl.]). The polite imperative forms follow certain rules of formation. Likewise, the placement of object pronouns (reflexive, indirect, direct) also follow a certain order depending on whether or not the imperatives are affirmative or negative. Again, we remind you that the rules for formation of the polite imperatives and the placement of object pronouns with relation to these imperative forms may seem complex. However, if you follow the step-by-step discussion below, you will have no problems.

Affirmative Polite Singular Imperative

First, we shall discuss the formation of the affirmative polite singular imperative (Ud. / *you*).

The Ud. / *you* imperative form is the same as the third person singular present subjunctive, as illustrated below.

> ¡Entre! / *Enter!*
> ¡Coma! / *Eat!*
> ¡Escriba! / *Write!*
> ¡Cierre! / *Close!*
> ¡Vuelva! / *Return!*
> ¡Pida! / *Order!*

Affirmative Polite Plural Imperative

The plural of the affirmative polite imperative (Uds. / *you*) is very simple to form.

To form an affirmative polite plural imperative form, use the third person plural present subjunctive form.

> ¡Entren! / *Enter!*
> ¡Coman! / *Eat!*
> ¡Escriban! / *Write!*
> ¡Cierren! / *Close!*
> ¡Vuelvan! / *Return!*
> ¡Pidan! / *Order!*

Negative Polite Singular Imperative

The negative form of the polite singular imperative (Ud. / *you*) is formed by using the third person singular form of the present subjunctive (see Chapter 15) plus the negative word no before the verb, as illustrated below.

> ¡No entre! / *Don't enter!*
> ¡No coma! / *Don't eat!*
> ¡No escriba! / *Don't write!*
> ¡No cierre! / *Don't close!*
> ¡No vuelva! / *Don't return!*
> ¡No pida! / *Don't order!*

Negative Polite Plural Imperative

The negative form of the polite plural imperative (Uds. / *you*) is formed by using the third person plural form of the present subjunctive (see Chapter 15) plus the negative word no before the verb, as illustrated below.

> ¡No entren! / *Don't enter!*
> ¡No coman! / *Don't eat!*
> ¡No escriban! / *Don't write!*
> ¡No cierren! / *Don't close!*
> ¡No vuelvan! / *Don't return!*
> ¡No pidan! / *Don't order!*

Irregular Affirmative Polite Singular and Plural Imperative

The polite imperative has a few irregular forms. In Chapter 15, we introduced the memory aid of the acronym DISHES, which we reproduce here for your convenience. The plural (Uds. / *you*) form is the same as the third person plural of the present subjunctive.

> <u>D</u>ar / *to give* → ¡Dé(n)! (Plural has no written accent)
> <u>I</u>r / *to go* → ¡Vaya(n)!
> <u>S</u>er / *to be* → ¡Sea(n)!
> <u>H</u>aber / *to have* → ¡Haya(n)!
> <u>E</u>star / *to be* → ¡Esté(n)!
> <u>S</u>aber / *to know* → ¡Sepa(n)!

Irregular Negative Polite Singular and Plural Imperative

The negative polite singular imperatives (Ud. / *you*) for the above verbs use the third person singular present subjunctive. The plural (Uds. / *you*) form is the same as the third person plural of the present subjunctive. Nevertheless, we illustrate them below to help you become familiar with them.

> <u>D</u>ar / *to give* → ¡No dé(n)! (Plural has no written accent)
> <u>I</u>r / *to go* → ¡No vaya(n)!
> <u>S</u>er / *to be* → ¡No sea(n)!
> <u>H</u>aber / *to have* → ¡No haya(n)!
> <u>E</u>star / *to be* → ¡No esté(n)!
> <u>S</u>aber / *to know* → ¡No sepa(n)!

EXERCISE **Set 19-3**

A. Supply the missing affirmative polite singular imperative (Ud.) forms of cantar, comer, asistir, ser, dar, giving the English equivalents.

1. _____ = _____

2. _____ = _____

3. _____ = _____

4. _____ = _____

5. _____ = _____

B. Supply the missing negative polite singular imperative (Ud.) forms of comprar, beber, vivir, saber, ir, giving the English equivalents.

1. _____ = _____

2. _____ = _____

3. _____ = _____

4. _____ = _____

5. _____ = _____

C. Supply the missing affirmative polite plural imperative (Uds.) forms of buscar, leer, abrir, estar, volver, giving the English equivalents.

1. _____ = _____

2. _____ = _____

3. _____ = _____

4. _____ = _____

5. _____ = _____

D. Supply the missing negative polite plural imperative (Uds.) forms of preparar, creer, admitir, comenzar, proteger, giving the English equivalents.

1. _____ = _____

2. _____ = _____

3. _____ = _____

4. _____ = _____

5. _____ = _____

Affirmative Polite Singular Imperative with Object Pronouns

As with other verbs, the polite singular imperative (Ud. / *you*) may be used with object pronouns (reflexive, indirect, direct). In this section, we shall consider first the affirmative polite imperatives. With polite imperatives, the object pronouns follow and are attached to the imperative form (see Chapter 6 for the section on object pronouns). We provide examples with direct object pronouns, indirect object pronouns, combinations of indirect and direct object pronouns (in that order), and reflexive pronouns below.

You will note that when you add one or two pronouns to an affirmative polite singular imperative (Ud. / *you*) form, you must write an accent mark over the <u>next to the last syllable </u>of the base imperative form (the verb before you add object pronoun(s)). We have examples of both below. The written accent means that you retain the stress in its original position. We have indicated the base imperative form of the verb (minus the object pronouns) with an underline. We have also used italic type to indicate the syllable that receives a written stress mark.

1. *Direct object pronoun*
    ¡<u>Cié*rre*la</u>! / *Close it!*
    ¡<u>*Có*ma</u>la! / *Eat it!*
    ¡<u>*Á*bra</u>la! / *Open it!*
    ¡<u>*Há*ga</u>lo! / *Do it!*
    ¡<u>*Pó*nga</u>lo aquí! / *Put it here!*

2. *Indirect object pronoun*
    ¡<u>*Há*ble</u>me! / *Speak to me!*
    ¡<u>Mu*é*stre</u>me! / *Show me!*

3. *Indirect and direct object pronouns*
    ¡<u>*Dí*ga</u>melo! / *Tell it to me!*
    ¡<u>*Cán*te</u>mela! / *Sing it to me!*

4. *Reflexive pronoun*
    ¡<u>Levá*n*te</u>se! / *Get up!*
    ¡<u>*Ví*sta</u>se! / *Get dressed!*

Negative Polite Singular Imperative with Object Pronouns

To form the negative polite singular imperative (Ud. / *you*) of the above verb examples, you use the third person singular present subjunctive (pol. sg.). First you place the negative word no before the verb. Next, you place the object pronouns immediately before the imperative form. The order of the words in a negative polite singular imperative is the following: No + object pronoun(s) + third person singular present subjunctive. We reproduce the examples from the previous section, but in a negative format. We have used an underline to indicate the imperative form.

1. *Direct object pronoun*
    ¡No la <u>cierre</u>! / *Don't close it!*
    ¡No la <u>coma</u>! / *Don't eat it!*
    ¡No la <u>abra</u>! / *Don't open it!*
    ¡No lo <u>haga</u>! / *Don't do it!*
    ¡No lo <u>ponga</u> aquí! / *Don't put it here!*

2. *Indirect object pronoun*
    ¡No me <u>hable</u>! / *Don't speak to me!*
    ¡No me <u>muestre</u>! / *Don't show me!*

3. *Indirect and direct object pronouns*
   ¡No me lo <u>diga</u>! / *Don't tell it to me!*
   ¡No me la <u>cante</u>! / *Don't sing it to me!*

4. *Reflexive pronoun*
   ¡No se <u>levante</u>! / *Don't get up!*
   ¡No se <u>vista</u>! / *Don't get dressed!*

Affirmative Polite Plural Imperative with Object Pronouns

As with other verbs, the polite plural imperative (Uds. / *you*) may be used with object pronouns (reflexive, indirect, direct). In this section, we shall consider first the affirmative polite plural imperatives. With polite imperatives, the object pronouns follow and are attached to the imperative form (see Chapter 6 for the section on object pronouns). We provide examples with direct object pronouns, indirect object pronouns, combinations of indirect and direct object pronouns (in that order), and reflexive pronouns below.

You will note that when you add one or two pronouns to a multi-syllable imperative form, you must write an accent mark over the next to the last syllable of the basic imperative form. We have examples of both below. The written accent means that you retain the stress in its original position. We have indicated the base imperative form (minus the object pronouns) with an underline. We have also used italic type to indicate the syllable that receives a written stress mark.

You will note that the affirmative polite plural imperative (Uds. / *you*) is the same as the third person plural present subjunctive plus the object pronoun.

We use the same verbs from the previous section, but this time they are in the Uds. / *you* form. We have used an underline to indicate the imperative form.

1. *Direct object pronoun*
   !<u>Ciérren</u>la! / *Close it!*
   ¡<u>Cóman</u>la! / *Eat it!*
   ¡<u>Ábran</u>la! / *Open it!*
   ¡<u>Hágan</u>lo! / *Do it!*
   ¡<u>Pónganlo</u> aquí! / *Put it here!*

2. *Indirect object pronoun*
   ¡<u>Háblen</u>me! / *Speak to me!*
   ¡<u>Muéstren</u>me! / *Show me!*

3. *Indirect and direct object pronouns*
   ¡<u>Dígan</u>melo! / *Tell it to me!*
   ¡<u>Cánten</u>mela! / *Sing it to me!*

4. *Reflexive pronoun*
   ¡<u>Levánten</u>se! / *Get up!*
   ¡<u>Vístan</u>se! / *Get dressed!*

Negative Polite Plural Imperative with Object Pronouns

Finally, to form the negative polite plural imperative (Uds. / *you*) of the verb examples we have seen, you use the third person plural present subjunctive (pol. pl.). First you place the negative word no before the verb. Next, you place the object pronouns immediately before the imperative form. The order of the words in a negative familiar plural imperative is the following: No + object pronoun(s) + third person plural present subjunctive. We reproduce the examples from the previous section, but in a negative format. We have used an underline to indicate the imperative form.

1. *Direct object pronoun*

¡No la <u>cierren</u>! / *Don't close it!*

¡No la <u>coman</u>! / *Don't eat it!*

¡No la <u>abran</u>! / *Don't open it!*

¡No lo <u>hagan</u>! / *Don't do it!*

¡No lo <u>pongan</u> aquí! / *Don't put it here!*

2. *Indirect object pronoun*

¡No me <u>hablen</u>! / *Don't speak to me!*

¡No me <u>muestren</u>! / *Don't show me!*

3. *Indirect and direct object pronouns*

¡No me lo <u>digan</u>! / *Don't tell it to me!*

¡No me la <u>canten</u>! / *Don't sing it to me!*

4. *Reflexive pronoun*

¡No se <u>levanten</u>! / *Don't get up!*

¡No se <u>vistan</u>! / *Don't get dressed!*

EXERCISE Set 19-4

A. How do you say the following sentences in Spanish? All are polite forms (**Ud., Uds.**). Pay attention to the placement of the object pronouns (reflexive, indirect, direct). Remember to use the redundant indirect object pronoun where necessary (see Chapter 6).

1. Go to bed! (pol. pl.)

_____

2. Buy it (novel) for me! (pol. sg.)

_____

3. Don't show it (book) to her! (pol. sg.)

_____

4. Sing it (song) to her! (pol. pl.)

_____

5. Get up! (pol. sg.)

_____

6. Don't look at me! (pol. pl.)

_____

7. Write it (letter) to them! (pol. sg.)

_____

8. Show them (books) to her! (pol. sg.)

_____

Let's Imperative

Imperatives may appear in the nosotros/-as / *we* form of the verb. The *let's* imperative form is identical to the first person plural of the present subjunctive (see Chapter 15).

Affirmative Let's *Imperative*

The following are selected examples of the affirmative form of this imperative.

> ¡Entremos! / *Let's enter!*
> ¡Comamos! / *Let's eat!*
> ¡Escribamos! / *Let's write!*
> ¡Cerremos! / *Let's close!*
> ¡Volvamos! / *Let's return!*
> ¡Pidamos! / *Let's order!*

Negative Let's *Imperative*

The following are selected examples of the negative form of this imperative. We use the same verbs as those above to illustrate this form of the verb.

> ¡No entremos! / *Let's not enter!*
> ¡No comamos! / *Let's not eat!*
> ¡No escribamos! / *Let's not write!*
> ¡No cerremos! / *Let's not close!*
> ¡No volvamos! / *Let's not return!*
> ¡No pidamos! / *Let's not order!*

GRAMMAR NOTE

The verb ir / *to go* may be used with an infinitive to express the meaning *let's,* as illustrated below in the affirmative and negative versions.

> Vamos a cantar. / *Let's sing.*
> No vamos a cantar. / *Let's not sing.*

EXERCISE Set 19-5

A. How do you say the following sentences in Spanish?

1. Let's begin!

_____

2. Let's not go!

_____

3. Let's play the guitar!

_____

4. Let's be nice!

_____

5. Let's not conjugate verbs in Spanish!

_____

Affirmative Let's Imperative with Object Pronouns

As with other verbs, the *let's* imperative may be used with object pronouns (reflexive, indirect, direct). In this section, we shall consider first the affirmative *let's* imperatives. With affirmative *let's* imperatives, the object pronouns follow and are attached to the *let's* imperative form (see Chapter 6 for the section on object pronouns).

You will note that when you add one or two pronouns to a *let's* imperative form, you must write an accent mark over the next to the last syllable of the basic imperative form. We have examples of both cases below. We have indicated the stressed syllable that must bear a written accent with italic type. The written accent means that you retain the stress in its original position. We have also underlined the verbal portion of the *let's* command form. You will note that with reflexive verbs, you remove the final -s of the verb and then add the reflexive pronoun -nos.

1. *Direct object pronoun*
    ¡Cerrémosla! / *Let's close it!*
    ¡Comámosla! / *Let's eat it!*
    ¡Abrámosla! / *Let's open it!*
    ¡Hagámoslo! / *Let's do it!*
    ¡Pongámoslo aquí! / *Let's put it here!*

2. *Indirect object pronoun*
    ¡Hablémosle a ella! / *Let's speak to her!*
    ¡Mostrémosle a ella! / *Let's show her!*

3. *Indirect and direct object pronouns*
   ¡<u>Digámo</u>selo a ellos! / *Let's tell it to them!* (Note: you only have one -s-)
   ¡<u>Cantémo</u>selo a él! / *Let's sing it to him!* (Note: you only have one -s-)

4. *Reflexive pronoun*
   ¡<u>Levantémo</u>nos! / *Let's get up!* (Note: you delete the -s- of the verb stem)
   ¡<u>Vistámo</u>nos! / *Let's get dressed!* (Note: you delete the -s- of the verb stem)

Negative *Let's* Imperative with Object Pronouns

To form the negative *let's* imperative of the above verb examples, you use the first person plural present subjunctive. First you place the negative word no before the verb. Next, you place the object pronouns immediately before the imperative form. The order of the words in a negative familiar singular imperative is the following: No + object pronoun(s) + first person plural present subjunctive. We reproduce the examples from the previous section, but in a negative format. We have also underlined the verbal portion of the *let's* command form.

1. *Direct object pronoun*
   ¡No la <u>cerremos</u>! / *Let's not close it!*
   ¡No la <u>comamos</u>! / *Let's not eat it!*
   ¡No la <u>abramos</u>! / *Let's not open it!*
   ¡No lo <u>hagamos</u>! / *Let's not do it!*
   ¡No lo <u>pongamos</u> aquí! / *Let's not put it here!*

2. *Indirect object pronoun*
   ¡No le <u>hablemos</u> a ella! / *Let's not speak to her!*
   ¡No le <u>mostremos</u> a ella! *Let's not show her!*

3. *Indirect and direct object pronouns*
   ¡No se lo <u>digamos</u> a ellos! / *Let's not tell it to them!*
   ¡No se lo <u>cantemos</u> a él! / *Let's not sing it to him!*

4. *Reflexive pronoun*
   ¡No nos <u>levantemos</u>! / *Let's not get up!*
   ¡No nos <u>vistamos</u>! / *Let's not get dressed!*

EXERCISE Set 19-6

A. How do you say the following sentences in Spanish? Pay attention to the position of the object pronouns. Remember to use the redundant indirect object pronoun where necessary (see Chapter 6).

1. Let's sing it (song) to her!

   _____

2. Let's not say anything to him!

   _____

3. Let's get up late!

_____

4. Let's do it (work)!

_____

5. Let's not give it (gift) to him!

_____

6. Let's show it (home) to them!

_____

7. Let's not go to bed!

_____

8. Let's not drink it (coffee)!

_____

EXERCISE Set 19-7

A. Provide the affirmative and negative familiar singular imperatives (tú) for the following Spanish infinitives.

1. comprar

2. beber

3. vivir

4. ser

5. estar

6. hacer

7. tener

8. ducharse

9. buscar

10. encontrar

B. Provide the affirmative and negative polite singular imperatives (Ud.) for the following Spanish infinitives.

1. comprar   _____   _____

2. beber   _____   _____

3. vivir   _____   _____

4. ser   _____   _____

5. estar   _____   _____

6. hacer   _____   _____

7. tener   _____   _____

8. ducharse   _____   _____

9. buscar   _____   _____

10. encontrar   _____   _____

C. Provide the affirmative and negative *let's* command for the following Spanish infinitives.

1. hablar   _____   _____

2. comer   _____   _____

3. escribir   _____   _____

4. divertirse (ie, i)   _____   _____

Crossword Puzzle 19

Use imperative forms based on the sense of each sentence.

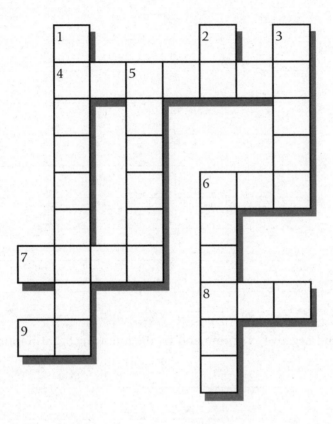

Horizontales

4. Señorita Pérez, ¡(escribir) . . . en la pizarra!
6. Alejandro, ¡(venir) . . . aquí!
7. Señora Martínez, ¡(hacer) . . . esta tarea!
8. Señora Rodríguez, ¡(leer) . . . este libro!
9. Claudia, ¡(ir) . . . a la tienda!

Verticales

1. Jorge, ¡(levantarse) . . . ahora!
2. Ana, ¡(decir) . . . la verdad!
3. Señores, ¡(ir) . . . !
5. Carlos, ¡(comprar) . . . los libros!
6. Señor González, ¡(volver) . . . !

20

The Passive Voice (*la voz pasiva*) and Non-Finite Verb Forms (*las formas no finitas del verbo*)

The True Passive Voice

Verbs can be in the active or passive voice. The active voice is used to indicate that the subject of the verb performs the action, whereas the passive voice, called **la voz pasiva** in Spanish, is used to indicate that the subject is the receiver of the action. It is sometimes called the "true passive."

> *Active*: **Mario compra los libros.** / *Mario buys the books.*
> *Passive*: **Los libros son comprados por Mario.** / *The books are bought by Mario.*

Passive sentences can be formed from corresponding active ones as follows:

1. Change the order of the subject and the object.

> **Mario** compra **los libros**. / *Mario buys the books.*
>
> **Los libros** (compra) **Mario.**

2. Change the verb into the passive form by introducing the verb **ser** / *to be* in the same tense. Next, change the verb into its past participle form (see Chapter 9). Recall that when you use the verb **ser** / *to be*, there is agreement (gender and number) of the adjective with the subject of the sentence (the past participle is the adjectival form of the verb).

> Los libros **son comprados**.

3. Put por / *by* in front of the passive object.

> Los libros son comprados por Mario. / *The books are bought by Mario.*

Here are a few additional examples of "passivization."

Active	Passive
La mujer <u>lee</u> la revista. / *The woman reads the magazine.*	La revista <u>es leída</u> por la mujer. / *The magazine is read by the woman.*
Él <u>vendió</u> el coche. / *He sold the car.*	El coche <u>fue vendido</u> por él. / *The car was sold by him.*

EXERCISE Set 20-1

A. Rewrite the following sentences. Change them to the "true passive" voice. Remember that the verb may be in any tense. Remember also that the past participle agrees in number and gender with the subject of a "true passive" voice.

1. José construyó la casa.

   _____

2. Los hombres abren las puertas.

   _____

3. Ana leerá la novela.

   _____

4. Los estudiantes cantaron la canción.

   _____

5. *Cervantes*[1] escribió *Don Quijote*[2].

   _____

[1]Miguel de Cervantes Saavedra, 1547–1616; [2]*Don Quijote*, novel in two parts, 1605, 1615.

B. How do you say the following sentences in Spanish? Remember that the past participle agrees in number and gender with the subject of a "true passive" voice.

1. The food was eaten by the children.

   _____

2. The house was built by the workers.

   _____

3. The window was broken by the men.

   _____

4. The bill was paid by Carlos.

   _____

5. The books were purchased by the students.

   _____

The *Se* Passive

There is another, more common way, of formulating the passive voice, when you don't want to express the original subject of the sentence. In this version of the passive voice, there are two possible verb forms: Third person singular and third person plural. These two verb forms are always preceded by the object pronoun se, as illustrated below. You will also note that the order of the words is as follows: Se + verb (singular/plural) + subject (singular/plural).

se +   verb in third person +   subject
(singular or plural)   (singular or plural)

The following examples illustrate how the above formula works.

Singular	Plural
Se canta la canción. / *The song is sung.*	Se cantan las canciones. / *The songs are sung.*

It should be noted that the English translation of the se passive is not always equivalent to the traditional passive voice (*the man was seen by his son*). The following are some examples of other ways of translating the se passive forms into English and vice-versa. We provide the most common English glosses for this construction, namely, non-referential "you," non-referential "they," and impersonal "one."

¿Cómo se dice "book" en español? /*How do you say book in Spanish?*
Se habla italiano en Suiza. / *They speak Italian in Switzerland.*
Se debe estudiar mucho. / *One must study a lot.*

Remember that the se passive may be used in any tense or mood just as with the "true passive" voice.

EXERCISE Set 20-2

A. How do you say the following sentences in Spanish? Use the **se** passive construction.

1. Spanish is spoken here.

   _____

2. They say that it is raining.

   _____

3. They sell newspapers here.

   _____

4. The bills are paid on Fridays.

   _____

5. You must eat three meals every day.

   _____

Summary

The passive voice may be expressed in two ways, as illustrated below.

1. The "true passive" voice involves a step-by-step process:
   a. Change the order of the subject and object.
   b. Introduce the verb **ser**.
   c. Make the verb **ser** the same tense as the original verb.
   d. Change the original verb to the past participle.
   e. Remember to make the past participle agree in number and gender with the new subject of the sentence.

   The following example shows the process in a nutshell.

   > Elena vende la casa. / *Elena sells the house.*
   > La casa <u>es vendida</u> por Elena. / *The house is sold by Elena.*

2. The **se** passive also has a formula for its use that we reproduce here. Remember that you do not express the agent (the person by whom the action of the verb is performed) in this construction.
   a. Use **se** and the third person (singular or plural) of the verb in any tense.
   b. Place the noun after the verb. The verb will be singular or plural depending on whether the noun is singular or plural.

   The following examples illustrate this process.

   > Se vende tabaco aquí. / *Tobacco is sold here.*
   > Se venden casas aquí. / *Houses are sold here (houses for sale).*

Non-Finite Verb Forms

You will recall that conjugated verbs have endings to indicate the following pieces of information:

1. Person (first, second, third).
2. Number (singular, plural).
3. Tense (past, present, future).
4. Mood (indicative, subjunctive, imperative).

Spanish also has three non-finite verb forms. This means that they have no subject expressed. You have already learned these three forms in previous chapters.

1. Infinitive (the form of the verb that ends in -r).
2. The present participle, or gerund (the form of the verb that ends in -ndo).
3. Past participle (the form of the verb that ends in -do, though there are irregular forms).

We provide examples of how these three non-finite verb forms may be used in Spanish.

1. The infinitive after a preposition.

    Al <u>llegar</u> a casa, preparé la cena. / *Upon arriving home, I prepared dinner.*

2. The infinitive when there is no change of subject in a sentence.

    Quiero <u>leer</u> esa novela. / *I want to read that novel.*

3. It should be noted also that a perfect infinitive also exists, as illustrated below.

    Debo <u>haber conjugado</u> esos verbos. / *I should have conjugated those verbs.*

4. Remember that object pronouns (reflexive, indirect, direct) may follow and may be attached to infinitives.

    Voy a ver<u>lo</u>. / *I am going to see him.*

5. Alternatively, object pronouns (reflexive, indirect, direct) may appear immediately before the conjugated verb, as shown below.

    <u>Lo</u> voy a ver. / *I am going to see him.*

6. The present participle, or gerund, is used to create progressive verb forms (see Chapter 6) but it is also used to modify a sentence as illustrated below. Remember that object pronouns (reflexive, direct, indirect) follow and are attached to a present participle.

    <u>Corriendo</u>, pierdo peso. / *By running, I lose weight.*
    <u>Viéndolo</u>, lo saludé. / *Upon seeing him, I greeted him.*

7. The past participle may also be used to modify a sentence, as shown below.

    <u>Hecho</u> el trabajo, regresé a casa. / *With the work completed, I returned home.*

A. How do you say the following sentences in Spanish? Use an infinitive, present participle, or past participle according to the meaning.

1. After reading the paper, Marisol started to work.

_____

2. While walking, I saw Pablo.

_____

3. With the game finished, we went to the restaurant.

_____

4. While reading the magazine, Lidia drank coffee.

_____

5. Before leaving, Juan bought a book.

_____

Crossword Puzzle 20

Provide an infinitive, present participle, or past participle according to the grammar and the meaning.

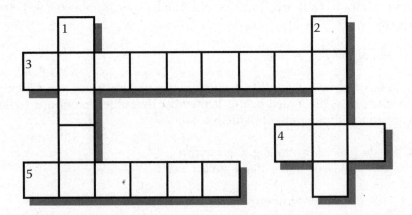

Horizontales
3. (Terminar) . . . la tarea, fui al cine.
4. Al (ver) . . . a Sara, la saludé.
5. Antes de (volver) . . . a casa, corrí en el parque.

Verticales
1. (Hacer) . . . el trabajo, él volvió a casa.
2. Después de (haber) . . . visto a María, él regresó a casa.

Review 5

(Chapters 19–20)

This final review chapter will allow you to go over and reinforce your ability to work with the imperative, the passive voice, and the non-finite verb forms, and to recognize their use in conversation and writing. There are, as in the previous review chapters, two specific types of exercise: (1) *Conjugation Review* and (2) *Usage Review*.

Conjugation Review

Review Exercise Set 5-1

A. Conjugate the following verbs in the affirmative imperative:

1. comprar, vender, asistir

(tú)		
(Ud.)		
(nosotros/-as)		
(vosotros/-as)		
(Uds.)		

2. decir, hacer, estar

(tú)		
(Ud.)		
(nosotros/-as)		
(vosotros/-as)		
(Uds.)		

3. ducharse, ser, tener

(tú)		
(Ud.)		
(nosotros/-as)		
(vosotros/-as)		
(Uds.)		

B. Conjugate the following verbs in the negative imperative:

1. comprar, vender, asistir

(tú)		
(Ud.)		
(nosotros/-as)		
(vosotros/-as)		
(Uds.)		

2. decir, hacer, estar

(tú)		
(Ud.)		
(nosotros/-as)		
(vosotros/-as)		
(Uds.)		

3. ducharse, ser, tener

(tú)		
(Ud.)		
(nosotros/-as)		
(vosotros/-as)		
(Uds.)		

Usage Review

Review Exercise Set 5-2

A. Choose the appropriate verb form, **a** or **b**, according to the grammar and the meaning:

1. Sofía, ¡… las verduras!
    a. come
    b. coma

2. Antonio, ¡no … ese libro!
    a. leas
    b. lea

3. Sara, ¡… aquí!
    a. venga
    b. ven

4. Señora, ¡… la verdad siempre!
    a. di
    b. diga

5. Señorita, ¡… esta canción!
    a. canta
    b. cante

6. Silvia, ¡… la carta!
    a. escriba
    b. escribe

7. Señores, ¡…! Es tarde.
    a. levantaos
    b. levántense

8. Salvador, ¡… algo!
    a. di
    b. diga

9. Carmen, ¡… ahora!
    a. despiértate
    b. despiértese

10. Benito, ¡ … a casa!
    a. vaya
    b. ve

B. Convert each of the following sentences into "true passive" sentences.

1. Cervantes escribió *Don Quijote*.

    _____

2. Pablo prepara la comida.

    _____

3. Teresa vendió los libros.

    _____

C. Provide the Spanish for the following English sentences. Use the "se passive."

1. They say that it is raining.

    _____

2. Italian is spoken here.

    _____

3. Cars are sold here.

    _____

D. Change the following English sentences to Spanish. Use an infinitive, or present participle.

1. While walking, I saw Eva.

    _____

2. Before studying, Sara listened to music.

    _____

3. After watching TV, I went to bed.

    _____

Answers

CHAPTER 1
Exercise Set 1-1

A.

1.	toco	=	I play, I am playing, I do play
2.	esperas	=	you (fam. sg.) hope/wait, you are hoping/waiting, you do hope/wait
3.	preparamos	=	we prepare, we are preparing, we do prepare
4.	llevan	=	they wear, they are wearing, they do wear
5.	pagáis	=	you (fam. pl.) pay for, you are paying for, you do pay for
6.	trabaja	=	you (pol. sg.) work, you are working, you do work
7.	miran	=	they look at, they are looking at, they do look at
8.	estudian	=	you (pol. pl.) study, you are studying, you do study
9.	viajo	=	I travel, I am traveling, I do travel
10.	bailas	=	you (fam. sg.) dance, you are dancing, you do dance
11.	cantamos	=	we sing, we are singing, we do sing
12.	compra	=	he buys, he is buying, he does buy
13.	hablan	=	they speak, they are speaking, they do speak
14.	entra	=	you (pol sg.) enter, you are entering, you do enter
15.	buscan	=	you (pol. pl.) look for, you are looking for, you do look for

B.

1. Perdón, ¿habla Ud. inglés?
2. Sí, hablo inglés muy bien.
3. Ellos no hablan español muy bien.
4. Hablamos español un poco.
5. Rafael, hablas español también, ¿verdad?
6. No hablo español, pero mi hija habla español muy bien.
7. No, no es verdad. El autobús no llega ahora.
8. Gracias. Ud. es muy amable. No hablo español bien.
9. Alejandro toca el violoncelo como *Pablo Casals* y Claudia pinta como *Diego Velázquez*.
10. Ella escucha la radio demasiado.
11. Deseo mirar la corrida de toros en la televisión.
12. Ellos tocan el piano bien.
13. Siempre miras la televisión.
14. Ud. lleva una chaqueta nueva, ¿verdad?
15. Uds. esperan el autobús, ¿verdad?

Exercise Set 1-2

A.

1.	aprendo	=	I learn, I am learning, I do learn
2.	comprendes	=	you (fam. sg.) understand, you are understanding, you do understand
3.	creemos	=	we believe, we are believing, we do believe
4.	meten	=	they put (into), they are putting (into), they do put (into)
5.	corréis	=	you (fam. pl.) run, you are running, you do run
6.	lee	=	you (pol. sg.) read, you are reading, you do read
7.	mi amiga teme	=	my friend (f.) fears, my friend is fearing, my friend does fear
8.	rompen	=	they (f.) break, they are breaking, they do break
9.	debo	=	I owe/ought/should, I am owing, I do owe

10. bebes	=	you (fam. sg.) drink, you are drinking, you do drink
11. vendemos	=	we sell, we are selling, we do sell
12. comen	=	you (pol. pl.) eat, you are eating, you do eat
13. aprende	=	he learns, he is learning, he does learn
14. comprenden	=	they understand, they are understanding, they do understand
15. cree	=	you (pol. sg.) believe, you are believing, you do believe

B.

1. ¿Lees *Don Quijote*?
2. No leo. Mando un correo electrónico.
3. Perdón, ¿manda Ud. un correo electrónico en español?
4. Sí, porque mi amiga habla, lee y escribe español muy bien.
5. Adiós. ¿Comprenden Uds.?
6. Debo mandar un correo electrónico en veinte minutos.
7. Mi amiga no vende el *Seat*.
8. Mi abuela bebe mucho café.
9. Temo los exámenes de español.
10. Mi hermano vende su coche.
11. Mi hermana siempre rompe algo.
12. Mi amiga mexicana lee *El País* con frecuencia.
13. Mi hijo debe leer más.
14. Mi hija aprende a hablar español en la Universidad de Salamanca.
15. ¿Comes mucho?

Exercise Set 1-3

A.

1. vivo	=	I live, I am living, I do live
2. asistes	=	you (fam. sg.) attend, you are attending, you do attend
3. describimos	=	we describe, we are describing, we do describe
4. cubren	=	they cover, they are covering, they do cover
5. sufrís	=	you (fam. pl.) suffer, you are suffering, you do suffer
6. admite	=	you (pol. sg.) admit, you are admitting, you do admit
7. mi amiga discute	=	my friend discusses, my friend is discussing, my friend does discuss
8. viven	=	they live, they are living, they do live
9. permito	=	I permit, I am permitting, I do permit
10. partes	=	you (fam. sg.) leave, you are leaving, you do leave
11. subimos	=	we go up, we are going up, we do go up
12. existen	=	you (pol. pl.) exist, you are existing, you do exist
13. escribe	=	he writes, he is writing, he does write
14. deciden	=	they decide, they are deciding, they do decide
15. recibe	=	you (pol. sg.) receive, you are receiving, you do receive

B.

1. ¿Recibes mucho correo electrónico?
2. Ellos discuten la película de *Luis Buñuel* ahora.
3. Asistimos a la clase ahora.
4. Ella parte para *Málaga* mañana.
5. Uds. viven cerca.
6. Escribo, leo y mando mucho correo electrónico.
7. Necesito asistir a la clase todos los días.
8. Ellos describen el cuadro de *Francisco Goya* ahora.
9. Mucha gente sufre hoy.

10. Decidís discutir el asunto.
11. Marta y yo abrimos las ventanas.
12. Descubro muchos secretos en clase.
13. Mi esposo escribe como *Calderón de la Barca*.
14. ¿Existen las hadas?
15. Cubres la mesa.

C.

1. a 2. a 3. a 4. a 5. b 6. a 7. b 8. a 9. b
10. a 11. b 12. a 13. b 14. a

Exercise Set 1-4

A.

1. toca 2. parten 3. vivimos 4. miran 5. llegan
6. limpiamos 7. comprendo 8. escucha 9. hablas

B.

1. b. 2. b 3. a 4. a 5. a 6. a 7. a 8. b 9. b

C.

1. ¿Baila Ud. el tango muy bien también?
2. ¿Qué leen Uds. en este momento?
3. ¿Qué estudia Ud.?
4. ¿Por qué mira Ud. la televisión tanto?
5. ¿Necesitan Uds. estudiar mucho?

D.

1. ¿Vivís en Madrid? (Spain)
2. Uds. viven en Barcelona. (Spain)
3. Uds. beben mucho café. (Latin America)
4. Uds. hablan español muy bien. (Latin America)
5. Uds. cantan muy bien. (Latin America)

Crossword Puzzle 1

CHAPTER 2
Exercise Set 2-1

A.

1. empiezo	=	I begin, I am beginning, I do begin
2. empiezas	=	you (fam. sg.) begin, you are beginning, you do begin
3. empezamos	=	we begin, we are beginning, we do begin
4. empiezan	=	they begin, they are beginning, they do begin
5. empezáis	=	you (fam. pl.) begin, you are beginning, you do begin
6. empieza	=	you (pol. sg.) begin, you are beginning, you do begin

1. entiendo	=	I understand, I am understanding, I do understand
2. entendemos	=	Raquel and I understand, Raquel and I are understanding, Raquel and I do understand
3. entienden	=	you (pol. pl.) understand, you are understanding, you do understand
4. entienden	=	they understand, they are understanding, they do understand
5. entendéis	=	you (fam. pl.) understand, you are understanding, you do understand
6. entiendes	=	you (fam. sg.) understand, you are understanding, you do understand

1. miento	=	I lie, I am lying, I do lie
2. mientes	=	you (fam. sg.) lie, you are lying, you do lie
3. mentimos	=	we lie, we are lying, we do lie
4. mienten	=	they lie, they are lying, they do lie
5. mentís	=	you (fam. pl.) lie, you are lying, you do lie
6. miente	=	you (pol. sg.) lie, you are lying, you do lie

B.

1. Empiezo a leer la poesía de *Alfonsina Storni.*
2. ¿Quieres leer las novelas de *Eduardo Mallea?*
3. Encendemos la luz todas las noches.
4. ¿Entiende Ud. la pregunta?
5. ¿Sientes no leer *El túnel* de *Ernesto Sábato?*
6. Perdemos nuestras llaves mucho.
7. Ella confiesa que mira muchas telenovelas.
8. Queremos leer *Mafalda.*
9. Ellos prefieren ir a la *Calle Florida* para comprar la ropa.
10. Él sugiere el libro de *Ana María Shua.*
11. No mientes.

Exercise Set 2-2

A.

1. encuentro	=	I find, I am finding, I do find
2. encuentras	=	you (fam. sg.) find, you are finding, you do find
3. encontramos	=	we find, we are finding, we do find
4. encuentran	=	they find, they are finding, they do find
5. encuentran	=	you (pol. pl.) find, you are finding, you do find
6. encuentra	=	you (pol. sg.) find, you are finding, you do find

1. devuelvo	=	I return, I am returning, I do return
2. devolvemos	=	Javier and I return, Javier and I are returning, Javier and I do return
3. devuelven	=	they return, they are returning, they do return
4. devuelven	=	you (pol. pl.) return, you are returning, you do return

| 5. devolvéis | = | you (fam. pl.) return, you are returning, you do return |
| 6. devuelves | = | you (fam. sg.) return, you are returning, you do return |

1. muero	=	I die, I am dying, I do die
2. mueres	=	you (fam. sg.) die, you are dying, you do die
3. morimos	=	we die, we are dying, we do die
4. mueren	=	they die, they are dying, they do die
5. morís	=	you (fam. pl.) die, you are dying, you do die
6. muere	=	you (pol. sg.) die, you are dying, you do die

B.

1. Un bistec cuesta mucho en *La Cabaña*.
2. Uds. pueden leer *El puente* de *Carlos Gorostiza*.
3. Ella encuentra las llaves en el sofá.
4. Volamos a Ushuaia mañana.
5. Sueñas con ganar la lotería.
6. Ellos duermen tarde si pueden.
7. Cuelgo el teléfono si ellos venden algo.
8. Volvemos a *Mendoza* mañana en *Aerolíneas Argentinas*.
9. Él recuerda el ensayo de *Domingo Fausto Sarmiento*.
10. El teléfono suena constantemente.

Exercise Set 2-3

A.

1. compito	=	I compete, I am competing, I do compete
2. compites	=	you (fam. sg.) compete, you are competing, you do compete
3. competimos	=	we compete, we are competing, we do compette
4. compiten	=	they compete, they are competing, they do compete
5. compiten	=	you (pol. pl.) compete, you are competing, you do compete
6. compite	=	you (pol. sg.) compete, you are competing, you do compete

1. mido	=	I measure, I am measuring, I do measure
2. miden	=	they measure, they are measuring, they do measure
3. medimos	=	Lydia and I measure, Lydia and I are measuring, Lydia and I do measure
4. miden	=	you (pol. pl.) measure, you are measuring, you do measure
5. medimos	=	we measure, we are measuring, we do measure
6. mides	=	you (fam. sg.) measure, you are measuring, you do measure

1. sigo	=	I follow, I am following, I do follow
2. sigue	=	you (pol. sg.) follow, you are following, you do follow
3. seguimos	=	we follow, we are following, we do follow
4. siguen	=	they follow, they are following, they do follow
5. seguís	=	you (fam. pl.) follow, you are following, you do follow
6. seguimos	=	Joaquín and I follow, Joaquín and I are following, Joaquín and I do follow

B.

1. Ellos compiten por el premio.
2. Los profesores necesitan corregir los exámenes hoy.
3. Siempre sigo las reglas.
4. Pido el *churrasco* en *Dora*.
5. Cuando repites las palabras en voz alta, recuerdas.
6. Ella mide los ingredientes con cuidado.

7. Ellos sirven vino excelente en el restaurante.
8. Él despide a los empleados.
9. Uds. ríen mucho.
10. Ellos siempre fríen los huevos aquí.

Exercise Set 2-4

A.

1. prefiero   2. entienden   3. cerramos   4. friega   5. sueñas
6. vuelvo   7. competimos   8. vuela   9. sirven

B.

1. a   2. b   3. a   4. b   5. b   6. b   7. a   8. b   9. b

C.

1. Vuelvo a Buenos Aires.
2. Almuerzo en *Güerrín*.
3. Cierro las puertas
4. Sigo la misma ruta.
5. Empiezo a estudiar.

Crossword Puzzle 2

CHAPTER 3
Exercise Set 3-1

A.

1. soy	=	I am
2. eres	=	you (fam. sg.) are
3. somos	=	we are
4. son	=	they are
5. sois	=	you (fam. pl.) are
6. es	=	you (pol. sg.) are

B.

1. Son las ocho y veinte de la noche.
2. Son las siete y media (treinta) de la mañana.
3. Son las cinco menos cuarto (quince) de la tarde.
4. Son las diez y dieciocho de la mañana.
5. Son las doce menos veinticinco de la noche.
6. Son las nueve en punto de la mañana.
7. Son las dos y diez de la tarde.
8. Son las cuatro y media (treinta) de la mañana.

C.

1. ¿De dónde eres?
2. Mi esposa es de Uruguay, pero yo soy de España.
3. Ellos son uruguayos y son simpáticos.
4. La mujer española es rubia.
5. ¿De qué es el bolígrafo rojo? Es de plástico.
6. ¿De quién es el reloj? Es de Pilar.
7. Es importante estudiar español hoy.
8. Silvia es pelirroja y alta.
9. Mi casa es de madera.
10. La película es a las ocho de la noche.

Exercise Set 3-2

A.

1. estás	=	you (fam. sg.) are
2. estoy	=	I am
3. estamos	=	we are
4. están	=	they are
5. estáis	=	you (fam. pl.) are
6. están	=	you (pol. pl.) are

B.

1. Estoy en casa ahora porque estoy enfermo/-a.
2. Mi esposo está para salir para Montevideo.
3. Ella está cansada porque trabaja mucho.
4. Mi hermana está casada con un hombre simpático.
5. Estoy de acuerdo con Pablo.
6. Estamos de vacaciones en Uruguay ahora.
7. Blanca, estás cansada porque estás de pie tanto.
8. Cuando estudio mucho, estoy de buen humor porque aprendo.
9. Estoy aburrido/a porque no estoy de vacaciones.
10. Este color es muy vivo.

Exercise Set 3-3

A.

1. Hay seis libros aquí.
2. Hay una mujer uruguaya en la clase.
3. Hay que estar aquí a las ocho de la mañana.
4. Hay que ir a Montevideo.
5. Hay muchos estudiantes en la clase.

Exercise Set 3-4

A.

1. tiene	=	she has, she does have
2. tengo	=	I have, I do have
3. tienes	=	you (fam. sg.) have, you do have
4. tienen	=	they have, they do have
5. tiene	=	you (pol. sg.) have, you do have
6. tienen	=	you (pol. pl.) have, you do have

B.

1. Tengo ganas de ir al *Museo del Gaucho y de la Moneda*.
2. Cuando estoy en el casino, tengo mucha suerte.
3. Él tiene cincuenta años.
4. Ella tiene vergüenza de sus acciones.
5. Uds. tienen que comer en *La Silenciosa*.
6. Tengo mucha sed hoy y quiero beber agua.
7. Cuando tengo mucha hambre, como salchichas.
8. Tengo miedo de las arañas.
9. Siempre tengo mucha prisa cuando tengo que trabajar.
10. Ella tiene mucho sueño y necesita dormir.

Exercise Set 3-5

A.

1. haces	=	you (fam. sg.) do/make, you are doing/making, you do do/make
2. hago	=	I do/make, I am doing/making, I do do/make
3. hacemos	=	we do/make, we are doing/making, we do do/make
4. hacen	=	they do/make, they are doing/making, they do do/make
5. hacéis	=	you (fam. pl.) do/make, you are doing/making, you do do/make
6. hacen	=	you (pol. pl.) do/make, you are doing/making, you do do/make

B.

1. ¿Cuánto tiempo hace que estudias español?
2. Hace una hora que estudio español.
3. Hace frío en Montevideo en junio.
4. Cuando llueve, está nublado.
5. Hago caso a los verbos cuando estudio español.
6. Hace calor en Montevideo en diciembre.
7. Hago un viaje a *Punta del Este*.
8. Siempre nieva en invierno.
9. Siempre hace buen tiempo en junio.
10. Hace mucho viento en Chicago.
11. Es el treinta y uno de marzo, dos mil seis.

Exercise Set 3-6

A.

1. sabes	=	you (fam. sg.) know, you do know
2. sé	=	I know, I do know
3. sabemos	=	we know, we do know
4. saben	=	they know, they do know
5. sabéis	=	you (fam. pl.) know, you do know
6. saben	=	you (pol. pl.) know, you do know

B.

1. Sabes nadar bien.
2. Ella sabe que Raquel está aquí.
3. Sé que es necesario dormir ocho horas.
4. Sabemos que hace frío en enero.
5. Uds. saben que tengo que estar en Montevideo mañana.
6. Sabes la fecha de hoy.
7. Él sabe que estoy cansado/a.
8. Ud. sabe que el tango es muy popular en Montevideo.
9. Sabemos que *Piriápolis* está en Uruguay.
10. Ellos saben que estoy de buen humor.

Exercise Set 3-7

A.

1. conoces	=	you (fam.sg.) know, you do know
2. conozco	=	I know, I do know
3. conocemos	=	we know, we do know
4. conocen	=	they know, they do know
5. conocéis	=	you (fam. pl.) know, you do know
6. conocen	=	you (pol. pl.) know, you do know

B.

1. Conozco un buen restaurante en *Punta del Este.*
2. Conozco a Julio Rodríguez bien.
3. Conozco los cuentos de *Horacio Quiroga.*
4. Él conoce a los Hernández.
5. Conozco la ciudad de Montevideo muy bien.

Exercise Set 3-8

A.

1. Estoy seguro/-a de que tengo razón.
2. Sé que hace frío hoy.
3. Tengo que estar aquí a las seis en punto de la tarde.
4. Hay que ser simpático.
5. Ellos tienen sueño y están cansados.
6. Somos argentinos pero ellos son uruguayos.
.7. Es la una y cuarto (quince) de la tarde.
8. Tengo veinte años de edad y soy estudiante.
9. Cristina Aguilera es rubia y bonita.
10. Cuando hace calor, tengo mucha sed.

Crossword Puzzle 3

CHAPTER 4
Exercise Set 4-1

A.

1. salgo	=	I leave, I am leaving, I do leave
2. sales	=	you (fam. sg.) leave, you are leaving, you do leave
3. salimos	=	she and I leave, she and I are leaving, she and I do leave
4. salen	=	they leave, they are leaving, they do leave
5. salís	=	you (fam. pl.) leave, you are leaving, you do leave
6. sale	=	you (pol. sg.) leave, you are leaving, you do leave
1. voy	=	I go, I am going, I do go
2. vamos	=	Isabel and I go, Isabel and I are going, Isabel and I do go
3. van	=	you (pol. pl.) go, you are going, you do go
4. van	=	they go, they are going, they do go
5. vamos	=	we go, we are going, we do go
6. vas	=	you (fam. sg.) go, you are going, you do go
1. vengo	=	I come, I am coming, I do come
2. vienes	=	you (fam. sg.) come, you are coming, you do come
3. venimos	=	Ignacio and I come, Ignacio and I are coming, Ignacio and I do come
4. vienen	=	they come, they are coming, they do come
5. venís	=	you (fam. pl.) come, you are coming, you do come
6. vienen	=	you (pol. pl.) come, you are coming, you do come
1. doy	=	I give, I am giving, I do give
2. das	=	you (fam. sg.) give, you are giving, you do give
3. damos	=	we give, we are giving, we do give
4. dan	=	they give, they are giving, they do give
5. dais	=	you (fam. pl.) give, you are giving, you do give
6: dan	=	you (pol. pl.) give, you are giving, you do give
1. oigo	=	I hear, I am hearing, I do hear
2. oyes	=	you (fam. sg.) hear, you are hearing, you do hear
3. oímos	=	we hear, we are hearing, we do hear
4. oyen	=	they hear, they are hearing, they do hear
5. oís	=	you (fam. pl.) hear, you are hearing, you do hear
6. oyen	=	you (pol. pl.) hear, you are hearing, you do hear

1.	digo	=	I say/tell, I am saying/telling, I do say/tell
2.	dices	=	you (fam. sg.) say/tell, you are saying/telling, you do say/tell
3.	decimos	=	Isabel and I say/tell, Isabel and I are saying/telling, Isabel and I do say/tell
4.	dicen	=	they say/tell, they are saying/telling, they do say/tell
5.	decís	=	you (fam. pl.) say/tell, you are saying/telling, you do say/tell
6.	dicen	=	you (pol. pl.) say/tell, you are saying/telling, you do say/tell

1.	pongo	=	I put/place, I am putting/placing, I do put/place
2.	pones	=	you (fam.sg.) put/place, you are putting/placing, you do put/place
3.	ponemos	=	we put/place, we are putting/placing, we do put/place
4.	ponen	=	they put/place, they are putting/placing, they do put/place
5.	ponéis	=	you (fam. pl.) put/place, you are putting/placing, you do put/place
6.	ponen	=	you (pol. pl.) put/place, you are putting/placing, you do put/place

1.	veo	=	I see, I am seeing, I do see
2.	ves	=	you (fam. sg.) see, you are seeing, you do see
3.	vemos	=	we see, we are seeing, we do see
4.	ven	=	they see, they are seeing, they do see
5.	veis	=	you (fam. pl.) see, you are seeing, you do see
6.	ven	=	you (pol. pl.) see, you are seeing, you do see

B.

1. Doy un paseo en el parque todos los días.
2. Salgo con mis amigos los viernes.
3. Vengo tarde a la universidad con frecuencia.
4. Veo el *Museo de Arte Indígena* ahora.
5. Pongo mi dinero en mi cartera.
6. Voy al *Chaco* mañana.
7. Oigo los sonidos de la selva.
8. No digo mentiras.

C.

1. c   2. a   3. b   4. c   5. b   6. c

Exercise Set 4-2

A.

1.	ofrezco	=	I offer, I am offering, I do offer
2.	ofreces	=	you (fam. sg.) offer, you are offering, you do offer
3.	ofrecemos	=	she and I offer, she and I are offering, she and I do offer
4.	ofrecen	=	they offer, they are offering, they do offer
5.	ofrecéis	=	you (fam. pl.) offer, you are offering, you do offer
6.	ofrece	=	you (pol. sg.) offer, you are offering, you do offer

1. produzco	=	I produce, I am producing, I do produce
2. producimos	=	we produce, we are producing, we do produce
3. producen	=	you (pol. pl.) produce, you are producing, you do produce
4. producen	=	they produce, they are producing, they do produce
5. producimos	=	we produce, we are producing, we do produce
6. produces	=	you (fam. sg.) produce, you are producing, you do produce

1. traigo	=	I bring, I am bringing, I do bring
2. traemos	=	Ignacio and I bring, Ignacio and I are bringing, Ignacio and I do bring
3. traen	=	you (pol. pl.) bring, you are bringing, you do bring
4. traen	=	they bring, they are bringing, they do bring
5. traemos	=	we bring, we are bringing, we do bring
6. traes	=	you (fam. sg.) bring, you are bringing, you do bring

1. incluyo	=	I include, I am including, I do include
2. incluimos	=	we include, we are including, we do include
3. incluyen	=	you (pol. pl.) include, you are including, you do include
4. incluyen	=	they include, they are including, they do include
5. incluye	=	she includes, she is including, she does include
6. incluyes	=	you (fam. sg.) include, you are including, you do include

1. venzo	=	I conquer/defeat, I am conquering/defeating, I do conquer/defeat
2. vencemos	=	Jorge and I conquer/defeat, Jorge and I are conquering/defeating, Jorge and I do conquer/defeat
3. vencen	=	you (pol. pl.) conquer/defeat, you are conquering/defeating, you do conquer/defeat
4. vencen	=	they conquer/defeat, they are conquering/defeating, they do conquer/defeat
5. vencemos	=	we conquer/defeat, we are conquering/defeating, we do conquer/defeat
6. vences	=	you (fam. sg.) conquer/defeat, you are conquering/defeating, you do conquer/defeat

1. protejo	=	I protect, I am protecting, I do protect
2. protegemos	=	we protect, we are protecting, we do protect
3. protegen	=	you (pol. pl.) protect, you are protecting, you do protect
4. protegen	=	they protect, they are protecting, they do protect
5. protege	=	he protects, he is protecting, he does protect
6. proteges	=	you (fam. sg.) protect, you are protecting, you do protect

B.

1. Conozco la ciudad de Asunción bien.
2. Este libro pertenece a Carmen.
3. Traduzco poesía del guaraní al español.
4. Voy a reducir mis horas de trabajo.
5. Traigo mis libros a la oficina hoy.
6. Incluyo un capítulo sobre la literatura paraguaya.
7. Ellos vencen a sus enemigos con alabanzas.
8. Protejo a mis niños.

C.

1. b   2. c   3. c   4. a   5. b   6. c

Crossword Puzzle 4

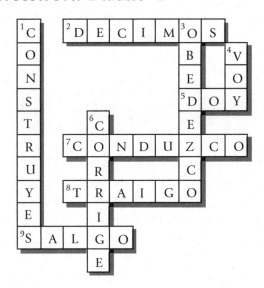

The crossword grid contains:
- 1 Down: CONSTRUYE
- 2 Across: DECIMOS
- 3 Down: OBEDECE
- 4 Down: VOY
- 5 Across: DOY
- 6 Down: CRIE
- 7 Across: CONDUZCO
- 8 Across: TRAIGO
- 9 Across: SALGO

CHAPTER 5
Exercise Set 5-1

A.

1. me levanto	=	I get up, I am getting up, I do get up
2. te levantas	=	you (fam. sg.) get up, you are getting up, you do get up
3. nos levantamos	=	we get up, we are getting up, we do get up
4. se levantan	=	they get up, they are getting up, they do get up
5. os levantáis	=	you (fam. pl.) get up, you are getting up, you do get up
6. se levanta	=	you (pol. sg.) get up, you are getting up, you do get up

1. me despierto	=	I wake up, I am waking up, I do wake up
2. nos despertamos	=	Isabel and I wake up, Isabel and I are waking up, Isabel and I do wake up
3. se despiertan	=	you (pol. pl.) wake up, you are waking up, you do wake up
4. se despiertan	=	they wake up, they are waking up, they do wake up
5. nos despertamos	=	we wake up, we are waking up, we do wake up
6. te despiertas	=	you (fam. sg.) wake up, you are waking up, you do wake up

1. me visto	=	I get dressed, I am getting dressed, I do get dressed
2. te vistes	=	you (fam. sg.) get dressed, you are getting dressed, you do get dressed
3. nos vestimos	=	we get dressed, we are getting dressed, we do get dressed
4. se visten	=	they get dressed, they are getting dressed, they do get dressed
5. os vestís	=	you (fam. pl.) get dressed, you are getting dressed, you do get dressed
6. se visten	=	you (pol. pl.) get dressed, you are getting dressed, you do get dressed

B.

1. a　　2. b　　3. b　　4. c　　5. a　　6. b　　7. c

C.

1. Ana se acuesta muy temprano.
2. El autor de *Raza de bronce* se llama *Alcides Arguedas*.

3. Margarita quiere casarse en La Paz.
4. Por la mañana me despierto, me levanto, me ducho y me visto.
5. Cuando estudio los verbos españoles mucho, me canso.
6. Después de bañarme, me seco.
7. Estoy contento cuando aprendo los verbos españoles.
8. Me preocupo cuando tengo un examen.
9. Ellos se duermen a las once de la noche.
10. Guillermo se mira en el espejo por la mañana.

Crossword Puzzle 5

CHAPTER 6
Exercise Set 6-1

A.

1. Me gusta este libro.
2. A mis amigos les gusta aquel restaurante.
3. Te gusta mirar las telenovelas.
4. Nos gusta ese programa.
5. A ella le gusta esta película.
6. A ellos les gustan estas revistas.
7. A él le gusta visitar *Antofagasta*.
8. A Rosa le gusta *Concepción*.
9. ¿A Ud. le gusta la comida chilena?
10. A ellos les gusta viajar a *Punta Arenas*.
11. Me gustas.
12. Nos gusta ella.
13. Me caes bien.
14. Me gusta ir al *Museo de Santiago*.
15. A Uds. les gusta nadar en el mar.

Exercise Set 6-2

A.

1. A ella le duele el diente.
2. Me caes bien.

3. Me faltan veinte *pesos*.
4. Me interesan los libros viejos.
5. Me importa el arte chileno.
6. A él le molesta la gente tonta.
7. A los turistas les interesa Valdivia.
8. Te conviene trabajar mucho ahora.

B.

1. ¿A Ud. le gusta la literatura chilena?
2. ¿A Ud. le gustan los museos de Santiago?
3. ¿A Ud. le interesa ir al teatro chileno?
4. ¿A Ud. le bastan cien pesos?
5. ¿A Ud. le importa leer *La Nación*?
6. ¿A Ud. le conviene dormir tarde todos los días?

Exercise Set 6-3

A.

1. estoy escribiendo	=	I am writing
2. estás escribiendo	=	you (fam. sg.) are writing
3. estamos escribiendo	=	we are writing
4. ellos están escribiendo	=	they are writing
5. estáis escribiendo	=	you (fam. pl.) are writing
6. Ud. está escribiendo	=	you (pol. sg.) are writing

1. estoy leyendo	=	I am reading
2. estamos leyendo	=	Isabel and I are reading
3. Uds. están leyendo	=	you (pol. pl.) are reading
4. ellos están leyendo	=	they are reading
5. estamos leyendo	=	we are reading
6. estás leyendo	=	you (fam. sg.) are reading

1. estoy sirviendo	=	I am serving
2. estás sirviendo	=	you (fam. sg.) are serving
3. estamos sirviendo	=	we are serving
4. están sirviendo	=	they are serving
5. estáis sirviendo	=	you (fam. pl.) are serving
6. está sirviendo	=	you (pol. sg.) are serving

1. estoy muriendo	=	I am dying
2. estás muriendo	=	you (fam. sg.) are dying
3. estamos muriendo	=	we are dying
4. están muriendo	=	they are dying
5. estáis muriendo	=	you (fam.pl.) are dying
6. están muriendo	=	you (pol. pl.) are dying

1. me estoy bañando	=	I am bathing myself
2. te estás bañando	=	you (fam. sg.) are bathing yourself
3. nos estamos bañando	=	we are bathing ourselves
4. se están bañando	=	they are bathing themselves
5. os estáis bañando	=	you (fam. pl) are bathing yourselves
6. se están bañando	=	you (pol. pl.) are bathing yourselves

1. estoy bañándome	=	I am bathing myself
2. estás bañándote	=	you (fam. sg.) are bathing yourself
3. estamos bañándonos	=	we are bathing ourselves
4. están bañándose	=	they are bathing themselves
5. estáis bañándoos	=	you (fam. pl) are bathing yourselves
6. están bañándose	=	you (pol. pl.) are bathing yourselves

B.

1. Ella está estudiando para su examen ahora mismo.
2. Ellos están practicando español en este momento.
3. Estamos sirviéndoles la cena a nuestros amigos.
4. Estoy jugando al fútbol en este momento.
5. Estás durmiendo ahora mismo.
6. Estoy diciendo la verdad.
7. Él está comiendo la comida chilena ahora.

Exercise Set 6-4

A.

1. Pablo las lee.
2. Pilar está bebiéndolo. Pilar lo está bebiendo.
3. Quiero cantarla. La quiero cantar.
4. Las escribimos.
5. Ella los come.

B.

1. La veo en el coche.
2. Quieres mirarla. La quieres mirar.
3. Ella está leyéndolo. Ella lo está leyendo.
4. Ellos lo necesitan ahora.

C.

1. Los leo.
2. Necesito hacerlo ahora. Lo necesito hacer ahora.
3. Estamos estudiándolo. Lo estamos estudiando.

Exercise Set 6-5

A.

1. Le digo la verdad a ella.
2. Ellos tienen que escribirles la carta a ellos. Ellos les tienen que escribir la carta a ellos.
3. Ellos están hablándonos en español. Ellos nos están hablando en español.

B.

1. Le doy los libros a ella.
2. Prefiero darle los regalos a ella. Le prefiero dar los regalos a ella.
3. Estoy entregándole el paquete a él. Le estoy entregando el paquete a él.

Exercise Set 6-6

A.

1. Aristófanes se las escribe a ellos.
2. Irene está contándoselo a ella. Irene se lo está contando a ella.
3. Francisco necesita vendérsela a ella. Francisco se la necesita vender.
4. Ellas están dándoselo a ellos. Ellas se lo están dando a ellos.
5. Carlos me la muestra.

B.

1. Ellos nos los venden.
2. Queremos mostrárselas a ellos. Se las queremos mostrar a ellos.
3. Él está dándoselo a ella. Él se lo está dando a ella.

C.

1. Se las muestro a ella.
2. Voy a escribírsela a ellos. Se la voy a escribir a ellos.
3. Estoy dándoselo a él. Se lo estoy dando a él.

Crossword Puzzle 6

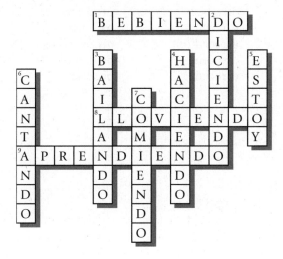

REVIEW 1
Review Exercise Set 1-1

A.

1.	2.	3.
hablo	bebo	vivo
hablas	bebes	vives
habla	bebe	vive
hablamos	bebemos	vivimos
habláis	bebéis	vivís
hablan	beben	viven

B.

1.	2.	3.	4.	5.
soy	estoy	tengo	hago	conozco
eres	estás	tienes	haces	conoces
es	está	tiene	hace	conoce
somos	estamos	tenemos	hacemos	conocemos
sois	estáis	tenéis	hacéis	conocéis
son	están	tienen	hacen	conocen

6.	7.	8.	9.	10.
sé	pongo	voy	digo	veo
sabes	pones	vas	dices	ves
sabe	pone	va	dice	ve
sabemos	ponemos	vamos	decimos	vemos
sabéis	ponéis	vais	decís	veis
saben	ponen	van	dicen	ven

11.	12.	13.	14.	15.
doy	salgo	vengo	ofrezco	produzco
das	sales	vienes	ofreces	produces
da	sale	viene	ofrece	produce
damos	salimos	venimos	ofrecemos	producimos
dais	salís	venís	ofrecéis	producís
dan	salen	vienen	ofrecen	producen

16.	17.
atraigo	huyo
atraes	huyes
atrae	huye
atraemos	huimos
atraéis	huís
atraen	huyen

C.

1.	2.	3.	4.
cierro	almuerzo	pierdo	pido
cierras	almuerzas	pierdes	pides
cierra	almuerza	pierde	pide
cerramos	almorzamos	perdemos	pedimos
cerráis	almorzáis	perdéis	pedís
cierran	almuerzan	pierden	piden

D.

1.	2.	3.
me levanto	me visto	me despierto
te levantas	te vistes	te despiertas
se levanta	se viste	se despierta
nos levantamos	nos vestimos	nos despertamos
os levantáis	os vestís	os despertáis
se levantan	se visten	se despiertan

E.

1.	2.	3.
estoy cantando	estoy comiendo	estoy escribiendo
estás cantando	estás comiendo	estás escribiendo
está cantando	está comiendo	está escribiendo
estamos cantando	estamos comiendo	estamos escribiendo
estáis cantando	estáis comiendo	estáis escribiendo
están cantando	están comiendo	están escribiendo

Review Exercise Set 1-2

A.

1. a   2. b   3. a   4. b   5. b   6. a   7. b   8. a   9. b   10. a
11. b   12. b   13. a   14. a   15. a   16. b   17. b   18. a   19. b   20. a

B.

1. juegan   2. vende   3. limpiamos   4. lee   5. habla
6. tengo   7. sabes   8. conocemos   9. gusta   10. salimos
11. llega   12. es   13. como   14. voy   15. está

CHAPTER 7
Execise Set 7-1

A.

1. canté	=	I sang, I did sing
2. cantaste	=	you (fam. sg.) sang, you did sing
3. cantamos	=	we sang, we did sing
4. cantaron	=	they sang, they did sing
5. cantasteis	=	you (fam. pl.) sang, you did sing
6. cantó	=	you (pol. sg.) sang, you did sing

1. vendí	=	I sold, I did sell
2. vendimos	=	Raquel and I sold, Raquel and I did sell
3. vendieron	=	you (pol. pl.) sold, you did sell
4. vendieron	=	they sold, they did sell
5. vendisteis	=	you (fam. pl.) sold, you did sell
6. vendiste	=	you (fam. sg.) sold, you did sell

1.	viví	=	I lived, I did live
2.	viviste	=	you (fam. sg.) lived, you did live
3.	vivimos	=	we lived, we did live
4.	vivieron	=	they lived, they did live
5.	vivisteis	=	you (fam. pl.) lived, you did live
6.	vivió	=	you (pol. sg.) lived, you did live

1.	me bañé	=	I bathed myself, I did bathe myself
2.	te bañaste	=	you (fam. sg.) bathed yourself, you did bathe yourself
3.	nos bañamos	=	we bathed ourselves, we did bathe ourselves
4.	se bañaron	=	they bathed themselves, they did bathe themselves
5.	os bañasteis	=	you (fam. pl.) bathed yourselves, you did bathe yourselves
6.	se bañó	=	you (pol. sg.) bathed yourself, you did bathe yourself

B.

1. Viajé de *Lima* a *Cuzco*.
2. Ellos comieron y bebieron en *Antaño*.
3. Visitamos *Arequipa* en el sur de Perú.
4. Viví en aquel barrio hace dos años.
5. Ella cantó la misma canción anoche.
6. Compré un coche nuevo ayer por la mañana.
7. Escribiste un correo electrónico anoche.
8. Ud. abrió la puerta.
9. Bebí mucho café esta mañana.
10. ¿Recibiste el regalo de Elena ayer?
11. Me gustó el viaje a *Huancayo*.
12. A él le dolió la cabeza anoche.

Exercise Set 7-2

A.

1.	morí	=	I died, I did die.
2.	moriste	=	you (fam. sg.) died, you did die
3.	morimos	=	Marta and I died, Marta and I did die
4.	murieron	=	they died, they did die
5.	moristeis	=	you (fam. pl.) died, you did die
6.	murió	=	you (pol. sg.) died, you did die

1.	preferí	=	I preferred, I did prefer
2.	preferimos	=	we preferred, we did prefer
3.	prefirieron	=	you (pol. pl.) preferred, you did prefer
4.	prefirieron	=	they preferred, they did prefer
5.	preferisteis	=	you (fam. pl.) preferred, you did prefer
6.	preferiste	=	you (fam. sg.) preferred, you did prefer

1.	repetí	=	I repeated, I did repeat
2.	repetimos	=	we repeated, we did repeat
3.	repitieron	=	you (pol. pl.) repeated, you did repeat
4.	repitieron	=	they repeated, they did repeat
5.	repetisteis	=	you (fam. pl.) repeated, you did repeat
6.	repetiste	=	you (fam. sg.) repeated, you did repeat

B.

1. Ellos sirvieron una buena comida en *Pisco*.
2. Inés durmió muy tarde hoy.
3. Mis amigos prefirieron ir al *Museo de la Nación* en Lima.
4. Repetí la conjugación del pretérito.
5. Medí el cuarto anoche.
6. Él siguió al profesor a la clase.
7. Su abuelo murió anoche.
8. Ellos frieron la carne en aceite de oliva.
9. Él despidió al empleado hace dos días.
10. Mis padres no mintieron nunca.

Exercise Set 7-3

A.

1. tuve	=	I had, I did have
2. tuviste	=	you (fam. sg.) had, you did have
3. tuvimos	=	Marta and I had, Marta and I did have
4. tuvieron	=	they had, they did have
5. tuvisteis	=	you (fam. pl.) had, you did have
6. tuvo	=	you (pol. sg.) had, you did have

1. quise	=	I wanted, I did want
2. quisimos	=	we wanted, we did want
3. quisieron	=	you (pol. pl.) wanted, you did want
4. quisieron	=	they wanted, they did want
5. quisisteis	=	you (fam. pl.) wanted, you did want
6. quisiste	=	you (fam. sg.) wanted, you did want

1. hice	=	I did, I did do
2. hiciste	=	you (fam. sg.) did, you did do
3. hicimos	=	we did, we did do
4. hicieron	=	you (pol. pl.) did, you did do
5. hicisteis	=	you (fam. pl.) did, you did do
6. hizo	=	you (pol. sg.) did, you did do

1. estuve	=	I was
2. estuviste	=	you (fam. sg.) were
3. estuvimos	=	we were
4. estuvieron	=	you (pol. pl.) were
5. estuvisteis	=	you (fam. pl.) were
6. estuvo	=	you (pol. sg.) were

1. pude	=	I could/was able
2. pudiste	=	you (fam. sg.) could/were able
3. pudimos	=	we could/were able
4. pudieron	=	you (pol. pl.) could/were able
5. pudisteis	=	you (fam. pl.) could/were able
6. pudo	=	you (pol. sg.) could/were able

1. vine	=	I came, I did come
2. viniste	=	you (fam. sg.) came, you did come
3. vinimos	=	we came, we did come
4. vinieron	=	you (pol. pl.) came, you did come

5. vinisteis	=	you (fam. pl.) came, you did come
6. vino	=	you (pol. sg.) came, you did come

1. fui	=	I was
2. fuiste	=	you (fam. sg.) were
3. fuimos	=	we were
4. fueron	=	you (pol. pl.) were
5. fuisteis	=	you (fam. pl.) were
6. fue	=	you (pol. sg.) were

1. traduje	=	I translated, I did translate
2. tradujiste	=	you (fam. sg.) translated, you did translate
3. tradujimos	=	we translated, we did translate
4. tradujeron	=	you (pol. pl.) translated, you did translate
5. tradujisteis	=	you (fam. pl.) translated, you did translate
6. tradujo	=	you (pol. sg.) translated, you did translate

1. fui	=	I went, I did go
2. fuiste	=	you (fam. sg.) went, you did go
3. fuimos	=	we went, we did go
4. fueron	=	you (pol. pl.) went, you did go
5. fuisteis	=	you (fam. pl.) went, you did go
6. fue	=	you (pol. sg.) went, you did go

1. conduje	=	I drove, I did drive
2. condujiste	=	you (fam. sg.) drove, you did drive
3. condujimos	=	we drove, we did drive
4. condujeron	=	you (pol. pl.) drove, you did drive
5. condujisteis	=	you (fam. pl.) drove, you did drive
6. condujo	=	you (pol. sg.) drove, you did drive

B.

1. Condujimos de *Lima* a *Tacna*.
2. Le di el dinero a mi amigo.
3. Raquel y yo fuimos al centro a cenar.
4. Ellos dieron un paseo en el *Parque Kennedy*.
5. Vine a clase tarde.
6. Caí en la calle.
7. Le dije la verdad a Marco.
8. Traduje los verbos del inglés al español.
9. Estuvimos en casa cuando la vi.
10. Fui presidente/a de la organización el año pasado.
11. Ayer hizo mal tiempo porque llovió mucho.
12. Hizo mucho frío en febrero porque nevó mucho.

Exercise Set 7-4

A.

1. jugué	=	I played, I did play
2. jugaste	=	you (fam. sg.) played, you did play
3. jugamos	=	we played, we did play
4. jugaron	=	you (pol. pl.) played, you did play
5. jugasteis	=	you (fam. pl.) played, you did play
6. jugó	=	you (pol. sg.) played, you did play

1. toqué	=	I played, I did play
2. tocaste	=	you (fam. sg.) played, you did play
3. tocamos	=	we played, we did play
4. tocaron	=	you (pol. pl.) played, you did play
5. tocasteis	=	you (fam. pl.) played, you did play
6. tocó	=	you (pol. sg.) played, you did play

1. empecé	=	I began, I did begin
2. empezaste	=	you (fam. sg.) began, you did begin
3. empezamos	=	we began, we did begin
4. empezaron	=	you (pol. pl.) began, you did begin
5. empezasteis	=	you (fam. pl.) began, you did begin
6. empezó	=	you (pol. sg.) began, you did begin

1. oí	=	I heard, I did hear
2. oíste	=	you (fam. sg.) heard, you did hear
3. oímos	=	we heard, we did hear
4. oyeron	=	you (pol. pl.) heard, you did hear
5. oísteis	=	you (fam. pl.) heard, you did hear
6. oyó	=	you (pol. sg.) heard, you did hear

1. construí	=	I built, I did build
2. constuiste	=	you (fam. sg.) built, you did build
3. construimos	=	we built, we did build
4. construyeron	=	you (pol. pl.) built, you did build
5. construisteis	=	you (fam. pl.) built, you did build
6. construyó	=	you (pol. sg.) built, you did build

B.

1. Almorcé con mi amigo en un buen restaurante peruano.
2. Leí *La República* temprano esta mañana.
3. Contribuí cien *soles* ayer.
4. Oímos a la mujer en la calle.
5. Ellos construyeron una casa cara.
6. El hombre culpable huyó de la policía.
7. Empezó a llover ayer.
8. Él se tropezó con la silla.
9. Toqué la guitarra para mi hermana.
10. La tormenta destruyó mi casa.

C.

1. hablamos
2. tuvieron
3. fueron
4. fuimos
5. estuviste
6. dijo
7. comimos
8. vivimos
9. me acosté
10. fui
11. durmieron
12. pidió
13. hizo
14. tuviste
15. entendí
16. pude
17. quisieron
18. empecé

Exercise Set 7-5

A.

1. Tuve un regalo de mi madre anoche.
2. No pude conjugar todos los verbos españoles.
3. Él conoció a su esposa en un ascensor.
4. Supimos la verdad el año pasado.
5. Pude encontrar mi libro en casa.
6. Ellos quisieron estudiar pero no pudieron.

Crossword Puzzle 7

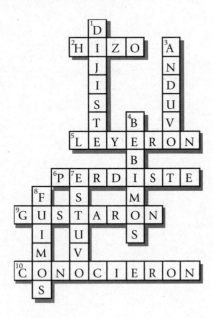

CHAPTER 8
Exercise Set 8-1

A.

1. cantaba	=	I was singing, I used to sing
2. cantabas	=	you (fam. sg.) were singing, you used to sing
3. cantábamos	=	we were singing, we used to sing
4. cantaban	=	they were singing, they used to sing
5. cantabais	=	you (fam. pl.) were singing, you used to sing
6. cantaba	=	you (pol. sg.) were singing, you used to sing

1. tenía	=	I was having, I used to have
2. teníamos	=	Raquel and I were having, Raquel and I used to have
3. tenían	=	you (pol. pl.) were having, you used to have
4. tenían	=	they were having, they used to have
5. teníais	=	you (fam. pl.) were having, you used to have
6. tenías	=	you (fam. sg.) were having, you used to have

1. decía	=	I was saying/telling, I used to say/tell
2. decías	=	you (fam. sg.) were saying/telling, you used to say/tell
3. decíamos	=	we were saying/telling, we used to say/tell

4. decían	=	they were saying/tellling, they used to say/tell
5. decíais	=	you (fam.pl.) were saying/telling, you used to say/tell
6. decía	=	you (pol. sg.) were saying/telling, you used to say/tell

1. era	=	I was, I used to be
2. eras	=	you (fam. sg.) were, you used to be
3. éramos	=	we were, we used to be
4. eran	=	they were, they used to be
5. erais	=	you (fam. pl.) were, you used to be
6. era	=	you (pol. sg.) were, you used to be

1. iba	=	I was going, I used to go
2. ibas	=	you (fam. sg.) were going, you used to go
3. íbamos	=	we were going, we used to go
4. iban	=	they were going, they used to go
5. ibais	=	you (fam. pl.) were going, you used to go
6. iba	=	you (pol. sg.) were going, you used to go

1. veía	=	I was seeing, I used to see
2. veías	=	you (fam. sg.) were seeing, you used to see
3. veíamos	=	we were seeing, we used to see
4. veían	=	they were seeing, they used to see
5. veíais	=	you (fam. pl.) were seeing, you used to see
6. veía	=	you (pol. sg.) were seeing, you used to see

1. me levantaba	=	I was getting up, I used to get up
2. te levantabas	=	you (fam. sg.) were getting up, you used to get up
3. nos levantábamos	=	we were getting up, we used to get up
4. se levantaban	=	they were getting up, they used to get up
5. os levantabais	=	you (fam. pl.) were getting up, you used to get up
6. se levantaba	=	you (pol. sg.) were getting up, you used to get up

B.

1. Yo vivía en Quito.
2. Yo era muy simpático/a de niño/a.
3. Eran las nueve de la noche.
4. Íbamos a la escuela todos los días.
5. De niña Isabel tenía el pelo rubio.
6. Llovía y estaba nublado.
7. Ellos querían ver la última película.
8. Me gustaba leer los libros de *Jorge Icaza*.
9. ¿Jugabas al fútbol?
10. Yo trabajaba en esa tienda.
11. Ellos estudiaban en la biblioteca.

Exercise Set 8-2

A.

1. estaba pagando
2. estabas empezando
3. estábamos comiendo
4. estaban prefiriendo
5. estabais jugando

6. estaba estudiando
7. estaban cantando
8. estábamos dando
9. estaba creyendo
10. estaban haciendo
11. estábamos escribiendo
12. estaba saliendo
13. te estabas levantando, estabas levantándote

B.

1. Estabas leyendo *Hoy*.
2. Sofía estaba estudiando los verbos españoles.
3. Roberto y yo estábamos mirando la televisión.
4. Mis amigos estaban jugando al fútbol.
5. Él estaba preparando la comida.

Exercise Set 8-3

A.

1. hablamos, hablábamos
2. tuve, tenía
3. fuimos, íbamos
4. fuimos, éramos
5. estuve, estaba
6. dije, decía
7. comimos, comíamos
8. vivimos, vivíamos
9. se acostó, se acostaba
10. fueron, eran
11. dormimos, dormíamos
12. pediste, pedías
13. hizo, hacía
14. tuvieron, tenían
15. entendió, entendía
16. pudo, podía
17. quisimos, queríamos
18. empecé, empezaba

B.

1. Yo estudiaba cuando fuiste a la escuela.
2. Gloria se duchaba cuando sonó el teléfono.
3. Fui a la tienda cuando llovía.
4. Francisco leía una revista cuando María entró en la casa.
5. Mi padre bebía café cuando nevaba.

C.

1. estudiaba
2. se afeitó
3. llegamos
4. eran me levanté
5. tocaba
6. leyó

Crossword Puzzle 8

CHAPTER 9
Exercise Set 9-1

A.

1. llegado
2. comido
3. recibido
4. sido
5. estado
6. tenido

7. hecho
8. sabido
9. conocido
10. mentido
11. perdido
12. podido

13. ofrecido
14. seguido
15. corregido
16. empezado
17. querido
18. almorzado

B.

1. romper
2. escribir
3. ver
4. abrir
5. poner
6. freír

7. decir
8. pudrir
9. morir
10. caer
11. hacer
12. volver

13. envolver
14. resolver
15. descubrir
16. creer
17. devolver
18. proveer

Exercise Set 9-2

A.

1. he cantado	=	I have sung
2. has cantado	=	you (fam. sg.) have sung
3. hemos cantado	=	we have sung
4. han cantado	=	they have sung
5. habéis cantado	=	you (fam. pl.) have sung
6. ha cantado	=	you (pol. sg.) have sung

1. he vendido	=	I have sold
2. hemos vendido	=	Raquel and I have sold
3. han vendido	=	you (pol. pl.) have sold
4. han vendido	=	they have sold
5. habéis vendido	=	you (fam. pl.) have sold
6. has vendido	=	you (fam. sg.) have sold

1. he recibido	=	I have received
2. has recibido	=	you (fam. sg.) have received
3. hemos recibido	=	we have received
4. han recibido	=	they have received
5. habéis recibido	=	you (fam. pl.) have received
6. ha recibido	=	you (pol. sg.) have received

1. me he bañado	=	I have bathed myself
2. te has bañado	=	you (fam. sg.) have bathed yourself
3. nos hemos bañado	=	we have bathed ourselves
4. se han bañado	=	they have bathed themselves
5. os habéis bañado	=	you (fam. pl.) have bathed yourselves
6. se ha bañado	=	you (pol. sg.) have bathed yourself

1. he vuelto	=	I have returned
2. has vuelto	=	you (fam. sg.) have returned
3. hemos vuelto	=	we have returned
4. han vuelto	=	they have returned
5. habéis vuelto	=	you (fam. pl.) have returned
6. ha vuelto	=	you (pol. sg.) have returned

1. he estado	=	I have been
2. has estado	=	you (fam. sg.) have been
3. hemos estado	=	we have been
4. han estado	=	they have been
5. habéis estado	=	you (fam. pl.) have been
6. ha estado	=	you (pol. sg.) have been

1. he sido	=	I have been
2. has sido	=	you (fam. sg.) have been
3. hemos sido	=	we have been
4. han sido	=	they have been
5. habéis sido	=	you (fam. pl.) have been
6. ha sido	=	you (pol. sg.) have been

B.

1. He visitado Bogotá muchas veces.
2. Hemos estado en *Cartagena*.
3. ¿Te has duchado?
4. ¿Ha visto Ud. a mi esposa?
5. Ha llovido mucho.
6. ¿Han resuelto ellos sus problemas?
7. Uds. han tenido sed todo el día.
8. Hemos visto *Leticia*.
9. Ella ha dicho la verdad.
10. Siempre me ha gustado esta playa.
11. Has tenido que trabajar mucho.

12. Él ha sido muy simpático.
13. Uds. han abierto todas las puertas.
14. He provisto toda la comida.
15. Ellos se han vestido.
16. Hemos creído a nuestro hijo siempre.
17. Has hecho un viaje a *Cali*.
18. Hemos leído todos los escritos de *José Eustacio Rivera*.
19. ¿Por qué no ha vuelto ella?
20. El teléfono ha sonado toda la noche y no he podido dormir.
21. Ha habido muchos exámenes en este libro.

Exercise Set 9-3

A.

1. Los he leído.
2. Pilar lo ha bebido.
3. Debo haberla cantado. La debo haber cantado.
4. Ella la ha escrito.

B.

1. Ramón se lo ha hablado a ella.
2. Marina debe habérsela escrito a él. Marina se la debe haber escrito a él.
3. Uds. se la han dicho a ellos.

C.

1. Le he vendido el coche a mi hermano.
2. Ellos deben habernos hablado. Ellos nos deben haber hablado.

D.

1. Vicente se lo ha mandado a ella.
2. Se lo he leído a ella.
3. Se la hemos dicho a él.
4. Berta se la ha enseñado a él.

E.

1. Se la has enviado a él.
2. Se los hemos dado a ellos.
3. Ellos se lo han vendido a ella.

F.

1. Se los he dado a ella.
2. Se lo he hablado a ellos.
3. Se lo he servido a ella.

Exercise Set 9-4

A.

1. comimos, comíamos, hemos comido
2. tuvo, tenía, ha tenido
3. fui, iba, he ido
4. fui, era, he sido

  5. estuve, estaba, he estado
  6. dijimos, decíamos, hemos dicho
  7. vivimos, vivíamos, hemos vivido
  8. hicimos, hacíamos, hemos hecho
  9. se bañó, se bañaba, se ha bañado
 10. hubo, había, ha habido
 11. murió, moría, ha muerto
 12. pidieron, pedían, han pedido
 13. hizo, hacía, ha hecho
 14. tuvieron, tenían, han tenido
 15. entendiste, entendías, has entendido
 16. pudieron, podían, han podido
 17. quise, quería, he querido
 18. empezó, empezaba, ha empezado

Crossword Puzzle 9

CHAPTER 10
Exercise Set 10-1

A.

1. había dado	=	I had given
2. habías dado	=	you (fam. sg.) had given
3. habíamos dado	=	we had given
4. habían dado	=	they had given
5. habíais dado	=	you (fam. pl.) had given
6. había dado	=	you (pol. sg.) had given

1. había aprendido	=	I had understood
2. habíamos aprendido	=	Raquel and I had understood
3. habían aprendido	=	you (pol. pl.) had understood
4. habían aprendido	=	they had understood
5. habíais aprendido	=	you (fam. pl.) had understood
6. habías aprendido	=	you (fam. sg.) had understood

1. había sufrido	=	I had suffered
2. habías sufrido	=	you (fam. sg.) had suffered
3. habíamos sufrido	=	we had suffered
4. habían sufrido	=	they had suffered
5. habíais sufrido	=	you (fam. pl.) had suffered
6. había sufrido	=	you (pol. sg.) had suffered

1. me había vestido	=	I had gotten dressed
2. te habías vestido	=	you (fam. sg.) had gotten dressed
3. nos habíamos vestido	=	we had gotten dressed
4. se habían vestido	=	they had gotten dressed
5. os habíais vestido	=	you (fam. pl.) had gotten dressed
6. se había vestido	=	you (pol. sg.) had gotten dressed

1. había cubierto	=	I had covered
2. habías cubierto	=	you (fam. sg.) had covered
3. habíamos cubierto	=	we had covered
4. habían cubierto	=	they had covered
5. habíais cubierto	=	you (fam. pl.) had covered
6. había cubierto	=	you (pol. sg.) had covered

1. había estado	=	I had been
2. habías estado	=	you (fam. sg.) had been
3. habíamos estado	=	we had been
4. habían estado	=	they had been
5. habíais estado	=	you (fam. pl.) had been
6. había estado	=	you (pol. sg.) had been

1. había sido	=	I had been
2. habías sido	=	you (fam. sg.) had been
3. habíamos sido	=	we had been
4. habían sido	=	they had been
5. habíais sido	=	you (fam. pl.) had been
6. había sido	=	you (pol. sg.) had been

B.

1. Yo había visto el *Museo Boliviariano* en Caracas.
2. Yo había oído la música folclórica de Venezuela.
3. Yo había comprado *El Diario de Caracas*.
4. Había habido muchas casas allí.
5. Había llovido anoche.
6. Pablo había vivido en Madrid antes de venir a Venezuela.
7. Yo había visto la última película venezolana.
8. Yo había tocado la guitarra.
9. Yo había viajado a *Mérida*.
10. Me había levantado muy tarde.
11. Habías estudiado los verbos españoles mucho.
12. Habíamos entrado en la capital de Venezuela.
13. Había empezado a llover.
14. Ellos habían conducido a Maracaibo.
15. ¿Dónde había encontrado él el dinero?
16. Yo había hecho el rompecabezas.
17. Ud. había tenido el libro antes.
18. ¿Habían descubierto Uds. el secreto?

19. Las flores habían muerto en el otoño.
20. Ella había reído mucho.

Exercise Set 10-2

A.

1. hemos vivido, habíamos vivido
2. ha llovido, había llovido
3. ha ido, había ido
4. has sido, habías sido
5. hemos estado, habíamos estado
6. han dicho, habían dicho
7. hemos bebido, habíamos bebido
8. he hecho, había hecho
9. se ha duchado, se había duchado
10. ha habido, había habido
11. ha muerto, había muerto
12. ha pedido, había pedido
13. ha hecho, había hecho
14. he tenido, había tenido
15. has entendido, habías entendido
16. ha podido, había podido
17. has querido, habías querido
18. ha comenzado, había comenzado

Crossword Puzzle 10

REVIEW 2-1
Review Exercise Set 2-1

A.

1. abierto
2. atraído
3. bebido
4. cantado
5. creído
6. cubierto
7. dicho
8. descrito
9. descubierto
10. devuelto
11. envuelto
12. escrito
13. estado
14. frito
15. hecho
16. muerto
17. oído
18. opuesto
19. puesto
20. provisto
21. podrido
22. resuelto
23. roto
24. sido
25. tenido
26. visto
27. vuelto

B.

1.
compré, corrí, abrí
compraste, corriste, abriste
compró, corrió, abrió
compramos, corrimos, abrimos
comprasteis, corristeis, abristeis
compraron, corrieron, abrieron

2.
dormí, mentí, pedí
dormiste, mentiste, pediste
durmió, mintió, pidió
dormimos, mentimos, pedimos
dormisteis, mentisteis, pedisteis
durmieron, mintieron, pidieron

3.
estuve, tuve, hube
estuviste, tuviste, hubiste
estuvo, tuvo, hubo
estuvimos, tuvimos, hubimos
estuvisteis, tuvisteis, hubisteis
estuvieron, tuvieron, hubieron

4.
pude, puse, supe
pudiste, pusiste, supiste
pudo, puso, supo
pudimos, pusimos, supimos
pudisteis, pusisteis, supisteis
pudieron, pusieron, supieron

5.
hice, quise, vine
hiciste, quisiste, viniste
hizo, quiso, vino
hicimos, quisimos, vinimos
hicisteis, quisisteis, vinisteis
hicieron, quisieron, vinieron

6.
fui, di, dije
fuiste, diste, dijiste
fue, dio, dijo
fuimos, dimos, dijimos
fuisteis, disteis, dijisteis
fueron, dieron, dijeron

7.
busqué, llegué, comencé
buscaste, llegaste, comenzaste
buscó, llegó, comenzó
buscamos, llegamos, comenzamos
buscasteis, llegasteis, comenzasteis
buscaron, llegaron, comenzaron

C.

1.	2.
estudiaba, creía, cubría	iba, era, veía
estudiabas, creías, cubrías	ibas, eras, veías
estudiaba, creía, cubría	iba, era, veía
estudiábamos, creíamos,	íbamos, éramos, veíamos
cubríamos	ibais, erais, veíais
estudiabais, creíais, cubríais	iban, eran, veían
estudiaban, creían, cubrían	

D.

he buscado, he vendido, me he vestido
has buscado, has vendido, te has vestido
ha buscado, ha vendido, se ha vestido
hemos buscado, hemos vendido, nos hemos vestido
habéis buscado, habéis vendido, os habéis vestido
han buscado, han vendido, se han vestido

E.

había bailado, había temido, me había sentido
habías bailado, habías temido, te habías sentido
había bailado, había temido, se había sentido
habíamos bailado, habíamos temido, nos habíamos sentido
habíais bailado, habíais temido, os habíais sentido
habían bailado, habían temido, se habían sentido

Review Exercise Set 2-2

A.

1. b   2. a   3. a   4. a   5. a   6. b   7. b   8. a   9. b   10. a

B.

1. Trabajaste   2. nació   3. estudiaba   4. hizo   5. corría
6. Llovió   7. miraba   8. compraron   9. fuimos   10. me acosté

CHAPTER 11
Exercise Set 11-1

A.

1. estudiaré	=	I will study
2. estudiarás	=	you (fam. sg.) will study
3. estudiaremos	=	we will study
4. estudiarán	=	they will study
5. estudiaréis	=	you (fam. pl.) will study
6. estudiará	=	you (pol. sg.) will study

1. aprenderé	=	I will learn
2. aprenderemos	=	Raquel and I will learn
3. aprenderán	=	you (pol. pl.) will learn
4. aprenderán	=	they will learn

| 5. aprenderéis | = | you (fam. pl.) will learn |
| 6. aprenderás | = | you (fam. sg.) will learn |

1. escribiré	=	I will write
2. escribirás	=	you (fam sg.) will write
3. escribiremos	=	we will write
4. escribirán	=	they will write
5. escribiréis	=	you (fam. pl.) will write
6. escribirá	=	you (pol. sg.) will write

1. me sentaré	=	I will sit down
2. te sentarás	=	you (fam. sg.) will sit down
3. nos sentaremos	=	we will sit down
4. se sentarán	=	they will sit down
5. os sentaréis	=	you (fam. pl.) will sit down
6. se sentará	=	you (pol. sg.) will sit down

B.

1. Viajaré a *David*.
2. Ese programa comenzará a las ocho de la noche.
3. Ella se duchará mañana.
4. Rosalba y yo compraremos nuestros libros mañana.
5. Me levantaré tarde mañana.
6. Veré el *Museo afro-antillano* el viernes.
7. A ella no le gustará esa película.
8. Él dormirá hasta el mediodía.
9. Asistiré a la universidad el año próximo.
10. Ellos llegarán a la una de la tarde.

Exercise Set 11-2

A.

1. cabré	=	I will fit
2. cabrás	=	you (fam. sg.) will fit
3. cabremos	=	we will fit
4. cabrán	=	they will fit
5. cabréis	=	you (fam. pl.) will fit
6. cabrá	=	you (pol. sg.) will fit

1. saldré	=	I will leave
2. saldremos	=	Raquel and I will leave
3. saldrán	=	you (pol. pl.) will leave
4. saldrán	=	they will leave
5. saldréis	=	you (fam. pl.) will leave
6. saldrás	=	you (fam. sg.) will leave

1. diré	=	I will say/tell
2. dirás	=	you (fam. sg.) will say/tell
3. diremos	=	we will say/tell
4. dirán	=	they will say/tell
5. diréis	=	you (fam. pl.) will say/tell
6. dirá	=	you (pol. sg.) will say/tell

1. habré	=	I will have	
2. habrás	=	you (fam. sg.) will have	
3. habremos	=	we will have	
4. habrán	=	they will have	
5. habréis	=	you (fam. pl.) will have	
6. habrá	=	you (pol. sg.) will have	

1. podré	=	I will be able
2. podrás	=	you (fam. sg.) will be able
3. podremos	=	we will be able
4. podrán	=	they will be able
5. podréis	=	you (fam. pl.) will be able
6. podrá	=	you (pol. sg.) will be able

1. vendré	=	I will come
2. vendrás	=	you (fam. sg.) will come
3. vendremos	=	we will come
4. vendrán	=	they will come
5. vendréis	=	you (fam. pl.) will come
6. vendrá	=	you (pol. sg.) will come

1. sabré	=	I will know
2. sabrás	=	you (fam. sg.) will know
3. sabremos	=	we will know
4. sabrán	=	they will know
5. sabréis	=	you (fam. pl.) will know
6. sabrá	=	you (pol. sg.) will know

1. pondré	=	I will put/place
2. pondrás	=	you (fam. sg.) will put/place
3. pondremos	=	we will put/place
4. pondrán	=	they will put/place
5. pondréis	=	you (fam. pl.) will put/place
6. pondrá	=	you (pol. sg.) will put/place

B.

1. ¿Cuándo llegará Elena?
2. Serán las seis pronto.
3. Habrá mucha gente allí.
4. Ellos tendrán que estar aquí.
5. Saldrás mañana.
6. Vendremos a las once de la mañana.
7. Cristina sabrá la respuesta.
8. Mis padres querrán ver las fotos de Panamá.
9. El *balboa* valdrá más en el futuro.
10. Uds. pondrán los libros en la mesa.
11. Hará frío en diciembre.
12. Ellos irán a *la Isla Contadora*.
13. Estará nublado mañana.
14. Diré la verdad.

Exercise Set 11-3

A.

1. f   2. a   3. e   4. b   5. h   6. c   7. d   8. g

B.

1. ¿Dónde estará él?
2. Habrá que conjugar más verbos.
3. Ellos saldrán mañana.
4. Tendré que trabajar por la tarde.
5. Querrás ver la última película.
6. Habrá muchos estudiantes en esta clase.
7. Le diremos la verdad a ella.
8. Uds. tendrán que comprar más comida.
9. ¿Qué día será?
10. Iré a la casa de Pablo.

C.

1. llegarán
2. romperé
3. cubrirás
4. será
5. estarán
6. irá
7. tendré
8. habrá
9. sabré
10. conoceré
11. podremos
12. querrá
13. hará
14. diré
15. valdrá
16. saldré
17. vendremos
18. te vestirás

Crossword Puzzle 11

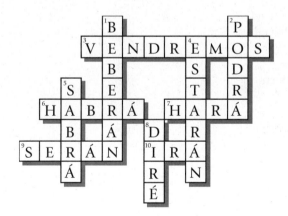

CHAPTER 12
Exercise Set 12-1

A.

1.	habré trabajado	=	I will have worked
2.	habrás trabajado	=	you (fam. sg.) will have worked
3.	habremos trabajado	=	we will have worked
4.	habrán trabajado	=	they will have worked
5.	habréis trabajado	=	you (fam. pl.) will have worked
6.	habrá trabajado	=	you (pol. sg.) will have worked

1.	habré creído	=	I will have believed
2.	habremos creído	=	Raquel and I will have believed
3.	habrán creído	=	you (pol. pl.) will have believed
4.	habrán creído	=	they will have believed
5.	habréis creído	=	you (fam. pl.) will have believed
6.	habrás creído	=	you (fam. sg.) will have believed

1.	habré decidido	=	I will have decided
2.	habrás decidido	=	you (fam. sg.) will have decided
3.	habremos decidido	=	we will have decided
4.	habrán decidido	=	they will have decided
5.	habréis decidido	=	you (fam. pl.) will have decided
6.	habrá decidido	=	you (pol. sg.) will have decided

1.	me habré afeitado	=	I will have shaved
2.	te habrás afeitado	=	you (fam. sg.) will have shaved
3.	nos habremos afeitado	=	we will have shaved
4.	se habrán afeitado	=	they will have shaved
5.	os habréis afeitado	=	you (fam. pl.) will have shaved
6.	se habrá afeitado	=	you (pol. sg.) will have shaved

1.	habré sido	=	I will have been
2.	habrás sido	=	you (fam. sg.) will have been
3.	habremos sido	=	we will have been
4.	habrán sido	=	they will have been
5.	habréis sido	=	you (fam. pl.) will have been
6.	habrá sido	=	you (pol. sg.) will have been

1.	habré estado	=	I will have been
2.	habrás estado	=	you (fam. sg.) will have been
3.	habremos estado	=	we will have been
4.	habrán estado	=	they will have been
5.	habréis estado	=	you (fam. pl.) will have been
6.	habrá estado	=	you (pol. sg.) will have been

1.	habré hecho	=	I will have done/made
2.	habrás hecho	=	you (fam. sg.) will have done/made
3.	habremos hecho	=	we will have done/made
4.	habrán hecho	=	they will have done/made
5.	habréis hecho	=	you (fam. pl.) will have done/made
6.	habrá hecho	=	you (pol. sg.) will have done/made

B.

1. Cuando ellos se habrán casado, vivirán en San José.
2. Cuando Uds. se habrán graduado, ¿dónde trabajarán Uds.?
3. Cuando habré aprendido muchos verbos españoles, podré hablar español.
4. Ellos habrán llegado mañana por la mañana.
5. Él habrá leído este libro para mañana.

C.

1. veré, habré visto
2. cubrirás, habrás cubierto
3. abrirán, habrán abierto
4. serán, habrán sido
5. estaré, habré estado
6. diré, habré dicho
7. venderemos, habremos vendido
8. escribiremos, habremos escrito
9. te bañarás, te habrás bañado
10. tendréis, habréis tenido
11. pedirán, habrán pedido
12. volveremos, habremos vuelto
13. hará, habrá hecho
14. tendrán, habrán tenido
15. cerrarás, habrás cerrado
16. morirá, habrá muerto
17. pondré, habré puesto
18. habrá, habrá habido

Crossword Puzzle 12

CHAPTER 13
Exercise Set 13-1

A.

1. entraría	=	I would enter
2. entrarías	=	you (fam. sg.) would enter
3. entraríamos	=	we would enter
4. entrarían	=	they would enter
5. entraríais	=	you (fam. pl.) would enter
6. entraría	=	you (pol. sg.) would enter

1. temería	=	I would fear
2. temeríamos	=	Raquel and I would fear
3. temerían	=	you (pol. pl.) would fear
4. temerían	=	they would fear
5. temeríais	=	you (fam. pl.) would fear
6. temerías	=	you (fam. sg.) would fear

1. descubriría	=	I would discover
2. descubrirías	=	you (fam. sg.) would discover
3. descubriríamos	=	we would discover
4. descubrirían	=	they would discover
5. descubriríais	=	you (fam. pl.) would discover
6. descubriría	=	you (pol. sg.) would discover

1. me casaría	=	I would marry
2. te casarías	=	you (fam. sg.) would marry
3. nos casaríamos	=	we would marry
4. se casarían	=	they would marry
5. os casaríais	=	you (fam. pl.) would marry
6. se casaría	=	you (pol. sg.) would marry

B.

1. Yo hablaría más español, pero debo estudiar los verbos.
2. ¿Vendrías aquí, por favor?
3. Ellos pagarían el café, pero no tienen el dinero.
4. ¿Dónde encontrarías una tienda abierta a esta hora?
5. ¿Quién lo vería?
6. Ellos irían a la *Reserva Natural Volcán Mombacho*.
7. Yo iría de compras, pero no tengo dinero.
8. ¿Me darías ese diario?
9. ¿Se casaría él con Carmen?
10. Me gustaría aprender más verbos españoles.

Exercise Set 13-2

A.

1. querría	=	I would want
2. querrías	=	you (fam. sg.) would want
3. querríamos	=	we would want
4. querrían	=	they would want
5. querríais	=	you (fam. pl.) would want
6. querría	=	you (pol. sg.) would want

1. cabría	=	I would fit
2. cabríamos	=	Raquel and I would fit
3. cabrían	=	you (pol. pl.) would fit
4. cabrían	=	they would fit
5. cabríais	=	you (fam. pl.) would fit
6. cabrías	=	you (fam. sg.) would fit

1. haría	=	I would do/make
2. harías	=	you (fam. sg.) would do/make
3. haríamos	=	we would do/make
4. harían	=	they would do/make
5. haríais	=	you (fam. pl.) would do/make
6. haría	=	you (pol. sg.) would do/make

1. habría	=	I would have
2. habrías	=	you (fam. sg.) would have
3. habríamos	=	we would have
4. habrían	=	they would have
5. habríais	=	you (fam. pl.) would have
6. habría	=	you (pol. sg.) would have

1. podría	=	I would be able
2. podrías	=	you (fam. sg.) would be able
3. podríamos	=	we would be able
4. podrían	=	they would be able
5. podríais	=	you (fam. pl.) would be able
6. podría	=	you (pol. sg.) would be able

1. vendría	=	I would come
2. vendrías	=	you (fam. sg.) would come
3. vendríamos	=	we would come
4. vendrían	=	they would come
5. vendríais	=	you (fam. pl.) would come
6. vendría	=	you (pol. sg.) would come

1. tendría	=	I would have
2. tendrías	=	you (fam. sg.) would have
3. tendríamos	=	we would have
4. tendrían	=	they would have
5. tendríais	=	you (fam. pl.) would have
6. tendría	=	you (pol. sg.) would have

B.

1. Yo haría los ejercicios, pero estoy muy cansado/a.
2. Ella podría hacer ese trabajo.
3. Pondríamos los platos en la mesa.
4. Yo saldría por la noche.
5. Ud. sabría la respuesta.
6. Él diría que es tarde.
7. Uds. tendrían que estar aquí a tiempo.
8. El coche valdría diez mil *córdobas*.
9. ¿Querrías ir al teatro?
10. Llovería por la noche.
11. Dirías la verdad.

12. Los libros cabrían en el estante.
13. Sabríamos conjugar el tiempo condicional.
14. Habría que levantarse temprano.

Exercise Set 13-3

A.

1. Serían las cinco de la tarde cuando Lidia llegó.
2. Habría que trabajar toda la noche.
3. ¿Qué harías durante una tormenta?
4. Costaría mucho dinero.
5. Yo compraría otro coche, pero no tengo el dinero.

B.

1. irían
2. haría
3. dirías
4. serían
5. estaría
6. cantaría

7. tendrías
8. habría
9. sabría
10. encontraría
11. podría
12. querríamos

13. haría
14. cerraría
15. valdría
16. saldrían
17. vendría
18. te afeitarías

Crossword Puzzle 13

CHAPTER 14
Exercise Set 14-1

A.

1. habría llegado	=	I would have arrived
2. habrías llegado	=	you (fam. sg.) would have arrived
3. habríamos llegado	=	we would have arrived
4. habrían llegado	=	they would have arrived

5. habríais llegado	=	you (fam. pl.) would have arrived
6. habría llegado	=	you (pol. sg.) would have arrived

1. habría comprendido	=	I would have understood
2. habríamos comprendido	=	Raquel and I would have understood
3. habrían comprendido	=	you (pol. pl.) would have understood
4. habrían comprendido	=	they would have understood
5. habríais comprendido	=	you (fam. pl.) would have understood
6. habrías comprendido	=	you (fam. sg.) would have understood

1. habría discutido	=	I would have discussed
2. habrías discutido	=	you (fam. sg.) would have discussed
3. habríamos discutido	=	we would have discussed
4. habrían discutido	=	they would have discussed
5. habríais discutido	=	you (fam. pl.) would have discussed
6. habría discutido	=	you (pol. sg.) would have discussed

1. me habría quitado	=	I would have taken off
2. te habrías quitado	=	you (fam. sg.) would have taken off
3. nos habríamos quitado	=	we would have taken off
4. se habrían quitado	=	they would have taken off
5. os habríais quitado	=	you (fam. pl.) would have taken off
6. se habría quitado	=	you (pol. sg.) would have taken off

1. habría sido	=	I would have been
2. habrías sido	=	you (fam. sg.) would have been
3. habríamos sido	=	we would have been
4. habrían sido	=	they would have been
5. habríais sido	=	you (fam. pl.) would have been
6. habría sido	=	you (pol. sg.) would have been

1. habría estado	=	I would have been
2. habrías estado	=	you (fam. sg.) would have been
3. habríamos estado	=	we would have been
4. habrían estado	=	they would have been
5. habríais estado	=	you (fam. pl.) would have been
6. habría estado	=	you (pol. sg.) would have been

1. habría hecho	=	I would have done/made
2. habrías hecho	=	you (fam. sg.) would have done/made
3. habríamos hecho	=	we would have done/made
4. habrían hecho	=	they would have done/made
5. habríais hecho	=	you (fam. pl.) would have done/made
6. habría hecho	=	you (pol. sg.) would have done/made

B.

1. Yo habría ido a la fiesta, pero yo no tenía el tiempo.
2. Mis padres habrían ido a Honduras, pero ellos no tenían el dinero.
3. Yo habría ido con ellos, pero yo tenía que estudiar.
4. Ellos se habrían levantado temprano, pero durmieron tarde.
5. Él habría comprado el coche, pero costó demasiado.

C.

1. iría, habría ido
2. escribirías, habrías escrito
3. dirían, habrían dicho
4. seríais, habríais sido
5. estarían, habrían estado
6. diría, habría dicho
7. comeríamos, habríamos comido
8. viviríamos, habríamos vivido
9. te lavarías, te habrías lavado
10. tendría, habría tenido
11. morirían, habrían muerto
12. volvería, habría vuelto
13. vendrías, habrías venido
14. sabría, habría sabido
15. conocería, habría conocido
16. resolvería, habría resuelto
17. pondríamos, habríamos puesto
18. habría, habría habido

Crossword Puzzle 14

REVIEW 3
Review Exercise Set 3-1

A.

1.
bailaré, leeré, asistiré
bailarás, leerás, asistirás
bailará, leerá, asistirá
bailaremos, leeremos, asistiremos
bailaréis, leeréis, asistiréis
bailarán, leerán, asistirán

2.
contaré, perderé, sugeriré
contarás, perderás, sugerirás
contará, perderá, sugerirá
contaremos, perderemos, sugeriremos
contaréis, perderéis, sugeriréis
contarán, perderán, sugerirán

3.
cabré, pondré, diré
cabrás pondrás, dirás
cabrá, pondrá, dirá
cabremos, pondremos, diremos
cabréis, pondréis, diréis
cabrán, pondrán, dirán

4.
habré, saldré, haré
habrás, saldrás, harás
habrá, saldrá, hará
habremos, saldremos, haremos
habréis, saldréis, haréis
habrán, saldrán, harán

5.
seré, estaré, me bañaré
serás, estarás, te bañarás
será, estará, se bañará
seremos, estaremos, nos bañaremos
seréis, estaréis, os bañaréis
serán, estarán, se bañarán

B.

habré hecho, habré sido, habré estado
habrás hecho, habrás sido, habrás estado
habrá hecho, habrá sido, habrá estado
habremos hecho, habremos sido, habremos estado
habréis hecho, habréis sido, habréis estado
habrán hecho, habrán sido, habrán estado

C.

1.
buscaría, metería, sufriría
buscarías, meterías, sufrirías
buscaría, metería, sufriría
buscaríamos, meteríamos, sufriríamos
buscaríais, meteríais, sufriríais
buscarían, meterían, sufrirían

2.
podría, tendría, querría
podrías, tendrías, querrías
podría, tendría, querría
podríamos, tendríamos, querríamos
podríais, tendríais, querríais
podrían, tendrían, querrían

3.
sabría, vendría, sería
sabrías, vendrías, serías
sabría, vendría, sería
sabríamos vendríamos, seríamos
sabríais, vendríais, seríais
sabrían, vendrían, serían

D.

habría estado, habría tenido, habría sido
habrías estado, habrías tenido, habrías sido
habría estado, habría tenido, habría sido
habríamos estado, habríamos tenido, habríamos sido
habríais estado, habríais tenido, habríais sido
habrían estado, habrían tenido, habrían sido

Review Exercise Set 3-2

A.

1. a   2. b   3. a   4. a   5. b   6. a   7. a   8. a   9. a   10. a

B.

1. valdrán   2. irán   3. hará   4. estará   5. tendrá
6. asistiría   7. regresarán   8. estudiaría

CHAPTER 15
Exercise Set 15-1

A.

1. … mire	=	… I look at, I am looking at, I may look at
2. … mires	=	… you (fam. sg.) look at, you are looking at, you may look at
3. … miremos	=	… we look at, we are looking at, we may look at
4. … miren	=	… they look at, they are looking at, they may look at
5. … miréis	=	… you (fam. pl.) look at, you are looking at, you may look at
6. … mire	=	… you (pol. sg.) look at, you are looking at, you may look at

1. … crea	=	… I believe, I am believing, I may believe
2. … creamos	=	… Raquel and I believe, Raquel and I are believing, Raquel and I may believe
3. … crean	=	… you (pol. pl.) believe, you are believing, you may believe
4. … crean	=	… they believe, they are believing, they may believe
5. … creáis	=	… you (fam. pl.) believe, you are believing, you may believe
6. … creas	=	… you (fam. sg.) believe, you are believing, you may believe

1. … discuta	=	… I discuss, I am discussing, I may discuss
2. … discutas	=	… you (fam. sg.) discuss, you are discussing, you may discuss
3. … discutamos	=	… we discuss, we are discussing, we may discuss
4. … discutan	=	… they discuss, they are discussing, they may discuss
5. … discutáis	=	… you (fam. pl.) discuss, you are discussing, you may discuss
6. … discuta	=	… you (pol. sg.) discuss, you are discussing, you may discuss

1. … me duche	=	… I take a shower, I am taking a shower, I may take a shower
2. … te duches	=	… you (fam. sg.) take a shower, you are taking a shower, you may take a shower
3. … nos duchemos	=	… we take a shower, we are taking a shower, we may take a shower
4. … se duchen	=	… they take a shower, they are taking a shower, they may take a shower
5. … os duchéis	=	… you (fam. pl.) take a shower, you are taking a shower, you may take a shower
6. … se duche	=	… you (pol. sg.) take a shower, you are taking a shower, you may take a shower

1. … cuente	=	… I count, I am couting, I may count
2. … cuentes	=	… you (fam. sg.) count, you are counting, you may count
3. … contemos	=	… we count, we are counting, we may count
4. … cuenten	=	… they count, they are counting, they may count
5. … contéis	=	… you (fam. pl.) count, you are counting, you may count
6. … cuente	=	… you (pol. sg.) count, you are counting, you may count

1. … niegue	=	… I deny, I am denying, I may deny
2. … niegues	=	… you (fam. sg.) deny, you are denying, you may deny
3. … neguemos	=	… we deny, we are denying, we may deny
4. … nieguen	=	… they deny, they are denying, they may deny
5. … neguéis	=	… you (fam. pl.) deny, you are denying, you may deny
6. … niegue	=	… you (pol. sg.) deny, you are denying, you may deny

1. … muera	=	… I die, I am dying, I may die
2. … mueras	=	… you (fam. sg.) die, you are dying, you may die
3. … muramos	=	… we die, we are dying, we may die
4. … mueran	=	… they die, they are dying, they may die
5. … muráis	=	… you (fam. pl.) die, you are dying, you may die
6. … muera	=	… you (pol. sg.) die, you are dying, you may die

1. … consiga	=	… I get/obtain, I am getting/obtaining, I may get/obtain
2. … consigas	=	… you (fam. sg.) get/obtain, you are getting/obtaining, you may get/obtain
3. … consigamos	=	… we get/obtain, we are getting/obtaining, we may get/obtain
4. … consigan	=	… they get/obtain, they are getting/obtaining, they may get/obtain
5. … consigáis	=	… you (fam. pl.) get/obtain, you are getting/obtaining, you may get/obtain
6. … consiga	=	… you (pol. sg.) get/obtain, you are getting/obtaining, you may get/obtain

1. … rija	=	… I rule, I am ruling, I may rule
2. … rijas	=	… you (fam. sg.) rule, you are ruling, you may rule
3. … rijamos	=	… we rule, we are ruling, we may rule
4. … rijan	=	… they rule, they are ruling, they may rule
5. … rijáis	=	… you (fam. pl.) rule, you are ruling, you may rule
6. … rija	=	… you (pol. sg.) rule, you are ruling, you may rule

1. … obtenga	=	… I obtain, I am obtaining, I may obtain
2. … obtengas	=	… you (fam. sg.) obtain, you are obtaining, you may obtain
3. … obtengamos	=	… we obtain, we are obtaining, we may obtain
4. … obtengan	=	… they obtain, they are obtaining, they may obtain
5. … obtengáis	=	… you (fam. pl.) obtain, you are obtaining, you may obtain
6. … obtenga	=	… you (pol. sg.) obtain, you are obtaining, you may obtain

1. … componga	=	… I compose, I am composing, I may compose
2. … compongas	=	… you (fam. sg.) compose, you are composing, you may compose
3. … compongamos	=	… we compose, we are composing, we may compose
4. … compongan	=	… they compose, they are composing, they may compose
5. … compongáis	=	… you (fam. pl.) compose, you are composing, you may compose
6. … componga	=	… you (pol. sg.) compose, you are composing, you may compose

1. … sea	=	… I am, I may be
2. … seas	=	… you (fam. sg.) are, you may be
3. … seamos	=	… we are, we may be
4. … sean	=	… they are, they may be
5. … seáis	=	… you (fam. pl.) are, you may be
6. … sea	=	… you (pol. sg.) are, you may be

1. … esté	=	… I am, I may be
2. … estés	=	… you (fam. sg.) are, you may be
3. … estemos	=	… we are, we may be
4. … estén	=	… they are, they may be
5. … estéis	=	… you (fam. pl.) are, you may be
6. … esté	=	… you (pol. sg.) are, you may be

1. … venza	=	… I conquer, I am conquering, I may conquer
2. … venzas	=	… you (fam. sg.) conquer, you are conquering, you may conquer
3. … venzamos	=	… we conquer, we are conquering, we may conquer
4. … venzan	=	… they conquer, they are conquering, they may conquer
5. … venzáis	=	… you (fam. pl.) conquer, you are conquering, you may conquer
6. … venza	=	… you (pol. sg.) conquer, you are conquering, you may conquer

Exercise Set 15-2

A.

1. Concepción duda que vaya a nevar.
2. Quiero que Oscar esté aquí a las nueve de la noche.
3. Sientes que el examen sea mañana.
4. A menos que trabajemos mucho, nunca terminaremos.
5. Es fácil que Rosa tenga el libro.
6. Él no cree que haya muchos estudiantes allí hoy.
7. Espero que Julio lea la novela.
8. No hay nadie que sepa usar esta computadora.
9. Ella escibirá la composición antes de que ella mire la televisión.
10. Es posible que él pague la cuenta.
11. Tan pronto como yo llegue a San Salvador, iré al *Museo Nacional de Antropología David F. Guzmán.*
12. Ellos no están seguros de que sus padres estén en El Salvador.
13. Es difícil que Laura conozca a Enrique.
14. Quiero que Salvador vea este programa.
15. Mis padres insisten en que mi hermano asista a la clase.

Exercise Set 15-3

A.

1. Es probable que ellos vayan a San Salvador.
2. Mi esposa niega que yo tenga sueño.
3. Temo que mis amigos beban mucha cerveza.
4. Espero que este libro sea muy bueno.
5. No creo que Pablo estudie demasiado.
6. Es una lástima que mis niños estén enfermos.
7. Prefiero que ellos jueguen al fútbol.
8. Tal vez Aurora venga mañana.
9. Es fácil que yo vaya a El Salvador.
10. No pienso que haga calor.

Exercise Set 15-4

A.

1. Con tal de que haga fresco, nadaremos en *La Libertad.*
2. Tal vez ellos vayan a Centroamérica. ¿Sabes?
3. Es posible que esté nublado.

4. Puede ser que ella esté cansada.
5. Iré a la biblioteca cuando Mario llegue.
6. Quiero que él escriba una carta.
7. Él no cree que haya una tormenta.
8. Temo que Esperanza no sepa la respuesta.

Exercise Set 15-5

A.

1. tenga
2. pongamos
3. pidáis
4. sean
5. estés
6. vayan

7. sepa
8. conozcamos
9. durmamos
10. corrijan
11. haya
12. digamos

13. traigas
14. te bañes
15. busque
16. salgan
17. venga
18. haga

Crossword Puzzle 15

CHAPTER 16
Exercise Set 16-1

A.

1. ... pagara	=	... I paid, I was paying, I might pay
2. ... pagaras	=	... you (fam sg.) paid, you were paying, you might pay
3. ... pagáramos	=	... we paid, we were paying, we might pay
4. ... pagaran	=	... they paid, they were paying, they might pay
5. ... pagarais	=	... you (fam. pl.) paid, you were paying, you might pay
6. ... pagara	=	... you (pol. sg.) paid, you were paying, you might pay

| 1. ... cometiera | = | ... I committed, I was committing, I might commit |
| 2. ... cometiéramos | = | ... Raquel and I committed, Raquel and I were committing, Raquel and I might commit |

3. ... cometieran   =   ... you (pol. pl.) committed, you were committing, you might commit
4. ... cometieran   =   ... they committed, they were committing, they might commit
5. ... cometierais   =   ... you (fam. pl.) committed, you were committing, you might commit
6. ... cometieras   =   ... you (fam. sg.) committed, you were committing, you might commit

1. ... permitiera   =   ... I permitted, I was permitting, I might permit
2. ... permitieras   =   ... you (fam sg.) permitted, you were permitting, you might permit
3. ... permitiéramos   =   ... we permitted, we were permitting, we might permit
4. ... permitieran   =   ... they permitted, they were permitting, they might permit
5. ... permitierais   =   ... you (fam. pl.) permitted, you were permitting, you might permit
6. ... permitiera   =   ... you (pol. sg.) permitted, you were permitting, you might permit

1. ... me quitara   =   ... I took off, I was taking off, I might take off
2. ... te quitaras   =   ... you (fam. sg.) took off, you were taking off, you might take off
3. ... nos quitáramos   =   ... we took off, we were taking off, we might take off
4. ... se quitaran   =   ... they took off, they were taking off, they might take off
5. ... os quitarais   =   ... you (fam. pl.) took off, you were taking off, you might take off
6. ... se quitara   =   ... you (pol. sg.) took off, you were taking off, you might take off

1. ... confesara   =   ... I confessed, I was confessing, I might confess
2. ... confesaras   =   ... you (fam. sg.) confessed, you were confessing, you might confess
3. ... confesáramos   =   ... we confessed, we were confessing, we might confess
4. ... confesaran   =   ... they confessed, they were confessing, they might confess
5. ... confesarais   =   ... you (fam. pl.) confessed, you were confessing, you might confess
6. ... confesara   =   ... you (pol. sg.) confessed, you were confessing, you might confess

1. ... volara   =   ... I flew, I was flying, I might fly
2. ... volaras   =   ... you (fam. sg.) flew, you were flying, you might fly
3. ... voláramos   =   ... we flew, we were flying, we might fly
4. ... volaran   =   ... they flew, they were flying, they might fly
5. ... volarais   =   ... you (fam. pl.) flew, you were flying, you might fly
6. ... volara   =   ... you (pol. sg.) flew, you were flying, you might fly

1. ... midiera   =   ... I measured, I was measuring, I might measure
2. ... midieras   =   ... you (fam. sg.) measured, you were measuring, you might measure
3. ... midiéramos   =   ... we measured, we were measuring, we might measure
4. ... midieran   =   ... they measured, they were measuring, they might measure
5. ... midierais   =   ... you (fam. pl.) measured, you were measuring, you might measure
6. ... midiera   =   ... you (pol. sg.) measured, you were measuring, you might measure

1. ... muriera   =   ... I died, I was dying, I might die
2. ... murieras   =   ... you (fam. sg.) died, you were dying, you might die
3. ... nuriéramos   =   ... we died, we were dying, we might die
4. ... murieran   =   ... they died, they were dying, they might die
5. ... murierais   =   ... you (fam. pl.) died, you were dying, you might die
6. ... muriera   =   ... you (pol. sg.) died, you were dying, you might die

1. ... fuera   =   ... I was, I might be
2. ... fueras   =   ... you (fam. sg.) were, you might be
3. ... fuéramos   =   ... we were, we might be
4. ... fueran   =   ... they were, they might be
5. ... fuerais   =   ... you (fam. pl.) were, you might be
6. ... fuera   =   ... you (pol. sg.) were, you might be

1. ... tuviera	=	... I had, I was having, I might have
2. ... tuvieras	=	... you (fam. sg.) had, you were having, you might have
3. ... tuviéramos	=	... we had, we were having, we might have
4. ... tuvieran	=	... they had, they were having, they might have
5. ... tuvierais	=	... you (fam. pl.) had, you were having, you might have
6. ... tuviera	=	... you (pol. sg.) had, you were having, you might have

1. ... hiciera	=	... I did/made, I was doing/making, I might do/make
2. ... hicieras	=	... you (fam. sg.) did/made, you were doing/making, you might do/make
3. ... hiciéramos	=	... we did/made, we were doing/making, we might do/make
4. ... hicieran	=	... they did/made, they were doing/making, they might do/make
5. ... hicierais	=	... you (fam. pl.) did/made, you were doing/making, you might do/make
6. ... hiciera	=	... you (pol. sg.) did/made, you were doing/making, you might do/make

1. ... fuera	=	... I went, I was going, I might go
2. ... fueras	=	... you (fam. sg.) went, you were going, you might go
3. ... fuéramos	=	... we went, we were going, we might go
4. ... fueran	=	... they went, they were going, they might go
5. ... fuerais	=	... you (fam. pl.) went, you were going, you might go
6. ... fuera	=	... you (pol. sg.) went, you were going, you might go

1. ... estuviera	=	... I was, I might be
2. ... estuvieras	=	... you (fam. sg.) were, you might be
3. ... estuviéramos	=	... we were, we might be
4. ... estuvieran	=	... they were, they might be
5. ... estuvierais	=	... you (fam. pl.) were, you might be
6. ... estuviera	=	... you (pol. sg.) were, you might be

1. ... condujera	=	... I drove, I was driving, I might drive
2. ... condujeras	=	... you (fam. sg.) drove, you were driving, you might drive
3. ... condujéramos	=	... we drove, we were driving, we might drive
4. ... condujeran	=	... they drove, they were driving, they might drive
5. ... condujerais	=	... you (fam. pl.) drove, you were driving, you might drive
6. ... condujera	=	... you (pol. sg.) drove, you were driving, you might drive

Exerise Set 16-2

A.

1. Si yo tuviera el dinero, yo compraría un boleto de lotería.
2. Yo leería *El señor presidente* de Miguel Ángel Asturias, si yo tuviera el tiempo.
3. Si no hiciera tanto calor, yo correría en el parque.
4. Si yo no estuviera tan cansado/a, yo limpiaría la casa.
5. Ella vendría si pudiera.
6. Compraríamos la casa si no fuera tan cara.
7. Iríamos a *Quetzaltenango*, si no trabajáramos.
8. Si ella estuviera aquí, ella estaría contenta.
9. Si Uds. vieran *Chichecastenango*, Uds no se irían.
10. Si hubiera más tiempo, yo iría a Guatemala más a menudo.

B.

1. Ellos dudaban que yo empezara a estudiar.
2. Él temía que quisieras ir a Guatemala.
3. Esperábamos que no hiciera mucho frío.

4. Yo no estaba seguro/a de que Ud. tuviera razón.
5. Era increíble que ellos no miraran la televisión.
6. Ella no creía que yo supiera hablar español.
7. Era fácil que fuéramos a la capital de Guatemala.
8. Yo no pensaba que lloviera mucho.

Exercise Set 16-3

A.

1. ¿Adónde quisieras ir?
2. ¿Quisiera Ud. mostrarme la novela del nuevo escritor guatemalteco?
3. ¿Pudiera Ud. conducirme a la universidad?
4. Mi esposa quisiera ver las ruinas mayas.
5. ¿Pudiera Ud. repetir la pregunta?

Exercise Set 16-4

A.

1. Me sentí como si yo estuviera enfermo/a.
2. Toqué la guitarra como si yo fuera *Andrés Segovia*.
3. Él pinta como si fuera *Pablo Picasso*.
4. Yo escribía como si fuera *Miguel Ángel Asturias*.
5. Hablas como si fueras de Guatemala.
6. Él condujo como si él estuviera borracho.

Exercise Set 16-5

A.

1. compre, comprara	7. conozca, conociera	13. caiga, cayera
2. crean, creyeran	8. sepa, supiera	14. se duche, se duchara
3. vivamos, viviéramos	9. muráis, murierais	15. ponga, pusiera
4. seamos, fuéramos	10. digan, dijeran	16. salgamos, saliéramos
5. esté, estuviera	11. haya, hubiera	17. vengas, vinieras
6. vaya, fuera	12. corrijas, corrigieras	18. haga, hiciera

Crossword Puzzle 16

CHAPTER 17
Exercise Set 17-1

A.

1.	... haya estudiado	=	... I have studied, I may have studied
2.	... hayas estudiado	=	... you (fam. sg.) have studied, you may have studied
3.	... hayamos estudiado	=	... we have studied, we may have studied
4.	... hayan estudiado	=	... they have studied, they may have studied
5.	... hayáis estudiado	=	... you (fam. pl.) have studied, you may have studied
6.	... haya estudiado	=	... you (pol. sg.) have studied, you may have studied

1.	... haya corrido	=	... I have run, I may have run
2.	... hayamos corrido	=	... Raquel and I have run, Raquel and I may have run
3.	... hayan corrido	=	... you (pol. pl.) have run, you may have run
4.	... hayan corrido	=	... they have run, they may have run
5.	... hayáis corrido	=	... you (fam. pl.) have run, you may have run
6.	... hayas corrido	=	... you (fam. sg.) have run, you may have run

1.	... haya sufrido	=	... I have suffered, I may have suffered
2.	... hayas sufrido	=	... you (fam. sg.) have suffered, you may have suffered
3.	... hayamos sufrido	=	... we have suffered, we may have suffered
4.	... hayan sufrido	=	... they have suffered, they may have suffered
5.	... hayáis sufrido	=	... you (fam. pl.) have suffered, you may have suffered
6.	... haya sufrido	=	... you (pol. sg.) have suffered, you may have suffered

1.	... me haya afeitado	=	... I have shaved, I may have shaved
2.	... te hayas afeitado	=	... you (fam. sg.) have shaved, you may have shaved
3.	... nos hayamos afeitado	=	... we have shaved, we may have shaved
4.	... se hayan afeitado	=	... they have shaved, they may have shaved
5.	... os hayáis afeitado	=	... you (fam. pl.) have shaved, you may have shaved
6.	... se haya afeitado	=	... you (pol. sg.) have shaved, you may have shaved

B.

1. Es difícil que ella haya leído *El laberinto de la soledad* de Octavio Paz.
2. Dudo que Eulalia haya llegado.
3. Antonio no conoce a nadie que haya visto esa película.
4. En caso de que Clara haya llegado, tendré que ir al aeropuerto.
5. Temes que ella ya haya vuelto a casa.
6. Es posible que ellos hayan comido todos los dulces.
7. No creo que Benito haya hecho su tarea.
8. Ellos niegan que Blas haya ido a México.
9. Espero que Gloria no haya estado enferma.
10. César no cree que Amalia haya hecho el trabajo.

C.

1. a   2. b   3. a   4. b   5. b

Exercise Set 17-2

A.

1. Es fantástico que yo haya comenzado a estudiar.
2. Dudo que mi hermana haya llegado.
3. Temo que haya hecho mal tiempo.
4. Mi esposo niega que yo haya leído esos poemas.
5. Espero que mi amiga haya visto esa película.
6. Es posible que haya estado nublado.
7. Ella no cree que me haya divertido mucho.
8. Es increíble que mi hermano haya pagado la cuenta.
9. Es improbable que te hayas levantado muy tarde.
10. Puede ser que ellos hayan estado aquí por dos semanas.

Exercise Set 17-3

A.

1. hayamos tenido	7. hayan sabido	13. hayan traído
2. hayáis podido	8. haya conocido	14. se haya duchado
3. haya pedido	9. hayas dormido	15. haya creído
4. haya sido	10. haya roto	16. haya abierto
5. hayamos estado	11. haya habido	17. hayas cubierto
6. haya ido	12. haya dicho	18. haya hecho

Crossword Puzzle 17

CHAPTER 18
Exercise Set 18-1

A.

1. ... hubiera dudado	=	... I had doubed, I might have doubted
2. ... hubieras dudado	=	... you (fam. sg.) had doubted, you might have doubted
3. ... hubiéramos dudado	=	... we had doubted, we might have doubted
4. ... hubieran dudado	=	... they had doubted, they might have doubted
5. ... hubierais dudado	=	... you (fam. pl.) had doubted, you might have doubted
6. ... hubiera dudado	=	... you (pol. sg.) had doubted, you might have doubted

1. ... hubiera bebido	=	... I had drunk, I might have drunk
2. ... hubiéramos bebido	=	... Raquel and I had drunk, Raquel and I might have drunk
3. ... hubieran bebido	=	... you (pol. pl.) had drunk, you might have drunk
4. ... hubieran bebido	=	... they had drunk, they might have drunk
5. ... hubierais bebido	=	... you (fam. pl.) had drunk, you might have drunk
6. ... hubiera bebido	=	... you (pol. sg.) had drunk, you might have drunk

1. ... hubiera escrito	=	... I had written, I might have written
2. ... hubiéramos escrito	=	... Raquel and I had written, Raquel and I might have written
3. ... hubieran escrito	=	... you (pol. pl.) had written, you might have written
4. ... hubieran escrito	=	... they had written, they might have written
5. ... hubierais escrito	=	... you (fam. pl.) had written, you might have written
6. ... hubiera escrito	=	... you (pol. sg.) had written, you might have written

1. ... me hubiera duchado	=	... I had showered, I might have showered
2. ... te hubieras duchado	=	... you (fam. sg.) had showered, you might have showered
3. ... nos hubiéramos duchado	=	... we had showered, we might have showered
4. ... se hubieran duchado	=	... they had showered, they might have showered
5. ... os hubierais duchado	=	... you (fam. pl.) had showered, you might have showered
6. ... se hubiera duchado	=	... you (pol. sg.) had showered, you might have showered

B.

1. Yo dudaba que hubieras leído *Tres tristes tigres* de Guillermo Cabrera Infante.
2. ¿Era fácil que ellos hubieran visto a mi hermana?
3. Yo no creía que Beatriz hubiera visitado La Habana.
4. El profesor esperaba que sus estudiantes hubieran conjugado los verbos en el pluscuamperfecto del subjuntivo.
5. Negaste que yo hubiera estado en Cuba.
6. No había nadie que hubiera visto las noticias en la televisión.
7. Era difícil que Julio hubiera estado muy ocupado.
8. Era posible que mis padres hubieran llegado tarde.
9. Inés no creía que mi hermano hubiera roto los platos.
10. Era probable que hubiera habido un accidente allí.

C.

1. Si yo hubiera tenido el tiempo, yo habría ido a Cuba.
2. Bárbara habría conducido a la universidad, si ella hubiera sabido conducir.
3. Si yo hubiera sabido del examen, yo habría leído el libro.
4. Si Oscar hubiera comprado un boleto, él habría ganado la lotería.
5. Si Rosa no hubiera estado cansada, ella no habría tenido un accidente.
6. Si no hubiera llovido tanto, habríamos ido a la fiesta.

7. Si Raúl no hubiera mentido, él no habría ido a la cárcel.
8. Si me hubieras dicho la verdad, no habría estado tan enojado/a.
9. Si no hubiera habido tantos problemas, habríamos llegado a tiempo.
10. Si yo hubiera recordado mi cartera, yo habría podido pagar la cuenta.

Exercise Set 18-2

A.

1. hayáis tenido, hubierais tenido
2. haya cantado, hubiera cantado
3. haya hecho, hubiera hecho
4. hayan estado, hubieran estado
5. hayamos sido, hubiéramos sido
6. hayan ido, hubieran ido
7. haya sabido, hubiera sabido
8. haya conocido, hubiera conocido
9. hayas muerto, hubieras muerto
10. hayamos abierto, hubiéramos abierto
11. haya habido, hubiera habido
12. hayas dicho, hubieras dicho
13. haya caído, hubiera caído
14. se haya bañado, se hubiera bañado
15. haya creído, hubiera creído
16. haya abierto, hubiera abierto
17. hayan cubierto, hubieran cubierto
18. haya medido, hubiera medido

Crossword Puzzle 18

REVIEW 4
Review Exercise Set 4-1

A.

1.	2.	3.
… tome, venda, abra	… tenga, salga, vea	… dé, vaya, sepa
… tomes, vendas, abras	… tengas, salgas, veas	… des, vayas, sepas
… tome, venda, abra	… tenga, salga, vea	… dé, vaya, sepa
… tomemos, vendamos, abramos	… tengamos, salgamos, veamos	… demos, vayamos, sepamos
… toméis, vendáis, abráis	… tengáis, salgáis, veáis	… deis, vayáis, sepáis
… tomen, vendan, abran	… tengan, salgan, vean	… den, vayan, sepan

4.
… haya, esté, sea
… hayas, estés, seas
… haya, esté, sea
… hayamos, estemos, seamos
… hayáis, estéis, seáis
… hayan, estén, sean

5.
… duerma, pida, me vista
… duermas, pidas, te vistas
… duerma, pida, se vista
… durmamos, pidamos, nos vistamos
… durmáis, pidáis, os vistáis
… duerman, pidan, se vistan

6.
… pague, saque, rece
… pagues, saques, reces
… pague, saque, rece
… paguemos, saquemos, recemos
… paguéis, saquéis, recéis
… paguen, saquen, recen

7.
… recoja, finja, siga
… recojas, finjas, sigas
… recoja, finja, siga
… recojamos, finjamos, sigamos
… recojáis, finjáis, sigáis
… recojan, finjan, sigan

B.

1.
… cantara, corriera, escribiera
… cantaras, corrieras, escribieras
… cantara, corriera, escribiera
… cantáramos, corriéramos, escribiéramos
… cantarais, corrierais, escribierais
… cantaran, corrieran, escribieran

2.
… hiciera, fuera, estuviera
… hicieras, fueras, estuvieras
… hiciera, fuera, estuviera
… hiciéramos, fuéramos, estuviéramos
… hicierais, fuerais, estuvierais
… hicieran, fueran, estuvieran

3.
… dijera, fuera, quisiera
… dijeras, fueras, quisieras
… dijera, fuera, quisiera
… dijéramos, fuéramos, quisiéramos
… dijerais, fuerais, quisierais
… dijeran, fueran, quisieran

C.
… haya corrido, haya admitido
… hayas corrido, hayas admitido
… haya corrido, haya admitido
… hayamos corrido, hayamos admitido
… hayáis corrido, hayáis admitido
… hayan corrido, hayan admitido

D.
… hubiera bailado, hubiera comido
… hubieras bailado, hubieras comido
… hubiera bailado, hubiera comido
… hubiéramos bailado, hubiéramos comido
… hubierais bailado, hubierais comido
… hubieran bailado, hubieran comido

Review Exercise Set 4-2

A.

1. b   2. a   3. a   4. a   5. a   6. b   7. a   8. a

B.

1. pueda   2. pudiera   3. tenga   4. tuviera   5. sepan
6. supieran   7. pudiera   8. hubiera podido

CHAPTER 19
Exercise Set 19-1

A.

1. ¡Compra!	=	Buy!
2. ¡Bebe!	=	Drink!
3. ¡Abre!	=	Open!
4. ¡Ten!	=	Have!
5. ¡Sal!	=	Leave!

B.

1. ¡No prepares!	=	Don't prepare!
2. ¡No corras!	=	Don't run!
3. ¡No cubras!	=	Don't cover!
4. ¡No hagas!	=	Don't do!
5. ¡No vengas!	=	Don't come!

C.

1. ¡Comprad!	=	Buy!
2. ¡Bebed!	=	Drink!
3. ¡Abrid!	=	Open!
4. ¡Tened!	=	Hold!
5. ¡Salid!	=	Leave!

D.

1. ¡No preparéis!	=	Don't prepare!
2. ¡No corráis!	=	Don't run!
3. ¡No cubráis!	=	Don't cover!
4. ¡No hagáis!	=	Don't do!
5. ¡No vengáis!	=	Don't come!

Exercise Set 19-2

A.

1. ¡Aféitate!
2. ¡No me lo des!
3. ¡Estúdiala!
4. ¡Léemelo!
5. ¡No te acuestes!
6. ¡ No me la digas!
7. ¡No la leas!
8. ¡Cómpralo!

Exercise Set 19-3

A.

1.	¡Cante!	=	Sing!
2.	¡Coma!	=	Eat!
3.	¡Asista!	=	Attend!
4.	¡Sea!	=	Be!
5.	¡Dé!	=	Give!

B.

1.	¡No compre!	=	Don't buy!
2.	¡No beba!	=	Don't drink!
3.	¡No viva!	=	Don't live!
4.	¡No sepa!	=	Don't know!
5.	¡No vaya!	=	Don't go!

C.

1.	¡Busquen!	=	Look for!
2.	¡Lean!	=	Read!
3.	¡Abran!	=	Open!
4.	¡Estén!	=	Be!
5.	¡Vuelvan!	=	Return!

D.

1.	¡No preparen!	=	Don't prepare!
2.	¡No crean!	=	Don't believe!
3.	¡No admitan!	=	Don't admit!
4.	¡No comiencen!	=	Don't begin!
5.	¡No protejan!	=	Don't protect!

Exercise Set 19-4

A.

1. ¡Acuéstense!
2. ¡Cómpremela!
3. ¡No se lo muestre a ella!
4. ¡Cántensela a ella!
5. ¡Levántese!
6. ¡No me miren!
7. ¡Escríbasela a ellos!
8. ¡Muéstreselos a ella!

Exercise Set 19-5

A.

1. ¡Comencemos!
2. ¡No vayamos!
3. ¡Toquemos la guitarra!
4. ¡Seamos simpáticos!
5. ¡No conjuguemos los verbos en español!

Exercise Set 19-6

A.

1. ¡Cantémosela a ella!
2. ¡No le digamos nada a él!
3. ¡Levantémonos tarde!
4. ¡Hagámoslo!
5. ¡No se lo demos a él!
6. ¡Mostrémosela a ellos!
7. ¡No nos acostemos!
8. ¡No lo bebamos!

Exercise Set 19-7

A.

1. ¡Compra!, ¡No compres!
2. ¡Bebe!, ¡No bebas!
3. ¡Vive!, ¡No vivas!
4. ¡Sé!, ¡No seas!
5. ¡Está!, ¡No estés!
6. ¡Haz!, ¡No hagas!
7. ¡Ten!, ¡No tengas!
8. ¡Dúchate!, ¡No te duches!
9. ¡Busca!, ¡No busques!
10. ¡Encuentra!, ¡No encuentres!

B.

1. ¡Compre!, ¡No compre!
2. ¡Beba!, ¡No beba!
3. ¡Viva!, ¡No viva!
4. ¡Sea!, ¡No sea!
5. ¡Esté!, ¡No esté!
6. ¡Haga!, ¡No haga!
7. ¡Tenga!, ¡No tenga!
8. ¡Dúchese!, No se duche!
9. ¡Busque!, ¡No busque!
10. ¡Encuentre!, ¡No encuentre!

C.

1. ¡Hablemos!, ¡No hablemos!
2. ¡Comamos!, ¡No comamos!
3. ¡Escribamos!, ¡No escribamos!
4. ¡Divirtámonos!, ¡No nos divirtamos!

Crossword Puzzle 19

CHAPTER 20
Exercise Set 20-1

A.

1. La casa fue construida por José.
2. Las puertas fueron abiertas por los hombres.
3. La novela será leída por Ana.
4. La canción fue cantada por los estudiantes.
5. *Don Quijote* fue escrito por Cervantes.

B.

1. La comida fue comida por los niños.
2. La casa fue construida por los obreros.
3. La ventana fue rota por los hombres.
4. La cuenta fue pagada por Carlos.
5. Los libros fueron comprados por los estudiantes.

Exercise Set 20-2

A.

1. Se habla español aquí.
2. Se dice que llueve.
3. Se venden periódicos aquí.
4. Se pagan las cuentas los viernes.
5. Se deben comer tres comidas todos los días.

Exercise Set 20-3

A.

1. Después de leer el periódico, Marisol comenzó a trabajar.
2. Caminando, vi a Pablo.
3. Terminado el partido, fuimos al restaurante.
4. Leyendo la revista, Lidia bebió café.
5. Antes de salir, Juan compró un libro.

Crossword Puzzle 20

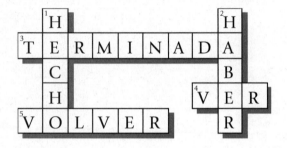

REVIEW 5
Review Exercise Set 5-1

A.

1.
compra, vende, asiste
compre, venda, asista
compremos, vendamos, asistamos
comprad, vended, asistid
compren, vendan, asistan

2.
di, haz, está
diga, haga, esté
digamos, hagamos, estemos
decid, haced, estad
digan, hagan, estén

3.
dúchate, sé, ten
dúchese, sea, tenga
duchémonos, seamos, tengamos
duchaos, sed, tened
dúchense, sean, tengan

B.

no compres, no vendas, no asistas
no compre, no venda, no asista
no compremos, no vendamos, no asistamos
no compréis, no vendáis, no asistáis
no compren, no vendan, no asistan

no digas, no hagas, no estés
no diga, no haga, no esté
no digamos, no hagamos, no estemos
no digáis, no hagáis, no estéis
no digan, no hagan, no estén

no te duches, no seas, no tengas
no se duche, no sea, no tenga
no nos duchemos, no seamos, no tengamos
no os duchéis, no seáis, no tengáis
no se duchen, no sean, no tengan

Review Exercise Set 5-2

A.

1. a   2. a   3. b   4. b   5. b   6. b   7. b   8. a   9. a   10. b

B.

1. *Don Quijote* fue escrito por Cervantes.
2. La comida es preparada por Pablo.
3. Los libros fueron vendidos por Teresa.

C.

1. Se dice que llueve.
2. Se habla italiano aquí.
3. Se venden coches aquí.

D.

1. Caminando, vi a Eva.
2. Antes de estudiar, Sara escuchó la música.
3. Después de mirar la televisión, me acosté.

ENGLISH-SPANISH VOCABULARY

A

a little bit   un poco
a lot   mucho
A.M.   de la mañana
about (concerning)   sobre
about to   para (with estar)
absent   ausente
accident   accidente (*m.*)
according to   según
accordion   acordeón (*m.*)
(to) ache   doler (ue)
action   acción (*f.*)
active   activo/-a
address   dirección (*f.*)
(to) admire   admirar
(to) admit   admitir
advisable (to be)   convenir
(to) advise   aconsejar
afraid (to be)   (tener) miedo
   (de)
after   después (de)
afternoon   tarde (*f.*)
afterwards   después
ago   hace
(to) agree (with)   (estar) de
   acuerdo (con)
airplane   avión (*m.*)
airport   aeropuerto (*m.*)
alert (to be)   (ser) despierto/-a
alive (to be)   (estar) vivo/-a
all   todo/-a
all day   todo el día
all night   toda la noche
almost   casi
aloud   en voz alta
already   ya
also   también
although   aunque
always   siempre
American   americano/-a
amused (to be)   (estar)
   divertido/-a
and   y
Andes   Andes (*m. pl.*)
angry   enojado/-a
animal   animal (*m.*)
(to) annoy   molestar
another   otro/-a

answer   respuesta (*f.*)
(to) appeal to (food)   apetecer
(to) appear   aparecer
(to) appear to   parecer
appetizing (to be)   apetecer
(to) approve   aprobar (ue)
April   abril
archaeology   arqueología (*f.*)
Argentinean   argentino/-a
(to) arrest   detener
(to) arrive   llegar (a)
art   arte (*m.*)
artichoke   alcachofa (*f.*)
as a child   de niño (*m.*); de
   niña (*f.*)
as soon as   en cuanto, tan
   pronto como
ashamed (to be)   (tener)
   vergüenza (de)
(to) ask for   pedir (i, i)
at   a, en
at home   en casa
at this moment   en este
   momento
at this time   a esta hora
At what time?   ¿A qué hora?
(to) attend   asistir (a)
attic   desván (*m.*)
(to) attract   atraer
attractive   atractivo/-a
August   agosto
author   autor (*m.*)
(to) authorize   autorizar
avenue   avenida (*f.*)
awake (to be)   (estar)
   despierto/-a

B

bad   malo/-a; mal (before *m. sg.*
   noun)
bad mood (to be in a)   (estar)
   de mal humor
bad weather   (hacer) mal
   tiempo
balboa   balboa (*m.*)
   (Panamanian unit of currency)
ballet   ballet (*m.*)
baseball   béisbol (*m.*)

basement   sótano (*m.*)
basketball   baloncesto (*m.*)
bathe (oneself)   bañarse
bathing suit   traje de baño (*m.*)
bathroom   cuarto de baño (*m.*)
bay   bahía (*f.*)
(to) be   estar (location, short
   duration)
(to) be   ser (enduring)
(to) be … years old   tener …
   años
(to) be able   poder (ue)
(to) be sufficient   bastar
(to) be sure (of)   estar seguro
   (de)
(to) be worth   valer
beach   playa (*f.*)
bean   frijol (*m.*)
beautiful   bello/-a; hermoso/-a
beauty   belleza (*f.*)
because   porque
bedroom   alcoba (*f.*)
beer   cerveza (*f.*)
before   antes (de); antes de
   que + clause
(to) beg   rogar (ue)
(to) begin   comenzar (ie);
   empezar (ie)
(to) believe   creer
(to) belong (to)   pertencer (a)
beloved   querido/-a
better   mejor
bill   cuenta (*f.*)
birthplace   lugar de nacimiento
   (*m.*)
(to) bite   morder (ue)
black   negro/-a
blackboard   pizarra (*f.*)
blond   rubio/-a
blue   azul
(to) boil   hervir (ie, i)
Bolivian   boliviano/-a
book   libro (*m.*)
border   frontera (*f.*)
bored (to be)   (ser) aburrido/-a
boring (to be)   (estar)
   aburrido/-a
(to) bother   molestar
boxer   boxeador (*m.*)

boyfriend   novio (*m.*)
brand-new (to be)   (ser) nuevo/-a
bread   pan (*m.*)
(to) break   romper
brick   ladrillo (*m.*)
bright (in color)   (ser) vivo/-a
(to) bring   traer
(to) bring back   retraer
brother   hermano (*m.*)
brown   marrón
brunette   moreno/-a
(to) brush (oneself)   cepillarse
(to) build   construir
bullfight   corrida de toros (*f.*)
(to) burst out laughing   dar una carcajada
bus   autobús (*m.*)
busy   ocupado/-a
but   pero
(to) buy   comprar
by   por, de

C

(to) call   llamar
(to) call (oneself)   llamarse
camera   cámara (*f.*)
(to) can   poder (ue)
canal   canal (*m.*)
capital   capital (*f.*)
car   coche (*m.*)
cards   naipes (*m. pl.*)
(to) care for   cuidar
carefully   con cuidado
Caribbean   caribe
(to) carry   llevar
casino   casino (*m.*)
castle   castillo (*m.*)
Catalan   catalán
cave   cueva (*f.*)
CD   disco compacto (*m.*)
cello   violoncelo (*m.*)
center   centro (*m.*)
Central America   Centroamérica
certain   cierto/-a
chair   silla (*f.*)
chapter   capítulo (*m.*)
(to) chat   charlar
checkers   damas (*f. pl.*)
chess   ajedrez (*m.*)
child   niño (*m.*); niña (*f.*)
Chilean   chileno/-a

church   iglesia (*f.*)
city   ciudad (*f.*)
civil   civil
class   clase (*f.*)
(to) classify   clasificar
classroom   aula de clase (*f.*)
(to) clean   limpiar
clever (to be)   (ser) listo/-a
(to) climb   subir (a)
(to) close   cerrar (ie)
clothes   ropa (*f.*)
clothing   ropa (*f.*)
cloudy (to be)   (estar) nublado
coffee   café (*m.*)
cold   frío (*m.*)
cold (to be)   (tener) frío
cold (to be) (weather)   (hacer) frío
Colombian   colombiano/-a
colón   colón (*m.*) (monetary unit in Costa Rica)
color   color (*m.*)
(to) comb (one's hair)   peinarse
(to) come   venir
(to) commit   cometer
(to) compete   competir (i, i)
(to) complete   acabar, terminar
(to) compose   componer
composition   composición (*f.*)
computer   computadora (*f.*)
concert   concierto (*m.*)
(to) conclude   concluir
condition   condición (*f.*)
(to) confess   confesar (ie)
congrio   congrio (*m.*) (Chilean eel)
(to) conjugate   conjugar
conjugation   conjugación (*f.*)
(to) conquer   vencer
(to) consent   consentir (ie, i)
constantly   constantemente
(to) contain   contener
contained (to be)   caber
(to) contract   contraer
(to) contribute   contribuir
(to) convert   convertir (ie, i)
(to) convince   convencer
convinced (to be) (of)   estar convencido/-a (de que)
(to) cook   cocinar
cool (to be) (weather)   (hacer) fresco

córdoba   córdoba (*m.*) (Nicaraguan unit of currency)
(to) correct   corregir (i, i)
corvina   corvina (*f.*) (Peruvian sea bass)
(to) cost   costar (ue)
Costa Rican   costarricense
(to) count (on)   contar (con) (ue)
country   país (*m.*)
court   corte (*f.*)
cousin   primo (*m.*); prima (*f.*)
(to) cover   cubrir
covered (with)   cubierto (de)
(to) create   crear
(to) create a good impression   caer bien a
crop   cosecha (*f.*)
Cuban   cubano/-a
culture   cultura (*f.*)

D

(to) dance   bailar
(to) darn   zurcir
date   fecha (*f.*)
daughter   hija (*f.*)
day   día (*m.*)
day before yesterday   anteayer
dead   muerto/-a
December   diciembre
(to) decide   decidir
(to) deduce   deducir
(to) defeat   vencer
(to) defend   defender (ie)
(to) delight   encantar
(to) demand   exigir (i, i)
(to) deny   negar (ie)
(to) describe   describir
(to) deserve   merecer
(to) destroy   destruir
(to) detain   detener
(to) die   morir (ue, u)
difficult   difícil
dining room   comedor (*m.*)
dinner   cena (*f.*)
(to) direct   dirigir (i, i)
direction   dirección (*f.*)
(to) disappear   desaparecer
(to) discover   descubrir
(to) discuss   discutir
dish   plato (*m.*)
(to) display   lucir
(to) dissuade   retraer

(to) distract distraer
divorced divorciado/-a
(to) do hacer
doctor doctor (*m.*); doctora (*f.*)
dog perro (*m.*)
dollar dólar (*m.*)
Dominican dominicano/-a
Dominican Republic La República Dominicana
Don't you? ¿Verdad?
door puerta (*f.*)
(to) doubt dudar
downtown centro (*m.*)
dream sueño (*m.*)
(to) dream (of) soñar (con) (ue)
(to) dress (oneself) vestirse (i, i)
dressed (in) vestido/-a (de)
(to) drink beber
(to) drive conducir, manejar
(to) drizzle lloviznar
drunk borracho/-a
(to) dry (oneself) secarse

E

e-mail correo electrónico (*m.*)
early temprano
easily fácilmente
East este (*m.*)
(to) eat comer
(to) eat breakfast desayunar
(to) eat dinner cenar
(to) eat lunch almorzar (ue)
Ecuadorean ecuatoriano/-a
efficient eficiente
egg huevo (*m.*)
eight ocho
eighteen dieciocho
eighty ochenta
(to) elect elegir (i, i)
elegant elegante
elevator ascensor (*m.*)
eleven once
(to) embrace abrazar
employee empleado (*m.*); empleada (*f.*)
enchanting to (to be) encantar
enemy enemigo (*m.*)
English inglés (*m.*)
(to) enjoy gozar (de)

(to) enjoy (oneself) divertirse (i, i)
enormous enorme
enough (to be) bastar
(to) enter entrar (en)
entertaining (to be) (ser) divertido/-a
essay ensayo (*m.*)
(to) establish establecer
even if aunque
even though aunque
every cada
every day todos los días
every month todos los meses
every night todas las noches
every week todas las semanas
every year todos los años
everything todo
evident evidente
evil malo/-a; mal (before *m. sg.* noun)
exactly en punto (time)
exam examen (*m.*); exámenes (*m. pl.*)
excellent excelente
Excuse me Perdón
exercise ejercicio (*m.*)
(to) exercise ejercer
(to) exert ejercer
exhaustive (to be) (ser) completo/-a
exhibition exhibición (*f.*)
(to) exist existir
expensive caro/-a

F

fácil easy
fairy hada (*f.*)
fall otoño (*m.*); caer
(to) fall asleep dormirse (ue, u)
(to) fall down caerse
falls cataratas (*f. pl.*)
familiar with (to be) conocer
famous famoso/-a
fantastic fantástico/-a
far (from) lejos de
(to) fascinate fascinar
fast rápido
fat gordo/-a
father padre (*m.*)
favorite favorito/-a
fear miedo (*m.*); temer

February febrero
(to) feel sentirse (ie, i)
(to) feel like tener ganas (de)
(to) feel sorry sentir (ie, i)
few pocos/-as
fifteen quince
fifty cincuenta
film película (*f.*)
(to) find encontrar (ue); hallar
(to) finish acabar; terminar
(to) fire despedir (i, i)
first primero/-a
fish pescado (*m.*)
(to) fit caber
five cinco
five hundred quinientos/-as
(to) flash (with lightning) relampaguear
(to) flee huir
flight vuelo (*m.*)
(to) flow fluir
flower flor (*f.*)
(to) fly volar (ue)
folkloric folclórico/-a
(to) follow seguir (i, i)
food comida (*f.*)
foolish tonto/-a
football fútbol americano (*m.*)
for para, por (see Chapter 5 use of para and por)
for that reason por eso
force fuerza (*f.*)
forty cuarenta
four cuatro
four hundred cuatrocientos/-as
fourteen catorce
French francés (*m.*)
frequently con frecuencia, frecuentemente
Friday viernes
friend amiga (*f.*); amigo (*m.*)
from de
(to) fry freír (i, i)
full lleno/-a
funny cómico/-a
furniture muebles (*m. pl.*)

G

gallery galería (*f.*)
game juego (*m.*); partido (*m.*)

garage   garaje (*m.*)
generally   generalmente
generous   generoso/-a
(to) get   conseguir (i, i); obtener
(to) get angry   enojarse
(to) get undressed   desvestirse (i, i)
(to) get up   levantarse
gift   regalo (*m.*)
girlfriend   novia (*f.*)
(to) give   dar
glad (to be)   alegrarse (de)
gladly   de buenas ganas
glass   copa (*f.*) (wine); vaso (*m.*) (drinking)
(to) go   ir (a)
(to) go away   irse
(to) go downtown   ir al centro
(to) go out with   salir (con)
(to) go shopping   ir de compras
(to) go to bed   acostarse (ue)
(to) go up   subir
golf   golf (*m.*)
good   bueno/-a; buen (before *m. sg.* noun)
good (by nature) (to be)   (ser) bueno/-a
good for (to be)   convenir
good mood (to be in a)   (estar) de buen humor
good weather   (hacer) buen tiempo
good-bye   adiós
(to) graduate   graduarse
grandfather   abuelo (*m.*)
grandmother   abuela (*f.*)
(to) grasp   coger
gray   gris
great   gran
green   verde
(to) greet   saludar
(to) grow   crecer
Guarani   guaraní
Guatemalan   guatemalteco/-a
guilty   culpable
guitar   guitarra (*f.*)

H

hair   pelo (*m.*)
half   medio/-a
hand   mano (*f.*)

(to) hand over   entregar
(to) hang (up)   colgar (ue)
happy   alegre
hardworking   trabajador/-a
hat   sombrero (*m.*)
hatred   odio (*m.*)
(to) have   haber (auxiliary); tener (possess)
(to) have dinner   cenar
(to) have just   acabar de (+ infinitive)
(to) have lunch   almorzar (ue)
(to) have to   tener que (+ infinitive)
head   cabeza (*f.*)
(to) hear   oír
heat   calor (*m.*)
(to) help   ayudar
her   su
here   aquí
(to) hinder   impedir (i, i)
his   su
historic; historical   histórico/-a
hockey   hockey (*m.*)
(to) hold   contener
home   casa (*f.*)
homework   tarea (*f.*)
Honduran   hondureño/-a
(to) hope   esperar
hot (to be)   tener calor
hot (to be) (weather)   hacer calor
hotel   hotel (*m.*)
hour   hora (*f.*)
house   casa (*f.*)
How long?   ¿Cuánto tiempo hace que …?; ¿Desde cuándo?
How long had…?   ¿Cuánto tiempo hacía que …?; ¿Desde cuándo …?
How many?   ¿Cuántos/-as?
How much?   ¿Cuánto/-a?
How nice!   ¡Qué bueno!
(to) hug   abrazar
humid (to be)   (estar) húmedo
hundred   cien(to)
hunger   hambre (*f.*)
hungry (to be)   (tener) hambre
hurry   prisa (*f.*)
hurry (to be in a)   (tener) prisa
husband   esposo (*m.*)

I

I hope that …   Ojalá que …
idea   idea (*f.*)
if   si
(to) impede   impedir (i, i)
importance   importancia (*f.*)
important   importante
important (to be)   (ser) importante; importar
impossible   imposible
improbable   improbable
in case that   en caso de que
in good health (to be)   (estar) bueno/-a
in order that   para que + clause
in order to   para
in surplus (to be)   sobrar
in the afternoon   por la tarde
in the evening   por la noche
in the habit of (to be)   soler (ue)
in the morning   por la mañana
Incan   incásico/-a
(to) include   incluir
incredible   increíble
(to) induce   inducir
(to) infer   deducir
(to) influence   influir
ingredient   ingrediente (*m.*)
intelligent   inteligente
intend   pensar (ie) (+ infinitive)
interesting   interesante
interesting (to be)   (ser) interesante
(to) introduce   introducir
irresponsible   irresponsable
island   isla (*f.*)
It is necessary   Hay que …
It may be   Puede ser …
Italian   italiano (*m.*)
itinerary   itinerario (*m.*)

J

jacket   chaqueta (*f.*)
jail   cárcel (*f.*)
January   enero
jewel   joya (*f.*)
job   puesto (*m.*); trabajo (*m.*); empleo (*m.*)
July   julio
(to) jump about   dar saltos
June   junio

jungle   selva (f.)
(to) justify   justificar

K

key   llave (f.)
kind   amable
(to) kiss   besar
kitchen   cocina (f.)
(to) know (fact)   saber
(to) know (someone)   conocer
(to) know how   saber (+
   infinitive)

L

lacking (to be)   faltar
lake   lago (m.)
language   idioma (m.); lengua
   (f.)
last month   el mes pasado
last night   anoche
last week   la semana pasada
last year   el año pasado
late   tarde
latest   último/-a
(to) laugh   reír (i, i)
lawyer   abogado (m.); abogada
   (f.)
lazy   perezoso/-a
(to) learn   aprender (a)
(to) leave   partir
(to) leave (from a place)   salir
   (de)
(to) leave (something)   dejar
left over (to be)   sobrar
lempira   lempira (m.)
   (monetary unit in Honduras)
lesson   lección (f.)
letter   carta (f.)
library   biblioteca (f.)
(to) lie   mentir (ie, i)
(to) lie down   yacer
lier   mentiroso/-a
light   luz (f.)
(to) light   encender (ie)
(to) light up   lucir
like   como; caer bien a
like new (to be)   (estar)
   nuevo/-a
likely (to be)   (ser) probable;
   (ser) fácil
(to) listen to   escuchar
literature   literatura (f.)

little   poco
(to) live   vivir
lively (to be)   (ser) vivo/-a
living room   sala de estar
   (f.)
long   largo/-a
(to) look at   mirar
(to) look at (oneself)   mirarse
(to) look for   buscar
(to) lose   perder (ie)
lottery   lotería (f.)
love   querer (ie) (a)
luck   suerte (f.)
lucky (to be)   (tener) suerte
lunch   almuerzo (m.)

M

magazine   revista (f.)
(to) maintain   mantener
(to) make   hacer
(to) make no difference   dar
   igual
man   hombre (m.)
many   muchos/-as
map   mapa (m.)
March   marzo
married (to)   casado/-a (con)
(to) marry   casarse (con)
marvelous   maravilloso
mate   mate (m.)
matter   asunto (m.)
May   mayo
Mayan   maya
meal   comida (f.)
(to) measure   medir (i, i)
(to) mend   zurcir
(to) merit   merecer
Mexican   mexicano/-a
midnight   medianoche (f.)
milk   leche (f.)
miner   minero/-a
mining   minero/-a
minute   minuto (m.)
mirror   espejo (m.)
Miss   señorita (f.)
missing (to be)   faltar
mixed grill   parillada (f.)
moment   momento (m.)
Monday   lunes
money   dinero (m.)
month   mes (m.)
Moorish   moro/-a
more   más

morning   mañana (f.)
mother   madre (f.)
(to) move   mover (ue)
movie   película (f.)
Mr.   señor (m.)
Mrs.   señora (f.)
museum   museo (m.)
music   música (f.)
my   mi

N

named (to be)   llamarse
nation   nación (f.)
natural   natural
near   cerca de
nearby   cerca
necessary   necesario
(to) need   necesitar
neighborhood   barrio (m.)
never   jamás, nunca
new   nuevo/-a
news   noticias (f. pl.)
newspaper   periódico (m.)
next week   la semana próxima
next year   el año próximo
Nicaraguan   nicaragüense
nice   amable; simpático/-a
night   noche (f.)
nine   nueve
nine hundred   novecientos/-as
nineteen   diecinueve
ninety   noventa
no   ningún(o)/-a; before m. sg.
   noun ningún; no
no one   nadie
noon   mediodía (m.)
North   norte (m.)
not   no
notebook   cuaderno (m.)
nothing   nada
(to) notice   advertir (ie, i)
novel   novela (f.)
November   noviembre
now   ahora
nowadays   hoy en día

O

obelisk   obelisco (m.)
(to) obey   obedecer
(to) obtain   conseguir (i, i);
   obtener
obvious   obvio

October   octubre
of   de
Of course!   ¡Claro que sí!
(to) offer   ofrecer
office   oficina (f.)
often   a menudo; muchas veces
old   viejo/-a
olive oil   aceite de oliva (m.)
on   en
on call (to be)   (estar) de
   guardia
on time   a tiempo
on vacation   de vacaciones
one   uno
one must   hay que
open   abierto/-a
(to) open   abrir
(to) oppose   oponerse (a)
orange   anaranjado/-a
(to) order   pedir (i, i)
organization   organización (f.)
other   otro/-a
ought   deber
our   nuestro/-a
(to) owe   deber

P

P.M.   de la tarde, de la
   noche
Pacific Ocean   Océano Pacífico
package   paquete (m.)
painful (to be)   doler (ue)
(to) paint   pintar
painting   cuadro (m.); pintura
   (f.)
palace   palacio (m.)
Panamanian   panameño/-a
paper   papel (m.)
Paraguayan   paraguayo/-a
parents   padres (m. pl.)
park   parque (m.)
party   fiesta (f.)
past   pasado (m.)
(to) pay attention to   hacer
   caso a
(to) pay for   pagar
peaceful   pacífico/-a
pen   bolígrafo
peninsula   península (f.)
people   gente (f. sg.); personas
   (f. pl.)
perfectly   perfectamente
perhaps   acaso, quizá(s), tal vez

(to) permit   permitir
(to) persuade   inducir
Peruvian   peruano/-a
peso   peso (m.) (unit of money
   in several countries)
phone   teléfono (m.); llamar
   por teléfono
photo   foto (f.)
piano   piano (m.)
(to) pick up   recoger
pink   rosado/-a
pity   lástima (f.)
pizza   pizza (f.)
place   lugar (m.)
(to) place   poner
plague   plaga (f.)
plain   llano (m.)
plan   plan (m.)
(to) plan   pensar (ie)
   (+ infinitive)
plane   avión (m.)
planet   planeta (m.)
plastic   plástico (m.)
(to) play (game)   jugar (a) (ue)
(to) play (instrument)   tocar
(to) play the role of   hacer el
   papel de
plaza   plaza (f.)
pleasant   agradable
(to) please   agradar
pleasing to (to be)   gustar (a)
pluperfect   pluscuamperfecto
   (m.)
poem   poema (m.)
poetry   poesía (f.)
point   punto (m.)
police (force)   policía (f.)
pool   billar (m.)
popular   popular
(to) possess   poseer
possible   posible
(to) practice   practicar
praise   alabanza (f.)
(to) pray   rezar; rogar (ue)
(to) prefer   preferir (ie, i)
(to) prepare   preparar
(to) pretend   fingir
preterit   pretérito (m.)
pretty   bonito/-a; lindo/-a
(to) prevent   impedir (i, i)
prize   premio (m.)
probable   probable
problem   problema (m.)
program   programa (m.)

(to) protect   proteger
(to) prove   probar (ue)
(to) provide   proveer
provided that   con tal de que
province   provincia (f.)
prudently   prudentemente
Puerto Rican   puertorriqueño/-a
pupil   alumno (m.); alumna (f.)
purse   bolsa (f.)
(to) put   poner
(to) put (into)   meter (en)
(to) put on (clothing)   ponerse
   (la ropa)
puzzle   rompecabezas (m.)
pyramid   pirámide (f.)

Q

quarter   cuarto (time)
question   pregunta (f.)
quickly   rápido
quiet (to be)   (ser) callado/-a

R

radio   radio (f.)
(to) rain   llover (ue)
rainy (to be)   (estar) lluvioso
(to) read   leer
ready (to be)   (estar) listo/-a
ready to   listo/-a para
(to) realize   darse cuenta (de)
reason   razón (f.)
(to) receive   recibir
(to) recognize   reconocer
(to) recommend   recomendar
   (ie)
red   rojo/-a
red-haired   pelirrojo/-a
(to) reduce   reducir
region   región (f.)
regional   regional
(to) regret   lamentar; sentir
   (ie, i)
regularly   regularmente
relative   pariente (m.)
(to) remain   quedarse
(to) remember   recordar (ue);
   acordarse (ue) (de)
(to) repeat   repetir (i, i)
(to) request   pedir (i, i); rogar
   (ue)
(to) require   exigir (i, i)
(to) resolve   resolver (ue)

responsible   responsable
(to) rest   descansar; resto (*m*.)
restaurant   restaurante (*m*.)
(to) return   regresar (a); volver (ue) (a)
(to) return (something) devolver (ue)
ridiculous   ridículo
right (to be)   tener razón
right now   ahora mismo
(to) ring   sonar (ue)
romance   romance
room   cuarto (*m*.)
route   ruta (*f*.)
routine   rutina (*f*.)
ruin   ruina (*f*.)
rule   regla (*f*.)
(to) run   correr

S

safe   seguro/-a
salsa (music)   salsa (*f*.)
Salvadoran   salvadoreño/-a
same   mismo/-a
Saturday   sábado
sausage   salchicha (*f*.)
(to) say   decir (i, i)
(to) scatter   esparcir
science fiction   ciencia ficción (*f*.)
(to) scream   dar voces
(to) scrub   fregar (ie)
sea   mar (*m*.)
season   estación (*f*.)
SEAT   SEAT (*m*.) (Spanish car)
secret   secreto (*m*.)
(to) see   ver
(to) see (oneself)   verse
(to) seem   parecer
(to) seize   coger
(to) select   escoger
selfish   egoísta
(to) sell   vender
(to) send   enviar; mandar
September   septiembre
serious   serio/-a
(to) serve   servir (i, i)
(to) set the table   poner la mesa
seven   siete
seven hundred   setecientos/-as
seventeen   diecisiete
seventy   setenta

several   varios/-as
(to) shake hands   dar la mano
shame   vergüenza (*f*.)
sharp   en punto (time)
(to) shave   afeitarse
shelf   estante (*m*.)
shop   tienda (*f*.)
short   bajo/-a
short story   cuento (*m*.)
should   deber
(to) shout   gritar
show   espectáculo (*m*.); cine (*m*.)
(to) show   mostrar (ue)
sick (to get)   enfermarse; enfermo/-a; malo/-a
side   lado (*m*.)
silent (to be)   (estar) callado/-a
similar (to)   semejante (a)
sincere   sincero/-a
(to) sing   cantar
sister   hermana (*f*.)
(to) sit down   sentarse (ie)
sitting   sentado/-a
six   seis
six hundred   seiscientos/-as
sixteen   dieciséis
sixty   sesenta
(to) ski   esquiar
(to) sleep   dormir (ue, u); sueño (*m*.)
sleepy (to be)   (tener) sueño
slender   delgado/-a
slowly   lentamente
(to) smoke   fumar
(to) snow   nevar (ie)
so much   tanto/-a; tanto (adverb)
soap opera   telenovela (*f*.)
soccer   fútbol (*m*.)
sofa   sofá (*m*.)
sol   sol (*m*.) (Peruvian monetary unit)
(to) solve   resolver (ue)
some   algun(o)/-a
someone   alguien
something   algo
somewhat   algo (with an adjective)
son   hijo (*m*.)
song   canción (*f*.)
(to) sound   sonar (ue); sonido (*m*.)
soup   sopa (*f*.)

South   sur (*m*.)
South America   Sudamérica
South American   sudamericano/-a
Southwest   suroeste (*m*.)
souvenir   recuerdo (*m*.)
Spaniard   español
Spanish   español
(to) speak   hablar
specific   específico/-a
(to) spend (money)   gastar
(to) spend (time)   pasar
spider   araña (*f*.)
spread   esparcir
spring   primavera (*f*.)
(to) spurt   surgir
(to) stand out   destacar
standing (to be)   (estar) de pie
(to) stay   quedarse
steak   churrasco (*m*.) (Argentina)
(to) stop   cesar (de)
store   tienda (*f*.)
storm   tormenta (*f*.); tempestad (*f*.)
street   calle (*f*.)
student   estudiante (*m*.); estudiante (*f*.)
(to) study   estudiar
(to) stumble (into)   tropezar (ie) (con)
stupendous   estupendo/-as
subject   tema (*m*.)
subjunctive   subjuntivo (*m*.)
(to) substitute   sustituir
(to) subtract   sustraer
subway   metro (*m*.)
(to) suffer   sufrir
(to) suggest   sugerir (ie, i)
(to) suit one's interest   convenir
suitcase   maleta (*f*.)
summer   verano (*m*.)
sun   sol (*m*.)
Sunday   domingo
sunny (weather) (to be)   (hacer) sol
(to) support   sostener
(to) suppose   suponer
sure of (to be)   (estar) seguro/-a (de)
sure to happen (to be)   (ser) seguro/-a
(to) surge   surgir
(to) sustain   sostener

T

(to) swallow   tragar
sweets   dulces (*m. pl.*)
(to) swim   nadar
Switzerland   Suiza

t-bone   bife de costilla (*m.*); biftec (*m.*)
table   mesa (*f.*)
(to) take (food)   tomar
(to) take a photo   sacar fotos
(to) take a shower   ducharse
(to) take a trip   hacer un viaje
(to) take a walk   dar un paseo
(to) take care of   cuidar
(to) take off (clothing)   quitarse
(to) take photos   sacar fotos
tall   alto/-a
tango   tango (*m.*)
task   tarea (*f.*)
(to) taste   probar (ue)
tea · té (*m.*)
teacher   profesor (*m.*); profesora (*f.*)
telephone   llamar por teléfono; teléono (*m.*)
(to) tell   decir (i, i)
(to) tell (a story)   contar (ue)
ten   diez
tennis   tenis (*m.*)
terrible   terrible
test   examen (*m.*) exámenes (*m. pl.*)
(to) test   probar (ue)
(to) thank   agradecer
Thank you   Gracias
that   aquel/-la (at a distance); ese/-a (near speaker and hearer); que (introduces a clause)
theater   teatro (*m.*)
their   su
then   entonces
there   allí
there are   hay
there is   hay
therefore   por eso
these   estos/-as
thing   cosa (*f.*)
(to) think (about)   pensar (ie) (en)
thirst   sed (*f.*)

thirsty (to be)   (tener) sed
thirteen   trece
thirty   treinta
thirty-one   treinta y un/o
this   este, esta
those   esos/-as (near speaker and hearer); aquellos/-as (at a distance)
thousand   mil
three   tres
three hundred   trescientos/-as
throat   garganta (*f.*)
(to) thunder   tronar (ue)
Thursday   jueves
ticket   boleto (*m.*)
time   tiempo (*m.*)
tired (to be)   (estar) cansado/-a
tired (to get)   cansarse
tiring (to be)   (ser) cansado/-a
(to) toast   tostar (ue)
tobacco   tabaco (*m.*)
today   hoy
tomorrow   mañana
too much   demasiado
tooth   diente (*m.*)
topic   tema (*m.*)
(to) touch   tocar
tourist   turista (*m./f.*)
(to) trace   trazar
(to) translate   traducir
(to) travel   viajar
trip   viaje (*m.*)
true   verdadero/-a
truth   verdad (*f.*)
Tuesday   martes
(to) turn on   encender (ie)
TV   telvisión (*f.*)
twelve   doce
twenty   veinte
twenty-eight   veintiocho
twenty-five   veinticinco
twenty-four   veinticuatro
twenty-nine   veintinueve
twenty-one   veintiun(o)/a
twenty-seven   veintisiete
twenty-six   veinteséis
twenty-three   veintitrés
twenty-two   veintidós
two   dos
two hundred   doscientos/-as

U

U.S. citizen   estadounidense
ugly   feo/-a

umbrella   paraguas (*m.*)
(to) understand   comprender; entender (ie)
(to) undo   deshacer
unfortunately   desafortunadamente
university   universidad (*f.*)
unless   a menos que
unlikely   difícil
unpleasant   antipático/-a
(to) untie (knot)   deshacer
until   hasta (que, with clause)
Uruguayan   uruguayo/-a

V

vacation   vacaciones (*f. pl.*)
vegetable   verdura (*f.*)
Venezuelan   venezolano/-a
verb   verbo (*m.*)
very   muy
visit   visita (*f.*)
(to) visit   visitar

W

(to) wait for   esperar
(to) wake up   despertarse (ie)
(to) walk   andar; caminar
wallet   cartera (*f.*)
(to) wander   vagar
(to) want   desear; querer (ie)
war   guerra (*f.*)
warm (to be)   (tener) calor
warmth   calor (*m.*)
(to) warn   advertir (ie, i)
(to) wash (dishes)   fregar (ie)
(to) wash (oneself)   lavarse
(to) watch   mirar; reloj (*m.*)
water   agua (*f.*)
(to) water   regar (ie)
waterfall   cascada (*f.*)
(to) wear   llevar
weather   tiempo (*m.*)
Wednesday   miércoles
week   semana (*f.*)
weight   peso (*m.*)
well   bien
What?   ¿Qué?
What time is it?   ¿Qué hora es?
When?   ¿Cuándo?
Where?   ¿Dónde?
Which (one)?   ¿Cuál?
Which (ones)?   ¿Cuáles?

while mientras
white blanco/-a
Who? ¿Quién? (*sg.*) ¿Quiénes?
  (*pl.*)
Why? ¿Por qué?
wife esposa (*f.*)
(to) win ganar
wind viento (*m.*)
window ventana (*f.*)
windy (to be) (hacer) viento
wine vino (*m.*)
winter invierno (*m.*)
(to) wish querer (ie)
with me conmigo
with you (*fam. sg.*) contigo
without sin que

witty (to be) (ser) listo/-a
woman mujer (*f.*)
wood madera (*f.*)
word palabra (*f.*)
work puesto (*m.*); trabajo (*m.*)
(to) work trabajar
worker obrero (*m.*); obrera (*f.*)
worried preocupado/-a
(to) worry (about)
  preocuparse (por)
(to) wrap (up) envolver (ue)
(to) write escribir
writer escritor (*m.*), escritora
  (*f.*)
writing escrito (*m.*)
wrong (to be) no tener razón

Y

year año (*m.*)
yellow amarillo/-a
yes sí
yesterday ayer
you (*fam. pl.*) vosotros/-as
you (*fam. sg.*) tú
you (*pol. pl.*) ustedes; Uds.
you (*pol. sg.*) usted; Ud.
young joven
your (*fam. pl.*) vuestro/-a
your (*fam. sg.*) tu
your (*pol. pl.*) su
your (*pol. sg.*) su

mindfulness practices

Cultivating Heart Centered Communities Where Students Focus and Flourish

Christine Mason

Michele M. Rivers Murphy

Yvette Jackson

foreword by Paul Liabenow

Solution Tree | Press

a division of

Solution Tree

555 North Morton Street
Bloomington, IN 47404
800.733.6786 (toll free) / 812.336.7700
FAX: 812.336.7790

email: info@SolutionTree.com
SolutionTree.com

Visit **go.SolutionTree.com/behavior** to download the free reproducibles in this book.

Printed in the United States of America

Library of Congress Cataloging-in-Publication Data

Names: Mason, Christine Y. (Christine Yvonne), 1949- author. | Rivers Murphy,
    Michele M., author. | Jackson, Yvette, author.
Title: Mindfulness practices : cultivating heart centered communities where
    students focus and flourish / Christine Mason, Michele M. Rivers Murphy,
    Yvette Jackson.
Description: Bloomington, IN : Solution Tree Press, 2018. | Includes
    bibliographical references and index.
Identifiers: LCCN 2018005654 | ISBN 9781947604063 (perfect bound)
Subjects: LCSH: Affective education. | School environment. | Behavior
    modification. | Mindfulness (Psychology)
Classification: LCC LB1072 .M37 2018 | DDC 370.15/34--dc23 LC record available at https://lccn.loc
    .gov/2018005654

Solution Tree
Jeffrey C. Jones, CEO
Edmund M. Ackerman, President

Solution Tree Press
President and Publisher: Douglas M. Rife
Editorial Director: Sarah Payne-Mills
Art Director: Rian Anderson
Managing Production Editor: Kendra Slayton
Senior Production Editor: Tonya Maddox Cupp
Senior Editor: Amy Rubenstein
Copy Editor: Ashante K. Thomas
Proofreader: Elisabeth Abrams
Text and Cover Designer: Laura Cox
Editorial Assistant: Sarah Ludwig

For all the children around the world:
may they be loved, may they be safe. This book is dedicated to
the thousands of children who valiantly persevere in spite of
the scars of the emotional trauma they experience because of
adverse experiences (physical, racial, social), coming to school
each and every day hoping to find a healing balm that will
strengthen their resilience and intellectual courage to achieve.
This book is also dedicated to the many selfless caregivers away
from home—our teachers, support staff, and educational leaders
who show up every day in our schools with strong conviction and
compassionate hearts, striving to make a difference.
These caregivers enrich the lives of those they teach through their
nurturing presence and unwavering love and care.

Acknowledgments

We like this quote by Kofi A. Annan (n.d.) and want to start with it:

> There is no trust more sacred than the one the world holds with children. There is no duty more important than ensuring that their rights are respected, that their welfare is protected, that their lives are free from fear and want and that they grow up in peace.

Let me begin by thanking my coauthors, with the foremost thanks to Michele M. Rivers Murphy for always believing in our work, for being a motivational coach, and for her gift of working by my side, so to speak, even at a distance of hundreds of miles away. There were many days when Michele and I began our morning with a conversation and ended our day with a quick text or email. Then, I believe Michele will echo my gratitude for the loving, caring attention that Yvette Jackson provided to us. Yvette, as the more experienced author, and internationally known educator, has shown us a path forward, helping us navigate the publishing process.

On a personal note, thanks too to my husband, John Wilhelm, for his unflagging support and encouragement, and to our daughters, Maria, Holly, and Amber, for their love, their amazing ability to check in at just the right time, and their practical advice. As many of you know, trauma is something that many of us have experienced, and I cherish the insights from family as I hold in my heart their belief that this book is important for children and schools.

—Chris Mason

Writing our book has been a long and exciting process. I am thankful to have shared this special journey with my coauthors and cherished friends, Chris Mason and Yvette Jackson. Chris is an amazingly gifted and natural writer who has inspired me every step of the way through her unwavering passion for educating with both heart and mind and a strong belief in a more compassionate and caring world. I have shared many morning calls and rapid-fire emails in our mutual desire to strike just the right chord with our readers as we strive to cultivate a more compassionate educational landscape. Yvette is an invaluable resource and inspiration, having touched countless lives through her lifelong work and focus on strengths-based education as the vehicle to high intellectual performance. She has created a ripple effect of change, transforming educators' belief about providing engaging and supportive environments so each and every child has the ability to maximize his or her potential. Yvette's insights, work, and accomplishments in the field of education, as well as contributions to our book, have been remarkable.

On a personal note, I am both grateful and blessed to have my best friend and husband, Tom Murphy, always by my side to extend unwavering love and support and provide family balance for any endeavor I may choose. And, our daughters, Julia and Abigail Murphy, who inspire me every day through their compassionate hearts and goodness—to do more and make this a better world for all children. Lastly, I am indebted to my parents, Dick and Paula Rivers (both former educators), for being my first teachers and the best role models, parents, and cheerleaders that a child could have. Thank you for the many lessons learned along the way, for being nonjudgmental, and opening your hearts to not only your own children but to our many friends so that they too could feel love and supported along the path of life.

—Michele M. Rivers Murphy

I thank Chris and Michele for their leadership in demonstrating the power of mindfulness practices to generate in schools that healing balm for which students hope and dedicated teachers search. I am honored to have been able to join with them to write this book to provide educators with the research that substantiates the vital power that integrating mindfulness practices into their pedagogy has for mitigating the impact of trauma and mediating learning so the innate potential of their students can surface and flourish.

This book is also dedicated to my husband, Howard, whose constant love and support enable me to stay focused on my passion, my drishti—building the confidence of teachers to inspire *all* their students to believe in, value, and demonstrate their innate potential for high achievement and contribution to our society.

—Yvette Jackson

In the production of this book, several interns and colleagues reviewed drafts at various stages of development. Thanks to Meghan Wenzel and Effie Cummings for their assistance with editing, and the following interns who assisted with background research: Mahnaz Ahrary, Sheri Brick, Rachel Kelly, Morgan Grant, Tess Renerie, Joanna Marzano, Andrew Davis, Madison Rogas, Dana Asby, and Marah Barrow. Thanks too to Linda Clearly, Cheryl Karoly, Melissa Patschke, Jillayne Flanders, and Nancy Phenis-Bourke for their early reviews. Additionally, Paul Liabenow was instrumental in making recommendations to ensure that our practical examples were embedded throughout; Paul also provided support for our research and helped us maintain a network of principals who learned with us, as we put the pieces of this puzzle together. Midway through our writing process, we also met Maud Schaafsma, a brilliant strategist, who helped us connect some of the dots between trauma, mindfulness, and community building.

While writing this book, we engaged in related research. Our thanks particularly to Melissa Patschke, Jillayne Flanders, Sue Mullane, Kate Retzel, Chris Dodge, Brian Aikens, Matt Bergey, and the teachers at Royersford Elementary School, Lee Elementary School, and Orange Elementary School for the hours spent in meetings and classrooms piloting many of the recommendations that are included in our approach to mindfulness.

We are also grateful to our editors at Solution Tree, particularly to Amy Rubenstein, for her editorial eye and how she helped us weave our insights into a powerful plan for schools, and to Tonya Cupp, who led us through the final editorial production process.

Solution Tree Press would like to thank the following reviewers:

Cathy Alland
Mathematics / Options Teacher
Twin Groves Middle School
Buffalo Grove, Illinois

Lisa Borowski
Mathematics Coach and Interventionist
North Greenville Elementary School
Hortonville Area School District
Greenville, Wisconsin

Terese Brennan-Marquez
Director of Counseling and Student
   Wellness
Castilleja School
Palo Alto, California

Vicky Galloway
Counselor
West Middle School
Sioux City, Iowa

A. Blaine Hawley
Principal
Red Pump Elementary School
Bel Air, Maryland

Diane Langworthy
Guidance Counselor
Woodland School
Warren, New Jersey

Sarah Trevino
Professional School Counselor
Mason Crest Elementary School
Annandale, Virginia

Kylie Warner
Second-Grade Teacher
Truman Elementary School
Kansas City, Missouri

Visit **go.SolutionTree.com/behavior** to download the free reproducibles in this book.

Table of Contents

About the Authors

Christine Mason, PhD, an educational psychologist, has over thirty years of experience as a classroom teacher; college professor; educational leader; and researcher; and seventeen years of experience as a yoga, mindfulness, and meditation teacher. She presents experiential workshops for school principals and teachers. Mason is the founder and executive director of the Center for Educational Improvement (CEI), a nonprofit organization whose mission is to uplift schools with teachers and principals who are caring, compassionate, and knowledgeable about learning and teaching. CEI focuses on mindfulness; social-emotional learning; and early childhood science, technology, engineering, and mathematics.

An expert in childhood trauma, Mason has experience teaching and developing teacher-mentor and youth dropout prevention programs in high-poverty urban areas. She is the developer of Heart Beaming®, a meditative practice for classroom mind breaks. Her workshops incorporate up-to-date research on brain neuroplasticity, scientific evidence, and practical activities to reduce stress, lessen the impact of trauma, and improve teacher morale and job satisfaction.

Mason has experience as a principal at an international boarding school in India. She served as executive director of research and professional development for the National Association of Elementary School Principals, where she conducted investigations to improve response to intervention, principal knowledge of the Common Core State Standards, and principal mentoring. As a senior scientist in disability education, she led research on quality of life for youth and adults with disabilities. As a senior research associate at the Council for Exceptional Children, she investigated student self-direction, teacher mentoring, and inclusive education. Mason has authored several books and research reports, including books on teacher mentoring and universal design for learning, and research reports on student self-determination, scenario-based planning, principal mentoring, urban schools, integrating the arts in schools, and inclusive education. She has presented internationally on mindfulness, trauma, Heart Centered Learning™, visions for 21st century instruction, yoga, meditation, and student self-determination.

Mason is credentialed through the International Kundalini Yoga Teachers Association and Radiant Child Yoga (a Yoga Alliance registered school). She has been a yoga practitioner for over twenty years and a yoga and meditation instructor since 2001, teaching classes at a local recreation center and offering workshops for teachers and students of all ages. She was trained directly by Yogi Bhajan, who brought Kundalini yoga to the West from India in 1968.

Early in her career, Mason received an award as researcher of the year from Montana State University. The Robert Wood Johnson Foundation and Ashoka named her a pioneer in children's well-being in 2016.

She received her doctorate in educational psychology at The Ohio State University, with post-doctoral research at the University of Washington and a fellowship to further inclusive education practices in India.

To learn more about Mason's work, visit www.edimprovement.org or follow @Edimprove on Twitter.

 **Michele M. Rivers Murphy, EdD,** is an independent educational consultant at KIDS FIRST! and a research associate and consultant for the Center for Educational Improvement (CEI). Rivers Murphy has served as a transformational change agent in some of the highest-needs neighborhoods and districts, cultivating a community education and shared responsibility approach. Through strong networking, positive relationship building, a laser-sharp focus on student strengths, and collective vision and action by stakeholders, she has maximized or redistributed resources and facilitated positive, compassionate school culture transformation.

Rivers Murphy coauthored the School Compassionate Culture Analytic Tool for Educators (S-CCATE) and created a 21st century, full-service, innovative school community model, supported by an equity framework and driven by the pedagogy principles of confidence, to inspire high intellectual performance. She presented her 21st century, high-performing public school solution for high-needs neighborhoods and districts to the Massachusetts secretary of education and facilitated a pilot study using the S-CCATE as an envisioning tool and guide for transformational school culture change. She also is facilitating CEI research regarding Heart Centered Learning, with the foundational practices of mindfulness and mindful leadership.

Rivers Murphy has over eight years of direct educational supervisory experience and several Massachusetts' certifications at all levels, in both administration (superintendent and principal) and teaching (K–12), including special education. She has developed an innovative, positive alternative to in-school and out-of-school suspension, eliminating in-school suspension completely and decreasing out-of-school suspension by 75 percent through positive relationship building and individual accountability. Rivers Murphy also expanded high-needs programming to a mainstream setting, with a focus on real-life practice, service, and community connection, authoring a paraprofessional manual and ten individual Massachusetts' disability manuals for school leaders, teachers, and support staff to utilize when servicing students.

Rivers Murphy obtained a doctorate in educational leadership (K–12) from Northeastern University. Her doctoral thesis specifically addresses the gap between what students are learning in school and what they need to know to prepare for college, career, and life in the 21st century.

To learn more about Rivers Murphy's work, follow @Rivers.Murphy on Twitter.

 **Yvette Jackson, EdD,** is an adjunct professor at Teachers College, Columbia University in New York and senior scholar for the National Urban Alliance for Effective Education. Jackson's passion is assisting educators in cultivating their confidence and competence to unlock the *giftedness* in all students. She is driven to provide and promote pedagogy that enables students who are disenfranchised and marginalized to demonstrate their strengths and innate intellectual potential. Jackson's approach, called Pedagogy of Confidence, helps educators believe in and value these students and optimize student success, which for Jackson, is the basis of equity consciousness.

Jackson is a former teacher and has served New York City Public Schools as director of gifted programs and executive director of instruction and professional development. She continues to work with school districts to customize and systemically deliver the collegial, strengths-based High Operational Practices of the Pedagogy of Confidence that integrate culture, language, and cognition to engage and elicit the innate potential of *all* students for self-actualization and contributions to our world. Jackson has been a visiting lecturer at Harvard University's Urban Superintendents Program, the Stanford Center for Opportunity Policy in Education at Stanford University, the Feuerstein Institute, and Thinking Schools International.

In 2012, the Academy of Education Arts and Sciences International honored Jackson with its Educators' Voice Awards for education policy/researcher of the year. She has applied her research in neuroscience, gifted education, literacy, and the cognitive mediation theory of the eminent cognitive psychologist, Dr. Reuven Feuerstein, to develop integrated processes that engage and elicit high-intellectual performances from students who are underachieving. This work is the basis for her award-winning book, *The Pedagogy of Confidence: Inspiring High Intellectual Performance in Urban Schools*. Jackson also coauthored *Aim High, Achieve More: How to Transform Urban Schools Through Fearless Leadership* and *Unlocking Student Potential: How Do I Identify and Activate Student Strengths?* with Veronica McDermott.

Jackson received a bachelor of arts from Queens College, City University of New York with a double major in French and education, and a master's degree in curriculum design, master of education, and doctor of education in educational administration all from Teachers College, Columbia University.

To book Christine Mason, Michele M. Rivers Murphy, or Yvette Jackson for professional development, contact pd@SolutionTree.com.

Foreword

by Paul Liabenow

Whether trauma stems from violence on the streets of high-crime cities like Detroit, New York, or Washington, D.C., or abuse within a child's own home, the impact on our students is significant. Trauma takes many forms, dramatic and subtle—the death of a grandparent, the loss of a pet, bullying at school, or the ongoing stress of living in poverty. It is pervasive. It is also more and more apparent to teachers that so many of our students exhibit signs of distress and trauma that impede learning, resulting in underachievement, loss of self-esteem, and arrested social-emotional development. Many educators are also suffering from chronic stress, pressure to raise student achievement, high expectations to turn around low-performing schools, and burnout. Trauma and toxic stress compromise students, teachers, and school leaders' health and well-being.

Trauma takes a toll on learning, instructing, and living. Christine Mason, distinguished elementary and secondary principals, and I executed focus groups, surveys, and discussions in which educators around the United States expressed a sense of helplessness and frustration trying to find antidotes to address the tragic reality of their students' challenges as well as their own. Teachers and school leaders recognize that traditional instruction is not adequate and that simply having high expectations and more test prep won't meet student needs, increase achievement, raise staff morale, or improve teacher performance.

Fortunately, there is an exciting knowledge base on the neuroscience of learning, evidence from MRIs, and the authors' empirical research illustrating how mindfulness practices and compassion can diminish stress and fortify focus, reflection, and higher-order cognitive functioning for both students and educators to mitigate the trauma of adverse childhood experiences' deleterious impact. Research on the brain's propensity shows that children are born with the innate potential for high levels of learning and achievement, and teachers are well positioned to help our children reclaim this potential. Human brains contain trillions of pathways, and from birth to age three neural connections continue to be generated at a rate of seven hundred connections per second (Shonkoff & Phillips, 2000; Roberts, 2017; Schiller, 2010). Early childhood educators can help children reclaim this potential using the strategies the authors reference (Bierman & Torres, 2016). Authors Christine Mason, Michele M. Rivers Murphy, and Yvette Jackson incorporated this research to provide us with *Mindfulness Practices: Cultivating Heart Centered Communities Where Students Focus and Flourish*, a practical guide for teachers and school leaders to effectively address the impact of trauma on social-emotional development, learning, and achievement.

Mindfulness Practices does *not* present yet another program to follow. It is not an add-on or one more thing to squeeze into our busy days. Rather, the authors advocate for and illustrate change in methods of both *being* and *doing*. They provide staff with advice, practices, and exercises to incorporate directly into their teaching, as well as support for activating the benefits of mindfulness for their students—and themselves. Teachers who participated in the Center for Educational Improvement's (CEI's) heart centered mindfulness pilot programs in 2017 report that as the foundational practice for cultivating compassionate school environments, mindfulness was a great stress reliever for them, as classroom climates became more positive, with a new calm and sense of renewed enthusiasm and purpose. This new way of being is a new beginning toward directly combating stress, leading to greater compassion, happiness, and success for teachers, administrators, staff, and students. Whether a physical education teacher, health educator, art teacher, special education teacher, school counselor, traditional classroom teacher, or school leader, this book has practical and natural lifelong strategies for you.

As important as spreading love and goodwill is, *Mindfulness Practices* also does much more. It provides a systematic approach to building persistence, grit, and resilience. In *How Children Succeed: Grit, Curiosity, and the Hidden Power of Character*, author Paul Tough (2012) says:

> What matters most in a child's development, they say, is not how much information we can stuff into her brain in the first few years. What matters, instead, is whether we are able to help her develop a very different set of qualities, a list that includes persistence, self-control, curiosity, conscientiousness, grit and self-confidence. (p. xv)

As a K–12 educator for thirty-two years, a former superintendent of schools, and the executive director of the Michigan Elementary and Middle School Principals Association, I have worked with thousands of principals and understand their needs as instructional leaders. *Mindfulness Practices* is a must-read. My prediction is that mindfulness and heart centeredness are not simply trending practices, but that they will be around for decades to come. These practices take pressure off students and teachers, advance well-being, and set the stage for increasing academic achievement.

With the Every Student Succeeds Act (2015), the pendulum is swinging back to a more holistic, whole-child approach to education. This will be a challenge for many as we combat the barriers of bureaucracy, time, and habits. It will take some intentional effort to add creativity and kindness back into our curriculum. *Mindfulness Practices* will help guide you on your way, with insights, stories, research, and practical exercises. George Leonard and Michael Murphy (1995), founding figures in the human potential movement, say, "To begin any strong practice is to turn the pages of your life to a new chapter" (p. 39). As you turn the pages of this book, will you invest the time and effort to break through for a transformational change? If you are ready and willing to undertake this challenge, this is the book for you.

Introduction

My hope and wish is that one day, formal education will pay attention to what I call education of the heart. Just as we take for granted the need to acquire proficiency in the basic academic subjects, I am hopeful that a time will come when we can take it for granted that children will learn, as part of the curriculum, the indispensability of inner values: love, compassion, justice, and forgiveness.

—The Dalai Lama

Imagine for a moment if we refined schools' focus through a cultivation of both the heart and the mind. What if we pay less attention to what isn't working, feel less pressure from the many mandates and demands that teaching and leading present, and develop a more caring lens of nonjudgment for ourselves, our coworkers, and our students?

Imagine recreating schools as compassionate learning environments, school cultures built on positive relationships that deepen and where cooperation expands, where students and teachers alike gain the confidence and courage to act in ways that enhance their own lives and the lives of others. Imagine schools where leaders, teachers, and students alike cultivate a compassionate, caring learning environment; where teachers once again enjoy the small teachable moments that pop up when room to breathe and to reflect on learning replaces the emphasis on record-breaking speed of learning; and where a natural balance emerges. Envision a balance of academics and conversations about life, a balance between doing well and feeling great, a balance between a focus on self and a focus on others. Imagine that you, your students, and your peers eagerly await Monday mornings. Then what would education look like? And, how would you feel about your job, your work, yourself, and your students?

Now imagine a conscious effort to refocus our schools and school cultures so that students become immersed in environments that consider social-emotional well-being and the needs of self and others. Envision this awareness and goodness extending to a wider school community of parents, families, and community stakeholders; embracing our ability to educate with both our hearts and minds. Imagine a school where caring matters; where teachers and administrators seek to learn more about their students and are more supportive of families; where students appreciate the extra effort teachers take to welcome and encourage students and support student success. This is a heart centered school community, a compassionate school community that balances well-being and learning.

Within the walls of a school is a community of students, teachers, and staff. To be a heart centered community, compassion is quintessential. Compassion is necessary to educate, lead, learn, and live with heart and be at our best. In this book, as we discuss compassion, we intentionally use the term *heart centered*. We do this in part with a nod to mindfulness and meditation. (See chapters 4–6, pages 61, 73, and 91.) As an introduction to this concept, we invite you to read the next few lines and then close your eyes and follow these steps.

1. Take a couple of breaths and consider compassion.
2. Visualize a scene with students at your school and picture the students feeling excited, engaged, kind, and considerate.
3. Consider what you pictured and how you felt.
4. Place your hands over your heart, take a couple of deep breaths, and picture the same scene.
5. Consider what you pictured and how you felt. Did you note any difference?

With your hands over your heart, you may have noticed a warmth in your heart, a sense of a more complete scene, or a feeling of being more fully present with the students, more connected to these students. (However, we are not suggesting that there is one correct response to this exercise—not everyone experiences the same feelings when placing his or her hand on his or her heart.) So, while we are focused on compassion, the term that more precisely reflects the spirit we are seeking to achieve in schools is *heart centered.* You will learn more about this in this book and will gain some experiences to deepen your understanding of both mindfulness and heart centeredness. In a compassionate, heart centered community, a spirit of cooperation helps develop the goodness and best in others and ourselves.

Education of the Heart Through Mindfulness

Remember the days before you taught, when you considered a teaching career, when you desired to teach to *make a difference in the life of a student*? Our wish for every teacher, staff member, and school leader who picks up this book is that the fire and passion that first drew you to teaching reignite. And that as you consciously address

what students really need most in the moment, that you also feel more t
We see mindfulness as the vehicle to bring us back to authentic, foundatior
compassionate relationships—relationships that cultivate the gift of *connect
being*, and the *goodness in all.*

Why Mindfulness Practice?

Far too many children and adults carry an insurmountable weight of stress or past
traumatic experiences that can negatively impact the way that they interact, learn,
teach, lead, and live (Center for Substance Abuse Treatment, 2014). *Mindfulness* is
an organic, practical, and accessible life tool that they can use to calm the mind and
body and counteract the high levels of stress and trauma associated with school, work,
and life. To be mindful is to be aware, to be sensitive to oneself, to how others are
feeling and behaving, and to one's environment. Mindfulness is also about balance
or equanimity—the feeling of ease, calm, acceptance, and nonreaction in that same
particular moment of awareness. Mindfulness is the opposite of absentmindedness.
When we are absentminded, we are distracted in thought and inattentive to what
is before us. When we are mindful, we take care—we are not careless or neglectful.
When we are mindful, we consider the well-being of others, ourselves, and our world,
the greater good, the needs of the planet, the best course of action for preserving the
environment, and the impact on children and others.

Cultivating an environment where we are mindful—where students, and the teachers on whom they depend, can focus and flourish—requires staff who have an ecologi-
cal perspective. That perspective is one where teachers develop a keen awareness of the
factors that affect themselves and their students inside and outside of school. Professor
and stress-reduction expert Jon Kabat-Zinn (2003) says that such awareness "emerges
through paying attention on purpose, in the present moment, and nonjudgmentally"
(p. 143). Such awareness or mindfulness involves turning inward to be more aware
of self; being more observant of the external world; and having a greater awareness
of self and others in various situations. Being mindful is to put in place the practices
and strategies that create an environment where students and staff "wake into a day
in which there is a possibility of grace, of being 'gifted,' of being surprised" (Jackson,
2011, p. 35) and of learning instead of waking into a day of stress or hopelessness
(Whyte, 2002).

Mindfulness is enhanced through a range of activities that elicit greater awareness
of one's environment, awareness of experiences, awareness of breath, and awareness
of emotions and how one is feeling. The use of activities that generate mindfulness
in schools is growing rapidly (Felver et al., 2016). A meta-analysis of twelve databases
of research conducted on the effectiveness of mindfulness activities in schools makes
apparent the accumulating evidence of the popularity of these activities (Zenn

Herrnleben-Kurz, & Walach, 2014). *Mindful attention to self and others is a powerful first step to creating schools that are more responsive to the needs of students and to our own needs.* With mindfulness, you can *become the change you seek* in your school community. Through developing a greater sense of calm and living life moment by moment on a deeper level, you can reduce stress and see the possibility of experiencing greater joy, insight, and understanding.

Why Is Mindfulness Important to Combating Trauma and Stress?

While mindfulness is an important component in improving well-being for all children and adults (Farrell & Barrett, 2007), it has particular significance for those who experienced trauma (Fischer, 2017). One of every four children experiences a trauma before the age of four. The Centers for Disease Control and Prevention (CDC, 2014) reports that many children live in a culture of violence, bullying, and trauma. And if children live with poverty, if children live in neighborhoods of high crime, if children experience racism and discrimination, the frequency and severity of their trauma will be even greater. Paul Gilbert (2009), the founder of compassion-focused therapy, describes the extent of harm that children experience: "Individuals subjected to early [traumatic] experiences can become highly sensitive to threats of rejection or criticism from the outside world and can quickly become self-attacking; they experience both their external and internal worlds as easily turning hostile" (p. 199). Children who are ashamed often "use a cold, bullying or aggressive inner tone to try to change their thoughts and behaviors" (Gilbert, 2009, p. 203). They often experience difficulties with learning, attention, memory, self-esteem, decision making, communication, fear, and impulsive behavior.

Through mindfulness practice, we can help build stronger connections between the areas of the brain that stress and traumatic experiences have compromised. Mindfulness helps to slow down reactivity and increase body awareness. It can contribute to greater emotional regulation and help us cope more easily with life's frustrations, setbacks, and relationship challenges (Siegel, 2010a). When considering the trauma children face and the impact of poverty and neighborhoods of violence, the importance of being more responsive to the needs of our students is obvious. Developing a greater awareness, understanding, and compassionate response to children's suffering is essential. In essence, we might be able to achieve greater compassion and greater academic gains if we pay more attention to what our hearts tell us. As Rollin McCraty (2015) indicates in *Science of the Heart, Volume 2*:

> The heart communicates to the brain in four major ways: *neurologically* (through the transmission of nerve impulses), biochemically (via hormones and neurotransmitters), biophysically (through pressure waves) and energetically (through

electromagnetic field interactions). . . . The heart-brain's neural
circuitry enables it to act independently of the cranial brain to
learn, remember, make decisions and even feel and sense. (p. 3)

Rollin McCraty's (2015) extensive research suggests that it may be worthwhile to pay attention to our hearts. When we focus solely on our intellectual understanding, we may miss out on important information that is readily available to us as it is processed at our heart level.

Why Should We Open Our Hearts Through Mindfulness Practice?

So, we are suggesting that you consider opening your heart, listening to your heart, and acting from a place that includes input from your heart—increasing your mindful awareness of what your heart is feeling. If you have ever felt that your heart was telling you one thing and your head another, you may understand the value of tuning into your heart. Mindfulness practices can help us increase our sensitivity to our feelings and help us make more balanced heart-head decisions.

We believe that to adequately prepare our students for college, career, and life, we must educate with both our minds and our hearts. Chapters 1 (page 13), 2 (page 21), and 3 (page 37) offer research to support this belief. However, before educators can open the minds of their students, they must open their hearts to understanding the magnitude of the stressors, trauma, and circumstances that surround their lives. It is not good enough for teachers and other school leaders to simply stay the course with a sole academic focus. If they are going to address the many challenges associated with trauma and stress that so many students and teachers endure, and how they impact both learning and teaching, then small steps are not enough. It is not enough to practice compassion one day a week or to celebrate success with an annual assembly. If we are to improve the lives and education for all students, it will require a paradigm shift in the way we think about education, our children, families, and our world. It will require a move toward educating the whole child, with a balanced focus of academics and health and well-being so that all students feel safe and are cared for. We are concerned about the trauma, the violence, and the stress that permeate society, our families, and our schools. However, we believe we can turn this around.

Today, schools can increase *protective factors*—factors that help protect students from both the short-term and long-term damage of stress and trauma (Howard, Dryden, & Johnson, 1999; Knight, 2007; Santos, 2012). Schools can also decrease risk factors when we use our hearts to educate our students and ourselves. Listening to our hearts is not always easy to do. In fact, we have been trained as professionals to not get too involved with our students' problems, to not care too deeply. Yet, with the approach we will outline in this book, we can achieve a balance—high expectations for students, research-supported pedagogy, and mindfulness.

We can help magnify protective factors in schools so long as there are caring and compassionate adults to help support students and parents during times of need. These supportive actions help to increase resilience and grit, making it easier for individuals to bounce back when experiencing stress and trauma. Using mindfulness practices in this book will guide us to achieve more favorable and positive outcomes for all students, helping to prevent child maltreatment and other social problems that complicate their lives.

What Do Students Need to Focus and Flourish?

Where would you begin if your task was not to ensure academic excellence, but to consider the ultimate well-being of each student, to give each student a toolbox to enhance skills, knowledge, and opportunities for individual feelings of success and being valued? If you think of students in your school who seem happy, successful, joy filled, and ready for the challenges of any particular day, what traits come to mind? Why do some students seem to be able to readily focus on tasks at hand, and others become easily distracted? Why do some gravitate toward high achievement, a healthy self-esteem, and happiness while others seem to walk under a cloud of doom? Substantial research suggests that we start with consciousness and mindfulness—something we consider to be two sides of the same coin (Diamond & Lee, 2011; Flook et al., 2010; Rempel, 2012; Schmalzl, Powers, & Henje Blom, 2015; Zelazo & Lyons, 2012). Mindfulness and the steps we recommend are research-based strategies for creating compassionate school communities where students, and the teachers on whom they depend, can flourish.

Mindfulness focuses our attention on the here and now. Meditation and yogic practices heighten our awareness of self and others by quieting our thoughts and creating a sense of calmness, and improving our awareness of the relationship between our physical feelings and our emotions. Research supports their value in a wide array of instances and for various subpopulations of students. It shows that mindfulness and yoga decrease anxiety and depression and increase self-esteem, mood, and ability to focus and control emotions (Büssing, Michaelsen, Khalsa, Telles, & Sherman, 2012; Felver, Butzer, Olson, Smith, & Khalsa, 2015; Raes, Griffith, Van der Gucht, & Williams, 2014; Semple, Droutman, & Reid, 2017).

Yoga, meditation, and mindfulness are being integrated into a growing number of U.S. schools, and teachers and students are adapting as they learn about these practices that used to be relegated to fitness centers and after-school programs. We find it useful for middle or high school student athletes, perhaps even some who participate in what some consider traditionally masculine sports such as football and wrestling, to talk with middle schoolers about their own yoga practices. Because athletes are sometimes revered, students are often surprised to find that these rough and tough student athletes are doing yoga. Using student leaders to guide activities also helps narrow the gap of discomfort some students associate with trying something new. Adolescents with depression or mental illness; children with learning disabilities, autism, or attention deficit hyperactivity disorder; students with conduct disorders, or students with high rates of truancy or school suspensions all benefit from mindfulness (Ehleringer, 2010; Frank, Kohler, Peal, & Bose, 2017; Malboeuf-Hurtubise, Lacourse, Taylor, Joussemet, & Ben Amor, 2017; Zenner et al., 2014).

Teachers and school leaders create mindful, compassionate communities when they have the foundational knowledge in part I of this book; personal and classroom experience with the exercises in part II; and the deeper collaborative understanding and experience that we present in part III. We present a package to help grades preK–12 teachers, school leaders, and school communities practice the steps we recommend.

Mindfulness Practices: About the Book

While developing *Mindfulness Practices*, we relied on our collective experience leading schools and districts to consider what was essential to set the stage for cultivating more responsive and compassionate school communities through mindfulness. Our experiences facilitating systemic change, focusing on student self-determination and strengths, and collaborating with neuroscientists and educational leaders provided an important backdrop for our recommendations. Our work with rural and urban, including high-poverty, schools rounded out our practical experience, grounding us in the realities that teachers and principals face. Our experience teaching and practicing yoga, mindfulness, and meditation gave us confidence in the instructions we provide for incorporating these into your lives and into your classrooms through compassionate, heart centered action and instruction. The CEI (n.d.) says Heart Centered Learning™:

> Equips students with the knowledge, attitudes, and skills necessary to understand and manage emotions, feel and show empathy for others, resolve conflicts nonviolently, think creatively, and overcome obstacles to succeed in the classroom and in life. Heart Centered Education is not overly dependent on rigid academic scheduling or expectations for academic growth—instead taking a holistic approach.

Note that the CEI is not alone in its connection of mindfulness to heart centeredness: many yogic and mindfulness traditions refer to listening to and acting from our hearts (Ruth, 2017). Hence, we use the term recognizing the importance of tuning into our hearts as we make decisions and help children heal from the trauma they have experienced. As a life-long student of metaphysics, mysticism, and spirituality

Kiyanush Kamrani (2017) states that a "mindfulness practice is only complete when it includes the heart, as awareness is not limited to the mind; the heart is the center of our consciousness" (p. 1).

This book is grounded in research, input from exemplary principals, and practical experiences in schools. The research-based principles and activities that follow are universal, and you can easily adapt them across grades preK–12 or apply them to multiple settings. Whether you are concerned with a preschooler who seems withdrawn, a fourth grader who is missing too much school, or a ninth grader who bullies others, you will find that the mindfulness practices we recommend can help you restructure learning expectations, give you tools to help establish a sense of calmness, and turn around the lives of that student and teachers.

While there is an urgency to provide mindful instruction to help students mediate immediate and long-term trauma and stress impact, mindfulness is a simple and useful life tool for everyone (including our own selves, parents, families, and the larger community). With this book, you will learn steps and strategies for creating compassionate communities of students, teachers, staff, and school leaders to alleviate the impact of trauma and toxic, daily stress. In our approach, we make apparent the value of helping all students become more aware of the needs of self and others, as well as becoming more attuned to being compassionate.

The research conducted to date on mindfulness confirms its overall effectiveness (Schmalzl et al., 2015; Zenner et al., 2014). While the techniques are meant for all schools and all classrooms—not just those with the most serious needs—the results will be especially significant for those trauma and stress most highly impacted. The topics we discuss throughout this book—trauma, neuroscience, mindfulness, and compassionate community building—have not been part of undergraduate or graduate teacher preparation programs. They have not been part of the curriculum for preparation of school administrators. They have also not been popular topics for teacher or administrator professional development. So, by reading this book, most of you will gain new insights and understanding. As presented in this book, you achieve mindfulness through practice of a carefully sequenced range of activities and processes that will result in greater awareness of self and others. Mindfulness practice is most effective when naturally infused into the curriculum and fully integrated into the course of the school day. In this three-part book, you will learn practical ways to easily implement mindfulness practice into your school community and lives.

Part I provides foundational background information. Part I is the *why*. We set the stage in chapters 1–3, describing why there is a sense of urgency to move toward a more compassionate and supportive learning environment as a direct response to combat trauma and toxic stress. We also provide information on developmental trauma and neuroscience, as well as the interconnectivity of our brain, our emotions, and trauma.

Part II contains information and exercises for you to practice by yourself and with your students to learn the mindfulness strategies we recommend. Part II is the *how*—how to transform classrooms into nurturing, caring, and compassionate learning environments through mindfulness practice to create caring, compassionate communities. This part explains how we use mindfulness and compassionate activities, exercises, and practice to combat trauma and stress. While individual teachers can implement this book's recommendations with good success, we believe that even greater and more long-term gains result with the consistency of schoolwide implementation. Principal leadership is key to creating heart centered school communities, as is consideration for schoolwide policies for discipline, celebrations of success, and welcoming families. Mindfulness is not something that you can read about and then just start implementing. With practice, you will become more mindful. Chapters 4–6 provide exercises to enhance breathing, practice yoga and meditation, and increase mindfulness. These mindfulness practices are mutually beneficial for students, teachers, staff, and leaders when they practice them individually or collectively with others. Because it is easy to forget to check in with yourself, we will remind you, at the end of most exercises, to ask yourself how you feel.

You will benefit the most by going beyond merely reading the material presented in part II to actually practicing the exercises. We recommend practicing a few of them yourself on a regular basis before bringing them to students. Students will also benefit the most if you implement these exercises routinely. Mindfulness is not a one-time event. You can practice the following exercises with one of three methods.

1. Having someone read them to you
2. Recording them and playing back the recording with your eyes closed
3. Reading them and then closing your eyes to go through the exercise

If you are using the third method, you can gain a lot by simply approximating the listed steps—you do not need to be exact. After you practice any of the breaths you are planning to introduce in the classroom, you can introduce them to your students. You will lead students through the exercises.

These chapters provide strategies for practical application of mindfulness, complete with teacher, staff, and student exercises and activities that help develop a greater consciousness and a compassionate mindset to combat trauma and stress.

Part III will help teachers and school leaders consider implications and procedures for infusing mindfulness practices into academic instruction and for schoolwide or districtwide implementation. Part III is the *now what*. It explains what you do after you practice the mindfulness exercises. You will find guidance on how to introduce mindfulness and compassion activities and strategies to impact not only your students' and your own well-being, but also to improve academic performance and resilience. Building on the exercises presented in part II, part III takes you another step forward with activities to become more mindful of your school, your students, and your classroom community. This includes how to reduce stress and address compassionate challenges—those times when it is difficult to be patient, understanding, and compassionate.

Part III provides insights into improving students' learning, memory, attention, and reasoning abilities and implementing empowering community-building strategies within your schools. Because the greatest and most lasting gains will be made with collaborative community building within schools, this final section of the book also offers an opportunity for you to learn from mindful leadership experts about what it means to be a mindful leader, and why mindful leadership is important to transformational change.

At the beginning of each chapter, you will find a key principle that highlights one essential point from that chapter. At the end of each chapter, you will find mindful reflection questions to help you connect the information to your own circumstances and experiences, as well as space to record your answers or any other thoughts you have during your practices or while reading this book. These questions, which are available as free reproducibles at **go.SolutionTree.com/behavior**, may also be useful for those of you who meet in small groups to study, learn, and practice mindfulness. You can easily form specific study groups for population groups, such as teachers or parents. The group might even provide an opportunity for parents, teachers, and staff to learn about mindfulness as a part of your larger school community.

Whether you are a teacher, parent, or community member, you may find it worthwhile to approach this book in three dedicated blocks of time—(1) setting aside a few hours for part I, (2) reading and practicing the exercises in part II over a period of several weeks, and (3) then reading and reflecting on part III when you are ready to advance broader collaborative use of the suggested techniques. While there are many reasons to approach this book sequentially, reading it front to back, if you want to know more about trauma or neurobiology, or have an interest in a specific technique, then you may opt to hone in on specific chapters. If you are an administrator, you may be most interested in part III—particularly chapter 9, which includes practical advice from a former school superintendent and several principals. Please note that chapters 4–6 (part II) are linked and that reading that set of chapters together can help you gain more complete information.

Let's get started on your journey toward mindfulness, and prepare for creating, and being a part of, a heart centered community.

PART I

THE URGENCY OF NOW

In part I, we build on the first of three streams of research that guide our work toward creating mindful, compassionate communities: pediatric neurobiology research on the impact of toxic stress and trauma (Ford & Courtois, 2009; Zelazo & Cunningham, 2007) on brain development. This research suggests that toxic stress and trauma are particularly damaging for preschool and elementary-age children during their early developmental years, and those early years are an important time for helping children recover from trauma due to the brain's neuroplasticity.

Chapters 1 (page 13), 2 (page 21), and 3 (page 37) provide context for the reader regarding the importance of changing the conversation and narrative of how we educate and the importance of beginning now. These three chapters provide the urgency for implementing mindfulness as the foundational practice for cultivating caring, compassionate school communities as a direct response to combat the escalating prevalence of trauma and toxic stress in our students' lives and in those who teach and lead. As we begin the journey toward healing, we also provide foundational information on developmental trauma and neuroscience, and information regarding the underlying structure of the brain that teachers must consider in developing classroom-based interventions, introducing mindfulness, and building caring, compassionate school communities. Note that chapter 3 contains overarching sections that explain the connection between our brains, our emotions, trauma, and stress.

We believe that by engaging in schoolwide mindfulness activities and creating caring, compassionate school communities, educators have a vehicle for strengthening executive functioning (EF), accelerating personalized learning, advancing student interest and strengths, and helping students heal from trauma.

CHAPTER 1

The Need to Care

I feel the capacity to care is the thing which gives life its deepest significance.

—Pablo Casals

key principle

Mindfulness practices can stimulate the paradigm shift in schools and the new societal mindset needed to overcome the impact of trauma and stress.

Children live with nightmares. Whether it is the trauma of living through a hurricane or earthquake, feeling uncertain of where one's loved ones are, or living in a neighborhood of poverty or neglect, their trauma surrounds us today. Whether it is domestic abuse, school shootings, or graphic displays of killing on television and in video games, violence is all too prevalent. All too often for young children living with fear, anxiety, or violence, their experiences and unvoiced reactions create layers of damage (National Scientific Council on the Developing Child, 2014).

Trauma touches the lives of children of all ages. It may be pre-traumatic, post-traumatic, or recurrent. It is not limited to youth who are in gangs or those who are of a certain age. While violence may not be the source of trauma for all children, the trauma could be related to abuse, or neglect, or simply losing a friend. While the impact of a traumatic event will not affect everyone equally, the impact of trauma resulting from each of these experiences could be significant. Sometimes teachers will be aware of the traumatic event the student brings into their classroom. We as teachers may hear about the death of a grandparent, for example. At other times, all we may see is that Christopher did not finish his homework or that Latosha seems to have withdrawn. Traumatic experiences are not left at home. Children come into classrooms and the school community every day carrying their school bags and the weight of their traumatic experiences.

There Is a Mounting Urgency

We know many teachers care deeply about children's emotional health and have the intention to nurture this emotional health even in a time of tremendous pressure to achieve academic gains. Many teachers understand that actualizing this intention requires being mindful that there is a myriad of impacting student realities to which they must pay attention (Feuerstein, 2006; Jackson, 2011; Kabat-Zinn, 2003). If you have cracked the cover of this book, you may already be aware of the realities and huge unmet needs that many students face on a daily basis. Factors such as poverty, racism, divorce, homelessness, and abuse, when coupled with the everyday stressors we all face, often lead to toxic or ongoing stress. Over time, this stress impedes brain development and creates blocks to learning, memory, and one's sense of security, safety, and happiness.

Trauma Causes Lifelong Damage

Potentially, the effects of profound, long-term damage that accompanies trauma permanently alter children's brain architecture, resulting in decreased learning and behavioral and emotional problems. According to an American Academy of Pediatrics (2003) report, the damage and cost of suffering extend well into adulthood, with social risk factors, mental health issues, substance abuse, violence, and risky adult behaviors increasing and parenting capabilities reduced, thereby continuing a cycle of adverse childhood experiences well into our next generation of children (Shonkoff, Garner, Committee on Psychosocial Aspects of Child and Family Health, Committee on Early Childhood, Adoption, and Dependent Care, & Section on Developmental and Behavioral Pediatrics, 2012). These consequences have far-reaching, damaging tentacles that can profoundly impact society as a whole, with the potential to cripple a whole generation of children if their needs are left unmet.

Alarming Statistics

The following statistics support the need to mitigate factors harmful to student well-being and development.

- Over seven million young children a year are referred to a child protective agency for trauma due to neglect, physical abuse, or sexual abuse. The U.S. Department of Health and Human Services (2016) cites this number as an underestimation because not all abuse is reported. The horrific reality is people do not automatically recover from childhood trauma, and 60 percent of adults report experiencing trauma during childhood. Stress from abuse distorts the brain's cognitive functioning, impairing judgment and contributing to slower academic progress and deflated test scores (Smith, 2010). The statistics of this reality are a cataclysmic foreboding for the future of the United States. (The website www.recognizetrauma.org has more information. Visit **go.SolutionTree.com/behavior** for live links to the websites mentioned in this book.)

- For students of color, especially African American males, the reality of racial abuse is an additional ignored reality. At very young ages, the reality of racism results in negative perceptions children have about themselves, affecting their psychological and cognitive development (Starr, 2015). Tragically, the confrontations children of color personally encounter or view through the media happen so regularly and are internalized so profoundly that the term *post* in post-traumatic stress disorder (PTSD) has been dropped in recognition that this cause of the trauma (racism) for African American males is ongoing. The designation is *traumatic stress disorder* (Kugler, 2013). Given the surge of police violence against African American males, particularly in the context of long-term racism, discrimination, oppression, and injustice, social work professor Samuel Aymer (2016) goes as far as to describe the fear and hyper-alertness as *pre-traumatic stress disorder*. Considered in the context of the number of African American males who are imprisoned, the number who are profiled, and the impact of such policies as stop and frisk, the urgency is great (Aymer, 2016).

- For indigenous students, whose people are native to America, the impact of the history of assault, abuse, and persecution has continued through centuries. Gone (2009) describes the "collective, cumulative, and intergenerational transmission of risk of adverse health outcomes that stem from the historically unresolved grief" (p. 2) for Native Americans. Contributing factors such as subjugation, forced cultural assimilation, and brutal corporal punishment have not been resolved and have led to alcohol and substance abuse as a means of escape.

- The misperception that students of color, including Native American students, construct about themselves due to the abuse of racism they live, reflects what Carol S. Dweck (2000) calls *entity theory*. As Dweck (2000) explains, tragically, individuals' beliefs about their own capabilities, their self-concept, motivation, goal setting, and tenacity in school are affected by these inaccurate perceptions of self that abuse and discrimination perpetuated. Such beliefs about self ravage students' learning potential and academic achievement. According to the entity theory, false and limiting beliefs about self that have been instilled as a result of racism and discrimination result in a *fixed mindset*, or a belief that indigenous students and students of color have that their intelligence is fixed and unchangeable (Dweck, 2000; Jackson, 2011).

The lifelong consequences of trauma are significant. According to the Adverse Childhood Experiences (ACEs) study, where over seventeen thousand patients were interviewed regarding childhood trauma and their current health, people don't just get over childhood experiences and trauma (Felitti et al., 1998). Rather, according to that watershed longitudinal study and subsequent research, "unhealed emotions have a profound impact on personal relationships, health choices and chronic diseases that subsequently develop from self-diminishing choices" such as smoking, using illicit drugs, or having multiple sexual partners (CDC, 2016). While you may find this information unsettling, what is most encouraging is that the presence of a caring adult can mitigate the negative impact of trauma and stress. And, this caring adult does not need to be the parent or other relative. More often than not, the stable, caring adult is a teacher, and his or her impact can be significantly ameliorating (Flanagan, 2015).

Shared Responsibility

The damage that students experience due to trauma happens during a critical time in their development. This is especially true for elementary-age students. According to the Kresge Foundation (2016):

> These early, formative years serve as the foundation for all of life's later endeavors. If, as a society, we fail to meet the needs of our young children, it is not just the children who suffer. We as a society suffer as well. Their success is our success.

In the life of a child, there is no greater time for action than *now*. It is, after all, the foundation of success developed in early and formative years. Multiple societal interventions to address long-standing and escalating problems facing students of color, including Native American students, are needed. For all students to attain strong cognitive development, educational achievement, economic productivity, and ultimately responsible citizenship, we must all bear a shared responsibility early in their development. For all students to obtain lifelong health, sound mental health, and ultimately the successful parenting skills for life success, we must all bear a shared responsibility early in their development. For all students to be welcomed members of communities, we must all bear a shared responsibility early in their development (Child First, n.d.).

Compassion Increases the Power of Protective Factors

Greater consciousness and more compassion in a school community can lead to increased protective factors to counteract what is missing for so many students as they experience unthinkable trauma and stress. Protective factors such as having a caring adult to turn to, teaching consciousness and compassion in schools, strengthening an array of social connections, and providing parents concrete support in times of need help combat trauma and stress.

We naturally decrease risk factors when we make conscious decisions as educators and leaders to increase protective factors like building adult and student relationships (through mindfulness and self and social awareness), supportive interactions with students and families, and increased compassion and understanding of the circumstances and experiences that children face. A buffering adult relationship is one of the most important deterrents to decreasing risk factors. Adult relationships provide the personalized sensitivity, support, and safety that help buffer children from developmental disruptions, which occur when the impact is severe enough to impede their development. Adult relationships also build resilience, which is their ability to recover quickly from difficult experiences. Such relationships help students to become more resilient and more likely to overcome challenges that come into their lives (Center on the Developing Child, n.d.a). Within the school community, we have a unique opportunity to promote and develop this buffer through developing strong and caring teacher and student relationships.

We believe that schools as social institutions serving children and youth have a significant role to play (Noddings, 1998, 2003; Wall, 2010). We agree that schools have a moral imperative to become involved, to consider what they can do as they plan and implement their curriculum and instruction. So, the question becomes, With what we know about trauma, where do educators go from here?

With Mindfulness, Imagine Compassionate Communities

Mindfulness is the first step we recommend to change the way we think (mindset) and educate. Mindfulness is a foundational and essential practice to create caring, compassionate school communities. However, it is important to note that while teachers can teach mindfulness, it is also critical that compassion be a key classroom theme as well. Otherwise, students might not get the help they need to overcome the impact of their traumatic experiences. Mindfulness without compassion in classrooms is like tea without honey or dinner without dessert; we lose the opportunity to savor the richness of it. Without a conscious effort to enhance compassionate interactions, protocols, and policies in schools, we fail to hit the sweet spot.

With the approach we suggest, mindfulness plus compassion, both parts of the equation are integral to the effectiveness and result of practice. Significant research on mindfulness, compassion, and community building supports our suggestions for a focus on mindfulness and compassion (Brock, 2015; Broderick, 2013; Brown &

Olson, 2015; Cole, et al., 2005; Davidson & Begley, 2012; Flook et al., 2010; Gilbert, 2010; Kohler-Evans & Barnes, 2015; Schmalzl et al., 2015; Singer & Bolz, 2013).

Children experiencing trauma need compassionate interactions and support every day. It is only when we develop a *heightened awareness*, greater *consciousness*, or *mindfulness* of our own self, surroundings, feelings, and others that we are capable of acting more compassionately toward ourselves and others (Kohler-Evans & Barnes, 2015). This holds true for everyone: teachers, principals, other staff, and students. It is when we take a deep breath, pause, and cultivate the awareness of any moment between an action and a reaction that we heighten our understanding of what is really happening (Siegel, 2012). As Siegel (2012) indicates, this consciousness starts with a simple deep breath and a pause (chapter 4, page 61). And, from the base of mindfulness or greater consciousness comes an increased capacity to demonstrate compassionate caring and understanding. This includes compassion for self and for others.

We can make a difference if we choose to act, to believe, to elevate our collective consciousness with compassion. As educators, we have an enormous charge before us. If we are to properly prepare the next generation for their future, helping all students develop into healthy, well-adjusted, caring, and contributing individuals for their success and ours, then a paradigm shift is critically needed: a paradigm shift in mindset, in the way we think and act regarding education, our children, families, and our world. Our collective and shared work on this shift begins now.

Mindful Reflection

As an individual or with your study group, respond to the mindful reflection questions, taking notes on the following page.

- What do you know about the trauma your students experience at home or at school?
- What steps, if any, is your school community taking to combat trauma and increase social well-being for students and teachers?
- Racism, intolerance, and prejudice are major factors contributing to trauma. How prevalent are these in your local area? Who is addressing them, and how?
- What do you know about mindfulness?
- Are you implementing any mindfulness practices in your classroom, your school, or your own life? If so, describe the practices and their impact to date.
- Describe your school community. How compassionate is it? Has there been a conscious effort to increase compassion? Explain how.

— Notes —

CHAPTER 2

The Journey—
Healing Along the Way

*Too often we underestimate the power of a touch, a smile, a kind
word, a listening ear, an honest compliment, or the smallest act
of caring, all of which have the potential to turn a life around.*

—Leo Buscaglia

key principle

Mindfulness and
compassionate learning
communities are critical
for alleviating the life-
altering impacts of stress
and trauma.

The reasons for writing this book are many, but none
are more important than our unwavering belief that
each and every school leader and teacher has the
amazing proclivity to demonstrate genuine caring and
compassion toward their students. Because of their
compassion, they also have the unique opportunity
to help students heal from the toxic repercussions of
the stress so many endure. We believe that through
developing higher consciousness and deeper compassion, teachers and school leaders can deliver healing as
an integral part of children's school experience. With
healing comes opportunities to thrive as children and
to later become positive, contributing adults in our
communities and world.

Through Mindfulness and Compassion
Comes Healing

As we developed this chapter and book, we took a hard look at the world before us.
We also considered the many lenses and perspectives that our experiences as humans
and as educators provide. We considered many terms to describe what schools need
to support all children's innate potential to succeed. Teachers and other educators

could provide nurturing environments, foster climates of success, or incorporate social-emotional learning in our schools. All these are good.

However, we decided on *healing*. Healing ("healing," 2018) is the "process of making or becoming sound or healthy again" and as such implies damage, action, and progress. We are intentional in our use of the word *healing* because it implies action and impact. For our students who have experienced trauma, there has been damage and with damage comes a deep need for healing.

With healing, we do not stop at nurturing or fostering but rather stimulate healing through a higher consciousness of deliberate actions, words, and caring. With healing, we take actions to further well-being, beginning with mindfulness exercises to help ourselves and the students we serve become more conscious or mindful of ourselves, others, and our environment.

Catalysts for Healing

We believe that educators not only have the capacity to help students' healing but have the ability to take the necessary action to create sustainable compassionate communities within their own schools. This is vital action because many students come to school needing to regain a sense of self-esteem, confidence, and courage. An important part of what teachers do goes far beyond the academics. The human connection is critical. A kind word or a caring presence is easily delivered in schools where children spend so many hours each year. And, as caregivers outside the home, teachers have a unique opportunity to become catalysts of healing and help students heal every day through mindful classroom routines, activities, and experiences.

Mindfulness is about seeking greater understanding through paying attention on purpose and gaining insight to respond to our students' needs and feelings from moment to moment throughout the day. When we mindfully respond with a caring and compassionate heart instead of reacting, we are sending the message, "I care about you, and I care about how you are feeling because your well-being matters." Compassionate actions open the door for deeper mindfulness experiences. Some mindful experiences that we can provide at school begin with helping students get more in touch with their bodies and their breath—how they feel when they are happy, sad, or stressed, for example. You create other experiences through our positive moment-to-moment interactions with children. Over time, these precious moments have a cumulative effect, and students who are stressed out and broken learn to count on you, creating a sense of security, safety, and trust.

This is where our journey begins as we begin to shift our thinking by focusing on healing instead of trauma, calm instead of agitation, pleasure instead of pain, and love instead of hate.

And, in doing so we capitalize on our potential as human beings to strive in achieving positive emotional health and well-being for our students and ourselves.

Restorative Healing and Relationships

Teachers can be at the heart of the solution, serving as the catalyst of protection and as healing agents for those students whom trauma, violence, and crisis affect. We see teachers as agents of mediation. *Mediation* is a process through which the teacher provides support and experiences to assist students in moving from coping with stress to thriving and flourishing.

For some students, an agent of mediation is someone listening to their fears and concerns; for others, it is someone helping them problem solve or learn new ways to handle situations and conflicts. In this book, you will learn how to naturally embed vital mindfulness and mediation into your classroom so that it becomes part of your common practice and daily routine. You will see evidence of healing already happening in classrooms and how true cultures of health and well-being can transcend the walls of the classroom and permeate throughout the school building to the playgrounds or athletic fields, bus rides, and beyond. And finally, we will provide information regarding why more healing is both required and possible.

Anchors of Support

As educators, we have the ability to not only attend to students' basic needs but also the capacity to mediate their overall desperations and ensure healthy growth and well-being. More important, we have the power to help circumvent the displacement, hurt, loss, and violence that threaten students' normal development when we learn to be more conscious of ourselves and in-tune to a student's circumstance on any given day.

A longitudinal study examining youth at risk from birth to age eighteen shows that even those with previous or ongoing trauma have much better chances of achieving success if they have a strong emotional bond with a role model in their community (Werner & Smith, 2001). For many youth at risk, this role model might not be someone in their family, in which case they need someone in the community to step up. Since teachers spend so much time with their students every day, they are primary candidates for this role.

Learning, teaching, and student engagement directorate Cecily Knight (2007) argues that all people have the trait of resilience but that protective factors enhance that trait. These protective factors as previously discussed in chapter 1 (page 13) include having a supportive relationship with an adult and a sense of optimism about the future.

A related review of literature from Howard et al. (1999) finds that the more protective factors a child has, the greater his or her odds of resilience. However, the risk factors work in the same cumulative fashion where the more risk factors present, the more resilient one needs to be. Knight (2007) also writes that risk factors are less influential in children's lives than protective factors.

In a review of resilience factors, Ryan Santos (2012) at San Diego State University finds that a compassionate, supportive school environment is of utmost importance. This kind of environment helps students learn how to trust, which is a necessary element in any relationship. Students who have experienced trauma often find themselves in a world of chaos, where they may not have set routines or be able to count on parents to be there and be protective. As trauma experts Margaret E. Blaustein and Kristine M. Kinniburgh (2010) explain, "Trauma often involves children being hurt by others [and] not protected by others. When early relationships are not consistently safe, children may develop a sense of mistrust in relationships" (p. 249). If adults in their world cannot be trusted, it becomes difficult to trust anyone. However, when teachers gain mindfulness skills, they become more responsive to individual students. Through their consistently compassionate interactions with students—including having consistent classroom rules and procedures—they establish predictability and trust.

One way to build more compassionate, supportive environments is to first become more mindful or conscious of students' needs, the needs they bring to school each day. It is important to note, however, that a school does not and should not have to choose between being caring and having high expectations for their students. In fact, Santos's (2012) review finds that a caring community and a culture of high expectations are both of vital importance as protective factors in schools.

Providing both nurturing and challenging school environments will help all students succeed. While some might lack this environment at home, it is absolutely necessary that they find it at their schools. Our school families have great potential and opportunity in the course of a school day and year to provide a safe haven for all students. Given the amount of time students spend at school on a daily, weekly, monthly, and yearly basis, it is possible and also critical that we create the best environment for our students. Consider a simple equation: How many hours do children spend in classrooms between the ages of five and eighteen, assuming nine months of schooling, with perhaps the equivalent of a month of vacation, and classes from 8:30 a.m. to 3:30 p.m.? Omitting preschool or summer sessions, look at the following numbers.

6 hours per day × 5 days per week × 4 weeks a month × 8 months a year × 13 years = 12,480 hours in class

Where else, other than at home, do children spend as much time? With 12,480 hours, a staggering amount of time, a precious gift, educators have such an opportunity. We cannot afford to forfeit any time we have with our students. When children are in crisis, when their egos are shattered, and their sense of self-worth is minimized, the most hazardous measure educators can take is to ignore their pain. Despite research showing the importance of a caring adult (Center on the Developing Child, n.d.a; Santos, 2012), too often children's anguish is ignored as we attend to our curriculum pacing guides, high academic standards, and preset agendas (Hargreaves, 2000; Jardine, 2017; Krashen, 2014; Ravitch, 2016). However, to begin the process of healing, we must provide students more time for mediation from a caring adult— some time to pursue something where they excel and some guidance to help them understand their pains, develop self-compassion, and empower them to heal from within (Cole et al., 2005; Ritchhart & Perkins, 2000; Semple, Reid, & Miller, 2005; Singer & Bolz, 2013).

Where and how do we begin to facilitate change?

Mindsight as the Beginning

For some of the concepts this book presents, we recommend that you begin with yourself. Sometimes it is a matter of pausing and mindfully reflecting, reexamining our beliefs, and looking more closely at our own roles and what we might be able to do in classrooms and schools. We ask that you start with yourself so that you will have sufficient perspective from your own frame of reference—and the insights that come from that direct knowledge and firsthand experiences. It is through this personal journey and expanded knowledge that we as educators gain a better understanding of the students and families we serve. After all, checking in with yourself is one of the first steps toward mindfulness.

Sometimes to truly understand the students we serve we need to take a step back to look more carefully at ourselves. We may have our own suppressed childhood experiences; sometimes for a variety of reasons, we may have compartmentalized our life experiences. However, it helps to turn inward and examine even those things that we find unpleasant, or frightening; perhaps even those things that give us a sense of remorse— the times when we wish we had behaved differently. As we do this, for those who are willing to put forth the effort, we may find that we develop what Daniel J. Siegel (2007) calls our *mindsight*, our capacity to be aware of what we are thinking, enabling us to truly begin to see our students and our world differently. When we do this, we realize that the depth of our understanding, empathy, and capabilities increases.

A View of Our Students

To reach students, it helps to begin with understanding something about them. As of fall 2016, approximately 98,300 U.S. public schools served over 50.4 million elementary and secondary students (National Center for Education Statistics [NCES], 2017a).

The United States is a land of great diversity, and the percentage of Caucasian students is declining. In 2013, 51 percent of students were Caucasian, 25 percent were Hispanic, 16 percent were Black, 3 percent were of two or more races, and 1 percent were American Indian or Alaska Native. NCES (2017b) expects the number of white students to continue declining, totaling 46 percent of enrollment in 2025, while the number of Hispanic students will continue to increase, totaling 29 percent of enrollment in 2025.

A report shows that 25 percent of U.S. twelfth graders are proficient in mathematics and 37 percent are proficient in reading. In earlier grades, academic proficiency is also disturbingly low (NCES, 2016).

- Forty percent of fourth-grade and thirty-three percent of eighth-grade students perform at or above the proficient level in mathematics.
- Thirty-six percent of fourth-grade and thirty-four percent of eighth-grade students perform at or above the proficient level in NAEP reading.
- Seventy-nine percent of eighth graders recognize the meaning of the words when reading them in a reading assessment.

Looking at the scores, there is more evidence supporting mindfulness. When we open the cognitive pathways that have been clogged with stress and trauma, students will be better prepared for mathematics and reading.

Contributors That Complicate a Student's World

Trauma, poverty, and numbers are compounding contributors that complicate a student's world. By as early as age four, over one-quarter of U.S. children experience trauma that impacts their lives and their learning (Costello, Erkanli, Fairbank, & Angold, 2002). Moreover, if children live in neighborhoods with high rates of violent crime, estimates increase to 83–91 percent (Breslau, Peterson, Poisson, Schultz, & Lucia, 2004). Results from a North Carolina study indicate that more than 68 percent of children and youth experience a potentially traumatic event by age sixteen (Copeland, Keeler, Angold, & Costello, 2007). Sixty-eight percent! That is over two-thirds of our students. And there is more. In 2014, more than two-thirds of children (ages seventeen and younger) were exposed to violence within the past year either directly (as victims) or indirectly (as witnesses; Finklehor, Turner, Shattuck, & Hamby, 2015). Exposure to violence can lead to enduring physical, mental, and emotional harm. Exposure to violence at a young age is associated with attachment problems, anxiety, aggression, and depression.

Additionally, even merely witnessing violence may negatively impact children's attentional and cognitive achievement (Child Trends, 2016). According to sociologist and researcher David Finkelhor and his colleagues Anne Shattuck, Heather Turner, and Sherry Hamby (2014), one in nine girls and one in fifty-three boys under the age of eighteen experience sexual abuse or assault at the hands of an adult. According to the U.S. Department of Health and Human Services (2016), fifty-seven thousand children were victims of sexual abuse in 2016.

The gap between potential and performance that is present in achievement tests for students living in the most and least affluent homes widened 40 percent since the 1960s (Reardon, 2011), leading to greater disparities in terms of not only demonstrated educational achievement but also post-school opportunities. Approximately 21 percent of children in the United States under age eighteen years old are from families living in poverty, and an alarming 43 percent of students are living in low-income homes (Jiang, Granja, & Koball, 2017). See figure 2.1 (page 28) for a state-by-state breakdown.

Figure 2.1 represents individuals with different histories, interests, capabilities, abilities, and needs. There is great diversity. Some students come from large families with a traditional mother and father. Others don't have siblings. Some students are raised by same-sex parents. Others are raised in single-parent homes, or by extended families. While some students are raised in families where one or both parents work, others come from families where parents have trouble finding or keeping jobs.

The research on socioeconomic status (SES), race, and the prevalence of child maltreatment and abuse is not definitive. While most studies (Dubow, Huesmann, Boxer, & Smith, 2016; Kim, Drake, & Johnson-Reid, 2018; Moore & Ramirez, 2016) show that poverty is definitely associated with more ACEs, other studies show that abuse and maltreatment cross SES conditions (Chiu et al., 2013; Steele et al., 2016). The relationship between race and abuse is also complex. Several studies find that abuse is higher among white people than other groups (Chiu et al., 2013; Kim et al., 2018; Mersky & Janczewski, 2018). Fewer studies report that abuse is higher among Latinos (Clark, Galano, Grogan-Kaylor, Montalvo-Liendo, & Graham-Bermann, 2016; Lee & Chen, 2017) or African Americans (Scher, Forde, McQuaid, & Stein, 2004). We conclude that although poverty is a significant contributing factor, abuse is not limited to specific SES levels, and maltreatment is perpetuated by adults across all races and cultural conditions.

Further, while we conclude that SES is a significant contributor to childhood trauma, other factors such as maternal stress, parenting skills, home environment, and school safety may offset the disadvantages associated with poverty (Aizer, Stroud, & Buka, 2016; Hackman, Gallop, Evans, & Farah, 2015; Moore & Ramirez, 2016). Students in so-called traditional families may feel the impact of abusive homes, while children raised by extended family members or by a single mother may find a high degree of support. Other students may be raised by a parent or parents who are

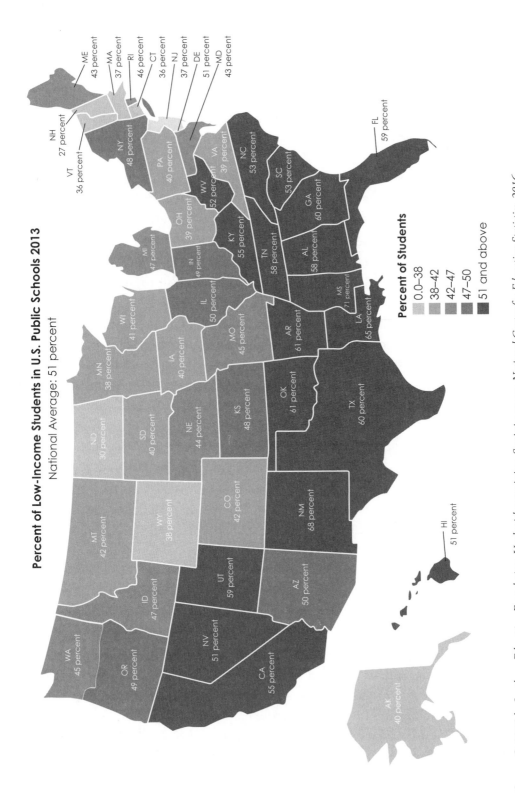

Percent of Low-Income Students in U.S. Public Schools 2013
National Average: 51 percent

NH 27 percent
VT 36 percent
ME 43 percent
MA 37 percent
RI 46 percent
CT 36 percent
NJ 37 percent
DE 51 percent
MD 43 percent
FL 59 percent

NY 48 percent
PA 40 percent
VA 39 percent
NC 53 percent
WV 52 percent
SC 53 percent
GA 60 percent
OH 39 percent
KY 55 percent
TN 58 percent
AL 58 percent
MI 47 percent
IN 49 percent
MS 71 percent
LA 65 percent
IL 50 percent
AR 61 percent
WI 41 percent
MO 45 percent
OK 61 percent
TX 60 percent
MN 38 percent
IA 40 percent
KS 48 percent
ND 30 percent
SD 40 percent
NE 44 percent
NM 68 percent
MT 42 percent
WY 38 percent
CO 42 percent
HI 51 percent
ID 47 percent
UT 59 percent
AZ 50 percent
WA 45 percent
OR 49 percent
NV 51 percent
CA 55 percent
AK 40 percent

Percent of Students
0.0–38
38–42
42–47
47–50
51 and above

Figure 2.1: U.S. families living in poverty.

stressed with the demands of parenting, and it may be hard for a parent or parents in any of the family constellations to provide the nurturing and caring a child needs (Walsh, 2016). Yet other students experience the instability and uncertainty of being moved from one foster family to another.

Students' interests, skills, abilities, and needs also vary widely. Some students are blessed with circumstances that allow them to explore a dream; others can only dream without having the opportunity to take dance lessons or attend a science camp. Despite the excellence in the United States, despite everything the country has achieved, many students have undeveloped or underdeveloped potential. We believe that significant contributing factors to this unused potential include lack of adequate nutrition, threats to the emotional and psychological well-being of children (including racism and low expectations), poverty, and an instructional paradigm that disregards the strengths and needs of the individual child.

Children living in poverty and lacking mediated, enriching experiences that cultivate interest and attention are more likely to display short attention spans, have difficulty monitoring the quality of their work, and struggle with problem solving. *Poor Students, Rich Teaching* author Eric Jensen (2009, 2016) provides substantial research on how to teach students, understanding what we know about the impact of poverty. He concludes the following about students in poverty.

- They enter school with a less developed vocabulary, resulting in barriers to learning.
- They are less likely to exercise, get proper diagnoses, receive appropriate and prompt medical attention, or be prescribed appropriate medications or interventions.
- They have a higher likelihood of ear infections resulting in hearing problems, undiagnosed vision problems, greater exposure to lead, higher exposure to asthma, and greater problems with their immune systems.
- They are less likely to have breakfast and more likely to eat less nutritious food.
- They are more likely to experience acute and chronic stress, often related to their parents' stress, poverty, and living conditions.

The Complexity of a Student's World

Each of the previously mentioned factors negatively affect attendance, attention, behavior, energy, reasoning, learning, memory, and cognition. For students, there are stressors associated with not going to school and stressors associated with being in school. There are peer group pressures and home and life pressures. Students also face a myriad of situations that can evolve to a high level of stress. These challenges may involve using good decision-making skills each day for the seemingly small decisions such as who to hang around with, when to speak out, or when to back down. Consider, for example, the stress that poverty or abuse creates. Students may wonder where their next meal will come from or whether their home will be safe when returning from school.

To reiterate our earlier point, many students live in a culture of violence, bullying, and trauma (CDC, 2014). Additionally, the epidemic of violence on streets and on elementary or secondary school campuses (McDaniel, Logan, & Schneiderman, 2014; Schoen & Schoen, 2010), and the pervasiveness of school and cyberbullying, further the urgency to find creative solutions to violence and stress that go beyond academic reforms (Adelman & Taylor, 2014; Sugai, Horner, & Gresham, 2002).

Understanding the realities of the stressors associated with young children and families is the beginning of our quest to understand the complexity of the world in which our students find themselves.

This Is a Conscious Shift to Reach All Students

While we have provided many statistics regarding violence, poverty, and trauma, the approaches we recommend are for all classes, all students, all teachers, and all school leaders. Without a unified, schoolwide approach, we can anticipate fragmented results. It is simply inadequate to only teach compassion to the students who are bullied, or to those who bully. Also, at a societal level, our need is to deepen an understanding of and commitment to compassion at all levels, in all districts, with students from different walks of life. And the research-based strategies we recommend are effective across the board.

The stakes are high. When we look at the world at large, and at neighborhoods in the United States, we believe that the role of compassion and mindfulness is foundational, and that high-stakes assessments, while important, cannot be a sole driver to further our educational agenda. Despite the pervasive trauma, educators have the opportunity to help students heal and overcome the obstacles to happiness, success, and well-being that stress, trauma, and daily challenges create. Educators, with the nuanced approach we are recommending, can achieve the mission of reaching all students so they not only learn, but also experience a higher quality of life. With our intentional support, even students who are difficult to reach can experience basic opportunities that are at the core of our democracy—greater happiness, more justice, and more equity—and lead more productive and fulfilled lives. Educators, by first being aware, or mindful, can then implement strategies that could make substantial differences for many students. It might even be a matter of a few moments of consideration a day—a few moments of planning, greater expressions of caring, and extended compassion.

from the classroom

Caring can be demonstrated with small gestures of kindness or understanding such as a kind greeting or explanation of how students feel on a five-point scale or a simple journal prompt. In Lori Curtin's first-grade classroom at Lee Elementary School, in Lee, Massachusetts, every day is a new beginning, with each first grader taking a turn as the morning greeter. These students stand alongside their teacher welcoming classmates with a smile, handshake, or high five.

When in the classroom, students follow a well-established and practiced routine: hanging their belongings, placing homework or notes from home into the teacher's bin on her desk, standing in line patiently, or talking quietly at their desks. Exchanges are pleasant and respectful. Students then fill in a small writing prompt at their desks, much like a short journal: "On a scale of one to five, where one is very sad and five is very happy, I feel like a _____ this morning" or "Dear Ms. Curtin, I wish you knew _____." This writing activity helps students identify how they are feeling and helps the teacher understand their feelings as well.

The short writing entry also helps alleviate any fear or anxiety that students may be feeling at that moment—maybe they didn't eat breakfast, maybe their parents had an argument, or maybe something consistent changed to upset them. Whatever the reason, students can start their day aware of how they feel and move forward. At the same time, the teacher is alerted (through the student lens) to any concerns she should know about to help students through the day (L. Curtin, personal communication, May 2, 2017).

We Can Take a More Holistic and All-Encompassing Approach

To quote Peter A. Levine (2008), "As individuals, families, communities, and even nations, we have the capacity to learn how to heal and prevent much of the damage done by trauma." All of us remember teachers who made a difference, teachers who elevated our sense of well-being. Educators will only optimize the learning success of children when they make this shift from a sole focus on academics and learning in academic environments to a more holistic, all-encompassing approach that also includes understanding the varied social-emotional and psychological needs of students in their classrooms and the trials they bear.

The approach we recommend has its roots in various cultural traditions, with individuals with mental health and medical concerns, and by organizations promoting healthy organizational climates that boost good health and well-being. For example, the National Child Traumatic Stress Network (2014) describes the need to build trust before the work of healing trauma can begin. In *Capacitar: Healing Trauma, Empowering Wellness*, Joan Rebmann Condon and Patricia Mathes Cane (2011) address trauma through a multicultural approach that addresses body, mind, spirit, and emotions, discussing the need to heal the brain, heal the person, and heal the community. Physician, neuroscientist, and author David Servan-Schreiber (2013) discusses a need to reprogram the brain to adapt to the present rather than to continuously call up past experiences. Mindfulness facilitates that work, and part II (page 59) introduces those practices step by step. Servan-Schreiber (2013) also discusses an approach to reduce stress and help heal stress through creating more coherence between the brain and the heart.

Jon Kabat-Zinn (2003), creator and researcher of the Stress Reduction Clinic and the Center for Mindfulness in Medicine, Health Care, and Society at the University of Massachusetts Medical School, suggests that our thoughts, emotions, and life experiences influence our overall health and well-being. While Jon Kabat-Zinn and Thich Nhat Hanh (2013) acknowledge "there are few outright cures for chronic diseases or for stress-related disorders" (p. 199), they believe it is possible for people to heal themselves when they learn to live and work with conditions in the present, moment to moment. Specifically, their research, work, and practice of mindfulness demonstrate the moment-to-moment awareness of cultivating just *being* and how this heightened awareness can boost our immune system, help regulate our emotions when under stress, reduce our pain, increase our energy, and allow us greater peace, calm, and happiness. According to Kabat-Zinn and Hanh (2013), healing "implies the possibility that we can relate differently to illness, disability, even death, as we learn to see with eyes of wholeness" (p. 199).

One of the primary reasons we recommend focusing on healing in classrooms is the wide-ranging extent and prevalence of trauma. There is simply too much work to be done to rely on organizations outside of schools to take on a lion's share of the work. Another simple reason is that the research continues to show that by addressing trauma and teaching mindfulness, we better situate students for learning and success (Bandura, 1991; Felver et al., 2015; Kauts & Sharma, 2009; Shunk & Ertmer, 2000; Zelazo & Lyons, 2012).

The students we are teaching will only focus and flourish when we meet them where they are, when we teach with a full realization of how to mindfully educate in a way that pulls each child into the excitement of learning and draws out his or her innate potential and confidence to learn. It isn't so much about teaching academics as shifting our focus to teaching students—paying attention to what impacts learning and how to nurture students so they learn well.

We Can Support Teacher Health and Well-Being Through Mindfulness

In attending to student stress, schools also need to be alert to ways to decrease teacher stress. High absenteeism or attrition rates for teachers may provide a small window of opportunity to better understand the prevalence or significance of how many teachers are actually suffering from their own personal stress or trauma or from secondary trauma in the classroom. Teaching is a high-stress occupation, and teacher stress and burnout are significant factors in teacher turnover (Greenberg, Brown, & Abenavoli; 2016; Ingersoll, 2001; Ingersoll & Strong, 2011). As Flook et al. (2010) find in research on the impact of mindfulness training for teachers over an eight-week period, mindfulness reduces teacher stress and improves classroom teaching performance. In Flook and colleagues' (2010) study, teachers were encouraged to practice mindfulness strategies for fifteen to forty-five minutes a day for six days a week. In 2011–2012, the Mindful Schools Research Study in conjunction with the University of California, Davis, conducted one of the largest randomized controlled studies to date on mindfulness (Fernando, 2013). Participating teachers report greater job satisfaction, an improved sense of efficacy, reduced stress, and greater self-compassion. Eighty percent of these teachers also reported that they were able to deliver the curriculum with "greater ease," and 82 percent reported that they had better connections with students (Fernando, 2013).

When we turn inward, we become mindful, or conscious, and more able to feel empathy for others. Siegel and Rutsch (n.d.) say:

> When we attune with others we allow our own internal state to shift, to come to resonate with the inner world of another. This resonance is at the heart of the important sense of "feeling felt" that emerges in close relationships. Children need attunement to feel secure and to develop well, and throughout our lives we need attunement to feel close and connected.

The ability to look inward emerges through reflection, and reflection is at the core of mindfulness. These are important life skills not only for students but also for adults, including teachers.

With mindfulness, we increase our focus and our capacity to observe and to serve. We act more intentionally and increase our ability to receive information and learn. As educators, when we become more mindful, we are better able to tune into the needs of the students sitting in our classrooms. We become more sensitive to their wounds, as well as their interests, their strengths, and their needs. With mindfulness, we also are able to be more present in the moment as we teach. Hence our pedagogy may become more relevant to the needs and interests of our students.

When we mediate mindfulness with our students, we help them channel their attention and sustain motivation even in the midst of their frustrations; students are better able to understand and manage their emotions as they become more mindful (Broderick, 2013). Mindfulness helps the brain reorganize thoughts and ideas. With mindful practices that reduce stress, students become better able to cope with their daily lives and improve their overall physical and mental health. (In chapter 6, page 91, we will provide concrete activities for educators to implement with their students to help them develop mindfulness.)

We Can Become More Conscious

When we spend more time helping students through their crises, we find that their brains function more optimally and their academic achievement comes more easily (Broderick, 2013; Cole et al., 2005; Jackson, 2011; Jensen, 2009). When we mediate the learning environment for our students and create a safe, supporting, and nurturing school climate with rich learning experiences, our students leave behind the daily stressors of life and may begin to experience trust and perhaps even delight. You might even begin to see students smiling more, beaming as they share their journeys, their exploration, in our classes.

All too often, we see adults who seem to never be happy or who are in a constant state of anxiety or anger, and we consider how all their negative emotions may escalate or infect the lives of those students who depend on them. We can see how vital teachers must be in helping students become resilient; and we are able to look at life through a different lens. With this new perspective, we understand that it is worth the extra effort to extend instruction beyond a standard textbook approach to reach the individual student.

We Can Create Compassionate Havens of Healing in Schools

Children who remain in stressful neighborhoods and homes benefit from whatever opportunities they have to experience a sense of safety, security, and trust. Even if only for a few hours of the day, teachers can help students heal by creating compassionate, safe havens for learning. It is perhaps then, through our conscious choice and action, that we can best serve the needs of the whole child—intellectually, physically, and social-emotionally. We can provide the life tools to navigate the tough seas that we all inevitably encounter as we make daily decisions and struggle to chart our own courses over our lifetimes.

Knowing what we know about mindfulness, we are urging a deliberate paradigm shift. We consider mindfulness not only as an essential 21st century skill but also as a foundational skill and practice that will be most potent when educators infuse it in compassionate learning environments.

Mindful Reflection

As an individual or with your study group, respond to the mindful reflection questions, taking notes on the following page.

- Do you agree that teachers can be agents of healing for students who have faced stress and trauma? If so, how? If not, why?
- Poverty contributes to trauma in numerous ways. What in your classroom, school, or community is helping lessen poverty's impact?
- Can you envision a paradigm shift toward more compassionate education? If so, what are some of the key factors in your vision for schools to become more compassionate? If not, why not?
- Do you agree that schools have been hyper-focused on academic growth to the exclusion of some factors needed to support students? Why or why not?
- As you look back on your own life, are there areas where you already experienced healing? Are there areas still in need of healing?

— Notes —

CHAPTER 3

Our Brain and the Mind-Body Connection

The greatest weapon against stress is our ability to choose one thought over another.

—William James

key principle

Neuroplasticity research shows that despite the impact of trauma, children's brains and brain functioning can improve with mindfulness practices.

As presented in chapters 1 (page 13) and 2 (page 21), school leaders and educators have the unique opportunity to become catalysts of protection and healing for students. When considering the overwhelming and stressful life conditions and circumstances of many students as well as teachers, one thing is for sure: no one is immune to stress. Many times each day we encounter what could be stressful situations. Consider teachers who are overwhelmed with too many tasks, expectations, and mandates to handle on a daily basis and not knowing where to begin or if the demands will ever end. Consider a student getting out the door on time to catch a school bus, making decisions about what to wear, remembering what is needed for the day, or even deciding when to ask a teacher for help.

Stress presents itself in different ways at different times. Some stress can be normal—even healthy—but other times, stress can be unbearable, or toxic. A certain amount of stress, such as stress associated with doing homework, trying out for an athletic team, making new friends, or attending a first dance, is normal. However, too much prolonged stress or toxic stress can cause brain overload or unhealthy brain development. In order for educators to fully understand how to deal with stress (their own as well as their students') and to strive toward healthy brain development through mindfulness practice, we first must understand the brain and its functions as they directly relate to our stress and our emotions. In this chapter, we will describe the impact of stress and the brain physiology and functions (the function junctions), the emotional toll of stress responses, and brain health and classroom implications.

The next time you are ready to give up on a student who seems so utterly unable to follow directions; the next time you contemplate leaving teaching because of the stress; or the next time you feel pulled in too many directions as a school leader, it might help to become a bit detached. Take an intentional pause. Step back from the situation and consider that what you are feeling is the cortisol (bad hormone) kicking in or the amygdala (your brain's guard dog) taking over. Mindfulness practices can help calm physiological functions. Simply taking a deep breath and pausing, refocusing, and recentering before responding to frustrating situations can help provide an intentional, rather than reactionary, response. When we notice how we are feeling and thinking, then take a deep breath, and relax, we are able to develop stronger self-awareness that translates into a more positive response.

This important information on how the brain functions provides educators with a different lens, which can lead to a deeper understanding of and empathy for our students, their families, and ourselves.

Function Junctions of Our Brain

As James Gordon, founder of the Center for Mind-Body Medicine, explains, the "brain and peripheral nervous system, the endocrine and immune systems, and indeed, all the organs of our body and all the emotional responses we have, share a common chemical language and are constantly communicating with one another" (University of Minnesota, n.d.). Our brain involves a complex, interconnected relationship between mind and body. The mind-body connection involves our mental outlook—thoughts, feelings, beliefs, and attitudes—that can either positively or negatively impact our physiology. Similarly, what we do with our physical body can positively or negatively impact our mental outlook (University of Minnesota, n.d.).

The Central Nervous System: Central Station for Emotions and Stress

So, is it Johnny who is unwilling to sit still, or rather is it Johnny's brain sending signals to escape? Or perhaps when Johnny is rocking back and forth, his nervous system actually engages in some self-soothing behavior that, contrary to outside observations, may have a calming impact on him.

The central nervous system is the central station for both our emotions and our stress. It comprises two parts: (1) the brain and (2) the spinal cord. Our emotions involve our entire nervous system. The limbic and autonomic nervous systems both play a significant role in regulating our emotions. The systems are especially influential over our emotional health, including our endocrine and visceral responses to external stimuli that we experience daily. Think of the limbic system as the center of your emotions, thoughts, and working memory, controlling and helping translate how you express your emotions. Think of the autonomic nervous system as the physical center of your reactions to stress, regulating reactions through pulse, heart rate, and blood pressure. Together, these two systems make up the mental and physical consequences of emotions and stress—reaction and response.

The Limbic System and Emotion Regulation

The limbic system, which is the center for regulating emotions, comprises a complex set of structures. This complex set of structures includes the prefrontal cortex, hippocampus, and amygdala as well as the hypothalamus, an area of the brain associated with the production of stress hormones such as adrenaline, noradrenaline, and cortisol (glucocorticoids).

Three Brain Parts Associated With Stress and Responses

The prefrontal cortex, hippocampus, and amygdala are highly involved in how we recognize and respond to stressors. These three areas of the brain also work with the hypothalamus to turn on or off the production of stress hormones that cause physical responses such as racing heart rates, quick breathing, or upset stomach. Those who have experienced long-term stress or numerous stressors are more likely to report that stress is impacting their family, social life, and health (National Public Radio, Robert Wood Johnson Foundation, & Harvard School of Public Health, 2014).

Think for a minute about how you feel when you are what we refer to as *stressed out*. Now, think about students in your classrooms who you know or may not know who have also experienced extended periods of chronic stress. They too may experience a lack of sleep, much worry, inadequate diet, and emotional distress that rattle the brain like a washer on the spin cycle. How can they function optimally in school? Are they attentive, ready to learn, or engaged? *Think again.*

Figure 3.1 (page 40) displays the prefrontal cortex, hippocampus, and amygdala.

The Prefrontal Cortex

As figure 3.1 indicates, the prefrontal cortex is the central processing unit of cognition and affect. Located near the front of our head is the prefrontal cortex of the brain, a large web of neurons and synaptic connections that intelligently regulate our thoughts, actions, and emotions. The prefrontal cortex links to sensory and memory centers throughout the brain, bringing to mind previously experienced and stored

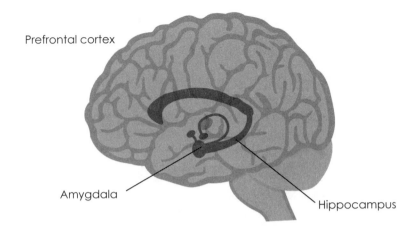

Prefrontal cortex

Amygdala

Hippocampus

Figure 3.1: The prefrontal cortex, hippocampus, and amygdala.

memories (in the hippocampus), helping regulate our thoughts, actions, and emotion. It is the part of the brain that creates a *mental sketch pad* (Baddeley, 2003, 2012), which assists our working memory (auditory and visual-spatial skills) by helping the brain keep in mind (attention skills) a recent event so it can bring to mind information from our long-term storage (memory), and use this information to decide how to moderate our thoughts, emotions, or behaviors (Goldman-Rakic, 1995). Working memory, long-term memory, and attention are all critical for academic learning, as are self-regulation and emotional control. For example, the ability to remember previously learned mathematics facts is critical for solving problems.

The prefrontal cortex is the center of our emotional intelligence. Emotional intelligence involves a set of competencies such as self-awareness, self-management, empathy, and social awareness and relationship management—many of the competencies that mindfulness develops. These competencies allow us to increase our ability to feel, understand, and differentiate gradually more complex emotions. A higher emotional intelligence also is associated with higher academic achievement, since the personal and social competencies such as self-motivation, self-regulation, and social skills contribute to greater focus and outcomes. The prefrontal cortex also helps us understand how we relate to others and regulate our emotions, feelings, and behaviors.

- These emotional intelligence skills involve a conscious awareness of our own and other people's feelings. The skills are directly related to our executive functioning—specifically the cognition we need to control our thoughts, emotions, and actions.
- Emotional intelligence and executive functioning skills are sometimes referred to as *soft skills* when in actuality they are the strong skills required for 21st century learning and social-emotional regulation.
- Our prefrontal cortex is the central processing unit that runs our brain's programs. It helps regulate anxiety and is involved in decision making in response to our emotions, serving as the center of cognition and affect.

- The prefrontal cortex dictates what decisions we will make when confronted by an emotional reaction, thus helping us to problem solve.
- The prefrontal cortex is also the center for regulating behavior, including suppressing inappropriate behaviors and processing complex thoughts.

See chapter 8 (page 131) for more on executive functioning.

The Hippocampus

As figure 3.1 shows, the hippocampus is our internal hard drive. It is correct to say that memories are made in the hippocampus. In our work in schools, we have found that teachers and students enjoy learning about the unusual shape of some parts of the brain, like the hippocampus. Described as two-horned and curved from the back of the amygdala, this portion of the brain plays an important role in converting things that are in or on our mind at the moment (short-term memory) into things that we will remember for a long time (long-term memory). One of the fascinating things about the brain is that as important as the hippocampus is, it takes up relatively little space. The hippocampus acts like an internal hard drive or filing cabinet. It also retrieves memories, processes stimuli (such as where objects are), provides context to the stimuli, and sends the amygdala that information.

The hippocampus is particularly important since applying memories of past threats or similar danger situations to the present means choosing the best choice to guarantee one's own survival. Stress can have a powerful effect on this region of the brain, changing the cellular makeup within the hippocampus and causing difficulties in attention, perception, short-term memory, learning, and word retrieval (Rahman, Callaghan, Kerskens, Chattarji, & O'Mara, 2016; Women's Health Network, n.d.).

The Amygdala

The amygdala is the emotional regulator and danger identification center. Described as the brain's gatekeeper, watchdog, or guard dog, the amygdala consists of two almond-shaped masses of neurons sitting at the base of the hippocampus. When we work with students and schools, we find that children not only learn to say "Oh, my amygdala is acting up" but also that they are able to draw pictures showing the relationship of the amygdala to the prefrontal cortex and hippocampus. The amygdala also helps us perceive other people's emotions, which is an essential part of compassion and one of the soft skills that lead to being a good team player. The amygdala does the following.

- Regulates emotions that mediate and control major affective activities like friendship, love, and affection; expression of moods; and fear, rage, and aggression
- Can give rise to fear, anxiety, or stress when something triggers it
- May take over to seek safety or security

The limbic system and the autonomic nervous system work in tandem. The limbic system helps regulate emotions, and the autonomic nervous system helps prepare us for action when under stress.

You can see the location and purpose of the prefrontal cortex, hippocampus, and amygdala in figure 3.2.

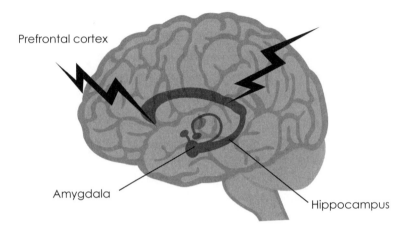

Prefrontal cortex
(decision making, working memory, self-regulatory behaviors, mood, and impulses) helps shut off the stress response, including:

- Dendrite shrinkage (part of neuron that receives information from other neurons)
- Loss of synapse

Hippocampus
(memory loss and mood dysregulation) assists in overactive stress response, specifically:

- Neuron shrinkage
- Synapse loss
- Reduced neuron generation

Amygdala
(anxiety, fear, and aggression):

- Turns on stress hormones
- Increases heart rate—
  - Increased volume and activity
  - Synapse increase

Figure 3.2: The human brain under stress.

The Autonomic Nervous System and Emotion

The autonomic nervous system sends messages from the central nervous system without conscious effort to trigger bodily functions in our internal organs such as the heart, lungs, sweat glands, and digestive glands.

It comprises two divisions.

1. The sympathetic nervous system reacts immediately with a fight, flight, or freeze response to threatening situations—through heart rate, blood pressure, breathing, and pupil dilation.
2. The parasympathetic system is involved in bodily reactions while at rest—digestion, saliva production, urination, and muscle relaxation—creating calming and balancing responses.

Preparation for Action

We can all recall terrifying instances in our lives when we have experienced moments of sheer terror, danger, or fright ripping and rushing through our body like a hotbed of lava. Can you also remember what you were thinking, feeling, or seeing, or how you reacted during these times? These sudden rushes of adrenaline or energy can cause different people to react differently in times of stress, trauma, or danger.

Fight-or-Flight Responses to Perceived Threats

When our mind experiences what it perceives to be some type of threat, whether it be an intrusion to our calm, a disruption to the flow of daily living, or an incitement of unintended fear, we respond through fight or flight. Seminal psychologist Walter Bradford Cannon (1914) describes this response as a reaction that makes an animal ready to run or fight during an emergency. The fight-or-flight response is an automatic survival reaction to a perceived, stressful, and potentially dangerous situation where there is hope of outrunning or outfighting an attacker. There is an animalistic instinct in every human that responds similar to the animal kingdom and its quest for survival. Figure 3.3 demonstrates the significance of the fight-or-flight physiological response of our mind.

Source: Adapted from Sourroubille Arnold, 2016.

Figure 3.3: Fight-or-flight response process.

Cortisol kicks in a few minutes after your body releases adrenaline and noradrenaline. If you are under chronic stress, your body will continue to release cortisol, whose elevated levels can weaken your immune system and decrease your energy.

One Stress Step Further: Freeze

Stress experts added the *freeze* response to the fight-or-flight schema to acknowledge that instead of fighting or fleeing in traumatic or stressful situations, we sometimes freeze up (Schmidt, Richey, Zyolensky, & Maner, 2008). When there is literally no hope of fighting off or fleeing from an attacker, sometimes our body simply goes still in order to survive. There is a direct correlation as to how our mind and our body work in unison to keep us safe, and the *fight-flight-or-freeze* mechanisms are examples of this. Simply said, our minds prepare our body for action.

How Stress May Impact Students

Table 3.1 demonstrates physiological responses of their mind and how students behave when they perceive a threat.

Table 3.1: Physiological Responses of Fight, Flight, or Freeze

Fight	Flight	Freeze
Student actions: <ul><li>Acting out</li><li>Behaving aggressively</li><li>Acting silly</li><li>Exhibiting defiance</li><li>Being hyperactive</li><li>Arguing</li><li>Screaming, yelling, or both</li></ul>	Student actions: <ul><li>Withdrawing</li><li>Fleeing the classroom</li><li>Skipping class</li><li>Daydreaming</li><li>Seeming to sleep</li><li>Avoiding others</li><li>Hiding or wandering</li><li>Becoming disengaged</li></ul>	Student actions: <ul><li>Exhibiting numbness</li><li>Refusing to answer</li><li>Refusing to get needs met</li><li>Giving a blank look</li><li>Feeling unable to move or act</li></ul>

Source: Adapted from Souers & Hall, 2016.

Children and adults manage stress in many ways, and their responses also may present differently as seen in table 3.1. Sometimes their actions may even betray their words. They may know the socially correct thing to say, but their gestures or facial expressions may portray a far different response. While it is important to remember that not all stress is bad, there is also no denying that the long-term toll of stress on the brain structure and function can be potentially catastrophic (Bremner et al., 1997; Hull, 2002; Kemeny, 2003; Koob, 2015; Yale University, 2012).

- Chronic stress may shrink your brain.
- Stress can disrupt memory by triggering the brain's threat response.
- Stress can trigger a chemical change or imbalance that makes you irritable.

Cortisol and the Domino Effect

At the University of California, Berkeley, neuroscientists find that long-lasting stress can have long-term effects on brain structure and function (Bergland, 2014; Sanders, 2014). Researchers are learning how cortisol, a stress hormone, can create paths between the hippocampus and amygdala that result in a vicious cycle that becomes predisposed to be in a constant state of fight, flight, or freeze (Bergland, 2014).

The Impact of Stress on Teachers

While teacher and student stress may present differently, both can be equally debilitating and interfere with learning and teaching. In order for teachers to be catalysts for healing for students, they must take care of their own stress levels, health, and well-being. Teacher signs of stress and burnout may present themselves in various ways (see table 3.2). Increased tasks, expectations, mandates, and demands in teaching may contribute to and magnify high teacher stress levels (Pillars, 2014).

Table 3.2: Teacher Signs of Stress and Burnout

State	May Look Like	May Feel Like
Exhaustion	Appears disconnected	Deep tiredness in bones and psyche
Depression or extreme graveness	Does not smile, laugh, or display joy in life for hours or days	Complete graveness and emptiness
Extreme anxiety	Appears worried and anxious	Constant nagging feeling that the teacher can never do enough while also feeling he or she needs to spend more time with family and loved ones
Being overwhelmed	Experiences shortage of time; always too many tasks to complete	Weight of the world on teacher's shoulders—too many tasks, expectations, and mandates to meet; energy depleted; dragging all the time
Seeking or irritability	Loses creativity, imagination, patience, and enthusiasm for daily challenges	Emptiness; feeling void of happiness and zest for teaching, maybe life in general Need to escape from the noise and chatter and self-reflect
Isolation	Removes himself or herself from the mainstream of school activity	Desire to hide and get away so no one sees the teacher's vulnerability; seeking to find quietness

Source: Pillars, 2014.

The Destructive Impact of Stress

Stress can physically change or compromise our brain's capacity for productive mood and impulse control, decision making, working memory, and self-regulatory behaviors. This may also be one explanation for why young people, including children to age seventeen years who are exposed to continued stress early in life, are more prone to mental illness, anxiety, mood disorders, and learning challenges when they are older (Bergland, 2014).

Stress overload with cortisol dominance can also negatively impact our attention span and how we learn, form memories, and even make decisions. Even more concerning is that "extensive research on the biology of stress now shows that healthy development can be derailed by excessive or prolonged activation of stress response systems in the body and brain" (Center on the Developing Child, 2016). This high level of prolonged stress response is referred to as toxic stress and "can have damaging effects on learning, behavior, and health across the lifespan" (Center on the Developing Child, 2016).

According to Harvard University's Center on the Developing Child (n.d.b), there are three distinct kinds of stress response systems: positive, tolerable, and toxic. These response systems are exclusive to our reaction to the stressful situation or events. Look at the three kinds of stress response systems as defined by the Center on the Developing Child (n.d.b).

1. **Positive:** Brief increases in heart rate and mild elevations in stress hormone levels
2. **Tolerable:** Serious, temporary stress responses that supportive relationships buffer
3. **Toxic:** Prolonged activation of stress response systems in the absence of protective relationships

Positive stress response is often associated with feelings that elicit some immediate, short-term anxiety or fear. When delivering a speech, shooting your first foul shot during a tied game, taking an entrance exam, or going to your first dance, you may feel positive stress as your body may experience mild elevations in stress hormone levels and brief increases in heart rate; however, in a short time, your body returns to its normal state.

Tolerable stress response results in the body's alert or guard dog system signaling a greater degree of more severe and longer-lasting challenges. This response can occur in situations like a natural disaster, an accident or injury, serious illness, or the loss of a loved one. Sometimes this tolerable stress even helps stimulate adrenaline to stay awake long hours to help those in need. For students in classrooms, tolerable stress may help provide the perseverance to spend extra hours studying for an important exam. Tolerable stress may also help students make decisions to spend hours conducting research for a paper rather than joining friends for a movie. However, students may experience serious or prolonged stress hormones if they encounter situations that are demanding and they have nowhere to turn for assistance. Teachers who are able to advise them about how to cope with a stressful situation, or perhaps even buffer them from stressful situations or intervene to help resolve stressful disputes, can mediate these situations. One of the most important things teachers can do is be kind and supportive.

Toxic stress response activates when an individual is exposed to chronic or ongoing conditions associated with frequent, prolonged, and strong adversity that threatens, shakes, or both, one to his or her core. Life conditions or situations at this high and unrelenting intensity can involve emotional, physical, or psychological abuse; chronic neglect; caregiver substance abuse or mental illness; exposure to violence, poverty, and economic hardship; or accumulated family challenges (Center on the Developing Child, n.d.b).

Adults as a Protective Buffer

Sometimes without even talking about a particular situation, adults can provide protective buffers. As discussed in the introductory paragraphs to this chapter, a certain amount of stress is a natural and important part of healthy development, especially in times of danger, in healthy anticipation of an event, or when coping with adversity. "While moderate, short-lived stress responses in the body can promote growth, toxic stress is the strong, unrelieved activation of the body's stress management system in the absence of protective adult support" (Center on the Developing Child, 2007).

Sometimes the impact of toxic stress becomes apparent within a matter of months or years. Students may display more bouts of anger, become confrontational, or grow quiet and withdrawn. Students may change their habits to avoid discussions or refuse to participate in normal routines or activities. In classrooms, as at home, stress can manifest itself in a variety of ways, such as being uncooperative or half-hearted in completing assignments. In addition, particularly with students in middle or high school, they may learn to hide their stress by acting tough or pretending not to care. Psychosis or schizophrenia may emerge in extreme cases as a way to cope with frightening or unpleasant memories as children dissociate from their trauma (Bremner & Marmar, 2002; Fonagy & Target, 1995; Read, van Os, Morrison, & Ross, 2005).

Without adult mediation, effects of stress on a student's brain and body can be catastrophic and lifelong. Stress impacts other parts of the brain and hormones as well. From what we now know about toxic stress, we can see that it is the missing link connecting our fight-flight-or-freeze response and unhealthy levels of the stress hormone cortisol with students' perplexing classroom behavior. Every day, students struggle to maintain, cope, learn, and even survive when facing unfathomable toxic stress and its effects. The adverse effects on the brain eventually take their toll, resulting in poor executive functioning, arrested self-regulatory skills development, and often lifelong damaging effects on the brain function and structure as a whole.

Emotional Toll of Stress Responses

In the section Function Junctions of Our Brain (page 38), we described the impact of stress in the brain. However, stress is not contained to the mind. Stress is felt throughout the body and impacts our ability to attend, relax, learn, and relate to others. Stress, whether it is positive, tolerable, or toxic is our *emotional unease* (McCraty & Tomasino, 2006).

Emotions associated with stress can range from a minor reaction and feeling uncomfortable about something like speaking in front of peers to feeling anger triggered by a very strong inner disturbance like past abuse. Stressful emotions rise from external variables that stem from relationships, events, or challenges to internal unresolved issues, attitudes, or perceptions.

Emotion is a mix of the following (Bradley & Lang, 2000; Niedenthal & Ric, 2017).

- Physiological activation of the sympathetic nervous system (heart rate, blood pressure, breathing, pupil dilation) and various parts of the brain (amygdala, frontal cortex)
- Expressive behaviors (quickened pace, clenched fists, smile, frown)
- Conscious experience, including thoughts and cognitive interpretation (wondering if someone is going to attack) and subjective feelings (a sense of fear)

Our emotions often automatically display as products of a synthesis of our internal reactions. When we are under stress the sympathetic nervous system takes over, sometimes interfering with the relaxation and bodily function responses of the parasympathetic system.

Recall times when you were particularly happy, sad, or angry. Consider your heart rate and breathing, as well as your memory of the time. What do you remember for each? You can also decide to pay more attention next time you experience these emotions—to check on your heart rate and breathing at these times.

Emotions Turning Inward

Turn your attention again to your own life. Do you remember being upset over an intellectual disagreement? Do you remember why you strongly disagreed with the conclusions someone else reached? Or perhaps you became upset in reaction to someone else's anger or hate? When have you experienced strong negative emotions (fear, anxiety, rage, hate)? Did you experience any physiological symptoms (sweating palms, upset stomach, tightening in your throat, perhaps even trembling)? Did you experience any digestive problems, insomnia, frequent urination, or muscle tension? Have you ever felt a fear that has returned time and time again? Have you ever experienced anger that is hard to turn off? Perhaps you have even felt your heart race only to take a deep breath when danger passes.

The combination of sympathetic and parasympathetic reactions operates to help keep our systems in balance. For individuals who experience significant or prolonged stress, there is often an imbalance where negative physiological reactions take over, urging us to act (fight, flight, or freeze). As teachers, it is important to know that just as we have experienced these symptoms, so have our students. For adults and children alike, sometimes emotions are so strong that it is hard to focus on anything other than our physiological response. Just as adults sometimes need someone to listen to them, to hear about their fear or anger, so do children.

Emotional Responses to Fight, Flight, or Freeze

Students who cry easily, are prone to anger, or appear frightened or even seem somewhat apathetic or uncaring, may be stressed. What are the culprit responses to toxic stress that stand in the way of learning, resilience, and success? Indicators of responses to toxic stress cover a wide territory, including the following.

- **Fear:** Fear paralyzes, whether it is fear of failure, fear of a class bully, or fear of a parent with a bad temper. That paralysis may block an individual from pursuing actions that might be healthier and more in the person's own best interest.
- **Anxiety:** Where there is fear there is often anxiety—anxiety over a situation becoming worse or anxiety over one's own health, safety, or well-being. Sometimes anxiety arises from repeated negative situations that involve approach-avoidance (coexisting desires to engage and to detach when faced with one goal; Weiten, 2017). Helping students overcome anxiety may require a multifaceted approach that is somewhat dependent on the student's age, history of anxiety, and life experiences.
- **Failure:** It may be somewhat a matter of the chicken and the egg. Sometimes anxiety sets the stage for failure. At other times failure may trigger feelings of incompetence leading to fear and anxiety.
- **Shame:** One consequence of trauma in particular can be a sense of shame.

This is particularly true for someone who has experienced bullying or physical or sexual abuse.

See How Students Exhibit Feelings of Fear, Anxiety, Failure, or Shame

While there may be external indicators of fear, anxiety, failure, and shame some students are also able to cover up their deeper, underlying issues. For example, we are all familiar with the student who is the class clown—the misbehavior and acting out may be covering up the student's difficulty with reading. Other students flee by disengaging; shutting down; and tuning out classrooms, teachers, and school.

Some abuse alcohol or drugs to address their pain, but many will internalize their emotions, suffering headaches, stomachaches, ulcers, or eventually hypertension. In some cases of chronic stress, the coping mechanism may be to shut out the everyday circumstances. In extreme cases, psychosis and other forms of mental illness may appear, presenting as delusions or loss of contact with reality (Bremner & Marmar, 2002; Fonagy & Target, 1995; Read et al., 2005).

Consider the Cumulative Impact of Trauma

Consider some of the urgent situations we described in chapter 1 (page 13), such as the impact of trauma on African American males or other urban children and youth who may be experiencing pre-traumatic stress (a constant state of alertness to possible danger) or recurrent stress. Consider the cumulative impact of generational issues that have involved oppression, inequality, and injustice for these children. Or perhaps some of you or your students have experienced frequent or prolonged stress from physical or emotional abuse, chronic neglect, violence, or hunger. These are all examples that generate a prolonged activation of stress responses that can have devastating and debilitating consequences.

Some students are under a constant state of hypervigilance, being prepared to react. For them, each loud noise may recreate an awareness of gunfire, each quick aggressive movement toward them may activate traumatic memories of abuse and result in a readiness to lash out with aggression, each negative comment from a teacher or peer may stimulate a reaction of shame or anger or guilt. Sometimes these students may also be passive aggressive—at times appearing to go along with the requirements of your class, and at other times reacting angrily. The solutions to these incidents of serious and prolonged trauma are not simple, and simply talking through the situations will usually be insufficient and ineffective. However, increasing your awareness—your consciousness of their reality and needs, is an important step in helping all students heal from prolonged or daily stress that impedes life and learning.

Brain Health and Classroom Implications

Our knowledge of brain development suggests that the early childhood years are undoubtedly the most critical in establishing the neural connections that provide the foundation for language, reasoning, problem solving, social skills, behavior, and emotional health. Quite simply put, we have but a small window of time to vitalize good brain health in the lives of children.

Significance of Early Brain Health

Our knowledge in neuroscience and neuroplasticity has increased exponentially. This knowledge has taught us much about our brains, our emotions, and their interconnectivity. We are learning how emotions impact how our brains work. We are learning how our cultural frames of reference (for instance, those things that are most relevant, meaningful, or have had deep impact on us) are laden with emotions, and we are learning how emotions affect learning either in a positive or not-so-positive manner. We are also learning about the significance of good brain health, and how easily pathways to learning can be blocked. We are learning that new cognitive pathways can be opened through natural and healthy brain strategies, exercises, and simple awareness of our emotions, others, our surroundings, and ourselves.

The first years of life set the stage for the rest of our years to come. Our first ten years of childhood experiences have great influence over how our brains will be wired and function when we reach our adult years. Shore (1997) explains that a two-year-old's brain is as active as an adult's. Children's brains also have more neurotransmitters, which increases learning efficiency. By age three, a child's brain is even more active and has more neurotransmitters, which help create synapses for efficient learning (Shore, 1997).

Neuroplasticity to the Rescue

Our brain in all its complexity is arguably the most fascinating and impressive organ in our body. When teachers learn about the brain, its malleability, and the activities that mediate learning and enable high intellectual performance from *all* students, they are more confident and competent about eliciting and nurturing students' innate capacity for high intellectual performances. With all our life experiences, you can imagine the impact of accumulating layer on layer of stress.

Brain Malleability and Molding

Neuroscience has taught us that our brains are malleable at any age. Under the right conditions (particularly when feeling safe and confident with an adult who acts as a protective factor) and when employing the right tools and learning supports (sometimes even providing research-based tools to facilitate rehabilitation and repair), the brain can grow new pathways and neurons for healthy connectivity and enhanced functioning (Siegel, 2010b; Willis, 2007).

Neuroscience has also taught us that our brains are not only malleable but that the structure of our brains is constantly undergoing changes through *neuroplasticity*, the ability of our brains to be molded or remain shaped after change. This is very encouraging considering the rise in mental illness, violence, and anxiety-ridden behaviors. "Mindset, behavior, and chronic stress are never fixed" according to Bergland (2014), a public health advocate. Every day provides us with an opportunity to improve our brain structure and connectivity. Teachers are instrumental in mediating support of student brain growth and connectivity. By helping students build confidence, providing opportunities for them to connect new learning with old concepts and skills, and structuring opportunities for individual challenge and success, teachers contribute to a positive mindset, reduce student stress, and further neuroplasticity. Mindfulness helps set the stage for personal growth, by cultivating one's dispositions toward optimism, self, and positivity, and removing doubts and feelings of inadequacy (Cayoun, 2014; Esposito, 2017). Even simple acts of kindness in a classroom can go far toward helping students experience more happiness, feel more secure, and be more likely to extend kindness to others, building a foundation of empathy, compassion, and caring.

Moreover, from a neuroscientific perspective, this practice of conscious reflection and mindsight also helps with our own neuroplasticity and supports our ability to use our brains more fully and efficiently, thus giving us greater insight. This amazing cycle of reflection, support, positivity, and kindness impacts teachers and students alike.

Mindfulness to Combat Trauma and Stress

Neuroscience clearly indicates that trauma can have debilitating effects on brain development, resulting in "smaller brain size, diminished IQ, anti-social behavior, aggression, and emotional numbness" (Williams-Carter, n.d.). While trauma can hinder brain development and functioning, mindfulness practice can help students combat trauma and stress. Mindfulness can help students connect with positive emotional and social experiences through stimulating the prefrontal cortex area of the brain associated with reflective awareness. When this happens, we slow down the reactivity and increase the sense of the body as a whole (Siegel, 2010b). This is why mindfulness practice can also be very effective in relieving a variety of symptoms of toxic stress as well, such as anxiousness or inability to focus for long periods of time. Regular maintenance of our brains, therefore, becomes significant to our health and healing.

Alleviate Stress With Regular Brain Maintenance

The brain is a muscle. Like a muscle, it needs exercise and nurturing for proper growth and development. There are many ways to organically and healthily lower cortisol to reduce stress and maintain brain health. According to Kang and colleagues' (2013) study, making a shift toward healthier mediations that combat stress can help improve brain structure and connectivity.

While mindfulness can improve brain structure and connectivity, we would be remiss not to note that teachers who implement part II's mindfulness, breathing, yoga, and meditation exercises but then humiliate or behave hypercritically to a student can easily undo all the good that the exercises created. Similarly, if teachers repeatedly give students assignments that are too difficult, these teachers' actions can lead to a sense of failure in their students and a reduction in students' sense of self-confidence. Instead, the most effective teachers will combine the information and exercises in this book with pedagogy that supports the development of a student's sense of well-being as well as their own.

Pay Attention to Our Own Health and Well-Being First

Practicing mindfulness provides teachers with a practical and natural way to manage their own stress, health, and well-being so that they can best serve and support their students. Teaching is a stressful job and even though schools and society in general may have paid little attention in the past to a teacher's social-emotional health and well-being, 21st century statistics indicate that teacher stress is a very real phenomenon, maybe even an international epidemic. In 2017, 61 percent of U.S. teachers reported they were always (23 percent) or often (38 percent) under stress, and 58 percent of U.S. teachers described their mental health as *not good* for at least seven of the previous thirty days—compared to 34 percent two years earlier (American Federation of Teachers, 2017). According to MetLife (2013), the morale of 69 percent of teachers has declined since they began teaching, and 55 percent report low or very low morale. Moreover, Richard Ingersoll and his colleagues Lisa Merrill and Daniel Stuckey (2014) report that 41 percent or more of teachers in the United States leave the profession after just five years of teaching.

As school leaders and community stakeholders, we have an obligation to take care of those who take care of our children. Just as teachers mediate support for their students, school leaders must also mediate support for their teachers' social-emotional health and well-being. Mindfulness practice can help teachers maintain better coping, self-regulation, and resilience skills to handle stress in the classroom as well as deliver higher-quality instruction and interact more positively and compassionately.

Ways to Reset Your Brain's Hard Drive

The more stressors a student encounters, or the more serious the student's circumstances, the more likely that it will take special efforts to provide the help and support the student needs. However, over time they can rebuild trust and neural pathways in the brain's hard drive to facilitate connections within the brain and facilitate learning.

Many factors contribute to how one reacts in stressful situations. Things like predisposition, life experience, and genetics can all play a part in the equation of stress response. Helping students discover how to respond to stress in healthy ways can potentially mean a world of difference in their daily lives and in learning. The following are some simple ideas for responding to stress and helping students heal.

- Engaging in physical activity like sports and walking in the woods or outdoors
- Getting plenty of sleep and nutrition, drinking plenty of water, and eating vegetables and fruits

- Relaxing, closing one's eyes, breathing slowly, observing thoughts in a detached manner, and then exhaling and letting go of thoughts one by one
- Focusing on a single thought or phrase to release the chaos in the mind
- Prioritizing time for hobbies or interests like listening to music, drawing, reading, or watching a comedy
- Getting a good laugh or maintaining a sense of humor
- Enjoying positive interactions with friends or family

Mindfulness to Mediate Toxic Stress

Ways in which adults in school environments can help mediate stress and help our students move from conditions of toxic to tolerable stress are many. All require teachers to be mindful or conscious of students' basic emotional needs. The following are a few strategies.

- If you suspect child abuse or neglect, document the incident, share it with counselors and appropriate school officials, and report the possible abuse or neglect to child protective services as the law requires.
- Consider what you can do to lighten a student's load. It may be a matter of giving a student a pass (or extra time) on an assignment. Or it may be a matter of incorporating high-interest activities in assignments, finding a volunteer mentor, or recommending a tutor to help a student academically.
- Find a quiet way to indicate to a student that you are available if he or she needs to talk to someone. In a group setting, you may be able to pause and say a few kind, healing words. In that case you model caring concern. It is important to not gloss over the situation. Depending on the student's age and the nature of the concern, consider the most appropriate action.
- Do what you can to help build the student's sense of trust and fairness, so he or she can see some consistency and have a caring role model. If you express confidence in your ability to help the student, follow through with competence, and ease the student's anxiety with academic scaffolds and emotional support, a student will learn that your actions match your words, and that you are trustworthy.

Classroom Considerations

Mindfulness requires that we deepen our understanding of ourselves and those around us. Sometimes we become better prepared to be a *mindful* teacher by first being more reflective of the stressors we have experienced and the impact of these stressors on our own lives. Once we better understand ourselves, we often become more sensitive to our students' needs.

While we provide further examples in chapters 6 (page 91) and 7 (page 115), we offer the following few simple strategies to connect information on the brain, stress, and implications for classrooms.

- Reflect on a time of prolonged or toxic stress, how you felt, and how you were able to reduce the stress.
- Recall a time of positive or tolerable stress, like the excitement of an upcoming event or of working long hours to meet deadlines. Remember how you felt in each instance.
- Try to identify students who have recently displayed positive, tolerable, and toxic stress.
- Consider students in your school or classroom. Identify what behaviors lead you to conclude that they may be experiencing prolonged trauma or facing anxiety, fear, shame, or failure.
- Reflect on your students' community, considering if there has been a traumatic event that has impacted the community or if the community is embroiled with ongoing violence.
- Consider the nature of the community events and needs, and how this may be impacting students and schools.

Helping students to understand and regulate their emotions is essential to mastery of both academic skills and social skills. Providing opportunities throughout the school day for students to learn and for students or teachers to practice together how to calm their anxieties and how to self-regulate through mindfulness helps to decrease high levels of arousal and fear (cortisol) that trigger inappropriate behaviors. As we have learned in this chapter, understanding that learning challenges may be a result of trauma or toxic stress is important to how we instruct. Often students who experience trauma or toxic stress are unable to find the words to describe their pain or are unable to express their experiences so that others understand. As a result, teachers and students may not understand *why* they are acting out at any given time. When this happens for the student, it may create a disconnect between his or her experience, emotions, and actions. Teachers who do not fully understand why a student is acting out tend to focus on a student's behavior rather than the emotions behind it. When this happens, teachers may react in ways that do not help resolve the issues, and at times can even add to a student's stress, sense of distrust, or anxiety.

Through the practice of mindfulness and better understanding how the brain, trauma or stress, and emotions interconnect, teachers can develop a heightened awareness and gain critical insights into how to respond to situations as they arise. With these insights, teachers can then consider a student's feelings and emotions, resulting in actions that would never be considered with a focus solely on the student's behavior.

Mindful Reflection

As an individual or with your study group, respond to the mindful reflection questions, taking notes on the following page.

- Are you implementing any instructional strategies to help students focus, feel secure, and be confident?
- What do your students know about neuroscience and their brains?
- How can you incorporate understanding of the interconnectivity of stress and emotions into your classroom?
- How comfortable do you feel teaching about the three major brain parts that are directly related to stress?
- When you sense that students are under considerable stress, what steps will you take to help relieve their stress?

— Notes —

PART II

MINDFULNESS PRACTICES— GETTING PRACTICAL

In part II, we address the *how*—how to practice mindfulness strategies and introduce them into your classroom. This part builds on the second of three streams of research that guide our work toward creating mindful, compassionate communities: trauma research and mindfulness practices in classrooms (The Hawn Foundation, 2011; Jennings & Greenberg, 2009). This research confirms the value of these practices in helping improve students' well-being, social skills, and academic achievement.

Mindfulness can begin with becoming more aware of one's breathing and bodily sensations and moving on to noticing shifts in how one feels when stretching, doing mindful yoga that incorporates inhaling and exhaling with movement, and then learning to meditate or participate in guided visualizations. Teachers can use mindfulness and the accompanying exercises in chapters 4–6 (pages 61, 73, and 91) as the foundational practice to help mitigate the significant social-emotional needs of students, alleviate the social-emotional demands of classroom teachers, and provide a nurturing and caring learning environment. We have geared our practices toward increasing social-emotional competencies such as self- and social awareness, positive relationship development, responsible decision making, stress management, self-regulation, and calming of the mind. Self-regulation, or the ability to monitor and control one's emotions, ideas, and behavior, is particularly important for success in academic settings (Bandura, 1991; Schunk & Ertmer, 2000).

While you can gain much by reading about mindfulness, if you take your journey one step further and follow our advice to engage in the exercises before introducing them to students, you will gain additional benefits. Substantial research supports these exercises, demonstrating a reduction in levels of stress, improvements in focus, and increases in prefrontal cortex activity of the brain. To gain the greatest impact, you will need to repeat most of the exercises, and in particular the breathing, meditation, and Heart Beaming (Mason & Banks, 2014) exercises. In fact, we repeat these exercises over and over again, year after year. The exercises will reduce your stress. Yet, we caution you that our experiences are individual—some people will experience an immediate *aha* moment and a deep sense of peace and calm, and others realize the impact over time.

The breathing, yoga, meditation, and mindfulness exercises will also be most potent if you keep up with what we call your practice. By *your practice*, we mean that you intentionally set aside time, perhaps as little as fifteen minutes four to five times a week, to keep up with the recommended exercises. We suggest that you also look for opportunities (transition times, lunch, or recess) to naturally infuse three to five minutes of practice within the course of the school day to help alleviate daily stressors and calm your own mind. Students will gain the most if you incorporate these exercises as a practice naturally embedded within the school day and classroom, with time set aside for students to learn and experience the impact, time after time, day after day.

CHAPTER 4

A Deep Breath

*Sometimes the most important thing in a whole day is the rest
we take between two deep breaths.*

—Etty Hillesum

key principle

*Breath work is essential
to balancing and
regulating one's
emotional state of mind,
health, and well-being.*

As introduced in chapter 3 (page 37), the connection between stress, our mind-body, and brain becomes undeniable once we better understand the complicated structure of the brain and the role it plays in regulating emotions. While trauma, stress, and crises can have short- and long-term negative effects on brain structure and function, we have the ability to make healthy lifestyle choices that will help maintain positive mind and body health. For our students, calming the mind and body can greatly mitigate stress and open healthy new neuropathways to learning.

This chapter presents an intimate view of key strategies for connecting with ourselves and others to overcome trauma, fear, and a sense of failure. It begins with every breath we take under stress, duress, or fear. With breath work, we focus on the conscious control of breathing "to change what is happening in your mind and body . . . . to experience calm and well-being" (The Chopra Center, n.d.).

This chapter introduces breath work. However, in chapter 5 (page 73) and chapter 6 (page 91), we consider components of breath work that you can practice and understand when you combine them with movement and meditation. With breathing exercises come opportunities to experience our breath and its impact. In essence, we become more mindful of our breath. With long, deep breathing we can expand and strengthen our lungs and calm our nerves.

To facilitate your practice, you could make an audio recording to guide you through the steps as you practice with a friend, family member, or peer teacher. We recommend that teachers practice breathing and mindfulness techniques together before they teach them to students. We recommend the following exercises when you instruct students in breathing. After practicing, be sure to reflect on the experience with the questions that follow.

Breath—A Natural Means to Handle Stress

When teachers learn to master simple breathing techniques, we can help regulate our own state of mind. With a bit of practice, we can teach our students the importance of breath and how to regulate their breath. If for some reason, you do not feel comfortable teaching breathing exercises even after practicing, continue to practice but investigate the many online videos (such as Breath Meditation for Kids by the Meditation Channel at https://bit.ly/2r74Vnj and TeensHealth at https://kidshealth.org/en/teens/relax-breathing.html) that teach breathing techniques for all different age groups. Practicing breathing exercises alongside your students is beneficial whether you or an online teacher leads the exercises. Either approach will provide the needed relief and calming you and your students seek.

Research demonstrates that taking deep breaths is not only one of the most effective tools to balancing the brain and returning the nervous system back to its ready emotional state, but is also one of the easiest and quickest forms of relief (Baghel & Shamkuwar, 2017; Kumar, 2014). You take in more oxygen during intentional deep breathing, which results in better circulation, respiration, and toxin elimination. For students in classrooms, this means that there is more oxygen available to their brains and that chemicals are reduced to increase brain efficiency, elevate their mood, and reduce pain (Chong, Tsunaka, Tsang, Chan, & Cheung, 2011; Jerath, Edry, Barnes, & Jerath, 2006). With these changes taking place in their brains, students are better prepared to focus on learning without being distracted. With stronger immune systems, student attendance is higher.

Deep breathing is also a simple tool that you can use anywhere and anytime, making it an ideal choice as a lifelong form of relief from stress and increased self-regulation.

Simply Breathing

Breath is amazing. By breathing we can calm or energize ourselves. When we are frightened we may find that our pulse is faster and our heartbeat is stronger. When we are scared our breath may be shallower, almost as if we are afraid to take a deep breath. Yet breath is the essence of life.

By focusing on breathing (breath awareness) we can connect to the very essence of our lives. Practice in breath awareness helps us to tune in and notice our breathing. Through practicing breath awareness, we can enter a state of relaxation and calm, releasing other thoughts and focusing on the simple rhythmic activity, the rise and fall of our chest, belly, and diaphragm.

Take a moment. Take a few deep breaths. Is your breathing deep or shallow? Is it fast or slow? Is it smooth or irregular? Notice. Are you breathing from your diaphragm? The diaphragm is a dome-shaped piece of muscle and tendons positioned on top of the stomach. When we inhale deeply into our bellies, the abdomen expands and the breath passes through the diaphragm. When we exhale deeply, the exhale also involves the abdomen and the diaphragm. A deep exhale pulls the navel point to the spine. In quiet breathing, the diaphragm only moves a few centimeters. With intentional deep breathing or exercise, the diaphragm can move up to ten centimeters, which increases the amount of oxygen that is available to our bodies. More oxygen means better circulation, respiration, and toxin elimination (Baghel & Shamkuwar; 2017; Kumar, 2014). Deeper breathing also makes more oxygen available to the brain. This deep breathing helps slow the heart rate, which can reduce cortisol and other stress hormones. (See chapter 2, page 21, for more information about that.) A few simple deep breaths may help reduce anxiety or fear for students who have experienced significant trauma or who are just stressed out because of their struggle with academic achievement.

Put your hands on your abdomen. Breathe through your nostrils, and take a few deep breaths. If you are taking deep yogic breaths, breathing from your abdomen, your fingers will spread apart slightly as your abdomen expands like a balloon. Sometimes it takes weeks of practice to feel comfortable with deep breathing. Most people who haven't received instruction in yogic breathing will breathe into their upper lungs, instead of bringing the breath all the way down into their abdomen. When you instruct students—particularly those who are ages ten and older—scan the room to see if students are actually breathing deep into their bellies. Gentle reminders such as "Remember to breathe deep into your belly," are helpful. It can be easier, initially, to practice this lying on your back with your hands on your abdomen. You may want to use this exercise on a regular basis, with these same reminders over a period of several weeks.

Teachers' Plates Are Full and Yet . . .

Teachers who are charged with teaching so many things to students may not be interested in bringing one more thing to their plates. However, if you knew that students would learn more readily, that instruction would be more enjoyable, and that students would gain greater insights into what they are studying, perhaps then you might be interested. Perhaps if you knew that taking a few moments to breathe would provide a lifetime of benefits for yourself and your students, you would consider taking on the challenge we present in this book.

Each day more and more research appears on the benefits of breathing, movement, mindfulness, and meditation (Davidson et al., 2003; Flook et al., 2010; Schmalzl et al., 2015; Streeter, Gerbarg, Saper, Ciraulo, & Brown, 2012). A synthesis of the literature by Schmalzl et al. (2015) shows evidence that yoga and meditation can help a wide array of ailments, illnesses, and stressors. These techniques have reduced cortisol levels, lowered depression, and increased gray matter volume in the brain. Self-reports of yoga practitioners, for example, have found increased levels of vitality. Other findings that Schmalzl and colleagues (2015) summarize include faster reaction times on a visual discrimination task, improved short-term and long-term memory, and fewer errors in everyday tasks of attention, memory, and motor skills.

Importantly, functional magnetic resonance imaging (fMRI) shows that yoga practitioners or those engaged in mindfulness activities also are able to view negative emotional situations with less likelihood of being pulled into the trauma and drama of the moment or becoming angry, sad, or fearful. There was also less activity from the amygdala as practitioners maintained a greater level of prefrontal cortex involvement than those in the control groups (Bremner et al., 1997). The implications for classrooms? Students will be less distracted and better able to focus on academic learning.

Breath Is Our Life Energy

In some ways, information on breathing is common knowledge. Many of us have heard the advice to take a few deep breaths. If we are feeling agitated, hurried, anxious, or scared, our breath becomes shallow and quick. When teaching relaxation, instructors often say something like, "Inhale deeply, circulate the energy, relax, and let go." With a few minutes of long, deep breathing, we are able to improve the functioning and efficiency of our heart, lungs, and other internal organs and systems. This deep breathing helps expand our lungs and slow our heart rate. We are able to help balance our emotions. We are able to transform our stress and negativity into the energy that we can use for self-healing and self-development. And we are better able to extract and absorb the energy we need for spiritual growth and independence.

Breathing correctly helps us to maintain positive emotions and keep our performance at its best in everyday activity (Chiang, Ma, Huang, Tseng, & Hsueh, 2009; Piquero, Jennings, Farrington, Diamond, & Gonzalez, 2016; Singh, Wisniewski, Britton, & Tattersfield, 1990).

Practical Exercises

Breathing exercises can produce an immediate sense of calm by slowing our heart rates and blood pressure and sharpening our focus. Several breathing exercises follow. Read through them prior to practicing the breathing. Then intentionally plan to practice these breaths every day for at least a week before teaching them to your students or electing to use an online video teacher as previously discussed.

You can teach students of all ages the breath exercises in this chapter. The exercises can be meaningful and fun for everyone, but sometimes we describe them differently for elementary students. For example, instead of saying "Take short, quick sniffs—or quick inhales—through your nose," you could say, "Now we're going to try bunny breath." Also for elementary students, combining breath and movement or references to animals helps them focus as they have fun.

Though breathing exercises can be calming, it may be challenging at first to focus on breathing without your mind wandering. Often, our minds become distracted with other thoughts. When your mind wanders, gently refocus and bring your awareness back to your breath each time. While following the steps, be patient with yourself. Remember that every time you practice breathing awareness, you are retraining your brain by focusing on your breathing rather than letting the emotional part of the brain (amygdala) hijack the thinking part of the brain (prefrontal cortex). In time and with practice, you will improve your ability to maintain awareness of breath, decrease competing thoughts, and increase your focused attention.

After a week of breath work, reflect on the following questions.

- Did you notice any changes in how you felt over the course of the week?
- Did you develop a preference for one of these breathing exercises? If so, which one, and why?

After you have practiced breathing for a while, you will find that you can extend the length of time you are able to hold your breath and the depth of your breath will also increase. When you are comfortable, the next step is to introduce breathing techniques in your classroom. You can introduce each of the techniques you practiced on the previous pages to students in a step-by-step fashion, demonstrating breathing to students and asking them to practice. When you instruct students in breathing, we recommend the following.

- Begin by helping students to become comfortable. Consider where they are—at their seats, in a group circle, standing, or sitting.
- Use a soft, calming voice.
- Speak somewhat slowly and meditatively, pausing between phrases so that students can absorb and stay with a thought before adding the next component.

Rotating Mind to Body Focus

Breathing exercises can produce an immediate sense of calm because it is generally hard to think of much else when focusing on breathing. Follow the seven steps to deep breathing.

1. Close your eyes.
2. Breathe deeply, inhaling (breath in) through your nose and exhaling (breath out) through your nose from your abdomen.
3. Inhale into your abdomen and imagine bringing the breath up to your forehead.
4. As you exhale, imagine rotating the breath back down to your abdomen and start again.
5. Practice for about three minutes.
6. Close your eyes, focus, and see how you feel.
7. Open your eyes and think about the following questions.
   - Were you able to imagine inhaling into your abdomen and bringing the breath up to your forehead?
   - As you exhaled, did you bring the breath back down to your abdomen?
   - Could you feel your abdomen expand on the inhale and contract on the exhale?
   - Were you able to stay focused on this?
   - Did you have other thoughts?

There are many different versions of how to focus on the inhale and exhale. Following are two more exercises that focus on the inhale (breathing in) and exhale of breath (breathing out).

Relaxing and Breathing

The following exercise, which originally appears in Christine Mason and Karen Lee Banks's (2014) *Heart Beaming*, focuses on seven steps to a different way to inhale and exhale.

1. Sit comfortably, with your back straight but relaxed.
2. Relax and notice your breathing when you're relaxed.
3. Inhale fully through your nose, thinking "One, two, three, four."
4. Hold for a count of three.
5. Exhale fully through the side of your mouth, thinking "One, two, three, four, five, six."
6. Repeat four or six times.
7. Check to see how you feel.

Hummingbird Vibrations

Consider a hummingbird. Its wings flutter at a very rapid rate, producing a humming sound. With this exercise you feel your lips vibrate.

1. Inhale through your nose.
2. As you exhale, say "Hummmmmm," starting with an open mouth for the *H* and then pressing your lips together for the *mmmmmm*.
3. Repeat several times for between one to three minutes. Try to work up to five minutes to help calm the autonomic system even further.

Buzzing Bee

Consider the hum of a buzzing bee. The finger positions, which you can see in figure 4.1, amplify the sound.

1. Place your thumbs over your ears.
2. Place your index fingers over your eyes.
3. Place your middle fingers on your nose.
4. Put your pinkie fingers lightly on your mouth.
5. Inhale deeply and slowly, thinking "One, two, three."
6. Exhale slowly for five seconds making a light humming sound.
7. Repeat until you feel a deep sense of relaxation and calm.

Figure 4.1: Buzzing bee.

Balloon Breathing

This exercise can help provide a better understanding of deep breathing. Repeat this exercise for two or three minutes. With elementary students, you may ask them to imagine the balloon as their favorite color, or that they are floating higher in the sky with each breath.

1. Get into a comfortable position.
2. Close your eyes.
3. Breathe in through your nose.
4. Breathe out through your mouth, with your lips slightly open.
5. As you inhale, imagine your abdomen is inflating with air, like a balloon.
6. As you exhale, imagine that the air is slowly leaving, like a deflating balloon. Remember, you do not need to force out your air; gently and slowly exhale.

Quick Sniffs

This breath is shallow and somewhat rapid. Nonetheless, it will increase the amount of oxygen in our bodies.

You can call this *bunny breath* to make this exercise more fun for elementary students. Add context to the exercise by asking K–2 students if they have ever seen a bunny sniff or asking one student to demonstrate, or hop like bunnies, stop, and show you how bunnies breathe. With grades K–3, make sure everyone exaggerates sniffing through their nose, perhaps even showing a little nose twitching. For grades 4 and up, you can follow the steps as is.

1. Take three quick sniffs in through your nose.
2. Take one long exhale out your nose.
3. Make the exhale slower and slower as the exercise continues.
4. Start sniffing and continue breathing like this for between one and three minutes.

Snake Breath

This simple exercise works for students of all ages.

1. Inhale slowly through your nose.
2. Exhale through your mouth with a long, slow, hissing sound.

Blow Out the Candle

This simple exercise works for students of all ages.

1. Imagine a birthday candle.
2. Take in a deep breath through your nose.
3. Exhale through your mouth to blow out the candle.

Lion's Roar

In the next chapter, we consider components of breath that you can practice and understand when you combine them with movement and meditation. You can modify this exercise for middle and high school students by omitting steps one and two.

1. Move like lions in the jungle.
2. Stop and roar. Keep roaring. (Continue for three minutes.)

3. Stick out your tongue and roar. (Continue for one or two minutes.)

4. Do you feel the roar in your throat?

After completing this exercise, you can ask middle or high school students to compare the bunny, snake, and lion breaths. You could ask them questions such as, "Where did you feel the breath?" or "Which breath would you use to relax your throat?" (The latter would be lion's roar breath.)

Practical Applications

You can use breath work and breathing exercises in a variety of ways with classes and groups of students to help regulate emotions and calm body and mind. Teachers or counselors could introduce these exercises. Here are a few examples.

- **Anger management:** When working with a group of students on anger issues, you could instruct students in the old adage to "take a deep breath." You could combine breathing with scenarios and role playing designed to help students address anger issues.
- **Exam or speaking anxiety:** You can practice deep breathing along with your whole class for two to three minutes prior to taking a test or speaking in front of a class to alleviate feelings of anxiety and fear. Insert "Take a couple of deep breaths" into test directions as a reminder for students to breathe, relax, and calm their minds throughout taking the test.
- **A student in distress:** If a student comes to you with a concern, whether it's fear, hurt, or sadness, you can suggest that the student take a few deep breaths to calm the mind and body before he or she explains the situation.
- **Disruptive classrooms:** Once your class has had some practice with long, deep breathing, you can signal that it's time to pause, stop, and breathe when you notice students getting louder. Use a signal like those that get students' attention, such as raising your hand and waiting for students to raise theirs. When you have their attention, breathe deeply as you move your hands palms up, sustain the breath with your palms still up, and then exhale as you lower your hands, palms down.

Only two to three minutes of breath work and breathing breaks spread out through the school day can help alleviate the several ten- to fifteen-minute periods of disruption and redirection time that it often takes to help students refocus and get back on task. The amount of breath work necessary to handle anger, anxiety, and distress varies person to person and situation to situation. However, even five minutes three times a week, or three minutes daily, can start making a difference. Within three or four weeks, you may notice a difference. Simple breathing practice offers both students and teachers the opportunity to maintain calm, balance, and equanimity throughout the school day.

from the classroom

Sixth-grade teacher Angela Worden-Corey, at Dexter Park Elementary in Orange, Massachusetts, says:

> Breathing activities have become especially important in the last few weeks of school. I used roller coaster breathing and found it really helped calm and center the class. When I worked one-to-one with students, starting with calming breathing really helped (personal communication, June 2017).

For roller coaster breathing, place a stuffed animal on the student's stomach. The stuffed animal moves up and down as he or she breathes (JoBea Kids, 2016).

Reading specialist Mia Darone, at Lee Elementary School in Massachusetts, works with a kindergarten tier three reading group on its understanding of the *air in our lungs* activity where students learned about the calming impact of breathing (the MindUP Curriculum; The Hawn Foundation, 2011).

> We talked about breathing and inhaling and exhaling. We used balloons to simulate the lungs expanding and contracting. We also painted trees with balloons, and the kids loved this! They really seemed to understand the vocabulary words and now when I say inhale and exhale, they know just what to do. It amazes me how quickly the students calm down when we start focusing on breathing. They really benefit from these exercises (M. Darone, personal communication, April 5, 2017).

Mindful Reflection

As an individual or with your study group, respond to the mindful reflection questions, taking notes on the following page.

- What did you notice most about how you felt before the deep breathing and after the deep breathing?
- What was the biggest obstacle to letting go of all other thoughts? How did you get over this obstacle?
- Did one of the breathing exercises have greater success than another in certain situations? If so, how did you come to this conclusion?
- How did students respond to the breathing exercises?

— Notes —

CHAPTER 5

Move and Stretch—
Yoga and Meditation Basics

The rhythm of the body, the melody of the mind, and the harmony of the soul create the symphony of life.

—B. K. S. Iyengar

key principle

Yoga and breath work can reduce stress, increase focus, and improve capacity to learn. However, practice is required. The benefits only come with practice.

♥

With yoga, we are consciously lifted from our daily experience to a deeper understanding of and appreciation for our bodies. As we explain in chapters 2 (page 21) and 3 (page 37), stress and trauma negatively impact our minds and bodies. Since our emotions and breathing are interconnected, we can better regulate our emotions through deep breathing, as we discussed in chapter 4 (page 61). Deep breathing is a simple but powerful life tool that can enhance our well-being, help regulate our emotions, and open new learning pathways for students. You can easily integrate deep breathing into the school day, at home, or in any life setting to help alleviate stress and the impact of trauma.

In this chapter, we present yoga and meditation techniques. In our teaching, we have found that breathing and yoga prepare the body and brain for meditation. Meditation often brings a greater feeling of calmness and well-being *if it follows* breathing and yoga exercises. In the previous chapter, we presented several breathing exercises to get you started. In this chapter, we continue the sequence with yoga and then move to meditation.

Yoga is trending. Each day more research appears on the benefits of breathing and also yoga, mindfulness, and meditation, either separately or in combination. Research shows that contemplative, yogic, or mindfulness programs that include a meditation component increase brain and learning capacity, reduce stress and anxiety, improve academic functioning, and increase a sense of well-being and social connectedness (Davidson et al., 2003; Flook et al., 2010; Hutcherson, Seppala, & Gross, 2008; Lazar et al., 2005; Lutz, Brefczynski-Lewis, Johnstone, & Davidson, 2008; Semple et al., 2017). Research on the impact of yoga shows it to be effective in treating post-traumatic stress disorder (Mitchell et al., 2014) and in improving feelings of self-efficacy, control, security, and confidence (Büssing et al., 2012; Franzblau, Smith, Echevarria, & Van Cantfort, 2006).

All these elements connect to academic success and suffer greatly when someone experiences trauma. A growing body of research shows that yoga is important to reducing the impact of stress and trauma and creating pathways that build resilience and expedite learning and academic achievement (Kauts & Sharma, 2009). Researchers find that participating in yoga is associated with higher mean increases in grade point average when compared to students in traditional physical education classes (Hagins & Rundle, 2016).

This chapter provides some ancient guidance from yoga and meditative practices, updated with several Heart Beaming (Mason & Banks, 2014) exercises adapted for schools as recommended by the CEI. For each of the exercises in this chapter, we first give teachers and administrators some practical experience. We follow this with exercises for students. Our practical exercises are life tools that you can use with students; students and teachers can do together while at school; and students can teach their parents and families together at home. Given the wide array of needs and circumstances involved with practicing yoga, we recommend first taking a yoga class in order to observe the instructors and learn *prior* to introducing yoga into the classroom.

While you may be able to introduce simple breathing or yoga postures after attending one class with a certified yoga instructor, many teachers report feeling more comfortable introducing components as they gain experience. Of course, this depends on the grade level and the exercises' difficulty level. Many of the yogic movements for prekindergarten and kindergarten students are similar to the movement exercises that are part of many early childhood classrooms. In these cases, it may be simply a matter of becoming familiar with the yoga practice.

Research demonstrates these healthy practices to be particularly important for victims of bullying, violence, and trauma, as well as those inflicting the pain and trauma who are living with their own trauma and emotional concerns (Frank, Jennings, & Greenberg, 2013; Heineberg, 2013).

Body Awareness From Sports and Yoga

Certainly, vigorous cardiovascular activities that increase the heart rate are important for people of all ages. Similarly, sports and team activities are important for many reasons—they can improve fitness and eye-hand coordination as well as skills such as listening, following directions, and making instantaneous decisions. On the ball field, we face decisions about whether to move to the left or right, backward, or forward and whether to jump, stretch to catch a ball, or block an opponent. Sports also give us an opportunity to learn about teamwork: taking turns, helping out a teammate, and even being aggressive in swooping in to take the ball from the other team. And as people play sports they often find that their minds focus on the game at hand, creating neural pathways to reinforce bodily movements and decisions. All of this is particularly true for individuals who are either born athletes or are making progress as they learn to play the game.

During these sports and cardiovascular activities, individuals learn about their bodies—their physical capabilities and their limitations. Over time, we learn from the feedback our bodies provide as we engage in sports, cardiovascular exercises, or other physical movements. This feedback helps us understand more about our individual fitness, strength, and endurance and helps us make decisions about how to up our practice or how to sustain the results we have obtained. For example, with sports, I may learn that I am better at shooting a basketball from a certain spot on the court, or that I am definitely better at sprinting rather than long-distance running. Over time with practice, I may gain skills to increase my capabilities.

Yoga's and Meditation's Introspection

Yoga and meditation provide opportunities to learn about our own bodies in a different, more introspective way.

- With breath work, yoga, and meditation, we may gain a sense of what a deep breath truly feels like—about how our abdomens expand and our chests rise on a truly deep inhale. In yoga, much of the attention on breath is on deep, diaphragmatic breathing—also called *yogic breathing*. Many of the breathing exercises we present in chapter 4 occur in yoga classes and integrate with yoga movements. With yogic breathing, we learn about the power of our lungs, and over time we can gain an understanding of ways to enhance our breath.
- With yoga and meditation, we may learn about our sense of balance, our flexibility, and our ability with practice to stretch farther and hold poses for longer periods of time. Many people can benefit from the fitness that results from yoga stretches. Athletes often find it loosens and lengthens muscles.

People who spend hours at computers find it counteracts the forward leaning posture.

- With yoga and meditation, we may learn to put stress aside, to stop a mind that wanders from topic to topic, and instead to focus on one thing, leading to better concentration and more insights into ourselves and others.

Imagine what this can do for your students!

Evidence of the Effectiveness of Yoga and Meditation in Schools

Amanda Machado (2014), in an article in *The Atlantic*, investigates the impact of yoga for students, reporting on the results from studies conducted in several schools, among them the following.

- New Haven Academy, a magnet high school in New Haven, Connecticut, requires yoga and meditation classes three times a week for first-year students. They measured stress levels with a saliva test and found significant reductions in cortisol, a stress hormone. Students also reported feeling calmer (Bailey, 2013).
- Visitacion Valley Middle School, located in a high-crime area in San Francisco known for its gun violence, had frequent fighting in the hallways and a high absenteeism rate. The implementation of Quiet Time, a program that has options for transcendental meditation, reduced suspensions by 45 percent in the first year. After four years, attendance rates have risen to 98 percent, grade point averages improved, and the school recorded the highest happiness levels in San Francisco on the annual California Healthy Kids Survey (http://chks.wested.org), which assesses health and safety risk and social-emotional health (Kirp, 2014).
- Research on the impact of Quiet Time demonstrated dramatic increases in academic achievement and also reduced school violence. (Suspensions for fighting dropped from twenty-six to nine in just two years of implementation [Kirp, 2014].) In this study, most students chose the meditation option.

With the increasing evidence of the association between improvements in academic achievement and stress reduction, behavioral disruptions, and violence, practices including yoga, mindfulness, and meditation are gaining greater acceptance as school-day tools. What experience do you have with such practices?

What You Bring to the Mat

To teach students about yoga and meditation, you need to have first practiced some yourself. Yoga is not something you read about and memorize but rather something to experience and only then understand. Following are a few questions to ask yourself before teaching students yoga.

- "What are my school and district policies?"
- "Have I removed any elements of religion, so that I am conveying no religious terminology?"
- "Should I talk with the principal before beginning?"
- "Are others in my school teaching yoga?"
- "How comfortable do I feel teaching yoga?"

It may be helpful to garner support and buy-in to convey that yoga is not a religion and there is no religion required in order to practice yoga. In the West, it was introduced as a secular practice, and many U.S. schools incorporate it into the school day in a way that increases families' acceptance and comfort.

Our comfort zones vary. If you have taken yoga courses or have been a yoga practitioner, you may already be incorporating some yoga in your classroom. Some people may feel comfortable teaching about breathing and stretching but not teaching yoga postures or poses. Some people may not have adequate experience to be an instructor.

Yoga Options: Teach or Find a Teacher

Many of these exercises are as simple and safe as the aerobics that are taught in physical education or in early childhood movement programs. Others are very simple meditations. According to a 2015 survey by the *Advances in Mind-Body Medicine* journal, 940 U.S. schools are offering yoga in 36 different programs (Butzer, Ebert, Telles, & Khalsa, 2015). Research finds that yoga in schools may contribute to a significant reduction in anger, depression, fatigue, confusion, tension, and negative affect, as well as positive improvements in resilience, self-esteem, and coping (Felver et al., 2015).

Teaching yoga in schools covers a vast area—from full-length classes that teachers might incorporate in gym class or in after-school classes, to spending a few minutes with breathing and stretching. The range also covers everything from teaching simple movements and exercises such as frog and lion pose to preschoolers to teaching warrior pose and shoulder stands to high schoolers.

Given the wide array of needs and circumstances, we recommend you do the following before introducing yoga into your classroom.

- Gain experience with yoga and meditation as a student so that you both observe teachers and learn.
- Try CEI's Heart Beaming program (www.edimprovement.org/heart -beaming-book-certification), which includes simple exercises that even those without a yoga background can teach.
- Consider whether you are comfortable teaching yoga for five to ten minutes during class breaks.
- Find out if there is someone in your community who has experience teaching yoga in schools or if your school could offer it in physical education classes. Another option is to use online videos of exercises guided by an online instructor.
- Make sure you have experience with the exercises that you will be teaching.

Yoga in the Classroom

Take notes, noticing the space needed, possible modifications, the time between poses, and the total time it takes to complete the exercise. When you instruct students in yoga, we recommend doing the following.

- Ensure that parents are aware of how yoga is being implemented. If you are introducing yoga in your school for the first time, or if there are families who are new to your school community, consider ways to help parents become informed and comfortable with how you are using yoga. You may even try to make arrangements for a yoga class for parents or families.
- Practice the session and timing prior to instructing students.
- Use a soft, calming voice. Speak somewhat slowly and meditatively, pausing between phrases so that students can absorb and stay with a thought before adding the next component. You can apply this protocol to all mindfulness practices.
- Begin by helping students become comfortable. Consider where they are— at their seats, in a group circle, standing, or sitting. Let students know that it is all right to do what they can; often it is best to focus on those who are participating and either ignore or gently suggest that others try it. Usually within a few sessions most students are comfortable and participating.
- Sit in a good yogic position, which you can see in figure 5.1. This posture allows breath and energy to flow more freely up and down the spine. Your back is straight, navel point pulled back to the spine, pelvic area is thrust forward, you are slightly lifting the heart and chest, your shoulder blades are together in back, and chin is tucked back slightly.

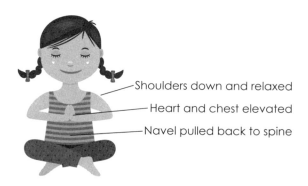

Shoulders down and relaxed
Heart and chest elevated
Navel pulled back to spine

Figure 5.1: Good yogic posture.

Refer to the following articles before leading students through the exercises. (Visit **go.SolutionTree.com/behavior** for live links to articles.)

- "4 Breathing Exercises for Kids" (Move With Me Yoga Adventures, 2014; http://bit.ly/2BMnzrk) has a video demonstrating four breathing exercises (bear, flower, hissing, and bunny breath) and describing the benefits of each.

- "Five Fun Breathing Exercises for Kids" (Cosmic Kids, 2013; www.cosmic kids.com/read/five-fun-breathing-practices-for-kids) describes five fun breathing exercises teachers use in student yoga classes. Some techniques help with asthma.

- "Pranayama—The Power of the Breath" (The School Counseling Yogi, 2014; http://bit.ly/2GYRNqp) gives a description of real-world applications using volcano breath for intention setting and school culture promotion.

- "5 Ways to Get Teenagers Practicing Yoga" (Wills, n.d.; www.mindbody green.com/0-5159/5-Ways-to-Get-Teenagers-Practicing-Yoga) lists five ways to engage teenagers in yoga practice by knowing when to give them more responsibility, and how and when to treat them as adults or preschoolers.

Practical Exercises: Yoga

Combining a conscious focus on breath with physical movement is a powerful way to accelerate the impact of stretching. Moving with the breath—often the exhale— often provides a way to stretch farther or to hold postures for a longer period of time. As you engage in the exercises that follow, make sure to maintain a conscious focus on the breath, letting the movement flow from the breath.

- As you engage in the following exercises, maintain a conscious focus on the breath, letting the movement flow from the breath. Follow two steps.
  a. Through your nostrils, breathe deeply into your abdomen, sustain your breath, extend the exhale, and hold the breath out, pausing and sustaining the breath before starting the next inhale. (This could

be considered a *4, 4, 4, 4 breath*: inhale for a count of four, sustain the inhale for a count of four, exhale for a count of four, hold the breath out for a count of four, and then begin another inhale. Breathe through your nostrils.)

    b. Complete two or three yogic or stretching postures. Pick one or do the forward bend or twisting that follow.

Forward Bend

The following exercise is a simple yoga stretch that you can do in a few minutes as a brain break. It is a good exercise because students are up, out of their seats, and the stretching and leaning forward provide good physical relief for anyone who has been sitting too long. You can repeat this exercise two or three times.

1. Stand. Breathe, exhaling through your nostrils, and pause to hold the breath out.
2. Inhale and stretch your arms over your head, pointing your fingers up.
3. Bend over, hands toward your toes, exhale, and hang as you think, slowly, "One, two, three, four, five."
4. Take a few deep breaths.
5. Inhale and slowly rise up.
6. Inhaling up, stretch your arms toward the ceiling and lean your head back slightly.
7. Exhale while going down.
8. Hang and breathe.

Twisting

The following four-step exercise is easy to implement with students standing beside their desks or chairs. As with the forward bend, the twist provides relief from sitting and increases flexibility in the spine.

1. Stand, feet together, with heels touching and toes pointing slightly out to the sides. Hands can hang loosely by your thighs or be on your hips.
2. Breathe deeply two or three times.
3. With hands by your sides, twist to the left and then to the right. Inhale as you turn left; exhale as you turn right.
4. Twist back and forth about five times.

from the classroom

Suzan Mullane, who teaches breathing exercises and yoga to preschoolers in Huntington, West Virginia, explains her work and its value for students and schools like this: "Preschoolers with emotional trauma have wounded hearts, and they react with their bodies." She has seen them cry, bite, and hit others, and crawl under tables from fear. A traumatized preschooler can fear a visiting classroom consultant (personal communication, 2017).

> When visiting a preschool in West Virginia, students got time to observe my tender care with a baby doll. Sensing my love and tenderness in the moment, my image of a safe adult prevailed. I later invited students to lie down in a circle to practice deep breathing with hands on their tummy. I instructed them to "feel your breath move up and down in your bodies and close your eyes. Now think about a time when you felt safe and happy. Wiggle your toes as you see your happy picture in your head and keep breathing" (S. Mullane, personal communication, 2017).

Mullane wanted to practice narrative yoga, so she let each student name his or her happy memory; the class practiced poses that matched those memories. If students didn't share a memory, Mullane invited them to share a memory they would like to have. An example is "'Dancing in a lake!' We swam in an imaginary lake while turning in circles. After seven minutes, we sat down in a circle with hands on our hearts so they could share what they love and wished for." The next day, the teacher said her students focused the best they ever had.

Meditation—Calming and Quieting Moments of the Mind

Imagine eliminating violence. The following quote, attributed to the Dalai Lama, suggests that "If every eight-year-old in the world is taught meditation, we will eliminate violence from the world within one generation." As a teacher, imagine teaching a room full of students who are bringing many different emotions and feelings not only to the quality of their work and ability to learn, but also to their social interactions. You can imagine a student who is upset with his parents, one who is immersed in peer-related decision making, and one who is frustrated with mathematics and dislikes school because of it. What if there was a way to calm their minds and tap into the potential creativity of each student using what we know about neurological functioning, physiology, and body chemistry to help them learn more effectively?

Meditation in the Classroom

There are various ways of describing the impact of meditation on the brain. Basically, it stimulates the frontal lobe. Focusing on the space between the brows, in particular, stimulates the hypothalamus and pituitary glands. When they are stimulated, these master glands stimulate other glands leading to a more powerful circulation of energy and impact. A number of National Institutes of Health–funded researchers at departments of complementary medicine or psychiatry in medical schools, as well as researchers in cancer and other medical centers, have reported on the positive impact of meditation for a wide array of conditions (Manjunath & Telles, 2001; Schmalzl et al., 2015; Seppälä et al., 2014; Streeter et al., 2012).

Practical Exercises: Meditation

Meditation. Often, we use the word as if there is only one way to meditate. Close your eyes and focus on nothing or focus on a candle flame. One thing. Let other thoughts go. Meditate and you will transcend physical reality and be transported to a place of calm and peace.

In actuality there is a variety of ways to meditate. You could meditate with eyes softly open, or closed, or by focusing on the tip of your nose or gently rolling your eyes upward as if looking right through the very top of the center of the head. You could meditate in silence. Or with music. Or by focusing on the breath, inhaling and exhaling. Inhaling as you fill your heart with love, exhaling as you exhale out fear or sadness, letting go. You can even use different hand placements (called *hand mudras*) for different impacts. You may want to pause here and try a few different eye positions. For each one, focus the eyes as recommended and take a few deep breaths.

We often use the term *meditation* as if there is an importance to really being able to meditate—to stop the influx of thoughts. However, some yogis suggest that by even defining the outcome and criteria we are adding ego and interfering with the process. Yogi Bhajan, a yoga master who brought yoga to the West in the 1960s, suggests that we not focus on the "goal of stopping thoughts or transcending life," but rather that we meditate for the practice of meditation, opening ourselves to the possibility of the experience. He also describes meditation as a way of clearing cluttered thoughts out of the brain (Y. Bhajan, personal communication, June 1997). We like to think of meditation partially as a way to free up space in the brain, providing more room, almost like deleting unnecessary files from your computer so that you have more memory and you can process at faster speeds.

from the classroom

From Chris's experience as a yoga and meditation teacher, she realizes that if she stretches and uses gentle yogic exercises to reach a stronger alignment of the body, that meditation will be more satisfying. There seems to be an amazing balance with breath, movement, symmetry, balance, and meditation. She also knows that there are a few things that support her meditation. Meditating in a calm environment, at a certain time of day, often helps. Pulling her navel point to her spine and pulling her chin back slightly so the back of her head is even with her spine help. Feeling symmetry between the left and right sides of her body helps. There are different ways to focus the eyes. With her eyes closed, she can focus on the area in the middle of her forehead right between the brows, or at the top of her skull, or she can meditate with her eyes one-tenth open, or with them focused on the tip of her nose, although this sometimes takes some practice.

Practice the following meditation exercises for at least three days.

Using Heart Beaming Yoga-Like Strategies

Heart Beaming (Mason & Banks, 2014) is one example of a simple but effective way to implement breathing, yoga-like, and meditation practices more widely in schools. Different schools and school districts are taking different positions on yoga in schools, and some communities are very happy to embrace yoga, mindfulness, and meditation, while others limit the inclusion to voluntary or after-school activities. Therefore, we urge teachers and administrators to use care as they introduce any of these practices into schools.

Unlike some forms of yoga, Heart Beaming does not include any postures that might be construed as praying or any reference to yogic terms such as *namaste*. Rather, Heart Beaming includes simple movements and postures that educators use with movement activities and *brain breaks*, also known as *brain gym* (movements, exercises, or activities that coax the two hemispheres of our brain to work in synchronicity, providing a whole body balance, revitalizing our healing mechanisms, and improving executive functioning areas such as cognitive function, physical coordination, memory, organization, and relationships) in schools, as well as instruction to reflect and meditate on positive values like peace, healing, and success (Alexander, 2011). Heart Beaming also provides a structure so that teachers can introduce three- to ten-minute mind breaks to help students refocus their attention and be better prepared to learn.

Read the following instructions aloud to guide students through this exercise. Make sure the students are seated. Proceed at a slow to medium pace for about three minutes.

1. Take a few deep breaths.
2. Put your right hand over your heart and your left hand over your right hand. Feel your heart beating.
3. Listen to your heart.
4. Imagine a friend you care about.
5. Send energy *beaming* from *your* heart to your friend and back again. You might even imagine this energy as a beam of light. Continue for one to three minutes.
6. Focus on breathing from your heart. As you end you may feel warmth, or a feeling of love in your heart.

Riding the Wind

Begin with a few minutes of stretching, Heart Beaming (Mason & Banks, 2014), or yoga exercises. Then, complete seven steps to riding the wind.

1. Bring your hands in front of your face. Cup your hands at the level of your chin. Place the edges of your little fingers together and point them away from you. See figure 5.2 for an example.
2. Looking into the cup in front of you; breathe in; imagine love, success, and healing; and gently blow these thoughts into your hands.
3. Take another breath.
4. Imagine peace, happiness, and health, and gently blow these thoughts into your hands.
5. Imagine someone at a distance who needs help. It could be someone you know or a stranger.
6. Look into your hands. Feel the peace, happiness, health, success, healing, and love in your hands. As you take a deep breath, exhale more forcefully, sending these on the wind to that person. Let your love and healing ride the wind to that person.
7. Repeat and continue for three to five minutes. Think about the following.
   • How did this work for you?
   • Were you able to visualize what was happening?

Figure 5.2: Riding the wind.

Traditional Meditation

Begin with the previous meditation exercises. This will help prepare you. Note that practice is good, even when you don't feel all that successful. We urge you not to concentrate on so-called *success*, but rather to keep letting your thoughts go and returning to your breath.

1. Rest the backs of your hands on your knees.
2. You can bring the thumb and index finger of each hand together in *gyan mudra*, shown in figure 5.3.
3. Close your eyes and focus on the area between your eyebrows.
4. Breathe deeply.
5. For any thought that comes, examine the thought briefly and then relax and let it go.
6. Continue for three to five minutes.
7. Inhale deeply and exhale. Were you able to let your thoughts go and return to your breath?
8. Open your eyes.

Figure 5.3: The *gyan mudra*, or hand position.

from the classroom

We have introduced a technique called *mind spinning* in several schools. Essentially, students close their eyes and draw imaginary circles. They can breathe deeply and imagine drawing circles that link the left and right hemispheres of the brain, or rotate circles diagonally or from the front of the brain to the back.

One teacher from Upper Providence Elementary in Royersford, Pennsylvania, says the following about the mind spinning exercise.

> I was working with a student who had been struggling greatly over the past few months. He was back in the safety corner, very upset and agitated. I reminded him of the Heart Beaming exercise that he had really liked a few days prior, mind spinning. For a brief moment, maybe four or five minutes, he was able to use this practice and de-escalate. At that point I felt that if I continued to be consistent with the practice it could help in the future (B. Aikens, personal communication, February 13, 2017).

Practical Applications

Experienced meditators will tell you that meditation starts to really take hold over time. What at first may seem to feel unnatural, with practice starts to become easier. Even experienced meditators may find that during a meditation session, it takes several minutes to slow down one's breath and center down into a meditative state. It is only with practice that one begins to feel the impact.

Some students will feel uncomfortable initially; they may feel self-conscious. This may be more apparent with middle and high school students. That is one reason it is important to insert the practice into a solid, consistent schedule—so students can adjust to the quiet that is at first a challenge. You may hear comments such as "This is awkward," or "I can't stop thinking or moving." This is also another reason movement prior to meditation is preferred; performing relaxing poses before the deeper relaxation that meditation can offer reduces mind wandering and fidgety feelings. Additionally, introducing more challenging yoga postures to high school students tends to increase their interest and desire to participate (R. Fajardo, personal communication, June 2017).

It is important to implement yoga and meditation practice as a natural part of your classroom routine or lesson. Rather than responding to inappropriate behavior with punitive consequences and reprimands, teachers can naturally infuse these practices into the school day to maintain and sustain students' interests and attention throughout, thus providing everyday relief and calm, rather than heightening student stress and anxiety. Here are some suggestions for doing so.

- It is easier to meditate after doing yoga or stretching. These both open pathways in the body for energy and breath to travel. They also help with alignment, including alignment of the spine.
- Sit in a good yogic position (back straight, navel point pulled to the spine, pelvic area thrust forward slightly lifting the heart and chest, shoulder blades together in back, and chin tucked back slightly) to allow breath and energy to flow more freely up and down the spine.
- Try yoga and meditation before or after the first morning lesson; plan for a longer session on Mondays to enhance student focus for the remainder of the week.
- Try yoga and meditation during transition from one subject to another; going into group work or prior to testing.
- Try yoga at those times when students are beginning to fidget and lose their concentration.
- Try yoga to help students engage with subjects like music and art; yoga can facilitate creativity as students experience combining art or music with movement and stretching.
- Take a schoolwide approach. Make it a part of the broadcast morning announcements.
- After all the announcements, have a teacher or an experienced student instruct students on three minutes of yogic stretching and three minutes of meditation. If you have time, starting every day in this manner and incorporating it simultaneously during class or various subjects (such as gym) can be very effective.
- Incorporate breath work, yogic, and meditation breaks during regular transition times during the school day such as when students arrive, after lunch, or at the end of the school day. When students and teachers take the time (two to five minutes) to gain calm, they find balance and equanimity in their day. They also gain more focused time because these practices decrease stress, distractions, and inattentiveness while also increasing self-regulation.
- Incorporate yoga or meditation before or after lunch to stimulate better digestion and regain focus to reenter the classroom.
- Play music at a low volume. Music can be popular songs related to peace, love, and perseverance. Students can move or practice yoga stretches with

the music, and then meditate as they listen to the inspiring words. This could occur during music classes and at other times during the day.

- Prior to a creative activity, whether it be in art or for writing, use meditation to help increase focus, insight, and the quality of the product.
- Prior to doing a problem-solving activity, use yoga and meditation to increase focus and the ability to connect ideas and consider implications of actions.
- Incorporate yoga and breath work in physical education classes. Teach stretching as part of the physical education curriculum.

The Impact of Meditation Over Time

Meditating for longer periods of time and over days, months, and years makes a difference. Research shows that those who spend more time meditating are likely to see more stimulation in parts of the brain such as the hypothalamus, pituitary glands, and prefrontal cortex (Schmalzl et al., 2015), resulting in stronger neuropathways that support learning and readiness to learn.

We recommend you pause at this point in your reading, practice the meditation exercises in this chapter for three to five days, and then answer the following questions. If you are able, you may want to keep a daily reflection log.

- What changes did you notice during or after the three to five days?
- At the end of the three to five days, which meditation do you prefer and why?

Mindful Reflection

As an individual or with your study group, respond to the mindful reflection questions, taking notes on the following page.

- Did you notice any difference in how you felt for the different exercises? Was one more natural to you?
- If you had difficulty, what was the difficulty? Was it boring, hard to keep focused, felt unpleasant?
- Did you feel better (calmer or more energetic) after the first three exercises in comparison to the others?
- What seemed to work most effectively for you, and what was the impact of your practice?
- Did you practice before you introduced the practice to students?

— Notes —

CHAPTER 6

Mindful Sensation, Presence, and Emotion

Mindfulness—moment to moment nonjudgmental attention and awareness.

—Richard Davidson

key principle

Conscious awareness of sensation, presence, and emotion leads to deeper understanding of self and sets the stage for healing and wiser decisions and actions.

Remember from the previous chapters: breath, meditation, and movement (particularly yoga) are mindfulness practices that reduce stress and increase awareness. Chapter 6 provides an introduction to mindfulness practices that include cognitive reflection, awareness of sensory input, and exercises that connect mindful awareness to feelings. This chapter also includes guided visualizations and meditations to help students with mindful exploration or problem solving. Because mindfulness is directly tied to sensation, presence, and emotion, and we explain that throughout the book, this chapter does not have a "Practical Applications" section. We encourage you to practice the exercises in this chapter before turning to chapter 7 (page 115), which focuses specifically on mindful instruction.

Mindfulness: What It Is and What It Does

Being present in the here and now is a step away from isolated breath work, yoga, and meditation. The use of mindfulness practices in schools is growing rapidly due to their positive outcomes. A meta-analysis of 1,348 students instructed in mindfulness finds the greatest positive results in those sites occurred with more frequent or extensive mindfulness practice (Zenner et al., 2014). Another meta-analysis of twenty-four studies found mindfulness treatments to be superior over control conditions, especially for students who displayed symptoms of long-term stress or psychological problems (Zoogman et al., 2015). All of this is promising news since as early as kindergarten, healthy social-emotional skills and general well-being are predictors of improved education and employment (Jones, Greenberg, & Crowley, 2015).

Mindfulness: Impressive Results in Schools

In the United States, the Mindful Schools program has helped K–12 schools set up mindfulness programs. Since 2007, the program has trained 170,000 students worldwide. The organization has produced guidelines for secular inclusion of mindfulness in schools (Brensilver, 2017). For school settings, we recommend adapting yoga in a way that removes references to religion or religious practices and that does not use it to advance or inhibit any specific religious practice.

Mindful Schools with the University of California, Davis conducted a large randomized controlled study with students and teachers in three high-poverty Oakland public elementary schools (Fernando, 2013). The study began with fifteen-minute mindfulness sessions, two to three times a week, over six weeks, and incorporated a sustainability plan. Instruction included sessions on mindful eating, breathing, listening, test taking, and empathizing. Each of the three schools had high crime rates (fourth-highest rate of any city in the United States), students receiving free and reduced lunch (91 percent overall), and English learners (68 percent on average; Fernando, 2013).

Results showed significant increases in behavioral indices over the six weeks; boys improved more than girls. The researchers concluded that among other things, "strong sustainability support is critical." (See figure 6.1.)

Research also supports the efficacy of mindfulness training for teachers as well as students. For example, in a study examining occupational stress and burnout, 113 elementary and secondary school teachers from the United States and Canada who participated in mindfulness training improved their focused attention and working memory and had lower levels of occupational stress (Roeser et al., 2013). Mindfulness is equally important to maintaining teacher health and well-being as it is for students. When teachers are calm and nonreactive, they can better focus through a heightened awareness of their own feelings and emotions as well as be more aware of the feelings and emotions of their students.

Kimberly Schonert-Reichl et al. (2015) investigated the impact of mindfulness with ninety-nine fourth and fifth graders, comparing a social-emotional learning (SEL) program that included mindfulness to a regular social responsibility program. They found significant differences in self-reported measures of well-being, executive functioning, and self- and peer-reported prosocial behavior. In all cases, improvements were greater for students in the SEL programs with mindfulness.

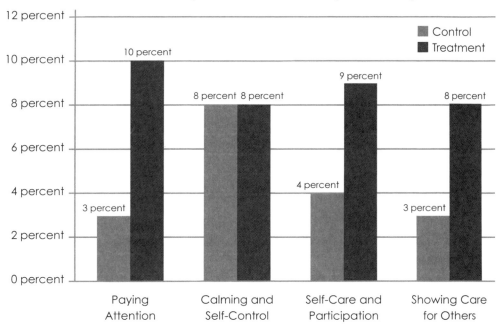

Behavioral Improvement in Six Weeks (780 Students)

Source: © Fernado, 2013. Used with permission.

Figure 6.1: Improvements in a large randomized controlled study in Oakland, California.

Mindfulness Replacing Punitive Action and Traditional Punishment

Schools have taken major steps to use breathing, yoga, meditation, and mindfulness in practical ways to relieve student stress and to directly address the ever-increasing social-emotional challenges of our students. The short documentary film *Room to Breathe* (www.mindfulschools.org) shows how infusing mindfulness practice into the course of the regular school day can help transform even the most challenging classrooms and help students self-regulate and control their own behaviors through breathing and mindfulness (Long & Mallimson, 2013). These mindfulness techniques can become an effective substitute for traditional means of punishment procedures such as sending the student to the principal's office or in- or out-of-school suspensions.

Another example is the Mindful Life Project (MLP), which is based out of Richmond, California. Instructors with MLP teach mindfulness, yoga, expressive arts, and hip hop and performing arts to elementary and middle school students in underserved schools and communities. They infuse two mindfulness programs within the school day to teach self-awareness, self-regulation, impulse control, confidence, and resilience, all executive functioning skills, or strong skills, needed for life success (Brensilver, 2017).

With mindfulness as the foundation of their program, students, through focused and specific awareness, develop "skills to navigate ALL thoughts, emotions, physical sensations, and experiences by strategically living in the here and now" (Mindful Life Project, n.d.b) Mindfulness was infused into the school day daily (http://mindfullife project.org). The results are staggering. All Mindful Life Project (n.d.a) schools report, on average, suspensions and referrals decreased by 70 percent. Along with decreased suspensions, teachers report an increase in positive social-emotional behaviors that include the following.

- Relating to peers (82 percent)
- Paying attention (75 percent)
- Settling oneself down (79 percent)
- Controlling impulses (73 percent)
- Showing self-awareness (86 percent)

The overall school community yielded an average of 22 minutes more per day, or 110 more minutes, of quality teaching time in a week (Mindful Life Project, n.d.a).

When teachers and principals infused a more proactive, kinder, and gentler approach like mindfulness throughout the day, the overall amount of discipline, referrals, and punitive measures decreased.

One other example is the Robert W. Coleman Elementary School in Baltimore, which uses a Mindful Moment Room—which is a cheerful, brightly lit room with purple pillows, yoga mats, and the scent of lavender essential oil. Created as a partnership with the Holistic Life Foundation, the collaboration centered around an afterschool mindfulness and yoga program. However, the Mindful Moment Room evolved so that it brings mindfulness strategies into the academic school day. In 2015, there were zero suspensions and increased attendance (Gaines, 2016).

As implemented at Coleman, students begin and end their day with fifteen minutes of yoga and a guided meditation. Students use the Mindful Moment Room to calm down. When students are disruptive, instead of being punished or sent to the principal's office, they proceed to the Mindful Moment Room. Once there, staff members help students relax and become more aware of their emotions and reactions with belly breathing (deep breathing) exercises. Then staff briefly dialogue with students about the incident with a focus on the emotions that led to the behavior—a cognitive reflection of the incident and themselves. The session ends with the student and staff coming up with a plan to use mindfulness in future situations (Gaines, 2016). At the high school level, using the same program, one school reported a decrease in suspensions from forty-nine in 2012–2013 to twenty-three in 2013–2014. At the same time, the number of students promoted from ninth to tenth grade increased from 45 percent to 64 percent.

Mindfulness and How Painful Memories May Play Out

Our experiences impact our individual mindfulness. Over the years, occasions arise where memories can be painful, and a defense mechanism that often works well in the moment is to turn our awareness elsewhere. We essentially opt to become less mindful. Rather than focusing on our pain, we may simply shift our attention elsewhere. Or we may even create a new version of the experience—highlighting our success and avoiding the painful memories. However, sometimes the opposite can also occur. We may elect to dwell on the painful and become enmeshed in a sense of doom and overwhelming sadness or depression. Sometimes we even numb ourselves as a matter of survival. While this is sometimes a very good short-term strategy for day-to-day functioning, over time, as we stay frozen, we lose something of our identity, our depth of emotion, our ability to be compassionate, and our insights into our own lives and the lives of those around us. This may lead us to be cold and uncaring, and perhaps even apathetic or violent (Lu, 2015).

Considerations as You Begin Mindful Sensation, Presence, and Emotion Exercises in the Classroom

Sensation, presence, and emotion are different windows into our experiences. By focusing on one of these at a time, we give students a richer, fuller experience that sets the foundation for expanding their consciousness.

- The sensation exercises can enhance science observations.
- The presence exercises can enhance listening and communication.
- The emotion exercises build empathy and kindness.

To build your understanding of mindfulness and how to implement it in classrooms, in this section we start with a few simple activities that we recommend you do first before introducing them to your students. As you engage in these activities we invite you to be mindful, or as Davidson and Begley (2012) suggest, be nonjudgmental as you focus on the here and now from moment to moment.

Most steps as written (except where noted specifically for elementary) will work for grades 5–12. Many of the exercises in this chapter can be implemented with little adaptation for most students. However, some exercises are most effective for students who are at least eight to ten years old. For prekindergarten and kindergarten students, alternative or simpler exercises may be more beneficial. To guide you in implementation with younger students, we have inserted alternative exercises several places. The remainder of chapter 6 presents exercises for you to practice on your own and then share with students. You should do the exercises in the following order and as shown in figure 6.2.

This chapter presents sensation, presence, and emotion exercises. The following steps show you in what order you should introduce practices as a whole.

1. As with all others, practice the exercises in this chapter yourself before introducing them to students.
2. Start with basic breathing exercises from chapter 4 (page 61), noticing how your body reacts to stimuli or events in the classroom. Alternatively, you may begin with sensory experiences. By beginning with basic exercises, students learn fundamentals. With these experiences, students then approach other mindfulness activities with new sensory input and neural pathways that are ready to enhance their perceptions and understanding.
3. Add guided visualizations.
4. Do exercises to become mindful of others (page 99).
5. Do exercises to become mindful of bodily sensations and emotions (page 99). Begin with body, then introduce happiness, sadness, and disappointment, in this order. This sequence helps you begin with emotions that are easier to process before proceeding to those that may possibly reintroduce trauma.
6. Do self-soothing behavior exercises (page 107). After students experience how disappointment impacts their bodily sensations, self-soothing behaviors will give them a tool to help reduce their stress or sadness.
7. After introducing several exercises to students, repeat them. Giving students an opportunity to experience the exercise again helps them reflect on the impact to their bodies, thinking, and emotions. Do exercises for mindful reflections after learning (page 110). After students practice the suggested exercises, consider what else you need to support students' understanding of their progress. It might be reading books about children who have had similar experiences. It could be journaling or writing stories about emotions. Mindful reflections will include questions such as, How did this feel? or How do you feel now that you have done this exercise? Other questions might be, Did anything feel uncomfortable? or What images came to mind? For exercises such as Eat an Orange Mindfully (page 98), the reflection would include questions such as, What did you notice? How did your orange taste? Was it bitter or sweet? Follow-up activities might include reading books about children who have had similar experiences, or journaling or writing stories about emotions.

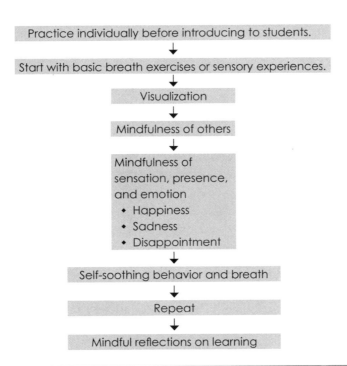

Figure 6.2: Steps to heart centered mindfulness.

*Visit **go.SolutionTree.com/behavior** for a free reproducible version of this figure.*

Practical Exercises: Sensation

When you have introduced a number of exercises to students, return to the exercises, repeating them, and giving students an opportunity to experience the exercise again and to once more reflect on the impact on their bodies, their thinking, and their emotions.

After students have practiced the suggested exercises, consider what else is necessary to support student understanding of progress. Journaling, writing stories about emotions, or reading books about children who share such experiences can be effective methods of checking in.

First try these exercises yourself, and then try them with students. Think about your students, their ages, and which activities might be more interesting to them. As you experience each activity, write down your observations in your journal or diary.

from the classroom

Sometimes it is nice to give students a break from the voices they hear all the time guiding the lessons, and instead use an online video, such as on YouTube (www .youtube.com), which is popular with lots of secondary students, or GoNoodle (www.gonoodle.com), which is popular with elementary students. Make sure you watch a video before playing it for students. There is a variety of mindfulness videos to explore that can be very beneficial and interesting to students.

Use Anchor of Awareness

This repeated recentering will train your brain to come back to and fully experience the present moment. Its three steps follow.

1. Close your eyes and begin long, deep breathing. Keep the focus on your breath.
2. Every time your mind begins to wander, refocus on the inhale and exhale of your breath. Let go and recenter your thoughts on the here and now.
3. Repeat for at least three minutes. For middle or high school students with more practice, extend it to ten or fifteen minutes.

Eat an Orange Mindfully

Many of you may be able to *imagine* doing this exercise. However, please pause, find an orange (or a small chunk of a banana, or some other fruit), and proceed with the following four steps to benefit fully from the mindfulness of this exercise.

1. Slowly eat an orange segment.
2. See if you can keep the segment in your mouth for five minutes.
3. Savor the flavor, the sweetness, the tartness, and the texture.
4. Describe what you notice.

Contemplate an Object

You can modify the following four-step exercise to fit with your students' interests and capacity. For example, with elementary students, you could lead exercises comparing two objects and asking questions such as, "Which ones are softer?" and "Which ones are bigger?"

1. Mindfully look around you.
2. Pick one object that you like. Perhaps it is a rock, a plant, a book, or a digital device.

3. Spend three or four minutes contemplating the object. Feel the texture, observe the color, and listen to any sounds it makes.

4. Describe the object or pair with another student and share.

Be Mindful of Others

Mindfulness needs to extend beyond self to mindfulness of our environment and of others. Sometimes we are so busy living our own lives that we haven't paused to consider how others are. The following emotion exercise will help intentionally increase mindfulness of others' emotions.

1. Consider people in your environment. Depending on where you are, it could be someone in the classroom, a friend, or a family member. Focus on one person.

2. Consider the person's general nature (happy, friendly, angry, fearful) and how the person appears in your imagination right at the moment.

3. Look at the person's face and imagine him or her speaking to you.
   - What is he or she saying?
   - What kind of voice is the person using?
   - How do you feel around that person?
   - Does the person need anything from you?

Another way to enhance our understanding of ourselves is to understand how we feel under various circumstances. As always, practice this first on yourself and then with your students. In the following sequence, depending on the ages of students and their understanding of vocabulary, you could substitute *inhale and exhale* for the word *breathe*. If you have instructed students in deep breathing as we recommend in chapter 4 (page 61), it may lead to deeper and more purposeful breathing to use *inhale and exhale*.

Do a Body Scan

You can repeat this exercise with lips, ears, eyes, cheeks, nose, forehead, and scalp if you desire. Slowly lead students through this nine-step exercise with a soft, calming voice, and take special note of all the moments where you will silently pause. Students can sit or lie on the floor.

1. Close your eyes (or lower your eyes toward your feet) and be aware of your hands, feet, arms, and legs. Inhale. Then exhale, relax, let go. (Pause.)

2. Inhale and focus on your feet. (Pause.) Exhale, relax, let go.

3. Inhale and focus on your legs. (Pause. Notice that breath occurs between every pause.)

4. Exhale, relax, let go.

5. Repeat with a focus on stomach (pause), heart (pause), and lungs (pause) using the same sequence: inhale, focus, relax, let go.

6. Inhale and focus on your arms. (Pause.) Exhale, relax, let go.
7. Move up to your face (pause), scalp (pause), and the top of your head. Exhale, relax, and let go.
8. Inhale deeply. Relax, sinking down onto your mat or the ground beneath you.
9. Remain in relaxaion for between three and five minutes.

Tighten and Release

You can easily add the following six-step tighten and release exercise to body scans. This exercise can help students relax and move away from negative feelings. Students can take off their shoes if they want.

1. Tighten your fists and the muscles in your legs and feet. Maybe curl your toes. Inhale and tighten, then exhale and relax.
2. Inhale and make a face (or wrinkle your nose) at the same time you make fists.
3. Exhale and relax.
4. Inhale, exhale, and relax one more time.
5. Sit up and close your eyes.
6. Consider how you feel.

from the classroom

Preschool and kindergarten teachers use body scans as part of their mindful daily classroom practice at Lee Elementary School, Massachusetts. After a few weeks of practice, teachers observed that "students are truly resting during the afternoon rest period" (G. Ardouin, March 16, 2017). Ginny Ardouin, a kindergarten teacher at Lee Elementary School in Lee, Massachusetts, notes that students who used to squirm are now falling asleep during this time.

Ginny describes the process she uses: she turns off the lights. Students lie down on towels or their jackets. She leads them through body scans and reads a script that focuses on empowering self-images (such as doing our best, being kind, or being in a safe place). She sees a student who has ADHD able to rest longer, and a student who is on the autism spectrum able to use body scans at home to calm him- or herself. Ardouin finds that students demonstrate greater empathy, and this is apparent even while they discuss characters in books she reads aloud to them (personal communication, March 16, 2017).

Drawing for Elementary Students

Use drawing in a variety of ways to help elementary students express their needs or feelings. Students from the ages of five to eight years old may appreciate the following experience.

Use drawing in a variety of ways to help elementary students express their needs or feelings. Developmentally, at this age, students can draw an outline; their self-awareness is such that this activity will typically fit in with their mindset (Santrock, 2012).

A variation of this activity for elementary school is to talk with students about their favorite colors and what those colors sometimes represent (yellow is cheerful, red is angry, green is calm, blue is sad) prior to them completing their drawings. Alternatively, students could first use paint, chalk, or crayons to color in the body outlines before placing their descriptive words or images.

You can perform this three-step exercise over two or three days.

1. Students can begin at their desks, drawing pictures or writing some facts about themselves, including their thoughts and feelings. Examples are *I love my cat*, *I live with my mom and two sisters*, and *I love the color green*. Adults can help with the writing and drawing; they can cut pictures from magazines if they'd rather not draw. It may help to have pictures of people with various emotions.
2. Let students pair up. In each pair, a student lies down on a piece of butcher paper and the partner traces an outline of the other; they then switch.
3. Students put their writings, drawings, and pictures on their body outline (or rewrite their thoughts directly on the body outline). Depending on your class, invite other students to write positive comments about the person on the outline. You can display the body drawings in the classroom and let students comment on their drawings.

Drawing for Secondary Students

Because middle and high schoolers may be particularly aware of their bodies, you might hear some giggling or refusals of certain activities. We recommend the following exercise as more age appropriate.

1. Close your eyes and begin deep breathing.
2. Reflect on who you are. (You could provide prompts such as, "Think about not only your physical characteristics, but your values and interests.")
3. Give the students options such as drawing a life-size picture of themselves, or drawing several pictures of themselves perhaps in a notebook. Another option would be to cut out pictures from magazines or download images to make a collage of who they are.

4. Once the images are there, students can add words, sentences, or other images to connate who they are.

Happiness for Elementary Students

We intentionally focus on happiness to help students get in touch with that emotion. Students between ages six and ten will be able to keep their eyes closed for longer and can visualize more details than preK students. Use the following five steps for this exercise. Visit **go.SolutionTree.com/behavior** to download a reproducible version of the handout for your students.

1. Close your eyes and think about a time you were happy. Perhaps it was at a birthday party, when you got a new toy, or during a picnic.
2. Now open your eyes and look at this picture. Can you find the child who is happy?
3. Now close your eyes again and think about a time when you were happy. It could be real or make-believe. Picture in your mind what was happening. Maybe it was when you had fun swimming, playing with a dog or cat, sledding in snow, or visiting grandparents.
4. Open your eyes. Who did you see in your mind's eye? Where were you? What was happening?
5. Talk about happiness and how we feel when we are happy.

Happiness for Secondary Students

The effort to experience happiness may be particularly important for middle school and high school students, who can often be moody and hypersensitive to the opinions (and slights) of others. Take a few minutes, and proceed slowly. Lead students through the following three-step exercise, reading the instructions aloud. Practice this exercise three to five times over the week.

1. Take a few deep breaths, inhaling and exhaling slowly.
2. Imagine a circumstance where you are very happy. It could be an actual event, something you are looking forward to, or even a fantasy.
3. Picture what is happening. See yourself in the picture. Keep your eyes closed but, in your imagination, look around. Notice who is in the picture, as well as the colors, sounds, smells, or tastes.
   - What emotions do you feel—happiness, excitement, joy, or something else?
   - Are you smiling? How does your heart feel?
   - How does your body feel? Do you have any tension or pain?

Sadness for Elementary Students

When discussing sadness with elementary students, we recommend using pictures or stories of others and asking questions about their emotions rather than going immediately to those for sadness. Visit **go.SolutionTree.com/behavior** for a free reproducible version of a handout showing emotions.

1. Look at these people. (Share a picture of people showing happiness, sadness, and anger.)
2. How do you think they might feel? (Discuss emotions such as happiness, sadness, grief, anger, and joy. Many online resources can help you with these discussions. You will find book recommendations and live links to online resources on this book's landing page.)

The Complexity of Emotions for Students Ages Eleven and Older

Psychotherapist Paul Gilbert has helped us to realize that when we introduce meditation to students, negative thoughts will sometimes emerge. While learning to recognize sadness and other basic emotions is foundational for our work with younger students, as children age, we can help them learn to differentiate between feeling sad, angry, guilty, or even feeling shame, regret, and jealousy. Gilbert (2010) puts it this way:

> We have seen that we have a very difficult brain because of the way it has evolved over many millions of years. Within us are different patterns and potential states of mind. There is the angry self, the anxious self, the "wanting to be loved self," the excited self, the proud self, the ashamed self—all of which come with slightly different emotions, ways of thinking and desires to behave. These can also be affected by our background bodily states—whether we're exhausted or have a physical problem. Powerful emotional memories can also be triggered in us that affect our bodies and emotions. If we come from difficult backgrounds, some of the states of mind we typically experience are rooted in anxiety and anger, because we haven't had the chance to develop other patterns and we've always been "on the defensive." (p. 68)

For students experiencing significant grief, loss, anger, or depression, teachers may wish to consult with counselors. We believe it is important for teachers to find time to have discussions about emotions with students and also to be aware that meditation may stir up emotions that have been repressed. If that happens, remind students that deep breaths are useful. How you proceed from there will depend in part on your training, background, and comfort level. We want students to be in touch with their emotions, so we can encourage them to observe how they are feeling—whether they are feeling pain or tension in any part of their body. If they are, they should inhale deeply, imagining a healing breath going to that part of the body, and then relaxing and letting go. Meditations on positive experiences or positive affirmations (page 123) may be helpful.

Considerations Before Practicing Guided Visualizations for Sadness and Disappointment

Guided visualizations, which are relaxation exercises that incorporate sounds, words, or images, can enhance mindfulness. With a guided visualization, the teacher leads the exercise aloud, usually speaking softly, reminding students to breathe, and periodically pausing between steps. To help students get in touch with their emotions, we recommend repeating exercises several times—perhaps two or three times for each, devoting several days to each one. As students get in touch with their breath, their emotions will bubble up. Students may experience sadness or anger, emotions that may have been frozen or repressed. The following four steps can be useful.

1. If this happens, find a way to have a brief, private conversation with the student.
2. Reassure the student that you are here to support him or her and that you are available if the student needs to talk.
3. If the student talks with you, listen mindfully. Focus on hearing the student and being supportive. Researchers advise against saying things like "You'll get over it," or "Only the strong survive" and warn educators not to probe for more details; doing so "can re-traumatize the student and may cause more emotional and psychological distress" (Kataoka, Langley, Wong, Baweja, & Stein, 2012).
4. Depending on the issue, and how equipped you feel handling this conversation yourself, you might consider contacting the parents, school counselor, a social worker, or your principal for advice or perhaps even a referral for services.

If your school or community has experienced a recent tragic event, or if students are aware of national or international tragedies, make sure to talk with counselors to gain their insights before you begin this work. For additional guidance, see "Responding to Students with PTSD in Schools" (Kataoka et al., 2012).

Begin with the Positive and Use Care With Negative Experiences

As stated earlier, to incorporate mindfulness into the classroom, begin with positive experiences. This holds true for visualizations. While mindfulness can be an important tool for helping individuals understand and cope with pain, grief, and disappointment, proceed cautiously—particularly for students who have experienced significant trauma. That is why, even for adults, with the following visualization and mindfulness exercises we chose an experience such as cancelling an expected outing, which would most likely be negative, but not as likely to trigger flashbacks to trauma. If instead of a cancelled event we described more serious rejection, an issue with family, or times when a person had been afraid or anxious, there is a greater likelihood that such a reflection could be a catalyst for more stressful emotions.

Try to Avoid Situations in Which a Student Might Flash Back to Trauma

If you know one or more students who are experiencing, or have recently experienced, significant trauma—including but not limited to abuse, divorcing parents, or a loved one's death—proceed carefully. In fact, because of trauma's prevalence, assume at least one student in your class has experienced a recent traumatic event. You may want a school counselor or a therapist's advice. Since trauma often stays in the body (Scaer, 2014), it is useful to involve movement. Movement activities release stress and help prepare the brain for meditative experiences (Arbeau, 2016; Khalsa & Gould, 2012; Khalsa & O'Keeffe, 2002; Stephens, 2012).

Practical Exercises

People handle painful emotions in different ways. Sometimes they stuff the pain, trying to ignore the hurt, and simply forge ahead. Sometimes they experience deep sadness or even depression. Sometimes built-up pain and hurt take people to a deeper level of sadness. The first disappointment may feel one way, but repeated disappointments may lead to other emotions taking over.

Begin With the Positive

Begin your practices with positive experiences.

1. Close your eyes, take a few deep breaths, and imagine eagerly awaiting an activity that you will do with a friend. Perhaps this is a memory of something you enjoyed with a family member or friend. Or, imagine that you plan to go to a movie, to the park, or on a walk. Choose any activity you like. (Pause.)
2. Imagine your happiness when spending time with your family member or friend, and visualize being there with that person. (Pause.)
3. Take a few minutes to appreciate how wonderful it might feel to do something positive with a friend.
4. Talk about how we feel when we have a pleasant experience or memory.

Disappointment

Disappointment impacts each of us in different ways, depending on our previous experiences and the degree of disappointment. Self-soothing behaviors can be used to help with disappointment, as can deep or self-soothing breaths.

Take a few minutes and slowly proceed through the following exercise, reading the instructions aloud. The class can discuss how the disappointment felt and how students problem solved.

1. Close your eyes, take a few deep breaths, and imagine eagerly awaiting an activity that you will do with a friend. Perhaps you plan to go to a movie, to the park, or on a walk. Choose any activity you like. (Pause.)
2. Imagine your happiness of spending time with your friend and visualize being there with that person. (Pause.)
3. You are looking forward to this adventure. Then, your friend calls to tell you the activity is cancelled. (Pause.)
4. Now picture yourself, the circumstance you were anticipating, and your friend. Use your five senses to see if you can smell popcorn, hear music, feel the air. Check to see how you are feeling first as you planned the outing. (Pause.) Then check how you feel after the cancellation.
5. Check your body language, facial expressions, and feelings.
   - Are you disappointed, angry, sad, or distrustful?
   - How does your body feel? Do you have any tightness or pain? You might feel your heart sinking in your chest; you might feel the sadness in your posture.
   - Open your eyes. How do you process hurt and disappointment?

Resolving Disappointment

Source: Adapted from Gilbert, 2009.

With emotions it is important to not rush into resolving feelings, but rather to get in touch with the emotion prior to problem solving and learning to get past our feelings. Practice the following six-step exercise only after doing the Disappointment exercise.

1. Sit comfortably with your eyes closed. Inhale and exhale deeply.
2. Consider once again the time when a friend let you down, when you were eagerly anticipating an event which your friend cancelled. Remember the excitement about your initial plan and then how you felt when your friend phoned to cancel.
   - Did you feel rejected, sad, or angry?
   - How did your body feel?
3. Now take some deep breaths and imagine yourself getting over this disappointment.

- What do you do?
- Are you able to get over it quickly, or does it take some time?
- Do you pick another movie, call another friend, stay in your room, or watch something online or on TV?

4. Imagine that you *did* do something else. Imagine that you are feeling better, and that you move past this disappointment. See yourself picking an option that makes you feel better. Open your eyes.

5. Were you able to move past this, or did the hurt and disappointment stay with you?

6. There is no right answer. Sometimes we can move on quickly, and sometimes the hurt stays with us longer. However, we have some tools that might help, like the self-soothing behavior exercise (see page 108). We'll do that next.

Self-Soothing Behavior and Breath

One way to handle disappointments is self-soothing behavior. Karyn Hall (n.d.) describes it this way:

> Self-soothing is part of finding a middle ground, a gray area, between being detached or numb and experiencing an emotional crisis or upheaval. Allowing yourself to experience the uncomfortable emotions (without feeding them and making them more intense) enables the emotions to pass. Soothing yourself helps you tolerate the experience without acting in ways that are not helpful in the long run, or blocking the emotions, which makes the emotions grow larger or come out in ways you didn't intend.

While self-soothing may involve doing something to make yourself feel better like lighting candles, soaking in a bubble bath, or having a cup of warm tea, it can also involve physical activity—such as going for a walk or a run. When elementary-age students suck their thumbs or carry around their favorite blanket or stuffed animal, they are engaging in self-soothing behavior. For children between four and eight years old, self-soothing behaviors may include running to a parent or teacher for comfort or even stomping around the house to release anger or frustration. It can also include positive self-talk: "I'll go to a movie next month," or even simple work with breath. Also, by doing something for others, sometimes we end up feeling better ourselves, so acts of kindness are another kind of self-soothing behavior.

Of course, sometimes we turn to self-soothing behaviors that have negative side effects. Alcohol, drugs, food, and sex are all examples of addictive behaviors that may be self-soothing and also harmful. Obsessive-compulsive disorder behaviors can also fall into this category. Sometimes we soothe ourselves with routines that ultimately end up interfering with our happiness, health, and well-being.

Looking at the brain, and what we know about fight-flight-or-freeze behaviors, sometimes our reactions to disappointments or even threatening or unpleasant situations are more a matter of the amygdala taking over and less about making conscious decisions. When the amygdala gets involved, we act from a lower, more instinctual part of the brain, a part of the brain that actually interferes with rational, logical thinking. However, the self-soothing breath is an example of a helpful self-soothing behavior that you can consciously substitute to rebuild neuropathways and responses to stress.

Paul Gilbert (2010), in *Compassion Focused Therapy*, describes deep yogic breathing as a self-soothing behavior that some people automatically turn to and also something that they sometimes need to learn, particularly for individuals who have experienced trauma.

Self-Soothing Behavior

Students who have experienced trauma often lack the ability to engage in self-soothing behaviors, something that is important to gaining control of the brain back from the hypothalamus, which might have taken over. This exercise can stand on its own, but should always be used following the resolving disappointment exercises (page 106).

1. Close your eyes, take some deep breaths. Right now, imagine a disappointment. Picture it. Feel it.
2. Turn your focus on your breath. You might even make a soft cooing sound like "Ahhh, ahhh, oh, oh." This sound is like a sigh.
3. Ask yourself the following questions.
   • "How did the breath work?"
   • "Did I try a sound? If so, how did I feel after that?"

Disappointment and Self-Soothing Breath

Deep breathing and self-soothing breaths can be useful for many types of disappointments.

1. Close your eyes. Breathe deeply. Imagine the disappointment of a friend cancelling an event. Feel the hurt, anguish, or pain.
2. Guide yourself through deep breathing. Focus on your breath for three or four minutes.
3. As you breathe, focus on your belly's rise and fall, on sustaining the breath between the inhale and exhale, and on holding the breath after you exhale. Keep the breath long and deep. (Pause.)
4. Now notice if the long, deep breathing produces a change in your body. How do you feel? Do you still feel tension, or are you relaxed? (Pause.)

5. Now inhale, circulate the energy, exhale, and think again about your friend's cancellation. When you reintroduced those thoughts, how did it feel this time? If the pain is still deep, return to the long, deep breathing.

Repeat, Refocus, Recenter

Repeat any of the previous exercises in this chapter at least three to five times over the next week. If you like, keep a diary or a journal—or use the ruled pages in this book—and note your reactions, including how these reactions may shift over the course of the week. Did you notice any changes as the week went by, either in the practice or how you felt in general?

Now that you have completed a variety of directed mindfulness exercises with your students, help guide them toward checking in on their own feelings.

Check In by Visualizing for Elementary Students

Some prekindergarten and elementary students may have difficulty with a multistep process, but the following five-step process is something you can guide them through. In step 4, you will gradually talk students through the next body part until you work your way to their heads.

1. How are you feeling?
2. Close your eyes and check again to see how you are feeling.
3. Check your stomach, your jaw, and face. Is your body relaxed?
4. Scan your body and check for tension. Starting with your feet, inhale, exhale, relax, let go. (Pause.) Now focus on your calves. Inhale, exhale, relax, let go. (Continue through body parts, ending with the head.)
5. Open your eyes. How did you feel? Do you feel different, or better, now?

Check In by Visualizing for Secondary Students

The following four-step visualizing exercise is fairly simple.

1. Close your eyes, reflect on your life and on your present situation. How are you feeling?
2. Check your breath, your body, your posture, your heart, and your facial expressions.
3. Notice what makes you feel hopeful or happy, and notice what may be producing feelings of stress, sadness, or anxiety.
4. Open your eyes and check to see how you are feeling.

Reflection After Learning

After each activity, students, depending on their ages and abilities, can reflect aloud or write about their experiences. Elementary students may want to draw pictures. Middle school and high school students may maintain a reflection log. Teachers will find that some students will experience more intense emotions such as sadness, grief, depression, and anger as they go through these activities. With these activities, students may find that they are remembering or reliving previous or ongoing trauma. While sometimes recalling trauma can help increase awareness and lead to important problem solving and the creation of new, happier endings or solutions, it can also be painful. We encourage you to find time for private discussions with these students; in some cases, you may want to make referrals to school counselors or others.

Natural Integration of Mindfulness in Our Lives Through Practice

The experiences students and teachers gain in practicing activities with being mindful of self, of body, of emotions, and of others will be most useful when we incorporate the teachings in our daily lives. With sufficient practice, we will reach the point where we begin to automatically be aware of self. We will learn to recognize our emotions, our hurts, and our fears. With that awareness, we can be in a better position to act from a centered place of knowledge rather than being blindsided by emotions, stress, or trauma.

Teachers can guide students through this process by helping them reflect on their feelings, fears, emotions, and hurts and encouraging them to name their emotions. Once we have this awareness, then we are better able to decide how to handle the ups and downs that we experience. From a place of consciousness, we can use our bodily wisdom to avoid harmful circumstances. We can also use our consciousness as a reminder that we can use self-soothing behaviors to comfort ourselves.

Mindful Reflection

As an individual or with your study group, respond to the mindful reflection questions, taking notes on the following page.

- What have you learned about mindfulness?
- What did you most enjoy?
- Did any students appear particularly impacted by the mindfulness exercises that focused on disappointment or feelings of grief, sadness, or anger? If so, how will you follow up?
- Which activities seemed to be most important for you and your students?
- What activities will you incorporate into an ongoing practice?

— Notes —

PART III
MINDFUL AND COMPASSIONATE CLASSROOMS AND SCHOOL COMMUNITIES

Part II provides exercises for teachers to do themselves and with students to build mindfulness skills (the *how*). Part III takes the reader to the next step—to address the *now what* questions related to classroom implementation, particularly of mindfulness and compassion exercises, to improve learning and academic achievement. This chapter focuses on organizational behavior research. From our experience with teachers and schools, we find that if schools go beyond individual teacher implementation in individual classrooms to collaboratively creating mindful and compassionate communities, they gain a unique advantage. Teachers realize the greatest benefits when they *implement the changes as schoolwide activities*, with corresponding changes in school policies and ways of engaging with the larger community, rather than attempting it as individuals or small groups. When we take the time and effort to create significant changes, we want them to be lasting. Sustainability is critical for transformational change. Peter M. Senge's (2006; Senge et al., 2012) organizational research suggests that real improvement only happens if the people who are responsible for implementing change actually *design* the change. Teachers, administrators, and other members of wider school communities must all be invested—and such investment is more likely when they collaborate in planning, sharing ideas and responsibility for the change that follows.

CHAPTER 7

Mindful Instruction—
Paying Attention to Your Students

Walk as if you are kissing the Earth with your feet.

—Thich Nhat Hanh

key principle

You can incorporate mindfulness exercises throughout the day. This will increase conscious awareness, a prerequisite to compassion.

Are you able to imagine the sensation of the ground giving way gently to the soft imprint your feet make, step by step? If not, we invite you to step outside, bare-footed, and feel the earth beneath your feet. Is it warm or cold? Do you feel the blades of grass or the texture of the dirt?

How does this translate to what happens in class-rooms as we teach? What would be the equivalent in your day at school? Is it the spark of interest in one stu-dent's eye? The smile that suddenly appears on a face? The air of excitement when students are truly engaged?

Mindfulness in the classroom is not only about teach-ing mindfulness; it involves being mindful. In chapter 6 (page 91), we take you through a series of exercises to increase your own mindfulness. We also introduce you to initial mindfulness exercises to use in classrooms. Chapter 7 furthers your understanding of mindfulness and its implementation in the classroom by including the following.

- Simple strategies to increase your mindfulness as you instruct
- Mindful activities to incorporate across academic subjects and grade levels
- Compassion challenges and activities
- Examples of how to extend mindfulness to increase compassion within the context of everyday events at school
- Considerations for mindful, compassionate communities

Consider Who You Are Teaching

Mindful instruction begins with mindful preparation, considering who you are teaching as you prepare your lessons and review material for the next class session. Mindful instruction includes being mindfully present, and listening with your heart and your ears, as you greet each student and help him or her prepare for the day ahead. The suggested activities that follow will help reduce stress and bring basic consciousness or mindfulness to the level of compassion in your classrooms and schools. In this section we start with some basic activities and end with some ways that you can practice handling the more challenging situations.

Build Compassion in Classrooms

All the activities in this chapter will help lead to more self-compassion and compassion for others. However, as we all know, sometimes being compassionate is more challenging than at other times. It is one thing to be compassionate when the cost is small and the ask is not too great. For example, it is usually simple to remember to look students in the eye and smile a warm, friendly smile that says, "I care." It is another thing to be compassionate when a student is noncompliant, disruptive, habitually tardy, or excuse-prone.

Mindful Greetings

As a student enters the classroom, he or she is on the threshold to a new school day. This threshold provides the opportunity to leave unnecessary baggage at the doorstep. A warm greeting from a teacher could be instrumental in setting the tone for a good day at school.

Practice the five-step mindful greeting each day for one week. Record what you discover either in a journal or here, in the pages offered in this book. We recommend that teachers practice this exercise first as a mindfulness meditation and then as they greet students and parents. Follow through by warmly greeting each student and parent with good eye contact and radiating kind, caring thoughts to them.

1. Take a few breaths.
2. Imagine warmly greeting each student and each parent with direct eye contact and complete attention.
3. Imagine being fully present and attentive to possible needs.
4. Imagine radiating light to each student and parent.
5. Close your eyes and visualize the day ahead.

Mindful Intention

We could say a lot about mindful instruction. As with mindful greetings, you could prepare by visualizing yourself successfully instructing a group of students who are rapt listeners, engaged, and learning. As you visualize this, you could note how you feel when you are connecting with your students. Over the next week, consider visualizing your class the night before you teach. Then as you instruct, take notes on what you learn. The following questions guide you.

- How effective was your hook?
- Did the hook pull students into the lesson?
- Which students were most and least engaged?
- When did your students show the greatest enthusiasm?
- When things did not go as well, what was happening?
- If any behavioral incidents occurred, what were likely catalysts (time of day, hunger, fatigue, boredom, students acting out, tests, disrespect or lack of bonding with you, or peer attention)? How was the timing and pacing of activities?
- How was your voice tone? What message did your voice tone and words convey?
- How was your rapport with students and staff?
- What message does the physical appearance of your room convey?
- What would you change?

Practice mindful instruction (pages 119–122) for a few weeks and see if it impacts your instruction. Perhaps you already considered all of these questions. Have you conducted visualization? Have you considered your body as you ask questions? (Do you feel a knot in your stomach? Fatigue? Impatience? Delight? Confusion?)

It's important to remember that the goal of mindfulness is not a state of perfection, but a constant ongoing practice of becoming self-aware. Improvement, whether it is in a particular setting, a subject, or during social interaction, takes practice and awareness. Keep in mind that the effectiveness of mindfulness practice stems from the attempt to detach from the daily distractions of everyday life, even our own emotions, and use our senses to live and feel in the present. By practicing this with students, we can help ourselves and our students to learn more about themselves by being able to assess an object, a person, or situation for what it truly is or isn't. Following are some recommendations of how you can introduce mindfulness across all school subjects to become part of classroom instruction.

Practical Exercises

At some point, after you have practiced a few exercises as introduced in chapters 4–6 (on pages 61, 73, and 91), we recommend that you introduce the terms *mindfulness* and *being mindful* to your students and explain their application to everyday life.

With students grades 1 to 4, you may want to use the Mindfulness for Children (n.d.) organization's definition: "Mindfulness means paying attention to what is happening right now with kindness and curiosity." With this definition, you could discuss kindness and curiosity, perhaps reading from children's books in which these are major themes. You might begin a class discussion by saying, "When you are mindful you are aware of others—of what is happening around you. Look around you, what do you see?" As students respond, you can prompt, "Yes, Jennifer is wearing an orange skirt," or "Kelly did build a really high tower with his bricks," and so on. Other natural opportunities to discuss mindfulness or being mindful may arise as you discuss seasons of the year with students. When you involve children in nature play or help them observe the seasons, for example, you help them to be more mindful.

You could ask elementary-aged students to spend some time on a daily basis observing their surroundings, perhaps in the neighborhoods where they live. It might help to make this a group activity for a few days. Count how many stores, parks, and cars they see. Or make observations, perhaps even with a graphic organizer as a part of an observational experience in science. Does their neighborhood have a lot of trees? What kind of trees? Are they healthy? Or ask them to observe the weather. What kind of weather do they prefer? Does weather affect how they feel? If so, ask them to try and answer why that is. If they are recording responses, make sure that there is time to share and discuss findings with others. As time goes by, check in with them periodically to get an idea about how they are following through, what they are continuing to observe about their surroundings, and whether you need to adjust your approach. For middle or high school students, consider using Jon Kabat-Zinn's (2003) definition of mindfulness: paying attention "on purpose, in the present moment, and nonjudgmentally" (p. 145).

You can ask students to help lead discussions about being purposeful, being in the present, and being nonjudgmental. From there, you can explore together with your students what you think mindfulness is and how it can help at school, home, and in life. Students can even conduct internet research on mindfulness, perhaps developing group projects to share back with others. For example, one group of students could investigate how some schools are using mindful moments in lieu of traditional disciplinary procedures. Another group could research what students appreciate about yoga, mindfulness, and meditation. You can provide students with suggestions to practice daily on their own using their senses and body scans.

Mindfulness might also be an ideal topic to mention in relation to world events, crises, or natural disasters. Asking simple questions about the impact of the events on people who are most traumatized will help to increase student awareness or consciousness. Following these questions with questions about how communities are responding, whether organizations such as the Red Cross, Habitat for Humanity, or Doctors Without Borders are helping, or whether celebrities have held a telethon to raise funds, will further understanding of compassionate action.

On a more personal level, teachers and psychologists or school counselors may want to work with students who are having difficulty with bullying, gang involvement, or anger management. After-school meetings, for example, could help these students increase their consciousness and compassion. And if yoga, meditation, breath work, or mindfulness exercises were a part of these meetings, then students may have much-needed opportunities for additional practice using these techniques and observing changes in how they feel, think, and act.

Learning and Feelings

We use most of the school day to teach and assess, but try asking your students (according to the age-appropriate lesson you're teaching or reviewing) how a particular subject, person in history, or discussion makes them feel. Ask them to pay attention and assess the importance of what they are learning and why. This also is a good way to get feedback. Ask students to share information about where they or their parents are from and some cultural or background information. This is when students can use the opportunity to be mindful of how learning about others, especially their peers, can cause them to feel. Ultimately, a lot of what we feel speaks volumes about ourselves, our hopes, and our fears.

Mindful Instruction Strategies

If students are confused or anxious about an assignment, providing a little extra academic support may reduce the student's anxiety. Supportive teachers incorporate not only the mindfulness strategies we recommend in part II, they also implement some best teaching practices that will help reduce the level of stress students feel by providing scaffolds or modifications in lesson plans. Consider the following.

- Go slowly and with a soft voice.
- Be clear about instructions.
- Write down the expectations for an assignment.
- Present the directions one step at a time so as not to overwhelm the student.
- Provide more frequent feedback; this can often be helpful.
- Sometimes modifying an assignment, inserting some questions where the student can show success, and linking classroom tasks to a student's interests can help increase a student's sense of academic security and further academic success.

If you observe that a student appears to have difficulty remembering information, following directions, or staying attentive, it could be that the hippocampus is not working efficiently or that cortisol is flooding his or her brain. Teachers may find it useful to repeat directions, present information sequentially, conduct a demonstration, or provide a glossary or study guide to facilitate memory and attention.

Playtime

Play is part of the preschool and kindergarten school day. Before dismissing students from a learning circle to a play activity, ask children to pay close attention to how they interact with others: to be kind and share. After playtime, bring students back to the circle and ask a few questions.

- "Were you respectful?"
- "Did you share?"
- "Were you able to make others smile?"
- "Did anyone become upset during play? If so, how did that person's emotions make you feel?"
- "What can you do to get along better?"

Physical Education

If we do not have a physical limitation, most of our movements are subconscious and automatic. Try these two steps for mindful walking after completing most of the rigorous activities and as class is coming to an end.

1. Ask students to walk slowly around the gymnasium, field, or track.
2. Tell them to pay attention to every footstep individually, feeling which part of the foot touches the ground first, and when the other foot rises.

Do this for between ten and fifteen minutes. Since mindfulness and balance, both physically and psychologically, are related, use balancing exercises to enhance mindfulness. Focusing on balance can truly increase mindfulness (McCall, 2013; Slovacek, Tucker, & Pantoja, 2003).

from the classroom

At Lee Elementary School in Lee, Massachusetts, physical education teachers Janet Warner and Jen Carlino regularly incorporate mindful movements and focused breathing (cleansing breaths) into their curriculum. In 2017, they also added a short, developmentally appropriate video to teach students about the three main parts of the brain associated with our mind, body, and emotions: (1) the prefrontal cortex, (2) hippocampus, and (3) amygdala. Children dance and sing along with the video and take turns being one of the three main parts of the brain. Following the video, they play the "Ha" song (that helps students use the playful art of laughing as a calming technique). Discussion, conversation, and a trivia game follow to reinforce the parts of the brain and use of brain vocabulary.

——— ♥ ———

It is helpful to remind students of the difference between being mindful and present and being on autopilot. Each day when students arrive to begin the school day, ask them to shift into mindful mode. Give them five to ten minutes to remember what that means and apply it presently as they sit in their seats. Combine it with some breathing exercises as we discuss in chapter 4 (page 61). You can create a symbol or use a word that represents a call to mindfulness, in which students understand that it's time to breathe and become self-aware. This is different from trying to quiet students down during lunch or recess. Ensure that students are well versed and fully aware of what mindfulness entails prior to implementing this.

Science

Students can have a hard time understanding the scientific method despite being taught it. Mindfulness practice can facilitate not only better observation, but also better understanding of why you are asking them to follow the method. Try the following two steps.

1. When conducting an experiment or building an innovation, as an individual or group, ask students to observe what is happening.
2. Think as freely as possible. (For example, "Use your imaginations when looking at cells under a microscope" or "Envision a process to increase energy efficiency.") Pay close attention to the following.
   + How does the order of events influence the outcome?
   + How much does each individual participate in the group? Focus mainly on your own contributions.

In an experiment, you can also ask them to pay attention to the smells and colors—even their emotions. Were they excited? Bored? Scared? Ask them why. Did it prompt any questions, besides the obvious? For example, you could use this technique with experiments where students are blind-folded and asked to identify food or drinks from smell and taste trials so they can focus on sensation.

Art

Have students follow these steps. You can ask the questions in step 5 of students ages five to eleven as part of verbal debriefing. Students grades 7 and up can write their individual responses to these questions, perhaps in their journals.

1. Tell students they will create a class painting on a large piece of paper from a variety of colors and supplies.
2. Depending on the class size, students may work in teams of six or eight on sheets of paper. You might organize these groups into between three and five workstations. Students move from one workstation to another every five minutes.

3. As students begin, ask them to use colors that make them happy and connect their next stroke to someone else's. Their goal is to examine their own thoughts as they move from group to group, choosing colors and trying to create images or abstractions.

4. During the last five minutes, gather the sheets together and ask students to find a way to connect their paintings with masking tape. Once the sheets are taped together, give students one last opportunity to connect strokes to merge the pictures.

5. Consider the following questions.

   - What colors were more fun to work with?
   - What was your favorite part of the painting?
   - What does the result look like? Does it remind you of anything? How is it representative of your classroom?
   - Does sharing space create any awkward feelings?
   - What emotions arose when you contributed to each other's work?
   - What emotions did you feel as you changed groups?

Writing

Writing is an effective way of becoming mindful (Siegel, 2007) and has been an important technique used with teacher preparation programs (Brookfield, 2017). Journal writing might seem a thing of the past, but it's a useful supplement to mindfulness practice. By writing daily or weekly, students will be able to organize their thoughts and emotions in written form. They could also use laptops, iPads, tablets, or phones for this purpose. Penzu (https://penzu.com) and Moodle's (https://moodle.org/plugins/mod_journal) activities journal are examples of online journaling options.

This activity is applicable and helpful, with modifications, for any grade. You can provide prompts like the following if they do not know what to write about.

- Invent and describe a new food.
- Describe your perfect day.
- What questions do you want answers to?

Mindfulness and Greater Consciousness Can Lead to Compassion, Confidence, and Courage

You can encourage students to express empathy and compassion. Participants can designate a wall of kindness, and teachers can intentionally embed a sense of kindness, calmness, and caring in classes by naming needs, demonstrating concern, and proposing actions. As students learn in history or current events, for example, about other parts of the world or even of recent actions in local neighborhoods, teachers can pause and take an extra minute or two to help students understand the far-reaching impact of violence, wars, food scarcity, poverty, illiteracy, homelessness, refugee camps, and brutality. Teachers and students can brainstorm about solutions, research these solutions, and weigh the pros and cons of alternative actions. Service learning projects may even develop as a result of these discussions. The following sections highlight some ways that mindfulness can facilitate compassion, confidence, and courage.

from the classroom

In a second-grade classroom at Lee Elementary School in Lee, Massachusetts, a second-grade teacher writes about incorporating journal writing into her civil rights unit by asking students to write about how they would feel or react to situations that were similar to those of the civil rights leaders they were studying. The teacher reports that most students were able to thoughtfully connect what they learned in this unit to their own feelings. She sometimes incorporates mindfulness into the curriculum that she is already teaching (such as journal writing) instead of mindfulness as its own separate activity. Because of mindfulness, her students are somewhat better able to handle situations that make them anxious or uncomfortable. She has noticed that her students have become more compassionate and understanding of others who may be going through a difficult time (J. Pollard, personal communication, May 19, 2017).

Positive Affirmation

We cannot dismiss the power of positive thought. Even in the worst and most challenging circumstances that so many of our children face every day, positive affirmation can be a game changer. Affirmations can lead to both greater confidence as students practice them over time and to courage, which they may strengthen with specific affirmations or positive talk.

As a former program director for juvenile delinquents in Florida, Michele M. Rivers Murphy recalls one of the most powerful, easiest, and most effective defenses she uses with youth who are up against grave circumstances and odds—the power of positive affirmation. Michele can still feel the power this verse elicited many years ago. The positive affirmation fills students with a feeling of positive energy, strong collective voices, and hope. Every day, morning meetings begin and end with the same strong verse that went something like this: "Repeat after me: I am somebody (I am somebody). If my mind can conceive it (if my mind can conceive it), and my heart can believe it (and my heart can believe it), then I can achieve it (then I can achieve it) because I am somebody (because I am somebody)."

These twenty-four simple but powerful words reaffirm that each and every student, no matter the circumstance, no matter the past history or battles, is worth all the hopes, dreams, and success in that student's heart. Simply awesome!

Ask yourself: "At school, how do I begin and end the day with my students?"

Live Life Large Jar

Students submit their favorite quotes into the Live Life Large jar in a centrally located place in the school, such as the lunchroom or main hallway. Pull a new quote every morning for a student to read during morning announcements. Students can develop confidence as they see that their opinions become part of the school ritual and routines.

Weave Magically

Throughout the day, teachers can weave an inspirational quote almost magically into their classroom instruction. Throughout the day, it is surprising how many opportunities may arise for reflection on a given quotation. For example, teachers could hold a brief class discussion about an inspirational quote. In cooperative learning groups or teams, students could explore the meaning of an inspirational quote. You could also provide students with opportunities to gain extra credit by using a quotation in context, perhaps as part of a paper on a specific topic or by sharing an example of the meaning of the quotation. As you weave inspirational quotes throughout the day and students practice them, they are more likely to remember these gems that provide useful advice for how to live our lives.

Half-Minute Confidence Boost

Teachers can challenge students in each classroom or grade level to create a class motto that is self-affirming just like Jess Bazinet, a technology specialist at Allendale Elementary School in Pittsfield, Massachusetts, has posted on her website (http://jbazinet.wixsite.com/baz14): "I Am Smart; I Am Important; I Can Do Anything If I Try; I Will Graduate; and I Will Be Somebody" Students can repeat their class motto often—before class, during class, and before leaving class. Begin and end with it every class and every day. Hang your class motto in your classroom, on your classroom door, and in nearby hallways. Live it and remind one another of it throughout the day.

Gratitude

One mindful activity involves the experience of being thankful. Sometimes simply saying "I am thankful for . . . " each day can change moods from negative to positive.

A simple attitude of gratitude is a life changer. Research favorably suggests that gratitude is something we can cultivate and, in turn, "increase our well-being and happiness by doing so. Gratefulness—and especially expression of it to others—is associated with increased energy, optimism, and empathy" ("The Benefits of Gratitude," n.d.).

Keeping a daily gratitude journal can also enhance our own lives and the lives of our students. A gratitude journal can be as easy as the following.

- Writing three new things each day that a student is thankful for
- Changing it up and asking students to write down one genuine compliment on a sticky note pertaining to a nearby student (rotate)
- Teaching the art of handwritten thank-you notes; write a hand-written note or card to someone as a form of recognition, gratitude, or encouragement
- Throwing a thank-you party for someone in the school setting who is not often recognized; consider the lunch personnel, bus drivers, custodians, or classroom volunteers

In an experimental study of gratitude and subjective well-being, Jeffrey Froh, William Sefick, and Robert Emmons (2008) find that a daily gratitude journal can help students achieve higher grades; higher goals; more satisfaction with relationships, life, and school; less materialism; and more willingness to give back. Adults who keep gratitude journals are able to be more optimistic, experience more social satisfaction, exercise more often, have less envy and depression, experience fewer physical complaints, and sleep better (Froh et al., 2008). In other words, don't just teach students to count; show them what counts.

Compassion Challenges

As you read through the following activities, consider your students and your classroom. Consider whether you could do anything to enhance your mindfulness or compassion and whether you could do anything to further students' understanding of compassion.

Compassion Challenge: Mindful Attention to an Unresponsive Student

Christine Mason spent three years as a middle school resource teacher in a high-poverty, multicultural school in a suburb of Washington, D.C. As you read, think about a student you instruct and make some notes about your student's needs.

> As a new co-teacher at Glasgow Middle School, I remember walking into the classroom and seeing Ahmed, slouched down at his desk . . . staring into space; disengaged, eyes glazed over, probably high and certainly lethargic. Ahmed was a tall lanky boy who didn't seem to fit with the other, seemingly

younger looking students. My job in this classroom was to "float" around, helping students get on task, stay on task, and complete their work. Ahmed was not one of my targeted students; he did not have an IEP, but he certainly seemed to need assistance. I remember walking up to Ahmed, with the intent of listening to him. Thoughts flashed through my mind—why was Ahmed so disengaged? Was it a language barrier? Reading problem? Boredom? Teenage hormones? Pride? How could we connect? My consciousness, my awareness, was that if connection with an adult at school did not happen soon, Ahmed would likely leave the system, either dropping out or being expelled. My awareness was that I needed to listen to Ahmed, to ask some basic questions, listen to his response, and try to engage with him.

Consider the following questions.

- Do you have a student like Ahmed in your classroom? Or have you had one in the past?
- What did you do to engage the student?
- Is there more you could do?

Compassion Challenge: Teachable Moments When Emotions Arise

A foremost opportunity to be mindful arises when teachers pause to take advantage of teachable moments. Sometimes the most important thing a teacher can do is deviate from the curriculum, pause in the midst of a planned lesson, and help students try to understand more about what is happening right at that moment. Teachers in these times can help students name and process their emotions, allow them to give voice to their fears, and provide reassurance that at school the teacher as a caring adult will listen and be someone who may make the phone call that needs to be made. Students need to feel confident that their teacher (an adult) will be the one who will help them handle some of the toughest issues that arise during these turbulent times, times that are filled with rapidly changing events and mass media portrayals of the ugliest side of human nature. They need reassurance, and they need to know someone cares so that they feel a greater sense of safety and well-being.

- How have you handled teachable moments? Do you find ways to deviate from the curriculum or your lesson when necessary?
- Do you find ways to reduce the stress that children face?
- Is there more you could do?

Compassion Challenge: Academic Learning and Feelings

We use most of the school day to teach and assess, but try asking your students how a particular subject, person in history, or discussion makes them feel. Or you may ask students to relate to the compassion that the lesson displays. A challenge sometimes arises when the students do not make the connections. Sometimes students need help in brainstorming how a character from a story or a person at a particular time and place in history may be feeling. This may take additional preparation; however, considering these feelings can also help lessons come alive.

- How could you incorporate questions about feelings and compassion into your academic lessons?
- If students have difficulty connecting with possible feelings, consider adding a visualization similar to the ones we present in chapter 6 (page 91). Students could close their eyes and imagine being with George Washington as he crossed the Delaware in an icy storm. They could imagine being a member of a Native American tribe, perhaps cooking over a fire when suddenly troops appear on horseback. They could imagine being a newcomer to the United States who has emigrated from a war-torn country.

Compassion Challenge: Cultural Competence

Ask students to share information about where they are from or about cultural traditions such as how they celebrate holidays. A good way to begin is to ask students to conduct some research or talk with parents or family members before sharing with their classmates. Or students could also talk with parents or grandparents to find out more about their heritage. With these activities, students can use the opportunity to be mindful of how others feel. What do you know about the culture, heritage, and traditions of your students and their families? How could you find out more in a positive, unobtrusive way?

Be aware of the concerns and vulnerability that students and families may feel—particularly for those who have immigrated to this country. It is important to note that schools are immune from Immigration and Customs Enforcement (ICE). While reporting requirements can be confusing, and schools should be alert as to changes in policy that may occur, as the South Carolina Appleseed Legal Justice Center (2012) explains:

> All children have a right to a public education for grades kindergarten through twelve, even if they are undocumented. Students cannot be stopped from attending a public school because they are undocumented. Schools cannot require undocumented students or their parents to tell their immigration status. School employees, like teachers and principals, have **no duty** to report undocumented students or their parents.

Compassion Challenge: Disruptive Behaviors, Habitual Tardiness, Excuses

Each of these situations involves behaviors that interfere with learning and the well-being of the self and others. We can increase compassion in classrooms by trying to understand more about the underlying factors that are influencing the behavior. Is it a stress reaction? A factor that is related to home life or a student's sense of insecurity? A learned behavior?

- Consider the students you teach. Are you currently addressing any of these concerns or related behaviors? How compassionate is your response?
- Imagine the factors that might be impacting the students to influence these behaviors.
- Close your eyes and visualize the situation. You are present with the student and are finding a compassionate response. What solution appears to you? How feasible is that solution? With mindfulness practice you may find that compassionate responses come to you, perhaps particularly during times of meditation.

Compassion Challenge: Bullying, Anger, and Gang Behaviors

On a personal level, teachers and psychologists or school counselors may want to work with students who are having difficulty with bullying, gang involvement, or anger management. After-school meetings, for example, could help these students increase their mindfulness and compassion. And if yoga, meditation, breath work, or mindfulness exercises are a part of these meetings, then students may have much-needed opportunities for additional practice using these techniques and observing changes in how they feel, think, and act.

- Do you have any special programs at your school for students who are victims of bullying or involved in gangs? Do you have any anger management groups or protocol?
- How effective are the current procedures? Do they have a mindfulness component?
- How could they be improved?

Creating Mindful, Compassionate Communities in Schools

In classrooms where teachers are practicing mindfulness and becoming more and more aware of feelings and emotional reactions of others and themselves, they are able to be more fully present to the needs of the students they teach. In classrooms where students are more conscious about their own emotions, their feelings, and the bodily reactions they are experiencing with their emotions, they are better able to handle emotions as they arise and to self-regulate, or to consciously choose to express their emotions in healthy ways (Flook, Goldberg, Pinger, & Davidson, 2015). When they are able to self-regulate, they can choose actions rather than be controlled by emotions (or the amygdala as it shifts into survival mode). Rather than striking out at another student, a mindful student may first observe his or her own emotions and then decide on a course of action that might involve being more compassionate or understanding.

Compassionate action follows from greater awareness and empathy or understanding about the self and others. This awareness can be increased through the yoga, breathing, meditation, and specific mindfulness strategies we present in part II (page 59). Teachers have many opportunities each day to demonstrate awareness or mindfulness and compassion. Classrooms are great learning labs for learning about one's emotions, increasing one's sensitivity, and practicing healthier ways of interacting with others. Such awareness can reduce uncertainty, and help a person envision his or her success. Visions of success and a positive future are steps toward self-efficacy and resilience. When students have a greater sense of self-efficacy and a growth mindset, then they are better able to take responsibility for their own learning (Dweck, 2006). Such experiences during childhood can lead to adults who are in better touch with their emotions and are able to find healthier ways to express their frustrations.

Mindful Reflection

As an individual or with your study group, respond to the mindful reflection questions, taking notes on the following page.

- How do you want to integrate breath work, meditation, and mindfulness into your life?
- During your trial period, did you gain insights that suggest that this could be a valuable practice?
- If you experienced any difficulties, where could you go for additional support?
- Do you have specific compassionate challenges? How are you addressing them?
- Sometimes it takes forty days of practice to make a good decision about a new activity. Are you willing to commit forty days to one or more of the exercises in this chapter? Which ones? If forty days seems like a long time, could you start with a month, perhaps completing the exercises three to four days a week?

— Notes —

CHAPTER 8

Executive Functioning

Obstacles, of course, are developmentally necessary: they teach kids strategy, patience, critical thinking, resilience and resourcefulness.

—Naomi Wolf

key principle

Teachers can help students improve executive functioning, which is critical for coping and learning, by introducing mindfulness exercises in classrooms.

Neuroscience and our knowledge of neuroplasticity provide important scientific information about ways to better support students as they are learning in our classrooms. For many, the compounded stress effect becomes intolerable, compromising important cognitive skills like executive functioning, wreaking havoc on their mind and bodies, and undermining their physical health with illness or *disease.* However, brains are malleable. Thankfully, teachers who work with students who have been damaged by trauma have tools to help them live healthier lives and support their healing and well-being. Some of these tools have been in our teaching toolbox for a long, long time. Other tools, with our 21st century technology, are emerging.

Teachers can use our expanding array of tools to help students sharpen memories, increase focus, enhance self-regulation, build resilience, and bring healing. Much like *emotional intelligence* and *21st century learning*, the term *executive functioning* may have a slightly fluid definition. Phil Zelazo (2015) describes executive functioning as "essential for goal-directed problem solving and reflective learning" (p. 55). Executive functioning skills assist with "goal-directed behavior, including planning, organized search, and impulse control" (Welsh, Pennington, & Groisser, 1991). Following your individual and classroom practice, you should begin to see improvements in executive functioning.

Mind Full Versus *Mindful*

When students are not sufficiently engaged or tuned into learning, their minds will wander during instruction. Some may be remembering a fun or exciting experience with family or friends. Others may be feeling the weight of the world as they continue to re-experience sorrows or tragedies they or a loved one has encountered. They may be reliving the look on a grandmother's face or the feeling of fear or anger that a parent or teacher has expressed. Students living with chronic stress may be in a state of numbness, shame, or depression in response to an interaction, striving to push down unwanted memories that keep re-emerging. Each of these responses affects learning. Positive interactions cause the release of hormones or neurotransmitters such as endorphins, dopamine, or oxytocin, which stimulate the efficiency and effectiveness of a learning experience. Negative interactions cause the release of cortisol (the body's natural chemical response to stress) that inhibit learning (Jackson, 2011).

Mindful Lens in the Classroom

From a mindfulness perspective, wise teachers are aware of the individual students in their classrooms. These teachers will realize that for many of the reasons we address in earlier chapters, students may not all be following the teacher note for note, footnote by footnote. Teachers who are attuned to mindfulness will be aware of a student who appears distracted or a student who looks confused or bored. Mindfulness can lead to a subtle fine-tuning in how teachers approach instruction. Sometimes pausing to repeat a direction for the student who is confused is the most mindful thing to do in the moment. Sometimes, suggesting that students stand up for a minute and take a Heart Beaming (see chapter 4, page 61) or stretch break may be the most mindful thing to do. After a breathing or stretch break, sometimes students are able to reconnect with the instruction.

As we revisit the key points in the book and consider how to use what we know of needs, our brains, breath, movement, meditation, and mindfulness, we pause to consider some key ways to aid with the healing of children in our classrooms. To provide the help that students most need, we believe teachers and schools will be well served to review the implications from a neuroscientific arena known as *executive functioning*.

How Our Brains Help Us Learn

Our brains are involved in learning in a thousand different ways. Our brains help regulate stress. They also alert us to danger. Communication, coordination of all muscle movements, regulation of hormones and glandular functions, sensory perceptions, and reaction to environmental stimuli all depend on firing neurons and the connection of synapses within our brains. Under optimal conditions, brains operate with efficiency, requiring few resources for basic sensory perception and information processing. However, many things can reduce this efficiency and set up barriers to learning. Students whose lives are overshadowed with trauma or who face the daily academic trials of trying to keep up with classmates even as they have trouble with memory, attention, or learning new tasks may benefit from classrooms where teachers intentionally add components that recent neuroscientific discoveries support. Exercises involving breathing, yoga, meditation, mindfulness, and Heart Centered Learning can assist these students.

Understand the Brain's Hardwire Complexity

Human brains are indeed complex. Informal estimates place neural firing rates in the <1–200 hertz (Hz) range, which is one to two-hundred times per second (AI Impacts, 2015). Since we have roughly one-hundred billion neurons (Herculano-Houzel, 2009), with an estimated eighty-six billion neurons in our brains (Voytek, 2013), that hard drive takes in gigabytes of stimuli simultaneously. However, some students may experience processing delays. Some may have trouble switching gears. For others, following an instructional thread may be challenging. They may be easily distracted. Others may have trouble retrieving what they have tried to remember. Teachers have many tools to help, including mindfulness practices.

Connect 21st Century Skills and Executive Functioning Neuroscience

Mindfulness is not only a foundational skill, it is also one that facilitates executive functioning and the 21st century skills and tools necessary for college, career, and life success. The field of neuroscience also provides us with research documenting ways to strengthen these same executive functioning skills (Diamond & Lee, 2011; Hölzel et al., 2011; Zelazo & Lyons, 2012). Two hundred fifty neuroscientists collaborated with the National Institutes of Health to develop the NIH Toolbox, which identifies ways to measure important cognitive, sensory, motor, and emotional functions of the brain (HealthMeasures, 2018). Within that arena are specific processes that neuroscientists have identified as executive functions, or mental skills that help our brain organize and act on information. Designed as a tool for researchers and clinicians, the NIH Toolbox includes a cognition battery specifically designed to measure executive functioning skills.

Executive functioning skills are the most crucial that students need to acquire for life success. These skills predict certain developmental outcomes such as school readiness, academic achievement, social functioning, and mental and physical health (Bierman, Nix, Greenberg, Blair, & Domitrovich, 2008; Clark, Pritchard, & Woodward, 2010; Moffitt et al., 2011; Zelazo & Lyons, 2012). The Partnership for 21st century skills (P21; 2007) has articulated some of the most important

21st century skills. P21, with a host of high-tech and educational organizations, developed a framework for incorporating many of the soft skills needed for success in the workforce. This includes collaboration, communication, critical thinking, and creativity, as well as leadership, problem solving, and adaptability. P21 developed and expanded its Patterns of Innovation program (www.p21.org/exemplar -program-case-studies/patterns-of-innovation) to showcase exemplary programs and empower learners, promote a climate conducive to achievement, and share 21st century learning practices.

Executive functioning skills complement 21st century skills that are required for success. (See table 8.1.)

Table 8.1: Executive Functioning Skills Needed to Develop 21st Century Skills

Executive Functioning Skills Necessary to Develop 21st Century Skill Set	21st Century (Soft) Skill Set Required for Success
Controlling impulses and emotions, planning, and prioritizing	Communicating
Controlling impulses and focusing attention	Making decisions
Planning and prioritizing	Showing commitment
Thinking flexibly	Adapting
Self-monitoring, focusing attention, organizing, planning, and prioritizing	Managing time
Organizing	Leading and collaborating
Thinking flexibly	Showing creativity, innovating, thinking critically, solving problems, and team building
Initiating tasks, planning, and prioritizing	Accepting responsibility
Controlling emotions and self-monitoring	Working under pressure

Source: Dawson & Guare, 2010; Partnership for 21st Century Skills, 2007.

Throughout preK to about seventh grade (age twelve), executive functioning skills are required to set a solid foundation for students to achieve school, career, and life success. For example, students are required to learn and work collaboratively, manage time, and share responsibility for team projects. Students who are adept at problem solving and innovation are likely to be flexible in their thinking and to have working memory skills that enable them to organize, remember, and plan for assignments. Consider task initiation, planning, and prioritizing as another example. To generate data (perhaps for school, business, corporate, or scientific reports), students need the ability to sift through information and prioritize data. Students with these skills are better prepared to complete classroom assignments in a timely way, and to assume job responsibilities when they are adults.

Executive functioning skills are necessary to handle, plan, organize, analyze, and break down multiple steps; follow directions; make adjustments; prioritize; pay attention; and get started on tasks. Look at this list and consider your class.

- Do you know any students who have trouble staying organized?
- Do you know any students who probably did their homework and then failed to bring it to school?
- Do you know any students who may get down to work and five minutes later be bouncing up and down in their seats, yelling across the room to their classmates, and perhaps even raising their hands as if to announce that they are giving up and can't possibly proceed without the teacher's undivided attention?
- From a mindfulness perspective, what might teachers do to assist students with the foregoing problems? Consider the Compassionate Challenge exercises in chapter 7 (page 115). If you do not find good solutions to these situations, try sitting down, closing your eyes, and visualizing what is happening. In your visualization consider the student, other students, and yourself. Imagine a solution that works. When you open your eyes, consider the possibilities of trying the solution that appeared in your meditation or visualization.

Reflect on Past Experiences

With mindfulness, we urge teachers to first consider whether they have ever experienced any of the circumstances that their students face (empathy).

- Have you ever misplaced your car keys or forgotten to stop by the grocery to pick up an ingredient that was critical to the dinner you planned?
- Have you ever tried to learn a complex new task—perhaps one that doesn't line up with your portfolio?
    - Perhaps something like reading a blueprint to assemble a piece of furniture or learning a task that involves unlearning first?
    - Perhaps something like learning to switch from using Microsoft Windows to using an Apple computer?

Next, go back and think through the steps you took with one of the dilemmas you faced. How did you resolve your dilemma? Was it a long, arduous process, or did you find a simple solution?

- Did you construct certain techniques to help yourself with these tasks?
- Perhaps you have certain prompts to assist with memory and retrieval of information? Sticky notes, for example?

- Have you learned to practice or use a verbal rehearsal prompt (even thinking about the steps as you proceed)?

Perhaps you decided to do something such as use sticky notes to enhance your memory. If so, were you able to immediately start using the new memory device, or did it take you awhile to get into the new routine?

Now, consider your students.

- What have you learned about yourself that might help you better understand your students?
- Did you gain any insights that have increased your empathy?
- Did you come up with strategies that you might be able to share with them to help them through similar circumstances?
- Did you construct certain techniques to help yourself with these tasks?
- Perhaps you have certain prompts to assist with memory and retrieval of information, such as sticky notes?
- Have you learned to practice or use a verbal rehearsal prompt (even thinking about the steps as you proceed)?

Retrieve Past Information and Experiences

Executive functioning also helps us use information and experiences from our past to solve current problems and make adjustments. How well one develops these crucial 21st century skills for learning and life depends on three main brain functions: (1) working memory, (2) mental flexibility, and (3) self-control. According to the Center on the Developing Child (2016), all three of these functions are "highly interrelated, and the successful application of executive functioning skills requires them to cooperate in coordination with each other."

Revisit and Reflect Again

When students show deficits in executive functioning, perhaps as a result of trauma or prolonged stress, these deficits present barriers to learning. Do you know students who do the following?

- Have trouble remembering the rules
- Protest when the rules are changed
- Seem unable to contain their excitement (or their anger)
- Seem forgetful
- Fail to retain over the summer what they learned the previous year
- Thrive on the attention of others and go the extra mile to get a laugh

From a mindfulness perspective, how could teachers address the needs of students who are characterized by their seeming need for personalized attention, prompts, and guidance?

Working memory, mental flexibility, and self-control are independent. The hippocampus largely handles working memory—it operates likes the switch that will direct a train onto another track. However, close by are areas of the brain that govern emotions, reactions, and responses (the amygdala and limbic system), and decision making and self-regulation (the prefrontal cortex). The implications for teaching and learning are significant. If students are having trouble remembering, for example, then this may stem from emotions and reactions that seize control of attention as part of our primitive instinct for survival. Students may improve their memory in a number of ways by strengthening the prefrontal cortex. Students can work on visualization skills (creating a mental picture), play games that include visualization, read aloud, underline and highlight essential information, use graphic organizers, and use multisensory memorization approaches (including say it, write it, map it).

Mindfulness, yoga, breath work, and meditation are efficient ways to get both long-term and sustainable improvements. You can also enhance these executive functioning skills by helping students feel more secure and working directly to develop self-regulation skills. You can do this through reducing chaos, increasing the positive predictability in a child's life through routines, and directly teaching children through clarifying simple rules. These rules might be related to academic tasks—"Here are the steps to follow"—or through codes of conduct—"We keep our hands to ourselves."

To increase mental flexibility, largely related to operations occurring in the prefrontal cortex, teachers add flexibility to the rules, so that in an overt way flexibility becomes part of the norm. For example, a rule may be that when you drive you should stop for stoplights. Flexibility enters the picture when you see that a police officer is at an intersection waving you through the red light to keep traffic flowing. The adage that rules are made to be broken has some merit and value. In classrooms, teachers can enhance mental flexibility by occasionally changing routines and expectations. However, for students who count on consistency it is important to introduce flexibility carefully, sometimes with accompanying explanations. You might help prepare students by saying something such as, "Today we are mixing it up a bit. We will have a shorter recess so that we have time for the assembly this afternoon." As with memory, students can also improve their mental flexibility with mindfulness, yoga, breath work, and meditation, as these strengthen the prefrontal cortex.

When it comes to self-control, the hippocampus rules. High levels of stress generate increased cortisol and activity in the area of the hippocampus, making it more difficult for reasoning and thought to govern behavior. As stated in chapter 3 (page 37), with increased stress, fewer neurons are available for learning; that is the result of hypervigilance due to fight-flight-or-freeze mode. Reducing stress and overtly teaching rules for self-control, as well as giving students opportunities for self-reflection, are critical to improving self-control. Students with enhanced abilities to reflect on how they are learning and behaving (metacognitive abilities) typically have greater self-control and are less likely to act in impulsive ways that are detrimental to their own good (Sodian & Frith, 2008). And they can rehearse and practice these metacognitive skills and, over time, use them frequently as individuals to engage in self-reflective behavior. The former might result in expectations you convey on the first day of school, including taking turns, sharing, or being compassionate to peers. Students with enhanced ability to reflect on how they are learning and behaving—their metacognitive abilities—typically have greater self-control and are less likely to be impulsive (Sodian & Frith, 2008). The good news is that executive functioning skills are developed, not inherited. It is important for educators to understand that students do not innately possess the required executive functioning skills necessary for life success—however, they are born with the potential to develop them:

> If children do not get what they need from their relationships with adults and the conditions in their environments—or (worse) if those influences are sources of toxic stress—their skill development can be seriously delayed or impaired. Adverse environments resulting from neglect, abuse, and/or violence may expose children to toxic stress, which disrupts brain architecture and impairs the development of executive function. (Center on the Developing Child, 2016)

Students who experience trauma over a prolonged period of time may exhibit a variety of symptoms such as defiance, hypersensitivity, or withdrawal. The following sections talk more about how important early intervention is, how crucial EF is for coping and learning, our ability to regenerate and restore good brain function, and how mindfulness works for improving executive functioning abilities.

Early Intervention

As our students' brains continue to develop and grow, executive functioning issues can also change (Cortiella & Horowitz, 2014). Finding ways to use individual students' strengths to their advantage and to combat weaknesses early on are the key to accelerated and restored brain health. The greatest and most accelerated brain growth takes place in a student's early years, so our work must begin early. At an early age, strengths may appear as language, gross motor, fine motor, or social skills. By the age of three, strengths such as reasoning, imagination, or even early reading or pre-mathematics skills may appear. Teachers who are aware of a student's strengths and interests can help promote brain growth by integrating these activities into lesson plans. They can, perhaps, take a cross-curricular approach. Some students may demonstrate a natural joy for movement and yoga, and this age is an ideal time to encourage children in these activities.

Classroom and Schoolwide Implications

In the school environment, poor executive functioning skills place any student at a severe disadvantage. Simply learning tasks such as following teacher directions, keeping track of time, paying attention, and managing time are challenging. However, more complex tasks such as completing a test, analyzing ideas, or planning for a project—even the rules for participating in schoolwide events such as celebrations and competitions—become intolerable for the student with executive functioning deficits and can challenge the teacher as well.

Consider the following steps that we adapted from the Understood Team (n.d.). It may help you understand how executive functioning skills work and the importance of developing them. Imagine that when a teacher asks students to complete a project in class, they must complete the following six steps in order.

1. Analyze the task at hand and decide what one needs to do.
2. Outline the steps on how to complete the task.
3. Organize oneself and break down the overall steps into a series of steps.
4. Manage one's time and decide how to use it.
5. Make adjustments as necessary.
6. Complete the task within the time outlined.

If executive functioning is working well and the task is fairly simple, the brain may go through these steps in autopilot mode in a matter of seconds. However, if a student has weak executive functioning skills, performing even a simple task such as remembering a key word may be highly challenging, taking several minutes to process and get started.

Crucial for Coping and Learning

Every classroom includes students who experience a variety of learning challenges, many specifically related to poor executive functioning skills. Executive functioning can greatly impact learning and one's ability to cope and succeed in the school environment. Poor executive functioning is not considered a defined disability in its own right but a variety of learning and intellectual challenges, mood disorders, autism, or acquired brain injuries can cause or impact it.

Our Ability to Regenerate and Restore Good Brain Function

Prefrontal cortex functioning issues in the brain, genes and heredity, and learning disabilities such as attention deficit disorder (with or without hyperactivity) and dyslexia can also contribute to or correlate with poor executive functioning (Cortiella & Horowitz, 2014). Some students have suffered trauma and also happen to have a disability. It is often difficult to distinguish whether a disability is the underlying issue or rather whether trauma is the primary source. Existing files may provide some assistance, and a completed cognitive test battery (such as the one used with the NIH Toolbox) completed by a therapist may provide further information on whether the child's executive functioning is impaired. And, while sometimes neuroscience cannot always provide a definitive reason or cause for poor executive functioning, we are encouraged by what we have learned regarding brain function and our ability to regenerate and restore good brain health.

Mindfulness for Improving Executive Functioning Abilities

How do we apply what we have learned about breathing, yoga, meditation, and mindfulness to assist students with deficits in working memory, attention, self-control, and cognitive flexibility? Is there value in teaching students about breathing and their brains and in leading students through breathing, yoga, meditation, and mindfulness exercises? A key to impacting students in positive ways, including improving executive functioning, may be to introduce in sequence all four components: (1) breathing, (2) yoga, (3) meditation, and (4) mindfulness. These exercises create new neural pathways, creating connections that help accelerate learning and overriding the neural pathways that have formed blockages and interfered with learning (Siegel, 2010a; Willis, 2007). While breath work, yoga, meditation, and mindfulness exercises will not result in specific executive functioning skill mastery, and no specific exercise facilitates, for example, impulse control or working memory, these activities will help strengthen specific parts of the brain that are connected with these executive functions.

Working Memory and Its Impact on Learning

Perhaps one of the most basic but important executive functioning skills necessary for learning is working memory. Our working memory is akin to a mental sticky note that we use to keep track of information until we need it. Working memory can have a profound impact on the learning process in general and directly affect all subject areas, especially the foundations for learning such as reading and math. Considering that working memory helps students retain information in the brain long enough to use it, plays a key role in concentrating and focusing, and is necessary to follow directions, it is essential to implement strategies to help develop and restore order to students' working memory (Morin, n.d.). We highlight the importance of working memory with the skills we outline in table 8.2.

Working memory is pivotal to success. One can consider it one of the central processors within the brain. Working memory helps students shift attention, wait for the right moment to ask a question, make and follow through with plans, and figure out strategic ways to complete assignments or meet their own individual needs. If students are overwhelmed with a task, or if they are bringing the pain of their world

Table 8.2: Cognitive, Behavioral, and Stress Tolerance Skills

Skill	Explanation
Skills Involving Thinking (Cognition)	
Working memory	The ability to hold information in memory while performing complex tasks; incorporates ability to draw on past learning or experience to apply to current situations
Planning and prioritization	The ability to create a road map to reach a goal or to complete a task; making decisions about what's important to focus on
Organization	The ability to create and maintain systems to keep track of information or materials
Time management	The capacity to estimate how much time one has, how to allocate it, and how to stay within time limits and deadlines
Metacognition	The ability to monitor oneself; the ability to ask oneself, "How am I doing?" or "How did I do?" (Dawson & Guare, 2010)
Skills Involving Doing (Behavior)	
Response inhibition	The capacity to think before you act
Emotional control	The ability to manage emotions to achieve goals, complete tasks, or control and direct behavior
Sustained attention	The capacity to keep paying attention to a situation or task in spite of distractions, fatigue, or boredom
Task initiation	The ability to begin a task or activity without undue procrastination and to independently generate ideas, responses, or problem-solving strategies
Goal-directed persistence	The capacity to have a goal, follow through to the completion of the goal, and not be distracted by competing interests
Cognitive flexibility	The ability to revise plans in the face of obstacles, setbacks, new information, or mistakes
Stress tolerance	The ability to thrive in stressful situations and to cope with uncertainty, change, and performance demands (Dawson & Guare, 2010)

to their classrooms, then roadblocks to learning emerge. At times, it is almost as if an emergency signal goes off in their brains and for survival's sake, students learn to ignore some of what is happening.

Given the importance of working memory for the academic tasks that have been so very much at the front and center of classroom learning, teachers may find it to their advantage to learn and implement mindfulness and related strategies for bolstering executive functioning. University of British Columbia's Adele Diamond (2015) warns:

> If we ignore that someone is stressed, lonely, or not healthy because of poor nutrition, lack of sleep or lack of exercise, those unmet needs will work against that person exercising the executive functions s/he needs to function properly at work and at home.

Some educators use brain-based games to boost executive functioning. The games are advertised to increase working memory, attention to task, response time, and more. The cost of these computer products varies widely, and their effectiveness isn't proven. Most of the games appear to increase student ability to perform specific tasks that are part of the game, showing instead short-term effects. Moreover, most of these games encourage rapid-fire responses, which can be useful at times. However, sometimes learners need to slow down and reflect before responding. Most brain-based games do not encourage such reflection, and most have not incorporated features for skills to transfer to learning academic tasks (Gibson et al., 2012; Melby-Lervåg & Hulme, 2013; Shipstead, Hicks, & Engle, 2012). These games are designed to entice players to repeatedly return to the game. Hence, some brain-based games are highly addictive (Wexler, 2012, 2013, 2017; Wexler, Anderson, Fullbright, & Gore, 2000). However, because this field has potential, we urge you to stay aware of changes that are bound to occur in the next several years.

If you are considering a brain-based game for your students, first research answers to the following questions.

- What research has been conducted on the game?
- Is there evidence of skills transfer outside the game?
- Which executive functions does the game support?
- Does the game have any disclaimers or acknowledged restrictions for age, prerequisite skills, or learning outside of playing the game?

Mindful Reflection

As an individual or with your study group, respond to the mindful reflection questions, taking notes on the following page.

- What are the implications of what we know about stress and executive functioning for improving teacher sensitivity, building student security, and helping students who have been traumatized?
- What are two to three tools, procedures, or activities that teachers can use to help alleviate stress and improve executive functioning?

- Are you implementing any brain-based games in your classrooms? If so, which ones and how are you using them? How useful are they?
- Of the activities mentioned, which are you considering for your classrooms?
- What additional information do you need to integrate the knowledge and strategies we present in this book into your instruction?

— Notes —

CHAPTER 9

Mindful Leadership From Within—A New Mindset

The world as we have created it is a process of our thinking. It cannot be changed without changing our thinking.

—Albert Einstein

key principle

Mindful leadership is critical to cultivating compassionate and heart centered school communities.

In the first chapter (page 13), we spoke of a sense of urgency and a necessary call to action to serve our students and families with open hearts and minds. We asked the question, "Are we doing enough?" In this final chapter, we take this question one step further and ask education leaders, "What will it take to do things differently and take care of the students that will someday become our future?"

We use a mindful leadership lens to help us develop a new mindset and the courage within to understand and act upon what it will take to help move the needle of change.

In this chapter, we look back and take in the view, as we present the voices of four leaders: Paul Liabenow, James Dierke, Melissa Patschke, and Kate Retzel. Consider the story that Paul Liabenow tells of five suicides in his district within five years (page 146), or James Dierke, who faced forty-one murders in his school community within a three-year span, and unfathomable student traumatic stress as a result (page 148). Yet, through the practice of mindfulness came a significant increase in academic performance and achievement and a significant reduction in school suspensions and student violence. Consider how Melissa Patschke, Kate Retzel, and Al Skrocki shared leadership and built staff capacity to further mindfulness and compassion in their schools (page 153). In each case, the leaders ventured to lead their schools with high expectations and cutting-edge practices. They shared leadership and took bold actions. And all are committed to continuing their journeys.

from the classroom

Paul Liabenow, executive director of Michigan Elementary and Middle School Principals Association (and former teacher, principal, and superintendent), knows that unexpected events can become the catalyst for systematic and transformational change. Cadillac Public Schools, a small district in northern Michigan, faced unspeakable tragedy with five student suicides during a short five-year period. Some parents blamed the school district for the student deaths. They said that bullying was the cause. The community was numb with fear of more of the same, and school leaders and teachers became defensive, as it seemed that a suicide cluster was on the horizon. Local radio and television boosted their ratings opining about the student losses and put the school administration in various stages of fight-flight-or-freeze mode.

But urgency to find answers brought together key teacher leaders, administrators, parents, and the community to find answers. A valiant effort to understand the *why* included bringing in experts like school psychologist Marcia McEvoy and anti-bullying advocate Kevin Epling to evaluate community needs. That information led to a comprehensive plan to educate the whole child, with attention to the affective (emotional) domain and not just academic skill and content. Students grades 6–12 learned suicide-prevention strategies. A parent-initiated bullying-prevention program called See It, Hear It, Stop It (www.seeithearitstopit.org), which supports students and families across the United States. A renewed focus on empathy, kindness, resilience, and grit led to a positive change of the entire community culture. Hence, it is imperative that every school leader embraces mindfulness as the foundation for educating every student. Leaders must not let tragedy drive urgency (P. Liabenow, personal communication, January 2018).

Staying the Course of Change

As most of us know only too well, change does not come easily. For every centimeter of progress, there is the opposite reaction as entities strive to maintain the status quo. How often have we heard, "Oh, this will never work" or "Oh, not again—why can't they leave us alone and let us teach?" How many of us know teachers who admittedly have been told, "Do this" and "Do that" so many times that the teachers have lost their bearings and sometimes their passion for their work? And, with a sense of discouragement, they often become disengaged.

So, what is the role of a school principal or district administrator in our proposed change process? How do the attitudes and actions of these local education leaders impact our challenge of creating compassionate schools? And, how do leaders begin to move toward a path of mindful leadership with purpose and by example, setting a tone for educating with both an open heart and clear mind?

Transforming Schools and Lives as Transformational Change Agents

Change cannot happen without transformational change agents. Great principals are change agents and, "school leaders, principals are the lynchpin of effective implementation of any school-level reform and are critical to student success" (New Leaders, 2013, p. 2). Principals who are transformational leaders are change makers, creative problem solvers, and innovators. They rise above the fray and mediocrity and make significant, substantial, and sustaining change that matters in the lives of students. Transformational leaders create waves. The waves may start, however, with a few ripples skimming the surface of the lives of students, staff, and families in their school communities.

Showing Fearless Leadership and a Drive for Change

Transformational school leaders have the courage, confidence, and fortitude to change with the changing times in education and in our world. They understand that this is the only option in the face of leaving too many children behind. They are fearless, understanding that fearlessness is necessary because the changes we are proposing and they are embracing are not simply trending add-ons. These changes cannot happen in a vacuum. Neither will they rise to the necessary level of effectiveness if teachers implement them only in a few grade levels, in a few schools. Implementation across grades, across schools, and across districts will result in the most impactful changes in education and the greatest good for the most students.

As with other change efforts, moving the needle toward more mindful, compassionate schools will take planning, strategy, persistence, and more. Administrators can anticipate that adding more compassion and empathy to classrooms may prompt some uneasiness from the community or their staff. Communities and teachers may hesitate to insert the unknown (that is, yoga, breathing, meditation, and mindfulness) into classrooms. For some, this will be as foreign as entering a country an ocean away. However, the research is clear—yoga, breathing, meditation, and mindfulness are expedient ways to not only improve students' well-being but also to accelerate learning. School leaders might even ask themselves, "What moral and professional responsibility do we have to introduce mindfulness tools that are so promising? And, how can we become more mindful leaders?"

from the classroom

When James Dierke started as principal of Visitacion Valley Middle School in San Francisco, in 2000, it carried the label *the fight school*. His students' and staff's fragile social-emotional states were a reaction to the continuous assault they were under—forty-one murders in the community surrounding the school within three years (Myers, 2012). One-fifth of the students had one parent in the penal system (Schreiber, 2011). There were Samoan students who were navigating the change from their oral, tribal culture (one in which a group of parents go through a chief to communicate with the school) to a U.S. system of print culture.

Dierke, a courageous and mindful leader, reached out to staff and community members who would collaborate with him to minimize neighborhood violence and mitigate students' trauma. He created a leadership team that focused on building, within the school, a community where all students felt valued and as if they belonged. Dierke researched the impact of meditation on stress reduction and cognitive repair. He was granted funding to integrate transcendental meditation into the school.

Each school day began and ended with a twelve-minute meditation period. In the first year, multiday suspensions dropped 45 percent, and within a four-year period, suspensions dropped to ten. Simultaneously, academic performance increased forty points on the Academic Performance Index (www.cde.ca.gov/ta/ac/ap) the same academic year (Dierke, 2012; Jackson & McDermott, 2015; Schreiber, 2011).

Using Mindfulness as a Tool of Opportunity

To be effective in using mindfulness tools in the classroom, school leaders and teachers will need to both learn about these tools and also try them out so they gain firsthand experiences. With mindfulness experiences, educators will not only be better equipped to introduce them in classrooms, they will also benefit from stress reduction, greater energy, and greater sensitivity to themselves and others that come with practicing the practice.

Being mindful requires that all staff, teachers, counselors, school leaders, families, and communities respond to the needs of the students as they arise day by day, week by week, month by month, and year by year. Melissa Patschke, a principal for thirty years and a national principal mentor and leader, indicates that mindfulness is an ongoing process (personal communication, 2017). Mindfulness practices in year one

from the classroom

To make mindfulness truly part of the schoolwide (not just the school day) culture, principals and other administrators should consider principal Melissa Patschke's ideas for weekly faculty and staff meetings and in-service days (personal communication, 2017).

- Open faculty meetings with a mindfulness practice or yoga in the classroom activity that teachers can use in classrooms.
- Dedicate time during an in-service day to introduce faculty to the practice and science behind mindfulness.
- Share research and pilot programs that prove the positive impact on student behaviors and classroom focus. Share those messages in every faculty meeting.

will set the stage for increasing mindfulness in year two. In a sense, with mindfulness we grow in our readiness and ability to respond to needs that arise. While mindfulness provides a tool to build 21st century skills including resilience, grit, and compassion, the process takes time and some fearlessness.

Getting to the Heart of the Matter

Earlier in this chapter we posed the question, What is the role of a school principal or district administrator, and how do they impact the challenge of creating compassionate school cultures? In this next section, we explore mindful leadership behavior and why it is at the heart of the matter in propelling change within. And, from the experiences related to us by experts in mindful leadership, we explore how we can enhance and transform the role of school leaders through cultivating our own mindfulness practice.

Mindful Leadership

Janice Marturano (2015), executive director for the Institute of Mindful Leadership and author of *Finding the Space to Lead: A Practical Guide to Mindful Leadership*, recognizes that leaders can only learn to lead with excellence when they learn to cultivate their innate capabilities to focus on what is important, see more clearly what is presenting itself, foster creativity, and embody compassion. Marturano (2015) describes this feeling as bringing "our mind, body and heart a kind warmth and ease." She goes on to explain that when we reflect and take a few moments to remember how we felt when we experienced the compassionate understanding that others extend, our capability to be compassionate and understanding ignites. In other words, compassion leads us to a small moment in time of just being and connecting, rather than doing and moving. And with this sense of just being, we have opportunities to reflect and engage in important problem solving as we become more aware of the options before us.

Mindful Leadership Development

With over two decades of experience in formal mindfulness training and working with all different people in leadership roles, Michael Bunting (2016a) recognizes that leading is challenging. School leaders often feel pressure from time constraints, comprehensive evaluative schedules, state and federal mandates, standardized testing requirements, and financial woes. At the same time, the community has charged them with educating students for the future and providing a healthy school environment. With these leadership challenges, we either discover the best of leadership behavior or expose our insecurities as we react rather than act and avoid rather than embrace the leadership we must assume.

Bunting (2016b) writes in *The Mindful Leader Companion Workbook*:

> Developing as a leader is about cultivating our inner strength to stay aware and balanced under fire, to inspire others with an inspirational purpose, to appreciate others' gifts, and to courageously hold ourselves and others [sic] accountable when we want to slop into avoidance and justification. (p. xx)

Leaders who are mindful take notice and deliberately look for opportunities to openly support, encourage, appreciate, and praise others. Mindful leaders recognize the magnitude and importance of their job and its far-reaching influence on others, themselves, and the school community.

Ignite a New Leadership Mindset

Mindfulness sets the tone and culture of the school community. It is through an intentionality of mindfulness practice that we develop a heightened awareness or consciousness that ignites a new mindset or way of thinking. With mindfulness, leaders begin to consider possibilities for schools as healing communities. Just as a growth mindset (Dweck, 2006) is important to envisioning oneself as capable and not limited by factors such as IQ or background, one's mindset also plays a significant role in freeing our minds to imagine a better future.

Mindfulness is most certainly a logical and thoughtful first step toward changing our vision for schools and the way we think, educate, and transform school cultures into compassionate learning communities. However, as Bunting (2016a) notes, even with a change of mindset, mindful leadership or practicing mindfulness alone is not enough. In other words, leaders can envision a better future and seriously practice mindfulness and still be ineffective leaders, unable to move the education needle of change. Just as we recommend to teachers that they naturally infuse and fully integrate mindfulness into classrooms, school communities, and beyond, so must leaders embed mindfulness in leadership behavior, actions, and practice. And, as we suggest in the introduction to this book, your school may wish to consider book study groups that include parents. If we reach out to families as we implement mindfulness, we may find that students will be better prepared to incorporate mindfulness practices into their lives outside of school. Another way to engage parents is to begin with a few parents to get their input, and perhaps even to offer after-school yoga classes for parents and students.

Integrating mindfulness in our lives will take time. Leaders are pushed and pulled in many directions. In "The 7 Habits of Highly Mindful Leaders," Ray Williams (2016) says that from the time leaders first awake, they are "bombarded with distractions and demands." Leaders, he explains, have so much on their plates before even walking out the door and into the whirlwind of the school day that their thinking is quickly triggered into a heightened state of fight-flight-or-freeze instinct. This constant state of alertness then releases cortisol (the stress hormone) into our bloodstream (as we explain in chapter 3, page 37), wreaking havoc on our minds and bodies and resulting in "scattered attention and focus, elevated stress levels and sped-up thinking" that continue throughout our day (Williams, 2016).

As leaders, we cannot afford to make decisions with distracted minds, always reacting instead of responding, and never really focusing our attention to what is most important (Williams, 2016). Mindfulness provides us a tool for allowing our minds to be free of distraction. Mindfulness supports our intention to live life with focus, purpose, clarity, creativity, and compassion, even in times of hurriedness, challenges, and complexity (Marturano, 2015).

Choices: Stand Still or Dance

Unless we courageously take the first step, we will never get on the dance floor of real change. As we previously outlined in this book, creating compassionate communities based on the foundational practice of mindfulness stems from three streams of research: (1) pediatric neurobiology, (2) trauma and mindfulness practices in the classroom, and (3) organizational behavior. Peter M. Senge, in a 1995 interview with the Association for Supervision and Curriculum Development, states, "Most teachers feel oppressed trying to conform to all kinds of rules, goals and objectives, many of which they don't believe in. Teachers don't work together; there's very little sense of collective learning going on in most schools" (as cited in O'Neil, 1995, p. 22).

We can no longer ignore the critical importance of teacher buy-in and support. If we are to succeed at preparing students for college, career, and most importantly, life, our approach to education can no longer be one size fits all, or we risk losing creative and innovative teachers, just as we risk losing too many children, marginalizing their potential and compromising their future.

As the principal at Upper Providence Elementary School, Melissa Patschke, reminds us, school leaders and educators can start small with simple acts of mindfulness, empowering staff, and slowly weaving compassion naturally into their school community. Patschke practiced and encouraged mindfulness, using the following tools to help students and staff practice mindfulness each day (personal communication, 2017).

- Setting intentions as you walk into class
- Using chill skills to help move through issues
- Sharing three grateful moments
- Taking three mindful breaths as you wait in line
- Taking a mindful walk from class to the lunchroom
- Using mindfulness jars
- Employing mirroring activities
- Snacking mindfully
- Engaging in guided mindfulness in groups
- Smiling, being grateful, and paying attention to people

Mindful Leadership Within

Cultivating mindful leadership within entails *practicing what you believe to be important*, not just having expectations of others; setting the example of best practices by incorporating mindfulness into your day and your interactions; and supporting the regular practice of mindfulness at your school so that teachers, staff, and students can see that you are infusing mindfulness into leadership as well as classrooms at your school. Bunting (2016a) characterizes this as *leadership presence*. Bunting (2016b), who combines mindfulness with the best leadership strategies, states that "being a leader means connecting with people, uplifting, ensuring people know they matter and that their opinions matter" (p. 17). In other words, you can't just show up—you must be present and fully awake in the moment to the people and circumstances before you can be an effective and mindful leader.

Just like teachers, leaders often become so overwhelmed with the enormity of tasks, expectations, demands, and mandates that they become more concerned with checking the boxes and rushing to finish rather than quality and the importance of what is before them. Mindful leaders are able to slow down the demands, reduce complexity, and counter the overwhelming feelings attached with doing rather than being. Mindfulness practice allows leaders to function and respond in a calmer, clearer, and more open-hearted manner. Bunting (2016a) suggests these practices, among others, for mindful leaders: be here now, lead from mindful values, and nourish others with love.

Senge and colleagues' (2012) research in organizational behavior specifically addresses how we get to where we want to be and just dance. Their findings suggest that real improvement only happens if the people who are responsible for implementing change actually design the change itself. What this means is that teachers, school leaders, and other members of wider school communities (students, parents, and school committees) must learn how to build their own capacity to facilitate change within rather than look for expertise from outside of school (learning organizational) systems.

from the classroom

School principal Kate Retzel and district superintendent Al Skrocki are examples of the capacity to facilitate change within a school. Lee Elementary School in Lee, Massachusetts, became a pilot site for Heart Centered Learning as the result of a teacher-led, schoolwide effort to purposely transform the school culture (and community) into a compassionate learning community. In response to the escalating social-emotional needs of students and the ongoing, job-related, daily stressors and vicarious trauma that many teachers experience, teachers petitioned Retzel and Skrocki for help. Teachers requested support and permission from the superintendent and school committee to create a more responsive school community so that they could meet the needs of the whole child, intellectually, physically, socially, and emotionally, and prevent teacher burnout at the same time. Already trained as a trauma sensitive school, staff requested specific training that would help combat the trauma, toxic stress, and daily stressors that were impeding both learning and teaching.

Retzel is an example of a compassionate and caring school leader. She readily responded to her staff and student needs, helping to facilitate the beginnings of schoolwide change. Teachers, in turn, were not afraid to take risks and initiate new mindfulness practices within their own classrooms or schoolwide. At Lee Elementary, Michele M. Rivers Murphy provided professional development for teachers and support staff over the course of a year in the use of a tool for measuring compassionate school culture and in the neurobiology of trauma, the interconnectivity of brain, emotions, and stress, and the foundational practice of mindfulness. This was the beginning of creating a schoolwide, compassionate, and heart centered community.

At year's end, an approximate 87 percent favorable rating from school staff indicated that mindfulness and their heart centered work, building compassionate learning environments schoolwide, were effective tools supporting their initial work in the process of change (K. Retzel & A. Skrocki, personal communication, May 2018).

Facilitating a Collective Community of Shared Vision and Leadership

We all must dance together. Once school leaders deeply understand the paradigm shift that is part of a Heart Centered Learning approach—and once administrators have had firsthand experiences with the integral components of mindfulness and creating compassionate school environments—then the next step is to seek a collective community education approach. We make the greatest gains when mindfulness becomes a way of *being* not only within the school walls, but as a part of the surrounding community. According to the Institute for Educational Leadership (2017), a fresh vision of school improvement and 21st century learning requires a move toward whole-child community education and a collective effort of shared vision and leadership among school systems, families, communities, business, and government if we hope to meet the needs and goals of every student.

Understanding the Need to Lead With Courageous Action

As we indicated in chapter 1 (page 13), there is substantial societal evidence that the type of change we are recommending is greatly needed and that many efforts have already fallen short of their desired impact. Our belief is that it will take changes over years and decades to decrease the levels of violence and abuse that are pervasive today. We consider creating mindful and compassionate school communities to represent a substantial paradigm shift that will require heartfelt efforts by many educators and school leaders in local communities. The data from neuroscience, to trauma, to mindfulness, yoga, and meditation are clear. Trauma comes in many forms and can be hard to overcome, and the mindfulness strategies we are recommending are research based; they can bring about significant changes for students and schools.

With this dance, let us remember that the task we have before us is huge and significant. We are not advocating for simply adding more character education or social-emotional learning into schools to meet federal requirements or other legal obligations. An hour or two of social-emotional learning a week, or even an hour after school, is totally inadequate. It will, however, take a collective community education approach to move things forward, and through the practice of mindfulness increase our capacity to help students heal and live healthy and happy lives.

Moving Forward

Mindfulness provides a solid base for developing caring, compassionate school communities, where teachers and staff help children heal, where students' well-being is a primary concern, and where school leaders fully integrate mindfulness into leadership behavior, actions, and practice. In this book, we have focused on the first steps to developing a new school community culture in which consciousness or mindfulness and compassion—being compassionate and encouraging compassion—are central to our interactions with students and each other. (See figure 9.1.) Now that you are beginning your journey, we encourage you to take time to savor your experience and to feel the joy that comes with stress reduction and renewed insights into yourself and others. Mindfulness can open doors to a new way of being, living, and educating. However, as you continue your journey, we also invite you to consider where you will go from the foundation of consciousness or mindfulness and compassion, to consider the additional steps that lead to compassionate action.

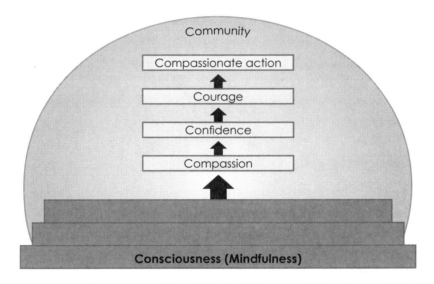

Figure 9.1: Steps to the future, taking in the view.

To reduce trauma and the impact of trauma and for people ultimately to treat each other more kindly, action is necessary. It is insufficient to stop at the levels of furthering mindfulness or consciousness and understanding compassion, as important as these steps are.

With this book you have a framework to guide you as you take the essential first steps—implementing mindfulness and building compassion. There will be more steps to take along the way. Thankfully, there are leaders who are stepping into the future and building compassionate, heart centered communities.

Inspiring Others to Move the Needle of Change

The way forward will require direct actions—walking the walk and talking the talk. As Nelson Mandela is quoted as saying, "Courage is not the absence of fear—it's inspiring others to move beyond it" (as cited in Friend, 2010). As we implement mindfulness skills, we anticipate that greater compassion will emerge. We can achieve much by acting with courage to take bold, transformational steps. Together, teachers, students, school leaders, families, and community members will build greater and more caring and compassionate school communities—communities necessary to heal generations of old wounds and create an inner core of strength.

Leaders, the steps you take are important. Plan to take mindful, conscious steps with full awareness and sensitivity of those who are with you and those who turn to you and are counting on you. For transformational healing, we need people to step to the front and others to follow. Have courage, take heart, and trust your breath and your awareness, to help educators, students, families, communities, and yourself to move beyond what has been, toward what could be and what might be, to what will be essential for our schools and for our future.

Mindful Reflection

As an individual or with your study group, respond to the mindful reflection questions, taking notes on the following page.

- What leadership activities at your school have facilitated compassion and reduced stress and trauma?
- How do you understand mindful leadership in the context of schools and change?
- How does becoming a mindful leader help build transformational change?
- What challenges have you faced, and how are you addressing them? What else could you do?

— Notes —

Epilogue

We are at what could be a magnificent time in the learning, growth, and high achievement of *all* our students. Neuroscience proves that all children are born with the propensity for engagement, motivation, high intellectual performance, self-determination, and self-transcendence (Sodian & Frith, 2008; Zelazo & Lyons, 2012). With these findings, educators can go beyond hope to real confidence in accepting these strengths as an underlying premise to guide instruction. And yet, our current reality illustrates that our schools are plagued by underperformance as we fail to adequately understand, support, and challenge our children—our most valuable resource.

If we were to truly invest in our students, we would take multiple steps to halt the unspeakable trauma and stress they experience on a daily basis. We would open neuropathways and reduce the blockages produced by fear and anxiety. We would apply practices to mitigate the barriers that impede their learning. We would strive to inspire a positive sense of self. We would move away from focusing on what is inherently wrong with a student and seeking to remediate deficits, and instead develop supportive environments with leadership that guides a growth mindset. All this could occur while strengthening focus, engagement, determination, and learning. These are mindfulness practices.

In *Mindfulness Practices*, we have sought to lay a firm foundation for a path to a future with less violence and trauma and more kindness and compassion for our students and their teachers. While there are numerous societal initiatives that we believe could slow down or reduce the overwhelming amount of trauma that children suffer, we are struck with the reality that the general U.S. population may not fully understand the scope of the challenge. However, we are encouraged by the reception that mindfulness is receiving in education. The number of schools implementing mindfulness is increasing, and a public without the will to adapt and make the many needed societal changes seems nonetheless supportive of introducing mindfulness in schools. To truly make a difference and combat the long-term harm created by layers of damage will take time.

As the neuroscientific evidence we have cited so many times throughout this book shows, trauma does indeed impact the mind, body, and spirit and it can be healed through breath and body work. An essential aspect of mindfulness in schools is ensuring that teachers are *practicing the practice* for their own benefit as they become the nurturing adults—the protective factors—mitigating childhood trauma. Imagine hundreds of thousands of teachers, school leaders, and school communities implementing mindfulness practices. As we examine the evidence supporting mindfulness practices, we have come to understand that if ever we could bottle a tonic for hope for our future, mindfulness in schools is that tonic.

We must choose whether to stay on the path we have been following or take steps in a new direction. Even in the midst of change, many people may be more comfortable leaving the trailblazing to others. Courage, confidence, and leadership are imperative to guide us toward a fundamental and needed transformation. We invite you to walk with us on a path to a future that expands horizons for youth, community, and all of humanity. This is a path to authenticity that will build on mindfulness and student strengths and interests. You hold the power to make this choice a reality!

References and Resources

Addy, S., Engelhardt, W., & Skinner, C. (2013). *Basic facts about low-income children: Children under 18 years, 2011*. New York: National Center for Children in Poverty. Accessed at www.nccp.org/publications/pdf/text_1074.pdf on July 30, 2018.

Adelman, H., & Taylor, L. (2014). Bringing new prototypes into practice: Dissemination, implementation, and facilitating transformation. *The F.M. Duffy Reports, 19*(3), 1–35.

AI Impacts. (2015, April 14). *Neuron firing rates in humans*. Accessed at https://aiimpacts.org/rate-of-neuron-firing on August 4, 2018.

Aizer, A., Stroud, L., & Buka, S. (2016). Maternal stress and child outcomes: Evidence from siblings. *Journal of Human Resources, 51*(3), 523–555.

Alexander, J. (2011, July 5). *Brain gym—simple exercises for a better mind and body* [Blog post]. Accessed at https://brutallyfrank.wordpress.com/2011/07/05/brain-gym-simple-exercises-for-a-better-mind-and-body on July 30, 2018.

American Academy of Pediatrics. (2003). Out-of-school suspension and expulsion. *Pediatrics, 112*(5), 1206–1209.

American Federation of Teachers. (2017). *2017 educator quality of work life survey*. Accessed at www.aft.org/sites/default/files/2017_eqwl_survey_web.pdf on July 30, 2018.

Aragón, K. (2017). *Immigrant aid*. Accessed at www.schoolcounselor.org/asca/media/PDFs/ImmigrantAid.pdf on February 8, 2018.

Arbeau, D. C. (2016). Take a breath: Yoga and meditation in the developmental classroom. *National Association for Developmental Education Digest, 8*(1), 35–38.

Arseneault, L., Cannon, M., Fisher, H. L., Polanczyk, G., Moffitt, T. E., & Caspi, A. (2011). Childhood trauma and children's emerging psychotic symptoms: A genetically sensitive longitudinal cohort study. *American Journal of Psychiatry, 168*(1), 65–72.

Aymer, S. R. (2016). "I can't breathe": A case study—Helping Black men cope with race-related trauma stemming from police killing and brutality. *Journal of Human Behavior in the Social Environment, 26*(3–4), 367–376.

Baddeley, A. D. (2003). Working memory and language: An overview. *Journal of Communication Disorders, 36*(3), 189–208.

Baddeley, A. D. (2012). Working memory: Theories, models, and controversies. *Annual Review of Psychology, 63*, 1–29.

Baghel, S. P., & Shamkuwar, S. S. (2017). Physiological review of qualitative impact of pranayama on respiration. *International Journal of Innovation and Research in Educational Sciences, 4*(1), 2349–5219.

Bailey, M. (2013, October 10). Newest required high school course: Yoga. *New Haven Independent*. Accessed at www.newhavenindependent.org/index.php/archives/entry/mandatory_yoga_classes_debut on July 6, 2018.

Bandura, A. (1991). Social cognitive theory of self-regulation. *Organizational Behavior and Human Decision Processes, 50*(2), 248–287.

The benefits of gratitude. (n.d.). *Psychology Today.* Accessed at www.psychologytoday.com/basics/gratitude on February 8, 2018.

Bergland, C. (2014, February 12). Chronic stress can damage brain structure and connectivity. *Psychology Today*. Accessed at www.psychologytoday.com/blog/the-athletes-way/201402/chronic-stress-can-damage-brain-structure-and-connectivity on January 31, 2018.

Bierman, K. L., Nix, R. L., Greenberg, M. T., Blair, C., & Domitrovich, C. E. (2008). Executive functions and school readiness intervention: Impact, moderation, and mediation in the Head Start REDI program. *Development and Psychopathology, 20*(3), 821–843.

Bierman, K. L., & Torres, M. (2016). Promoting the development of executive functions through early education and prevention programs. In J. A. Griffin, P. McCardle, & L. S. Freund (Eds.), *Executive function in preschool-age children: Integrating measurement, neurodevelopment, and translational research* (pp. 299–326). Washington, DC: American Psychological Association.

Blaustein, M. E., & Kinniburgh, K. M. (2010). *Treating traumatic stress in children and adolescents: How to foster resilience through attachment, self-regulation, and competency.* New York: Guilford Press.

Borchard, T. (2014). *Mind your health: Using mindfulness to heal your body.* Accessed at www.everydayhealth.com/columns/therese-borchard-sanity-break/mind-your-health-using-mindfulness-to-heal-your-body on January 31, 2018.

Bradley, M. M., & Lang, P. J. (2000). Measuring emotion: Behavior, feeling, and physiology. In R. D. Lane & L. Nadel, *Cognitive neuroscience of emotion* (pp. 242–276). New York: Oxford University Press.

Bremner, J. D., & Marmar, C. R. (2002). *Trauma, memory, and dissociation.* Washington, DC: American Psychiatric.

Bremner, J. D., Randall, P., Vermetten, E., Staib, L., Bronen, R. A., Mazure, C., et al. (1997). Magnetic resonance imaging-based measurement of hippocampal volume in posttraumatic stress disorder related to childhood physical and sexual abuse—A preliminary report. *Biological Psychiatry, 41*(1), 23–32.

Brennan, D. S. (2018, July 1). School districts affirm: Undocumented students safe on campus. *The San Diego Union-Tribune.* Accessed at www.sandiegouniontribune.com/news/immigration/sd-no-immigrant-students-20180625-story.html on July 30, 2018.

Brensilver, M. (2017). *Guidelines for secular teaching of mindfulness.* Accessed at www.mindfulschools.org/foundational-concepts/secularity on February 8, 2018.

Breslau, N., Peterson, E. L., Poisson, L. M., Schultz, L. R., & Lucia, V. C. (2004). Estimating post-traumatic stress disorder in the community: Lifetime perspective and the impact of typical traumatic events. *Psychological Medicine, 34*(5), 889–898.

Brock, A. (2015, March 5). Kundalini Yoga used to reach youth in underserved communities and juvenile detention centers. *Huffington Post.* Accessed at www.huffingtonpost.com /antoinette-brock/kundalini- yoga-used-to- reach-youth-in-underserved_b_6812934.html on July 26, 2016.

Broderick, P. C. (2013). *Learning to breathe: A mindfulness curriculum for adolescents to cultivate emotion regulation, attention, and performance.* Oakland, CA: New Harbinger.

Brookfield, S. D. (2017). *Becoming a critically reflective teacher.* Hoboken, NJ: John Wiley & Sons.

Brown, V., & Olson, K. (2015). *The mindful school leader: Practices to transform your leadership and school.* Thousand Oaks, CA: Corwin Press.

Bunting, M. (2016a). *The mindful leader: 7 practices for transforming your leadership, your organisation and your life.* Milton, Queensland, Australia: John Wiley & Sons.

Bunting, M. (2016b). *The mindful leader companion workbook: 7 practices for transforming your leadership, your organisation and your life.* Milton, Queensland, Australia: John Wiley & Sons.

Büssing, A., Michalsen, A., Khalsa, S. B. S., Telles, S., & Sherman, K. J. (2012). Effects of yoga on mental and physical health: A short summary of reviews. *Evidence-Based Complementary and Alternative Medicine.* Accessed at www.hindawi.com/journals /ecam/2012/165410 on August 5, 2018.

Butzer, B., Ebert, M., Telles, S., & Khalsa, S. B. S. (2015). School-based yoga programs in the United States: A survey. *Advances in Mind-Body Medicine, 29*(4), 18–26.

C8 Sciences. (n.d.). *How executive function impacts your classroom.* Accessed at www.c8 schools.com/executive-function on February 1, 2018.

Campbell, E. (2013, October 10). Research round-up: Mindfulness in schools. *Greater Good Magazine.* Accessed at http://greatergood.berkeley.edu/article/item/research _round_up_school_based_mindfulness_programs on February 1, 2018.

Cannon, W. B. (1914). Recent studies of bodily effects of fear, rage, and pain. *Journal of Philosophy, Psychology and Scientific Methods, 11*(6), 162–165.

Cayoun, B. A. (2014). *Mindfulness-integrated CBT for well-being and personal growth: Four steps to enhance inner calm, self-confidence and relationships.* Hoboken, NJ: Wiley.

Centeio, E. E., Whalen, L., Thomas, E., Kulik, N., & McCaughtry, N. (2017). Using yoga to reduce stress and bullying behaviors among urban youth. *Health, 9*, 409–424.

Center for Educational Improvement. (n.d.). *Considering social emotional learning.* Accessed at www.edimprovement.org/heart-centered-education on February 6, 2018.

Center on the Developing Child. (n.d.a). *Resilience.* Accessed at https://developingchild .harvard.edu/science/key-concepts/resilience on February 6, 2018.

Center on the Developing Child. (n.d.b). *Toxic stress.* Accessed at https://developingchild .harvard.edu/science/key-concepts/toxic-stress on July 2, 2018.

Center on the Developing Child. (2007). *InBrief: The science of early childhood development.* Accessed at https://developingchild.harvard.edu/resources/inbrief-the-science-of-early -childhood-development on February 1, 2018.

Center on the Developing Child. (2016). *Brain architecture.* Accessed at http://developing child.harvard.edu/science/key-concepts/brain-architecture on February 1, 2018.

Centers for Disease Control and Prevention. (2014). Youth risk behavior surveillance—United States, 2013. *Morbidity and Mortality Weekly Report, 63*(SS04), 1–168.

Centers for Disease Control and Prevention. (2016). *About the CDC-Kaiser ACE study.* Accessed at www.cdc.gov/violenceprevention/acestudy/about.html on February 1, 2018.

Chiang, L. C., Ma, W. F., Huang, J. L., Tseng, L. F., & Hsueh, K. C. (2009). Effect of relaxation-breathing training on anxiety and asthma signs/symptoms of children with moderate-to-severe asthma: A randomized controlled trial. *International Journal of Nursing Studies, 46*(8), 1061–1070.

Child First. (n.d.). *Needs.* Accessed at www.childfirst.org/about-us/needs on February 1, 2018.

Child Trends. (2016). *Children's exposure to violence: Indicators of child and youth well-being.* Accessed at www.childtrends.org/wp-content/uploads/2016/05/118_Exposure_to_Violence -1.pdf on February 1, 2018.

Children International. (n.d.). *Child poverty in the U.S.: Facts & stats about child poverty in the United States.* Accessed at www.children.org/global-poverty/global-poverty-facts/ facts-about-poverty-in-usa on July 30, 2018.

Chiu, G. R., Lutfey, K. E., Litman, H. J., Link, C. L., Hall, S. A., & McKinlay, J. B. (2013). Prevalence and overlap of childhood and adult physical, sexual, and emotional abuse: A descriptive analysis of results from the Boston Area Community Health (BACH) survey. *Violence and Victims, 28*(3), 381–402.

Chong, C. S., Tsunaka, M., Tsang, H. W., Chan, E. P., & Cheung, W. M. (2011). Effects of yoga on stress management in healthy adults: A systematic review. *Alternative Therapies in Health and Medicine, 17*(1), 32–38.

The Chopra Center. (n.d.). *Breathwork: Pranayama techniques to enhance vitality.* Accessed at https://chopra.com/online-courses/breathwork/on-demand on August 4, 2018.

Clark, C. A., Pritchard, V. E., & Woodward, L. J. (2010). Preschool executive functioning abilities predict early mathematics achievement. *Developmental Psychology, 46*(5), 1176–1191.

Clark, H. M., Galano M. M., Grogan-Kaylor, A. C., Montalvo-Liendo, N., & Graham-Bermann, S. A. (2016). Ethnoracial variation in women's exposure to intimate partner violence. *Journal of Interpersonal Violence, 31*(3), 531–552.

Cohen, S., Kamarck, T., & Mermelstein, R. (1983). A global measure of perceived stress. *Journal of Health and Social Behavior, 24*(4), 385–396.

Colchete, N., & Mason, C. (2017). *Ending DACA: Resources for principals, counselors, and teachers.* Accessed at www.edimprovement.org/2017/10/ending-daca-resources-principals -counselors-teachers on February 8, 2018.

Cole, S. F., O'Brien, J. G., Gadd, M. G., Ristuccia, J., Wallace, D. L., & Gregory, M. (2005). *Helping traumatized children learn: Supportive school environments for children traumatized by family violence—A report and policy agenda.* Boston Massachusetts Advocates for Children. Accessed at https://traumasensitiveschools.org/wp-content /uploads/2013/06/Helping-Traumatized-Children-Learn.pdf on September 27, 2018.

Colino, S. (2017, May 24). Fearing the future: Pre-traumatic stress reactions. *U.S. News & World Report.* Accessed at https://health.usnews.com/wellness/mind/articles/2017-05-24 /fearing-the-future-pre-traumatic-stress-reactions on July 2, 2018.

Condon, J. R., & Cane, P. M. (2011). *Capacitar: Healing trauma, empowering wellness: A multicultural population education approach to transforming trauma.* Santa Cruz, CA: Capacitar International.

Copeland, W. E., Keeler, G., Angold, A., & Costello, E. J. (2007). Traumatic events and posttraumatic stress in childhood. Archives of General Psychiatry, 64(5), 577–584.

Cortiella, C., & Horowitz, S. H. (2014). *The state of learning disabilities: Facts, trends and emerging issues* (3rd ed.). New York: National Center for Learning Disabilities. Accessed at www.ncld.org/wp-content/uploads/2014/11/2014-State-of-LD.pdf on February 1, 2018.

Cosmic Kids. (2013, March 6). *Five fun breathing exercises for kids.* Accessed at www .cosmickids.com/read/five-fun-breathing-practices-for-kids on February 8, 2018.

Costello, E. J., Erkanli, A., Fairbank, J. A., & Angold, A. (2002). The prevalence of potentially traumatic events in childhood and adolescence. *Journal of Traumatic Stress,* *15*(2), 99–112.

Crenshaw, D. (2006). Neuroscience and trauma treatment: Implications for creative arts therapists. In L. Carey (Ed.), *Expressive and creative arts methods for trauma survivors* (pp. 21–38). Philadelphia: Jessica Kingsley.

Davidson, R. J., & Begley, S. (2012). *The emotional life of your brain: How its unique patterns affect the way you think, feel, and live—and how you can change them.* London: Penguin.

Davidson, R. J., Kabat-Zinn, J., Schumacher, J., Rosenkranz, M., Muller, D., Santorelli, S. F., et al. (2003). Alterations in brain and immune function produced by mindfulness meditation. *Psychosomatic Medicine, 65*(4), 564–570.

Dawson, P., & Guare, R. (2010). *Executive skills in children and adolescents: A practical guide to assessment and intervention* (2nd ed.). New York: Guilford Press.

Diamond, A. (2015). *Factors that aid and factors that hinder the development of executive functions* [Presentation]. Accessed at www.neuroplasticityandeducation.com/wp-content/ uploads/2015/10/adele-diamond.pdf on August 20, 2018.

Diamond, A., & Lee, K. (2011). Interventions shown to aid executive function development in children 4 to 12 years old. *Science, 333*(6045), 959–964.

Dierke, J. E. (2012). A quiet transformation. *Leadership,* 14–17.

Dubow, E. F., Huesmann, L. R., Boxer, P., & Smith, C. (2016). Childhood and adolescent risk and protective factors for violence in adulthood. *Journal of Criminal Justice, 45,* 26–31.

Dweck, C. S. (2000). *Self-theories: Their role in motivation, personality, and development.* Philadelphia: Psychology Press.

Dweck, C. S. (2006). *Mindset: The new psychology of success.* New York: Ballantine Books.

Edutopia. (2012, February 22). *Infographic: Meditation in schools across America.* Accessed at www.edutopia.org/stw-student-stress-meditation-schools-infographic on February 1, 2018.

Ehleringer, J. (2010). Yoga for children on the autism spectrum. *International Journal of Yoga Therapy, 20*(1), 131–139.

Eres, F., & Atanasoska, T. (2011, June). Occupational stress of teachers: A comparative study between Turkey and Macedonia. *International Journal of Humanities and Social Science, 1*(7), 59–65. Accessed at https://pdfs.semanticscholar.org/1bb3/e18d9abd6136 d647fbc84bf95ec4ef3e2e91.pdf on May 29, 2018.

Esch, P., Bocquet, V., Pull, C., Couffignal, S., Lehnert, T., Graas, M., et al. (2014). The downward spiral of mental disorders and educational attainment: A systematic review on early school leaving. *BMC Psychiatry, 14*(237).

Esposito, L. (2017, November 21). The space between mindfulness and self-confidence. *Psychology Today.* Accessed at www.psychologytoday.com/us/blog/anxiety-zen/201711 /the-space-between-mindfulness-and-self-confidence on August 4, 2018.

Evans, G. W., & Kim, P. (2013). Childhood poverty, chronic stress, self-regulation, and coping. *Child Development Perspectives, 7*(1), 43–48. Accessed at https://onlinelibrary .wiley.com/doi/abs/10.1111/cdep.12013 on July 2, 2018.

Every Student Succeeds Act of 2015, Pub. L. No. 114-95, 20 U.S.C. § 1177 (2015).

Farrell, L. J., & Barrett, P. M. (2007). Prevention of childhood emotional disorders: Reducing the burden of suffering associated with anxiety and depression. *Child and Adolescent Mental Health, 12*(2), 58–65.

Feeding America. (2017, September). *Child hunger fact sheet.* Accessed at www.feeding america.org/assets/pdfs/fact-sheets/child-hunger-fact-sheet.pdf on July 30, 2018.

Felitti, V. J., Anda, R. F., Nordenberg, D., Williamson, D. F., Spitz, A. M., Edwards, V., et al. (1998). Relationship of childhood abuse and household dysfunction to many of the leading causes of death in adults: The Adverse Childhood Experiences (ACES) Study. *American Journal of Preventive Medicine, 14*(4), 245–258.

Felver, J. C., Butzer, B., Olson, K. J., Smith, I. M., & Khalsa, S. B. S. (2015). Yoga in public school improves adolescent mood and affect. *Contemporary School Psychology, 19*(3), 184–192.

Felver, J. C., Jones, R., Killam, M. A., Kryger, C., Race, K., & McIntyre, L. L. (2016). Contemplative intervention reduces physical interventions for children in residential psychiatric treatment. *Prevention Science, 18*(2), 164–173.

Fernando, R. (2013). *Measuring the efficacy and sustainability of a mindfulness-based in-class intervention* [PowerPoint]. Accessed at www.mindfulschools.org/pdf/Mindful-Schools-Study -Highlights.pdf on February 8, 2018.

Feuerstein, R. (2006). *Feuerstein Instrumental Enrichment Program (IE-1).* Jerusalem: ICELP Publications.

Finkelhor, D., Shattuck, A., Turner, H. A., & Hamby, S. L. (2014). The lifetime prevalence of child sexual abuse and sexual assault assessed in late adolescence. *Journal of Adolescent Health, 55*(3), 329–333.

Finkelhor, D., Turner, H., Shattuck, A., & Hamby, S. L. (2015). Prevalence of childhood exposure to violence, crime, and abuse: Results from the National Survey of Children's Exposure to Violence. *Journal of the American Medical Association Pediatrics*, *169*(8), 746–754. Accessed at www.ncbi.nlm.nih.gov/pubmed/26121291 on July 2, 2018.

Fischer, M. (2017). *Mindfulness practice with children who have experienced trauma* (Master of Social Work Clinical Research Papers #736). Accessed at http://sophia.stkate.edu/msw_papers/736 on February 1, 2018.

Flanagan, L. (2015). *How schools can help nurture students' mental health*. Accessed at www.kqed.org/mindshift/40583/how-schools-can-help-nurture-students-mental-health on May 27, 2018.

Flook, L., Goldberg, S. B., Pinger, L., & Davidson, R. J. (2015). Promoting prosocial behavior and regulatory skills in preschool children through a mindfulness-based kindness curriculum. *Developmental Psychology*, *55*(1), 44–51.

Flook, L., Smalley, S. L., Kitil, M. J., Galla, B. M., Kaiser-Greenland, S., Locke, J., et al. (2010). Effects of mindful awareness practices on executive functions in elementary school children. *Journal of Applied School Psychology*, *26*(1), 70–95.

Fonagy, P., & Target, M. (1995). Dissociation and trauma. *Current Opinion in Psychiatry*, *8*(3), 161–166.

Ford, J. D., & Courtois, C. A. (2009). Defining and understanding complex trauma and complex traumatic stress disorders. In C. A. Courtois & J. D. Ford (Eds.), *Treating complex traumatic stress disorders: An evidence-based guide* (pp. 13–30). New York: Guilford Press.

Forman, M. (2015). A trauma-sensitive approach to meditation: Part I. *Certified Integral Therapist*. Accessed at https://citintegral.com/2015/10/02/a-trauma-sensitive-approach-to-meditation-part-I on July 2, 2018.

Frank, J. L., Jennings, P. A., & Greenberg, M. T. (2013). Mindfulness-based interventions in school settings: An introduction to the special issue. *Research in Human Development*, *10*(3), 205–210.

Frank, J. L., Kohler, K., Peal, A., & Bose, B. (2017). Effectiveness of a school-based yoga program on adolescent mental health and school performance: Findings from a randomized controlled trial. *Mindfulness*, *8*(3), 544–553.

Franzblau, S. H., Smith, M., Echevarria, S., & Van Cantfort, T. E. (2006). Take a breath, break the silence: The effects of yogic breathing and testimony about battering on feelings of self-efficacy in battered women. *International Journal of Yoga Therapy*, *16*(1), 49–57.

Friend, J. (2010, February 27). *Mandela's 8 rules of leadership* [Blog post]. Accessed at www.smallstepsbigchanges.com/nelson-mandelas-8-rules-of-leadership on July 30, 2018.

Froh, J. J., Sefick, W. J., & Emmons, R. A. (2008). Counting blessings in early adolescents: An experimental study of gratitude and subjective well-being. *Journal of School Psychology*, *46*, 213–233.

Funk, R. R., McDermeit, M., Godley, S. H., & Adams, L. (2003). Maltreatment issues by level of adolescent substance abuse treatment: The extent of the problem at intake and relationship to early outcomes. *Child Maltreatment*, *8*(1), 36–45.

Gaines, J. (2016). *This school replaced detention with meditation: The results are stunning*. Accessed at www.upworthy.com/this-school-replaced-detention-with-meditation-the-results-are-stunning on August 5, 2018.

Gatens, B. (2015, May 14). *Five requirements for building trust in the classroom* [Blog post]. Accessed at https://education.cu-portland.edu/blog/curriculum-teaching-strategies /building-trust-classroom on July 31, 2018.

Gibson, B. S., Kronenberger, W. G., Gondoli, D. M., Johnson, A. C., Morrissey, R. A., & Steeger, C. M. (2012). Component analysis of simple span vs. complex span adaptive working memory exercises: A randomized controlled trial. *Journal of Applied Research in Memory and Cognition, 1*(3), 179–184.

Gilbert, P. (2009). Introducing compassion-focused therapy. *Advances in Psychiatric Treatment, 15*(3), 199–208.

Gilbert, P. (2010). *Compassionate focused therapy: Distinctive features (CBT distinctive features).* Abingdon, England: Routledge.

Goldman-Rakic, P. S. (1995). Cellular basis of working memory. *Neuron, 14*(3), 477–485.

Goleman, D., & Davidson, R. J. (2017). *Altered traits: Science reveals how meditation changes your mind, brain, and body.* London: Penguin.

Gone, J. P. (2009). Encountering professional psychology: Re-envisioning mental health services for Native North America. In L. J. Kirmayer & G. G. Valaskakis (Eds.), *Healing traditions: The mental health of Aboriginal peoples in Canada* (pp. 419–439). Vancouver, British Columbia, Canada: UBC Press.

Graham-Bermann, S. A. & Seng, J. (2005). Violence exposure and traumatic stress symptoms as additional predictors of health problems in high-risk children. *Journal of Pediatrics, 146*(3), 349–354.

Greenberg, M. T., Brown, J. L., & Abenavoli, R. M. (2016). *Teacher stress and health: Effects on teachers, students, and schools.* University Park, PA: Edna Bennett Pierce Prevention Research Center.

Hackman, D. A., Gallop, R., Evans, G. W., & Farah, M. J. (2015). Socioeconomic status and executive function: Developmental trajectories and mediation. *Developmental Science, 18*(5), 686–702.

Hagins, M., & Rundle, A. (2016). Yoga improves academic performance in urban high school students compared to physical education: a randomized controlled trial. *Mind, Brain, and Education, 10*(2), 105–116.

Hall, K. (n.d.). *Self-soothing: Calming the amygdala and reducing the effects of trauma* [Blog post]. Accessed at http://blogs.psychcentral.com/emotionally-calming-the-amgydala on February 1, 2018.

Hargreaves, A. (2000). Mixed emotions: Teachers' perceptions of their interactions with students. *Teaching and Teacher Education, 16*(8), 811–826.

Hattie, J. (2012). *Visible learning for teachers: Maximizing impact on learning.* Abingdon, England: Routledge.

The Hawn Foundation. (2011). *The MindUP curriculum: Grades 3–5.* New York: Scholastic Teaching Resources.

Hawn, G. (2011). *10 mindful minutes: Giving our children—and ourselves—the social and emotional skills to reduce stress and anxiety for healthier, happier lives.* New York: Perigee Books.

healing. (2018). In *Oxford English Dictionary.* Accessed at https://en.oxforddictionaries.com /definition/healing on June 15, 2018.

HealthMeasures. (2018). *NIH toolbox*. Accessed at www.nihtoolbox.org/Pages/default.aspx on June 29, 2018.

Heineberg, B. L. (2013, March 5). Training kids for kindness. *Greater Good Magazine*. Accessed at http://greatergood.berkeley.edu/article/item/training_kids_for_kindness on February 1, 2018.

Herculano-Houzel, S. (2009). The human brain in numbers: A linearly scaled-up primate brain. *Frontiers in Human Neuroscience, 3*(31), 1–11. Accessed at www.ncbi.nlm.nih.gov/pmc/articles/PMC2776484 on July 30, 2018.

Hölzel, B. K., Lazar, S. W., Gard, T., Schuman-Olivier, Z., Vago, D. R., & Ott, U. (2011). How does mindfulness meditation work? Proposing mechanisms of action from a conceptual and neural perspective. *Perspectives on Psychological Science, 6*(6), 537–559.

Howard, S., Dryden, J., & Johnson, B. (1999). Childhood resilience: Review and critique of literature. *Oxford Review of Education, 25*(3), 307–323.

Hull, A. M. (2002). Neuroimaging findings in post-traumatic stress disorder: Systematic review. *British Journal of Psychiatry, 181*(2), 102–110.

Hutcherson, C. A., Seppala, E. M., & Gross, J. J. (2008). Loving-kindness meditation increases social connectedness. *Emotion, 8*(5), 720–724.

Ingersoll, R. M. (2001). Teacher turnover and teacher shortages: An organizational analysis. *American Educational Research Journal, 38*(3), 499–534.

Ingersoll, R. M., Merrill, L., & Stuckey, D. (2014). *Seven trends: The transformation of the teaching force* (CPRE Report #RR-80). Philadelphia: Consortium for Policy Research in Education.

Ingersoll, R. M., & Strong, M. (2011). The impact of induction and mentoring programs for beginning teachers: A critical review of the research. *Review of Educational Research, 81*(2), 201–233.

Institute for Educational Leadership. (2017). *Community schools: A whole-child framework for school improvement.* Washington, DC: Author. Accessed at www.communityschools.org/assets/1/AssetManager/Community-Schools-A-Whole-Child-Approach-to-School-Improvement.pdf on August 4, 2018.

Jackson, Y. (2011). *The pedagogy of confidence: Inspiring high intellectual performance in urban schools.* New York: Teachers College Press.

Jackson, Y., & McDermott, V. (2015). *Unlocking student potential: How do I identify and activate student strengths?* Alexandria, VA: Association for Supervision and Curriculum Development.

Jardine, D. W., Clifford, P., & Friesen, S. (2017). *Back to the basics of teaching and learning: Thinking the world together.* Abingdon, England: Routledge.

Javnbakht, M., Kenari, R. H., & Ghasemi, M. (2009). Effects of yoga on depression and anxiety of women. *Complementary Therapies in Clinical Practice, 15*(2), 102–104.

Jennings, P. A., & Greenberg, M. T. (2009). The prosocial classroom: Teacher social and emotional competence in relation to student and classroom outcomes. *Review of Educational Research, 79*(1), 491–525.

Jensen, E. (2009). *Teaching with poverty in mind: What being poor does to kids' brains and what schools can do about it.* Alexandria, VA: Association for Supervision and Curriculum Development.

Jensen, E. (2016). *Poor students, rich teaching: Mindsets for change.* Bloomington, IN: Solution Tree Press.

Jerath, R., Edry, J. W., Barnes, V. A., & Jerath, V. (2006). Physiology of long pranayamic breathing: Neural respiratory elements may provide a mechanism that explains how slow deep breathing shifts the autonomic nervous system. *Medical Hypotheses, 67*(3), 566–571.

Jiang, Y., Granja, M. R., & Koball, H. (2017). *Basic facts about low-income children: Children under 18 years, 2015.* New York: National Center for Children in Poverty. Accessed at www.nccp.org/publications/pub_1170.html on January 31, 2018.

JoBea Kids. (2016, October 13). *Rollercoaster breathing with JoBea Kids* [Video file]. Accessed at www.youtube.com/watch?v=YzQod8vCtEE on February 6, 2018.

Jones, D. E., Greenberg, M., & Crowley, M. (2015). Early social-emotional functioning and public health: The relationship between kindergarten social competence and future wellness. *American Journal of Public Health, 105*(11), 2283–2290.

Junttila, H. (n.d.). *7 obstacles to mindfulness and how to overcome them* [Blog post]. Accessed at http://tinybuddha.com/blog/7-obstacles-to-mindfulness-and-how-to-overcome-them on January 31, 2018.

Kabat-Zinn, J. (1994). *Wherever you go, there you are: Mindfulness meditation in everyday life.* New York: Hyperion.

Kabat-Zinn, J. (2003). Mindfulness-based interventions in context: Past, present, and future. *Clinical Psychology: Science and Practice, 10*(2), 144–156.

Kabat-Zinn, J., & Hanh, T. N. (2013). *Full catastrophe living: Using the wisdom of your body and mind to face stress, pain, and illness* (Rev. ed.). New York: Bantam.

Kamrani, K. (2017, August 13). *From mindful to heart-full: Mindfully cultivating heart-centered awareness.* Accessed at www.seedsoftheheart.com/mindful-heart-full-mindfully-cultivating -heart-consciousness on February 1, 2018.

Kang, D.-H., Jo, H. J., Jung, W. H., Kim, S. H., Jung, Y.-H., Choi, C.-H., et al. (2013). The effect of meditation on brain structure: Cortical thickness mapping and diffusion tensor imaging. *Social Cognitive and Affective Neuroscience, 8*(1), 27–33.

Kataoka, S., Langley, A., Wong, M., Baweja, S., & Stein, B. (2012). Responding to students with PTSD in schools. *Child and Adolescent Psychiatric Clinics of North America, 21*(1), 119–133.

Kauts, A., & Sharma, N. (2009). Effect of yoga on academic performance in relation to stress. *International Journal of Yoga, 2*(1), 39–43.

Kemeny, M. E. (2003). The psychobiology of stress. *Current Directions in Psychological Science, 12*(4), 124–129.

Kena, G., Musu-Gillette, L., Robinson, J., Wang, X., Rathbun, A., Zhang, J., et al. (2015). *The condition of education 2015* (NCES 2015–144). Washington, DC: National Center for Education Statistics. Accessed at http://nces.ed.gov/pubsearch on January 31, 2018.

Khalsa, S. B. S., & Gould, J. (2012). *Your brain on yoga.* Rosetta Books.

Khalsa, G. D. S., & O'Keeffe, D. (2002). *The kundalini yoga experience: Bringing body, mind, and spirit together.* New York: Simon & Schuster.

Kim, H., Drake, B., & Jonson-Reid, M. (2018). An examination of class-based visibility bias in national child maltreatment reporting. *Children and Youth Services Review, 85,* 165–173.

Kirp, D. L. (2014, January 12). Meditation transforms roughest San Francisco schools. *SFGate.* Accessed at www.sfgate.com/opinion/openforum/article/Meditation-transforms -roughest-San-Francisco-5136942.php on September 27, 2018.

Klassen, R. M., Bong, M., Usher, E. L., Chong, W. H., Huan, V. S., Wong, I. Y., et al. (2009). Exploring the validity of a teachers' self-efficacy scale in five countries. *Contemporary Educational Psychology, 34*(1), 67–76.

Knight, C. (2007). A resilience framework: Perspectives for educators. *Health Education, 107*(6), 543–555.

Kohler-Evans, P., & Barnes, C. D. (2015). *Civility, compassion, and courage in schools today: Strategies for implementing in K–12 classrooms.* Lanham, MD: Rowman & Littlefield.

Koob, G. F. (2015). The darkness within: Individual differences in stress. *Cerebrum, 4.* Accessed at www.ncbi.nlm.nih.gov/pmc/articles/PMC4445593 on August 5, 2018.

Kotter, J. P. (2007). Leading change: Why transformation efforts fail. *Harvard Business Review, 73*(2), 59–67.

Kotter, J. P. (2012). *The 8-step process for leading change.* Accessed at www.kotterinternational .com/ourprinciples/changesteps on February 1, 2018.

Krashen, S. (2014). The Common Core: A disaster for libraries, a disaster for language arts, a disaster for American education. *Knowledge Quest, 42*(3), 37–45.

The Kresge Foundation. (2016). *Early childhood development: From building blocks to action.* Accessed at https://kresge.org/library/early-childhood-development-building-blocks-action on August 5, 2018.

Kugler, S. (2013, December 18). *Oakland residents suffering from PTSD due to urban violence.* Accessed at www.msnbc.com/melissa-harris-perry/oaklands-urban-violence-causing-ptsd on January 31, 2018.

Kumar, R. (2014). Care and cure: Power of yoga. *International Journal of Science and Research, 3*(2), 176–178.

Lazar, S. W., Kerr, C. E., Wasserman, R. H., Gray, J. R., Greve, D. N., Treadway, M. T., et al. (2005). Meditation experience is associated with increased cortical thickness. *NeuroReport, 16*(17), 1893–1897.

Lebron, D., Morrison, L., Ferris, D., Alcantara, A., Cummings, D., Parker, G., et al. (2015). *Facts matter! Black lives matter! The trauma of racism.* New York: McSilver Institute for Poverty Policy and Research.

Lee, R. D., & Chen, J. (2017). Adverse childhood experiences, mental health, and excessive alcohol use: Examination of race/ethnicity and sex differences. *Child Abuse & Neglect, 69,* 40–48.

Levine, P. A. (2008). *Healing trauma: A pioneering program for restoring the wisdom of your body.* Louisville, CO: Sounds True.

Long, R. (Producer/Director), & Mallimson, G. (Producer). (2013). Room to breathe [Motion picture]. United States: ZAP Zoetrope Aubry Productions.

Longobardi, C., Prino, L. E., Marengo, D., & Settanni, M. (2016). Student-teacher relationships as a protective factor for school adjustment during the transition from middle to high school. *Frontiers in Psychology, 7*, 1988.

Lu, S. (2015). *Mindfulness holds promise for treating depression.* Accessed at www.apa.org/monitor/2015/03/cover-mindfulness.aspx on August 5, 2018.

Lutz, A., Brefczynski-Lewis, J., Johnstone, T., & Davidson, R. J. (2008). Regulation of the neural circuitry of emotion by compassion meditation: Effects of meditative expertise. *PloS ONE, 3*(3), e1897.

Machado, A. (2014, January 27). Should schools teach kids to meditate? *The Atlantic.* Accessed at www.theatlantic.com/education/archive/2014/01/should-schools-teach-kids-to-meditate/283229 on January 31, 2018.

Malboeuf-Hurtubise, C., Lacourse, E., Taylor, G., Joussemet, M., & Ben Amor, L. (2017). A mindfulness-based intervention pilot feasibility study for elementary school students with severe learning difficulties: Effects on internalized and externalized symptoms from an emotional regulation perspective. *Journal of Evidence-Based Complementary and Alternative Medicine, 22*(3), 473–481.

Manjunath, N. K., & Telles, S. (2001). Improved performance in the Tower of London test following yoga. *Indian Journal of Physiology and Pharmacology, 45*(3), 351–354.

Maridesich, J. (2008). Yoga in schools. *Yoga Journal.* Accessed at www.yogajournal.com/forteachers/2008 on January 31, 2018.

Marturano, J. (2011). *The definition of a leader.* Accessed at www.mindful.org/the-definition-of-a-leader on September 26, 2018.

Marturano, J. (2015). *Finding the space to lead: A practical guide to mindful leadership.* London: Bloomsbury Press.

Mason, C., & Banks, K. L. (2014). *Heart Beaming: Positive, stress relieving exercises for use in the classroom.* Vienna, VA: Center for Educational Improvement.

McCall, M. C. (2013). How might yoga work? An overview of potential underlying mechanisms. *Journal of Yoga & Physical Therapy, 3*(1), 1–6.

McCraty, R. (2015). *Science of the heart: Exploring the role of the heart in human performance* (Vol. 2). Boulder Creek, CA: HeartMath.

McCraty, R., & Tomasino, D. (2006). Emotional stress, positive emotions, and psychophysiological coherence. In B. B. Arnetz & R. Ekman (Eds.), *Stress in health and disease* (pp. 342–365). Weinheim, Germany: Wiley–VCH.

McDaniel, D. D., Logan, J. E., & Schneiderman, J. U. (2014). Supporting gang violence prevention efforts: A public health approach for nurses. *Online Journal of Issues in Nursing, 19*(1), 3.

Melby-Lervåg, M., & Hulme, C. (2013). Is working memory training effective? A meta-analytic review. *Developmental Psychology, 49*, 270–291.

Mersky, J. P., & Janczewski, C. E. (2018). Racial and ethnic differences in the prevalence of adverse childhood experiences: Findings from a low-income sample of U.S. women. *Child Abuse and Neglect, 76*, 480–487.

MetLife. (2013). *The MetLife Survey of the American Teacher: Challenges for school leadership.* Accessed at www.metlife.com/assets/cao/foundation/MetLife-Teacher-Survey-2012.pdf on February 6, 2018.

Milam, A. J., Furr-Holden, C. D. M., & Leaf, P. J. (2010). Perceived school and neighborhood safety, neighborhood violence and academic achievement in urban school children. *Urban Review, 42*(5), 458–467. Accessed at https://link.springer.com/article/10.1007/s11256-010 -0165-7 on July 2, 2018.

Mindful Life Project. (n.d.a). *Mindful Life Project 2015–2016 end of year report.* Accessed at www.mindfullifeproject.org/annualreport.html on September 7, 2018.

Mindful Life Project. (n.d.b). *Try a Mindful Sit below!* Accessed at www.mindfullifeproject .org/mindful-sits.html on August 3, 2018.

Mindfulness for Children. (n.d.). *How to explain mindfulness to young children.* Accessed at http://mindfulnessforchildren.org/for-parents/how-to-explain-mindfulness-to-young -children on February 8, 2018.

Mitchell, K. S., Dick, A. M., DiMartino, D. M., Smith, B. N., Niles, B., Koenen, K. C., et al. (2014). A pilot study of a randomized controlled trial of yoga as an intervention for PTSD symptoms in women. *Journal of Traumatic Stress, 27*(2), 121–128.

Moffitt, T. E., Arseneault, L., Belsky, D., Dickson, N., Hancox, R. J., Harrington, H., et al. (2011). A gradient of childhood self-control predicts health, wealth, and public safety. *Proceedings of the National Academy of Sciences, 108*(7), 2693–2698.

Moore, K. A., & Ramirez, A. N. (2016). Adverse childhood experience and adolescent well-being: Do protective factors matter? *Child Indicators Research, 9*(2), 299–316.

Morin, A. (n.d.). *8 working memory boosters.* Accessed at www.understood.org/en/school -learning/learning-at-home/homework-study-skills/8-working-memory-boosters on January 31, 2018.

Move with Me Yoga Adventures. (2014, November 8). *4 breathing exercises for kids* [Video title.]. Accessed at http://bit.ly/2BMnzrk on September 20, 2018.

Myers, A. (2012, June 11). Golf helping rough neighborhood near San Francisco's Olympic Club. *Golf Digest.* Accessed at www.golfdigest.com/story/golf-helping-rough-neighborhood -near-san-franciscos-olympic on July 30, 2018.

National Center for Education Statistics. (2016). Table 203.50: Enrollment and percentage distribution of enrollment in public elementary and secondary schools, by race/ethnicity and region: Selected years, fall 1995 through fall 2025 [Table]. *Digest of Education Statistics.* Accessed at https://nces.ed.gov/programs/digest/d15/tables/dt15_203.50.asp on February 6, 2018.

National Center for Education Statistics. (2017a). *Fast facts: Back to school statistics.* Accessed at https://nces.ed.gov/fastfacts/display.asp?id=372 on January 31, 2018.

National Center for Education Statistics. (2017b). *Status and trends in the education of racial and ethnic groups: Indicator 6—Elementary and secondary enrollment.* Accessed at https://nces.ed.gov/programs/coe/indicator_cge.asp on January 31, 2018.

National Child Traumatic Stress Network. (2014). Conversations about historical trauma: Part three. *Spotlight on Culture.* Accessed at www.nctsnet.org/sites/default/files/assets/pdfs /historical_trauma_pt_3.pdf on February 1, 2018.

National Public Radio, Robert Wood Johnson Foundation, & Harvard School of Public Health. (2014). *The burden of stress in America*. Accessed at http://media.npr.org /documents/2014/july/npr_rwjf_harvard_stress_poll.pdf on January 31, 2018.

National Scientific Council on the Developing Child. (2014). *Excessive stress disrupts the architecture of the developing brain* (Working Paper No. 3). Cambridge, MA: Harvard University, Center on the Developing Child. Accessed at https://developingchild .harvard.edu/wp-content/uploads/2005/05/Stress_Disrupts_Architecture_Developing _Brain-1.pdf on July 2, 2018.

New Leaders. (2013). *Change agents: How states can develop effective school leaders—Concept paper*. Accessed at http://newleaders.org/wp-content/uploads/2016/09/Change-Agents -Concept-Paper.pdf on January 31, 2018.

Niedenthal, P. M., & Ric, F. (2017). *Psychology of emotion: Interpersonal, experiential, and cognitive approaches (2nd ed.)*. Abingdon, England: Routledge.

Noddings, N. (1998). Thoughts on John Dewey's "Ethical Principles Underlying Education." *Elementary School Journal, 98*(5), 479–488.

Noddings, N. (2003). *Happiness and education*. New York: Cambridge University Press.

O'Neil, J. (1995). On schools as learning organizations: A conversation with Peter Senge. *Educational Leadership, 52*(7), 20–23. Accessed at www.ascd.org/publications/educational -leadership/apr95/vol52/num07/On-Schools-as-Learning-Organizations@-A -Conversation-with-Peter-Senge.aspx on January 31, 2018.

Ortiz, R., & Sibinga, E. M. (2017). The role of mindfulness in reducing the adverse effects of childhood stress and trauma. *Children, 4*(3).

Partnership for 21st Century Learning. (2007). *Framework for 21st century learning*. Accessed at www.ncpublicschools.org/docs/profdev/resources/skills/framework.pdf on August 4, 2018.

Perry, B. D. (2001). The neuroarcheology of childhood maltreatment: The neurodevelopmental costs of adverse childhood events. In K. Franey, R. Geffner, & R. Falconer (Eds.), *The cost of child maltreatment: Who pays? We all do* (pp. 15–37). San Diego: Family Violence & Sexual Assault Institute.

Pillars, W. (2014, May 20). Six signs of—and solutions for—teacher burnout. *Education Week Teacher*. Accessed at www.edweek.org/tm/articles/2014/05/20/ctq-pillars-signs-of -solutions-for-burnout.html?print=1 on January 31, 2018.

Pink, D. H. (2005). *A whole new mind: Why right-brainers will rule the future*. New York: Riverhead Books.

Piquero, A. R., Jennings, W. G., Farrington, D. P., Diamond, B., & Gonzalez, J. M. R. (2016). A meta-analysis update on the effectiveness of early self-control improvement programs to improve self-control and reduce delinquency. *Journal of Experimental Criminology, 12*(2), 249–264.

Pithers, R., and Soden, R. (1998). Scottish and Australian teacher stress and strain: A comparative study. *British Journal of Educational Psychology, 68*, 269–279.

Poon, A., & Danoff-Burg, S. (2011). Mindfulness as a moderator in expressive writing. *Journal of Clinical Psychology, 67*(9), 881–895.

Raes, F., Griffith, J. W., Van der Gucht, K., & Williams, J. M. G. (2014). School-based prevention and reduction of depression in adolescents: A cluster-randomized controlled trial of a mindfulness group program. *Mindfulness, 5*(5), 477–486.

Raes, F., Pommier, E., Neff, K. D., & Van Gucht, D. (2011). Construction and factorial validation of a short form of the self-compassion scale. *Clinical Psychology and Psychotherapy, 18*(3), 250–255.

Rahman, M. M., Callaghan, C. K., Kerskens, C. M., Chattarji, S., & O'Mara, S. M. (2016). Early hippocampal volume loss as a marker of eventual memory deficits caused by repeated stress. *Scientific Reports, 6*(29127).

Rama, S. (n.d.). *The real meaning of meditation* [Blog post]. Accessed at https://yoga international.com/article/view/the-real-meaning-of-meditation on May 31, 2018.

Ravitch, D. (2016). *The death and life of the great American school system: How testing and choice are undermining education (Rev. ed.)*. New York: Basic Books.

Read, J., van Os, J., Morrison, A. P., & Ross, C. A. (2005). Childhood trauma, psychosis and schizophrenia: A literature review with theoretical and clinical implications. *Acta Psychiatrica Scandinavica, 112*(5), 330–350.

Reardon, S. F. (2011). The widening academic achievement gap between the rich and the poor: New evidence and possible explanations. In G. J. Duncan & R. J. Murnane (Eds.), *Whither opportunity? Rising inequality, schools, and children's life chances.* (pp. 91–116). New York: Russell Sage Foundation.

Rempel, K. D. (2012). Mindfulness for children and youth: A review of the literature with an argument for school-based implementation. *Canadian Journal of Counselling and Psychotherapy, 46*(3), 201–220.

Ritchhart, R., & Perkins, D. N. (2000). Life in the mindful classroom: Nurturing the disposition of mindfulness. *Journal of Social Issues, 56*(1), 27–47.

Roberts, M. (2017, May 10). Baby brain scans reveal trillions of neural connections. *BBC News Online.* Accessed at www.bbc.com/news/health-39854654 on May 31, 2017.

Roeser, R. W., Schonert-Reichl, K. A., Jha, A., Cullen, M., Wallace, L., Wilensky, R., et al. (2013). Mindfulness training and reductions in teacher stress and burnout: Results from two randomized, waitlist-control field trials. *Journal of Educational Psychology, 105*(3), 787–804.

Rowe, R. A. (2015, November 5). Protecting America's black community. *The Baltimore Sun.* Accessed at www.baltimoresun.com/news/opinion/oped/bs-ed-black-victims-2015 1105-story.html on January 31, 2018.

Ruth. (2017, June 9). *Using mindfulness to make heart centered choices* [Blog post]. Accessed at http://feedingtheheart.com/using-mindfulness-to-make-heart-centered-choices on February 6, 2018.

Sanders, R. (2014, February 11). New evidence that chronic stress predisposes brain to mental illness. *Berkeley News.* Accessed at http://news.berkeley.edu/2014/02/11/chronic -stress-predisposes-brain-to-mental-illness on June 12, 2018.

Santos, R. S. (2012). *"Why resilience?" A review of literature of resilience and implications for further educational research.* Accessed at http://go.sdsu.edu/education/doc/files/01370 -reiliencyliteraturereview(sdsu).pdf on January 31, 2018.

Scaer, R. (2014). *The body bears the burden: Trauma, dissociation, and disease* (3rd ed.). Abingdon, England: Routledge.

Scher, C. D., Forde, D. R., McQuaid, J. R., & Stein, M. B. (2004). Prevalence and demographic correlates of childhood maltreatment in an adult community sample. *Child Abuse & Neglect, 28*(2), 167–180.

Schiller, P. (2010). Early brain development research review and update. *Exchange, 196,* 26–30.

Schmalzl, L., Powers, C., & Henje Blom, E. (2015). Neurophysiological and neurocognitive mechanisms underlying the effects of yoga-based practices: Towards a comprehensive theoretical framework. *Frontiers in Human Neuroscience, 9,* 235.

Schmidt, N. B., Richey, J. A., Zvolensky, M. J., & Maner, J. K. (2008). Exploring human freeze responses to a threat stressor. *Journal of Behavior Therapy and Experimental Psychiatry, 39*(3), 292–304. Accessed at www.ncbi.nlm.nih.gov/pmc/articles/PMC2489204 on July 30, 2018.

Schoen, S., & Schoen, A. (2010). Bullying and harassment in the United States. *The Clearing House, 83*(2), 68–72.

Schonert-Reichl, K. A., Oberle, E., Lawlor, M. S., Abbott, D., Thomson, K., Oberlander, T. F., et al. (2015). Enhancing cognitive and social–emotional development through a simple-to-administer mindfulness-based school program for elementary school children: A randomized controlled trial. *Developmental Psychology, 51*(1), 52–66.

The School Counseling Yogi. (2014, August 1). *Pranayama: The power of the breath* [Blog post]. Accessed at https://schoolcounselingyogi.wordpress.com/tag/volcano-breath on February 8, 2018.

Schreiber, D. (2011, May 8). Meditation program mends troubled Visitacion Valley Middle School. *San Francisco Examiner.* Accessed at www.sfexaminer.com/meditation -program-mends-troubled-visitacion-valley-middle-school on July 30, 2018.

Schreiber, T. A., & Niemeier, B. S. (2013). Exploring the health benefits of yoga: A review. *World Journal of Medical Research, 2*(1).

Schunk, D. H., & Ertmer, P. A. (2000). Self-regulation and academic learning: Self-efficacy enhancing interventions. In M. Boekaerts, P. R. Pintrich, & M. Zeidner (Eds.), *Handbook of self-regulation* (pp. 631–649). San Diego, CA: Academic Press.

Schwartz, K. (2014, January 17). Low-income schools see big benefits in teaching mindfulness. *KQED News.* Accessed at www.kqed.org/mindshift/33463/low-income -schools-see-big-benefits-in-teaching-mindfulness on June 1, 2018.

Semple, R. J., Droutman, V., & Reid, B. A. (2017). Mindfulness goes to school: Things learned (so far) from research and real-world experiences. *Psychology in the Schools, 54*(1), 29–52.

Semple, R. J., Reid, E. F., & Miller, L. (2005). Treating anxiety with mindfulness: An open trial of mindfulness training for anxious children. *Journal of Cognitive Psychotherapy, 19*(4), 379–392.

Senge, P. M. (2006). *The fifth discipline: The art and practice of the learning organization.* New York: Doubleday.

Senge, P. M., Cambron-McCabe, N., Lucas, T., Smith, B., Dutton, J., & Kleiner, A. (2012). *Schools that learn: A fifth discipline fieldbook for educators, parents, and everyone who cares about education.* New York: Crown Business.

Seppälä, E. M., Nitschke, J. B., Tudorascu, D. L., Hayes, A., Goldstein, M. R., Nguyen, D. T., et al. (2014). Breathing-based meditation decreases posttraumatic stress disorder symptoms in U.S. military veterans: A randomized controlled longitudinal study. *Journal of Traumatic Stress, 27*(4), 397–405.

Servan-Schreiber, D. (2013). *Healing without Freud or Prozac: Natural approaches to curing stress, anxiety and depression.* London: Rodale.

Shipstead, Z., Hicks, K. L., & Engle, R. W. (2012). Cogmed working memory training: Does the evidence support the claims? *Journal of Applied Research in Memory and Cognition, 1*(3), 185–193.

Shonkoff, J. P., Garner, A. S., Committee on Psychosocial Aspects of Child and Family Health, Committee on Early Childhood, Adoption, and Dependent Care, & Section on Developmental and Behavioral Pediatrics. (2012). The lifelong effects of early childhood adversity and toxic stress. *Pediatrics, 129*(1), e232–e246.

Shonkoff, J. P., & Phillips, D. A. (Eds.). (2000). *From neurons to neighborhoods: The science of early childhood development.* Washington, DC: National Academies Press.

Shore, R. (1997). *Rethinking the brain: New insights into early development.* New York: Families and Work Institute.

Sibinga, E. M., Perry-Parrish, C., Chung, S. E., Johnson, S. B., Smith, M., & Ellen, J. M. (2013). School-based mindfulness instruction for urban male youth: A small randomized controlled trial. *Preventive Medicine, 57*(6), 799–801.

Sibinga, E. M., Webb, L., Ghazarian, S. R., & Ellen, J. M. (2016). School-based mindfulness instruction: An RCT. *Pediatrics, 137*(1), e20152532.

Siegel, D. J. (2007). *The mindful brain: Reflection and attunement in the cultivation of well-being.* New York: Norton.

Siegel, D. J. (2010a). *Mindsight: The new science of personal transformation.* New York: Bantam Books.

Siegel, D. J. (2010b). *The mindful therapist: A clinician's guide to mindsight and neural integration.* New York: Norton.

Siegel, D. J. (2012). *The developing mind: How relationships and the brain interact to shape who we are* (2nd ed.). New York: Guilford Press.

Siegel, D. J. & Rutsch, E. (n.d.). *Dialogs on how to build a culture of empathy.* Accessed at http://cultureofempathy.com/References/Experts/Daniel-Siegel.htm on August 3, 2018.

Singer, T., & Bolz, M. (Eds.). (2013). *Compassion: Bridging practice.* Munich, Germany: Max Planck Society.

Singh, V., Wisniewski, A., Britton, J., & Tattersfield, A. (1990). Effect of yoga breathing exercises (pranayama) on airway reactivity in subjects with asthma. *The Lancet, 335*(8702), 1381–1383.

Slovacek, S. P., Tucker, S. A., & Pantoja, L. (2003). *A study of the yoga ed program at the accelerated school.* Los Angeles: Program Evaluation and Research Collaborative.

Smith, S. (2010, June 14). *Violence weighs heavy on a child's mind* [Blog post]. Accessed at http://thechart.blogs.cnn.com/2010/06/14/embargoed-monday-614-3pm-violence-weighs-heavy-on-a-childs-mind on February 1, 2018.

Sodian, B., & Frith, U. (2008). Metacognition, theory of mind, and self-control: The relevance of high-level cognitive processes in development, neuroscience, and education. *Mind, Brain, and Education, 2*(3), 111–113.

Souers, K., & Hall, P. (2016). *Fostering resilient learners: Strategies for creating a trauma-sensitive classroom.* Alexandria, VA: Association for Supervision and Curriculum Development.

Sourroubille Arnold, A. (2016, May 19). *Understand YOUR biology. Maximize YOUR productivity.* LinkedIn. Accessed at www.linkedin.com/pulse/understand-your-biology -maximize-productivity-sourroubille-arnold on September 27, 2018.

Sousa, D. A. (Ed.). (2010). *Mind, brain, and education.* Bloomington, IN: Solution Tree Press.

South Carolina Appleseed Legal Justice Center. (2012). *Reporting requirements: Who has a duty to report undocumented immigrants?—Fact sheet.* Accessed at http://scjustice.org/wp-content /uploads/2012/07/reporting-requirements-factsheet-2012.pdf on July 30, 2018.

Starr, T. J. (2015, May 8). *7 ways racism affects the lives of black children* [Blog post]. Accessed at www.alternet.org/civil-liberties/7-ways-racism-affects-lives-black-children on July 31, 2018.

Steele, H., Bate, J., Steele, M., Dube, S. R., Danskin, K., Knafo, H., et al. (2016). Adverse childhood experiences, poverty, and parenting stress. *Canadian Journal of Behavioural Science, 48*(1), 32–38.

Stephens, M. (2012). *Yoga Sequencing: Designing transformative yoga classes.* Berkeley, CA: North Atlantic Books.

Streeter, C. C., Gerbarg, P. L., Saper, R. B., Ciraulo, D. A., & Brown, R. P. (2012). Effects of yoga on the autonomic nervous system, gamma-aminobutyric-acid, and allostasis in epilepsy, depression, and post-traumatic stress disorder. *Medical Hypotheses, 78*(5), 571–579.

Substance Abuse and Mental Health Services Administration. (2014). Understanding the impact of trauma. In *Trauma-informed care in behavioral health services.* Rockville, MD: Author. Accessed at www.ncbi.nlm.nih.gov/books/NBK207191 on February 1, 2018.

Sugai, G., Horner, R. H., & Gresham, F. M. (2002). Behaviorally effective school environments. In M. R. Shinn, H. M. Walker, & G. Stoner (Eds.), *Interventions for academic and behavior problems II: Preventive and remedial approaches* (pp. 315–350). Bethesda, MD: National Association of School Psychologists.

Teicher, M. H. (2002). Scars that won't heal: The neurobiology of child abuse. *Scientific American, 286*(3), 68–75.

Tomporowski, P. D., Davis, C. L., Miller, P. H., & Naglieri, J. A. (2008). Exercise and children's intelligence, cognition, and academic achievement. *Educational psychology review, 20*(2), 111–131.

Tough, P. (2012). *How children succeed: Grit, curiosity, and the hidden power of character.* Boston: Houghton Mifflin.

Trafton, A., & MIT News. (2017). *Why stress can lead to poor decisions.* Accessed at www .weforum.org/agenda/2017/11/why-stress-can-lead-to-making-poor-decisions on May 26, 2018.

The Understood Team. (n.d.). *3 areas of executive function.* Accessed at www.understood .org/en/learning-attention-issues/child-learning-disabilities/executive-functioning -issues/3-areas-of-executive-function on February 6, 2018.

United Nations Children's Fund (with Annan, K. A.). (n.d.). *The state of the world's children: 2000.* Accessed at www.unicef.org/sowc00/foreword.htm on July 24, 2018.

University of Minnesota. (n.d.) *What is the mind-body connection?* Accessed at www .takingcharge.csh.umn.edu/what-is-the-mind-body-connection on July 17, 2018.

U.S. Department of Health and Human Services (2016). *Child maltreatment 2016.* Accessed at www.acf.hhs.gov/sites/default/files/cb/cm2016.pdf#page=10 on July 30, 2018.

Vassar, G. (2014). *Does your brain state make you smarter?* Accessed at https://lakesidelink .com/blog/lakeside/does-your-brain-state-make-you-smarter on February 8, 2018.

Vedhara, K., Hyde, J., Gilchrist, I. D., Tytherleigh, M., & Plummer, S. (2000). Acute stress, memory, attention and cortisol. *Psychoneuroendocrinology, 25*(6), 535–549.

Voytek, B. (2013, May 20). *Brain metrics: How measuring brain biology can explain the phenomena of mind* [Blog post]. Accessed at www.nature.com/scitable/blog/brain-metrics /are_there_really_as_many on August 5, 2018.

Wall, J. (2010). *Ethics in light of childhood.* Washington, DC: Georgetown University Press.

Walsh, F. (2016). *Strengthening family resilience* (3rd. ed.). New York: Guilford Press.

Weiten, W. (2017). *Psychology: Themes and variations* (10th ed.). Boston: Cengage Learning.

Welsh, M. C., Pennington, B. F., & Groisser, D. B. (1991). A normative-developmental study of executive function: A window on prefrontal function in children. *Developmental Neuropsychology, 7*(2), 131–149.

Werner, E. E., & Smith, R. S. (2001). *Journeys from childhood to midlife: Risk, resilience, and recovery.* New York: Cornell University Press.

Wexler, B. E. (2012, May). *Integrated brain and body exercises to increase core cognitive capacities.* Paper presented at the Learning and the Brain Conference, Arlington, VA.

Wexler, B. E. (2013). *Executive function skills to improve academic performance.* Paper presented at the Learning and the Brain Conference, Arlington, VA.

Wexler, B. E. (2017). Computer-presented and physical brain-training exercises for school children: Improving executive functions and learning. In *Transforming gaming and computer simulation technologies across industries* (pp. 206–224). Hershey, PA: IGI Global.

Wexler, B. E., Anderson, M., Fulbright, R. K., & Gore, J. C. (2000). Preliminary evidence of improved verbal working memory performance and normalization of task-related frontal lobe activation in schizophrenia following cognitive exercises. *American Journal of Psychiatry, 157*(10), 1694–1697.

Whyte, D. (2002). *Clear mind, wild heart: Finding courage and clarity through poetry* [CD]. Louisville, CO: Sounds True.

Williams, R. (2016, May 4). *The 7 habits of highly mindful leaders: Successful mindful leaders exhibit greater productivity and well-being* [Blog post]. Accessed at www.psychologytoday.com /blog/wired-success/201605/the-7-habits-highly-mindful-leaders on February 1, 2018.

Williams-Carter, H. (n.d.). *Trauma resolution: What is mindfulness?* Accessed at http://healingtraumacenter.com/mindfulness-2 on February 6, 2018.

Willis, J. (2007). Brain-based teaching strategies for improving students' memory, learning, and test-taking success. *Childhood Education, 83*(5), 310–315.

Wills, A. (n.d.). *5 ways to get teenagers practicing yoga*. Accessed at www.mindbodygreen.com /0-5159/5-Ways-to-Get-Teenagers-Practicing-Yoga.html on February 8, 2018.

Women's Health Network. (n.d.). *The link between stress and forgetfulness*. Accessed at www.womenshealthnetwork.com/adrenal-fatigue-and-stress/the-link-between-stress-and -forgetfulness.aspx on August 4, 2018.

Yale University. (2012). *How stress and depression can shrink the brain*. ScienceDaily. Accessed at www.sciencedaily.com/releases/2012/08/120812151659.htm on May 26, 2018.

Zelazo, P. D. (2015). Executive function: Reflection, iterative reprocessing, complexity, and the developing brain. *Developmental Review, 38*, 55–68.

Zelazo, P. D., & Cunningham, W. A. (2007). Executive function: Mechanisms underlying emotion regulation. In J. J. Gross (Ed.), *Handbook of emotion regulation* (pp. 135–158). New York: Guilford Press.

Zelazo, P. D., & Lyons, K. E. (2012). The potential benefits of mindfulness training in early childhood: A developmental social cognitive neuroscience perspective. *Child Development Perspectives, 6*(2), 154–160.

Zenner, C., Herrnleben-Kurz, S., & Walach, H. (2014). Mindfulness-based interventions in schools: A systematic review and meta-analysis. *Frontiers in Psychology, 5*, 603.

Zoogman, S., Goldberg, S. B., Hoyt, W. T., & Miller, L. (2015). Mindfulness interventions with youth: A meta-analysis. *Mindfulness, 6*(2), 290–302.

Index

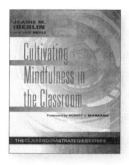

Cultivating Mindfulness in the Classroom
Jeanie M. Iberlin
Discover practical tools that align to the five key categories of mindfulness benefits—stress reduction, attention, emotional control, positive self-concept, and positive interactions—and explore a step-by-step process for establishing a formal school or classroom mindfulness program.
BKL035

Take Time for You
Tina H. Boogren
The key to thriving as a human and an educator rests in self-care. With *Take Time for You*, you'll discover a clear path to well-being. The author offers manageable strategies, reflection questions, and surveys that will guide you in developing an individualized self-care plan.
BKF813

Mindful Assessment
Lee Watanabe Crockett and Andrew Churches
It is time to rethink the relationship between teaching and learning and assess the crucial skills students need to succeed in the 21st century. Educators must focus assessment on mindfulness and feedback, framing assessment around six fluencies students need to cultivate.
BKF717

Behavior: The Forgotten Curriculum
Chris Weber
Discover how to fully prepare students for college, careers, and life by nurturing their behavioral skills along with their academic skills. Learn how to employ the most effective behavioral-skill exercises for your particular class and form unique relationships with every learner.
BKF828

Solution Tree | Press
a division of

Solution Tree

Visit SolutionTree.com or call 800.733.6786 to order.

GL⬤BAL PD

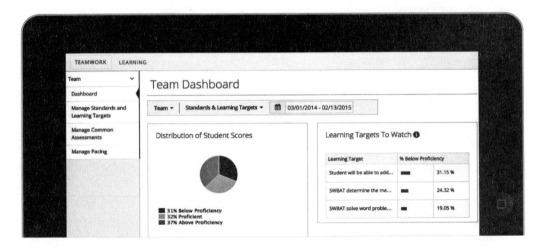

The **Power to Improve**
Is in Your Hands

Global PD gives educators focused and goals-oriented training from top experts. You can rely on this innovative online tool to improve instruction in every classroom.

- Get unlimited, on-demand access to guided video and book content from top Solution Tree authors.

- Improve practices with personalized virtual coaching from PLC-certified trainers.

- Customize learning based on skill level and time commitments.